TIME WITH GOD

KING JAMES VERSION

TIME WITH GOD

KING JAMES VERSION

WORD
BIBLES

Dallas · London · Vancouver · Melbourne

TIME WITH GOD
The New Testament for Busy People

Scripture text taken from the King James Version.

Library of Congress Cataloging-in-Publication Data:

Bible. English. N.T. Authorized. 1992.
    Time with God: King James Version.
      p. cm.
    Arranged for daily readings.
    ISBN 0–8499–1000–5 (HB).
    ISBN 0–8499–3411–7 (TP).
    ISBN 0–8499–1040–4 (Burgundy leather).
    ISBN 0–8499–1041–2 (Black leather).
    1. Devotional calendars. I. Word Bibles (Publisher) II. Title.
    BS2085   1992.I68
    225.5'2034—dc20   92–26729
                                                    CIP

2 3 4 9 RRD 9 8 7 6 5 4 3 2 1

Printed in the United States of America

INTRODUCTION

*W*ould you like to know God better . . . to explore exciting Scriptural truths each day and still meet your other demands and responsibilities . . . to be challenged (at a comfortable pace) to grow deeper in your faith?

Time with God has been designed for you! In fifteen minutes a day, you can systematically explore the treasures of Scripture. You may begin any time you wish, and at the end of the year you will have read the entire New Testament and related sections from the Old Testament. Plus you will have received insights from classical and contemporary writers.

There's a reading for Monday, Tuesday, Wednesday, Thursday, Friday, and one for Saturday/Sunday. (We know how busy weekends can be.)

Each two-page reading begins with the New Testament passage for the day and is followed by at least one Old Testament passage that reinforces the theme. This unique format allows you to see Scripture's truths unfold and to gain a new understanding of God's love and mercy throughout history.

If you wish, you may read thematically. Maybe you're wrestling with a problem at work, an issue of faith, or some type of suffering. Or maybe you would like to study a particular biblical theme. Whatever your need, the index that begins on page 627 will guide you to just the right reading.

Not only is *Time with God* a valuable aid in personal growth and meditative study, it is helpful for small groups and Sunday school classes.

Time with God features the King James Version, a beautiful and much-loved translation that is presented here in a contemporary and accessible format.

Most likely, you will recognize many of the authors' quotations we've included. Their insights—gleaned from more than one hundred seventy books—will challenge your thinking, broaden your understanding, and guide you to an even deeper relationship with God. The credits at the end of the book show the source of each quotation so you may pursue further reading.

Questions at the end of each reading will help you evaluate and apply what you've read. They are also excellent discussion starters for small group settings. We invite you now to spend time with God and discover what He has in store for you!

Amanda and Stephen Sorenson
Editors

MONDAY

The Savior of God's People Is Born

Matthew 1:1–25

The Family History of Jesus

1 The book of the generation of Jesus Christ, the son of David, the son of Abraham.

2 Abraham begat Isaac; and Isaac begat Jacob; and Jacob begat Judah and his brethren;

3 and Judah begat Pharez and Zerah of Tamar; and Pharez begat Hezron; and Hezron begat Ram;

4 and Ram begat Amminadab; and Amminadab begat Nahshon; and Nahshon begat Salmon;

5 and Salmon begat Boaz of Rachab; and Boaz begat Obed of Ruth; and Obed begat Jesse;

6 and Jesse begat David the king; and David the king begat Solomon of her *that had been the wife* of Uriah;

7 and Solomon begat Rehoboam; and Rehoboam begat Abijah; and Abijah begat Asa;

8 and Asa begat Jehoshaphat; and Jehoshaphat begat Jehoram; and Jehoram begat Uzziah;

9 and Uzziah begat Jotham; and Jotham begat Ahaz; and Ahaz begat Hezekiah;

10 and Hezekiah begat Manasseh; and Manasseh begat Amon; and Amon begat Josiah;

11 and Josiah begat Jeconiah and his brethren, about the time they were carried away to Babylon:

12 and after they were brought to Babylon, Jeconiah begat Shealtiel; and Shealtiel begat Zerubbabel;

13 and Zerubbabel begat Abiud; and Abiud begat Eliakim; and Eliakim begat Azor;

14 and Azor begat Zadok; and Zadok begat Achim; and Achim begat Eliud;

15 and Eliud begat Eleazar; and Eleazar begat Matthan; and Matthan begat Jacob;

16 and Jacob begat Joseph the husband of Mary, of whom was born Jesus, who is called Christ.

17 So all the generations from Abraham to David *are* fourteen generations; and from David until the carrying away into Babylon *are* fourteen generations; and from the carrying away into Babylon unto Christ *are* fourteen generations.

The Birth of Jesus Christ

*N*ow the birth of Jesus Christ was on this wise: When as his mother Mary was espoused to Joseph, before they came together, she was found with child of the Holy Ghost.

19 Then Joseph her husband, being a just *man*, and not willing to make her a public example, was minded to put her away privily.

20 But while he thought on these things, behold, the angel of the Lord appeared unto him in a dream, saying, Joseph, thou son of David, fear not to take unto thee Mary thy wife: for that which is conceived in her is of the Holy Ghost.

21 And she shall bring forth a son, and thou shalt call his name Jesus: for he shall save his people from their sins.

22 Now all this was done, that it might be fulfilled which was spoken of the Lord by the prophet, saying,

23 Behold, a virgin shall be with child,

and shall bring forth a son, and they shall call his name Immanuel, which being interpreted is, God with us.

²⁴ Then Joseph being raised from sleep did as the angel of the Lord had bidden him, and took unto him his wife:

²⁵ and knew her not till she had brought forth her firstborn son: and he called his name JESUS.

OLD TESTAMENT READING

*A*nd he said, Hear ye now, O house of David; *Is it* a small thing for you to weary men, but will ye weary my God also?

¹⁴ Therefore the Lord himself shall give you a sign; Behold, a virgin shall conceive, and bear a son, and shall call his name Immanuel.

Isaiah 7:13–14

*A*nd the LORD said, Shall I hide from Abraham that thing which I do;

¹⁸ Seeing that Abraham shall surely become a great and mighty nation, and all the nations of the earth shall be blessed in him?

Genesis 18:17–18

INSIGHTS

*T*he doctrine of the virgin birth is crucial to our faith. The incarnation of the Son of God was accomplished by a creative act of the Holy Spirit in the body of Mary, a virgin. It was a special miracle performed by the third person of the Holy Trinity—the Holy Spirit—which enabled the second person of the Trinity—the eternal Son of God—to take upon Himself a genuine, although sinless, human nature. He was born of a virgin, as a man, without surrendering

any aspect of His deity. . . .

. . . This may be difficult to understand, but we can understand the concept even if we can't grasp it in our minds. Jesus was fully human and fully divine. He was not just a prophet, He was God.

. . . One with us, yet one with God. He had to become man because man was the one who had sinned. He had to be God because God was the only One who could do anything about the sin of man. Humanity had tried for centuries, and the situation only got worse! The only way God could bring about the salvation of the fallen human race was to assume the form of the race He was to redeem.

God has given us the means to know the truth. Jesus is the way to the Father, because He is our Redeemer. He is the truth because He is the fulfillment of all the prophecies concerning Him. He is the life because He overcame death. . . . Jesus has the fullness of God dwelling in Him bodily forever and ever. The Son of God became the Son of man so that the sons of men might become the sons of God.

Terry Fullam

PAUSE FOR REFLECTION

*W*hat does the virgin birth of Jesus signify for all people? In what ways have all nations been blessed through the children of Abraham? How has Jesus, son of Abraham and son of God, blessed your life?

TUESDAY

God Guides and Protects Us

Matthew 2:1–23

Wise Men Come to Visit Jesus

2 Now when Jesus was born in Bethlehem of Judea in the days of Herod the king, behold, there came wise men from the east to Jerusalem,

² saying, Where is he that is born King of the Jews? for we have seen his star in the east, and are come to worship him.

³ When Herod the king had heard *these things*, he was troubled, and all Jerusalem with him.

⁴ And when he had gathered all the chief priests and scribes of the people together, he demanded of them where Christ should be born.

⁵ And they said unto him, In Bethlehem of Judea: for thus it is written by the prophet,

⁶ And thou Bethlehem, *in* the land of Judah, art not the least among the princes of Judah: for out of thee shall come a Governor, that shall rule my people Israel.

⁷ Then Herod, when he had privily called the wise men, inquired of them diligently what time the star appeared.

⁸ And he sent them to Bethlehem, and said, Go and search diligently for the young child; and when ye have found *him*, bring me word again, that I may come and worship him also.

⁹ When they had heard the king, they departed; and, lo, the star, which they saw in the east, went before them, till it came and stood over where the young child was.

¹⁰ When they saw the star, they rejoiced with exceeding great joy.

¹¹ And when they were come into the house, they saw the young child with Mary his mother, and fell down, and worshipped him: and when they had opened their treasures, they presented unto him gifts; gold, and frankincense, and myrrh.

¹² And being warned of God in a dream that they should not return to Herod, they departed into their own country another way.

Jesus' Parents Take Him to Egypt

*A*nd when they were departed, behold, the angel of the Lord appeareth to Joseph in a dream, saying, Arise, and take the young child and his mother, and flee into Egypt, and be thou there until I bring thee word: for Herod will seek the young child to destroy him.

¹⁴ When he arose, he took the young child and his mother by night, and departed into Egypt:

¹⁵ and was there until the death of Herod: that it might be fulfilled which was spoken of the Lord by the prophet, saying, Out of Egypt have I called my son.

Herod Kills the Baby Boys

*T*hen Herod, when he saw that he was mocked of the wise men, was exceeding wroth, and sent forth, and slew all the children that were in Bethlehem, and in all the coasts thereof, from two years old and under, according to the time which he had diligently inquired of the wise men.

¹⁷ Then was fulfilled that which was spoken by Jeremiah the prophet, saying,

¹⁸ In Ramah was there a voice heard, lamentation, and weeping, and great mourning, Rachel weeping *for* her children, and would not be comforted, because they are not.

Joseph and Mary Return

*B*ut when Herod was dead, behold, an angel of the Lord appeareth in a dream to Joseph in Egypt,

²⁰ saying, Arise, and take the young child and his mother, and go into the land of Israel: for they are dead which sought the young child's life.

²¹ And he arose, and took the young child and his mother, and came into the land of Israel.

²² But when he heard that Archelaus did reign in Judea in the room of his father Herod, he was afraid to go thither: notwithstanding, being warned of God in a dream, he turned aside into the parts of Galilee:

²³ and he came and dwelt in a city called Nazareth: that it might be fulfilled which was spoken by the prophets, He shall be called a Nazarene.

OLD TESTAMENT READING

*B*ut thou, Bethlehem Ephratah, *though* thou be little among the thousands of Judah, *yet* out of thee shall he come forth unto me *that is* to be ruler in Israel; whose goings forth *have been* from of old, from everlasting.

³ Therefore will he give them up, until the time *that* she which travaileth hath brought forth: then the remnant of his brethren shall return unto the children of Israel.

⁴ And he shall stand and feed in the strength of the LORD, in the majesty of the name of the LORD his God; and they shall abide: for now shall he be great unto the ends of the earth.

⁵ And this *man* shall be the peace, when the Assyrian shall come into our land.

Micah 5:2–5a

INSIGHTS

*G*od has led. This is history's testimony. Looking back over lives, we can see how beautifully, wonderfully, lovingly God has led. "As for me, the LORD has led me," testified the servant of Abraham (Genesis 24:27).

God will lead. This is the testimony of doctrine. The Scriptures teach it by precept and example throughout Old and New Testaments. The word of God declares it to be so. Looking ahead—before the need, before the crunch—we can testify that God will lead.

God is leading! This is the testimony of faith, where the rubber meets the road. God has promised to lead, and I seek to be led—an unbeatable combination. God's promise, my submission.

God has led, for which I am grateful.

I know God will lead, and for this I praise and thank Him.

God is leading! This is my confidence and joy . . . my rest.

Richard Halverson

PAUSE FOR REFLECTION

*N*ote the instances in which God protected the child Jesus and how each of those also fulfilled prophecy. What does this reveal about God's faithfulness in protecting his own?

WEDNESDAY

Change Your Hearts and Lives

Matthew 3:1—4:11

The Work of John the Baptist

3 In those days came John the Baptist, preaching in the wilderness of Judea,

² and saying, Repent ye: for the kingdom of heaven is at hand.

³ For this is he that was spoken of by the prophet Isaiah, saying, The voice of one crying in the wilderness, Prepare ye the way of the Lord, make his paths straight.

⁴ And the same John had his raiment of camel's hair, and a leathern girdle about his loins; and his meat was locusts and wild honey.

⁵ Then went out to him Jerusalem, and all Judea, and all the region round about Jordan,

⁶ and were baptized of him in Jordan, confessing their sins.

⁷ But when he saw many of the Pharisees and Sadducees come to his baptism, he said unto them, O generation of vipers, who hath warned you to flee from the wrath to come?

⁸ Bring forth therefore fruits meet for repentance:

⁹ and think not to say within yourselves, We have Abraham to *our* father: for I say unto you, that God is able of these stones to raise up children unto Abraham.

¹⁰ And now also the axe is laid unto the root of the trees: therefore every tree which bringeth not forth good fruit is hewn down, and cast into the fire.

¹¹ I indeed baptize you with water unto repentance: but he that cometh after me is mightier than I, whose shoes I am not worthy to bear: he shall baptize you with the Holy Ghost, and *with* fire:

¹² whose fan *is* in his hand, and he will thoroughly purge his floor, and gather his wheat into the garner; but he will burn up the chaff with unquenchable fire.

Jesus Is Baptized by John

*T*hen cometh Jesus from Galilee to Jordan unto John, to be baptized of him.

¹⁴ But John forbade him, saying, I have need to be baptized of thee, and comest thou to me?

¹⁵ And Jesus answering said unto him, Suffer *it to be so* now: for thus it becometh us to fulfil all righteousness. Then he suffered him.

¹⁶ And Jesus, when he was baptized, went up straightway out of the water: and, lo, the heavens were opened unto him, and he saw the Spirit of God descending like a dove, and lighting upon him:

¹⁷ and lo a voice from heaven, saying, This is my beloved Son, in whom I am well pleased.

The Temptation of Jesus

4 Then was Jesus led up of the Spirit into the wilderness to be tempted of the devil.

² And when he had fasted forty days and forty nights, he was afterward ahungered.

³ And when the tempter came to him, he said, If thou be the Son of God, command that these stones be made bread.

⁴But he answered and said, It is written, Man shall not live by bread alone, but by every word that proceedeth out of the mouth of God.

⁵Then the devil taketh him up into the holy city, and setteth him on a pinnacle of the temple,

⁶and saith unto him, If thou be the Son of God, cast thyself down: for it is written, He shall give his angels charge concerning thee: and in *their* hands they shall bear thee up, lest at any time thou dash thy foot against a stone.

⁷Jesus said unto him, It is written again, Thou shalt not tempt the Lord thy God.

⁸Again, the devil taketh him up into an exceeding high mountain, and showeth him all the kingdoms of the world, and the glory of them;

⁹and saith unto him, All these things will I give thee, if thou wilt fall down and worship me.

¹⁰Then saith Jesus unto him, Get thee hence, Satan: for it is written, Thou shalt worship the Lord thy God, and him only shalt thou serve.

¹¹Then the devil leaveth him, and, behold, angels came and ministered unto him.

OLD TESTAMENT READING

*C*ome, ye children, hearken unto me: I will teach you the fear of the LORD.

¹²What man *is he that* desireth life, *and* loveth *many* days, that he may see good?

¹³Keep thy tongue from evil, and thy lips from speaking guile.

¹⁴Depart from evil, and do good; seek peace, and pursue it.

Psalm 34:11–14

INSIGHTS

*J*ean, a small shopkeeper in Bordeaux, worked long hours with virtually nothing to show for his labors. Even his best efforts to beguile the Paris tax collector left him very little for his family. His life was depressing and without purpose, until the day when a missionary entered his shop to make a purchase.

Before leaving the shop, this foreigner shared his faith with Jean, and for the first time the shopkeeper realized that there was more to life than he had ever supposed. . . .

As he grew in faith, Jean became convinced that his lifestyle must be radically altered and that he could no longer lie about how much income he was making at his little shop. When the time came to submit his tax forms, he filled them out in full and paid the required amount of taxes. The local tax clerk was stunned, and word spread like wildfire among the shopkeepers. Jean's wife was outraged, and his neighbors were convinced that he had lost his mind. When they inquired about his foolish actions, he could only explain that God had made him a different man.

Ruth Tucker

PAUSE FOR REFLECTION

*W*hat message from God did John bring to the people of his day? Was it different from the message of the Old Testament? Was it different from Jesus' message? What does it mean to have a changed heart and live a changed life today?

THURSDAY

"Follow Me"

Matthew 4:12—5:12

Jesus Begins Work in Galilee

*N*ow when Jesus had heard that John was cast into prison, he departed into Galilee;
[13] and leaving Nazareth, he came and dwelt in Capernaum, which is upon the seacoast, in the borders of Zebulun and Naphtali:
[14] that it might be fulfilled which was spoken by Isaiah the prophet, saying,
[15] The land of Zebulun, and the land of Naphtali, *by* the way of the sea, beyond Jordan, Galilee of the Gentiles;
[16] the people which sat in darkness saw great light; and to them which sat in the region and shadow of death light is sprung up.

Jesus Chooses Some Disciples

*F*rom that time Jesus began to preach, and to say, Repent: for the kingdom of heaven is at hand.
[18] And Jesus, walking by the sea of Galilee, saw two brethren, Simon called Peter, and Andrew his brother, casting a net into the sea: for they were fishers.
[19] And he saith unto them, Follow me, and I will make you fishers of men.
[20] And they straightway left *their* nets, and followed him.
[21] And going on from thence, he saw other two brethren, James *the son* of Zebedee, and John his brother, in a ship with Zebedee their father, mending their nets; and he called them.
[22] And they immediately left the ship and their father, and followed him.

Jesus Teaches and Heals People

*A*nd Jesus went about all Galilee, teaching in their synagogues, and preaching the gospel of the kingdom, and healing all manner of sickness and all manner of disease among the people.
[24] And his fame went throughout all Syria: and they brought unto him all sick people that were taken with divers diseases and torments, and those which were possessed with devils, and those which were lunatic, and those that had the palsy; and he healed them.
[25] And there followed him great multitudes of people from Galilee, and *from* Decapolis, and *from* Jerusalem, and *from* Judea, and *from* beyond Jordan.

Jesus Teaches the People

5 And seeing the multitudes, he went up into a mountain: and when he was set, his disciples came unto him:
[2] and he opened his mouth, and taught them, saying,
[3] Blessed *are* the poor in spirit: for theirs is the kingdom of heaven.
[4] Blessed *are* they that mourn: for they shall be comforted.
[5] Blessed *are* the meek: for they shall inherit the earth.
[6] Blessed *are* they which do hunger and thirst after righteousness: for they shall be filled.
[7] Blessed *are* the merciful: for they shall obtain mercy.

⁸ Blessed *are* the pure in heart: for they shall see God.

⁹ Blessed *are* the peacemakers: for they shall be called the children of God.

¹⁰ Blessed *are* they which are persecuted for righteousness' sake: for theirs is the kingdom of heaven.

¹¹ Blessed are ye, when *men* shall revile you, and persecute *you*, and shall say all manner of evil against you falsely, for my sake.

¹² Rejoice, and be exceeding glad: for great *is* your reward in heaven: for so persecuted they the prophets which were before you.

OLD TESTAMENT READING

*N*ow the LORD had said unto Abram, Get thee out of thy country, and from thy kindred, and from thy father's house, unto a land that I will show thee:

² and I will make of thee a great nation, and I will bless thee, and make thy name great; and thou shalt be a blessing:

³ and I will bless them that bless thee, and curse him that curseth thee: and in thee shall all families of the earth be blessed.

⁴ So Abram departed, as the LORD had spoken unto him; and Lot went with him: and Abram *was* seventy and five years old when he departed out of Haran.

Genesis 12:1–4

INSIGHTS

*T*oday, in principle, the call of the Lord Jesus has not changed. He still says 'Follow me', and adds, 'whoever of you does not renounce all that he has cannot be my disciple'. In practice, however, this does not mean for the majority of Christians a physical departure from their home or their job. It implies rather an inner surrender of both, and a refusal to allow either family or ambition to occupy the first place in our lives.

First, there must be a renunciation of sin. This, in a word, is repentance. It is the first part of Christian conversion. It can in no circumstances be bypassed. Repentance and faith belong together. We cannot follow Christ without forsaking sin. . . .

Second, there must be a renunciation of self. In order to follow Christ we must not only forsake isolated sins, but renounce the very principle of self-will which lies at the root of every act of sin. To follow Christ is to surrender to him the rights over our own lives. It is to abdicate the throne of our heart and do homage to him as our King. . . .

The full, inexorable demand of Jesus Christ is now laid bare. He does not call us to a sloppy half-heartedness, but to a vigorous, absolute commitment. He calls us to make him our Lord.

John Stott

ACTION POINT

*W*hat did the men mentioned in these passages forsake in order to follow God? What have you had to forsake in order to follow Jesus? Think about what occupies first place in your life now. Pray that you will make following Jesus most important.

F R I D A Y

Take God's Light into the World

Matthew 5:13–37

You Are like Salt and Light

*Y*e are the salt of the earth: but if the salt have lost his savor, wherewith shall it be salted? it is thenceforth good for nothing, but to be cast out, and to be trodden under foot of men. ¹⁴ Ye are the light of the world. A city that is set on a hill cannot be hid. ¹⁵ Neither do men light a candle, and put it under a bushel, but on a candlestick; and it giveth light unto all that are in the house. ¹⁶ Let your light so shine before men, that they may see your good works, and glorify your Father which is in heaven.

The Importance of the Law

*T*hink not that I am come to destroy the law, or the prophets: I am not come to destroy, but to fulfil. ¹⁸ For verily I say unto you, Till heaven and earth pass, one jot or one tittle shall in no wise pass from the law, till all be fulfilled. ¹⁹ Whosoever therefore shall break one of these least commandments, and shall teach men so, he shall be called the least in the kingdom of heaven: but whosoever shall do and teach *them*, the same shall be called great in the kingdom of heaven. ²⁰ For I say unto you, That except your righteousness shall exceed *the righteousness* of the scribes and Pharisees, ye shall in no case enter into the kingdom of heaven.

Jesus Teaches About Anger

*Y*e have heard that it was said by them of old time, Thou shalt not kill; and whosoever shall kill shall be in danger of the judgment: ²² but I say unto you, That whosoever is angry with his brother without a cause shall be in danger of the judgment: and whosoever shall say to his brother, Raca, shall be in danger of the council: but whosoever shall say, Thou fool, shall be in danger of hell fire. ²³ Therefore if thou bring thy gift to the altar, and there rememberest that thy brother hath ought against thee; ²⁴ leave there thy gift before the altar, and go thy way; first be reconciled to thy brother, and then come and offer thy gift. ²⁵ Agree with thine adversary quickly, while thou art in the way with him; lest at any time the adversary deliver thee to the judge, and the judge deliver thee to the officer, and thou be cast into prison. ²⁶ Verily I say unto thee, Thou shalt by no means come out thence, till thou hast paid the uttermost farthing.

Jesus Teaches About Sexual Sin

*Y*e have heard that it was said by them of old time, Thou shalt not commit adultery: ²⁸ but I say unto you, That whosoever looketh on a woman to lust after her hath committed adultery with her already in his heart. ²⁹ And if thy right eye offend thee, pluck it out, and cast *it* from thee: for it is profitable for thee that one of thy members should perish, and not *that* thy whole body should be cast into hell.

[30] And if thy right hand offend thee, cut it off, and cast *it* from thee: for it is profitable for thee that one of thy members should perish, and not *that* thy whole body should be cast into hell.

Jesus Teaches About Divorce

*I*t hath been said, Whosoever shall put away his wife, let him give her a writing of divorcement:

[32] but I say unto you, That whosoever shall put away his wife, saving for the cause of fornication, causeth her to commit adultery: and whosoever shall marry her that is divorced committeth adultery.

Make Promises Carefully

*A*gain, ye have heard that it hath been said by them of old time, Thou shalt not forswear thyself, but shalt perform unto the Lord thine oaths:

[34] but I say unto you, Swear not at all; neither by heaven; for it is God's throne:

[35] nor by the earth; for it is his footstool: neither by Jerusalem; for it is the city of the great King.

[36] Neither shalt thou swear by thy head, because thou canst not make one hair white or black.

[37] But let your communication be, Yea, yea; Nay, nay: for whatsoever is more than these cometh of evil.

OLD TESTAMENT READING

*Y*e that love the LORD, hate evil: he preserveth the souls of his saints; he delivereth them out of the hand of the wicked.

[11] Light is sown for the righteous, and gladness for the upright in heart.

Psalm 97:10–11

*F*or thou wilt light my candle: the LORD my God will enlighten my darkness.

Psalm 18:28

INSIGHTS

*N*owhere in the Bible are we commanded to bring non-Christians into the church to get saved. In fact, there is not one instance in the Bible of anyone who ever got converted in a church or synagogue. For instance, in Luke 19, our Lord did not ask Zaccheus to meet Him at the synagogue on the Sabbath. Instead, he went to Zaccheus' home. The misconception is that the pagan is supposed to come and hear; the Biblical mandate for the believer is to go and tell.*

If we are to be salt and light in our world, we need to go where the lost are. That might mean inviting them into your home for dinner, going next door to visit with them, playing miniature golf together, or doing something else with them. The Holy Spirit will start working in their lives as they watch our lives and try to figure out why we are different.

Robert Tamasy

APPLICATION

*T*hink about what it means to be salt and light in the world today. What kind of lifestyle shines as a light to the world and shows people how to be saved? How do you need to change your life in order to be the salt and light God wants you to be?*

WEEKEND
The Wonder of God's Forgiveness

Matthew 5:38—6:15

Don't Fight Back

*Y*e have heard that it hath been said, An eye for an eye, and a tooth for a tooth:

³⁹ but I say unto you, That ye resist not evil: but whosoever shall smite thee on thy right cheek, turn to him the other also.

⁴⁰ And if any man will sue thee at the law, and take away thy coat, let him have *thy* cloak also.

⁴¹ And whosoever shall compel thee to go a mile, go with him twain.

⁴² Give to him that asketh thee, and from him that would borrow of thee turn not thou away.

Love All People

*Y*e have heard that it hath been said, Thou shalt love thy neighbor, and hate thine enemy.

⁴⁴ But I say unto you, Love your enemies, bless them that curse you, do good to them that hate you, and pray for them which despitefully use you, and persecute you;

⁴⁵ that ye may be the children of your Father which is in heaven: for he maketh his sun to rise on the evil and on the good, and sendeth rain on the just and on the unjust.

⁴⁶ For if ye love them which love you, what reward have ye? do not even the publicans the same?

⁴⁷ And if ye salute your brethren only, what do ye more *than others*? do not even the publicans so?

⁴⁸ Be ye therefore perfect, even as your Father which is in heaven is perfect.

Jesus Teaches About Giving

6 Take heed that ye do not your alms before men, to be seen of them: otherwise ye have no reward of your Father which is in heaven.

² Therefore when thou doest *thine* alms, do not sound a trumpet before thee, as the hypocrites do in the synagogues and in the streets, that they may have glory of men. Verily I say unto you, They have their reward.

³ But when thou doest alms, let not thy left hand know what thy right hand doeth:

⁴ that thine alms may be in secret: and thy Father which seeth in secret himself shall reward thee openly.

Jesus Teaches About Prayer

*A*nd when thou prayest, thou shalt not be as the hypocrites *are*: for they love to pray standing in the synagogues and in the corners of the streets, that they may be seen of men. Verily I say unto you, They have their reward.

⁶ But thou, when thou prayest, enter into thy closet, and when thou hast shut thy door, pray to thy Father which is in secret; and thy Father which seeth in secret shall reward thee openly.

⁷ But when ye pray, use not vain repetitions, as the heathen *do*: for they think that they shall be heard for their much speaking.

[8] Be not ye therefore like unto them: for your Father knoweth what things ye have need of, before ye ask him.
[9] After this manner therefore pray ye: Our Father which art in heaven, Hallowed be thy name.
[10] Thy kingdom come. Thy will be done in earth, as *it is* in heaven.
[11] Give us this day our daily bread.
[12] And forgive us our debts, as we forgive our debtors.
[13] And lead us not into temptation, but deliver us from evil: For thine is the kingdom, and the power, and the glory, for ever. Amen.
[14] For if ye forgive men their trespasses, your heavenly Father will also forgive you:
[15] but if ye forgive not men their trespasses, neither will your Father forgive your trespasses.

sin when he is converted, because he never gets beyond the reach of temptation. True, he has experienced the joy of forgiveness. He revels in the assurance that his guilt has been removed, but he is nowhere promised exemption from the lure of temptation or the possibility of sinning. . . .

Then how is it possible for a God who hates sin and requires purity, to continue having dealings with a sin-prone believer, to say nothing of permitting a deepening intimacy? The answer is that in the multi-faceted death of His Son, provision is made for a cleaning so deep, so radical, so continuous that a believer can walk with God in unbroken communion and deepening fellowship.

J. Oswald Sanders

OLD TESTAMENT READING

Show me thy ways, OLORD; teach me thy paths.
[5] Lead me in thy truth, and teach me: for thou *art* the God of my salvation; on thee do I wait all the day.
[6] Remember, O LORD, thy tender mercies and thy loving-kindnesses; for they *have been* ever of old.
[7] Remember not the sins of my youth, nor my transgressions: according to thy mercy remember thou me for thy goodness' sake, O LORD.

Psalm 25:4–7

ACTION POINT

In your own words, describe how God wants his people to pray. Why do you think seeking God's forgiveness is an essential part of prayer? Approach God now in prayer. Make yourself pure before him and share with him all that is in your heart.

INSIGHTS

Scripture is realistic in its treatment of sin, whether in the believer or unbeliever. It recognizes that sin is a continuing problem, even for the believer. He is not forever done with

MONDAY

God Wants Us to Seek, Honor, and Trust Him

Matthew 6:16—7:6

Jesus Teaches About Worship

*M*oreover when ye fast, be not, as the hypocrites, of a sad countenance: for they disfigure their faces, that they may appear unto men to fast. Verily I say unto you, They have their reward.

¹⁷ But thou, when thou fastest, anoint thine head, and wash thy face;

¹⁸ that thou appear not unto men to fast, but unto thy Father which is in secret: and thy Father, which seeth in secret, shall reward thee openly.

God Is More Important than Money

*L*ay not up for yourselves treasures upon earth, where moth and rust doth corrupt, and where thieves break through and steal:

²⁰ but lay up for yourselves treasures in heaven, where neither moth nor rust doth corrupt, and where thieves do not break through nor steal:

²¹ for where your treasure is, there will your heart be also.

²² The light of the body is the eye: if therefore thine eye be single, thy whole body shall be full of light.

²³ But if thine eye be evil, thy whole body shall be full of darkness. If therefore the light that is in thee be darkness, how great *is* that darkness!

²⁴ No man can serve two masters: for either he will hate the one, and love the other; or else he will hold to the one, and despise the other. Ye cannot serve God and mammon.

Don't Worry

*T*herefore I say unto you, Take no thought for your life, what ye shall eat, or what ye shall drink; nor yet for your body, what ye shall put on. Is not the life more than meat, and the body than raiment?

²⁶ Behold the fowls of the air: for they sow not, neither do they reap, nor gather into barns; yet your heavenly Father feedeth them. Are ye not much better than they?

²⁷ Which of you by taking thought can add one cubit unto his stature?

²⁸ And why take ye thought for raiment? Consider the lilies of the field, how they grow; they toil not, neither do they spin:

²⁹ and yet I say unto you, That even Solomon in all his glory was not arrayed like one of these.

³⁰ Wherefore, if God so clothe the grass of the field, which today is, and tomorrow is cast into the oven, *shall he* not much more *clothe* you, O ye of little faith?

³¹ Therefore take no thought, saying, What shall we eat? or, What shall we drink? or, Wherewithal shall we be clothed?

³² (For after all these things do the Gentiles seek:) for your heavenly Father knoweth that ye have need of all these things.

³³ But seek ye first the kingdom of God, and his righteousness; and all these things shall be added unto you.

³⁴ Take therefore no thought for the morrow: for the morrow shall take thought for the things of itself. Sufficient unto the day *is* the evil thereof.

Be Careful About Judging Others

7 Judge not, that ye be not judged.
² For with what judgment ye judge, ye shall be judged: and with what measure ye mete, it shall be measured to you again.

³ And why beholdest thou the mote that is in thy brother's eye, but considerest not the beam that is in thine own eye?

⁴ Or how wilt thou say to thy brother, Let me pull out the mote out of thine eye; and, behold, a beam *is* in thine own eye?

⁵ Thou hypocrite, first cast out the beam out of thine own eye; and then shalt thou see clearly to cast out the mote out of thy brother's eye.

⁶ Give not that which is holy unto the dogs, neither cast ye your pearls before swine, lest they trample them under their feet, and turn again and rend you.

OLD TESTAMENT READING

*N*ow in the twenty and fourth day of this month the children of Israel were assembled with fasting, and with sackclothes, and earth upon them.
² And the seed of Israel separated themselves from all strangers, and stood and confessed their sins, and the iniquities of their fathers.
³ And they stood up in their place, and read in the book of the law of the LORD their God *one* fourth part of the day; and *another* fourth part they confessed, and worshipped the LORD their God.

Nehemiah 9:1–3

*T*herefore also now, saith the LORD, turn ye *even* to me with all your heart, and with fasting, and with weeping, and with mourning:

¹³ And rend your heart, and not your garments, and turn unto the LORD your God.

Joel 2:12–13a

INSIGHTS

*O*ur problem is that we want to test God rather than trust him. We want to experiment with him rather than rely on him. We're like the boy who tests the doubtful ice instead of skating confidently where God is leading. What is our faith worth if we don't trust completely? It is perfectly natural to trust in our own understanding, to rely on our own natural strengths, gifts, or talents (and indeed some modern prophets tell us to do so!). But it is the walk of faith to trust his teaching and direction. Give him first place and let him have precedence. This is the secret of safe guidance and peaceful progression. Simple dependence upon him, committing our all to him, obeying him implicitly—this is how to acknowledge him "in all thy ways."

Al Bryant

APPLICATION

*D*escribe the kind of life that truly honors God. What are God's people to trust him to provide? In what ways do you trust and seek God on a daily basis?

TUESDAY

There Is Wisdom and Goodness in Walking in God's Ways

Matthew 7:7—8:4

Ask God for What You Need

*A*sk, and it shall be given you; seek, and ye shall find; knock, and it shall be opened unto you:

[8] for every one that asketh receiveth; and he that seeketh findeth; and to him that knocketh it shall be opened.

[9] Or what man is there of you, whom if his son ask bread, will he give him a stone?

[10] Or if he ask a fish, will he give him a serpent?

[11] If ye then, being evil, know how to give good gifts unto your children, how much more shall your Father which is in heaven give good things to them that ask him?

The Most Important Rule

*T*herefore all things whatsoever ye would that men should do to you, do ye even so to them: for this is the law and the prophets.

The Way to Heaven Is Hard

*E*nter ye in at the strait gate: for wide *is* the gate, and broad *is* the way, that leadeth to destruction, and many there be which go in thereat:

[14] because strait *is* the gate, and narrow *is* the way, which leadeth unto life, and few there be that find it.

People Know You by Your Actions

*B*eware of false prophets, which come to you in sheep's clothing, but inwardly they are ravening wolves.

[16] Ye shall know them by their fruits. Do men gather grapes of thorns, or figs of thistles?

[17] Even so every good tree bringeth forth good fruit; but a corrupt tree bringeth forth evil fruit.

[18] A good tree cannot bring forth evil fruit, neither *can* a corrupt tree bring forth good fruit.

[19] Every tree that bringeth not forth good fruit is hewn down, and cast into the fire.

[20] Wherefore by their fruits ye shall know them.

[21] Not every one that saith unto me, Lord, Lord, shall enter into the kingdom of heaven; but he that doeth the will of my Father which is in heaven.

[22] Many will say to me in that day, Lord, Lord, have we not prophesied in thy name? and in thy name have cast out devils? and in thy name done many wonderful works?

[23] And then will I profess unto them, I never knew you: depart from me, ye that work iniquity.

Two Kinds of People

*T*herefore whosoever heareth these sayings of mine, and doeth them, I will liken him unto a wise man, which built his house upon a rock:

[25] and the rain descended, and the floods came, and the winds blew, and beat upon that house; and it fell not: for it was founded upon a rock.

[26] And every one that heareth these sayings of mine, and doeth them not,

shall be likened unto a foolish man, which built his house upon the sand: 27 and the rain descended, and the floods came, and the winds blew, and beat upon that house; and it fell: and great was the fall of it.

28 And it came to pass, when Jesus had ended these sayings, the people were astonished at his doctrine:

29 for he taught them as *one* having authority, and not as the scribes.

Jesus Heals a Sick Man

8 When he was come down from the mountain, great multitudes followed him.

2 And, behold, there came a leper and worshipped him, saying, Lord, if thou wilt, thou canst make me clean.

3 And Jesus put forth *his* hand, and touched him, saying, I will; be thou clean. And immediately his leprosy was cleansed.

4 And Jesus saith unto him, See thou tell no man; but go thy way, show thyself to the priest, and offer the gift that Moses commanded, for a testimony unto them.

OLD TESTAMENT READING

*B*lessed *is* the man that walketh not in the counsel of the ungodly, nor standeth in the way of sinners, nor sitteth in the seat of the scornful.

2 But his delight *is* in the law of the LORD; and in his law doth he meditate day and night.

3 And he shall be like a tree planted by the rivers of water, that bringeth forth his fruit in his season; his leaf also shall not wither; and whatsoever he doeth shall prosper.

Psalm 1:1–3

INISIGHTS

*I*t must be admitted that, in its first stages, the broad way is generally easy and rather delightful. The boat launched on the flowing stream sweeps merrily and pleasantly along, the gradient of the road slopes so as to make walking easy, the sun shines, and the path is filled with bright flowers. But to a life given up to self-indulgence, there is only one end—destruction.

There is a more excellent way, but it is too narrow to admit the trailing garments of passionate desire, too narrow for pride, self-indulgence, greed, and avarice—it is the Way of the Cross, but it leads to Life! We all want to see life—and the remarkable thing is that those who expect to get most out of it by self-indulgence miss everything; whilst those who seem to curtail their lives by following Christ, win everything. Few find and enter this path, is the lament of our Lord. Let us put our hand in His, that He may lead us into the path of life, "that shineth more and more unto the perfect day."

F. B. Meyer

APPLICATION

*W*hat good things does God promise to those who search for him and walk in his ways? What kind of person makes the decision to walk through the narrow gate and build on the Rock? What kind of person are you? On what path do you walk? What will be the reward of that path?

WEDNESDAY
Jesus' Amazing Authority

Matthew 8:5–27

Jesus Heals a Soldier's Servant

*A*nd when Jesus was entered into Capernaum, there came unto him a centurion, beseeching him,

⁶ and saying, Lord, my servant lieth at home sick of the palsy, grievously tormented.

⁷ and Jesus saith unto him, I will come and heal him.

⁸ The centurion answered and said, Lord, I am not worthy that thou shouldest come under my roof: but speak the word only, and my servant shall be healed.

⁹ For I am a man under authority, having soldiers under me: and I say to this *man*, Go, and he goeth; and to another, Come, and he cometh; and to my servant, Do this, and he doeth *it*.

¹⁰ When Jesus heard *it*, he marveled, and said to them that followed, Verily I say unto you, I have not found so great faith, no, not in Israel.

¹¹ And I say unto you, That many shall come from the east and west, and shall sit down with Abraham, and Isaac, and Jacob, in the kingdom of heaven:

¹² but the children of the kingdom shall be cast out into outer darkness: there shall be weeping and gnashing of teeth.

¹³ And Jesus said unto the centurion, Go thy way; and as thou hast believed, *so* be it done unto thee. And his servant was healed in the self-same hour.

Jesus Heals Many People

*A*nd when Jesus was come into Peter's house, he saw his wife's mother laid, and sick of a fever.

¹⁵ And he touched her hand, and the fever left her: and she arose, and ministered unto them.

¹⁶ When the even was come, they brought unto him many that were possessed with devils: and he cast out the spirits with *his* word, and healed all that were sick:

¹⁷ that it might be fulfilled which was spoken by Isaiah the prophet, saying, Himself took our infirmities, and bare *our* sicknesses.

People Want to Follow Jesus

*N*ow when Jesus saw great multitudes about him, he gave commandment to depart unto the other side.

¹⁹ And a certain scribe came, and said unto him, Master, I will follow thee whithersoever thou goest.

²⁰ And Jesus saith unto him, The foxes have holes, and the birds of the air *have* nests; but the Son of man hath not where to lay *his* head.

²¹ And another of his disciples said unto him, Lord, suffer me first to go and bury my father.

²² But Jesus said unto him, Follow me; and let the dead bury their dead.

Jesus Calms a Storm

*A*nd when he was entered into a ship, his disciples followed him.

²⁴ And, behold, there arose a great tempest in the sea, insomuch that the ship was covered with the waves: but he was asleep.

25 And his disciples came to *him*, and awoke him, saying, Lord, save us: we perish.

26 And he saith unto them, Why are ye fearful, O ye of little faith? Then he arose, and rebuked the winds and the sea; and there was a great calm.

27 But the men marveled, saying, What manner of man is this, that even the winds and the sea obey him!

OLD TESTAMENT READING

*B*less the LORD, O my soul. O LORD my God, thou art very great; thou art clothed with honor and majesty.

2 Who coverest *thyself* with light as *with* a garment: who stretchest out the heavens like a curtain:

3 who layeth the beams of his chambers in the waters: who maketh the clouds his chariot: who walketh upon the wings of the wind:

4 who maketh his angels spirits; his ministers a flaming fire.

31 The glory of the LORD shall endure for ever: the LORD shall rejoice in his works.

32 He looketh on the earth, and it trembleth: he toucheth the hills, and they smoke.

33 I will sing unto the LORD as long as I live: I will sing praise to my God while I have my being.

Psalm 104:1–4, 31–33

INSIGHTS

*W*hen Jesus was on earth He displayed remarkable powers. He raised Lazarus from the dead and performed many other miracles. His contemporaries noted an element of His power that we sometimes do not—the power of His speaking. The gospel writers reported that Jesus did not speak like the scribes and the Pharisees but as one "having authority" (see Matt. 7:29). . . .

Behind the authority of Jesus stood the omnipotent power of God, the link to Jesus' divine authority. The very word authority hints at a connection to the word authorship. God is the omnipotent author of His creation. He is the omnipotent redeemer of His creation. He exercises omnipotent authority over His creation.

R. C. Sproul

PAUSE FOR REFLECTION

*I*n what ways did Jesus' followers see his powerful authority demonstrated? In what did the psalmist recognize his authority? What reveals his authority to you? Is his authority as real to you as to the army officer?

THURSDAY
God Forgives and Saves

Matthew 8:28—9:17

Jesus Heals Two Men with Demons

*A*nd when he was come to the other side into the country of the Gergesenes, there met him two possessed with devils, coming out of the tombs, exceeding fierce, so that no man might pass by that way.

²⁹ And, behold, they cried out, saying, What have we to do with thee, Jesus, thou Son of God? art thou come hither to torment us before the time?

³⁰ And there was a good way off from them a herd of many swine feeding.

³¹ So the devils besought him, saying, If thou cast us out, suffer us to go away into the herd of swine.

³² And he said unto them, Go. And when they were come out, they went into the herd of swine: and, behold, the whole herd of swine ran violently down a steep place into the sea, and perished in the waters.

³³ And they that kept them fled, and went their ways into the city, and told every thing, and what was befallen to the possessed of the devils.

³⁴ And, behold, the whole city came out to meet Jesus: and when they saw him, they besought *him* that he would depart out of their coasts.

Jesus Heals a Palsied Man

9 And he entered into a ship, and passed over, and came into his own city.

² And, behold, they brought to him a man sick of the palsy, lying on a bed: and Jesus seeing their faith said unto the sick of the palsy; Son, be of good cheer; thy sins be forgiven thee.

³ And, behold, certain of the scribes said within themselves, This *man* blasphemeth.

⁴ And Jesus knowing their thoughts said, Wherefore think ye evil in your hearts?

⁵ For whether is easier, to say, *Thy* sins be forgiven thee; or to say, Arise, and walk?

⁶ But that ye may know that the Son of man hath power on earth to forgive sins, (then saith he to the sick of the palsy,) Arise, take up thy bed, and go unto thine house.

⁷ And he arose, and departed to his house.

⁸ But when the multitudes saw *it*, they marveled, and glorified God, which had given such power unto men.

Jesus Chooses Matthew

*A*nd as Jesus passed forth from thence, he saw a man, named Matthew, sitting at the receipt of custom: and he saith unto him, Follow me. And he arose, and followed him.

¹⁰ And it came to pass, as Jesus sat at meat in the house, behold, many publicans and sinners came and sat down with him and his disciples.

¹¹ And when the Pharisees saw *it*, they said unto his disciples, Why eateth your Master with publicans and sinners?

¹² But when Jesus heard *that*, he said unto them, They that be whole need not a physician, but they that are sick.

¹³ But go ye and learn what *that*

meaneth, I will have mercy, and not sacrifice: for I am not come to call the righteous, but sinners to repentance.

Jesus' Disciples Are Criticized

Then came to him the disciples of John, saying, Why do we and the Pharisees fast oft, but thy disciples fast not?

15 And Jesus said unto them, Can the children of the bridechamber mourn, as long as the bridegroom is with them? but the days will come, when the bridegroom shall be taken from them, and then shall they fast.

16 No man putteth a piece of new cloth unto an old garment, for that which is put in to fill it up taketh from the garment, and the rent is made worse.

17 Neither do men put new wine into old bottles: else the bottles break, and the wine runneth out, and the bottles perish: but they put new wine into new bottles, and both are preserved.

OLD TESTAMENT READING

The LORD *is* merciful and gracious, slow to anger, and plenteous in mercy.

9 He will not always chide: neither will he keep *his anger* for ever.

10 He hath not dealt with us after our sins; nor rewarded us according to our iniquities.

11 For as the heaven is high above the earth, *so* great is his mercy toward them that fear him.

12 As far as the east is from the west, *so* far hath he removed our transgressions from us.

13 Like as a father pitieth *his* children, *so* the LORD pitieth them that fear him.

Psalm 103:8–13

INSIGHTS

Other faiths assume our ability to secure and retain God's favor by right action and give us detailed guidance as to how to do it; but Christianity has said that sin has so ruined us that we cannot do this. It is beyond our power to keep the law of God as we should; we are guilty and helpless, wholly unable to save ourselves, and so must be saved, if at all, by the action of another.

Other faiths direct us to follow the teaching of their founders—famous men long deceased; but Christianity, identifying its founder as God incarnate, who died for our sins and rose again to bestow forgiveness, proclaims him as alive and calls on us to trust him and his atoning work, making him the object of our worship and service. Redemption through the love of the Son of God, who became man, bore his Father's judgment on our sins, and rose from death to reign forever, is a theme without parallel in the world's religions.

Christianity proclaims that those who repent of sin and trust in Jesus Christ are created anew at the heart of their being by the Holy Spirit. They are united to Jesus Christ in his risen life, their inner nature is changed, so that their deepest impulse is not now to disobey God and serve self, but to deny self and obey God. There is nothing like this in any other religion.

J. I. Packer

APPLICATION

If Jesus is our example, what should our attitude toward sinners be?

21

FRIDAY

Jesus' Great Compassion for His Lost Sheep

Matthew 9:18—10:10

Jesus Gives Life to a Dead Girl and Heals a Sick Woman

*W*hile he spake these things unto them, behold, there came a certain ruler, and worshipped him, saying, My daughter is even now dead: but come and lay thy hand upon her, and she shall live.

¹⁹ And Jesus arose, and followed him, and *so did* his disciples.

²⁰ And, behold, a woman, which was diseased with an issue of blood twelve years, came behind *him*, and touched the hem of his garment:

²¹ for she said within herself, If I may but touch his garment, I shall be whole.

²² But Jesus turned him about, and when he saw her, he said, Daughter, be of good comfort; thy faith hath made thee whole. And the woman was made whole from that hour.

²³ And when Jesus came into the ruler's house, and saw the minstrels and the people making a noise,

²⁴ he said unto them, Give place: for the maid is not dead, but sleepeth. And they laughed him to scorn.

²⁵ But when the people were put forth, he went in, and took her by the hand, and the maid arose.

²⁶ And the fame hereof went abroad into all that land.

Jesus Heals More People

*A*nd when Jesus departed thence, two blind men followed him, crying,

and saying, *Thou* Son of David, have mercy on us.

²⁸ And when he was come into the house, the blind men came to him: and Jesus saith unto them, Believe ye that I am able to do this? They said unto him, Yea, Lord.

²⁹ Then touched he their eyes, saying, According to your faith be it unto you.

³⁰ And their eyes were opened; and Jesus straitly charged them, saying, See *that* no man know *it*.

³¹ But they, when they were departed, spread abroad his fame in all that country.

³² As they went out, behold, they brought to him a dumb man possessed with a devil.

³³ And when the devil was cast out, the dumb spake: and the multitudes marveled, saying, It was never so seen in Israel.

³⁴ But the Pharisees said, He casteth out devils through the prince of the devils.

³⁵ And Jesus went about all the cities and villages, teaching in their synagogues, and preaching the gospel of the kingdom, and healing every sickness and every disease among the people.

³⁶ But when he saw the multitudes, he was moved with compassion on them, because they fainted, and were scattered abroad, as sheep having no shepherd.

³⁷ Then saith he unto his disciples, The harvest truly *is* plenteous, but the laborers *are* few;

³⁸ pray ye therefore the Lord of the harvest, that he will send forth laborers into his harvest.

Jesus Sends Out His Apostles

10 And when he had called unto *him* his twelve disciples, he gave them power *against* unclean spirits, to cast them out, and to heal all manner of sickness and all manner of disease.

2 Now the names of the twelve apostles are these; The first, Simon, who is called Peter, and Andrew his brother; James *the son* of Zebedee, and John his brother;

3 Philip, and Bartholomew; Thomas, and Matthew the publican; James *the son* of Alpheus, and Lebbeus, whose surname was Thaddeus;

4 Simon the Canaanite, and Judas Iscariot, who also betrayed him.

5 These twelve Jesus sent forth, and commanded them, saying, Go not into the way of the Gentiles, and into *any* city of the Samaritans enter ye not:

6 But go rather to the lost sheep of the house of Israel.

7 And as ye go, preach, saying, The kingdom of heaven is at hand.

8 Heal the sick, cleanse the lepers, raise the dead, cast out devils: freely ye have received, freely give.

9 Provide neither gold, nor silver, nor brass in your purses;

10 nor scrip for *your* journey, neither two coats, neither shoes, nor yet staves: for the workman is worthy of his meat.

OLD TESTAMENT READING

I will feed my flock, and I will cause them to lie down, saith the Lord GOD. 16 I will seek that which was lost, and bring again that which was driven away, and will bind up *that which was* broken, and will strengthen that which was sick: but I will destroy the fat and strong; I will feed them with judgment.

Ezekiel 34:15–16

INSIGHTS

*T*he nature of God is to seek and to save sinners. From the opening pages of human history, it was God who sought the fallen couple in the garden. . . . The Almighty was portrayed as a Savior throughout the Old Testament (Psalm 106:21; Isaiah 43:11; Hosea 13:4), so it is appropriate that when Christ entered the world of men as God in human flesh, He was known first of all as a Savior.

Even His name was divinely chosen to be the name of a Savior. An angel told Joseph in a dream, "You shall call His name Jesus, for it is He who will save His people from their sins" (Matthew 1:21). The very heart of all redemptive teaching is that Jesus entered this world on a search-and-rescue mission for sinners. That truth is what characterizes the gospel as good news.

But it is good news only for those who perceive themselves as sinners. The unequivocal teaching of Jesus is that those who will not acknowledge and repent of their sin are beyond the reach of saving grace. All are sinners, but not all are willing to admit their depravity. If they do, He becomes their friend (cf. Matthew 11:19). Those who will not can know Him only as a Judge.

John F. MacArthur, Jr.

ACTION POINT

*I*n what ways is God's compassion for the lost expressed in these passages of Scripture? How does God want to care for his people? Thank him for the ways he has shown his compassion to you.

WEEKEND

The Price of Following Jesus

Matthew 10:11–40

*A*nd into whatsoever city or town ye shall enter, inquire who in it is worthy; and there abide till ye go thence.

12 And when ye come into an house, salute it.

13 And if the house be worthy, let your peace come upon it: but if it be not worthy, let your peace return to you.

14 And whosoever shall not receive you, nor hear your words, when ye depart out of that house or city, shake off the dust of your feet.

15 Verily I say unto you, It shall be more tolerable for the land of Sodom and Gomorrah in the day of judgment, than for that city.

Jesus Warns His Apostles

*B*ehold, I send you forth as sheep in the midst of wolves: be ye therefore wise as serpents, and harmless as doves.

17 But beware of men: for they will deliver you up to the councils, and they will scourge you in their synagogues;

18 And ye shall be brought before governors and kings for my sake, for a testimony against them and the Gentiles.

19 But when they deliver you up, take no thought how or what ye shall speak: for it shall be given you in that same hour what ye shall speak.

20 For it is not ye that speak, but the Spirit of your Father which speaketh in you.

21 And the brother shall deliver up the brother to death, and the father the child: and the children shall rise up against *their* parents, and cause them to be put to death.

22 And ye shall be hated of all *men* for my name's sake: but he that endureth to the end shall be saved.

23 But when they persecute you in this city, flee ye into another: for verily I say unto you, Ye shall not have gone over the cities of Israel, till the Son of man be come.

24 The disciple is not above *his* master, nor the servant above his lord.

25 It is enough for the disciple that he be as his master, and the servant as his lord. If they have called the master of the house Beelzebub, how much more *shall they call* them of his household?

Fear God, Not People

*F*ear them not therefore: for there is nothing covered, that shall not be revealed; and hid, that shall not be known.

27 What I tell you in darkness, *that* speak ye in light: and what ye hear in the ear, *that* preach ye upon the housetops.

28 And fear not them which kill the body, but are not able to kill the soul: but rather fear him which is able to destroy both soul and body in hell.

29 Are not two sparrows sold for a farthing? and one of them shall not fall on the ground without your Father.

30 But the very hairs of your head are all numbered.

31 Fear ye not therefore, ye are of more value than many sparrows.

Tell People About Your Faith

Whosoever therefore shall confess me before men, him will I confess also before my Father which is in heaven.

[33] But whosoever shall deny me before men, him will I also deny before my Father which is in heaven.

[34] Think not that I am come to send peace on earth: I came not to send peace, but a sword.

[35] For I am come to set a man at variance against his father, and the daughter against her mother, and the daughter-in-law against her mother-in-law.

[36] And a man's foes *shall be* they of his own household.

[37] He that loveth father or mother more than me is not worthy of me: and he that loveth son or daughter more than me is not worthy of me.

[38] And he that taketh not his cross, and followeth after me, is not worthy of me.

[39] He that findeth his life shall lose it: and he that loseth his life for my sake shall find it.

[40] He that receiveth you receiveth me; and he that receiveth me receiveth him that sent me.

OLD TESTAMENT READING

For since I spake, I cried out, I cried violence and spoil; because the word of the LORD was made a reproach unto me, and a derision, daily.

[9] Then I said, I will not make mention of him, nor speak any more in his name. But *his word* was in mine heart as a burning fire shut up in my bones, and I was weary with forbearing, and I could not *stay*.

Jeremiah 20:8–9

INSIGHTS

In the Sermon on the Mount Jesus said that those who suffer unjust treatment will have a "great" reward in heaven (see Matt. 5:10). The elect who have been abused, abandoned, stolen from, taken advantage of—all will be rewarded for their pain. . . .

God knows when we suffer unjustly. . . . God has not abandoned you to the whims and wishes of those who are more powerful. He knows when His children are overlooked for advancement because of their religious views. Young lady, He knows when less talented women are advanced past you because you refuse to compromise morally. He sees the abandoned mother who never knows from month to month if her estranged husband is going to send a check. God is taking it all in. He has already appointed a prosecuting attorney, a jury, and a judge. And they are all the same person—the Lord Jesus. On that court date He will bring about justice for His elect.

Charles Stanley

PAUSE FOR REFLECTION

How intensely does the desire to speak about Jesus burn within you? What price are you willing to pay to follow Jesus? What gives you comfort as you seek to follow him? What is your reward?

MONDAY

God Has Sent His Kingdom; Don't Reject It Foolishly!

Matthew 10:41—11:24

*H*e that receiveth a prophet in the name of a prophet shall receive a prophet's reward; and he that receiveth a righteous man in the name of a righteous man shall receive a righteous man's reward.

⁴²And whosoever shall give to drink unto one of these little ones a cup of cold *water* only in the name of a disciple, verily I say unto you, he shall in no wise lose his reward.

Jesus and John the Baptist

11 And it came to pass, when Jesus had made an end of commanding his twelve disciples, he departed thence to teach and to preach in their cities.

²Now when John had heard in the prison the works of Christ, he sent two of his disciples,

³and said unto him, Art thou he that should come, or do we look for another?

⁴Jesus answered and said unto them, Go and show John again those things which ye do hear and see:

⁵the blind receive their sight, and the lame walk, the lepers are cleansed, and the deaf hear, the dead are raised up, and the poor have the gospel preached to them.

⁶And blessed is *he*, whosoever shall not be offended in me.

⁷And as they departed, Jesus began to say unto the multitudes concerning John, What went ye out into the wilderness to see? A reed shaken with the wind?

⁸But what went ye out for to see? A man clothed in soft raiment? behold, they that wear soft *clothing* are in kings' houses.

⁹But what went ye out for to see? A prophet? yea, I say unto you, and more than a prophet.

¹⁰For this is *he*, of whom it is written, Behold, I send my messenger before thy face, which shall prepare thy way before thee.

¹¹Verily I say unto you, Among them that are born of women there hath not risen a greater than John the Baptist: notwithstanding he that is least in the kingdom of heaven is greater than he.

¹²And from the days of John the Baptist until now the kingdom of heaven suffereth violence, and the violent take it by force.

¹³For all the prophets and the law prophesied until John.

¹⁴And if ye will receive *it*, this is Elijah, which was for to come.

¹⁵He that hath ears to hear, let him hear.

¹⁶But whereunto shall I liken this generation? It is like unto children sitting in the markets, and calling unto their fellows,

¹⁷and saying, We have piped unto you, and ye have not danced; we have mourned unto you, and ye have not lamented.

¹⁸For John came neither eating nor drinking, and they say, He hath a devil.

¹⁹The Son of man came eating and drinking, and they say, Behold a man gluttonous, and a winebibber, a friend of publicans and sinners. But wisdom is justified of her children.

Jesus Warns Unbelievers

*T*hen began he to upbraid the cities wherein most of his mighty works were done, because they repented not:

²¹ Woe unto thee, Chorazin! woe unto thee, Bethsaida! for if the mighty works, which were done in you, had been done in Tyre and Sidon, they would have repented long ago in sackcloth and ashes.

²² But I say unto you, It shall be more tolerable for Tyre and Sidon at the day of judgment, than for you.

²³ And thou, Capernaum, which art exalted unto heaven, shalt be brought down to hell: for if the mighty works, which have been done in thee, had been done in Sodom, it would have remained until this day.

²⁴ But I say unto you, That it shall be more tolerable for the land of Sodom in the day of judgment, than for thee.

OLD TESTAMENT READING

*H*ow long, ye simple ones, will ye love simplicity? and the scorners delight in their scorning, and fools hate knowledge?

²⁴ Because I have called, and ye refused; I have stretched out my hand, and no man regarded;

²⁵ But ye have set at nought all my counsel, and would none of my reproof:

²⁶ I also will laugh at your calamity; I will mock when your fear cometh;

²⁸ Then shall they call upon me, but I will not answer; they shall seek me early, but they shall not find me:

²⁹ for that they hated knowledge, and did not choose the fear of the LORD:

³⁰ They would none of my counsel:

they despised all my reproof.

³¹ Therefore shall they eat of the fruit of their own way, and be filled with their own devices.

Proverbs 1:22, 24–26, 28–31

INSIGHTS

*G*enerally speaking, God's kingdom is a synonym for God's rule. Those who choose to live in His kingdom (though still very much alive on Planet Earth) choose to live under His authority. . . .

. . . The kingdom is the invisible realm where God rules as supreme authority. That's helpful news. The bad news is that we, by nature, don't want Him to rule over us; we much prefer to please ourselves. . . .

. . . To put it bluntly, we don't want anybody other than ourselves ruling over us! Much like those people in a story Jesus once told, "We do not want this man to reign over us!" (Luke 19:14). Not until we experience a spiritual rebirth will we submit to God's rule.

Charles Swindoll

PAUSE FOR REFLECTION

*W*hat is the penalty for rejecting God's wisdom and knowledge? What does God promise to those who listen to him? What change occurs in those who accept God's kingdom? Has that change occurred in you?

TUESDAY

God Wants Faithful Love More than Sacrifices

Matthew 11:25—12:21

Jesus Offers Rest to People

At that time Jesus answered and said, I thank thee, O Father, Lord of heaven and earth, because thou hast hid these things from the wise and prudent, and hast revealed them unto babes.

²⁶ Even so, Father: for so it seemed good in thy sight.

²⁷ All things are delivered unto me of my Father: and no man knoweth the Son, but the Father; neither knoweth any man the Father, save the Son, and *he* to whomsoever the Son will reveal *him*.

²⁸ Come unto me, all *ye* that labor and are heavy laden, and I will give you rest.

²⁹ Take my yoke upon you, and learn of me; for I am meek and lowly in heart: and ye shall find rest unto your souls.

³⁰ For my yoke *is* easy, and my burden is light.

Jesus Is Lord of the Sabbath

12 At that time Jesus went on the sabbath day through the corn; and his disciples were ahungered, and began to pluck the ears of corn, and to eat.

² But when the Pharisees saw *it*, they said unto him, Behold, thy disciples do that which is not lawful to do upon the sabbath day.

³ But he said unto them, Have ye not read what David did, when he was ahungered, and they that were with him;

⁴ how he entered into the house of God, and did eat the showbread, which was not lawful for him to eat, neither for them which were with him, but only for the priests?

⁵ Or have ye not read in the law, how that on the sabbath days the priests in the temple profane the sabbath, and are blameless?

⁶ But I say unto you, That in this place is *one* greater than the temple.

⁷ But if ye had known what *this* meaneth, I will have mercy, and not sacrifice, ye would not have condemned the guiltless.

⁸ For the Son of man is Lord even of the sabbath day.

Jesus Heals a Man's Hand

And when he was departed thence, he went into their synagogue:

¹⁰ and, behold, there was a man which had *his* hand withered. And they asked him, saying, Is it lawful to heal on the sabbath days? that they might accuse him.

¹¹ And he said unto them, What man shall there be among you, that shall have one sheep, and if it fall into a pit on the sabbath day, will he not lay hold on it, and lift *it* out?

¹² How much then is a man better than a sheep? Wherefore it is lawful to do well on the sabbath days.

¹³ Then saith he to the man, Stretch forth thine hand. And he stretched *it* forth; and it was restored whole, like as the other.

¹⁴ Then the Pharisees went out, and held a council against him, how they might destroy him.

Jesus Is God's Chosen Servant

*B*ut when Jesus knew *it*, he withdrew himself from thence: and great multitudes followed him, and he healed them all;

¹⁶ and charged them that they should not make him known:

¹⁷ that it might be fulfilled which was spoken by Isaiah the prophet, saying,

¹⁸ Behold my servant, whom I have chosen; my beloved, in whom my soul is well pleased: I will put my spirit upon him, and he shall show judgment to the Gentiles.

¹⁹ He shall not strive, nor cry; neither shall any man hear his voice in the streets.

²⁰ A bruised reed shall he not break, and smoking flax shall he not quench, till he send forth judgment unto victory.

²¹ And in his name shall the Gentiles trust.

OLD TESTAMENT READING

*T*he sacrifices of God *are* a broken spirit: a broken and a contrite heart, O God, thou wilt not despise.

Psalm 51:17

INSIGHTS

*L*ord," I said, "I want to be your man, not my own.
So to you I give my money, my car—even my home."
Then, smug and content, I relaxed with a smile
And whispered to God, "I bet it's been a while,
Since anyone has given so much —so freely?"
His answer surprised me. He replied, "Not really."

"Not a day has gone by since the beginning of time,
That someone hasn't offered meager nickels and dimes,
Golden altars and crosses, contributions and penance,
Stone monuments and steeples; but why not repentance?

"Your lips know no prayers. Your eyes, no compassion.
But you will go to church (when church-going's in fashion).

"Just give me a tear—a heart ready to mold.
And I'll give you a mission, a message so bold—
That a fire will be stirred where there was only death,
And your heart will be flamed by my life and my breath."

I stuck my hands in my pockets and kicked at the dirt.
It's tough to be corrected (I guess my feelings were hurt).
But it was worth the struggle to realize the thought.
That the cross isn't for sale and Christ's blood can't be bought.

Max Lucado

APPLICATION

*W*hat does God want from his people? Be specific! Think about what it means for God to want those things from you. Pray that you will understand what he wants and that your heart will be open to obey him.

WEDNESDAY

*Our Words Reveal What Is
in Our Hearts*

Matthew 12:22–45

Jesus' Power Is from God

*T*hen was brought unto him one possessed with a devil, blind, and dumb: and he healed him, insomuch that the blind and dumb both spake and saw.

23 And all the people were amazed, and said, Is not this the Son of David?

24 But when the Pharisees heard *it*, they said, This *fellow* doth not cast out devils, but by Beelzebub the prince of the devils.

25 And Jesus knew their thoughts, and said unto them, Every kingdom divided against itself is brought to desolation; and every city or house divided against itself shall not stand:

26 And if Satan cast out Satan, he is divided against himself; how shall then his kingdom stand?

27 And if I by Beelzebub cast out devils, by whom do your children cast *them* out? therefore they shall be your judges.

28 But if I cast out devils by the Spirit of God, then the kingdom of God is come unto you.

29 Or else how can one enter into a strong man's house, and spoil his goods, except he first bind the strong man? and then he will spoil his house.

30 He that is not with me is against me; and he that gathereth not with me scattereth abroad.

31 Wherefore I say unto you, All manner of sin and blasphemy shall be forgiven unto men: but the blasphemy *against* the *Holy* Ghost shall not be forgiven unto men.

32 And whosoever speaketh a word against the Son of man, it shall be forgiven him: but whosoever speaketh against the Holy Ghost, it shall not be forgiven him, neither in this world, neither in the *world* to come.

People Know You by Your Words

*E*ither make the tree good, and his fruit good; or else make the tree corrupt, and his fruit corrupt: for the tree is known by *his* fruit.

34 O generation of vipers, how can ye, being evil, speak good things? for out of the abundance of the heart the mouth speaketh.

35 A good man out of the good treasure of the heart bringeth forth good things: and an evil man out of the evil treasure bringeth forth evil things.

36 But I say unto you, That every idle word that men shall speak, they shall give account thereof in the day of judgment.

37 For by thy words thou shalt be justified, and by thy words thou shalt be condemned.

The People Ask for a Miracle

*T*hen certain of the scribes and of the Pharisees answered, saying, Master, we would see a sign from thee.

39 But he answered and said unto them, An evil and adulterous generation seeketh after a sign; and there shall no sign be given to it, but

the sign of the prophet Jonah:
40 for as Jonah was three days and three nights in the whale's belly; so shall the Son of man be three days and three nights in the heart of the earth.
41 The men of Nineveh shall rise in judgment with this generation, and shall condemn it: because they repented at the preaching of Jonah; and, behold, a greater than Jonah *is* here.
42 The queen of the south shall rise up in the judgment with this generation, and shall condemn it: for she came from the uttermost parts of the earth to hear the wisdom of Solomon; and, behold, a greater than Solomon *is* here.

People Today Are Full of Evil

When the unclean spirit is gone out of a man, he walketh through dry places, seeking rest, and findeth none.
44 Then he saith, I will return into my house from whence I came out; and when he is come, he findeth *it* empty, swept, and garnished.
45 The he goeth, and taketh with himself seven other spirits more wicked than himself, and they enter in and dwell there: and the last *state* of that man is worse than the first. Even so shall it be also unto this wicked generation.

OLD TESTAMENT READING

The tongue of the just *is as* choice silver: the heart of the wicked *is* little worth.
21 The lips of the righteous feed many: but fools die for want of wisdom.

Proverbs 10:20–21

INSIGHTS

The tongue is the indicator of the person. What we talk about all the time is what we love. The words we use and the words we don't use define what we are thinking, feeling, and becoming. . . .

We Christians must learn to undergo rigorous self-examination; we must honestly discern what we are really saying if we are going to understand who we are. . . .

We must listen closely to the inner reminder of this Holy Spirit. In essence, what we are doing is sticking out our tongues for the Great Physician to examine. . . . If some symptoms indicate mouth disease, we must confess to him the words that were unpleasing to him and ask forgiveness. Then we should take a dose of medicine and read from those Scriptures that emphasize healthy mouth habits. We should place the medicinal verses dealing with word usage under our tongues nightly, and let them accomplish a cathartic cleaning as we sleep so that tomorrow we can begin the day with renewed strength to speak words of life.

Karen Burton Mains

ACTION POINT

Are you intimidated by the thought of explaining every careless word you have said? Listen to your words today and write down what they reveal about your heart. Pray that your words will prove your heart to be innocent before God.

THURSDAY

Not Everyone Who Hears Understands

Matthew 12:46—13:17

Jesus' True Family

*W*hile he yet talked to the people, behold, *his* mother and his brethren stood without, desiring to speak with him.

⁴⁷ Then one said unto him, Behold, thy mother and thy brethren stand without, desiring to speak with thee.

⁴⁸ But he answered and said unto him that told him, Who is my mother? and who are my brethren?

⁴⁹ And he stretched forth his hand toward his disciples, and said, Behold my mother and my brethren!

⁵⁰ For whosoever shall do the will of my Father which is in heaven, the same is my brother, and sister, and mother.

A Parable About Planting Seed

13 The same day went Jesus out of the house, and sat by the sea side.

² And great multitudes were gathered together unto him, so that he went into a ship, and sat; and the whole multitude stood on the shore.

³ And he spake many things unto them in parables, saying, Behold, a sower went forth to sow;

⁴ and when he sowed, some *seeds* fell by the wayside, and the fowls came and devoured them up:

⁵ some fell upon stony places, where they had not much earth: and forth-

with they sprung up, because they had no deepness of earth:

⁶ and when the sun was up, they were scorched; and because they had no root, they withered away.

⁷ And some fell among thorns; and the thorns sprung up, and choked them:

⁸ but other fell into good ground, and brought forth fruit, some a hundredfold, some sixtyfold, some thirtyfold.

⁹ Who hath ears to hear, let him hear.

Why Jesus Used Parables to Teach

*A*nd the disciples came, and said unto him, Why speakest thou unto them in parables?

¹¹ He answered and said unto them, Because it is given unto you to know the mysteries of the kingdom of heaven, but to them it is not given.

¹² For whosoever hath, to him shall be given, and he shall have more abundance: but whosoever hath not, from him shall be taken away even that he hath.

¹³ Therefore speak I to them in parables: because they seeing see not; and hearing they hear not, neither do they understand.

¹⁴ And in them is fulfilled the prophecy of Isaiah, which saith, By hearing ye shall hear, and shall not understand; and seeing ye shall see, and shall not perceive:

¹⁵ for this people's heart is waxed gross, and *their* ears are dull of hearing, and their eyes they have closed; lest at any time they should see with *their* eyes and hear with *their* ears, and should understand with *their* heart, and should be converted, and I should heal them.

¹⁶ But blessed *are* your eyes, for they see: and your ears, for they hear.

[17] For verily I say unto you, That many prophets and righteous *men* have desired to see *those things* which ye see, and have not seen *them*; and to hear *those things* which ye hear, and have not heard *them*.

O how love I thy law! It *is* my meditation all the day.
[102] I have not departed from thy judgments: for thou hast taught me.
[103] How sweet are thy words unto my taste! *yea, sweeter* than honey to my mouth.
[104] Through thy precepts I get understanding: therefore I hate every false way.
[105] Thy word *is* a lamp unto my feet, and a light unto my path.
[106] I have sworn, and I will perform *it*, that I will keep thy righteous judgments.

Psalm 119:97, 102–106

*B*ut they refused to hearken, and pulled away the shoulder, and stopped their ears, that they should not hear.
[12] Yea, they made their hearts *as* an adamant stone, lest they should hear the law, and the words which the LORD of hosts hath sent in his Spirit by the former prophets: therefore came a great wrath from the LORD of hosts.

Zechariah 7:11–12

*O*ur Lord warns that the human heart can be so pounded and beaten down with the traffic of sin that it becomes completely insensitive to the gospel. This is the heart that knows no repentance, no sorrow over sin, no guilt, and no concern for the things of God. It allows itself to be trampled by an endless procession of evil thoughts, cherished sins, and ungodly activities. It is careless, callous, indifferent, never broken up or softened by conviction or sorrow for wrongdoing. This is the heart of the fool described in Proverbs. The fool hates knowledge, and resists instruction. The fool despises wisdom and says in his heart there is no God. He will not hear. His mind is closed. And he does not want to be bothered with a gospel invitation.

Many people have hearts like that. You can shower them with seed, but it just lies there. It does not penetrate. And it does not stay very long before Satan comes and takes it away completely. Each time you try to witness to such a person, you must start again at the beginning.

Dry, hard, soil on the edge of the field does not necessarily signify someone who is anti-religious. Some of the hardest individuals in the world remain on the fringes of true religion. But because sin has so hardened their hearts, they are utterly unproductive and unresponsive to God.

John F. MacArthur, Jr.

*H*ow are the teachings of Jesus received by those who follow him? By those who reject him? Why is it that some people are unable to understand God's words? Pray for a soft heart that wants to understand all that God teaches.

FRIDAY

Hide God's Teachings in Your Heart

Matthew 13:18–43

Jesus Explains the Parable

*H*ear ye therefore the parable of the sower.

¹⁹ When any one heareth the word of the kingdom, and understandeth *it* not, then cometh the wicked one, and catcheth away that which was sown in his heart. This is he which received seed by the wayside.

²⁰ But he that received the seed into stony places, the same is he that heareth the word, and anon with joy receiveth it;

²¹ yet hath he not root in himself, but dureth for a while: for when tribulation or persecution ariseth because of the word, by and by he is offended.

²² He also that received seed among the thorns is he that heareth the word; and the care of this world, and the deceitfulness of riches, choke the word, and he becometh unfruitful.

²³ But he that received seed into the good ground is he that heareth the word, and understandeth *it*; which also beareth fruit, and bringeth forth, some a hundredfold, some sixty, some thirty.

A Parable About Wheat and Weeds

*A*nother parable put he forth unto them, saying, The kingdom of heaven is likened unto a man which sowed good seed in his field:

²⁵ But while men slept, his enemy came and sowed tares among the wheat, and went his way.

²⁶ But when the blade was sprung up, and brought forth fruit, then appeared the tares also.

²⁷ So the servants of the householder came and said unto him, Sir, didst not thou sow good seed in thy field? from whence then hath it tares?

²⁸ He said unto them, An enemy hath done this. The servants said unto him, Wilt thou then that we go and gather them up?

²⁹ But he said, Nay; lest while ye gather up the tares, ye root up also the wheat with them.

³⁰ Let both grow together until the harvest: and in the time of harvest I will say to the reapers, Gather ye together first the tares, and bind them in bundles to burn them: but gather the wheat into my barn.

Parables of Mustard Seed and Yeast

*A*nother parable put he forth unto them, saying, The kingdom of heaven is like to a grain of mustard seed, which a man took, and sowed in his field:

³² which indeed is the least of all seeds: but when it is grown, it is the greatest among herbs, and becometh a tree, so that the birds of the air come and lodge in the branches thereof.

³³ Another parable spake he unto them; The kingdom of heaven is like unto leaven, which a woman took, and hid in three measures of meal, till the whole was leavened.

³⁴ All these things spake Jesus unto the multitude in parables; and without a parable spake he not unto them:

³⁵ that it might be fulfilled which was

spoken by the prophet, saying, I will open my mouth in parables; I will utter things which have been kept secret from the foundation of the world.

Jesus Explains About the Weeds

Then Jesus sent the multitude away, and went into the house: and his disciples came unto him, saying, Declare unto us the parable of the tares of the field.

[37] He answered and said unto them, He that soweth the good seed is the Son of man;

[38] the field is the world; the good seed are the children of the kingdom; but the tares are the children of the wicked one;

[39] the enemy that sowed them is the devil; the harvest is the end of the world; and the reapers are the angels.

[40] As therefore the tares are gathered and burned in the fire; so shall it be in the end of this world.

[41] The Son of man shall send forth his angels, and they shall gather out of his kingdom all things that offend, and them which do iniquity;

[42] and shall cast them into a furnace of fire: there shall be wailing and gnashing of teeth.

[43] Then shall the righteous shine forth as the sun in the kingdom of their Father. Who hath ears to hear, let him hear.

OLD TESTAMENT READING

Therefore shall ye lay up these my words in your heart and in your soul, and bind them for a sign upon your hand, that they may be as frontlets between your eyes.

[19] And ye shall teach them your children, speaking of them when thou sittest in thine house, and when thou walkest by the way, when thou liest down, and when thou risest up.

[20] And thou shalt write them upon the doorposts of thine house, and upon thy gates:

[21] that your days may be multiplied, and the days of your children, in the land which the LORD sware unto your fathers to give them, as the days of heaven upon the earth.

Deuteronomy 11:18–21

INSIGHTS

H. A. Ironside told of a godly man named Andrew Frazer who had come to southern California to recover from a serious illness. Though this Irishman was quite weak, he opened his worn Bible and began expounding the truths of God's Word in a way that Ironside had never heard before. So moved by Frazer's words was Ironside that his curiosity drove him to ask, "Where did you learn these things? Did you learn them in some college or seminary?" The sickly man said, "My dear young man, I learned these things on my knees on the mud floor of a little sod cottage in the north of Ireland. There with my open Bible before me I used to kneel for hours at a time and ask the Spirit of God to reveal Christ to my soul and to open the Word to my heart. He taught me more on my knees on that mud floor than I ever could have learned in all the seminaries or colleges in the world."

Woodrow Kroll

APPLICATION

What are you willing to do in order to remember God's Word with your whole heart?

WEEKEND

Jesus Tells His Followers About God's Kingdom

Matthew 13:44—14:12

Parables of a Treasure and a Pearl

*A*gain, the kingdom of heaven is like unto treasure hid in a field; the which when a man hath found, he hideth, and for joy thereof goeth and selleth all that he hath, and buyeth that field.

⁴⁵ Again, the kingdom of heaven is like unto a merchantman, seeking goodly pearls:

⁴⁶ who, when he had found one pearl of great price, went and sold all that he had, and bought it.

A Parable of a Fishing Net

*A*gain, the kingdom of heaven is like unto a net, that was cast into the sea, and gathered of every kind:

⁴⁸ which, when it was full, they drew to shore, and sat down, and gathered the good into vessels, but cast the bad away.

⁴⁹ So shall it be at the end of the world: the angels shall come forth, and sever the wicked from among the just,

⁵⁰ and shall cast them into the furnace of fire: there shall be wailing and gnashing of teeth.

⁵¹ Jesus saith unto them, Have ye understood all these things? They say unto him, Yea, Lord.

⁵² Then said he unto them, Therefore every scribe *which is* instructed unto the kingdom of heaven is like unto a man *that is* a householder, which bringeth forth out of his treasure *things* new and old.

Jesus Goes to His Hometown

*A*nd it came to pass, *that* when Jesus had finished these parables, he departed thence.

⁵⁴ And when he was come into his own country, he taught them in their synagogue, insomuch that they were astonished, and said, Whence hath this *man* this wisdom, and *these* mighty works?

⁵⁵ Is not this the carpenter's son? is not his mother called Mary? and his brethren, James, and Joses, and Simon, and Judas?

⁵⁶ And his sisters, are they not all with us? Whence then hath this *man* all these things?

⁵⁷ And they were offended in him. But Jesus said unto them, A prophet is not without honor, save in his own country, and in his own house.

⁵⁸ And he did not many mighty works there because of their unbelief.

How John the Baptist Was Killed

14 At that time Herod the tetrarch heard of the fame of Jesus,

² and said unto his servants, This is John the Baptist; he is risen from the dead; and therefore mighty works do show forth themselves in him.

³ For Herod had laid hold on John, and bound him, and put *him* in prison for Herodias' sake, his brother Philip's wife.

⁴ For John said unto him, It is not lawful for thee to have her.

⁵ And when he would have put him to death, he feared the multitude, because they counted him as a prophet.

⁶ But when Herod's birthday was kept, the daughter of Herodias danced before them, and pleased Herod.

⁷ Whereupon he promised with an oath to give her whatsoever she would ask.

⁸ And she, being before instructed of her mother, said, Give me here John Baptist's head in a charger.

⁹ And the king was sorry: nevertheless for the oath's sake, and them which sat with him at meat, he commanded *it* to be given *her*.

¹⁰ And he sent, and beheaded John in the prison.

¹¹ And his head was brought in a charger, and given to the damsel: and she brought *it* to her mother.

¹² And his disciples came, and took up the body, and buried it, and went and told Jesus.

OLD TESTAMENT READING

*A*ll thy works shall praise thee, O Lord; and thy saints shall bless thee.

¹¹ They shall speak of the glory of thy kingdom, and talk of thy power;

¹² to make known to the sons of men his mighty acts, and the glorious majesty of his kingdom.

¹³ Thy kingdom *is* an everlasting kingdom.

Psalm 145:10–13a

INSIGHTS

*D*uring the Civil War, the army of the Union and the army of the Confederacy were locked in a vicious battle to the death just outside the city of Richmond. As night fell after the first day of the battle, cheers were heard from the Confederate lines. When General Grant asked what was going on behind the enemy's line, he was told that the wife of General George Pickett had given birth to a baby boy, and that his troops were celebrating. . . .

Upon receiving the news, General Grant ordered bonfires to be lit and a toast to be given. Cheers and hoorahs rang out all night long. For a few hours, the shooting stopped and warring soldiers were drawn together for a birthday party. The birth of Pickett's son only temporarily stopped a war. But it stands as evidence of what a good birthday party can do. . . .

The good news is that another Son was born, and there were some who stopped what they were doing and enjoyed a little bit of peace for just a little while. There was singing in the sky—at least some shepherds said there was. And some strange visitors came looking for a baby whom they nicknamed the Prince of Peace. Everyone has not gotten the message, so not everyone knows about the baby. But the baby started a movement and we know that someday everyone will come to His party and call Him the Lord of the feast.

There's a great day coming when the world will change. What started as a birthday party will end with a wedding feast. We will call it the "Kingdom of God." We must pray for it, and we must work for it.

Tony Campolo

PAUSE FOR REFLECTION

*W*hat do you understand about God's kingdom from the three images Jesus presented to his followers? Is the coming of God's kingdom exciting enough for you to stop doing your own thing and celebrate?

MONDAY

Trust in God
to Meet Our Needs

Matthew 14:13–36

More than Five Thousand Fed

When Jesus heard *of it*, he departed thence by ship into a desert place apart: and when the people had heard *thereof*, they followed him on foot out of the cities.

¹⁴ And Jesus went forth, and saw a great multitude, and was moved with compassion toward them, and he healed their sick.

¹⁵ And when it was evening, his disciples came to him, saying, This is a desert place, and the time is now past; send the multitude away, that they may go into the villages, and buy themselves victuals.

¹⁶ But Jesus said unto them, They need not depart; give ye them to eat.

¹⁷ And they say unto him, We have here but five loaves, and two fishes.

¹⁸ He said, Bring them hither to me.

¹⁹ And he commanded the multitude to sit down on the grass, and took the five loaves, and the two fishes, and looking up to heaven, he blessed, and brake, and gave the loaves to *his* disciples, and the disciples to the multitude.

²⁰ And they did all eat, and were filled: and they took up of the fragments that remained twelve baskets full.

²¹ And they that had eaten were about five thousand men, beside women and children.

Jesus Walks on the Water

And straightway Jesus constrained his disciples to get into a ship, and to go before him unto the other side, while he sent the multitudes away.

²³ And when he had sent the multitudes away, he went up into a mountain apart to pray: and when the evening was come, he was there alone.

²⁴ But the ship was now in the midst of the sea, tossed with waves: for the wind was contrary.

²⁵ And in the fourth watch of the night Jesus went unto them, walking on the sea.

²⁶ And when the disciples saw him walking on the sea, they were troubled, saying, It is a spirit; and they cried out for fear.

²⁷ But straightway Jesus spake unto them, saying, Be of good cheer; it is I; be not afraid.

²⁸ And Peter answered him and said, Lord, if it be thou, bid me come unto thee on the water.

²⁹ And he said, Come. And when Peter was come down out of the ship, he walked on the water, to go to Jesus.

³⁰ But when he saw the wind boisterous, he was afraid; and beginning to sink, he cried, saying, Lord, save me.

³¹ And immediately Jesus stretched forth *his* hand, and caught him, and said unto him, O thou of little faith, wherefore didst thou doubt?

³² And when they were come into the ship, the wind ceased.

³³ Then they that were in the ship came and worshipped him, saying, Of a truth thou art the Son of God.

³⁴ And when they were gone over, they came into the land of Gennesaret.

35 And when the men of that place had knowledge of him, they sent out into all that country round about, and brought unto him all that were diseased;

36 and besought him that they might only touch the hem of his garment: and as many as touched were made perfectly whole.

---

*T*hou wilt keep *him* in perfect peace, *whose* mind *is* stayed *on thee*: because he trusteth in thee.

4 Trust ye in the LORD for ever: for in the LORD JEHOVAH *is* everlasting strength.

Isaiah 26:3–4

*G*racious is the LORD, and righteous; yea, our God *is* merciful.

6 The LORD preserveth the simple: I was brought low, and he helped me.

7 Return unto thy rest, O my soul; for the LORD hath dealt bountifully with thee.

8 For Thou hast delivered my soul from death, mine eyes from tears, *and* my feet from falling.

9 I will walk before the LORD in the land of the living

Psalm 116:5–9

his situation to the Lord. *Faith replaced fear. He PUT his trust in the Lord. This was an act of his will. "In God have I put my trust: I will not be afraid what man can do unto me" (Ps. 56:11).*

Freedom from fear is the result of confidence and trust in God. We may be helpless against fear, but God is not. When trusting God, there is nothing to fear.

Faith is more than believing what God can do. It is trust in the Person of God Himself. "But without faith it is impossible to please him: for he that cometh to God must believe that He IS, and that He is a rewarder of them that diligently seek Him" (Heb. 11:6). . . .

One day a father discovered his little boy had climbed an old tree. The limbs were beginning to break under the boy's weight. The father held up his arms and called, "Jump! I'll catch you." The little son considered the offer for a moment. Then, as more limbs began to break, he said, "Shall I let go of everything, Daddy, and trust you?"

What a lesson for us. Our Heavenly Father wants us to let go of everything and trust Him.

Millie Stamm

---

*T*oday many fears fill our lives. We fear poverty, sickness, loneliness, death. We fear the dangers of the night and the pressures of the day.

David learned that the only way to be released from fears was to TRUST the Lord. "What time I am afraid, I will trust in thee." He changed the focus of his eyes from

*T*hink about the fears and needs in your life. In what ways have you "let go of everything" and put your trust in God to meet those needs? Pray or write your own psalm of trust to God. Praise him for his faithfulness to you.

TUESDAY

Warnings Against Hypocrisy

Matthew 15:1–31

Obey God's Law

15 Then came to Jesus scribes and Pharisees, which were of Jerusalem, saying,

2 Why do thy disciples transgress the tradition of the elders? for they wash not their hands when they eat bread.

3 But he answered and said unto them, Why do ye also transgress the commandment of God by your tradition?

4 For God commanded, saying, Honor thy father and mother: and, He that curseth father or mother, let him die the death.

5 But ye say, Whosoever shall say to *his* father or *his* mother, *It is* a gift, by whatsoever thou mightest be profited by me;

6 and honor not his father or his mother, *he shall be free.* Thus have ye made the commandment of God of none effect by your tradition.

7 *Ye* hypocrites, well did Isaiah prophesy of you, saying,

8 This people draweth nigh unto me with their mouth, and honoreth me with *their* lips; but their heart is far from me.

9 But in vain they do worship me, teaching *for* doctrines the commandments of men.

10 And he called the multitude, and said unto them, Hear, and understand:

11 Not that which goeth into the mouth defileth a man; but that which cometh out of the mouth, this defileth a man.

12 Then came his disciples, and said unto him, Knowest thou that the Pharisees were offended, after they heard this saying?

13 But he answered and said, Every plant, which my heavenly Father hath not planted, shall be rooted up.

14 Let them alone: they be blind leaders of the blind. And if the blind lead the blind, both shall fall into the ditch.

15 Then answered Peter and said unto him, Declare unto us this parable.

16 And Jesus said, Are ye also yet without understanding?

17 Do not ye yet understand, that whatsoever entereth in at the mouth goeth into the belly, and is cast out into the draught?

18 But those things which proceed out of the mouth come forth from the heart; and they defile the man.

19 For out of the heart proceed evil thoughts, murders, adulteries, fornications, thefts, false witness, blasphemies:

20 these are *the things* which defile a man: but to eat with unwashen hands defileth not a man.

Jesus Helps a Canaanite Woman

*T*hen Jesus went thence, and departed into the coasts of Tyre and Sidon.

22 And, behold, a woman of Canaan came out of the same coasts, and cried unto him, saying, Have mercy on me, O Lord, *thou* Son of David; my daughter is grievously vexed with a devil.

23 But he answered her not a word. And his disciples came and besought him, saying, Send her away; for she crieth after us.

24 But he answered and said, I am not sent but unto the lost sheep of the house of Israel.

25 Then came she and worshipped him, saying, Lord, help me.

26 But he answered and said, It is not meet to take the children's bread, and to cast *it* to dogs.

27 And she said, Truth, Lord: yet the dogs eat of the crumbs which fall from their masters' table.

28 Then Jesus answered and said unto her, O woman, great *is* thy faith: be it unto thee even as thou wilt. And her daughter was made whole from that very hour.

Jesus Heals Many People

*A*nd Jesus departed from thence, and came nigh unto the sea of Galilee; and went up into a mountain, and sat down there.

30 And great multitudes came unto him, having with them *those that were* lame, blind, dumb, maimed, and many others, and cast them down at Jesus' feet; and he healed them:

31 insomuch that the multitude wondered, when they saw the dumb to speak, the maimed to be whole, the lame to walk, and the blind to see: and they glorified the God of Israel.

OLD TESTAMENT READING

*H*e that hateth dissembleth with his lips, and layeth up deceit within him;

25 when he speaketh fair, believe him not: for *there are* seven abominations in his heart.

26 *Whose* hatred is covered by deceit, his wickedness shall be showed before the *whole* congregation.

Proverbs 26:24–26

INSIGHTS

*I*n the ancient Greek plays, the actors were called hypocrites. On the stage they professed to be something they weren't. Unfortunately, there are many people who go through life playacting. They profess to be something they are not. They are hypocrites. They fool no one with this false veneer, this facade, this hypocrisy, except themselves. What they really are is well-known to God and their acquaintances with the result that they are displeasing to both. . . .

. . . Through the years innumerable people have gone to a Christless grave to spend eternity in hell because of the hypocrisy of many who call themselves Christians.

It is said that Thomas K. Beecher could not stand deceit of any kind. When he discovered that the clock in his church ran habitually either too slow or too fast, he reportedly put a placard on the wall above it that read in large letters, "Don't blame my hands—the trouble lies deeper." Don't make the mistake of promising to be a better Christian. The trouble is not on the outside; it is in the inner recesses of a person's being. Only Christ can cure this malady. This He will do if a person in genuine repentance seeks His forgiveness and turns himself over to Him in simple childlike faith.

Harold Fickett

APPLICATION

*W*hy is hypocrisy so displeasing to God? Where does hypocrisy originate? What is the cure for hypocrisy? What hypocrisy in your life needs to be healed by Christ's forgiveness?

WEDNESDAY

Jesus Offers Real Food

Matthew 15:32—16:20

More than Four Thousand Fed

*T*hen Jesus called his disciples *unto him*, and said, I have compassion on the multitude, because they continue with me now three days, and have nothing to eat: and I will not send them away fasting, lest they faint in the way.

33 And his disciples say unto him, Whence should we have so much bread in the wilderness, as to fill so great a multitude?

34 And Jesus saith unto them, How many loaves have ye? And they said, Seven, and a few little fishes.

35 And he commanded the multitude to sit down on the ground.

36 And he took the seven loaves and the fishes, and gave thanks, and brake *them*, and gave to his disciples, and the disciples to the multitude.

37 And they did all eat, and were filled: and they took up of the broken *meat* that was left seven baskets full.

38 And they that did eat were four thousand men, beside women and children.

39 And he sent away the multitude, and took ship, and came into the coasts of Magdala.

The Leaders Ask for a Miracle

16 The Pharisees also with the Sadducees came, and tempting desired him that he would show them a sign from heaven.

2 He answered and said unto them, When it is evening, ye say, *It will be* fair weather: for the sky is red.

3 And in the morning, *It will be* foul weather today: for the sky is red and lowering. O *ye* hypocrites, ye can discern the face of the sky; but can ye not *discern* the signs of the times?

4 A wicked and adulterous generation seeketh after a sign; and there shall no sign be given unto it, but the sign of the prophet Jonah. And he left them, and departed.

Guard Against Wrong Teachings

*A*nd when his disciples were come to the other side, they had forgotten to take bread.

6 Then Jesus said unto them, Take heed and beware of the leaven of the Pharisees and of the Sadducees.

7 And they reasoned among themselves, saying, *It is* because we have taken no bread.

8 *Which* when Jesus perceived, he said unto them, O ye of little faith, why reason ye among yourselves, because ye have brought no bread?

9 Do ye not yet understand, neither remember the five loaves of the five thousand, and how many baskets ye took up?

10 neither the seven loaves of the four thousand, and how many baskets ye took up?

11 How is it that ye do not understand that I spake *it* not to you concerning bread, that ye should beware of the leaven of the Pharisees and of the Sadducees?

12 Then understood they how that he bade *them* not beware of the leaven of bread, but of the doctrine of the Pharisees and of the Sadducees.

Peter Says Jesus Is the Christ

*W*hen Jesus came into the coasts of Caesarea Philippi, he asked his disciples, saying, Whom do men say that I, the Son of man, am?

[14] And they said, Some *say that thou art* John the Baptist; some, Elijah; and others, Jeremiah, or one of the prophets.

[15] He saith unto them, But whom say ye that I am?

[16] And Simon Peter answered and said, Thou art the Christ, the Son of the living God.

[17] And Jesus answered and said unto him, Blessed art thou, Simon Bar-jona: for flesh and blood hath not revealed *it* unto thee, but my Father which is in heaven.

[18] And I say also unto thee, That thou art Peter, and upon this rock I will build my church; and the gates of hell shall not prevail against it.

[19] And I will give unto thee the keys of the kingdom of heaven: and whatsoever thou shalt bind on earth shall be bound in heaven; and whatsoever thou shalt loose on earth shall be loosed in heaven.

[20] Then charged he his disciples that they should tell no man that he was Jesus the Christ.

OLD TESTAMENT READING

*H*o, every one that thirsteth, come ye to the waters, and he that hath no money; come ye, buy, and eat; yea, come, buy wine and milk without money and without price.

[2] Wherefore do ye spend money for *that which is* not bread? and your labor for *that which* satisfieth not? hearken diligently unto me, and eat ye *that which is* good, and let your soul delight itself in fatness.

Isaiah 55:1–2

INSIGHTS

*O*ur Lord's mission of grace and truth was at its height. His help was sought with the utmost eagerness. Large numbers of sick were cast at his feet in hot haste. The crumb was given to the woman of Canaan, but whole loaves were distributed to the crowds of Jews, because it was befitting that they should have a full chance to appreciate and accept Christ. For a brief moment they glorified the God of Israel, but the spasm of gratitude was transient. "His own" rejected Jesus. They would have his miracles, but would not own his claims. Take care that you do not become content with getting his help; love him for himself.

Do not suppose that these miracles were confined to his earthly life. He is still the great storehouse of divine and healing energy. He is still moved with compassion, and longs to help each weary and sin-sick soul. His thought still is "lest they faint in the way." The wilderness can place no bar on "the saving strength of his right hand."

F. B. Meyer

APPLICATION

*W*hat does the "real food" that Jesus offers satisfy? How does a person receive that food? Why do you want to be close to Jesus? Do you want his miracles or his claims? Physical food or spiritual food?

THURSDAY

Jesus' Suffering Will Be Followed by His Judgment

Matthew 16:21—17:13

Jesus Says that He Must Die

*F*rom that time forth began Jesus to show unto his disciples, how that he must go unto Jerusalem, and suffer many things of the elders and chief priests and scribes, and be killed, and be raised again the third day.

²² Then Peter took him, and began to rebuke him, saying, Be it far from thee, Lord: this shall not be unto thee.

²³ But he turned, and said unto Peter, Get thee behind me, Satan: thou art an offense unto me: for thou savorest not the things that be of God, but those that be of men.

²⁴ Then said Jesus unto his disciples, If any *man* will come after me, let him deny himself, and take up his cross, and follow me.

²⁵ For whosoever will save his life shall lose it: and whosoever will lose his life for my sake shall find it.

²⁶ For what is a man profited, if he shall gain the whole world, and lose his own soul? or what shall a man give in exchange for his soul?

²⁷ For the Son of man shall come in the glory of his Father with his angels; and then he shall reward every man according to his works.

²⁸ Verily I say unto you, There be some standing here, which shall not taste of death, till they see the Son of man coming in his kingdom.

Jesus Talks with Moses and Elijah

17 And after six days Jesus taketh Peter, James, and John his brother, and bringeth them up into an high mountain apart,

² and was transfigured before them: and his face did shine as the sun, and his raiment was white as the light.

³ And, behold, there appeared unto them Moses and Elijah talking with him.

⁴ Then answered Peter, and said unto Jesus, Lord, it is good for us to be here: if thou wilt, let us make here three tabernacles; one for thee, and one for Moses, and one for Elijah.

⁵ While he yet spake, behold, a bright cloud overshadowed them: and behold a voice out of the cloud, which said, This is my beloved Son, in whom I am well pleased; hear ye him.

⁶ And when the disciples heard *it*, they fell on their face, and were sore afraid.

⁷ And Jesus came and touched them, and said, Arise, and be not afraid.

⁸ And when they had lifted up their eyes, they saw no man, save Jesus only.

⁹ And as they came down from the mountain, Jesus charged them, saying, Tell the vision to no man, until the Son of man be risen again from the dead.

¹⁰ And his disciples asked him, saying, Why then say the scribes that Elijah must first come?

¹¹ And Jesus answered and said unto them, Elijah truly shall first come, and restore all things.

¹² But I say unto you, That Elijah is come already, and they knew him not, but have done unto him whatsoever they listed. Likewise shall

also the Son of man suffer of them. [13] Then the disciples understood that he spake unto them of John the Baptist.

OLD TESTAMENT READING

*A*ll we like sheep have gone astray; we have turned every one to his own way; and the LORD hath laid on him the iniquity of us all.

[7] He was oppressed, and he was afflicted, yet he opened not his mouth: he is brought as a lamb to the slaughter, and as a sheep before her shearers is dumb, so he openeth not his mouth.

[8] He was taken from prison and from judgment: and who shall declare his generation? for he was cut off out of the land of the living: for the transgression of my people was he stricken.

[9] And he made his grave with the wicked, and with the rich in his death; because he had done no violence, neither *was any* deceit in his mouth.

[10] Yet it pleased the LORD to bruise him; he hath put *him* to grief: when thou shalt make his soul an offering for sin, he shall see *his* seed, he shall prolong *his* days, and the pleasure of the LORD shall prosper in his hand.

Isaiah 53:6–10

*A*nd they that be wise shall shine as the brightness of the firmament; and they that turn many to righteousness, as the stars for ever and ever.

Daniel 12:3

INSIGHTS

*W*e are all of us judged every day. We are judged by the face that looks back at us from the bathroom mirror. We are judged by the faces of the people we love and by the faces and lives of our children and by our dreams. Each day finds us at the junction of many roads, and we are judged as much by the roads we have not taken as by the roads we have.

The New Testament proclaims that at some unforeseeable time in the future God will ring down the final curtain on history, and there will come a Day on which all our days and all the judgments upon us and all our judgments upon each other will themselves be judged. The judge will be Christ. In other words, the one who judges us most finally will be the one who loves us most fully.

Romantic love is blind to everything except what is lovable and lovely, but Christ's love sees us with terrible clarity and sees us whole. Christ's love so wishes our joy that it is ruthless against everything in us that diminishes our joy. The worst sentence Love can pass is that we behold the suffering which Love has endured for our sake, and that is also our acquittal. The justice and mercy of the judge are ultimately one.

Frederick Buechner

ACTION POINT

*W*hat was most important to Jesus when he suffered and died for us? What did he promise would follow? Think about the statement, "the one who judges us most finally will be the one who loves us most fully." Pray now and thank God that our Judge is also our Savior!

FRIDAY

*Greatness in God's Kingdom
Begins with Humility*

Matthew 17:14—18:9

Jesus Heals a Boy

*A*nd when they were come to the multitude, there came to him a *certain* man, kneeling down to him, and saying,

¹⁵ Lord, have mercy on my son; for he is lunatic, and sore vexed: for ofttimes he falleth into the fire, and oft into the water.

¹⁶ And I brought him to thy disciples, and they could not cure him.

¹⁷ Then Jesus answered and said, O faithless and perverse generation, how long shall I be with you? how long shall I suffer you? bring him hither to me.

¹⁸ And Jesus rebuked the devil; and he departed out of him: and the child was cured from that very hour.

¹⁹ Then came the disciples to Jesus apart, and said, Why could not we cast him out?

²⁰ And Jesus said unto them, Because of your unbelief: for verily I say unto you, If ye have faith as a grain of mustard seed, ye shall say unto this mountain, Remove hence to yonder place; and it shall remove: and nothing shall be impossible unto you.

²¹ Howbeit this kind goeth not out but by prayer and fasting.

Jesus Talks About His Death

*A*nd while they abode in Galilee, Jesus said unto them, The Son of man shall be betrayed into the hands of men:

²³ and they shall kill him, and the third day he shall be raised again. And they were exceeding sorry.

Jesus Talks About Paying Taxes

*A*nd when they were come to Capernaum, they that received tribute *money* came to Peter, and said, Doth not your master pay tribute?

²⁵ He saith, Yes. And when he was come into the house, Jesus prevented him, saying, What thinkest thou, Simon? of whom do the kings of the earth take custom or tribute? of their own children, or of strangers?

²⁶ Peter saith unto him, Of strangers. Jesus saith unto him, Then are the children free.

²⁷ Notwithstanding, lest we should offend them, go thou to the sea, and cast a hook, and take up the fish that first cometh up; and when thou hast opened his mouth, thou shalt find a piece of money: that take, and give unto them for me and thee.

Who Is the Greatest?

18 At the same time came the disciples unto Jesus, saying, Who is the greatest in the kingdom of heaven?

² And Jesus called a little child unto him, and set him in the midst of them,

³ and said, Verily I say unto you, Except ye be converted, and become as little children, ye shall not enter into the kingdom of heaven.

⁴ Whosoever therefore shall humble himself as this little child, the same is greatest in the kingdom of heaven.

⁵ And whoso shall receive one such

little child in my name receiveth me. [6] But whoso shall offend one of these little ones which believe in me, it were better for him that a millstone were hanged about his neck, and *that* he were drowned in the depth of the sea. [7] Woe unto the world because of offenses! for it must needs be that offenses come; but woe to that man by whom the offense cometh! [8] Wherefore if thy hand or thy foot offend thee, cut them off, and cast *them* from thee: it is better for thee to enter into life halt or maimed, rather than having two hands or two feet to be cast into everlasting fire. [9] And if thine eye offend thee, pluck it out, and cast *it* from thee: it is better for thee to enter into life with one eye, rather than having two eyes to be cast into hell fire.

OLD TESTAMENT READING

A man's pride shall bring him low: but honor shall uphold the humble in spirit.

Proverbs 29:23

*A*nd when he was in affliction, he besought the LORD his God, and humbled himself greatly before the God of his fathers, [13] and prayed unto him: and he was entreated of him, and heard his supplication, and brought him again to Jerusalem into his kingdom. Then Manasseh knew that the LORD he *was* God.

2 Chronicles 33:12–13

INSIGHTS

I was once considering what the reason was our Lord loved humility in us so much. I suddenly remem-

bered that He is essentially the supreme truth and that humility is just our walking in truth. For it is a very great truth that we have no good in us; we have only misery and nothingness. He who does not understand this walks in lies. But he who understands this the best is the most pleasing to the Supreme Truth. May God grant us this favor, sisters, never to be without the humbling knowledge of ourselves. . . .

His Majesty seeks and loves courageous souls. But they must be humble in all their ways and have no confidence in themselves. . . .

. . . I often used to think of those words of the Apostle Paul: "All things are possible with God" (Philippians 4:13). I saw clearly that I could do nothing of myself. This was of great help to me to see this. So also was the saying of Augustine: "Give me, Lord, what You command, and command what You desire." . . .

. . . But it is necessary that we should understand what this humility is like. For I believe Satan will try to do great harm. He hinders those who begin to pray from going forward by suggesting to them false notions of humility. He makes them think that it is pride to have spiritual ambitions, desires to imitate the saints, and longings to be like martyrs.

St. Teresa of Avila

ACTION POINT

*H*ow does God view pride? Why do you think he places such a high value on humility? In your own words, describe the attitudes and actions of true humility, and pray that God will cause you to want to be humble.

WEEKEND
The Magnitude of God's Forgiveness

Matthew 18:10–35

A Lost Sheep

Take heed that ye despise not one of these little ones; for I say unto you, That in heaven their angels do always behold the face of my Father which is in heaven.

11 For the Son of man is come to save that which was lost.

12 How think ye? if a man have a hundred sheep, and one of them be gone astray, doth he not leave the ninety and nine, and goeth into the mountains, and seeketh that which is gone astray?

13 And if so be that he find it, verily I say unto you, he rejoiceth more of that *sheep*, than of the ninety and nine which went not astray.

14 Even so it is not the will of your Father which is in heaven, that one of these little ones should perish.

When a Person Sins Against You

Moreover if thy brother shall trespass against thee, go and tell him his fault between thee and him alone: if he shall hear thee, thou hast gained thy brother.

16 But if he will not hear *thee, then* take with thee one or two more, that in the mouth of two or three witnesses every word may be established.

17 And if he shall neglect to hear them, tell it unto the church: but if he neglect to hear the church, let him be unto thee as an heathen man and a publican.

18 Verily I say unto you, Whatsoever ye shall bind on earth shall be bound in heaven: and whatsoever ye shall loose on earth shall be loosed in heaven.

19 Again I say unto you, That if two of you shall agree on earth as touching any thing that they shall ask, it shall be done for them of my Father which is in heaven.

20 For where two or three are gathered together in my name, there am I in the midst of them.

An Unforgiving Servant

Then came Peter to him, and said, Lord, how oft shall my brother sin against me, and I forgive him? till seven times?

22 Jesus saith unto him, I say not unto thee, Until seven times: but, Until seventy times seven.

23 Therefore is the kingdom of heaven likened unto a certain king, which would take account of his servants.

24 And when he had begun to reckon, one was brought unto him, which owed him ten thousand talents.

25 But forasmuch as he had not to pay, his lord commanded him to be sold, and his wife, and children, and all that he had, and payment to be made.

26 The servant therefore fell down, and worshipped him, saying, Lord, have patience with me, and I will pay thee all.

27 Then the lord of that servant was moved with compassion, and loosed him, and forgave him the debt.

28 But the same servant went out, and found one of his fellow servants, which owed him a hundred pence:

48

and he laid hands on him, and took *him* by the throat, saying, Pay me that thou owest.

²⁹ And his fellow servant fell down at his feet, and besought him, saying, Have patience with me, and I will pay thee all.

³⁰ And he would not: but went and cast him into prison, till he should pay the debt.

³¹ So when his fellow servants saw what was done, they were very sorry, and came and told unto their lord all that was done.

³² Then his lord, after that he had called him, said unto him, O thou wicked servant, I forgave thee all that debt, because thou desiredst me:

³³ shouldest not thou also have had compassion on thy fellow servant, even as I had pity on thee?

³⁴ And his lord was wroth, and delivered him to the tormentors, till he should pay all that was due unto him.

³⁵ So likewise shall my heavenly Father do also unto you, if ye from your hearts forgive not every one his brother their trespasses.

OLD TESTAMENT READING

*B*ut if the wicked will turn from all his sins that he hath committed, and keep all my statutes, and do that which is lawful and right, he shall surely live, he shall not die.

²² All his transgressions that he hath committed, they shall not be mentioned unto him: in his righteousness that he hath done he shall live.

²³ Have I any pleasure at all that the wicked should die? saith the Lord GOD: *and* not that he should return from his ways, and live?

Ezekiel 18:21–23

INSIGHTS

*F*orgiving and being forgiven are all of one piece. They cannot be separated. In giving we receive. In accepting those who have injured us we open ourselves to God's acceptance.

It is not a matter of which comes first. There is no sequence of time or priority. The two are one. Anyone who loves God must also love his neighbor. Anyone who hates another does not and cannot love God. Love of God and our neighbor are interlocking and indivisible. We only learn to love as we learn to know God. And we truly learn to know God as we learn to love our brother and sister. It's all of a piece. The life that is open to the love of God is loving to others. The person who truly receives the forgiveness of God is truly forgiving of others. . . .

God's forgiveness gives us the freedom to love and live creatively. The rush of God's strength, which brings forgiveness, gives in turn the ability to forgive, and forgive, and forgive, not just seven times, as the apostle Peter once volunteered, but seventy times seven. . . .

The contrast between our debt to God and the debts others may owe us is immeasurable.

And when God has forgiven us the debt we owe Him, how can we be unforgiving to others who owe us so little in comparison?

David Augsburger

APPLICATION

*W*hich of your debts that God has forgiven can serve as a model of how you ought to forgive others?

MONDAY

Jesus Talks About Marriage and Divorce

Matthew 19:1-26

Jesus Teaches About Divorce

19 And it came to pass, *that* when Jesus had finished these sayings, he departed from Galilee, and came into the coasts of Judea beyond Jordan;

² and great multitudes followed him; and he healed them there.

³ The Pharisees also came unto him, tempting him, and saying unto him, Is it lawful for a man to put away his wife for every cause?

⁴ And he answered and said unto them, Have ye not read, that he which made *them* at the beginning made them male and female,

⁵ and said, For this cause shall a man leave father and mother, and shall cleave to his wife: and they twain shall be one flesh?

⁶ Wherefore they are no more twain, but one flesh. What therefore God hath joined together, let not man put asunder.

⁷ They say unto him, Why did Moses then command to give a writing of divorcement, and to put her away?

⁸ He saith unto them, Moses because of the hardness of your hearts suffered you to put away your wives: but from the beginning it was not so.

⁹ And I say unto you, Whosoever shall put away his wife, except *it be* for fornication, and shall marry another, committeth adultery: and whoso marrieth her which is put away doth commit adultery.

¹⁰ His disciples say unto him, If the case of the man be so with *his* wife, it is not good to marry.

¹¹ But he said unto them, All *men* cannot receive this saying, save *they* to whom it is given.

¹² For there are some eunuchs, which were so born from *their* mother's womb: and there are some eunuchs, which were made eunuchs of men: and there be eunuchs, which have made themselves eunuchs for the kingdom of heaven's sake. He that is able to receive *it*, let him receive *it*.

Jesus Welcomes Children

*T*hen were there brought unto him little children, that he should put *his* hands on them, and pray: and the disciples rebuked them.

¹⁴ But Jesus said, Suffer little children, and forbid them not, to come unto me; for of such is the kingdom of heaven.

¹⁵ And he laid *his* hands on them, and departed thence.

A Rich Young Man's Question

*A*nd, behold, one came and said unto him, Good Master, what good thing shall I do, that I may have eternal life?

¹⁷ And he said unto him, Why callest thou me good? *there is* none good but one, *that is*, God: but if thou wilt enter into life, keep the commandments.

¹⁸ He saith unto him, Which? Jesus said, Thou shalt do no murder, Thou shalt not commit adultery, Thou shalt not steal, Thou shalt not bear false witness,

¹⁹ Honor thy father and *thy* mother:

and, Thou shalt love thy neighbor as thyself.

20 The young man saith unto him, All these things have I kept from my youth up: what lack I yet?

21 Jesus said unto him, If thou wilt be perfect, go *and* sell that thou hast, and give to the poor, and thou shalt have treasure in heaven: and come *and* follow me.

22 But when the young man heard that saying, he went away sorrowful: for he had great possessions.

23 Then said Jesus unto his disciples, Verily I say unto you, That a rich man shall hardly enter into the kingdom of heaven.

24 And again I say unto you, It is easier for a camel to go through the eye of a needle, than for a rich man to enter into the kingdom of God.

25 When his disciples heard *it*, they were exceedingly amazed, saying, Who then can be saved?

26 But Jesus beheld *them*, and said unto them, With men this is impossible; but with God all things are possible.

OLD TESTAMENT READING

*A*nd this have ye done again, covering the altar of the LORD with tears, with weeping, and with crying out, insomuch that he regardeth not the offering any more, or receiveth *it* with good will at your hand.

14 Yet ye say, Wherefore? Because the LORD hath been witness between thee and the wife of thy youth, against whom thou hast dealt treacherously: yet *is* she thy companion, and the wife of thy covenant.

15 And did not he make one? Yet had he the residue of the Spirit. And wherefore one? That he might seek a godly seed. Therefore take heed to your spirit, and let none deal treacherously against the wife of his youth.

16 For the LORD the God of Israel, saith that he hateth putting away: for *one* covereth violence with his garment, saith the LORD of hosts: therefore take heed to your spirit, that ye deal not treacherously.

Malachi 2:13–16

INSIGHTS

*T*he marriage law must conform with the purpose for which marriage was instituted by God. It was instituted to create a new unity of two persons, and no provision was made for the dissolving of that unity. Jesus does not idealize marriage. He does not say that every marriage is made in heaven; he says that marriage itself is made in heaven—that is, instituted by God. To the question, 'Is it lawful for a man to divorce his wife?' his answer, in effect, is 'No; not for any cause.' . . .

Is it wise to take Jesus's rulings on this or other practical issues and give them legislative force? Perhaps not. It is better probably, to let his words stand in the uncompromising rigour as the ideal at which his followers ought to aim. Legislation has to make provision for the hardness of men's hearts, but Jesus showed a more excellent way than the way of legislation and supplies the power to change the human heart and make his ideal a practical possibility.

F. F. Bruce

PAUSE FOR REFLECTION

*I*n what ways does knowing God's purpose for marriage affect your view of marriage and divorce?

TUESDAY
God's View of Fairness

Matthew 19:27—20:19

*T*hen answered Peter and said unto him, Behold, we have forsaken all, and followed thee; what shall we have therefore?

²⁸ And Jesus said unto them, Verily I say unto you, That ye which have followed me, in the regeneration when the Son of man shall sit in the throne of his glory, ye also shall sit upon twelve thrones, judging the twelve tribes of Israel.

²⁹ And every one that hath forsaken houses, or brethren, or sisters, or father, or mother, or wife, or children, or lands, for my name's sake, shall receive a hundredfold, and shall inherit everlasting life.

³⁰ But many *that are* first shall be last; and the last *shall be* first.

A Parable About Workers

20 For the kingdom of heaven is like unto a man *that is* a householder, which went out early in the morning to hire laborers into his vineyard.

² And when he had agreed with the laborers for a penny a day, he sent them into his vineyard.

³ And he went out about the third hour, and saw others standing idle in the marketplace,

⁴ and said unto them; Go ye also into the vineyard, and whatsoever is right I will give you. And they went their way.

⁵ Again he went out about the sixth and ninth hour, and did likewise.

⁶ And about the eleventh hour he went out, and found others standing idle, and saith unto them, Why stand ye here all the day idle?

⁷ They say unto him, Because no man hath hired us. He saith unto them, Go ye also into the vineyard; and whatsoever is right, *that* shall ye receive.

⁸ So when even was come, the lord of the vineyard saith unto his steward, Call the laborers, and give them *their* hire, beginning from the last unto the first.

⁹ And when they came that *were hired* about the eleventh hour, they received every man a penny.

¹⁰ But when the first came, they supposed that they should have received more; and they likewise received every man a penny.

¹¹ And when they had received *it*, they murmured against the goodman of the house,

¹² saying, These last have wrought *but* one hour, and thou hast made them equal unto us, which have borne the burden and heat of the day.

¹³ But he answered one of them, and said, Friend, I do thee no wrong: didst not thou agree with me for a penny?

¹⁴ Take *that* thine *is*, and go thy way: I will give unto this last, even as unto thee.

¹⁵ Is it not lawful for me to do what I will with mine own? Is thine eye evil, because I am good?

¹⁶ So the last shall be first, and the first last: for many be called, but few chosen.

Jesus Talks About His Death

*A*nd Jesus going up to Jerusalem

took the twelve disciples apart in the way, and said unto them,

18 Behold, we go up to Jerusalem; and the Son of man shall be betrayed unto the chief priests and unto the scribes, and they shall condemn him to death,

19 and shall deliver him to the Gentiles to mock, and to scourge, and to crucify *him*: and the third day he shall rise again.

OLD TESTAMENT READING

There is none holy as the LORD: for *there is* none besides thee: neither *is there* any rock like our God.

6 The LORD killeth, and maketh alive: he bringeth down to the grave, and bringeth up.

7 The LORD maketh poor, and maketh rich: he bringeth low and lifteth up.

8 He raiseth up the poor out of the dust, *and* lifteth up the beggar from the dunghill, to set *them* among princes, and to make them inherit the throne of glory: for the pillars of the earth *are* the LORD's and he hath set the world upon them.

1 Samuel 2:2, 6–8

INSIGHTS

The message of the parable is that the revolution of God brought by Jesus is a marvellously generous revolution, offering a full place and reward even to the late-comer or outsider. For the rich and the religious such egalitarian salvation did not always seem good news, since it meant giving up their present advantage and special position. . . . In the parable those who had worked all day complained of the master's unfair generosity. But for those in need of employment at the eleventh hour the master's generosity was good news indeed. . . .

. . . The revolution of God is a levelling revolution; not, however, a negatively levelling revolution bringing everyone down, but a positively levelling revolution in which God's amazing generosity welcomes even late-comers . . . and gives them the full day's wage. . . .

. . . To put it simply: entry into the kingdom of God is through God's generosity to sinners; being in the kingdom of God entails running the race to obtain the prize (1 Cor 9:24). There is truth in the old saying that the entry fee to Christianity is completely free, but the annual subscription is everything we've got. No one will be in the coming kingdom of God on the basis of his or her own achievements, but only on the basis of God's generosity; but everyone will be called to account on the day of judgement and will be rewarded according to his or her response to the Lord's generosity.

David Wenham

ACTION POINT

Think about God's fairness and mercy. In what ways are you tempted to be jealous of his generosity shown to others? Pray for a greater understanding of his goodness, and extend his generosity to others.

WEDNESDAY

Jerusalem Honors Jesus as King

Matthew 20:20—21:11

A Mother Asks Jesus a Favor

*T*hen came to him the mother of Zebedee's children with her sons, worshipping *him*, and desiring a certain thing of him.

²¹ And he said unto her, What wilt thou? She saith unto him, Grant that these my two sons may sit, the one on thy right hand, and the other on the left, in thy kingdom.

²² But Jesus answered and said, Ye know not what ye ask. Are ye able to drink of the cup that I shall drink of, and to be baptized with the baptism that I am baptized with? They say unto him, We are able.

²³ And he saith unto them, Ye shall drink indeed of my cup, and be baptized with the baptism that I am baptized with: but to sit on my right hand, and on my left, is not mine to give, but *it shall be given to them* for whom it is prepared of my Father.

²⁴ And when the ten heard *it*, they were moved with indignation against the two brethren.

²⁵ But Jesus called them *unto him*, and said, Ye know that the princes of the Gentiles exercise dominion over them, and they that are great exercise authority upon them.

²⁶ But it shall not be so among you: but whosoever will be great among you, let him be your minister;

²⁷ and whosoever will be chief among you, let him be your servant:

²⁸ Even as the Son of man came not to be ministered unto, but to minister, and to give his life a ransom for many.

Jesus Heals Two Blind Men

*A*nd as they departed from Jericho, a great multitude followed him.

³⁰ And, behold, two blind men sitting by the wayside, when they heard that Jesus passed by, cried out, saying, Have mercy on us, O Lord, *thou* Son of David.

³¹ And the multitude rebuked them, because they should hold their peace: but they cried the more, saying, Have mercy on us, O Lord, *thou* Son of David.

³² And Jesus stood still, and called them, and said, What will ye that I shall do unto you?

³³ They say unto him, Lord, that our eyes may be opened.

³⁴ So Jesus had compassion *on them,* and touched their eyes: and immediately their eyes received sight, and they followed him.

Jesus Enters Jerusalem as a King

21 And when they drew nigh unto Jerusalem, and were come to Bethphage, unto the mount of Olives, then sent Jesus two disciples,

² saying unto them, Go into the village over against you, and straightway ye shall find an ass tied, and a colt with her: loose *them*, and bring *them* unto me.

³ And if any *man* say aught unto you, ye shall say, The Lord hath need of them; and straightway he will send them.

⁴ All this was done, that it might be fulfilled which was spoken by the prophet, saying,

⁵Tell ye the daughter of Zion, Behold, thy King cometh unto thee, meek, and sitting upon an ass, and a colt the foal of an ass.

⁶And the disciples went, and did as Jesus commanded them,

⁷and brought the ass, and the colt, and put on them their clothes, and they set *him* thereon.

⁸And a very great multitude spread their garments in the way; others cut down branches from the trees, and strewed *them* in the way.

⁹And the multitudes that went before, and that followed, cried, saying, Hosanna to the Son of David: Blessed *is* he that cometh in the name of the Lord; Hosanna in the highest.

¹⁰And when he was come into Jerusalem, all the city was moved, saying, Who is this?

¹¹And the multitude said, This is Jesus the prophet of Nazareth of Galilee.

OLD TESTAMENT READING

O come, let us sing unto the Lord: let us make a joyful noise to the rock of our salvation.

²Let us come before his presence with thanksgiving, and make a joyful noise unto him with psalms.

³For the Lord *is* a great God, and a great King above all gods.

Psalm 95:1–3

*T*his *is* the day *which* the Lord hath made; we will rejoice and be glad in it.

Psalm 118:24

INSIGHTS

*Y*ou can almost hear the roar of the crowds as Jesus proceeds slowly into *Jerusalem, like a triumphant general returning from a great victory.* . . .

From the dusty roads of this earth, where the lips of little children sang his praises, to the very throne of heaven where surely angel anthems rolled, this was Jesus' moment. . . .

Not only on this day of days, but down through the centuries, Jesus has reigned in triumph in the hearts of men and women who have accepted his glorious life and teaching. The Pharisees could hardly have realized how prophetic their words would be: "Look how the whole world has gone after him!"

And why wouldn't we follow Jesus? He leads us in triumph! Just when we think we have had all the trouble we can handle, Jesus reaches down and lifts us gently onto the colt he is riding into Jerusalem. Just when we think nobody cares, he opens our ears and we can hear the crowds shout, "Look who's riding with the King!" And just when we think there is no reward for being righteous, Jesus smiles and quietly reassures us, "My Father will honor the one who serves me."

Not all of our hurt will go away, and our problems won't magically disappear. But through faith we can be a child of the King—a king of triumph!

F. LaGard Smith

ACTION POINT

*L*ist the ways Jesus has shown himself to be a king of triumph in your life. Spend some time in prayer, celebrating your praise to him. If you would like, write down your praises, or express them in another visible way.

THURSDAY

God Seeks Sincere Worship

Matthew 21:12–32

Jesus Goes to the Temple

*A*nd Jesus went into the temple of God, and cast out all them that sold and bought in the temple, and over threw the tables of the money changers, and the seats of them that sold doves,

[13] and said unto them, It is written, My house shall be called the house of prayer; but ye have made it a den of thieves.

[14] And the blind and the lame came to him in the temple; and he healed them.
[15] And when the chief priests and scribes saw the wonderful things that he did, and the children crying in the temple, and saying, Hosanna to the Son of David; they were sore displeased,

[16] and said unto him, Hearest thou what these say? And Jesus saith unto them, Yea; have ye never read, Out of the mouth of babes and sucklings thou hast perfected praise?
[17] And he left them, and went out of the city into Bethany; and he lodged there.

The Power of Faith

*N*ow in the morning as he returned into the city, he hungered.
[19] And when he saw a fig tree in the way, he came to it, and found nothing thereon, but leaves only, and said unto it, Let no fruit grow on thee henceforward for ever. And presently the fig tree withered away.

[20] And when the disciples saw it, they marveled, saying, How soon is the fig tree withered away!
[21] Jesus answered and said unto them, Verily I say unto you, If ye have faith, and doubt not, ye shall not only do this *which is done* to the fig tree, but also if ye shall say unto this mountain, Be thou removed, and be thou cast into the sea; it shall be done.
[22] And all things, whatsoever ye shall ask in prayer, believing, ye shall receive.

Leaders Doubt Jesus' Authority

*A*nd when he was come into the temple, the chief priests and the elders of the people came unto him as he was teaching, and said, By what authority doest thou these things? and who gave thee this authority?
[24] And Jesus answered and said unto them, I also will ask you one thing, which if ye tell me, I in like wise will tell you by what authority I do these things.
[25] The baptism of John, whence was it? from heaven, or of men? And they reasoned with themselves, saying, If we shall say, From heaven; he will say unto us, Why did ye not then believe him?
[26] But if we shall say, Of men; we fear the people; for all hold John as a prophet.
[27] And they answered Jesus, and said, We cannot tell. And he said unto them, Neither tell I you by what authority I do these things.

A Parable About Two Sons

*B*ut what think ye? A *certain* man had two sons; and he came to the first, and said, Son, go work today in my vineyard.

²⁹ He answered and said, I will not; but afterward he repented, and went.

³⁰ And he came to the second, and said likewise. And he answered and said, I *go*, sir: and went not.

³¹ Whether of them twain did the will of *his* father? They say unto him, The first. Jesus saith unto them, Verily I say unto you, That the publicans and the harlots go into the kingdom of God before you.

³² For John came unto you in the way of righteousness, and ye believed him not; but the publicans and the harlots believed him: and ye, when ye had seen *it*, repented not afterward, that ye might believe him.

OLD TESTAMENT READING

*L*ORD, I have loved the habitation of thy house, and the place where thine honor dwelleth.

Psalm 26:8

*A*nd come and stand before me in this house, which is called by my name, and say, We are delivered to do all these abominations?

¹¹ Is this house, which is called by my name, become a den of robbers in your eyes? Behold, even I have seen *it*, saith the LORD.

¹² But go ye now unto my place which *was* in Shiloh, where I set my name at the first, and see what I did to it for the wickedness of my people Israel.

¹³ And now, because ye have done all these works, saith the LORD, and I spake unto you, rising up early and speaking, but ye heard not; and I called you, but ye answered not;

¹⁴ therefore will I do unto *this* house, which is called by my name.

Jeremiah 7:10–14a

INSIGHTS

*I*n both the Old and New Testaments, God's purpose in revealing himself, in redeeming, and in bringing a people into existence was to create a worshiping community to be a sign of his redeeming work. For example, when God entered into a covenant with the people of Israel, they met him at Mt. Sinai in the first public meeting between God and his people. This meeting with God became the prototype for public worship in Israel. And it was through public worship that God's revelation, redemption, and covenant were remembered and passed down in history. . . .

. . . . We go to worship in praise and thank God for what he has done, is doing, and will do.

Robert Webber

PAUSE FOR REFLECTION

*I*n God's eyes, worship is no casual, Sunday-morning time filler! How does your worship experience stand as a continuing reminder of God's redeeming work in your life? How might it be made stronger and more meaningful?

FRIDAY

The Kingdom of Heaven Is for All Who Obey

Matthew 21:33—22:14

A Parable About God's Son

*H*ear another parable: There was a certain householder, which planted a vineyard, and hedged it round about, and digged a winepress in it, and built a tower, and let it out to husbandmen, and went into a far country:

34 and when the time of the fruit drew near, he sent his servants to the husbandmen, that they might receive the fruits of it.

35 And the husbandmen took his servants, and beat one, and killed another, and stoned another.

36 Again, he sent other servants more than the first: and they did unto them likewise.

37 But last of all he sent unto them his son, saying, They will reverence my son.

38 But when the husbandmen saw the son, they said among themselves, This is the heir; come, let us kill him, and let us seize on his inheritance.

39 And they caught him, and cast *him* out of the vineyard, and slew *him*.

40 When the lord therefore of the vineyard cometh, what will he do unto those husbandmen?

41 They say unto him, He will miserably destroy those wicked men, and will let out *his* vineyard unto other husbandmen, which shall render him the fruits in their seasons.

42 Jesus saith unto them, Did ye never read in the Scriptures, The stone which the builders rejected, the same is become the head of the corner: this is the Lord's doing, and it is marvelous in our eyes?

43 Therefore say I unto you, The kingdom of God shall be taken from you, and given to a nation bringing forth the fruits thereof.

44 And whosoever shall fall on this stone shall be broken: but on whomsoever it shall fall, it will grind him to powder.

45 And when the chief priests and Pharisees had heard his parables, they perceived that he spake of them.

46 But when they sought to lay hands on him, they feared the multitude, because they took him for a prophet.

A Parable About a Wedding Feast

22 And Jesus answered and spake unto them again by parables, and said,

2 The kingdom of heaven is like unto a certain king, which made a marriage for his son,

3 and sent forth his servants to call them that were bidden to the wedding: and they would not come.

4 Again, he sent forth other servants, saying, Tell them which are bidden, Behold, I have prepared my dinner: my oxen and *my* fatlings *are* killed, and all things *are* ready: come unto the marriage.

5 But they made light of *it*, and went their ways, one to his farm, another to his merchandise:

6 And the remnant took his servants, and entreated *them* spitefully, and slew *them*.

7 But when the king heard *thereof*, he was wroth: and he sent forth his armies, and destroyed those murder-

ers, and burned up their city.

⁸ Then saith he to his servants, The wedding is ready, but they which were bidden were not worthy.

⁹ Go ye therefore into the highways, and as many as ye shall find, bid to the marriage.

¹⁰ So those servants went out into the highways, and gathered together all as many as they found, both bad and good: and the wedding was furnished with guests.

¹¹ And when the king came in to see the guests, he saw there a man which had not on a wedding garment:

¹² and he saith unto him, Friend, how camest thou in hither not having a wedding garment? And he was speechless.

¹³ Then said the king to the servants, Bind him hand and foot, and take him away, and cast *him* into outer darkness; there shall be weeping and gnashing of teeth.

¹⁴ For many are called, but few *are* chosen.

OLD TESTAMENT READING

*N*either let the son of the stranger, that hath joined himself to the LORD, speak, saying, The LORD hath utterly separated me from his people: neither let the eunuch say, Behold, I *am* a dry tree.

⁴ For thus saith the LORD unto the eunuchs that keep my sabbaths, and choose *the things* that please me, and take hold of my covenant;

⁵ Even unto them will I give in mine house and within my walls a place and a name better than of sons and of daughters: I will give them an everlasting name, that shall not be cut off.

Isaiah 56:3–5

INSIGHTS

*W*ho can became a Christian? The answer in a nutshell is that anyone can. Anyone who wants to can "take the free gift of the water of life" (Revelation 22:17). Whosoever will may come. Everyone has an invitation to the marriage supper of the Lamb (Matthew 22:9). . . .

. . . It is certainly true that not all do make the decision to give their lives over to God. Some stubbornly insist on going their own way. "Whoever rejects the Son will not see life, for God's wrath remains on him" (John 3:36). Such people will not enjoy the salvation God has for the world. "Yet to all who received him, to those who believed in his name, he gave the right to become children of God" (John 1:12). . . .

Who can become a Christian? Anyone can, because God's grace closes nobody out. There are no limits to his grace except those that sinners impose upon themselves. Jesus Christ, our Advocate, has become "the atoning sacrifice for our sins, and not only for ours but also for the sins of the whole world" (1 John 2:2). Salvation is so broad as to encompass potentially the entire human race.

Clark H. Pinnock

APPLICATION

*T*o whom is God's kingdom given? For what reasons do people refuse God's invitation? Are there ways by which you limit God's grace in your life? Pray that you will obey and keep your agreement with God.

WEEKEND

The Most Important Command

Matthew 22:15–40

Is It Right to Pay Taxes or Not?

*T*hen went the Pharisees, and took counsel how they might entangle him in *his* talk.

16 And they sent out unto him their disciples with the Herodians, saying, Master, we know that thou art true, and teachest the way of God in truth, neither carest thou for any *man*: for thou regardest not the person of men.

17 Tell us therefore, What thinkest thou? Is it lawful to give tribute unto Caesar, or not?

18 But Jesus perceived their wickedness, and said, Why tempt ye me, *ye* hypocrites?

19 Show me the tribute money. And they brought unto him a penny.

20 And he saith unto them, Whose *is* this image and superscription?

21 They say unto him, Caesar's. Then saith he unto them, Render therefore unto Caesar the things which are Caesar's; and unto God the things that are God's.

22 When they had heard *these words*, they marveled, and left him, and went their way.

Some Sadducees Try to Trick Jesus

*T*he same day came to him the Sadducees, which say that there is no resurrection, and asked him,

24 saying, Master, Moses said, If a man die, having no children, his brother shall marry his wife, and raise up seed unto his brother.

25 Now there were with us seven brethren: and the first, when he had married a wife, deceased, and, having no issue, left his wife unto his brother:

26 likewise the second also, and the third, unto the seventh.

27 And last of all the woman died also.

28 Therefore in the resurrection whose wife shall she be of the seven? for they all had her.

29 Jesus answered and said unto them, Ye do err, not knowing the Scriptures, nor the power of God.

30 For in the resurrection they neither marry, nor are given in marriage, but are as the angels of God in heaven.

31 But as touching the resurrection of the dead, have ye not read that which was spoken unto you by God, saying,

32 I am the God of Abraham, and the God of Isaac, and the God of Jacob? God is not the God of the dead, but of the living.

33 And when the multitude heard *this*, they were astonished at his doctrine.

The Most Important Command

*B*ut when the Pharisees had heard that he had put the Sadducees to silence, they were gathered together.

35 Then one of them, *which was* a lawyer, asked *him a question*, tempting him, and saying,

36 Master, which *is* the great commandment in the law?

37 Jesus said unto him, Thou shalt love the Lord thy God with all thy heart, and with all thy soul, and with all thy mind.

38 This is the first and great commandment.

³⁹ And the second *is* like unto it, Thou shalt love thy neighbor as thyself.

⁴⁰ On these two commandments hang all the law and the prophets.

OLD TESTAMENT READING

*H*ear, O Israel: The LORD our God is one LORD:

⁵ And thou shalt love the LORD thy God with all thine heart, and with all thy soul, and with all thy might.

⁶ And these words, which I command thee this day, shall be in thine heart:

⁷ And thou shalt teach them diligently unto thy children, and shalt talk of them when thou sittest in thine house, and when thou walkest by the way, and when thou liest down, and when thou risest up.

⁸ And thou shalt bind them for a sign upon thine hand, and they shall be as frontlets between thine eyes.

Deuteronomy 6:4–8

*T*hen Joshua called the Reubenites, and the Gadites, and the half tribe of Manasseh,

² and said unto them, Ye have kept all that Moses the servant of the LORD commanded you, and have obeyed my voice in all that I commanded you:

⁵ But take diligent heed to do the commandment and the law, which Moses the servant of the LORD charged you, to love the LORD your God, and to walk in all his ways, and to keep his commandments, and to cleave unto him, and to serve him with all your heart and with all your soul.

Joshua 22:1–2, 5

INSIGHTS

I have tried giving myself to other gods—the gods of education and knowledge, success and money, accomplishment and work. I have given good works First Place in my affection. I have tried to get other people to be god for me; I have even let the church assume top priority in my time and energy. I have placed my neck in other worldly nooses and yokes, but only the yoke of Christ grants me freedom.

Surrendering my will to His yoke is a constant process. As I continue to allow the presence of God to permeate the various parts of my life, I am understanding more clearly that anything or anyone, other than God, to whom I turn for meaning, purpose, or strength will ultimately disappoint me or destroy me. God affirmed the first commandment for my benefit; He knew I would never be whole as long as I worshiped anything or anyone besides Himself. I have tried to fill my life with other people, pleasure, work, and acquisition, but these things only partially satisfy.

. . . I am learning that the God of Abraham, Joseph, and Isaac is indeed the Source of everything I need and that His intent is always for good.

Jeanie Miley

APPLICATION

*H*ow do we demonstrate that we love God with all our heart, soul, and mind? How are you loving God today?

MONDAY

Judgment Against
False Spiritual Leaders

Matthew 22:41—23:22

Jesus Questions the Pharisees

*W*hile the Pharisees were gathered together, Jesus asked them, ⁴² saying, What think ye of Christ? whose son is he? They say unto him, *The son* of David.

⁴³ He saith unto them, How then doth David in spirit call him Lord, saying, ⁴⁴ The Lord said unto my Lord, Sit thou on my right hand, till I make thine enemies thy footstool?

⁴⁵ If David then call him Lord, how is he his son?

⁴⁶ And no man was able to answer him a word, neither durst any *man* from that day forth ask him any more *questions*.

Jesus Accuses Some Leaders

23 Then spake Jesus to the multitude, and to his disciples, ² saying, The scribes and the Pharisees sit in Moses' seat:

³ all therefore whatsoever they bid you observe, *that* observe and do; but do not ye after their works: for they say, and do not.

⁴ For they bind heavy burdens and grievous to be borne, and lay *them* on men's shoulders; but they *themselves* will not move them with one of their fingers.

⁵ But all their works they do for to be seen of men: they make broad their phylacteries, and enlarge the borders of their garments,

⁶ and love the uppermost rooms at feasts, and the chief seats in the synagogues,

⁷ and greetings in the markets, and to be called of men, Rabbi, Rabbi.

⁸ But be not ye called Rabbi: for one is your Master, *even* Christ; and all ye are brethren.

⁹ And call no *man* your father upon the earth: for one is your Father, which is in heaven.

¹⁰ Neither be ye called masters: for one is your Master, *even* Christ.

¹¹ But he that is greatest among you shall be your servant.

¹² And whosoever shall exalt himself shall be abased; and he that shall humble himself shall be exalted.

¹³ But woe unto you, scribes and Pharisees, hypocrites! for ye shut up the kingdom of heaven against men: for ye neither go in *yourselves*, neither suffer ye them that are entering to go in.

¹⁴ Woe unto you, scribes and Pharisees, hypocrites! for ye devour widows' houses, and for a pretence make long prayer: therefore ye shall receive the greater damnation.

¹⁵ Woe unto you, scribes and Pharisees, hypocrites! for ye compass sea and land to make one proselyte; and when he is made, ye make him twofold more the child of hell than yourselves.

¹⁶ Woe unto you, *ye* blind guides, which say, Whosoever shall swear by the temple, it is nothing; but whosoever shall swear by the gold of the temple, he is a debtor!

¹⁷ *Ye* fools and blind: for whether is greater, the gold, or the temple that sanctifieth the gold?

¹⁸ And, Whosoever shall swear by the altar, it is nothing; but whosoever

sweareth by the gift that is upon it, he is guilty.

19 *Ye* fools and blind: for whether *is* greater, the gift, or the altar that sanctifieth the gift?

20 Whoso therefore shall swear by the altar, sweareth by it, and by all things thereon.

21 And whoso shall swear by the temple, sweareth by it, and by him that dwelleth therein.

22 And he that shall swear by heaven, sweareth by the throne of God, and by him that sitteth thereon.

OLD TESTAMENT READING

A wonderful and horrible thing is committed in the land;

31 the prophets prophesy falsely, and the priests bear rule by their means; and my people love *to have it* so: and what will ye do in the end thereof?

Jeremiah 5:30–31

INSIGHTS

*F*rom the Hallmark-card theology of a thousand churches to the nauseating nonsense of PTL, American evangelicalism is awash in a sloppy, sentimental, superficial theology that wouldn't empower a clockwork mouse, let alone a disciple of Christ in the tough, modern world. . . .

. . . Having visited almost all the countries in the English-speaking world, I would say that I know none where the churches are more full and the sermons more empty than in America. There are magnificent exceptions, of course. But by and large, I am never hungrier and rarely angrier than when I come out of an American evangelical church after what passes for the preaching of the Word of God.

The problem is not just the heresy, though doubtless there is some of that. Nor is it just the degree of entertainment, and there is lots of that. Nor is it even the appalling gaps in the theology, for there is far too much of that. The real problem is that in what is said there is almost no sense of announcement from God; and in what is shown, there is almost no sense of anointing by God.

Jeremiah attacked the false prophets of his day with the damning question, "Which of them has stood in the council of the LORD, seen him and heard his word?" (Jer 23:18). Are we who profess a high view of authority much better in practice? Is such a standard too demanding?

Os Guinness

PAUSE FOR REFLECTION

*S*tudy these readings and list the things that God's teachers are supposed to do. Why will God punish false spiritual leaders? How well do you think today's religious leaders measure up?

TUESDAY

God Will Punish Those Who Persecute His Messengers

Matthew 23:23—24:8

*W*oe unto you, scribes and Pharisees, hypocrites! for ye pay tithe of mint and anise and cummin, and have omitted the weightier *matters* of the law, judgment, mercy, and faith: these ought ye to have done, and not to leave the other undone.
24 Ye blind guides, which strain at a gnat, and swallow a camel.
25 Woe unto you, scribes and Pharisees, hypocrites! for ye make clean the outside of the cup and of the platter, but within they are full of extortion and excess.
26 *Thou* blind Pharisee, cleanse first that *which is* within the cup and platter, that the outside of them may be clean also.
27 Woe unto you, scribes and Pharisees, hypocrites! for ye are like unto whited sepulchres, which indeed appear beautiful outward, but are within full of dead *men's* bones, and of all uncleanness.
28 Even so ye also outwardly appear righteous unto men, but within ye are full of hypocrisy and iniquity.
29 Woe unto you, scribes and Pharisees, hypocrites! because ye build the tombs of the prophets, and garnish the sepulchres of the righteous,
30 and say, If we had been in the days of our fathers, we would not have been partakers with them in the blood of the prophets.
31 Wherefore ye be witnesses unto yourselves, that ye are the children of them which killed the prophets.
32 Fill ye up then the measure of your fathers.
33 *Ye* serpents, *ye* generation of vipers, how can ye escape the damnation of hell?
34 Wherefore, behold, I send unto you prophets, and wise men, and scribes: and *some* of them ye shall kill and crucify; and *some* of them shall ye scourge in your synagogues, and persecute *them* from city to city:
35 that upon you may come all the righteous blood shed upon the earth, from the blood of righteous Abel unto the blood of Zechariah son of Berechiah, whom ye slew between the temple and the altar.
36 Verily I say unto you, All these things shall come upon this generation.

Jesus Feels Sorry for Jerusalem

O Jerusalem, Jerusalem, *thou* that killest the prophets, and stonest them which are sent unto thee, how often would I have gathered thy children together, even as a hen gathereth her chickens under *her* wings, and ye would not!
38 Behold, your house is left unto you desolate.
39 For I say unto you, Ye shall not see me henceforth, till ye shall say, Blessed *is* he that cometh in the name of the Lord.

The Temple Will Be Destroyed

24 And Jesus went out, and departed from the temple: and his disciples came to *him* for to show him the buildings of the temple.
2 And Jesus said unto them, See ye not all these things? verily I say unto you, There shall not be left here one

stone upon another, that shall not be thrown down.

³ And as he sat upon the mount of Olives, the disciples came unto him privately, saying, Tell us, when shall these things be? and what *shall be* the sign of thy coming, and of the end of the world?

⁴ And Jesus answered and said unto them, Take heed that no man deceive you.

⁵ For many shall come in my name, saying, I am Christ; and shall deceive many.

⁶ And ye shall hear of wars and rumors of wars: see that ye be not troubled: for all *these things* must come to pass, but the end is not yet.

⁷ For nation shall rise against nation, and kingdom against kingdom: and there shall be famines, and pestilences, and earthquakes, in divers places.

⁸ All these *are* the beginning of sorrows.

OLD TESTAMENT READING

Shall the throne of iniquity have fellowship with thee, which frameth mischief by a law?

²¹ They gather themselves together against the soul of the righteous, and condemn the innocent blood.

²² But the LORD is my defense; and my God *is* the rock of my refuge.

²³ And he shall bring upon them their own iniquity, and shall cut them off in their own wickedness; *yea*, the LORD our God shall cut them off.

Psalm 94:20–23

INSIGHTS

A young man came to D. L. Moody and said, "Mr. Moody, I want to be a Christian; but must I give up the world?" Moody characteristically replied, "Young man, if you live the out-and-out Christian life, the world will soon give you up." If we are popular with the crowd of worldlings, or if we are not penalised in some way for our attachment to Christ, we have good cause to inspect our discipleship. . . .

The world varies its ways of persecuting us. Sometimes it uses the sword, and sometimes the lip of scorn. Most of us can stand the sword far better than derision or sarcasm. . . .

Let us remember, also, that there is another side to this being penalised for Christian godliness. It is equally true that all who live ungodly, and persecute God's people, shall suffer punishment. Old Testament incidents, as Paul tells us, were recorded for our admonition, as warnings and examples to us. Under the old dispensation God frequently visited punishment upon persons immediately after their committing of wrongs, so that the connection between the sin and the punishment might be clearly seen. In this present age, the judgment of the ungodly may be deferred; but it is none the less certain, and will be awful when at last it falls.

J. Sydlow Baxter

PAUSE FOR REFLECTION

What are Jesus' accusations against the teachers and Pharisees? What are his warnings to them? How can we be sure that God will punish those who persecute his servants?

WEDNESDAY

The Unmistakable and Terrible Signs of the End Times

Matthew 24:9–35

*T*hen shall they deliver you up to be afflicted, and shall kill you: and ye shall be hated of all nations for my name's sake.

[10] And then shall many be offended, and shall betray one another, and shall hate one another.

[11] And many false prophets shall rise, and shall deceive many.

[12] And because iniquity shall abound, the love of many shall wax cold.

[13] But he that shall endure unto the end, the same shall be saved.

[14] And this gospel of the kingdom shall be preached in all the world for a witness unto all nations; and then shall the end come.

[15] When ye therefore shall see the abomination of desolation, spoken of by Daniel the prophet, stand in the holy place, (whoso readeth, let him understand,)

[16] then let them which be in Judea flee into the mountains:

[17] let him which is on the housetop not come down to take any thing out of his house:

[18] neither let him which is in the field return back to take his clothes.

[19] And woe unto them that are with child, and to them that give suck in those days!

[20] But pray ye that your flight be not in the winter, neither on the sabbath day:

[21] for then shall be great tribulation, such as was not since the beginning of the world to this time, no, nor ever shall be.

[22] And except those days should be shortened, there should no flesh be saved: but for the elect's sake those days shall be shortened.

[23] Then if any man shall say unto you, Lo, here *is* Christ, or there; believe *it* not.

[24] For there shall arise false Christs, and false prophets, and shall show great signs and wonders; insomuch that, if *it were* possible, they shall deceive the very elect.

[25] Behold, I have told you before.

[26] Wherefore if they shall say unto you, Behold, he is in the desert; go not forth: behold, *he is* in the secret chambers; believe *it* not.

[27] For as the lightning cometh out of the east, and shineth even unto the west; so shall also the coming of the Son of man be.

[28] For wheresoever the carcass is, there will the eagles be gathered together.

[29] Immediately after the tribulation of those days shall the sun be darkened, and the moon shall not give her light, and the stars shall fall from heaven, and the powers of the heavens shall be shaken:

[30] and then shall appear the sign of the Son of man in heaven: and then shall all the tribes of the earth mourn, and they shall see the Son of man coming in the clouds of heaven with power and great glory.

[31] And he shall send his angels with a great sound of a trumpet, and they shall gather together his elect from the four winds, from one end of heaven to the other.

[32] Now learn a parable of the fig tree; When his branch is yet tender, and

putteth forth leaves, ye know that summer *is* nigh:

³³ so likewise ye, when ye shall see all these things, know that it is near, *even* at the doors.

³⁴ Verily I say unto you, This generation shall not pass, till all these things be fulfilled.

³⁵ Heaven and earth shall pass away, but my words shall not pass away.

OLD TESTAMENT READING

*B*ehold, the day of the LORD cometh, cruel both with wrath and fierce anger, to lay the land desolate: and he shall destroy the sinners thereof out of it.

¹⁰ For the stars of heaven and the constellations thereof shall not give their light: the sun shall be darkened in his going forth, and the moon shall not cause her light to shine.

Isaiah 13:9–10

INSIGHTS

*T*o a unique degree this generation has witnessed the universal and dramatic fulfillment of prophecy. Many of the signs Jesus said would herald His return have developed before our eyes.

There is the evangelistic sign: "This gospel of the kingdom will be preached in the whole world as a testimony to all nations, and then the end will come" (Matthew 24:14).

This prophecy has been fulfilled in our generation to a degree that has never before been the case. There is now no major nation in which there is no Christian witness. . . .

There is the religious sign: "That day will not come until the rebellion

occurs and the man of lawlessness is revealed" (2 Thessalonians 2:3).

Unfortunately, we can see this sign being fulfilled all around us. As Jesus foretold, the love of the many is growing cold (Matthew 24:12). . . .

Political signs abound. Could prevailing world conditions have been more accurately and comprehensively described than in our Lord's words in Luke 21:25–26? "There will be signs. . . . On the earth, nations will be in anguish and perplexity. . . . Men will faint from terror, apprehensive of what is coming on the world."

There is the Jewish sign: "Jerusalem will be trampled on by the Gentiles until the times of the Gentiles are fulfilled" (Luke 21:24). . . .

. . . For the first time in 2,500 years, Jerusalem is not dominated by Gentiles. . . .

Whatever view we hold regarding the details surrounding the second coming of Christ, history is moving rapidly—not to cataclysm merely, but to consummation.

J. Oswald Sanders

PAUSE FOR REFLECTION

*W*hy did Jesus warn his followers about the end times? What event will be perfectly clear to all people? Despite the horror of these events, what glorious hope does Jesus promise to his people at the end?

THURSDAY

*Always Be Ready
for the Lord's Coming*

Matthew 24:36—25:13

When Will Jesus Come Again?

*B*ut of that day and hour knoweth no *man*, no, not the angels of heaven, but my Father only.

[37] But as the days of Noah *were*, so shall also the coming of the Son of man be.

[38] For as in the days that were before the flood they were eating and drinking, marrying and giving in marriage, until the day that Noah entered into the ark,

[39] and knew not until the flood came, and took them all away; so shall also the coming of the Son of man be.

[40] Then shall two be in the field; the one shall be taken, and the other left.

[41] Two *women shall be* grinding at the mill; the one shall be taken, and the other left.

[42] Watch therefore: for ye know not what hour your Lord doth come.

[43] But know this, that if the goodman of the house had known in what watch the thief would come, he would have watched, and would not have suffered his house to be broken up.

[44] Therefore be ye also ready: for in such an hour as ye think not the Son of man cometh.

[45] Who then is a faithful and wise servant, whom his lord hath made ruler over his household, to give them meat in due season?

[46] Blessed *is* that servant, whom his lord when he cometh shall find so doing.

[47] Verily I say unto you, That he shall make him ruler over all his goods.

[48] But and if that evil servant shall say in his heart, My lord delayeth his coming;

[49] and shall begin to smite *his* fellow servants, and to eat and drink with the drunken;

[50] the lord of that servant shall come in a day when he looketh not for *him*, and in an hour that he is not aware of,

[51] and shall cut him asunder, and appoint *him* his portion with the hypocrites: there shall be weeping and gnashing of teeth.

A Parable About Ten Bridesmaids

25 Then shall the kingdom of heaven be likened unto ten virgins, which took their lamps, and went forth to meet the bridegroom.

[2] And five of them were wise, and five *were* foolish.

[3] They that *were* foolish took their lamps, and took no oil with them:

[4] but the wise took oil in their vessels with their lamps.

[5] While the bridegroom tarried, they all slumbered and slept.

[6] And at midnight there was a cry made, Behold, the bridegroom cometh; go ye out to meet him.

[7] Then all those virgins arose, and trimmed their lamps.

[8] And the foolish said unto the wise, Give us of your oil; for our lamps are gone out.

[9] But the wise answered, saying, *Not so*; lest there be not enough for us and you: but go ye rather to them that sell, and buy for yourselves.

[10] And while they went to buy, the bridegroom came; and they that were ready went in with him to the marriage: and the door was shut.

¹¹ Afterward came also the other virgins, saying, Lord, Lord, open to us. ¹² But he answered and said, Verily I say unto you, I know you not. ¹³ Watch therefore; for ye know neither the day nor the hour wherein the Son of man cometh.

OLD TESTAMENT READING

*B*ehold, I will send my messenger, and he shall prepare the way before me: and the Lord, whom ye seek, shall suddenly come to his temple, even the messenger of the covenant, whom ye delight in: behold, he shall come, saith the LORD of hosts. ² But who may abide the day of his coming? and who shall stand when he appeareth? for he *is* like a refiner's fire, and like fullers' soap: ⁵ And I will come near to you to judgment; and I will be a swift witness against the sorcerers, and against the adulterers, and against false swearers, and against those that oppress the hireling in *his* wages, the widow, and the fatherless, and that turn aside the stranger *from his right*, and fear not me, saith the LORD of hosts. ¹⁶ Then they that feared the LORD spake often one to another: and the LORD hearkened, and heard *it,* and a book of remembrance was written before him for them that feared the LORD, and that thought upon his name. ¹⁷ And they shall be mine, saith the LORD of hosts, in that day when I make up my jewels; and I will spare them, as a man spareth his own son that serveth him. ¹⁸ Then shall ye return, and discern between the righteous and the wicked, between him that serveth God and him that serveth God not.

Malachi 3:1–2, 5, 16–18

INSIGHTS

*W*e look for the return of the Lord because He said many times that He would come—and because it is one of the most frequently mentioned subjects in the Bible. Christ is with us today through His Holy Spirit, and He will be with Christians and with the church down to the end of the age. When He ascended up into heaven, the disciples were told by two angels standing by that He would return again as they were now seeing Him go (see Acts 1:11).

The climactic event of history is yet in the future. It will be sudden and final—the culmination of the ages. It will take the unbelieving world by surprise, and people will try to hide from His holy presence. At the return of Christ the resurrection of believers will take place. They will be gathered together to be with the Lord forever. We can only speculate about the exact details of His return. The important thing is that He is coming again and that we yet have time to trust in Him as our Savior and Lord. The Bible says all people must face Him at that time—as either Savior or Judge: "When the Son of Man comes in his glory . . . he will sit on his throne in heavenly glory" (Matthew 25:31).

Billy Graham

APPLICATION

*W*hat do you want to be doing when Jesus comes again? Will you be with those who say it is useless to serve God, or will you stand with those who honor the Lord? Pray that you will remain faithful.

FRIDAY
God Rewards Kindness

Matthew 25:14–40

A Parable About Three Servants

*F*or *the kingdom of heaven is* as a man traveling into a far country, *who* called his own servants, and delivered unto them his goods.

¹⁵ And unto one he gave five talents, to another two, and to another one; to every man according to his several ability; and straightway took his journey.

¹⁶ Then he that had received the five talents went and traded with the same, and made *them* other five talents.

¹⁷ And likewise he that *had received* two, he also gained other two.

¹⁸ But he that had received one went and digged in the earth, and hid his lord's money.

¹⁹ After a long time the lord of those servants cometh, and reckoneth with them.

²⁰ And so he that had received five talents came and brought other five talents, saying, Lord, thou deliveredst unto me five talents: behold, I have gained beside them five talents more.

²¹ His lord said unto him, Well done, *thou* good and faithful servant: thou hast been faithful over a few things, I will make thee ruler over many things: enter thou into the joy of thy lord.

²² He also that had received two talents came and said, Lord, thou deliveredst unto me two talents: behold, I have gained two other talents beside them.

²³ His lord said unto him, Well done, good and faithful servant; thou hast been faithful over a few things, I will make thee ruler over many things: enter thou into the joy of thy lord.

²⁴ Then he which had received the one talent came and said, Lord, I knew thee that thou art a hard man, reaping where thou hast not sown, and gathering where thou hast not strewed:

²⁵ and I was afraid, and went and hid thy talent in the earth: lo, *there* thou hast *that is* thine.

²⁶ His lord answered and said unto him, *Thou* wicked and slothful servant, thou knewest that I reap where I sowed not, and gather where I have not strewed:

²⁷ thou oughtest therefore to have put my money to the exchangers, and *then* at my coming I should have received mine own with usury.

²⁸ Take therefore the talent from him, and give *it* unto him which hath ten talents.

²⁹ For unto every one that hath shall be given, and he shall have abundance: but from him that hath not shall be taken away even that which he hath.

³⁰ And cast ye the unprofitable servant into outer darkness: there shall be weeping and gnashing of teeth.

The King Will Judge All People

*W*hen the Son of man shall come in his glory, and all the holy angels with him, then shall he sit upon the throne of his glory:

³² and before him shall be gathered all nations: and he shall separate them one from another, as a shepherd divideth *his* sheep from the goats:

33 and he shall set the sheep on his right hand, but the goats on the left. 34 Then shall the King say unto them on his right hand, Come, ye blessed of my Father, inherit the kingdom prepared for you from the foundation of the world:

35 for I was ahungered, and ye gave me meat: I was thirsty, and ye gave me drink: I was a stranger, and ye took me in:

36 naked, and ye clothed me: I was sick, and ye visited me: I was in prison, and ye came unto me.

37 Then shall the righteous answer him, saying, Lord, when saw we thee ahungered, and fed *thee*? or thirsty, and gave *thee* drink?

38 When saw we thee a stranger, and took *thee* in? or naked, and clothed *thee*?

39 Or when saw we thee sick, or in prison, and came unto thee?

40 And the King shall answer and say unto them, Verily I say unto you, Inasmuch as ye have done *it* unto one of the least of these my brethren, ye have done *it* unto me.

OLD TESTAMENT READING

*B*lessed *is* he that considereth the poor: the LORD will deliver him in time of trouble.

2 The LORD will preserve him, and keep him alive; *and* he shall be blessed upon the earth: and thou wilt not deliver him unto the will of his enemies.

3 The LORD will strengthen him upon the bed of languishing: thou wilt make all his bed in his sickness.

Psalm 41:1–3

INSIGHTS

*O*ne kind word can warm three winter months," says a Japanese proverb.

Kind words indeed warm the human spirit. Kindness is literally love in action, showing genuine friendship to others by regarding them as important in God's sight and worthy of dignity and respect. It involves treating others with courtesy, lending encouragement, and freely offering yourself or your resources to help a person in need, no strings attached. . . .

In the book of Proverbs, we read that kindness is a prime quality of a virtuous woman: "When she speaks, her words are wise, and kindness is the rule for everything she says" (Proverbs 31:26). Men, these virtues are for us, too!

Jim has discovered the pleasure of kindness. He makes a special effort to brighten someone's day with an unexpected kind word or gesture. . . . At work, he frequently expresses appreciation to others for the jobs they do. With his neighbors, he is quick to lend a helping hand or offer encouragement.

Imagine the impact Christians could have on the world if kindness were the rule in all we do!

Bill Bright

APPLICATION

*W*hat in these readings shows that God considers mistreatment of the poor, homeless, sick, and downtrodden to be a personal insult? How does that inspire you to be merciful, kind, and generous?

WEEKEND

*Honoring God Is
a Beautiful Thing*

Matthew 25:41—26:19

*T*hen shall he say also unto them on the left hand, Depart from me, ye cursed, into everlasting fire, prepared for the devil and his angels:

⁴² for I was ahungered, and ye gave me no meat: I was thirsty, and ye gave me no drink:

⁴³ I was a stranger, and ye took me not in: naked, and ye clothed me not: sick, and in prison, and ye visited me not.

⁴⁴ Then shall they also answer him, saying, Lord, when saw we thee ahungered, or athirst, or a stranger, or naked, or sick, or in prison, and did not minister unto thee?

⁴⁵ Then shall he answer them, saying, Verily I say unto you, Inasmuch as ye did *it* not to one of the least of these, ye did *it* not to me.

⁴⁶ And these shall go away into everlasting punishment: but the righteous into life eternal.

The Plan to Kill Jesus

26 And it came to pass, when Jesus had finished all these sayings, he said unto his disciples,

² Ye know that after two days is *the feast of* the passover, and the Son of man is betrayed to be crucified.

³ Then assembled together the chief priests, and the scribes, and the elders of the people, unto the palace of the high priest, who was called Caiaphas,

⁴ and consulted that they might take Jesus by subtilty, and kill *him*.

⁵ But they said, Not on the feast *day*, lest there be an uproar among the people.

Perfume for Jesus' Burial

*N*ow when Jesus was in Bethany, in the house of Simon the leper,

⁷ there came unto him a woman having an alabaster box of very precious ointment, and poured it on his head, as he sat at meat.

⁸ But when his disciples saw *it*, they had indignation, saying, To what purpose *is* this waste?

⁹ For this ointment might have been sold for much, and given to the poor.

¹⁰ When Jesus understood *it*, he said unto them, Why trouble ye the woman? for she hath wrought a good work upon me.

¹¹ For ye have the poor always with you; but me ye have not always.

¹² For in that she hath poured this ointment on my body, she did *it* for my burial.

¹³ Verily I say unto you, Wheresoever this gospel shall be preached in the whole world, *there* shall also this, that this woman hath done, be told for a memorial of her.

Judas Becomes an Enemy of Jesus

*T*hen one of the twelve, called Judas Iscariot, went unto the chief priests,

¹⁵ and said *unto them*, What will ye give me, and I will deliver him unto you? And they covenanted with him for thirty pieces of silver.

¹⁶ And from that time he sought opportunity to betray him.

Jesus Eats the Passover Meal

Now the first *day* of the *feast of* unleavened bread the disciples came to Jesus, saying unto him, Where wilt thou that we prepare for thee to eat the passover?

¹⁸ And he said, Go into the city to such a man, and say unto him, The Master saith, My time is at hand; I will keep the passover at thy house with my disciples.

¹⁹ And the disciples did as Jesus had appointed them; and they made ready the passover.

OLD TESTAMENT READING

And Manoah said unto the angel of the LORD, I pray thee, let us detain thee, until we shall have made ready a kid for thee.

¹⁶ And the angel of the LORD said unto Manoah, Though thou detain me, I will not eat of thy bread: and if thou wilt offer a burnt offering, thou must offer it unto the LORD. For Manoah knew not that he *was* an angel of the LORD.

¹⁷ And Manoah said unto the angel of the LORD, What *is* thy name, that when thy sayings come to pass we may do thee honor?

¹⁸ And the angel of the LORD said unto him, Why askest thou thus after my name, seeing it *is* secret?

¹⁹ So Manoah took a kid with a meat offering, and offered *it* upon a rock unto the LORD: and *the angel* did wondrously; and Manoah and his wife looked on.

²⁰ For it came to pass, when the flame went up toward heaven from off the altar, that the angel of the LORD ascended in the flame of the altar: and Manoah and his wife looked on *it*,

and fell on their faces to the ground. ²¹ But the angel of the LORD did no more appear to Manoah and to his wife. Then Manoah knew that he *was* an angel of the LORD.

²² And Manoah said unto his wife, We shall surely die, because we have seen God.

²³ But his wife said unto him, If the LORD were pleased to kill us, he would not have received a burnt offering and a meat offering at our hands, neither would he have showed us all these *things*, nor would as at this time have told us *such things* as these.

Judges 13:15–23

INSIGHTS

It was said of the soldiers of the first Napoleon that they were content to die in the ditch if only he rode over them to victory. With their last breath they cried, "Long live the Emperor!" It seemed as though they had lost all thought and care of their own interests, so long as glory was given to his name. So should it be of us. Higher than our own comfort, or success, or popularity, should be the one thought of the glory of our God. Let Christ be honored, loved, exalted, at whatever cost to us. . . .

. . . Live to please God, and He will breathe on you His peace. Seek His glory, and He will make your heart His home. Do His will, and thereby good shall come to you.

F. B. Meyer

ACTION POINT

Review the ways people honored God in these readings. Spend some time honoring God in prayer today.

MONDAY

God Cares for
His Scattered Sheep

Matthew 26:20–46

ow when the even was come, he sat down with the twelve.

²¹ And as they did eat, he said, Verily I say unto you, that one of you shall betray me.

²² And they were exceeding sorrowful, and began every one of them to say unto him, Lord, is it I?

²³ And he answered and said, He that dippeth *his* hand with me in the dish, the same shall betray me.

²⁴ The Son of man goeth as it is written of him: but woe unto that man by whom the Son of man is betrayed! it had been good for that man if he had not been born.

²⁵ Then Judas, which betrayed him, answered and said, Master, is it I? He said unto him, Thou hast said.

The Lord's Supper

And as they were eating, Jesus took bread, and blessed *it*, and brake *it*, and gave *it* to the disciples, and said, Take, eat; this is my body.

²⁷ And he took the cup, and gave thanks, and gave *it* to them, saying, Drink ye all of it;

²⁸ for this is my blood of the new testament, which is shed for many for the remission of sins.

²⁹ But I say unto you, I will not drink henceforth of this fruit of the vine, until that day when I drink it new with you in my Father's kingdom.

³⁰ And when they had sung a hymn, they went out into the mount of Olives.

Jesus' Disciples Will Leave Him

³¹ Then saith Jesus unto them, All ye shall be offended because of me this night: for it is written, I will smite the shepherd, and the sheep of the flock shall be scattered abroad.

³² But after I am risen again, I will go before you into Galilee.

³³ Peter answered and said unto him, Though all *men* shall be offended because of thee, *yet* will I never be offended.

³⁴ Jesus said unto him, Verily I say unto thee, That this night, before the cock crow, thou shalt deny me thrice.

³⁵ Peter said unto him, Though I should die with thee, yet will I not deny thee. Likewise also said all the disciples.

Jesus Prays Alone

Then cometh Jesus with them unto a place called Gethsemane, and saith unto the disciples, Sit ye here, while I go and pray yonder.

³⁷ And he took with him Peter and the two sons of Zebedee, and began to be sorrowful and very heavy.

³⁸ Then saith he unto them, My soul is exceeding sorrowful, even unto death: tarry ye here, and watch with me.

³⁹ And he went a little further, and fell on his face, and prayed, saying, O my Father, if it be possible, let this cup pass from me: nevertheless not as I will, but as thou *wilt*.

⁴⁰ And he cometh unto the disciples, and findeth them asleep, and saith unto Peter, What, could ye not watch with me one hour?

⁴¹ Watch and pray, that ye enter not into temptation: the spirit indeed *is* willing, but the flesh *is* weak.

⁴² He went away again the second

time, and prayed, saying, O my Father, if this cup may not pass away from me, except I drink it, thy will be done.

43 And he came and found them asleep again: for their eyes were heavy.

44 And he left them, and went away again, and prayed the third time, saying the same words.

45 Then cometh he to his disciples, and saith unto them, Sleep on now, and take *your* rest: behold, the hour is at hand, and the Son of man is betrayed into the hands of sinners.

46 Rise, let us be going: behold, he is at hand that doth betray me.

OLD TESTAMENT READING

*F*or thus saith the Lord GOD; Behold, I, *even* I, will both search my sheep, and seek them out.

12 As a shepherd seeketh out his flock in the day that he is among his sheep *that are* scattered; so will I seek out my sheep, and will deliver them out of all places where they have been scattered in the cloudy and dark day.

16 I will seek that which was lost.

Ezekiel 34:11–12, 16a

INSIGHTS

*L*ambs are wont to lag behind, prone to wander, and apt to grow weary, but from all the danger of these infirmities the Shepherd protects them with His arm of power. He finds new-born souls, like young lambs, ready to perish—He nourishes them till life becomes vigorous; He finds weak minds ready to faint and die—He consoles them and renews their strength. All the little ones He gathers, for it is not the will of our heavenly Father that one of them should perish. What a quick eye He must have to see them all! What a tender heart to care for them all! What a far-reaching and potent arm, to gather them all! In His lifetime on earth He was a great gatherer of the weaker sort, and now that He dwells in heaven, His loving heart yearns towards the meek and contrite, the timid and feeble, the fearful and fainting here below. How gently did He gather me to Himself, to His truth, to His blood, to His love, to His church! With what effectual grace did He compel me to Himself! Since my first conversion, how frequently has He restored me from my wanderings, and once again folded me within the circle of His everlasting arm! The best of all is, that He does it all Himself personally, not delegating the task of love, but condescending Himself to rescue and preserve His most unworthy servant.

Charles Spurgeon

APPLICATION

*W*hen have you felt discouraged or abandoned—perhaps ready to lose your faith? What prompted those feelings? How do these readings comfort you? Thank God that he promises to care for you.

TUESDAY

The Pain of Being Betrayed by Friends

Matthew 26:47–68

Jesus Is Arrested

And while he yet spake, lo, Judas, one of the twelve, came, and with him a great multitude with swords and staves, from the chief priests and elders of the people.

⁴⁸ Now he that betrayed him gave them a sign, saying, Whomsoever I shall kiss, that same is he: hold him fast.

⁴⁹ And forthwith he came to Jesus, and said, Hail, Master; and kissed him.

⁵⁰ And Jesus said unto him, Friend, wherefore art thou come? Then came they, and laid hands on Jesus, and took him.

⁵¹ And, behold, one of them which were with Jesus stretched out *his* hand, and drew his sword, and struck a servant of the high priest's, and smote off his ear.

⁵² Then said Jesus unto him, Put up again thy sword into his place: for all they that take the sword shall perish with the sword.

⁵³ Thinkest thou that I cannot now pray to my Father, and he shall presently give me more than twelve legions of angels?

⁵⁴ But how then shall the scriptures be fulfilled, that thus it must be?

⁵⁵ In that same hour said Jesus to the multitudes, Are ye come out as against a thief with swords and staves for to take me? I sat daily with you teaching in the temple, and ye laid no hold on me.

⁵⁶ But all this was done, that the Scriptures of the prophets might be fulfilled. Then all the disciples forsook him, and fled.

Jesus Before the Leaders

And they that had laid hold on Jesus led *him* away to Caiaphas the high priest, where the scribes and the elders were assembled.

⁵⁸ But Peter followed him afar off unto the high priest's palace, and went in, and sat with the servants, to see the end.

⁵⁹ Now the chief priests, and elders, and all the council, sought false witness against Jesus, to put him to death;

⁶⁰ but found none: yea, though many false witnesses came, *yet* found they none. At the last came two false witnesses,

⁶¹ and said, This *fellow* said, I am able to destroy the temple of God, and to build it in three days.

⁶² And the high priest arose, and said unto him, Answerest thou nothing? what *is it which* these witness against thee?

⁶³ But Jesus held his peace. And the high priest answered and said unto him, I adjure thee by the living God, that thou tell us whether thou be the Christ, the Son of God.

⁶⁴ Jesus saith unto him, Thou hast said: nevertheless I say unto you, Hereafter shall ye see the Son of man sitting on the right hand of power, and coming in the clouds of heaven.

⁶⁵ Then the high priest rent his clothes, saying, He hath spoken blasphemy; what further need have we of witnesses? behold, now ye have heard his blasphemy.

66 What think ye? They answered and said, He is guilty of death.

67 Then did they spit in his face, and buffeted him; and others smote *him* with the palms of their hands,

68 saying, Prophesy unto us, thou Christ, Who is he that smote thee?

OLD TESTAMENT READING

*F*or *it was* not an enemy *that* reproached me; then I could have borne *it*: neither *was it* he that hated me *that* did magnify *himself* against me; then I would have hid myself from him:

13 but *it was* thou, a man mine equal, my guide, and my acquaintance.

14 We took sweet counsel together, *and* walked unto the house of God in company.

20 He hath put forth his hands against such as be at peace with him: he hath broken his covenant.

21 *The words* of his mouth were smoother than butter, but war *was* in his heart: his words were softer than oil, yet *were* they drawn swords.

Psalm 55:12–14, 20–21

INSIGHTS

*H*ave you ever been betrayed by a friend? If so, you know the pain of separation which resembles the grief of death. When Judas agreed to betray Jesus, he might as well have hammered the spikes that would later be driven through Jesus' hands.

Have you ever wondered how it was possible for one of the apostles (who had witnessed Jesus' power, teaching, and love) to turn him over to his enemies for any amount of money? This, of course, was not Judas' first act of betrayal. As trea-surer for the disciples, Judas had been dipping into the till all along. He was a dishonest and greedy man. Even so, the mind races: How in the world could he have betrayed Jesus? . . .

Perhaps we have a clue when we are told about others who refused to accept Jesus as the Christ: "Even after Jesus had done all these miraculous signs in their presence, they still would not believe in him." Judas was not the only one to betray Jesus. All those who refused to believe on him despite the overwhelming evidence of his deity might as well have picked up their own 30 silver coins when Judas did.

Even today there are those who, despite the evidence, continue to betray Jesus through disbelief. How is it possible? Why do they choose to ignore him? . . .

. . . We can choose Christ, or we can choose the world with its false allure. Yet it is not a choice that we make just once in a lifetime. Each day that Judas robbed Jesus was a day of betrayal. And for those who heard Jesus teach, and watched his miracles, yet refused to believe—for them, every day was a day of betrayal.

Do we believe in Jesus, yet live our lives as if we didn't? If so, we too betray Jesus. Will today be a day of faith or a day of betrayal?

F. LaGard Smith

PAUSE FOR REFLECTION

*J*esus showed that he knew exactly what was in Judas' heart. If Jesus spoke to you today about your plans, how would you be affected?

WEDNESDAY

God Can Speak to Powerful Leaders Through Dreams

Matthew 26:69—27:20

Peter Denies Jesus

Now Peter sat without in the palace: and a damsel came unto him, saying, Thou also wast with Jesus of Galilee. 70 But he denied before *them* all, saying, I know not what thou sayest. 71 And when he was gone out into the porch, another *maid* saw him, and said unto them that were there, This *fellow* was also with Jesus of Nazareth. 72 And again he denied with an oath, I do not know the man. 73 And after a while came unto *him* they that stood by, and said to Peter, Surely thou also art *one* of them; for thy speech betrayeth thee. 74 Then began he to curse and to swear, *saying*, I know not the man. And immediately the cock crew. 75 And Peter remembered the word of Jesus, which said unto him, Before the cock crow, thou shalt deny me thrice. And he went out, and wept bitterly.

Jesus Is Taken to Pilate

27 When the morning was come, all the chief priests and elders of the people took counsel against Jesus to put him to death: 2 and when they had bound him, they led *him* away, and delivered him to Pontius Pilate the governor.

Judas Kills Himself

Then Judas, which had betrayed him, when he saw that he was condemned, repented himself, and brought again the thirty pieces of silver to the chief priests and elders, 4 saying, I have sinned in that I have betrayed the innocent blood. And they said, What *is that* to us? see thou *to that.* 5 And he cast down the pieces of silver in the temple, and departed, and went and hanged himself. 6 And the chief priests took the silver pieces, and said, It is not lawful for to put them into the treasury, because it is the price of blood. 7 And they took counsel, and bought with them the potter's field, to bury strangers in. 8 Wherefore that field was called, The field of blood, unto this day. 9 Then was fulfilled that which was spoken by Jeremiah the prophet, saying, And they took the thirty pieces of silver, the price of him that was valued, whom they of the children of Israel did value; 10 and gave them for the potter's field, as the Lord appointed me.

Pilate Questions Jesus

And Jesus stood before the governor: and the governor asked him, saying, Art thou the King of the Jews? And Jesus said unto him, Thou sayest. 12 And when he was accused of the chief priests and elders, he answered nothing. 13 Then said Pilate unto him, Hearest thou not how many things they witness against thee? 14 And he answered him to never a word; insomuch that the governor marveled greatly.

Pilate Tries to Free Jesus

*N*ow at *that* feast the governor was wont to release unto the people a prisoner, whom they would.
[16] And they had then a notable prisoner, called Barabbas.
[17] Therefore when they were gathered together, Pilate said unto them, Whom will ye that I release unto you? Barabbas, or Jesus which is called Christ?
[18] For he knew that for envy they had delivered him.
[19] When he was set down on the judgment seat, his wife sent unto him, saying, Have thou nothing to do with that just man: for I have suffered many things this day in a dream because of him.
[20] But the chief priests and elders persuaded the multitude that they should ask Barabbas, and destroy Jesus.

OLD TESTAMENT READING

*T*he king answered and said to Daniel, whose name *was* Belteshazzar, Art thou able to make known unto me the dream which I have seen, and the interpretation thereof?
[27] Daniel answered in the presence of the king, and said, The secret which the king hath demanded cannot the wise *men*, the astrologers, the magicians, the soothsayers, show unto the king;
[28] but there is a God in heaven that revealeth secrets, and maketh known to the king Nebuchadnezzar what shall be in the latter days.

Daniel 2:26–28a

INSIGHTS

*O*n one occasion when I was in prayer, I had a vision in which I saw how all things are seen in God. I cannot explain what I saw, but what I saw remains to this day, deeply imprinted upon my soul. It was a great act of grace in God to give me that vision. It puts me to unspeakable confusion, shame, and horror whenever I recall that magnificent sight, and then think of my sin. I believe that had the Lord been pleased to send me that great revelation of Himself earlier in my life, it would have kept me back from much sin. . . .

. . . To make use of an illustration, it was something like what follows.

Suppose the Godhead to be like a vast globe of light, a globe larger than the whole world, and that all our actions are seen in that all-embracing globe. . . . I saw all my most filthy actions gathered up and reflected back upon me from that world of light. I tell you it was the most pitiful and dreadful thing to see. I did not know where to hide myself, for that shining light, in which there was no darkness at all, held the whole world within it, and all worlds. . . .

. . . Oh that those who commit deeds of darkness could be made to see this! . . . Oh, the madness of committing sin in the immediate presence of a Majesty so great.

St. Teresa of Avila

PAUSE FOR REFLECTION

*W*as it normal to interrupt Pilate while he was judging? Why did he ignore his wife's urgent warning? What important messages from God are you ignoring?

THURSDAY

The Wicked Insult the Righteous

Matthew 27:21–44

*T*he governor answered and said unto them, Whether of the twain will ye that I release unto you? They said, Barabbas.

²² Pilate saith unto them, What shall I do then with Jesus which is called Christ? *They* all say unto him, Let him be crucified.

²³ And the governor said, Why, what evil hath he done? But they cried out the more, saying, Let him be crucified.

²⁴ When Pilate saw that he could prevail nothing, but *that* rather a tumult was made, he took water, and washed *his* hands before the multitude, saying, I am innocent of the blood of this just person: see ye *to it.*

²⁵ Then answered all the people, and said, His blood *be* on us, and on our children.

²⁶ Then released he Barabbas unto them: and when he had scourged Jesus, he delivered *him* to be crucified.

²⁷ Then the soldiers of the governor took Jesus into the common hall, and gathered unto him the whole band *of soldiers.*

²⁸ And they stripped him, and put on him a scarlet robe.

²⁹ And when they had platted a crown of thorns, they put *it* upon his head, and a reed in his right hand: and they bowed the knee before him, and mocked him, saying, Hail, King of the Jews!

³⁰ And they spit upon him, and took the reed, and smote him on the head.

³¹ And after that they had mocked him, they took the robe off from him, and put his own raiment on him, and led him away to crucify *him.*

Jesus Is Crucified

*A*nd as they came out, they found a man of Cyrene, Simon by name: him they compelled to bear his cross.

³³ And when they were come unto a place called Golgotha, that is to say, a place of a skull,

³⁴ they gave him vinegar to drink mingled with gall: and when he had tasted *thereof,* he would not drink.

³⁵ And they crucified him, and parted his garments, casting lots: that it might be fulfilled which was spoken by the prophet, They parted my garments among them, and upon my vesture did they cast lots.

³⁶ And sitting down they watched him there;

³⁷ and set up over his head his accusation written, THIS IS JESUS THE KING OF THE JEWS.

³⁸ Then were there two thieves crucified with him, one on the right hand, and another on the left.

³⁹ And they that passed by reviled him, wagging their heads,

⁴⁰ and saying, Thou that destroyest the temple, and buildest *it* in three days, save thyself. If thou be the Son of God, come down from the cross.

⁴¹ Likewise also the chief priests mocking *him*, with the scribes and elders, said,

⁴² He saved others; himself he cannot save. If he be the King of Israel, let him now come down from the cross, and we will believe him.

⁴³ He trusted in God; let him deliver him now, if he will have him: for he said, I am the Son of God.

⁴⁴The thieves also, which were crucified with him, cast the same in his teeth.

*B*ut I *am* a worm, and no man; a reproach of men, and despised of the people.
⁷All they that see me laugh me to scorn: they shoot out the lip, they shake the head, *saying,*
⁸He trusted on the LORD *that* he would deliver him: let him deliver him, seeing he delighted in him.

Psalm 22:6–8

*W*ho hath believed our report? and to whom is the arm of the LORD revealed?
²For he shall grow up before him as a tender plant, and as a root out of a dry ground: he hath no form nor comeliness; and when we shall see him, *there is* no beauty that we should desire him.
³He is despised and rejected of men; a man of sorrows, and acquainted with grief: and we hid as it were *our* faces from him; he was despised, and we esteemed him not.
⁵But he *was* wounded for our transgressions, *he was* bruised for our iniquities: the chastisement of our peace *was* upon him; and with his stripes we are healed.

Isaiah 53:1–3, 5

*H*ave you ever been persecuted because of your faith in Christ? If so, how did you respond?

While Francis Xavier was preaching one day in one of the cities of Japan, a man walked up to him as if he had something to say to him privately. As the missionary leaned closer to hear what he had to say, the man spat on his face.

Without a word or the least sign of annoyance, Xavier pulled out a handkerchief and wiped his face. Then he went on with his important message as if nothing had happened. The scorn of the audience was turned to admiration.

The most learned doctor of the city happened to be present.

"A law which teaches men such virtue, inspires them with such courage, and gives them such complete mastery over themselves," he said, "could not but be from God."

Supernatural power and enablement by God's Holy Spirit make that kind of behavior possible for every believer. Furthermore, that kind of behavior probably will do more to attract and influence an unbelieving world than words ever can.

With Christ as our example, love as our motive, and humility as our covering, let us depend on God's Holy Spirit for the wisdom and strength required to respond to mistreatment in a Christlike way. Then, and only then, are we in a position to reflect honor and glory to the Lord Jesus Christ.

Bill Bright

*D*o these readings indicate that we don't feel the pain of insults and suffering we bear for God's sake? Study the model of grace Christ provides by not lashing out against his tormentors. Pray that God will give you grace to bear the pain of whatever insults come your way.

FRIDAY

The Eternal Impact of Jesus'
Death and Resurrection

Matthew 27:45—28:10

Jesus Dies

*N*ow from the sixth hour there was darkness over all the land unto the ninth hour.

⁴⁶ And about the ninth hour Jesus cried with a loud voice, saying, Eli, Eli, lama sabachthani? that is to say, My God, my God, why hast thou forsaken me?

⁴⁷ Some of them that stood there, when they heard *that*, said, This *man* calleth for Elijah.

⁴⁸ And straightway one of them ran, and took a sponge, and filled *it* with vinegar, and put *it* on a reed, and gave him to drink.

⁴⁹ The rest said, Let be, let us see whether Elijah will come to save him.

⁵⁰ Jesus, when he had cried again with a loud voice, yielded up the ghost.

⁵¹ And, behold, the veil of the temple was rent in twain from the top to the bottom; and the earth did quake, and the rocks rent;

⁵² and the graves were opened; and many bodies of the saints which slept arose,

⁵³ and came out of the graves after his resurrection, and went into the holy city, and appeared unto many.

⁵⁴ Now when the centurion, and they that were with him, watching Jesus, saw the earthquake, and those things that were done, they feared greatly, saying, Truly this was the Son of God.

⁵⁵ And many women were there be-holding afar off, which followed Jesus from Galilee, ministering unto him:

⁵⁶ among which was Mary Magdalene, and Mary the mother of James and Joses, and the mother of Zebedee's children.

Jesus Is Buried

*W*hen the even was come, there came a rich man of Arimathea, named Joseph, who also himself was Jesus' disciple:

⁵⁸ he went to Pilate, and begged the body of Jesus. Then Pilate commanded the body to be delivered.

⁵⁹ And when Joseph had taken the body, he wrapped it in a clean linen cloth,

⁶⁰ and laid it in his own new tomb, which he had hewn out in the rock: and he rolled a great stone to the door of the sepulchre, and departed.

⁶¹ And there was Mary Magdalene, and the other Mary, sitting over against the sepulchre.

The Tomb of Jesus Is Guarded

*N*ow the next day, that followed the day of the preparation, the chief priests and Pharisees came together unto Pilate,

⁶³ saying, Sir, we remember that that deceiver said, while he was yet alive, After three days I will rise again.

⁶⁴ Command therefore that the sepulchre be made sure until the third day, lest his disciples come by night, and steal him away, and say unto the people, He is risen from the dead: so the last error shall be worse than the first.

⁶⁵ Pilate said unto them, Ye have a watch: go your way, make *it* as sure as ye can.

⁶⁶ So they went, and made the sepulchre sure, sealing the stone, and setting a watch.

Jesus Rises from the Dead

28 In the end of the sabbath, as it began to dawn toward the first *day* of the week, came Mary Magdalene and the other Mary to see the sepulchre.

² And, behold, there was a great earthquake: for the angel of the Lord descended from heaven, and came and rolled back the stone from the door, and sat upon it.

³ His countenance was like lightning, and his raiment white as snow:

⁴ and for fear of him the keepers did shake, and became as dead *men.*

⁵ And the angel answered and said unto the women, Fear not ye: for I know that ye seek Jesus, which was crucified.

⁶ He is not here: for he is risen, as he said. Come, see the place where the Lord lay.

⁷ And go quickly, and tell his disciples that he is risen from the dead; and, behold, he goeth before you into Galilee; there shall ye see him: lo, I have told you.

⁸ And they departed quickly from the sepulchre with fear and great joy; and did run to bring his disciples word.

⁹ And as they went to tell his disciples, behold, Jesus met them, saying, All hail. And they came and held him by the feet, and worshipped him.

¹⁰ Then said Jesus unto them, Be not afraid: go tell my brethren that they go into Galilee, and there shall they see me.

OLD TESTAMENT READING

I have set the LORD always before me: because *he is* at my right hand, I shall not be moved.

⁹ Therefore my heart is glad, and my glory rejoiceth: my flesh also shall rest in hope.

¹¹ Thou wilt show me the path of life: in thy presence *is* fulness of joy; at thy right hand *there are* pleasures for evermore.

Psalm 16:8–9, 11

INSIGHTS

*T*he power of the resurrection is the power of personal regeneration. Resurrection spells regeneration. The two things must always be kept together: the new world and the new person. Resurrection is not just a passport to heaven, but a power to change us now. Paul says he wants to know Christ and the power of his resurrection. The two are the same. To know Christ today is to come under the influence of the same power that raised Him from the dead. What a cruel thing an example is without the power to live it. Christ is the best of all examples, but more than that, He can come within us and give us His own Spirit to fulfill the example. The result is we actually become like Him, we are able to do the things He did, and most of all, we are able to love as He loved.

Lloyd Ogilvie

PAUSE FOR REFLECTION

*W*hy did the Pharisees fear the possibility of Jesus' resurrection? When he rose again, what did Jesus destroy forever? How has his resurrection regenerated your life?

WEEKEND
Tell the Good News!

Matthew 28:11—Mark 1:20

Soldiers Report to the Leaders

Now when they were going, behold, some of the watch came into the city, and shewed unto the chief priests all the things that were done. [12] And when they were assembled with the elders, and had taken counsel, they gave large money unto the soldiers, [13] saying, Say ye, His disciples came by night, and stole him *away* while we slept. [14] And if this come to the governor's ears, we will persuade him, and secure you. [15] So they took the money, and did as they were taught: and this saying is commonly reported among the Jews until this day.

Jesus Talks to His Disciples

Then the eleven disciples went away into Galilee, into a mountain where Jesus had appointed them. [17] And when they saw him, they worshipped him: but some doubted. [18] And Jesus came and spake unto them, saying, All power is given unto me in heaven and in earth. [19] Go ye therefore, and teach all nations, baptizing them in the name of the Father, and of the Son, and of the Holy Ghost: [20] teaching them to observe all things whatsoever I have commanded you: and, lo, I am with you alway, *even* unto the end of the world. Amen.

John Prepares for Jesus

1 The beginning of the gospel of Jesus Christ, the Son of God. [2] As it is written in the prophets, Behold, I send my messenger before thy face, which shall prepare thy way before thee. [3] The voice of one crying in the wilderness, Prepare ye the way of the Lord, make his paths straight. [4] John did baptize in the wilderness, and preach the baptism of repentance for the remission of sins. [5] And there went out unto him all the land of Judea, and they of Jerusalem, and were all baptized of him in the river of Jordan, confessing their sins. [6] And John was clothed with camel's hair, and with a girdle of a skin about his loins; and he did eat locusts and wild honey; [7] and preached, saying, There cometh one mightier than I after me, the latchet of whose shoes I am not worthy to stoop down and unloose. [8] I indeed have baptized you with water: but he shall baptize you with the Holy Ghost.

Jesus Is Baptized

And it came to pass in those days, that Jesus came from Nazareth of Galilee, and was baptized of John in Jordan. [10] And straightway coming up out of the water, he saw the heavens opened, and the Spirit like a dove descending upon him: [11] and there came a voice from heaven, *saying*, Thou art my beloved Son, in whom I am well pleased. [12] And immediately the Spirit driveth him into the wilderness. [13] And he was there in the wilderness forty days, tempted of Satan; and was with the wild beasts; and the angels ministered unto him.

Jesus Chooses Some Disciples

*N*ow after that John was put in prison, Jesus came into Galilee, preaching the gospel of the kingdom of God,

¹⁵ And saying, The time is fulfilled, and the kingdom of God is at hand: repent ye, and believe the gospel.

¹⁶ Now as he walked by the sea of Galilee, he saw Simon and Andrew his brother casting a net into the sea: for they were fishers.

¹⁷ And Jesus said unto them, Come ye after me, and I will make you to become fishers of men.

¹⁸ And straightway they forsook their nets, and followed him.

¹⁹ And when he had gone a little farther thence, he saw James the *son* of Zebedee, and John his brother, who also were in the ship mending their nets.

²⁰ And straightway he called them: and they left their father Zebedee in the ship with the hired servants, and went after him.

OLD TESTAMENT READING

*S*ing unto the LORD, all the earth; show forth from day to day his salvation.

²⁴ Declare his glory among the heathen; his marvelous works among all nations.

²⁵ For great *is* the LORD, and greatly to be praised: he also *is* to be feared above all gods.

1 Chronicles 16:23–25

INSIGHTS

*F*or the New Testament Christians, witness was not a sales pitch.

They simply shared, each in his own way, what they had received. Theirs was not a formally prepared, carefully worked-out presentation with a gimmick to manipulate conversation, and a "closer" for an on-the-spot-decision . . . but the spontaneous, irrepressible, effervescent enthusiasm of those who had met the most fascinating Person who ever lived.

The gospel is not theology. It's a Person. Theology doesn't save. Jesus Christ saves. The first-century disciples were totally involved with a Person. They were followers of Jesus. They were learners of Jesus. They were committed to Jesus. They were filled with Jesus.

They had encountered Jesus Christ and it simply could not be concealed. They witnessed not because they had to, but because they could not help it.

Their school of witnessing was the school of the Spirit where they learned continuously. Authentic Christian witness is born of the Spirit.

Madison Avenue, with all its sophisticated know-how, can't improve on the strategy. Nothing is more convincing than the simple, unembellished word of a satisfied customer.

Richard Halverson

ACTION POINT

*I*s your salvation real enough to boldly announce the Good News? Pray that God's salvation will be so real to you that you will tell others.

MONDAY

God Is Compassionate and Brings Healing to Body and Soul

Mark 1:21–45

A Man with an Unclean Spirit

*A*nd they went into Capernaum; and straightway on the sabbath day he entered into the synagogue, and taught. [22] And they were astonished at his doctrine: for he taught them as one that had authority, and not as the scribes. [23] And there was in their synagogue a man with an unclean spirit; and he cried out,

[24] saying, Let *us* alone; what have we to do with thee, thou Jesus of Nazareth? art thou come to destroy us? I know thee who thou art, the Holy One of God.

[25] And Jesus rebuked him, saying, Hold thy peace, and come out of him. [26] And when the unclean spirit had torn him, and cried with a loud voice, he came out of him.

[27] And they were all amazed, insomuch that they questioned among themselves, saying, What thing is this? what new doctrine *is* this? for with authority commandeth he even the unclean spirits, and they do obey him.

[28] And immediately his fame spread abroad throughout all the region round about Galilee.

Jesus Heals Many People

*A*nd forthwith, when they were come out of the synagogue, they entered into the house of Simon and Andrew, with James and John.

[30] But Simon's wife's mother lay sick of a fever; and anon they tell him of her.

[31] And he came and took her by the hand, and lifted her up; and immediately the fever left her, and she ministered unto them.

[32] And at even, when the sun did set, they brought unto him all that were diseased, and them that were possessed with devils.

[33] And all the city was gathered together at the door.

[34] And he healed many that were sick of divers diseases, and cast out many devils; and suffered not the devils to speak, because they knew him.

[35] And in the morning, rising up a great while before day, he went out, and departed into a solitary place, and there prayed.

[36] And Simon and they that were with him followed after him.

[37] And when they had found him, they said unto him, All *men* seek for thee.

[38] And he said unto them, Let us go into the next towns, that I may preach there also: for therefore came I forth.

[39] And he preached in their synagogues throughout all Galilee, and cast out devils.

Jesus Heals a Leper

*A*nd there came a leper to him, beseeching him, and kneeling down to him, and saying unto him, If thou wilt, thou canst make me clean.

[41] And Jesus, moved with compassion, put forth *his* hand, and touched him, and saith unto him, I will; be thou clean.

[42] And as soon as he had spoken, im-

mediately the leprosy departed from him, and he was cleansed.

[43] And he straitly charged him, and forthwith sent him away;

[44] and saith unto him, See thou say nothing to any man: but go thy way, show thyself to the priest, and offer for thy cleansing those things which Moses commanded, for a testimony unto them.

[45] But he went out, and began to publish *it* much, and to blaze abroad the matter, insomuch that Jesus could no more openly enter into the city, but was without in desert places: and they came to him from every quarter.

OLD TESTAMENT READING

*C*ome, and let us return unto the LORD: for he hath torn, and he will heal us; he hath smitten, and he will bind us up.

[2] After two days will he revive us: in the third day he will raise us up, and we shall live in his sight.

[3] Then shall we know, *if* we follow on to know the LORD: his going forth is prepared as the morning; and he shall come unto us as the rain, as the latter *and* former rain unto the earth.

Hosea 6:1–3

*H*eal me, O LORD, and I shall be healed; save me, and I shall be saved: for thou *art* my praise.

Jeremiah 17:14

INSIGHTS

*B*ethlehem, Galilee, Gethsemane—He walked there. But today Christ walks the concrete sidewalks of Times Square, 47th Street, and Broadway. And as He walks, His feet are soiled—not with the sand of the seashore or the reddish dust of the Emmaus Road, but with the soot and filth of the city.

He walks the "Great White Way," and His face is lit by the gaudy neon signboards of materialism. He walks in the shadows of the dark alleyways, where faces are not lit at all. . . .

He is pushed and shoved through Grand Central Station, elbowed and ignored, yet in the crowd He feels a measure of virtue flow from His being and searches through the faces for an honest seeker passing by. . . .

Christ walks the city and . . . weaves the cloth that transforms rags into a lovely tapestry. . . . He acts the part that tells the story of how that Love invaded humankind, for only story tells the Story. Christ incarnate. Christ the living, walking parable, takes the stage to be the Story. . . .

. . . He is the broken, and He is the healer. He is the hungry, and He is the Bread of Life. He is the homeless, yet it is He who says "Come to Me all you who are overloaded, and I will be your resting place." He is the loser who makes losing the only way to win. He is the omnipotent who calls all who follow to choose powerlessness and teaches us by laying down all power in heaven and in earth. He is the sick, and He is the wholeness.

Gloria Gaither

ACTION POINT

*C*an you imagine any greater compassion than that shown in the love of the Son? Meditate on one of these readings today.

TUESDAY

Jesus Has the Authority to Forgive

Mark 2:1–22

Jesus Heals a Palsied Man

2 And again he entered into Capernaum, after *some* days; and it was noised that he was in the house.

2 And straightway many were gathered together, insomuch that there was no room to receive *them*, no, not so much as about the door: and he preached the word unto them.

3 And they come unto him, bringing one sick of the palsy, which was borne of four.

4 And when they could not come nigh unto him for the press, they uncovered the roof where he was: and when they had broken *it* up, they let down the bed wherein the sick of the palsy lay.

5 When Jesus saw their faith, he said unto the sick of the palsy, Son, thy sins be forgiven thee.

6 But there were certain of the scribes sitting there, and reasoning in their hearts,

7 Why doth this *man* thus speak blasphemies? who can forgive sins but God only?

8 And immediately, when Jesus perceived in his spirit that they so reasoned within themselves, he said unto them, Why reason ye these things in your hearts?

9 whether is it easier to say to the sick of the palsy, *Thy* sins be forgiven thee; or to say, Arise, and take up thy bed, and walk?

10 But that ye may know that the Son of man hath power on earth to forgive sins, (he saith to the sick of the palsy,)

11 I say unto thee, Arise, and take up thy bed, and go thy way into thine house.

12 And immediately he arose, took up the bed, and went forth before them all; insomuch that they were all amazed, and glorified God, saying, We never saw it on this fashion.

13 And he went forth again by the sea side; and all the multitude resorted unto him, and he taught them.

14 And as he passed by, he saw Levi the *son* of Alphaeus sitting at the receipt of custom, and said unto him, Follow me. And he arose and followed him.

15 And it came to pass, that, as Jesus sat at meat in his house, many publicans and sinners sat also together with Jesus and his disciples; for there were many, and they followed him.

16 And when the scribes and Pharisees saw him eat with publicans and sinners, they said unto his disciples, How is it that he eateth and drinketh with publicans and sinners?

17 When Jesus heard *it*, he saith unto them, They that are whole have no need of the physician, but they that are sick: I came not to call the righteous, but sinners to repentance.

Jesus' Disciples Are Criticized

And the disciples of John and of the Pharisees used to fast: and they come and say unto him, Why do the disciples of John and of the Pharisees fast, but thy disciples fast not?

19 And Jesus said unto them, Can the children of the bridechamber fast, while the bridegroom is with them?

as long as they have the bridegroom with them, they cannot fast. ²⁰ But the days will come, when the bridegroom shall be taken away from them, and then shall they fast in those days. ²¹ No man also seweth a piece of new cloth on an old garment; else the new piece that filled it up taketh away from the old, and the rent is made worse. ²² And no man putteth new wine into old bottles; else the new wine doth burst the bottles, and the wine is spilled, and the bottles will be marred: but new wine must be put into new bottles.

OLD TESTAMENT READING

*Y*et it pleased the LORD to bruise him; he hath put *him* to grief: when thou shalt make his soul an offering for sin, he shall see *his* seed, he shall prolong *his* days, and the pleasure of the LORD shall prosper in his hand. ¹¹ He shall see of the travail of his soul, *and* shall be satisfied: by his knowledge shall my righteous servant justify many; for he shall bear their iniquities. ¹² Therefore will I divide him *a portion* with the great, and he shall divide the spoil with the strong; because he hath poured out his soul unto death: and he was numbered with the transgressors: and he bare the sin of many, and made intercession for the transgressors.

Isaiah 53:10–12

INSIGHTS

*F*orgiveness is one of the first and most glorious blessings we receive from God. It is the transition from the old to the new life; the sign and pledge of God's love: with it we receive the right to all the spiritual gifts which are prepared for us in Christ. The believer can never forget, either here or in eternity, that he is a forgiven sinner. Nothing more inflames his love, awakens his joy, or strengthens his courage than the continually renewed experience of God's forgiving love. Every day, yes, every thought of God reminds him: I owe all to pardoning grace.

This forgiving love is one of the greatest manifestations of the divine nature. In it God finds His glory and blessedness and wants to share this with His redeemed people.

Andrew Murray

APPLICATION

*W*hat is the most important characteristic of the good servant promised in Isaiah 53? Is it then surprising that Jesus forgave sins while he was on earth? Has your spirit been healed by Jesus' forgiveness of your sins?

WEDNESDAY

Jesus Teaches About the Rules of the Sabbath

Mark 2:23—3:27

Jesus Is Lord of the Sabbath

*A*nd it came to pass, that he went through the corn fields on the sabbath day; and his disciples began, as they went, to pluck the ears of corn.

24 And the Pharisees said unto him, Behold, why do they on the sabbath day that which is not lawful?

25 And he said unto them, Have ye never read what David did, when he had need, and was ahungered, he, and they that were with him?

26 How he went into the house of God in the days of Abiathar the high priest, and did eat the showbread, which is not lawful to eat but for the priests, and gave also to them which were with him?

27 And he said unto them, The sabbath was made for man, and not man for the sabbath:

28 therefore the Son of man is Lord also of the sabbath.

Jesus Heals a Man's Hand

3 And he entered again into the synagogue; and there was a man there which had a withered hand.

2 And they watched him, whether he would heal him on the sabbath day; that they might accuse him.

3 And he saith unto the man which had the withered hand, Stand forth.

4 And he saith unto them, Is it lawful to do good on the sabbath days, or to do evil? to save life, or to kill? But they held their peace.

5 And when he had looked round about on them with anger, being grieved for the hardness of their hearts, he saith unto the man, Stretch forth thine hand. And he stretched *it* out: and his hand was restored whole as the other.

6 And the Pharisees went forth, and straightway took counsel with the Herodians against him, how they might destroy him.

Many People Follow Jesus

*B*ut Jesus withdrew himself with his disciples to the sea: and a great multitude from Galilee followed him, and from Judea,

8 and from Jerusalem, and from Idumea, and *from* beyond Jordan; and they about Tyre and Sidon, a great multitude, when they had heard what great things he did, came unto him.

9 And he spake to his disciples, that a small ship should wait on him because of the multitude, lest they should throng him.

10 For he had healed many; insomuch that they pressed upon him for to touch him, as many as had plagues.

11 And unclean spirits, when they saw him, fell down before him, and cried, saying, Thou art the Son of God.

12 And he straitly charged them that they should not make him known.

Jesus Chooses His Apostles

*A*nd he goeth up into a mountain, and calleth *unto him* whom he would: and they came unto him.

14 And he ordained twelve, that they

should be with him, and that he might send them forth to preach,

¹⁵ and to have power to heal sicknesses, and to cast out devils:

¹⁶ and Simon he surnamed Peter;

¹⁷ and James the *son* of Zebedee, and John the brother of James; and he surnamed them Boanerges, which is, The sons of thunder:

¹⁸ And Andrew, and Philip, and Bartholomew, and Matthew, and Thomas, and James the *son of* Alphaeus, and Thaddaeus, and Simon the Canaanite,

¹⁹ and Judas Iscariot, which also betrayed him: and they went into a house.

Some Say Jesus Has a Devil

*A*nd the multitude cometh together again, so that they could not so much as eat bread.

²¹ And when his friends heard *of it,* they went out to lay hold on him: for they said, He is beside himself.

²² And the scribes which came down from Jerusalem said, He hath Beelzebub, and by the prince of the devils casteth he out devils.

²³ And he called them *unto him*, and said unto them in parables, How can Satan cast out Satan?

²⁴ And if a kingdom be divided against itself, that kingdom cannot stand.

²⁵ And if a house be divided against itself, that house cannot stand.

²⁶ And if Satan rise up against himself, and be divided, he cannot stand, but hath an end.

²⁷ No man can enter into a strong man's house, and spoil his goods, except he will first bind the strong man; and then he will spoil his house.

*T*hus saith the LORD, Keep ye judgment, and do justice: for my salvation *is* near to come, and my righteousness to be revealed.

² Blessed *is* the man *that* doeth this, and the son of man *that* layeth hold on it; that keepeth the sabbath from polluting it, and keepeth his hand from doing any evil.

Isaiah 56:1–2

---

*S*abbath rest means worship with the Christian family. In proper worship we will have a chance to exercise all three aspects that lead to the rest of our private worlds: looking backward, upward, and ahead. Such worship is non-negotiable to the person committed to walking with God. . . .

. . . Sabbath means a deliberate acceptance of personal rest and tranquility within the individual life. Sabbath means a rest that brings peace into the private world. As Christ pressed stillness into a storm, order into a being of a demon-possessed maniac, health into a desperately sick woman, and life into a dead friend, so He seeks to press peace into the harried private world of the man or woman who has been in the marketplace all week. But there is a condition. We must accept this peace as a gift and take the time to receive it.

Gordon MacDonald

---

*H*ow do you think Jesus feels about the way you keep the Sabbath?

THURSDAY

Those Who Obey God Belong to Him

Mark 3:28—4:20

*V*erily I say unto you, All sins shall be forgiven unto the sons of men, and blasphemies wherewith soever they shall blaspheme:

²⁹ but he that shall blaspheme against the Holy Ghost hath never forgiveness, but is in danger of eternal damnation:

³⁰ because they said, He hath an unclean spirit.

Jesus' True Family

*T*here came then his brethren and his mother, and, standing without, sent unto him, calling him.

³² And the multitude sat about him, and they said unto him, Behold, thy mother and thy brethren without seek for thee.

³³ And he answered them, saying, Who is my mother, or my brethren?

³⁴ And he looked round about on them which sat about him, and said, Behold my mother and my brethren!

³⁵ For whosoever shall do the will of God, the same is my brother, and my sister, and mother.

A Parable About Planting Seed

4 And he began again to teach by the sea side: and there was gathered unto him a great multitude, so that he entered into a ship, and sat in the sea; and the whole multitude was by the sea on the land.

² And he taught them many things by parables, and said unto them in his doctrine,

³ Hearken; Behold, there went out a sower to sow:

⁴ and it came to pass, as he sowed, some fell by the wayside, and the fowls of the air came and devoured it up.

⁵ And some fell on stony ground, where it had not much earth; and immediately it sprang up, because it had no depth of earth:

⁶ but when the sun was up, it was scorched; and because it had no root, it withered away.

⁷ And some fell among thorns, and the thorns grew up, and choked it, and it yielded no fruit.

⁸ And other fell on good ground, and did yield fruit that sprang up and increased, and brought forth, some thirty, and some sixty, and some a hundred.

⁹ And he said unto them, He that hath ears to hear, let him hear.

Why Jesus Used Parables

*A*nd when he was alone, they that were about him with the twelve asked of him the parable.

¹¹ And he said unto them, Unto you it is given to know the mystery of the kingdom of God: but unto them that are without, all *these* things are done in parables:

¹² that seeing they may see, and not perceive; and hearing they may hear, and not understand; lest at any time they should be converted, and *their* sins should be forgiven them.

¹³ And he said unto them, Know ye not this parable? and how then will ye know all parables?

¹⁴ The sower soweth the word.

¹⁵ And these are they by the wayside, where the word is sown; but when

they have heard, Satan cometh immediately, and taketh away the word that was sown in their hearts.

¹⁶ And these are they likewise which are sown on stony ground; who, when they have heard the word, immediately receive it with gladness;

¹⁷ and have no root in themselves, and so endure but for a time: afterward, when affliction or persecution ariseth for the word's sake, immediately they are offended.

¹⁸ And these are they which are sown among thorns; such as hear the word,

¹⁹ and the cares of this world, and the deceitfulness of riches, and the lusts of other things entering in, choke the word, and it becometh unfruitful.

²⁰ And these are they which are sown on good ground; such as hear the word, and receive *it*, and bring forth fruit, some thirtyfold, some sixty, and some a hundred.

OLD TESTAMENT READING

*A*nd Moses went up unto God, and the Lᴏʀᴅ called unto him out of the mountain, saying, Thus shalt thou say to the house of Jacob, and tell the children of Israel;

⁴ Ye have seen what I did unto the Egyptians, and *how* I bare you on eagles' wings, and brought you unto myself.

⁵ Now therefore, if ye will obey my voice indeed, and keep my covenant, then ye shall be a peculiar treasure unto me above all people: for all the earth *is* mine.

Exodus 19:3–5

INSIGHTS

*T*he source of Christ's victory, the secret of His power, and of ours, lies in obedience. . . . In an obedient heart there is a way prepared for God. There are many Christians who always seek pleasure and satisfaction for themselves. These have not yet learned that only obedient children are happy children. That which in truth brings abiding happiness is nothing else than obedience toward God. For a healthy soul there is only one thing that counts—to be obedient. . . .

Why have so many of God's lambs so little assurance of salvation? Why are their souls not satisfied with the peace of God? God gives us the answer in Isaiah 48:18: "Oh, that thou hadst hearkened to my commandments! Then had thy peace been as a river, and thy righteousness as the waves of the sea." People say, "I lack faith. I have too little faith; therefore I have no assurance of salvation, no peace." But in most instances it is not faith which is lacking, for even with a trembling hand one can receive costly gifts. It is rather obedience which is lacking. There is something in their lives which they will not let go, and which hinders the Holy Spirit from giving them the assurance that they are God's children. . . . No one who is disobedient to God can have confidence in Him. Confidence is a result of obedience.

G. Steinberger

APPLICATION

*W*hat one thing does God require of those who would be his people? What do those who obey God receive from him? How's your obedience? Is it obvious that you belong to God?

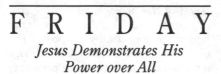

FRIDAY

*Jesus Demonstrates His
Power over All*

Mark 4:21—5:10

Use What You Have

*A*nd he said unto them, Is a candle brought to be put under a bushel, or under a bed? and not to be set on a candlestick?
²² For there is nothing hid, which shall not be manifested; neither was any thing kept secret, but that it should come abroad.
²³ If any man have ears to hear, let him hear.
²⁴ And he said unto them, Take heed what ye hear. With what measure ye mete, it shall be measured to you; and unto you that hear shall more be given.
²⁵ For he that hath, to him shall be given; and he that hath not, from him shall be taken even that which he hath.

Jesus' Parable About Seed

*A*nd he said, So is the kingdom of God, as if a man should cast seed into the ground;
²⁷ and should sleep, and rise night and day, and the seed should spring and grow up, he knoweth not how.
²⁸ For the earth bringeth forth fruit of herself; first the blade, then the ear, after that the full corn in the ear.
²⁹ But when the fruit is brought forth, immediately he putteth in the sickle, because the harvest is come.

A Parable About Mustard Seed

*A*nd he said, Whereunto shall we liken the kingdom of God? or with what comparison shall we compare it?
³¹ *It is* like a grain of mustard seed, which, when it is sown in the earth, is less than all the seeds that be in the earth:
³² but when it is sown, it groweth up, and becometh greater than all herbs, and shooteth out great branches; so that the fowls of the air may lodge under the shadow of it.
³³ And with many such parables spake he the word unto them, as they were able to hear *it*.
³⁴ But without a parable spake he not unto them: and when they were alone, he expounded all things to his disciples.

Jesus Calms a Storm

*A*nd the same day, when the even was come, he saith unto them, Let us pass over unto the other side.
³⁶ And when they had sent away the multitude, they took him even as he was in the ship. And there were also with him other little ships.
³⁷ And there arose a great storm of wind, and the waves beat into the ship, so that it was now full.
³⁸ And he was in the hinder part of the ship, asleep on a pillow: and they awake him, and say unto him, Master, carest thou not that we perish?
³⁹ And he arose, and rebuked the wind, and said unto the sea, Peace, be still. And the wind ceased, and there was a great calm.
⁴⁰ And he said unto them, Why are ye so fearful? how is it that ye have no faith?
⁴¹ And they feared exceedingly, and said one to another, What manner of man is this, that even the wind and the sea obey him?

A Man with Demons Inside Him

5 And they came over unto the other side of the sea, into the country of the Gadarenes.

² And when he was come out of the ship, immediately there met him out of the tombs a man with an unclean spirit,

³ who had *his* dwelling among the tombs; and no man could bind him, no, not with chains:

⁴ because that he had been often bound with fetters and chains, and the chains had been plucked asunder by him, and the fetters broken in pieces: neither could any *man* tame him.

⁵ And always, night and day, he was in the mountains, and in the tombs, crying, and cutting himself with stones.

⁶ But when he saw Jesus afar off, he ran and worshipped him,

⁷ and cried with a loud voice, and said, What have I to do with thee, Jesus, *thou* Son of the most high God? I adjure thee by God, that thou torment me not.

⁸ For he said unto him, Come out of the man, *thou* unclean spirit.

⁹ And he asked him, What *is* thy name? And he answered, saying, My name *is* Legion: for we are many.

¹⁰ And he besought him much that he would not send them away out of the country.

OLD TESTAMENT READING

*T*he voice of the LORD *is* powerful; the voice of the LORD *is* full of majesty.

¹⁰ The LORD sitteth upon the flood; yea, the LORD sitteth King for ever.

Psalm 29:4, 10

INSIGHTS

*T*here is a power that destroys. There is also a power that creates. The power that creates gives life and joy and peace. It is freedom and not bondage, life and not death, transformation and not coercion. The power that creates restores relationship and gives the gift of wholeness to all. The power that creates is spiritual power, the power that proceeds from God. . . .

In the crucifixion the power that creates reached its apex. At the cross Satan sought to use all the power at his disposal to destroy Christ, but God turned it into the ultimate act of creative power. The penalty for sin was paid; the justice of God was satisfied. Through the cross of Christ, you and I can receive forgiveness and know the restoring of our relationship to God. Christ died for our sins, and in that death we see the power that creates.

Our response to this supreme act of power is gratitude. It is "love divine, all loves excelling." We can never hope or want to duplicate this act of power. We simply thank God for what he has done.

Richard Foster

ACTION POINT

*T*hink about the many kinds of awesome power God has at his disposal. How has he used his power to draw you to himself? Thank him for saving you by his power.

WEEKEND

The Power of Faith

Mark 5:11–36

Now there was there nigh unto the mountains a great herd of swine feeding.

¹² And all the devils besought him, saying, Send us into the swine, that we may enter into them.

¹³ And forthwith Jesus gave them leave. And the unclean spirits went out, and entered into the swine; and the herd ran violently down a steep place into the sea, (they were about two thousand,) and were choked in the sea.

¹⁴ And they that fed the swine fled, and told *it* in the city, and in the country. And they went out to see what it was that was done.

¹⁵ And they come to Jesus, and see him that was possessed with the devil, and had the legion, sitting, and clothed, and in his right mind; and they were afraid.

¹⁶ And they that saw *it* told them how it befell to him that was possessed with the devil, and *also* concerning the swine.

¹⁷ And they began to pray him to depart out of their coasts.

¹⁸ And when he was come into the ship, he that had been possessed with the devil prayed him that he might be with him.

¹⁹ Howbeit Jesus suffered him not, but saith unto him, Go home to thy friends, and tell them how great things the Lord hath done for thee, and hath had compassion on thee.

²⁰ And he departed, and began to publish in Decapolis how great things Jesus had done for him: and all *men* did marvel.

Jesus Gives Life to a Dead Girl and Heals a Sick Woman

And when Jesus was passed over again by ship unto the other side, much people gathered unto him; and he was nigh unto the sea.

²² And, behold, there cometh one of the rulers of the synagogue, Jairus by name; and when he saw him, he fell at his feet,

²³ and besought him greatly, saying, My little daughter lieth at the point of death: *I pray thee*, come and lay thy hands on her, that she may be healed; and she shall live.

²⁴ And *Jesus* went with him; and much people followed him, and thronged him.

²⁵ And a certain woman, which had an issue of blood twelve years,

²⁶ and had suffered many things of many physicians, and had spent all that she had, and was nothing bettered, but rather grew worse,

²⁷ when she had heard of Jesus, came in the press behind, and touched his garment.

²⁸ For she said, If I may touch but his clothes, I shall be whole.

²⁹ And straightway the fountain of her blood was dried up; and she felt in *her* body that she was healed of that plague.

³⁰ And Jesus, immediately knowing in himself that virtue had gone out of him, turned him about in the press, and said, Who touched my clothes?

³¹ And his disciples said unto him, Thou seest the multitude thronging thee, and sayest thou, Who touched me?

³² And he looked round about to see her that had done this thing.

³³ But the woman fearing and trembling, knowing what was done in her, came and fell down before him, and told him all the truth.

³⁴ And he said unto her, Daughter, thy faith hath made thee whole; go in peace, and be whole of thy plague.

³⁵ While he yet spake, there came from the ruler of the synagogue's *house certain* which said, Thy daughter is dead; why troublest thou the Master any further?

³⁶ As soon as Jesus heard the word that was spoken, he saith unto the ruler of the synagogue, Be not afraid, only believe.

OLD TESTAMENT READING

*A*nd when the Philistine looked about, and saw David, he disdained him: for he was *but* a youth, and ruddy, and of a fair countenance.

⁴³ And the Philistine said unto David, *Am* I a dog, that thou comest to me with staves? And the Philistine cursed David by his gods.

⁴⁴ And the Philistine said to David, Come to me, and I will give thy flesh unto the fowls of the air, and to the beasts of the field.

⁴⁵ Then said David to the Philistine, Thou comest to me with a sword, and with a spear, and with a shield: but I come to thee in the name of the LORD of hosts, the God of the armies of Israel, whom thou hast defied.

⁴⁶ This day will the LORD deliver thee into mine hand; and I will smite thee, and take thine head from thee; and I will give the carcasses of the host of the Philistines this day unto the fowls of the air, and to the wild beasts of the earth; that all the earth may know that there is a God in Israel.

⁴⁷ And all this assembly shall know that the LORD saveth not with sword and spear: for the battle *is* the LORD's, and he will give you into our hands.

⁵⁰ So David prevailed over the Philistine with a sling and with a stone, and smote the Philistine, and slew him; but *there was* no sword in the hand of David.

1 Samuel 17:42–47, 50

INSIGHTS

*T*he doctrine of the Bible is that Christ saves His people from sin through faith; that Christ's Spirit is received by faith to dwell in the heart. It is faith that works by love. Love is wrought and sustained by faith. By faith, Christians "overcome the world, the flesh, and the devil." It is by faith that they "quench all the fiery darts of the wicked." It is by faith that they "put on the Lord Jesus Christ, and put off the old man, with his deeds." It is by faith that we "stand," by resolutions we fall. This is the victory that overcometh the world, even our faith.

. . . When we open the door by implicit trust, He enters in and takes up His abode with us and in us. By shedding abroad His love, He quickens our souls into sympathy with himself, and in this way, and in this way alone, He purifies our hearts through faith.

Charles Finney

PAUSE FOR REFLECTION

*W*hat has the Lord done for you? How has he responded to your faith in him? With whom does he want you to share your faith?

MONDAY

The Consequences of Unbelief

Mark 5:37—6:20

*A*nd he suffered no man to follow him, save Peter, and James, and John the brother of James.

38 And he cometh to the house of the ruler of the synagogue, and seeth the tumult, and them that wept and wailed greatly.

39 And when he was come in, he saith unto them, Why make ye this ado, and weep? the damsel is not dead, but sleepeth.

40 And they laughed him to scorn. But when he had put them all out, he taketh the father and the mother of the damsel, and them that were with him, and entereth in where the damsel was lying.

41 And he took the damsel by the hand, and said unto her, Talitha cumi; which is, being interpreted, Damsel, (I say unto thee,) arise.

42 And straightway the damsel arose, and walked; for she was *of the age* of twelve years. And they were astonished with a great astonishment.

43 And he charged them straitly that no man should know it; and commanded that something should be given her to eat.

Jesus Goes to His Hometown

6 And he went out from thence, and came into his own country; and his disciples follow him.

2 And when the sabbath day was come, he began to teach in the synagogue: and many hearing *him* were astonished, saying, From whence hath this *man* these things? and what wisdom *is* this which is given unto him, that even such mighty works are wrought by his hands?

3 Is not this the carpenter, the son of Mary, the brother of James, and Joses, and of Judas, and Simon? and are not his sisters here with us? And they were offended at him.

4 But Jesus said unto them, A prophet is not without honor, but in his own country, and among his own kin, and in his own house.

5 And he could there do no mighty work, save that he laid his hands upon a few sick folk, and healed *them*.

6 And he marveled because of their unbelief. And he went round about the villages, teaching.

7 And he called *unto him* the twelve, and began to send them forth by two and two; and gave them power over unclean spirits;

8 and commanded them that they should take nothing for *their* journey, save a staff only; no scrip, no bread, no money in *their* purse:

9 but *be* shod with sandals; and not put on two coats.

10 And he said unto them, In what place soever ye enter into a house, there abide till ye depart from that place.

11 And whosoever shall not receive you, nor hear you, when ye depart thence, shake off the dust under your feet for a testimony against them. Verily I say unto you, It shall be more tolerable for Sodom and Gomorrah in the day of judgment, than for that city.

12 And they went out, and preached that men should repent.

13 And they cast out many devils, and anointed with oil many that were sick, and healed *them*.

How John the Baptist Was Killed

*A*nd king Herod heard *of him*; (for his name was spread abroad;) and he said, That John the Baptist was risen from the dead, and therefore mighty works do show forth themselves in him.

¹⁵ Others said, That it is Elijah. And others said, That it is a prophet, or as one of the prophets.

¹⁶ But when Herod heard *thereof*, he said, It is John, whom I beheaded: he is risen from the dead.

¹⁷ For Herod himself had sent forth and laid hold upon John, and bound him in prison for Herodias' sake, his brother Philip's wife; for he had married her.

¹⁸ For John had said unto Herod, It is not lawful for thee to have thy brother's wife.

¹⁹ Therefore Herodias had a quarrel against him, and would have killed him; but she could not:

²⁰ for Herod feared John, knowing that he was a just man and a holy, and observed him; and when he heard him, he did many things, and heard him gladly.

OLD TESTAMENT READING

*A*nd the LORD said unto me, Say unto them, Go not up, neither fight; for I *am* not among you; lest ye be smitten before your enemies.

⁴³ So I spake unto you; and ye would not hear, but rebelled against the commandment of the LORD, and went presumptuously up into the hill.

⁴⁴ And the Amorites, which dwelt in that mountain, came out against you, and chased you, as bees do, and destroyed you in Seir, *even* unto Hormah.

⁴⁵ And ye returned and wept before the LORD; but the LORD would not hearken to your voice, nor give ear unto you.

Deuteronomy 1:42–45

INSIGHTS

*G*od had told the people to enter and possess the land, but they preferred to spy it out just to see if God was really telling the truth! Well, He was—it was a rich land, a beautiful land, and a fruitful land. But there were giants! "We are not able to overcome!" This was the majority report.

The minority report came from Caleb and Joshua, and Moses agreed with them: "We are well able to overcome it!" This is the Old Testament version of Romans 8:31: "If God be for us, who can be against us?" The majority saw the obstacles, and they were bigger than their God. The minority saw God, and the obstacles disappeared! . . .

Christians do not fight for victory; we fight from victory. Jesus said, "In the world ye shall have tribulation: but be of good cheer; I have overcome the world" (John 16:33). John said, "This is the victory that overcometh the world, even our faith" (1 John 5:4).

Either we are overcomers—or overcome.

Warren Wiersbe

APPLICATION

*L*ist the consequences of unbelief and the rewards of faith. Will you be an overcomer or be overcome?

TUESDAY

Trust God for His Provision

Mark 6:21–44

*A*nd when a convenient day was come, that Herod on his birthday made a supper to his lords, high captains, and chief *estates* of Galilee;

22 and when the daughter of the said Herodias came in, and danced, and pleased Herod and them that sat with him, the king said unto the damsel, Ask of me whatsoever thou wilt, and I will give *it* thee.

23 And he sware unto her, Whatsoever thou shalt ask of me, I will give *it* thee, unto the half of my kingdom.

24 And she went forth, and said unto her mother, What shall I ask? And she said, The head of John the Baptist.

25 And she came in straightway with haste unto the king, and asked, saying, I will that thou give me by and by in a charger the head of John the Baptist.

26 And the king was exceeding sorry; *yet* for his oath's sake, and for their sakes which sat with him, he would not reject her.

27 And immediately the king sent an executioner, and commanded his head to be brought: and he went and beheaded him in the prison,

28 and brought his head in a charger, and gave it to the damsel: and the damsel gave it to her mother.

29 And when his disciples heard *of it,* they came and took up his corpse, and laid it in a tomb.

More than Five Thousand Fed

*A*nd the apostles gathered themselves together unto Jesus, and told him all things, both what they had done, and what they had taught.

31 And he said unto them, Come ye yourselves apart into a desert place, and rest a while: for there were many coming and going, and they had no leisure so much as to eat.

32 And they departed into a desert place by ship privately.

33 And the people saw them departing, and many knew him, and ran afoot thither out of all cities, and outwent them, and came together unto him.

34 And Jesus, when he came out, saw much people, and was moved with compassion toward them, because they were as sheep not having a shepherd: and he began to teach them many things.

35 And when the day was now far spent, his disciples came unto him, and said, This is a desert place, and now the time *is* far passed:

36 send them away, that they may go into the country round about, and into the villages, and buy themselves bread: for they have nothing to eat.

37 He answered and said unto them, Give ye them to eat. And they say unto him, Shall we go and buy two hundred pennyworth of bread, and give them to eat?

38 He saith unto them, How many loaves have ye? go and see. And when they knew, they say, Five, and two fishes.

39 And he commanded them to make all sit down by companies upon the green grass.

40 And they sat down in ranks, by hundreds, and by fifties.

41 And when he had taken the five loaves and the two fishes, he looked up to heaven, and blessed, and brake the loaves, and gave *them* to his disciples to set before them; and

the two fishes divided he among them all.

[42] And they did all eat, and were filled.

[43] And they took up twelve baskets full of the fragments, and of the fishes.

[44] And they that did eat of the loaves were about five thousand men.

OLD TESTAMENT READING

I will extol thee, my God, O King; and I will bless thy name for ever and ever.

[2] Every day will I bless thee; and I will praise thy name for ever and ever.

[3] Great *is* the LORD, and greatly to be praised; and his greatness *is* unsearchable.

[4] One generation shall praise thy works to another, and shall declare thy mighty acts.

[5] I will speak of the glorious honor of thy majesty, and of thy wondrous works.

[6] And *men* shall speak of the might of thy terrible acts: and I will declare thy greatness.

Psalm 145:1–6

*O*h that *men* would praise the LORD *for* his goodness, and *for* his wonderful works to the children of men!

[9] For he satisfieth the longing soul, and filleth the hungry soul with goodness.

Psalm 107:8–9

INSIGHTS

*I*t is better to trust in God than to accumulate riches. . . .

Trust in God gives clearness of vision. When we are thinking partly of doing God's work in the world, and partly of lining our own nest, we are in the condition of the man whose eyes do not look in the same direction. . . . We are endeavouring to serve two masters, and our judgment is therefore distorted. Who has not often experienced this? You have tried to ascertain God's will, or to form a right judgment about your life, but constantly your perception of duty has been obscured by the thought that, if you decided in a certain direction, you would interfere with your interests in another. Your eye has not been single, and you have walked in darkness. When, however, you feel so absorbed in God's interests that you are indifferent to your own, all becomes clear, and you leave Him to care for all results. . . .

Let us not think that God is niggardly and stinting in His gifts. He gives fish as well as bread when He feeds the crowds; colours as well as leaves when He clothes the flowers. You have been adopted into His Family, and may call Him "Abba, Father." Surely this act of grace shows a special love on His part. Would He have taken such care of the spiritual, and have none for the physical? The ungodly may worry about the maintenance; but a child of God may be sure that His needs will be supplied.

F. B. Meyer

APPLICATION

*W*hat is the difference between Jesus' perspective on feeding the crowd and his disciples' perspective? Do you face similar conflict between feeling a need to provide for yourself and trusting God to provide? Let these psalms be your prayer of trust and thanks for God's provision!

WEDNESDAY

God Is Merciful,
Even to Those Who
Do Not Understand

Mark 6:45—7:13

Jesus Walks on the Water

*A*nd straightway he constrained his disciples to get into the ship, and to go to the other side before unto Bethsaida, while he sent away the people.

⁴⁶ And when he had sent them away, he departed into a mountain to pray.

⁴⁷ And when even was come, the ship was in the midst of the sea, and he alone on the land.

⁴⁸ And he saw them toiling in rowing; for the wind was contrary unto them: and about the fourth watch of the night he cometh unto them, walking upon the sea, and would have passed by them.

⁴⁹ But when they saw him walking upon the sea, they supposed it had been a spirit, and cried out:

⁵⁰ for they all saw him, and were troubled. And immediately he talked with them, and saith unto them, Be of good cheer: it is I; be not afraid.

⁵¹ And he went up unto them into the ship; and the wind ceased: and they were sore amazed in themselves beyond measure, and wondered.

⁵² For they considered not *the miracle* of the loaves: for their heart was hardened.

⁵³ And when they had passed over, they came into the land of Gennesaret, and drew to the shore.

⁵⁴ And when they were come out of the ship, straightway they knew him,

⁵⁵ and ran through that whole region round about, and began to carry about in beds those that were sick, where they heard he was.

⁵⁶ And whithersoever he entered, into villages, or cities, or country, they laid the sick in the streets, and besought him that they might touch if it were but the border of his garment: and as many as touched him were made whole.

Obey God's Law

7 Then came together unto him the Pharisees, and certain of the scribes, which came from Jerusalem.

² And when they saw some of his disciples eat bread with defiled, that is to say, with unwashen hands, they found fault.

³ For the Pharisees, and all the Jews, except they wash *their* hands oft, eat not, holding the tradition of the elders.

⁴ And *when they come* from the market, except they wash, they eat not. And many other things there be, which they have received to hold, *as* the washing of cups, and pots, brazen vessels, and of tables.

⁵ Then the Pharisees and scribes asked him, Why walk not thy disciples according to the tradition of the elders, but eat bread with unwashen hands?

⁶ He answered and said unto them, Well hath Isaiah prophesied of you hypocrites, as it is written, This people honoreth me with *their* lips, but their heart is far from me.

⁷ Howbeit in vain do they worship me, teaching *for* doctrines the commandments of men.

[8] For laying aside the commandment of God, ye hold the tradition of men, *as* the washing of pots and cups: and many other such like things ye do.

[9] And he said unto them, Full well ye reject the commandment of God, that ye may keep your own tradition.

[10] For Moses said, Honor thy father and thy mother; and, Whoso curseth father or mother, let him die the death:

[11] but ye say, If a man shall say to his father or mother, *It is* Corban, that is to say, a gift, by whatsoever thou mightest be profited by me; *he shall be free.*

[12] And ye suffer him no more to do ought for his father or his mother;

[13] making the word of God of none effect through your tradition, which ye have delivered: and many such like things do ye.

OLD TESTAMENT READING

*F*or all this they sinned still, and believed not for his wondrous works.

[33] Therefore their days did he consume in vanity, and their years in trouble.

[34] When he slew them, then they sought him: and they returned and inquired early after God.

[35] And they remembered that God *was* their rock, and the high God their redeemer.

[36] Nevertheless they did flatter him with their mouth, and they lied unto him with their tongues.

[37] For their heart was not right with him, neither were they steadfast in his covenant.

[38] But he, *being* full of compassion, forgave *their* iniquity, and destroyed *them* not: yea, many a time turned he his anger away, and did not stir up all his wrath.

[39] For he remembered that they *were but* flesh; a wind that passeth away, and cometh not again.

Psalm 78:32–39

INSIGHTS

*I*n Christ, God has broken the cycle of judgment and retaliation. We have received mercy—undeserved and unearned love. In the fifth Beatitude, Jesus invites us to share His character trait of mercy. But inflow and outgo must be matched. Mercy must be given away if we want to live in its flow. . . .

The test of the greatness Christ offers us is to be merciful to those who do not return it. When we've endured disappointments, injustice, or hurts, we do not become bitter or sour but draw on and express mercy. This is not easy—not until we remember how merciful Christ has been to us. We are called to be a channel of divine mercy flowing through us to others. This is the source of the silent strength of greatness.

Lloyd Ogilvie

ACTION POINT

*D*id Jesus condemn his followers for their lack of faith and understanding? What did he do for those who wanted his healing and miracles, but little else? How was Jesus merciful to the Pharisees and teachers of the law? In what way is God merciful, even to those who don't live by his teachings? Write your own psalm of praise to God for his unending mercy.

THURSDAY

*Evil Comes from
Within*

Mark 7:14–37

*A*nd when he had called all the people *unto him*, he said unto them, Hearken unto me every one *of you*, and understand:

¹⁵ there is nothing from without a man, that entering into him can defile him: but the things which come out of him, those are they that defile the man.

¹⁶ If any man have ears to hear, let him hear.

¹⁷ And when he was entered into the house from the people, his disciples asked him concerning the parable.

¹⁸ And he saith unto them, Are ye so without understanding also? Do ye not perceive, that whatsoever thing from without entereth into the man, *it* cannot defile him;

¹⁹ because it entereth not into his heart, but into the belly, and goeth out into the draught, purging all meats?

²⁰ And he said, That which cometh out of the man, that defileth the man.

²¹ For from within, out of the heart of men, proceed evil thoughts, adulteries, fornications, murders,

²² thefts, covetousness, wickedness, deceit, lasciviousness, an evil eye, blasphemy, pride, foolishness:

²³ all these evil things come from within, and defile the man.

Jesus Helps a Woman

²⁴ And from thence he arose, and went into the borders of Tyre and Sidon, and entered into a house, and would have no man know *it*: but he could not be hid.

²⁵ For a *certain* woman, whose young daughter had an unclean spirit, heard of him, and came and fell at his feet:

²⁶ the woman was a Greek, a Syrophoenician by nation; and she besought him that he would cast forth the devil out of her daughter.

²⁷ But Jesus said unto her, Let the children first be filled: for it is not meet to take the children's bread, and to cast *it* unto the dogs.

²⁸ And she answered and said unto him, Yes, Lord: yet the dogs under the table eat of the children's crumbs.

²⁹ And he said unto her, For this saying go thy way; the devil is gone out of thy daughter.

³⁰ And when she was come to her house, she found the devil gone out, and her daughter laid upon the bed.

Jesus Heals a Deaf Man

*A*nd again, departing from the coasts of Tyre and Sidon, he came unto the sea of Galilee, through the midst of the coasts of Decapolis.

³² And they bring unto him one that was deaf, and had an impediment in his speech; and they beseech him to put his hand upon him.

³³ And he took him aside from the multitude, and put his fingers into his ears, and he spit, and touched his tongue;

³⁴ and looking up to heaven, he sighed, and saith unto him, Ephphatha, that is, Be opened.

³⁵ And straightway his ears were opened, and the string of his tongue

was loosed, and he spake plain.

³⁶ And he charged them that they should tell no man: but the more he charged them, so much the more a great deal they published *it*;

³⁷ and were beyond measure astonished, saying, He hath done all things well: he maketh both the deaf to hear, and the dumb to speak.

OLD TESTAMENT READING

A naughty person, a wicked man, walketh with a froward mouth.

¹³ He winketh with his eyes, he speaketh with his feet, he teacheth with his fingers;

¹⁴ frowardness *is* in his heart, he deviseth mischief continually; he soweth discord.

¹⁵ Therefore shall his calamity come suddenly; suddenly shall he be broken without remedy.

¹⁶ These six *things* doth the LORD hate: yea, seven *are* an abomination unto him:

¹⁷ a proud look, a lying tongue, and hands that shed innocent blood,

¹⁸ an heart that deviseth wicked imaginations, feet that be swift in running to mischief,

¹⁹ a false witness *that* speaketh lies, and he that soweth discord among brethren.

Proverbs 6:12–19

T he heart *is* deceitful above all *things*, and desperately wicked: who can know it?

Jeremiah 17:9

INSIGHTS

A friend received a significant honor. I can't remember struggling

with envy and jealousy before, but on that day, I was swept up into a whirlwind of envy. I drove back to my office in a complete state of shock. Where in creation did that come from? It leaked through the pinholes of my otherwise good character. A Christian's good character is the character of Jesus breathed into each of us by the Holy Spirit. Once we stop allowing the Spirit to fill us with power, the pinholes leak sin from our old nature.

Accepting our total depravity— our capacity to sin, that our character is filled with pinholes—is essential to living a victorious Christian life. If we presume that when we become Christian we are now good, we have missed the point. Jesus Christ shed His blood to forgive our sin, not to remove our sin. We have a continuing sinful nature which requires us to guard our heart and mind. We must post a twenty-four-hour guard at the gate to our mind.

Patrick Morley

APPLICATION

W hat evil things does Jesus say come from within a person? Why is it necessary to have a clean heart? Does your life show any evidence of "heart" trouble? What commitment will you make to guard those areas of weakness?

FRIDAY

Miracles Won't Soften Hard Hearts

Mark 8:1–26

More than Four Thousand Fed

8 In those days the multitude being very great, and having nothing to eat, Jesus called his disciples *unto him,* and saith unto them,

[2] I have compassion on the multitude, because they have now been with me three days, and have nothing to eat:

[3] and if I send them away fasting to their own houses, they will faint by the way: for divers of them came from far.

[4] And his disciples answered him, From whence can a man satisfy these *men* with bread here in the wilderness?

[5] And he asked them, How many loaves have ye? And they said, Seven.

[6] And he commanded the people to sit down on the ground: and he took the seven loaves, and gave thanks, and brake, and gave to his disciples to set before *them*; and they did set *them* before the people.

[7] And they had a few small fishes: and he blessed, and commanded to set them also before *them*.

[8] So they did eat, and were filled: and they took up of the broken *meat* that was left seven baskets.

[9] And they that had eaten were about four thousand: and he sent them away.

[10] And straightway he entered into a ship with his disciples, and came into the parts of Dalmanutha.

The Leaders Ask for A Miracle

And the Pharisees came forth, and began to question with him, seeking of him a sign from heaven, tempting him.

[12] And he sighed deeply in his spirit, and saith, Why doth this generation seek after a sign? verily I say unto you, There shall no sign be given unto this generation.

[13] And he left them, and entering into the ship again departed to the other side.

Guard Against Wrong Teachings

Now *the disciples* had forgotten to take bread, neither had they in the ship with them more than one loaf.

[15] And he charged them, saying, Take heed, beware of the leaven of the Pharisees, and *of* the leaven of Herod.

[16] And they reasoned among themselves, saying, *It is* because we have no bread.

[17] And when Jesus knew *it*, he saith unto them, Why reason ye, because ye have no bread? perceive ye not yet, neither understand? have ye your heart yet hardened?

[18] Having eyes, see ye not? and having ears, hear ye not? and do ye not remember?

[19] When I brake the five loaves among five thousand, how many baskets full of fragments took ye up? They say unto him, Twelve.

[20] And when the seven among four thousand, how many baskets full of fragments took ye up? And they said, Seven.

[21] And he said unto them, How is it that ye do not understand?

Jesus Heals a Blind Man

*A*nd he cometh to Bethsaida; and they bring a blind man unto him, and besought him to touch him.

²³ And he took the blind man by the hand, and led him out of the town; and when he had spit on his eyes, and put his hands upon him, he asked him if he saw ought.

²⁴ And he looked up, and said, I see men as trees, walking.

²⁵ After that he put *his* hands again upon his eyes, and made him look up; and he was restored, and saw every man clearly.

²⁶ And he sent him away to his house, saying, Neither go into the town, nor tell *it* to any in the town.

OLD TESTAMENT READING

*H*ow oft did they provoke him in the wilderness, *and* grieve him in the desert!

⁴¹ Yea, they turned back and tempted God, and limited the Holy One of Israel.

⁴² They remembered not his hand, *nor* the day when he delivered them from the enemy:

⁴³ how he had wrought his signs in Egypt, and his wonders in the field of Zoan.

Psalm 78:40–43

INSIGHTS

*F*or three years, day in and day out, he Judas occupied himself with Jesus Christ. He saw the Lord's miracles, heard His words, even participated in His ministry. In all that time, no one ever questioned his faith. He had the same status as the other disciples. Except for the Savior Himself, who knew the thoughts of Judas's heart, no one ever suspected that this man would betray Christ.

Yet, while the others were growing into apostles, Judas was quietly becoming a vile, calculating tool of Satan. Whatever his character seemed to be at the beginning, his faith was not real (John 13:10–11). He was unregenerate, and his heart gradually hardened so that he became the treacherous man who sold the Savior for a fistful of coins. . . .

It was not the will of God apart from Judas's own choice that he should betray Christ. At every opportunity, Jesus warned Judas and entreated him to repent and be saved, but at every point Judas turned away. Judas had heard the gospel according to Jesus, yet he refused to turn from his sin and selfishness. Jesus' words in John 13 represent His final, loving appeal to this man. In the end, however, the Savior's merciful entreaty would condemn Judas in the hardness of his heart.

John F. MacArthur, Jr.

PAUSE FOR REFLECTION

*W*ho has witnessed more miracles of God than the Israelites or those who walked with Jesus while he was on earth? Do miracles lead people to salvation? What is more important than miracles in causing a person to turn toward God?

WEEKEND

Learn to Value
What God Values

Mark 8:27—9:13

Peter Says Jesus Is the Christ

And Jesus went out, and his disciples, into the towns of Caesarea Philippi: and by the way he asked his disciples, saying unto them, Whom do men say that I am?

28 And they answered, John the Baptist: but some *say,* Elijah; and others, One of the prophets.

29 And he saith unto them, But whom say ye that I am? And Peter answereth and saith unto him, Thou art the Christ.

30 And he charged them that they should tell no man of him.

31 And he began to teach them, that the Son of man must suffer many things, and be rejected of the elders, and *of* the chief priests, and scribes, and be killed, and after three days rise again.

32 And he spake that saying openly. And Peter took him, and began to rebuke him.

33 But when he had turned about and looked on his disciples, he rebuked Peter, saying, Get thee behind me, Satan: for thou savorest not the things that be of God, but the things that be of men.

34 And when he had called the people *unto him* with his disciples also, he said unto them, Whosoever will come after me, let him deny himself, and take up his cross, and follow me.

35 For whosoever will save his life shall lose it; but whosoever shall lose his life for my sake and the gospel's, the same shall save it.

36 For what shall it profit a man, if he shall gain the whole world, and lose his own soul?

37 Or what shall a man give in exchange for his soul?

38 Whosoever therefore shall be ashamed of me and of my words, in this adulterous and sinful generation, of him also shall the Son of man be ashamed, when he cometh in the glory of his Father with the holy angels.

9 And he said unto them, Verily I say unto you, That there be some of them that stand here, which shall not taste of death, till they have seen the kingdom of God come with power.

Jesus Talks with Moses and Elijah

And after six days Jesus taketh *with him* Peter, and James, and John, and leadeth them up into a high mountain apart by themselves: and he was transfigured before them.

3 And his raiment became shining, exceeding white as snow; so as no fuller on earth can white them.

4 And there appeared unto them Elijah with Moses: and they were talking with Jesus.

5 And Peter answered and said to Jesus, Master, it is good for us to be here: and let us make three tabernacles; one for thee, and one for Moses, and one for Elijah.

6 For he wist not what to say; for they were sore afraid.

7 And there was a cloud that overshadowed them: and a voice came out of the cloud, saying, This is my beloved Son: hear him.

8 And suddenly, when they had looked round about, they saw no

man any more, save Jesus only with themselves.

⁹ And as they came down from the mountain, he charged them that they should tell no man what things they had seen, till the Son of man were risen from the dead.

¹⁰ And they kept that saying with themselves, questioning one with another what the rising from the dead should mean.

¹¹ And they asked him, saying, Why say the scribes that Elijah must first come?

¹² And he answered and told them, Elijah verily cometh first, and restoreth all things; and how it is written of the Son of man, that he must suffer many things, and be set at nought.

¹³ But I say unto you, That Elijah is indeed come, and they have done unto him whatsoever they listed, as it is written of him.

OLD TESTAMENT READING

*A*nd whatsoever mine eyes desired I kept not from them, I withheld not my heart from any joy; for my heart rejoiced in all my labor: and this was my portion of all my labor.

¹¹ Then I looked on all the works that my hands had wrought, and on the labor that I had labored to do: and, behold, all *was* vanity and vexation of spirit, and *there was* no profit under the sun.

Ecclesiastes 2:10–11

INSIGHTS

I will hear what God the Lord will speak" (Ps. 85:8). Blessed is the soul which hears the Lord speaking within, and from His mouth receives the word of consolation. Blessed are the ears that catch the pulses of the divine whisper (Matt. 13:16, 17), and give no heed to the whisperings of this world. Blessed indeed are those ears which listen not after the voice which is sounding without, but for the truth teaching inwardly. Blessed are the eyes that are shut to outward things, but intent on things inward. Blessed are they that enter far into things within, and endeavor to prepare themselves more and more, by daily exercises, for the receiving of heavenly secrets. Blessed are they who are glad to have time to spare for God, and who shake off all worldly hindrances.

Consider these things, O my soul, and shut up the door of your sensual desires, that you may hear what the Lord your God speaks in you (Ps. 85:8).

Thus says your Beloved, "I am thy salvation," your Peace, and your Life: keep yourself with Me, and you shall find peace. Let go all transitory things, and seek the things eternal. What are all transitory objects but seductive things? And what can all creatures avail, if you are forsaken by the Creator?

Renounce therefore all things, and labor to please your Creator, and to be faithful unto Him, that you may be able to attain unto true blessedness.

Thomas à Kempis

ACTION POINT

*L*ist and evaluate the things in your life that seem worth pursuing. Might Jesus criticize you in the same way he criticized Peter (Mark 8:33–38)? If you want to follow Jesus, what priorities do you need to rearrange?

MONDAY

God Wants to Teach Us His Ways

Mark 9:14–37

Jesus Heals a Boy

*A*nd when he came to *his* disciples, he saw a great multitude about them, and the scribes questioning with them.

¹⁵ And straightway all the people, when they beheld him, were greatly amazed, and running to *him* saluted him.

¹⁶ And he asked the scribes, What question ye with them?

¹⁷ And one of the multitude answered and said, Master, I have brought unto thee my son, which hath a dumb spirit;

¹⁸ and wheresoever he taketh him, he teareth him; and he foameth, and gnasheth with his teeth, and pineth away: and I spake to thy disciples that they should cast him out; and they could not.

¹⁹ He answereth him, and saith, O faithless generation, how long shall I be with you? how long shall I suffer you? bring him unto me.

²⁰ And they brought him unto him: and when he saw him, straightway the spirit tare him; and he fell on the ground, and wallowed foaming.

²¹ And he asked his father, How long is it ago since this came unto him? And he said, Of a child.

²² And ofttimes it hath cast him into the fire, and into the waters, to destroy him: but if thou canst do any thing, have compassion on us, and help us.

²³ Jesus said unto him, If thou canst believe, all things *are* possible to him that believeth.

²⁴ And straightway the father of the child cried out, and said with tears, Lord, I believe; help thou mine unbelief.

²⁵ When Jesus saw that the people came running together, he rebuked the foul spirit, saying unto him, *Thou* dumb and deaf spirit, I charge thee, come out of him, and enter no more into him.

²⁶ And *the spirit* cried, and rent him sore, and came out of him: and he was as one dead; insomuch that many said, He is dead.

²⁷ But Jesus took him by the hand, and lifted him up; and he arose.

²⁸ And when he was come into the house, his disciples asked him privately, Why could not we cast him out?

²⁹ And he said unto them, This kind can come forth by nothing, but by prayer and fasting.

Jesus Talks About His Death

*A*nd they departed thence, and passed through Galilee; and he would not that any man should know *it*.

³¹ For he taught his disciples, and said unto them, The Son of man is delivered into the hands of men, and they shall kill him; and after that he is killed, he shall rise the third day.

³² But they understood not that saying, and were afraid to ask him.

Who Is the Greatest?

*A*nd he came to Capernaum: and being in the house he asked them, What was it that ye disputed among yourselves by the way?

³⁴ But they held their peace: for by the way they had disputed among themselves, who *should be* the greatest.

³⁵ And he sat down, and called the twelve, and saith unto them, If any man desire to be first, *the same* shall be last of all, and servant of all.

³⁶ And he took a child, and set him in the midst of them: and when he had taken him in his arms, he said unto them,

³⁷ Whosoever shall receive one of such children in my name, receiveth me; and whosoever shall receive me, receiveth not me, but him that sent me.

OLD TESTAMENT READING

*A*nd Moses took the tabernacle, and pitched it without the camp, afar off from the camp, and called it the Tabernacle of the congregation. And it came to pass, *that* every one which sought the LORD went out unto the tabernacle of the congregation, which *was* without the camp.

⁸ And it came to pass, when Moses went out unto the tabernacle, *that* all the people rose up and stood every man *at* his tent door, and looked after Moses, until he was gone into the tabernacle.

⁹ And it came to pass, as Moses entered into the tabernacle, the cloudy pillar descended, and stood *at* the door of the tabernacle, and *the* LORD talked with Moses.

¹⁰ And all the people saw the cloudy pillar stand *at* the tabernacle door: and all the people rose up and worshipped, every man *in* his tent door.

¹¹ And the LORD spake unto Moses face to face, as a man speaketh unto his friend. And he turned again into the camp; but his servant Joshua, the son of Nun, a young man, departed not out of the tabernacle.

Exodus 33:7–11

INSIGHTS

*T*he Father in heaven is so interested in His child, and so longs to have his life in step with His will and His love, that He is willing to keep the child's guidance entirely in His own hand. He knows so well that we do not do what is really holy and heavenly, except when He works it in us, that He intends His very demands to become promises of what He will do, in watching over and leading us all day long. We may count on Him to teach us His way and show us His path not only in special trials and hard times, but in everyday life. . . .

. . . So simple and delightful can it become to a soul that has practiced waiting on God, to walk all day in the enjoyment of God's light and leading. What is needed to help us find such a life is one thing: the real knowledge and faith of God as the only source of wisdom and goodness, as always ready and longing to be to us all that we can possibly need. Yes, this is the one thing we need.

Andrew Murray

ACTION POINT

*W*hat special teaching did Jesus want to give his followers when they were alone? As you read Old Testament passages, think about how much God wants to teach his people. Thank him for his great outpouring of love. Pray that your heart will listen for his wisdom.

TUESDAY

Flee All Evil

Mark 9:38—10:16

Anyone Not Against Us Is for Us

*A*nd John answered him, saying, Master, we saw one casting out devils in thy name, and he followeth not us; and we forbade him, because he followeth not us.

³⁹ But Jesus said, Forbid him not: for there is no man which shall do a miracle in my name, that can lightly speak evil of me.

⁴⁰ For he that is not against us is on our part.

⁴¹ For whosoever shall give you a cup of water to drink in my name, because ye belong to Christ, verily I say unto you, he shall not lose his reward.

⁴² And whosoever shall offend one of *these* little ones that believe in me, it is better for him that a millstone were hanged about his neck, and he were cast into the sea.

⁴³ And if thy hand offend thee, cut it off: it is better for thee to enter into life maimed, than having two hands to go into hell, into the fire that never shall be quenched:

⁴⁴ where their worm dieth not, and the fire is not quenched.

⁴⁵ And if thy foot offend thee, cut it off: it is better for thee to enter halt into life, than having two feet to be cast into hell, into the fire that never shall be quenched:

⁴⁶ where their worm dieth not, and the fire is not quenched.

⁴⁷ And if thine eye offend thee, pluck it out: it is better for thee to enter into the kingdom of God with one eye, than having two eyes to be cast into hell fire:

⁴⁸ where their worm dieth not, and the fire is not quenched.

⁴⁹ For every one shall be salted with fire, and every sacrifice shall be salted with salt.

⁵⁰ Salt *is* good: but if the salt have lost his saltness, wherewith will ye season it? Have salt in yourselves, and have peace one with another.

Jesus Teaches About Divorce

10 And he arose from thence, and cometh into the coasts of Judea by the farther side of Jordan: and the people resort unto him again; and, as he was wont, he taught them again.

² And the Pharisees came to him, and asked him, Is it lawful for a man to put away *his* wife? tempting him.

³ And he answered and said unto them, What did Moses command you?

⁴ And they said, Moses suffered to write a bill of divorcement, and to put *her* away.

⁵ And Jesus answered and said unto them, For the hardness of your heart he wrote you this precept.

⁶ But from the beginning of the creation God made them male and female.

⁷ For this cause shall a man leave his father and mother, and cleave to his wife;

⁸ and they twain shall be one flesh: so then they are no more twain, but one flesh.

⁹ What therefore God hath joined together, let not man put asunder.

¹⁰ And in the house his disciples asked him again of the same *matter.*

¹¹ And he saith unto them, Whosoever shall put away his wife, and

marry another, committeth adultery against her.

[12] And if a woman shall put away her husband, and be married to another, she committeth adultery.

Jesus Blesses Children

*A*nd they brought young children to him, that he should touch them; and *his* disciples rebuked those that brought *them*.

[14] But when Jesus saw *it*, he was much displeased, and said unto them, Suffer the little children to come unto me, and forbid them not; for of such is the kingdom of God.

[15] Verily I say unto you, Whosoever shall not receive the kingdom of God as a little child, he shall not enter therein.

[16] And he took them up in his arms, put *his* hands upon them, and blessed them.

OLD TESTAMENT READING

*A*nd Joseph was a goodly person, and well–favored.

[7] And it came to pass after these things, that his master's wife cast her eyes upon Joseph; and she said, Lie with me.

[8] But he refused, and said unto his master's wife, Behold, my master wotteth not what *is* with me in the house, and he hath committed all that he hath to my hand;

[9] *there is* none greater in this house than I; neither hath he kept back any thing from me but thee, because thou *art* his wife: how then can I do this great wickedness, and sin against God?

[10] And it came to pass, as she spake to Joseph day by day, that he hear-

kened not unto her, to lie by her, *or* to be with her.

[11] And it came to pass about this time, that *Joseph* went into the house to do his business; and *there was* none of the men of the house there within.

[12] And she caught him by his garment, saying, Lie with me: and he left his garment in her hand, and fled, and got him out.

Genesis 39:6b-12

INSIGHTS

*R*epentance is a definite turn from every thought, word, deed and habit which is known to be wrong. It is not sufficient to feel pangs of remorse or to make some kind of apology to God. Fundamentally, repentance is . . . an inward change of mind and attitude towards sin which leads to a change of behaviour.

. . . There may be sins in our lives which we do not think we ever could renounce; but we must be willing to let them go as we cry to God for deliverance from them. If you are in doubt regarding what is right and what is wrong, . . . do not be too greatly influenced by the customs and conventions of Christians you may know. Go by the clear teaching of the Bible and by the prompting of your conscience, and Christ will gradually lead you further along the path of righteousness. When he puts his finger on anything, give it up.

John Stott

APPLICATION

*D*o you vigorously run from sin or politely coexist with it? What sin needs to be purged from your life?

WEDNESDAY

The Righteous Will Be Rewarded in Heaven

Mark 10:17–41

A Rich Man's Question

*A*nd when he was gone forth into the way, there came one running, and kneeled to him, and asked him, Good Master, what shall I do that I may inherit eternal life?

18 And Jesus said unto him, Why callest thou me good? *there is* none good but one, *that is*, God.

19 Thou knowest the commandments, Do not commit adultery, Do not kill, Do not steal, Do not bear false witness, Defraud not, Honor thy father and mother.

20 And he answered and said unto him, Master, all these have I observed from my youth.

21 Then Jesus beholding him loved him, and said unto him, One thing thou lackest: go thy way, sell whatsoever thou hast, and give to the poor, and thou shalt have treasure in heaven: and come, take up the cross, and follow me.

22 And he was sad at that saying, and went away grieved: for he had great possessions.

23 And Jesus looked round about, and saith unto his disciples, How hardly shall they that have riches enter into the kingdom of God!

24 And the disciples were astonished at his words. But Jesus answereth again, and saith unto them, Children, how hard is it for them that trust in riches to enter into the kingdom of God!

25 It is easier for a camel to go through the eye of a needle, than for a rich man to enter into the kingdom of God.

26 And they were astonished out of measure, saying among themselves, Who then can be saved?

27 And Jesus looking upon them saith, With men *it is* impossible, but not with God: for with God all things are possible.

28 Then Peter began to say unto him, Lo, we have left all, and have followed thee.

29 And Jesus answered and said, Verily I say unto you, There is no man that hath left house, or brethren, or sisters, or father, or mother, or wife, or children, or lands, for my sake, and the gospel's,

30 but he shall receive a hundredfold now in this time, houses, and brethren, and sisters, and mothers, and children, and lands, with persecutions; and in the world to come eternal life.

31 But many *that are* first shall be last; and the last first.

Jesus Talks About His Death

*A*nd they were in the way going up to Jerusalem; and Jesus went before them: and they were amazed; and as they followed, they were afraid. And he took again the twelve, and began to tell them what things should happen unto him,

33 *saying*, Behold, we go up to Jerusalem; and the Son of man shall be delivered unto the chief priests, and unto the scribes; and they shall condemn him to death, and shall deliver him to the Gentiles:

34 and they shall mock him, and shall scourge him, and shall spit upon

him, and shall kill him; and the third day he shall rise again.

Two Disciples Ask Jesus a Favor

*A*nd James and John, the sons of Zebedee, come unto him, saying, Master, we would that thou shouldest do for us whatsoever we shall desire.

³⁶ And he said unto them, What would ye that I should do for you?

³⁷ They said unto him, Grant unto us that we may sit, one on thy right hand, and the other on thy left hand, in thy glory.

³⁸ But Jesus said unto them, Ye know not what ye ask: can ye drink of the cup that I drink of? and be baptized with the baptism that I am baptized with?

³⁹ And they said unto him, We can. And Jesus said unto them, Ye shall indeed drink of the cup that I drink of; and with the baptism that I am baptized withal shall ye be baptized:

⁴⁰ but to sit on my right hand and on my left hand is not mine to give; but *it shall be given to them* for whom it is prepared.

⁴¹ And when the ten heard *it*, they began to be much displeased with James and John.

But let My promise strengthen and comfort you under every circumstance. I am well able to reward you, above all measure and degree. . . .

Do in earnest what you do; labor faithfully in My vineyard (Matt. 20:7); I will be your recompense. Write, read, chant, mourn, keep silence, pray, endure crosses manfully. Life everlasting is worth all these battles, and greater than these. Peace shall come in one day which is known unto the Lord, and there shall be "not day, nor night" (Zech. 14:7) (that is, of this present time), but unceasing light, infinite brightness, steadfast peace, and secure rest. Then you shall not say: "Who shall deliver me from the body of this death?" (Rom. 7:24); nor cry: "Woe is me, that I sojourn in Mesech" (Ps. 120:5). For death shall be cast down headlong, and there shall be salvation which can never fail, no more anxiety, blessed joy, companionship sweet and noble. . . .

Lift up your face therefore to Heaven. Behold, I and all My saints with Me, who in this world had great conflict, do now rejoice, now are comforted, now secure, now at rest, and shall remain with Me everlastingly in the kingdom of My Father!

Thomas à Kempis

OLD TESTAMENT READING

*S*o that a man shall say, Verily *there is* a reward for the righteous: verily he is a God that judgeth in the earth.

Psalm 58:11

INSIGHTS

*B*e not wearied by the labors which you have undertaken for my sake, nor let tribulations cast you down.

APPLICATION

*W*hat areas of personal commitment to God's kingdom do you find difficult? What is hard for you to leave behind? Pray that you will truly believe—deep inside—that God will reward your faithfulness far above what you can even imagine.

115

THURSDAY

Being a Servant of God

Mark 10:42—11:14

*B*ut Jesus called them *to him*, and saith unto them, Ye know that they which are accounted to rule over the Gentiles exercise lordship over them; and their great ones exercise authority upon them.

43 But so shall it not be among you: but whosoever will be great among you, shall be your minister:

44 and whosoever of you will be the chiefest, shall be servant of all.

45 For even the Son of man came not to be ministered unto, but to minister, and to give his life a ransom for many.

Jesus Heals a Blind Man

*A*nd they came to Jericho: and as he went out of Jericho with his disciples and a great number of people, blind Bartimeus, the son of Timeus, sat by the highway side begging.

47 And when he heard that it was Jesus of Nazareth, he began to cry out, and say, Jesus, *thou* Son of David, have mercy on me.

48 And many charged him that he should hold his peace: but he cried the more a great deal, *Thou* Son of David, have mercy on me.

49 And Jesus stood still, and commanded him to be called. And they call the blind man, saying unto him, Be of good comfort, rise; he calleth thee.

50 And he, casting away his garment, rose, and came to Jesus.

51 And Jesus answered and said unto him, What wilt thou that I should do unto thee? The blind man said unto him, Lord, that I might receive my sight.

52 And Jesus said unto him, Go thy way; thy faith hath made thee whole. And immediately he received his sight, and followed Jesus in the way.

Jesus Enters Jerusalem as a King

11 And when they came nigh to Jerusalem, unto Bethphage and Bethany, at the mount of Olives, he sendeth forth two of his disciples,

2 and saith unto them, Go your way into the village over against you: and as soon as ye be entered into it, ye shall find a colt tied, whereon never man sat; loose him, and bring *him*.

3 And if any man say unto you, Why do ye this? say ye that the Lord hath need of him; and straightway he will send him hither.

4 And they went their way, and found the colt tied by the door without in a place where two ways met; and they loose him.

5 And certain of them that stood there said unto them, What do ye, loosing the colt?

6 And they said unto them even as Jesus had commanded: and they let them go.

7 And they brought the colt to Jesus, and cast their garments on him; and he sat upon him.

8 And many spread their garments in the way; and others cut down branches off the trees, and strewed *them* in the way.

9 And they that went before, and they that followed, cried, saying, Hosanna; Blessed *is* he that cometh in the name of the Lord:

¹⁰ Blessed *be* the kingdom of our father David, that cometh in the name of the Lord: Hosanna in the highest. ¹¹ And Jesus entered into Jerusalem, and into the temple: and when he had looked round about upon all things, and now the eventide was come, he went out unto Bethany with the twelve.

¹² And on the morrow, when they were come from Bethany, he was hungry: ¹³ and seeing a fig tree afar off having leaves, he came, if haply he might find any thing thereon: and when he came to it, he found nothing but leaves; for the time of figs was not *yet*.

¹⁴ And Jesus answered and said unto it, No man eat fruit of thee hereafter for ever. And his disciples heard *it*.

OLD TESTAMENT READING

*A*nd it came to pass after these things, that God did tempt Abraham, and said unto him, Abraham: and he said, Behold, *here* I *am*.

² And he said, Take now thy son, thine only *son* Isaac, whom thou lovest, and get thee into the land of Moriah; and offer him there for a burnt offering upon one of the mountains which I will tell thee of.

¹⁰ And Abraham stretched forth his hand, and took the knife to slay his son.

¹¹ And the angel of the LORD called unto him out of heaven, and said, Abraham, Abraham: and he said, Here *am* I.

¹² And he said, Lay not thine hand upon the lad, neither do thou any thing unto him: for now I know that thou fearest God, seeing thou hast not withheld thy son, thine only *son,* from me.

Genesis 22:1–2, 10–12

INSIGHTS

*W*e *must squarely face the fact that the thought of service, except as a token or temporary activity, is distasteful. To accept a lower place is bad enough, but to choose a lower place—preposterous!*

Words like obey, submit, serve, or worse, the expression "know your place," are met with defiance from a people who are obsessed with their "rights." Of course these rights are not wrong, and it is appropriate that there is legislation to protect rights. The problem is that legislation can only protect us from the bad; it cannot produce good in us. And it certainly cannot suggest to us that there might be some value in renouncing our rights for something or someone else. The Cross is the best evidence that there is much more to love than justice, much more to right than rights. A person who has won a public battle for human rights has done a good thing. But a person who has won a personal battle and given up human rights in the interest of human obligation has done a great thing. More often than not, the action will be labeled demeaning or ridiculous. So was the Cross.

Thomas Schmidt

APPLICATION

*W*ho *is our greatest example of being a servant of God? How far was he willing to go in serving others? What did God call his servant Abraham to do? How is God calling you to serve him? Are you willing to be his servant?*

FRIDAY

Pray with Conviction

Mark 11:15—12:12

Jesus Goes to the Temple

*A*nd they come to Jerusalem: and Jesus went into the temple, and began to cast out them that sold and bought in the temple, and overthrew the tables of the moneychangers, and the seats of them that sold doves;

¹⁶ and would not suffer that any man should carry *any* vessel through the temple.

¹⁷ And he taught, saying unto them, Is it not written, My house shall be called of all nations the house of prayer? but ye have made it a den of thieves.

¹⁸ And the scribes and chief priests heard *it*, and sought how they might destroy him: for they feared him, because all the people was astonished at his doctrine.

¹⁹ And when even was come, he went out of the city.

The Power of Faith

*A*nd in the morning, as they passed by, they saw the fig tree dried up from the roots.

²¹ And Peter calling to remembrance saith unto him, Master, behold, the fig tree which thou cursedst is withered away.

²² And Jesus answering saith unto them, Have faith in God.

²³ For verily I say unto you, That whosoever shall say unto this mountain, Be thou removed, and be thou cast into the sea; and shall not doubt in his heart, but shall believe that those things which he saith shall come to pass; he shall have whatsoever he saith.

²⁴ Therefore I say unto you, What things soever ye desire, when ye pray, believe that ye receive *them*, and ye shall have *them*.

²⁵ And when ye stand praying, forgive, if ye have ought against any: that your Father also which is in heaven may forgive you your trespasses.

²⁶ But if ye do not forgive, neither will your Father which is in heaven forgive your trespasses.

Leaders Doubt Jesus' Authority

*A*nd they come again to Jerusalem: and as he was walking in the temple, there come to him the chief priests, and the scribes, and the elders,

²⁸ and say unto him, By what authority doest thou these things? and who gave thee this authority to do these things?

²⁹ And Jesus answered and said unto them, I will also ask of you one question, and answer me, and I will tell you by what authority I do these things.

³⁰ The baptism of John, was *it* from heaven, or of men? answer me.

³¹ And they reasoned with themselves, saying, If we shall say, From heaven; he will say, Why then did ye not believe him?

³² But if we shall say, Of men; they feared the people: for all *men* counted John, that he was a prophet indeed.

³³ And they answered and said unto Jesus, We cannot tell. And Jesus answering saith unto them, Neither do I tell you by what authority I do these things.

A Parable About God's Son

12 And he began to speak unto them by parables. A *certain* man planted a vineyard, and set a hedge about *it*, and digged *a place for* the winevat, and built a tower, and let it out to husbandmen, and went into a far country.

² And at the season he sent to the husbandmen a servant, that he might receive from the husbandmen of the fruit of the vineyard.

³ And they caught *him*, and beat him, and sent *him* away empty.

⁴ And again he sent unto them another servant; and at him they cast stones, and wounded *him* in the head, and sent *him* away shamefully handled.

⁵ And again he sent another; and him they killed, and many others; beating some, and killing some.

⁶ Having yet therefore one son, his wellbeloved, he sent him also last unto them, saying, They will reverence my son.

⁷ But those husbandmen said among themselves, This is the heir; come, let us kill him, and the inheritance shall be ours.

⁸ And they took him, and killed *him*, and cast *him* out of the vineyard.

⁹ What shall therefore the lord of the vineyard do? he will come and destroy the husbandmen, and will give the vineyard unto others.

¹⁰ And have ye not read this Scripture; The stone which the builders rejected is become the head of the corner:

¹¹ this was the Lord's doing, and it is marvelous in our eyes?

¹² And they sought to lay hold on him, but feared the people; for they knew that he had spoken the parable against them: and they left him, and went their way.

OLD TESTAMENT READING

*T*he Lord *is* nigh unto all them that call upon him, to all that call upon him in truth.

Psalm 145:18

INSIGHTS

*H*ow do you pray a prayer so filled with faith that it can move a mountain? By shifting the focus from the size of your mountain to the sufficiency of the mountain mover, and by stepping forward in obedience. . . .

While the children of Israel are perched on the edge of the Promised Land, twelve spies go out to survey it. Ten come back saying, "You wouldn't believe the size of the cities, the armies, the giants. We'd better look somewhere else." Two come back saying, "The God who is faithful promised he would give us the land, so let's go in his strength." Ten looked at the size of the mountain and fell back; only two looked at the sufficiency of the mountain mover and wanted to move forward. . . .

I challenge you to shift the focus of your prayer. Don't spend a lot of time describing your mountain to the Lord. He knows what it is. Instead, focus your attention on the mountain mover—his glory, power and faithfulness. Then start walking in faith, following his leading, and watch that mountain step aside.

Bill Hybels

ACTION POINT

*H*ow does God want us to ask him for what we need? In what remarkable ways has God answered your prayers?

WEEKEND

The Wicked Persecute the Righteous

Mark 12:13–31

Is It Right To Pay Taxes or Not?

*A*nd they send unto him certain of the Pharisees and of the Herodians, to catch him in *his* words.

¹⁴ And when they were come, they say unto him, Master, we know that thou art true, and carest for no man; for thou regardest not the person of men, but teachest the way of God in truth: Is it lawful to give tribute to Caesar, or not?

¹⁵ Shall we give, or shall we not give? But he, knowing their hypocrisy, said unto them, Why tempt ye me? bring me a penny, that I may see *it*.

¹⁶ And they brought *it*. And he saith unto them, Whose *is* this image and superscription? And they said unto him, Caesar's.

¹⁷ And Jesus answering said unto them, Render to Caesar the things that are Caesar's, and to God the things that are God's. And they marveled at him.

Some Sadducees Try to Trick Jesus

*T*hen come unto him the Sadducees, which say there is no resurrection; and they asked him, saying,

¹⁹ Master, Moses wrote unto us, If a man's brother die, and leave *his* wife *behind him*, and leave no children, that his brother should take his wife, and raise up seed unto his brother.

²⁰ Now there were seven brethren: and the first took a wife, and dying left no seed.

²¹ And the second took her, and died, neither left he any seed: and the third likewise.

²² And the seven had her, and left no seed: last of all the woman died also.

²³ In the resurrection therefore, when they shall rise, whose wife shall she be of them? for the seven had her to wife.

²⁴ And Jesus answering said unto them, Do ye not therefore err, because ye know not the Scriptures, neither the power of God?

²⁵ For when they shall rise from the dead, they neither marry, nor are given in marriage; but are as the angels which are in heaven.

²⁶ And as touching the dead, that they rise; have ye not read in the book of Moses, how in the bush God spake unto him, saying, I *am* the God of Abraham, and the God of Isaac, and the God of Jacob?

²⁷ He is not the God of the dead, but the God of the living: ye therefore do greatly err.

The Most Important Command

*A*nd one of the scribes came, and having heard them reasoning together, and perceiving that he had answered them well, asked him, Which is the first commandment of all?

²⁹ And Jesus answered him, The first of all the commandments *is*, Hear, O Israel; The Lord our God is one Lord:

³⁰ and thou shalt love the Lord thy God with all thy heart, and with all thy soul, and with all thy mind, and with all thy strength: this *is* the first commandment.

³¹ And the second *is* like, *namely* this, Thou shalt love thy neighbor as thyself. There is none other commandment greater than these.

---

*W*hoso causeth the righteous to go astray in an evil way, he shall fall himself into his own pit: but the upright shall have good *things* in possesion.

Proverbs 28:10

*D*eliver me, O LORD, from the evil man: preserve me from the violent man;

² which imagine mischiefs in *their* heart; continually are they gathered together *for* war.

³ They have sharpened their tongues like a serpent; adders' poison *is* under their lips. Selah.

⁴ Keep me, O LORD, from the hands of the wicked; preserve me from the violent man; who have purposed to overthrow my goings.

⁵ The proud have hid a snare for me, and cords; they have spread a net by the wayside; they have set gins for me. Selah.

⁶ I said unto the LORD, Thou *art* my God: hear the voice of my supplications, O LORD.

⁷ O GOD the Lord, the strength of my salvation, thou hast covered my head in the day of battle.

⁸ Grant not, O LORD, the desires of the wicked: further not his wicked device; *lest* they exalt themselves. Selah.

Psalm 140:1–8

---

*T*he reproach we experience is the natural resentment in the hearts of men toward all that is godly and righteous. This is the cross we are to bear. This is why Christians are often persecuted. . . .

Let us not forget that there is happiness and blessing in persecution. As George MacDonald puts it, we become "hearty through hardship." . . .

Our Lord instructs the persecuted to be happy. "Rejoice," He said, "and be exceeding glad: for great is your reward in heaven: for so persecuted they the prophets which were before you" (Matthew 5:12).

The word joy has all but disappeared from our current Christian vocabulary. One of the reasons is that we have thought that joy and happiness were found in comfort, ease and luxury. James did not say, "Count it all joy when you fall into an easy chair," but he said, "Count it all joy when you fall into divers temptations" (James 1:2).

The persecuted are happy because they are being processed for heaven. Persecution is one of the natural consequences of living the Christian life. It is to the Christian what "growing pains" are to the growing child. No pain, no development. No suffering, no glory. No struggle, no victory. No persecution, no reward! Jesus predicted that if they persecuted Him, they would persecute you who follow Him, too.

Billy Graham

---

*H*ave you ever felt that you've unwittingly walked into a trap designed to test your Christian commitment? If so, be glad—you must be an effective witness! Pray that God will give you the strength and wisdom to face such encounters.

MONDAY

*Give Generously,
Even Sacrificially, to God*

Mark 12:32—13:10

*A*nd the scribe said unto him, Well, Master, thou hast said the truth: for there is one God; and there is none other but he:

33 and to love him with all the heart, and with all the understanding, and with all the soul, and with all the strength, and to love *his* neighbor as himself, is more than all whole burnt offerings and sacrifices.

34 And when Jesus saw that he answered discreetly, he said unto him, Thou art not far from the kingdom of God. And no man after that durst ask him *any question.*

35 And Jesus answered and said, while he taught in the temple, How say the scribes that Christ is the son of David?

36 For David himself said by the Holy Ghost, The LORD said to my Lord, Sit thou on my right hand, till I make thine enemies thy footstool.

37 David therefore himself calleth him Lord; and whence is he *then* his son? And the common people heard him gladly.

38 And he said unto them in his doctrine, Beware of the scribes, which love to go in long clothing, and *love* salutations in the marketplaces,

39 and the chief seats in the synagogues, and the uppermost rooms at feasts:

40 which devour widows' houses, and for a pretense make long prayers: these shall receive greater damnation.

True Giving

*A*nd Jesus sat over against the treasury, and beheld how the people cast money into the treasury: and many that were rich cast in much.

42 And there came a certain poor widow, and she threw in two mites, which make a farthing.

43 And he called *unto him* his disciples, and saith unto them, Verily I say unto you, That this poor widow hath cast more in, than all they which have cast into the treasury:

44 for all *they* did cast in of their abundance; but she of her want did cast in all that she had, *even* all her living.

The Temple Will be Destroyed

13 And as he went out of the temple, one of his disciples saith unto him, Master, see what manner of stones and what buildings *are here!*

2 And Jesus answering said unto him, Seest thou these great buildings? there shall not be left one stone upon another, that shall not be thrown down.

3 And as he sat upon the mount of Olives, over against the temple, Peter and James and John and Andrew asked him privately,

4 Tell us, when shall these things be? and what *shall be* the sign when all these things shall be fulfilled?

5 And Jesus answering them began to say, Take heed lest any *man* deceive you:

6 for many shall come in my name, saying, I am *Christ*; and shall deceive many.

7 And when ye shall hear of wars and rumours of wars, be ye not troubled:

for *such things* must needs be; but the end *shall* not *be* yet.

[8] For nation shall rise against nation, and kingdom against kingdom: and there shall be earthquakes in divers places, and there shall be famines and troubles: these *are* the beginnings of sorrows.

[9] But take heed to yourselves: for they shall deliver you up to councils; and in the synagogues ye shall be beaten: and ye shall be brought before rulers and kings for my sake, for a testimony against them.

[10] And the gospel must first be published among all nations.

OLD TESTAMENT READING

*A*nd they brought yet unto him free offerings every morning.

[4] And all the wise men, that wrought all the work of the sanctuary, came every man from his work which they made;

[5] and they spake unto Moses, saying, The people bring much more than enough for the service of the work, which the LORD commanded to make.

[6] And Moses gave commandment, and they causeth it to be proclaimed throughout the camp, saying, Let neither man nor woman make any more work for the offering of the sanctuary. So the people were restrained from bringing.

[7] For the stuff they had was sufficient for all the work to make it, and too much.

Exodus 36:3b–7

INSIGHTS

*M*any beloved saints are depriving themselves of wondrous spiritual blessing by not giving as stewards what is entrusted to them. They act

as if it were their own, as if all belonged to them, as if already they were in possession of the inheritance incorruptible and undefiled; forgetting that they have nothing whatever which is their own, that they are bought by the precious blood of Christ, and all they possess—their bodily strength, their time, their talents, their business, their professions, their eyes, their hands, their feet, all belong to the Lord Jesus Christ; because He has bought them with his precious blood. . . .

Just as we are constrained by the love of Christ, so God condescends to use us; and as we give, He is pleased to entrust to us more and more. . . .

My advice is this: if the reader has as yet but little knowledge and little grace, let him accordingly begin with a small percentage, yea, though it were ever so small a percentage, only let him be true to God, and put aside for Him habitually as He may be pleased to prosper him. In this way blessing for the soul will be reaped, will be abundantly reaped, and soon will the desire spring up in the heart to increase the proportion of returns to the Lord. This way will more and more lead the heart to such a state to be only a steward for the Lord, and to be willing to stand with all we have and are before the Lord as His stewards.

George Müller

PAUSE FOR REFLECTION

*W*hat does God promise to those who give generously to him? To those who do not? Reread the Exodus passage. Can you imagine God's people today giving so much that they would have to be told to stop?

TUESDAY

Be Strong
During the End Times

Mark 13:11–37

*B*ut when they shall lead *you*, and deliver you up, take no thought beforehand what ye shall speak, neither do ye premeditate: but whatsoever shall be given you in that hour, that speak ye: for it is not ye that speak, but the Holy Ghost.

¹² Now the brother shall betray the brother to death, and the father the son; and children shall rise up against *their* parents, and shall cause them to be put to death.

¹³ And ye shall be hated of all *men* for my name's sake: but he that shall endure unto the end, the same shall be saved.

¹⁴ But when ye shall see the abomination of desolation, spoken of by Daniel the prophet, standing where it ought not, (let him that readeth understand,) then let them that be in Judea flee to the mountains:

¹⁵ and let him that is on the housetop not go down into the house, neither enter *therein*, to take any thing out of his house:

¹⁶ and let him that is in the field not turn back again for to take up his garment.

¹⁷ But woe to them that are with child, and to them that give suck in those days!

¹⁸ And pray ye that your flight be not in the winter.

¹⁹ For *in* those days shall be affliction, such as was not from the beginning of the creation which God created unto this time, neither shall be.

²⁰ And except that the Lord had shortened those days, no flesh should be saved: but for the elect's sake, whom he hath chosen, he hath shortened the days.

²¹ And then if any man shall say to you, Lo, here *is* Christ; or, lo, *he is* there; believe *him* not:

²² for false Christs and false prophets shall rise, and shall show signs and wonders, to seduce, if *it were* possible, even the elect.

²³ But take ye heed: behold, I have foretold you all things.

²⁴ But in those days, after that tribulation, the sun shall be darkened, and the moon shall not give her light,

²⁵ and the stars of heaven shall fall, and the powers that are in heaven shall be shaken.

²⁶ And then shall they see the Son of man coming in the clouds with great power and glory.

²⁷ And then shall he send his angels, and shall gather together his elect from the four winds, from the uttermost part of the earth to the uttermost part of heaven.

²⁸ Now learn a parable of the fig tree: When her branch is yet tender, and putteth forth leaves, ye know that summer is near:

²⁹ so ye in like manner, when ye shall see these things come to pass, know that it is nigh, *even* at the doors.

³⁰ Verily I say unto you, that this generation shall not pass, till all these things be done.

³¹ Heaven and earth shall pass away: but my words shall not pass away.

³² But of that day and *that* hour knoweth no man, no, not the angels which are in heaven, neither the Son, but the Father.

³³ Take ye heed, watch and pray: for

ye know not when the time is.
³⁴ *For the Son of man is* as a man taking a far journey, who left his house, and gave authority to his servants, and to every man his work, and commanded the porter to watch.
³⁵ Watch ye therefore: for ye know not when the master of the house cometh, at even, or at midnight, or at the cockcrowing, or in the morning:
³⁶ Lest coming suddenly he find you sleeping.
³⁷ And what I say unto you I say unto all, Watch.

OLD TESTAMENT READING

*A*nd they that understand among the people shall instruct many: yet they shall fall by the sword, and by flame, by captivity, and by spoil, *many* days.
³⁴ Now when they shall fall, they shall be helped with a little help: but many shall cleave to them with flatteries.
³⁵ And *some* of them of understanding shall fall, to try them, and to purge, and to make *them* white, *even* to the time of the end: because *it is* yet for a time appointed.

Daniel 11:33–35

INSIGHTS

*M*y hope is built on nothing less
Than Jesus' blood and righteousness;
I dare not trust the sweetest frame,
But wholly lean on Jesus' name.
On Christ, the solid Rock, I stand:
All other ground is sinking sand.

When darkness veils His lovely face,
I rest on His unchanging grace;
In ev'ry high and stormy gale,
My anchor holds within the veil.

On Christ, the solid Rock, I stand:
All other ground is sinking sand.

His oath, His covenant, His blood,
Support me in the whelming flood;
When all around my soul gives way,
He then is all my hope and stay.
On Christ, the solid Rock I stand:
All other ground is sinking sand.

When He shall come with trumpet
sound,
O may I then in Him be found:
Dressed in His righteousness alone,
Faultless to stand before the throne.
On Christ, the solid Rock, I stand:
All other ground is sinking sand.

Edward Mote

PAUSE FOR REFLECTION

*W*hat are God's people to be and do *during the end times? What is the purpose of their suffering during that time? On what can God's righteous ones depend during that time?*

WEDNESDAY

The Passover and the Lord's Supper

Mark 14:1–26

The Plan to Kill Jesus

14 After two days was *the feast of* the passover, and of unleavened bread: and the chief priests and the scribes sought how they might take him by craft, and put *him* to death.

[2] But they said, Not on the feast *day*, lest there be an uproar of the people.

A Woman with Perfume for Jesus

*A*nd being in Bethany, in the house of Simon the leper, as he sat at meat, there came a woman having an alabaster box of ointment of spikenard very precious; and she brake the box, and poured *it* on his head.

[4] And there were some that had indignation within themselves, and said, Why was this waste of the ointment made?

[5] For it might have been sold for more than three hundred pence, and have been given to the poor. And they murmured against her.

[6] And Jesus said, Let her alone; why trouble ye her? she hath wrought a good work on me.

[7] For ye have the poor with you always, and whensoever ye will ye may do them good: but me ye have not always.

[8] She hath done what she could: she is come aforehand to anoint my body to the burying.

[9] Verily I say unto you, Wheresoever this gospel shall be preached throughout the whole world, *this* also that she hath done shall be spoken of for a memorial of her.

Judas Becomes an Enemy of Jesus

*A*nd Judas Iscariot, one of the twelve, went unto the chief priests, to betray him unto them.

[11] And when they heard *it*, they were glad, and promised to give him money. And he sought how he might conveniently betray him.

Jesus Eats the Passover Meal

*A*nd the first day of unleavened bread, when they killed the passover, his disciples said unto him, Where wilt thou that we go and prepare that thou mayest eat the passover?

[13] And he sendeth forth two of his disciples, and saith unto them, Go ye into the city, and there shall meet you a man bearing a pitcher of water: follow him.

[14] And wheresoever he shall go in, say ye to the goodman of the house, The Master saith, Where is the guest chamber, where I shall eat the passover with my disciples?

[15] And he will show you a large upper room furnished *and* prepared: there make ready for us.

[16] And his disciples went forth, and came into the city, and found as he had said unto them: and they made ready the passover.

[17] And in the evening he cometh with the twelve.

[18] And as they sat and did eat, Jesus said, Verily I say unto you, One of you which eateth with me shall betray me.

[19] And they began to be sorrowful, and to say unto him one by one, *Is* it I? and another *said, Is* it I?

[20] And he answered and said unto them, *It is* one of the twelve, that dippeth with me in the dish.

[21] The Son of man indeed goeth, as it is written of him: but woe to that man by whom the Son of man is betrayed! good were it for that man if he had never been born.

The Lord's Supper

*A*nd as they did eat, Jesus took bread, and blessed, and brake *it*, and gave to them, and said, Take, eat; this is my body.

[23] And he took the cup, and when he had given thanks, he gave *it* to them: and they all drank of it.

[24] And he said unto them, This is my blood of the new testament, which is shed for many.

[25] Verily I say unto you, I will drink no more of the fruit of the vine, until that day that I drink it new in the kingdom of God.

[26] And when they had sung a hymn, they went out into the mount of Olives.

OLD TESTAMENT READING

*A*nd this day shall be unto you for a memorial; and ye shall keep it a feast to the LORD throughout your generations: ye shall keep it a feast by an ordinance for ever.

[25] And it shall come to pass, when ye be come to the land which the LORD will give you, according as he hath promised, that ye shall keep this service.

[26] And it shall come to pass, when your children shall say unto you, What mean ye by this service?

[27] That ye shall say, It *is* the sacrifice of the LORD's passover, who passed over the houses of the children of Israel in Egypt, when he smote the Egyptians, and delivered our houses. And the people bowed the head and worshipped.

Exodus 12:14, 25–27

INSIGHTS

*R*ight down to the present, Jews re-enact the Passover-event in celebration of their redemption from Egypt. . . .

In this service, words are connected with ritual, symbol, and gesture. It is a drama, a reenactment of the flight of Israel from the land of Pharaoh. It is not only a past event, but a present reality. For, although the Exodus happened in the past, its power and meaning reach down into history and change the lives of people now as did the original event. Reenactment of the action still has the power to change lives. . . .

The church has also retained the Old Testament principle that the event being celebrated becomes contemporaneous: Paul referred to the Table as a "participation" in Christ (1 Cor. 10:16). It is important to understand, though, that the death and resurrection of Jesus Christ is not an event which we memorialize. Its power, like that of the Exodus, reaches down through history and becomes a present reality to the people who celebrate it in faith.

Robert Webber

PAUSE FOR REFLECTION

*R*ead Exodus 12:1–27 and try to feel the drama and significance of the Passover celebration. What feelings related to the Lord's Supper does this stir within you?

THURSDAY

*Kneel Before God
in Prayer*

Mark 14:27–52

Jesus' Disciples Will Leave Him

*A*nd Jesus saith unto them, All ye shall be offended because of me this night: for it is written, I will smite the shepherd, and the sheep shall be scattered.

²⁸ But after that I am risen, I will go before you into Galilee.

²⁹ But Peter said unto him, Although all shall be offended, yet *will* not I.

³⁰ And Jesus saith unto him, Verily I say unto thee, That this day, *even* in this night, before the cock crow twice, thou shalt deny me thrice.

³¹ But he spake the more vehemently, If I should die with thee, I will not deny thee in any wise. Likewise also said they all.

Jesus Prays Alone

*A*nd they came to a place which was named Gethsemane: and he saith to his disciples, Sit ye here, while I shall pray.

³³ And he taketh with him Peter and James and John, and began to be sore amazed, and to be very heavy;

³⁴ and saith unto them, My soul is exceeding sorrowful unto death: tarry ye here, and watch.

³⁵ And he went forward a little, and fell on the ground, and prayed that, if it were possible, the hour might pass from him.

³⁶ And he said, Abba, Father, all things *are* possible unto thee; take away this cup from me: nevertheless not what I will, but what thou wilt.

³⁷ And he cometh, and findeth them sleeping, and saith unto Peter, Simon, sleepest thou? couldest not thou watch one hour?

³⁸ Watch ye and pray, lest ye enter into temptation. The spirit truly *is* ready, but the flesh *is* weak.

³⁹ And again he went away, and prayed, and spake the same words.

⁴⁰ And when he returned, he found them asleep again, (for their eyes were heavy,) neither wist they what to answer him.

⁴¹ And he cometh the third time, and saith unto them, Sleep on now, and take *your* rest: it is enough, the hour is come; behold, the Son of man is betrayed into the hands of sinners.

⁴² Rise up, let us go; lo, he that betrayeth me is at hand.

Jesus Is Arrested

*A*nd immediately, while he yet spake, cometh Judas, one of the twelve, and with him a great multitude with swords and staves, from the chief priests and the scribes and the elders.

⁴⁴ And he that betrayed him had given them a token, saying, Whomsoever I shall kiss, that same is he; take him, and lead *him* away safely.

⁴⁵ And as soon as he was come, he goeth straightway to him, and saith, Master, Master; and kissed him.

⁴⁶ And they laid their hands on him, and took him.

⁴⁷ And one of them that stood by drew a sword, and smote a servant of the high priest, and cut off his ear.

⁴⁸ And Jesus answered and said unto them, Are ye come out, as against a thief, with swords and *with* staves to take me?

⁴⁹ I was daily with you in the temple teaching, and ye took me not: but the Scriptures must be fulfilled.
⁵⁰ And they all forsook him, and fled.
⁵¹ And there followed him a certain young man, having a linen cloth cast about *his* naked *body*; and the young men laid hold on him:
⁵² and he left the linen cloth, and fled from them naked.

OLD TESTAMENT READING

*A*nd it was *so*, that when Solomon had made an end of praying all this prayer and supplication unto the LORD, he arose from before the altar of the LORD, from kneeling on his knees with his hands spread up to heaven.
⁵⁵ And he stood, and blessed all the congregation of Israel with a loud voice, saying,
⁵⁶ Blessed *be* the LORD, that hath given rest unto his people Israel, according to all that he promised: there hath not failed one word of all his good promise, which he promised by the hand of Moses his servant.
⁵⁷ The LORD our God be with us, as he was with our fathers: let him not leave us, nor forsake us:
⁵⁸ that he may incline our hearts unto him, to walk in all his ways, and to keep his commandments, and his statutes, and his judgments, which he commanded our fathers.
⁵⁹ And let these my words, wherewith I have made supplication before the LORD, be nigh unto the LORD our God day and night, that he maintain the cause of his servant, and the cause of his people Israel at all times, as the matter shall require.

1 Kings 8:54–59

*H*e kneeled upon his knees three times a day, and prayed, and gave thanks before his God, as he did aforetime.

Daniel 6:10b

INSIGHTS

*T*he powerful reality grips me, Lord
That when I kneel in Your presence
To ask Your forgiveness
I am utterly stripped of facade.
You accept no big-name references
No high-caliber recommendations.
Extenuating circumstances
Crumble to dust
In Your court of appeal . . .
I am forgiven never
Because of inherited tendencies
Or emotional discomfort
Or nagging weakness . . .
I can never plead
Corrupt environment
Or life's strange twistings
Or my own unbelievable stupidity . . .
Ultimately I have one solitary defense.
Only one—
But always one:
Forgive me, God
For Jesus' sake.
Like a song unending
The words keep singing . . .
I am totally forgiven
I am continually cleansed
Just for Jesus' sake.

Ruth Calkin

PAUSE FOR REFLECTION

*D*o you think there is a difference between kneeling, sitting, or standing before God in prayer? How do you pray most earnestly to God?

129

FRIDAY

Accused by the Wicked,
the Blameless Stand
Innocent Before God

Mark 14:53—15:5

Jesus Before the Leaders

*A*nd they led Jesus away to the high priest: and with him were assembled all the chief priests and the elders and the scribes.

⁵⁴ And Peter followed him afar off, even into the palace of the high priest: and he sat with the servants, and warmed himself at the fire.

⁵⁵ And the chief priests and all the council sought for witness against Jesus to put him to death; and found none.

⁵⁶ For many bare false witness against him, but their witness agreed not together.

⁵⁷ And there arose certain, and bare false witness against him, saying,

⁵⁸ We heard him say, I will destroy this temple that is made with hands, and within three days I will build another made without hands.

⁵⁹ But neither so did their witness agree together.

⁶⁰ And the high priest stood up in the midst, and asked Jesus, saying, Answerest thou nothing? What *is it which* these witness against thee?

⁶¹ But he held his peace, and answered nothing. Again the high priest asked him, and said unto him, Art thou the Christ, the Son of the Blessed?

⁶² And Jesus said, I am: and ye shall see the Son of man sitting on the right hand of power, and coming in the clouds of heaven.

⁶³ Then the high priest rent his clothes, and saith, What need we any further witnesses?

⁶⁴ Ye have heard the blasphemy: what think ye? And they all condemned him to be guilty of death.

⁶⁵ And some began to spit on him, and to cover his face, and to buffet him, and to say unto him, Prophesy: and the servants did strike him with the palms of their hands.

Peter Denies Knowing Jesus

*A*nd as Peter was beneath in the palace, there cometh one of the maids of the high priest:

⁶⁷ and when she saw Peter warming himself, she looked upon him, and said, And thou also wast with Jesus of Nazareth.

⁶⁸ But he denied, saying, I know not, neither understand I what thou sayest. And he went out into the porch; and the cock crew.

⁶⁹ And a maid saw him again, and began to say to them that stood by, This is *one* of them.

⁷⁰ And he denied it again. And a little after, they that stood by said again to Peter, Surely thou art *one* of them: for thou art a Galilean, and thy speech agreeth *thereto*.

⁷¹ But he began to curse and to swear, *saying*, I know not this man of whom ye speak.

⁷² And the second time the cock crew. And Peter called to mind the word that Jesus said unto him, Before the cock crow twice, thou shalt deny me thrice. And when he thought thereon, he wept.

Pilate Questions Jesus

15 And straightway in the morning the chief priests held a consultation with the elders and scribes and the whole council, and bound Jesus, and carried *him* away, and delivered *him* to Pilate.

[2] And Pilate asked him, Art thou the King of the Jews? And he answering said unto him, Thou sayest *it*.

[3] And the chief priests accused him of many things; but he answered nothing.

[4] And Pilate asked him again, saying, Answerest thou nothing? behold how many things they witness against thee.

[5] But Jesus yet answered nothing; so that Pilate marveled.

OLD TESTAMENT READING

*J*udge me, O LORD; for I have walked in mine integrity: I have trusted also in the LORD; *therefore* I shall not slide.

[2] Examine me, O LORD, and prove me; try my reins and my heart.

Psalm 26:1–2

INSIGHTS

*H*ere is a secret to the spiritual strength that willingly suffers wrong: accustom yourself in everything that happens to recognize the hand and will of God. Whether it be some great wrong that is done you, or some little offense that you meet in daily life, before you consider the person who did it, first be still and remember, God allows me to come into this trouble to see if I will glorify Him in it. This trial, be it great or small, is allowed by God and is His will concerning me. Let me first recognize and submit to God's will in it. Then with the peace of God which this gives, I will receive wisdom to know how to behave in it. With my eye turned from man to God, suffering wrong takes on this new dimension.

. . . Jesus saw beyond the temporal injustice and was satisfied to leave the vindication of His rights and honor in God's hands; He knew they were safe with Him. Peter writes, "He committed himself to him that judgeth righteously" (2:23). It was settled between the Father and the Son: the Son was not to care for His own honor, but only for the Father's. The Father would care for the Son's honor. Let the believer follow Christ's example in this; it will give him such rest and peace. Commit your right and your honor into God's keeping. Meet every offense that man commits against you with the firm trust that God will watch over and care for you.

Andrew Murray

PAUSE FOR REFLECTION

*H*ow important is innocence in God's eyes? Think about the total trust Jesus had in his Father—a trust that enabled him to stand innocent before God without having to prove his innocence to his accusers.

WEEKEND

Jesus Suffered for Us

Mark 15:6–32

Pilate Tries to Free Jesus

Now at *that* feast he released unto them one prisoner, whomsoever they desired.

⁷ And there was *one* named Barabbas, *which lay* bound with them that had made insurrection with him, who had committed murder in the insurrection.
⁸ And the multitude crying aloud began to desire *him to do* as he had ever done unto them.
⁹ But Pilate answered them, saying, Will ye that I release unto you the King of the Jews?
¹⁰ For he knew that the chief priests had delivered him for envy.
¹¹ But the chief priests moved the people, that he should rather release Barabbas unto them.
¹² And Pilate answered and said again unto them, What will ye then that I shall do *unto him* whom ye call the King of the Jews?
¹³ And they cried out again, Crucify him.
¹⁴ Then Pilate said unto them, Why, what evil hath he done? And they cried out the more exceedingly, Crucify him.
¹⁵ And *so* Pilate, willing to content the people, released Barabbas unto them, and delivered Jesus, when he had scourged *him*, to be crucified.
¹⁶ And the soldiers led him away into the hall, called Pretorium; and they call together the whole band.
¹⁷ And they clothed him with purple, and platted a crown of thorns, and put it about his *head*,

¹⁸ and began to salute him, Hail, King of the Jews!
¹⁹ And they smote him on the head with a reed, and did spit upon him, and bowing *their* knees worshipped him.
²⁰ And when they had mocked him, they took off the purple from him, and put his own clothes on him, and led him out to crucify him.

Jesus Is Crucified

And they compel one Simon a Cyrenian, who passed by, coming out of the country, the father of Alexander and Rufus, to bear his cross.
²² And they bring him unto the place Golgotha, which is, being interpreted, The place of a skull.
²³ And they gave him to drink wine mingled with myrrh: but he received *it* not.
²⁴ And when they had crucified him, they parted his garments, casting lots upon them, what every man should take.
²⁵ And it was the third hour, and they crucified him.
²⁶ And the superscription of his accusation was written over, THE KING OF THE JEWS.
²⁷ And with him they crucify two thieves; the one on his right hand, and the other on his left.
²⁸ And the Scripture was fulfilled, which saith, And he was numbered with the transgressors.
²⁹ And they that passed by railed on him, wagging their heads, and saying, Ah, thou that destroyest the temple, and buildest *it* in three days,
³⁰ save thyself, and come down from the cross.
³¹ Likewise also the chief priests mocking said among themselves

with the scribes, He saved others; himself he cannot save.

32 Let Christ the King of Israel descend now from the cross, that we may see and believe. And they that were crucified with him reviled him.

OLD TESTAMENT READING

*F*or dogs have compassed me: the assembly of the wicked have inclosed me: they pierced my hands and my feet.

17 I may tell all my bones: they look *and* stare upon me.

18 They part my garments among them, and cast lots upon my vesture.

Psalm 22:16–18

INSIGHTS

Think of the love that God must have had when He gave His son to die for the world! I used to think a good deal more of Christ than I did of the Father. Somehow or other I had the idea that God was a stern judge; that Christ came between me and God, and appeased the anger of God. But after I became a father, and for years had an only son, as I looked at my boy I thought of the Father giving His Son to die, and it seemed to me as if it required more love for the Father to give His Son than for the Son to die. Oh, the love that God must have had for the world when He gave His Son to die for it! "God so loved the world, that He gave His only begotten Son, that whosoever believeth in Him should not perish, but have everlasting life" (John 3:16). I have never been able to preach from that text. I have often thought I would, but it is so high that I can never climb to its height,

I have just quoted it and passed on. Who can fathom the depth of those words: "God so loved the world"? We can never scale the heights of His love, or fathom its depths. Paul prayed that he might know the height, the depth, the length, and the breadth of the love of God; but it was past his finding out. . . .

Nothing speaks to us of the love of God like the Cross of Christ. Come with me to Calvary, and look upon the Son of God as He hangs there. Can you hear that piercing cry from His dying lips: "Father, forgive them; for they know not what they do!" and say that He does not love you? "Greater love hath no man than this, that a man lay down his life for his friends" (John 15:13). But Jesus Christ laid down His life for His enemies.

Another thought is this: He loved us long before we ever thought of Him. The idea that He does not love us until we first love Him is not to be found in Scripture. In 1 John 4:10 it is written: "Herein is love, not that we love God, but that He loved us, and sent His Son to be the propitiation for our sins." He loved us before we ever thought of loving Him. You loved your children before they knew anything about your love. And so, long before we ever thought of God, we were in His thoughts.

D. L. Moody

PAUSE FOR REFLECTION

How does your image of God's love change as you read about the way Jesus suffered injury, insult, and degradation in order to save you? Perhaps now would be a good time for a thoughtful prayer of thanks for God's love.

MONDAY

Jesus Dies,
but Rises as He Promised

Mark 15:33—16:8

Jesus Dies

*A*nd when the sixth hour was come, there was darkness over the whole land until the ninth hour.
³⁴ And at the ninth hour Jesus cried with a loud voice, saying, Eloi, Eloi, lama sabachthani? which is, being interpreted, My God, my God, why hast thou forsaken me?
³⁵ And some of them that stood by, when they heard *it*, said, Behold, he calleth Elijah.
³⁶ And one ran and filled a sponge full of vinegar, and put *it* on a reed, and gave him to drink, saying, Let alone; let us see whether Elijah will come to take him down.
³⁷ And Jesus cried with a loud voice, and gave up the ghost.
³⁸ And the veil of the temple was rent in twain from the top to the bottom.
³⁹ And when the centurion, which stood over against him, saw that he so cried out, and gave up the ghost, he said, Truly this man was the Son of God.
⁴⁰ There were also women looking on afar off: among whom was Mary Magdalene, and Mary the mother of James the less and of Joses, and Salome;
⁴¹ who also, when he was in Galilee, followed him, and ministered unto him; and many other women which came up with him unto Jerusalem.

Jesus Is Buried

*A*nd now when the even was come, because it was the preparation, that is, the day before the sabbath,
⁴³ Joseph of Arimathea, and honorable counselor, which also waited for the kingdom of God, came, and went in boldly unto Pilate, and craved the body of Jesus.
⁴⁴ And Pilate marveled if he were already dead: and calling *unto him* the centurion, he asked him whether he had been any while dead.
⁴⁵ And when he knew *it* of the centurion, he gave the body to Joseph.
⁴⁶ And he bought fine linen, and took him down, and wrapped him in the linen, and laid him in a sepulchre which was hewn out of a rock, and rolled a stone unto the door of the sepulchre.
⁴⁷ And Mary Magdalene and Mary *the mother* of Joses beheld where he was laid.

Jesus Rises from the Dead

16 And when the sabbath was past, Mary Magdalene, and Mary the *mother* of James, and Salome, had bought sweet spices, that they might come and anoint him.
² And very early in the morning the first *day* of the week, they came unto the sepulchre at the rising of the sun.
³ And they said among themselves, Who shall roll us away the stone from the door of the sepulchre?
⁴ And when they looked, they saw that the stone was rolled away: for it was very great.
⁵ And entering into the sepulchre, they saw a young man sitting on the right side, clothed in a long white

garment; and they were affrighted.

⁶And he saith unto them, Be not affrighted: ye seek Jesus of Nazareth, which was crucified: he is risen; he is not here: behold the place where they laid him.

⁷But go your way, tell his disciples and Peter that he goeth before you into Galilee: there shall ye see him, as he said unto you.

⁸And they went out quickly, and fled from the sepulchre; for they trembled and were amazed: neither said they any thing to any *man*; for they were afraid.

OLD TESTAMENT READING

*A*nd the parched ground shall become a pool, and the thirsty land springs of water: in the habitation of dragons, where each lay, *shall be* grass with reeds and rushes.

⁸And a highway shall be there, and a way, and it shall be called The way of holiness; the unclean shall not pass over it; but it *shall be* for those: the wayfaring men, though fools, shall not err *therein*.

⁹No lion shall be there, nor *any* ravenous beast shall go up thereon, it shall not be found there; but the redeemed shall walk *there*:

¹⁰and the ransomed of the LORD shall return, and come to Zion with songs and everlasting joy upon their heads: they shall obtain joy and gladness, and sorrow and sighing shall flee away.

Isaiah 35:7–10

INSIGHTS

I will never forget the day that I looked into the tomb. It changed my whole ministry. It came to me that my Savior was really alive, that His work on the cross for sinners so satisfied divine justice and divine character and divine righteousness, that I would never see my sins again. God raised Him from the dead as a guarantee to me personally that death has no more authority over the man in Christ. It has been shorn of its power. . . . At the cross we see His love, but in resurrection we see His power.

We've been joined to a risen Savior. That is why the apostles gave witness with such great power in the book of Acts. Paul stood before Felix, before Festus, before Agrippa, before the Sanhedrin, before the philosophers of Athens, and before the corrupt Corinthians with only one message. He preached the risen Christ.

. . . The cross is a tragedy if there is no resurrection. Would to God that His people would continually rejoice that our Savior is alive forevermore.

John G. Mitchell

ACTION POINT

*M*editate on the Isaiah 35 reading until you begin to understand the awesome reality of Christ's resurrection. Pray now and thank God that Jesus not only died, but that he lives today!

135

TUESDAY

*Those Who Don't Believe Will
Be Judged Guilty*

Mark 16:9—Luke 1:13

Jesus Appears to Several

*N*ow when *Jesus* was risen early the first *day* of the week, he appeared first to Mary Magdalene, out of whom he had cast seven devils.

[10] *And* she went and told them that had been with him, as they mourned and wept.

[11] And they, when they had heard that he was alive, and had been seen of her, believed not.

[12] After that he appeared in another form unto two of them, as they walked, and went into the country.

[13] And they went and told *it* unto the residue: neither believed they them.

Jesus Talks to the Apostles

*A*fterward he appeared unto the eleven as they sat at meat, and upbraided them with their unbelief and hardness of heart, because they believed not them which had seen him after he was risen.

[15] And he said unto them, Go ye into all the world, and preach the gospel to every creature.

[16] He that believeth and is baptized shall be saved; but he that believeth not shall be damned.

[17] And these signs shall follow them that believe; In my name shall they cast out devils; they shall speak with new tongues;

[18] they shall take up serpents; and if they drink any deadly thing, it shall not hurt them; they shall lay hands on the sick, and they shall recover.

[19] So then, after the Lord had spoken unto them, he was received up into heaven, and sat on the right hand of God.

[20] And they went forth, and preached everywhere, the Lord working with *them*, and confirming the word with signs following. Amen.

Luke Writes About Jesus' Life

1 Forasmuch as many have taken in hand to set forth in order a declaration of those things which are most surely believed among us,

[2] even as they delivered them unto us, which from the beginning were eyewitnesses, and ministers of the word;

[3] it seemed good to me also, having had perfect understanding of all things from the very first, to write unto thee in order, most excellent Theophilus,

[4] that thou mightest know the certainty of those things, wherein thou hast been instructed.

Zechariah and Elisabeth

*T*here was in the days of Herod, the king of Judea, a certain priest named Zechariah, of the course of Abijah: and his wife *was* of the daughters of Aaron, and her name *was* Elisabeth.

[6] And they were both righteous before God, walking in all the commandments and ordinances of the Lord blameless.

[7] And they had no child, because that Elisabeth was barren; and they both were *now* well stricken in years.

8 And it came to pass, that, while he executed the priest's office before God in the order of his course,

9 according to the custom of the priest's office, his lot was to burn incense when he went into the temple of the Lord.

10 And the whole multitude of the people were praying without at the time of incense.

11 And there appeared unto him an angel of the Lord standing on the right side of the altar of incense.

12 And when Zechariah saw *him*, he was troubled, and fear fell upon him.

13 But the angel said unto him, Fear not, Zechariah: for thy prayer is heard; and thy wife Elisabeth shall bear thee a son, and thou shalt call his name John.

OLD TESTAMENT READING

*A*nd the LORD said unto Moses, How long will this people provoke me? and how long will it be ere they believe me, for all the signs which I have showed among them?

22 Because all those men which have seen my glory, and my miracles, which I did in Egypt and in the wilderness, and have tempted me now these ten times, and have not hearkened to my voice;

23 surely they shall not see the land which I sware unto their fathers, neither shall any of them that provoked me see it:

24 but my servant Caleb, because he had another spirit with him, and hath followed me fully, him will I bring into the land whereinto he went; and his seed shall possess it.

Numbers 14:11, 22–24

INSIGHTS

*Y*ou may ask how people wind up in hell if God is a loving God. People wind up in hell by trampling the love of God instead of treasuring it. They ignore it, spurn it, yawn over it, close their hearts to it, keep saying "someday, someday, someday."

The Bible says there will be a someday. It's a day of reckoning. To those who have spurned His love, God will say in effect, "I loved you every day of your life. I loved you with a perfect love. I extended Myself to you. I made My wisdom available to you. I made My comfort and My strength and My Spirit available to you. I made My offer of salvation to you. But you trampled and spurned My love. You had it your way on earth, so now you can have it your way in eternity."

Are you facing that scenario? Will you continue to trample the love of God? That's the question of the ages, and it is one you yourself must answer.
Bill Hybels

PAUSE FOR REFLECTION

*W*hat is the essential message of the Good News? After Jesus returned to heaven, how did he prove that the Good News was true? Is it really easier to believe God when we see his miracles? What is the fate of all those who choose to reject God?

WEDNESDAY

God Sends
Special Messengers

Luke 1:14–45

*A*nd thou shalt have joy and gladness; and many shall rejoice at his birth.

[15] For he shall be great in the sight of the Lord, and shall drink neither wine nor strong drink; and he shall be filled with the Holy Ghost, even from his mother's womb.

[16] And many of the children of Israel shall he turn to the Lord their God.

[17] And he shall go before him in the spirit and power of Elijah, to turn the hearts of the fathers to the children, and the disobedient to the wisdom of the just; to make ready a people prepared for the Lord.

[18] And Zechariah said unto the angel, Whereby shall I know this? for I am an old man, and my wife well stricken in years.

[19] And the angel answering said unto him, I am Gabriel, that stand in the presence of God; and am sent to speak unto thee, and to show thee these glad tidings.

[20] And, behold, thou shalt be dumb, and not able to speak, until the day that these things shall be performed, because thou believest not my words, which shall be fulfilled in their season.

[21] And the people waited for Zechariah, and marveled that he tarried so long in the temple.

[22] And when he came out, he could not speak unto them: and they perceived that he had seen a vision in the temple; for he beckoned unto them, and remained speechless.

[23] And it came to pass, that, as soon as the days of his ministration were accomplished, he departed to his own house.

[24] And after those days his wife Elisabeth conceived, and hid herself five months, saying,

[25] Thus hath the Lord dealt with me in the days wherein he looked on *me,* to take away my reproach among men.

An Angel Appears to Mary

*A*nd in the sixth month the angel Gabriel was sent from God unto a city of Galilee, named Nazareth,

[27] To a virgin espoused to a man whose name was Joseph, of the house of David; and the virgin's name *was* Mary.

[28] And the angel came in unto her, and said, Hail, *thou that art* highly favoured, the Lord *is* with thee: blessed *art* thou among women.

[29] And when she saw *him*, she was troubled at his saying, and cast in her mind what manner of salutation this should be.

[30] And the angel said unto her, Fear not, Mary: for thou hast found favour with God.

[31] And, behold, thou shalt conceive in thy womb, and bring forth a son, and shalt call his name JESUS.

[32] He shall be great, and shall be called the Son of the Highest; and the Lord God shall give unto him the throne of his father David:

[33] and he shall reign over the house of Jacob for ever; and of his kingdom there shall be no end.

[34] Then said Mary unto the angel, How shall this be, seeing I know not a man?

[35] And the angel answered and said unto her, The Holy Ghost shall come

upon thee, and the power of the Highest shall overshadow thee: therefore also that holy thing which shall be born of thee shall be called the Son of God.

³⁶ And, behold, thy cousin Elisabeth, she hath also conceived a son in her old age; and this is the sixth month with her, who was called barren.

³⁷ For with God nothing shall be impossible.

³⁸ And Mary said, Behold the handmaid of the Lord; be it unto me according to thy word. And the angel departed from her.

Mary Visits Elisabeth

*A*nd Mary arose in those days, and went into the hill country with haste, into a city of Judah;

⁴⁰ and entered into the house of Zechariah, and saluted Elisabeth.

⁴¹ And it came to pass, that, when Elisabeth heard the salutation of Mary, the babe leaped in her womb; and Elisabeth was filled with the Holy Ghost:

⁴² and she spake out with a loud voice, and said, Blessed *art* thou among women, and blessed *is* the fruit of thy womb.

⁴³ And whence *is* this to me, that the mother of my Lord should come to me?

⁴⁴ For, lo, as soon as the voice of thy salutation sounded in mine ears, the babe leaped in my womb for joy.

⁴⁵ And blessed *is* she that believed: for there shall be a performance of those things which were told her from the Lord.

OLD TESTAMENT READING

*B*ehold, I will send you Elijah the prophet before the coming of the great and dreadful day of the LORD:

⁶ and he shall turn the heart of the fathers to the children, and the heart of the children to their fathers, lest I come and smite the earth with a curse.

Malachi 4:5–6

INSIGHTS

*D*emonic activity and Satan worship are on the increase in all parts of the world. The devil is alive and more at work than at any other time. The Bible says that since he realizes his time is short, his activity will increase. Through his demonic influences he does succeed in turning many away from true faith; but we can still say that his evil activities are countered for the people of God by His ministering spirits, the holy ones of the angelic order. They are vigorous in delivering the heirs of salvation from the stratagems of evil men. They cannot fail.

Believers, look up—take courage. The angels are nearer than you think. For after all, God has given "his angels charge of you, to guard you in all your ways. On their hands they will bear you up, lest you dash your foot against a stone" (Psalm 91:11, 12 RSV).

Billy Graham

APPLICATION

*W*hen an angel delivers God's message to a person, what response does God expect? What are the consequences of believing or doubting God's message? Are you open to receiving his message for you?

THURSDAY

*God Is Merciful
to His People*

Luke 1:46–79

Mary Praises God

*A*nd Mary said, My soul doth magnify the Lord,

⁴⁷ and my spirit hath rejoiced in God my Saviour.

⁴⁸ For he hath regarded the low estate of his handmaiden: for, behold, from henceforth all generations shall call me blessed.

⁴⁹ For he that is mighty hath done to me great things; and holy *is* his name.

⁵⁰ And his mercy *is* on them that fear him from generation to generation.

⁵¹ He hath showed strength with his arm; he hath scattered the proud in the imagination of their hearts.

⁵² He hath put down the mighty from *their* seats, and exalted them of low degree.

⁵³ He hath filled the hungry with good things; and the rich he hath sent empty away.

⁵⁴ He hath holpen his servant Israel, in remembrance of *his* mercy;

⁵⁵ as he spake to our fathers, to Abraham, and to his seed for ever.

⁵⁶ And Mary abode with her about three months, and returned to her own house.

The Birth of John

*N*ow Elisabeth's full time came that she should be delivered; and she brought forth a son.

⁵⁸ And her neighbors and her cousins heard how the Lord had showed great mercy upon her; and they rejoiced with her.

⁵⁹ And it came to pass, that on the eighth day they came to circumcise the child; and they called him Zechariah, after the name of his father.

⁶⁰ And his mother answered and said, Not *so*; but he shall be called John.

⁶¹ And they said unto her, There is none of thy kindred that is called by this name.

⁶² And they made signs to his father, how he would have him called.

⁶³ And he asked for a writing table, and wrote, saying, His name is John. And they marveled all.

⁶⁴ And his mouth was opened immediately, and his tongue *loosed*, and he spake, and praised God.

⁶⁵ And fear came on all that dwelt round about them: and all these sayings were noised abroad throughout all the hill country of Judea.

⁶⁶ And all they that heard *them* laid *them* up in their hearts, saying, What manner of child shall this be? And the hand of the Lord was with him.

Zechariah Praises God

*A*nd his father Zechariah was filled with the Holy Ghost, and prophesied, saying,

⁶⁸ Blessed *be* the Lord God of Israel; for he hath visited and redeemed his people,

⁶⁹ and hath raised up a horn of salvation for us in the house of his servant David;

⁷⁰ as he spake by the mouth of his holy prophets, which have been since the world began:

⁷¹ that we should be saved from our

enemies, and from the hand of all that hate us;

⁷² to perform the mercy *promised* to our fathers, and to remember his holy covenant;

⁷³ the oath which he sware to our father Abraham,

⁷⁴ that he would grant unto us, that we, being delivered out of the hand of our enemies, might serve him without fear,

⁷⁵ in holiness and righteousness before him, all the days of our life.

⁷⁶ And thou, child, shalt be called the prophet of the Highest: for thou shalt go before the face of the Lord to prepare his ways;

⁷⁷ to give knowledge of salvation unto his people by the remission of their sins,

⁷⁸ through the tender mercy of our God; whereby the dayspring from on high hath visited us,

⁷⁹ to give light to them that sit in darkness and *in* the shadow of death, to guide our feet into the way of peace.

OLD TESTAMENT READING

*T*his I recall to my mind, therefore have I hope.

²² *It is of* the LORD's mercies that we are not consumed, because his compassions fail not.

²³ *They are* new every morning: great *is* thy faithfulness.

²⁴ The LORD *is* my portion, saith my soul; therefore will I hope in him.

²⁵ The LORD *is* good unto them that wait for him, to the soul *that* seeketh him.

²⁶ *It is* good that *a man* should both hope and quietly wait for the salvation of the LORD.

Lamentations 3:21–26

INSIGHTS

*T*he Israelites were always worshiping the idols of the peoples around them in spite of the warning and the pleadings of the prophets. It wasn't until their captivity in Babylon that they were cured of these dangerous liaisons with "other gods." From the days of their captivity until now— two-and-a-half millennia—the Jews have never again been guilty of this sin. But in many places in Scripture, the Holy Spirit takes up the refrain to make sure the people of God would never slip back. . . .

God is still dealing mercifully with those who wander away in rebellion and pride, but return in humility and faith. We have our Golden Calves, our substitutes for the living God. We have things in our lives that seem more important because they promise more immediate gratification. We, too, grow discouraged in a wilderness—a treadmill of monotonous busyness without tangible or meaningful results. To banish our sense of emptiness and lostness in this secular world, we may have looked for satisfaction in lesser gods, although we would never call them Golden Calves. Even so, God is patiently waiting for us to forsake these idols. He may discipline us, but in His mercy, He will never forsake us.

William Stoddard

PAUSE FOR REFLECTION

*T*hank God that no matter how greatly we sin he is merciful and forgiving to everyone who repents!

FRIDAY

*Praise God
for His Salvation!*

Luke 1:80—2:26

*A*nd the child grew, and waxed strong in spirit, and was in the deserts till the day of his showing unto Israel.

The Birth of Jesus

2 And it came to pass in those days, that there went out a decree from Caesar Augustus, that all the world should be taxed.

2 (*And* this taxing was first made when Cyrenius was governor of Syria.)

3 And all went to be taxed, every one into his own city.

4 And Joseph also went up from Galilee, out of the city of Nazareth, into Judea, unto the city of David, which is called Bethlehem, (because he was of the house and lineage of David,)

5 to be taxed with Mary his espoused wife, being great with child.

6 And so it was, that, while they were there, the days were accomplished that she should be delivered.

7 And she brought forth her firstborn son, and wrapped him in swaddling clothes, and laid him in a manger; because there was no room for them in the inn.

8 And there were in the same country shepherds abiding in the field, keeping watch over their flock by night.

9 And, lo, the angel of the Lord came upon them, and the glory of the Lord shone round about them; and they were sore afraid.

10 And the angel said unto them, Fear not: for, behold, I bring you good tidings of great joy, which shall be to all people.

11 For unto you is born this day in the city of David a Saviour, which is Christ the Lord.

12 And this *shall be* a sign unto you; Ye shall find the babe wrapped in swaddling clothes, lying in a manger.

13 And suddenly there was with the angel a multitude of the heavenly host praising God, and saying,

14 Glory to God in the highest, and on earth peace, good will toward men.

15 And it came to pass, as the angels were gone away from them into heaven, the shepherds said one to another, Let us now go even unto Bethlehem, and see this thing which is come to pass, which the Lord hath made known unto us.

16 And they came with haste, and found Mary and Joseph, and the babe lying in a manger.

17 And when they had seen *it*, they made known abroad the saying which was told them concerning this child.

18 And all they that heard *it* wondered at those things which were told them by the shepherds.

19 But Mary kept all these things, and pondered *them* in her heart.

20 And the shepherds returned, glorifying and praising God for all the things that they had heard and seen, as it was told unto them.

21 And when eight days were accomplished for the circumcising of the child, his name was called JESUS, which was so named of the angel before he was conceived in the womb.

Jesus Is Presented in the Temple

*A*nd when the days of her purification according to the law of Moses were accomplished, they brought him to Jerusalem, to present *him* to the Lord;

23 (as it is written in the law of the Lord, Every male that openeth the womb shall be called holy to the Lord;)

24 and to offer a sacrifice according to that which is said in the law of the Lord, A pair of turtledoves, or two young pigeons.

Simeon Sees Jesus

*A*nd, behold, there was a man in Jerusalem, whose name *was* Simeon; and the same man *was* just and devout, waiting for the consolation of Israel: and the Holy Ghost was upon him.

26 And it was revealed unto him by the Holy Ghost, that he should not see death, before he had seen the Lord's Christ.

OLD TESTAMENT READING

I will trust, and not be afraid: for the LORD JEHOVAH *is* my strength and *my* song; he also is become my salvation.

3 Therefore with joy shall ye draw water out of the wells of salvation.

4 And in that day shall ye say, Praise the LORD, call upon his name, declare his doings among the people, make mention that his name is exalted.

Isaiah 12:2b–4

INSIGHTS

*I*n His holiness and love God could not wink at sin. He could not compromise either His justice or His

mercy. Therefore, out of grace He sent His Son. . . . By God's mercy, He came in Christ to pay the full price, and at the cross, exposed His heart. God abhors, condemns, and judges sin, and yet by the power of the cross, He forgives sinners— people like you and me! . . .

. . . We have all gone over the line in breaking the Ten Commandments and Jesus' commandment to love. We've brought hurt, pain and suffering to ourselves and others by what we've done or said or refused to be. We've broken His heart. And even before we asked Him, He forgave us. He reconciled us. He exonerated us. We stutter out our yearning to be free in response to His cross, melted by His love, and healed by His forgiveness.

The same voice that cried, "Father forgive them," from Calvary, says to us with the commanding power of His cross-shaped heart, "The ransom has been paid for all time. And now in this propitious moment in your time it is a pardon for you. You are forgiven. You are free!"

Lloyd Ogilvie

ACTION POINT

*T*hink about all the things Jesus' birth represented to his parents, the shepherds, and Simeon. What does Jesus' coming to earth signify to you? Meditate on the wonder of it all. Thank him for his salvation.

WEEKEND

*Called to Do
the Father's Work*

Luke 2:27–52

*A*nd he came by the Spirit into the temple: and when the parents brought in the child Jesus, to do for him after the custom of the law, [28] then took he him up in his arms, and blessed God, and said,

[29] Lord, now lettest thou thy servant depart in peace, according to thy word:

[30] for mine eyes have seen thy salvation, [31] which thou hast prepared before the face of all people;

[32] a light to lighten the Gentiles, and the glory of thy people Israel.

[33] And Joseph and his mother marvelled at those things which were spoken of him.

[34] And Simeon blessed them, and said unto Mary his mother, Behold, this *child* is set for the fall and rising again of many in Israel; and for a sign which shall be spoken against;

[35] (yea, a sword shall pierce through thy own soul also;) that the thoughts of many hearts may be revealed.

Anna Sees Jesus

*A*nd there was one Anna, a prophetess, the daughter of Phanuel, of the tribe of Asher: she was of a great age, and had lived with a husband seven years from her virginity;

[37] and she *was* a widow of about fourscore and four years, which departed not from the temple, but served *God* with fastings and prayers night and day.

[38] And she coming in that instant gave thanks likewise unto the Lord, and spake of him to all them that looked for redemption in Jerusalem.

Joseph and Mary Return Home

*A*nd when they had performed all things according to the law of the Lord, they returned into Galilee, to their own city Nazareth.

[40] And the child grew, and waxed strong in spirit, filled with wisdom; and the grace of God was upon him.

Jesus As a Boy

*N*ow his parents went to Jerusalem every year at the feast of the passover.

[42] And when he was twelve years old, they went up to Jerusalem after the custom of the feast.

[43] And when they had fulfilled the days, as they returned, the child Jesus tarried behind in Jerusalem; and Joseph and his mother knew not *of it*.

[44] But they, supposing him to have been in the company, went a day's journey; and they sought him among *their* kinsfolk and acquaintance.

[45] And when they found him not, they turned back again to Jerusalem, seeking him.

[46] And it came to pass, that after three days they found him in the temple, sitting in the midst of the doctors, both hearing them, and asking them questions.

[47] And all that heard him were astonished at his understanding and answers.

[48] And when they saw him, they were amazed: and his mother said unto him, Son, why hast thou thus dealt

with us? behold, thy father and I have sought thee sorrowing.

⁴⁹ And he said unto them, How is it that ye sought me? wist ye not that I must be about my Father's business?

⁵⁰ And they understood not the saying which he spake unto them.

⁵¹ And he went down with them, and came to Nazareth, and was subject unto them: but his mother kept all these sayings in her heart.

⁵² And Jesus increased in wisdom and stature, and in favor with God and man.

OLD TESTAMENT READING

Samuel Is Called to Do God's Work

And when she had weaned him, she took him up with her, with three bullocks, and one ephah of flour, and a bottle of wine, and brought him unto the house of the LORD in Shiloh: and the child *was* young.

²⁶ And she said, Oh my lord, as thy soul liveth, my lord, I *am* the woman that stood by thee here, praying unto the LORD.

²⁷ For this child I prayed; and the LORD hath given me my petition which I asked of him:

²⁸ therefore also I have lent him to the LORD; as long as he liveth he shall be lent to the LORD. And he worshipped the LORD there.

1 Samuel 1:24, 26–28

INSIGHTS

Many people have the idea that God only calls preachers and missionaries, and the rest of us can do whatever we want to. But God has a calling for all of His children. . . .

. . . God's work is going to be done primarily not through the superstar preachers, evangelists, or celebrities; God's work is going to be done through His ordinary everyday run-of-the-mill people. . . .

. . . God called a timid man with a stutter—a speech impediment—by the name of Moses and made him the greatest leader in the Old Testament. God called David, a little shepherd boy, right out of the pasture and made him the greatest king who ever ruled over Israel. . . .

When I think of the weak I recall the life of Jonathan Edwards. He was one of the greatest revival preachers America or the world has ever known. . . .

He was an asthmatic. Whenever he would preach he would cough and hack and wheeze during most of the message. He was a very thin, frail man. He had horrible eyesight. . . .

. . . Jonathan Edwards' sermons, despite his disabilities, caused people to come writhing in anguish down the aisles wanting to get right with God. . . .

. . . The people that God uses and chooses, God's all-stars, are not people of ability; they are people of availability who have learned the secret of giving their praise to God. If you use your life for the glory of God, God will use your life for His glory.

James Merritt

ACTION POINT

Jesus knew he was called to do the Father's work. So did Samuel. What about you? Do you long for His clear call? Why not begin today to offer yourself to God and pray that you will be made useful for his glory?

MONDAY

*The Hope of the
Coming Christ*

Luke 3:1–22

The Preaching of John

3 Now in the fifteenth year of the reign of Tiberius Caesar, Pontius Pilate being governor of Judea, and Herod being tetrarch of Galilee, and his brother Philip tetrarch of Ituraea and of the region of Trachonitis, and Lysanias the tetrarch of Abilene,

² Annas and Caiaphas being the high priests, the word of God came unto John the son of Zechariah in the wilderness.

³ And he came into all the country about Jordan, preaching the baptism of repentance for the remission of sins;

⁴ as it is written in the book of the words of Isaiah the prophet, saying, The voice of one crying in the wilderness, Prepare ye the way of the Lord, make his paths straight.

⁵ Every valley shall be filled, and every mountain and hill shall be brought low; and the crooked shall be made straight, and the rough ways *shall be* made smooth;

⁶ and all flesh shall see the salvation of God.

⁷ Then said he to the multitude that came forth to be baptized of him, O generation of vipers, who hath warned you to flee from the wrath to come?

⁸ Bring forth therefore fruits worthy of repentance, and begin not to say within yourselves, We have Abraham to *our* father: for I say unto you, That God is able of these stones to raise up children unto Abraham.

⁹ And now also the axe is laid unto the root of the trees: every tree therefore which bringeth not forth good fruit is hewn down, and cast into the fire.

¹⁰ And the people asked him, saying, What shall we do then?

¹¹ He answereth and saith unto them, He that hath two coats, let him impart to him that hath none; and he that hath meat, let him do likewise.

¹² Then came also publicans to be baptized, and said unto him, Master, what shall we do?

¹³ And he said unto them, Exact no more than that which is appointed you.

¹⁴ And the soldiers likewise demanded of him, saying, And what shall we do? And he said unto them, Do violence to no man, neither accuse *any* falsely; and be content with your wages.

¹⁵ And as the people were in expectation, and all men mused in their hearts of John, whether he were the Christ, or not;

¹⁶ John answered, saying unto *them* all, I indeed baptize you with water; but one mightier than I cometh, the latchet of whose shoes I am not worthy to unloose: he shall baptize you with the Holy Ghost and with fire:

¹⁷ whose fan *is* in his hand, and he will thoroughly purge his floor, and will gather the wheat into his garner; but the chaff he will burn with fire unquenchable.

¹⁸ And many other things in his exhortation preached he unto the people.

¹⁹ But Herod the tetrarch, being reproved by him for Herodias his brother Philip's wife, and for all the evils which Herod had done,

20 added yet this above all, that he shut up John in prison.

Jesus Is Baptized by John

Now when all the people were baptized, it came to pass, that Jesus also being baptized, and praying, the heaven was opened,
22 and the Holy Ghost descended in a bodily shape like a dove upon him, and a voice came from heaven, which said, Thou art my beloved Son; in thee I am well pleased.

OLD TESTAMENT READING

The voice said, Cry. And he said, What shall I cry? All flesh *is* grass, and all the goodliness thereof *is* as the flower of the field:
8 The grass withereth, the flower fadeth: but the word of our God shall stand for ever.
9b O Jerusalem, that bringest good tidings, lift up thy voice with strength; lift *it* up, be not afraid; say unto the cities of Judah, Behold your God!
10 Behold, the Lord GOD will come with strong *hand*, and his arm shall rule for him: behold, his reward *is* with him, and his work before him.

Isaiah 40:6, 8, 9b–10

INSIGHTS

Is it a waste to focus on the Lord's descent? Quite the contrary. It's biblical; it's the very thing Titus 2:13 says we ought to do.

When's the last time you—on your own—meditated on that fact? If you're like me it's been too long. People who are more practical than mystical, who are realistic rather than idealistic, tend to shove that
stuff to times like funerals or near-death experiences. . . . Listen, this Bible of ours is full and running over with promises and encouragements directly related to the return of our Lord Christ. . . .

Critics have denied it. Cynics have laughed at it. Scholars have ignored it. Liberal theologians have explained it away (they call that "rethinking" it) and fanatics have perverted it. . . . But there it stands, solid as a stone, soon to be fulfilled, ready to offer us hope and encouragement amidst despair and unbelief.

"Okay, swell. But what do I do in the meantime?" I can hear a dozen or more pragmatists asking that question. First, it might be best for you to understand what you don't do. You don't sit around, listening for some bugle call. You don't keep staring up into the sky, looking for the rapture cloud. . . .

You do get your act together. You do live every day (as if it's your last) for His glory. You do work diligently on your job and in your home (as if He isn't coming for another ten years) for His Name's sake. You do shake salt out every chance you get . . . and do shine the light . . . and remain balanced, cheerful, winsome, and stable, anticipating His return day by day.

Charles Swindoll

APPLICATION

Do you feel the excitement of John's listeners? They truly believed Christ was coming and wanted to know what to do to be ready. How about you? Do you await Christ's second coming with a yawn, or are you living each day as he wants you to?

TUESDAY

*Jesus: The Promised King
in David's Line*

Luke 3:23–38

The Family History of Jesus

*A*nd Jesus himself began to be about thirty years of age, being (as was supposed) the son of Joseph, which was *the son* of Heli,
²⁴ which was *the son* of Matthat, which was *the son* of Levi, which was *the son* of Melchi, which was *the son* of Janna, which was *the son* of Joseph,
²⁵ which was *the son* of Mattathias, which was *the son* of Amos, which was *the son* of Nahum, which was *the son* of Esli, which was *the son* of Naggai,
²⁶ which was *the son* of Maath, which was *the son* of Mattathias, which was *the son* of Semei, which was *the son* of Joseph, which was *the son* of Judah,
²⁷ which was *the son* of Joanna, which was *the son* of Rhesa, which was *the son* of Zerubbabel, which was *the son* of Shealtiel, which was *the son* of Neri,
²⁸ which was *the son* of Melchi, which was *the son* of Addi, which was *the son* of Cosam, which was *the son* of Elmodam, which was *the son* of Er,
²⁹ which was *the son* of Jose, which was *the son* of Eliezer, which was *the son* of Jorim, which was *the son* of Matthat, which was *the son* of Levi,
³⁰ which was *the son* of Simeon, which was *the son* of Judah, which was *the son* of Joseph, which was *the son* of Jonan, which was *the son* of Eliakim,
³¹ which was *the son* of Melea, which was *the son* of Menan, which was *the son* of Mattatha, which was *the son* of Nathan, which was *the son* of David,
³² which was *the son* of Jesse, which was *the son* of Obed, which was *the son* of Boaz, which was *the son* of Salmon, which was *the son* of Nahshon,
³³ which was *the son* of Amminadab, which was *the son* of Ram, which was *the son* of Hezron, which was *the son* of Pharez, which was *the son* of Judah,
³⁴ which was *the son* of Jacob, which was *the son* of Isaac, which was *the son* of Abraham, which was *the son* of Terah, which was *the son* of Nahor,
³⁵ which was *the son* of Serug, which was *the son* of Reu, which was *the son* of Peleg, which was *the son* of Eber, which was *the son* of Salah,
³⁶ which was *the son* of Cainan, which was *the son* of Arphaxad, which was *the son* of Shem, which was *the son* of Noah, which was *the son* of Lamech,
³⁷ which was *the son* of Methuselah, which was *the son* of Enoch, which was *the son* of Jared, which was *the son* of Mahalaleel, which was *the son* of Cainan,
³⁸ which was *the son* of Enos, which was *the son* of Seth, which was *the son* of Adam, which was *the son* of God.

OLD TESTAMENT READING

*A*nd there shall come forth a rod out of the stem of Jesse, and a Branch shall grow out of his roots:
² and the spirit of the LORD shall rest upon him, the spirit of wisdom and understanding, the spirit of counsel and might, the spirit of knowledge and of the fear of the LORD;

³ and shall make him of quick understanding in the fear of the LORD: and he shall not judge after the sight of his eyes, neither reprove after the hearing of his ears:

⁴ but with righteousness shall he judge the poor, and reprove with equity for the meek of the earth: and he shall smite the earth with the rod of his mouth, and with the breath of his lips shall he slay the wicked.

⁵ And righteousness shall be the girdle of his loins, and faithfulness the girdle of his reins.

Isaiah 11:1–5

INSIGHTS

In coming to the kingdom-phase of Satan's antagonism, we believe that he was aware of Jacob's prophetic utterance in Genesis 49:10.

With the abandonment of Saul, the throne of Israel is transferred from Benjamin to Judah (1 Sam. 16). David, a man after God's own heart, is chosen and anointed king (1 Sam. 16:13; 2 Sam. 2:4; 5:2). And with such a change, there commences the desperate and determined attack of Satan upon "the seed royal," that is, the house of Judah, from which the Messiah must spring. . . .

Saul, the God-forsaken, Satan-possessed monarch (1 Sam. 16:14), tried his utmost to destroy the Lord's anointed one, and thus David is obliged to flee as a fugitive, hiding in caves and holes from his father-in-law. . . .

In the union of Jehoram and Athaliah, the daughter of Ahab, king of Israel, Satan continues his assault upon the house of Judah. . . .

At this critical moment, God's word appears to be at stake. Those of the royal seed are becoming fewer and fewer. In fact, the light was almost quenched, for Athaliah "arose and destroyed all the seed royal of the house of Judah" (2 Chron. 22:10). What followed?

Carefully he is hid and cared for while Athaliah reigns on in blissful ignorance until the day dawns when Joash is presented and crowned as king over Judah and Athaliah is slain (2 Kings 11:4–16; 2 Chron. 23:11, 15). Thus God, in a marvelous way, defeated the evil tactics of the devil, thereby fulfilling the promise of giving a light forever (2 Chron. 21:7).

Herbert Lockyer

PAUSE FOR REFLECTION

Although family history may not be very important to you, a king must be able to prove his royal heritage. What do these prophetic and genealogical verses tell you about the nature of Jesus' kingship?

WEDNESDAY

Jesus Claims to Be the One of Whom Isaiah Spoke

Luke 4:1–31

Jesus Is Tempted by the Devil

4 And Jesus being full of the Holy Ghost returned from Jordan, and was led by the Spirit into the wilderness,

2 being forty days tempted of the devil. And in those days he did eat nothing: and when they were ended, he afterward hungered.

3 And the devil said unto him, If thou be the Son of God, command this stone that it be made bread.

4 And Jesus answered him, saying, It is written, That man shall not live by bread alone, but by every word of God.

5 And the devil, taking him up into an high mountain, showed unto him all the kingdoms of the world in a moment of time.

6 And the devil said unto him, All this power will I give thee, and the glory of them: for that is delivered unto me; and to whomsoever I will, I give it.

7 If thou therefore wilt worship me, all shall be thine.

8 And Jesus answered and said unto him, Get thee behind me, Satan: for it is written, Thou shalt worship the Lord thy God, and him only shalt thou serve.

9 And he brought him to Jerusalem, and set him on a pinnacle of the temple, and said unto him, If thou be the Son of God, cast thyself down from hence:

10 for it is written, He shall give his angels charge over thee, to keep thee:

11 and in *their* hands they shall bear thee up, lest at any time thou dash thy foot against a stone.

12 And Jesus answering said unto him, It is said, Thou shalt not tempt the Lord thy God.

13 And when the devil had ended all the temptation, he departed from him for a season.

Jesus Teaches the People

And Jesus returned in the power of the Spirit into Galilee: and there went out a fame of him through all the region round about.

15 And he taught in their synagogues, being glorified of all.

16 And he came to Nazareth, where he had been brought up: and, as his custom was, he went into the synagogue on the sabbath day, and stood up for to read.

17 And there was delivered unto him the book of the prophet Isaiah. And when he had opened the book, he found the place where it was written,

18 The Spirit of the Lord *is* upon me, because he hath anointed me to preach the gospel to the poor; he hath sent me to heal the brokenhearted, to preach deliverance to the captives, and recovering of sight to the blind, to set at liberty them that are bruised,

19 to preach the acceptable year of the Lord.

20 And he closed the book, and he gave *it* again to the minister, and sat down. And the eyes of all them that were in the synagogue were fastened on him.

21 And he began to say unto them, This day is this Scripture fulfilled in your ears.

150

22 And all bare him witness, and wondered at the gracious words which proceeded out of his mouth. And they said, Is not this Joseph's son? 23 And he said unto them, Ye will surely say unto me this proverb, Physician, heal thyself: whatsoever we have heard done in Capernaum, do also here in thy country. 24 And he said, Verily I say unto you, No prophet is accepted in his own country. 25 But I tell you of a truth, many widows were in Israel in the days of Elijah, when the heaven was shut up three years and six months, when great famine was throughout all the land; 26 but unto none of them was Elijah sent, save unto Zarephath, *a city* of Sidon, unto a woman *that was* a widow. 27 And many lepers were in Israel in the time of Elisha the prophet; and none of them was cleansed, saving Naaman the Syrian. 28 And all they in the synagogue, when they heard these things, were filled with wrath, 29 and rose up, and thrust him out of the city, and led him unto the brow of the hill whereon their city was built, that they might cast him down headlong. 30 But he, passing through the midst of them, went his way, 31 and came down to Capernaum, a city of Galilee, and taught them on the sabbath days.

OLD TESTAMENT READING

*T*he Spirit of the Lord GOD *is* upon me; because the LORD hath anointed me to preach good tidings unto the meek; he hath sent me to bind up the brokenhearted, to proclaim liberty to the captives, and the opening of the prison to *them that are* bound; 2 to proclaim the acceptable year of the LORD, and the day of vengeance of our God; to comfort all that mourn;

Isaiah 61:1–2

INSIGHTS

*J*esus' words in the synagogue at Nazareth, spoken near the beginning of his public ministry, throb with hope for the poor. . . . Jesus informed his audience that this Scripture was now fulfilled in himself. The mission of the Incarnate One was to free the oppressed. . . .

Jesus' actual ministry corresponded precisely to the words of Luke 4. He spent most of his time not among the rich and powerful in Jerusalem, but among the poor in the cultural and economic backwater of Galilee. He healed the sick and blind. He fed the hungry. And he warned his followers in the strongest possible words that those who do not feed the hungry, clothe the naked, and visit the prisoners will experience eternal damnation (Matt. 25:31–46).

At the supreme moment of history when God took on human flesh, the God of Israel was still liberating the poor and oppressed and summoning his people to do the same.

Ronald Sider

PAUSE FOR REFLECTION

*W*hy do you think Jesus so clearly proclaimed who he was in the synagogue at Nazareth? How was his message received? Why did he identify himself with these passages?

THURSDAY

Obedience Leads to Blessing and Faith

Luke 4:32—5:11

Jesus Forces Out a Devil

*A*nd they were astonished at his doctrine: for his word was with power. ³³ And in the synagogue there was a man, which had a spirit of an unclean devil, and cried out with a loud voice, ³⁴ saying, Let *us* alone; what have we to do with thee, *thou* Jesus of Nazareth? art thou come to destroy us? I know thee who thou art; the Holy One of God.

³⁵ And Jesus rebuked him, saying, Hold thy peace, and come out of him. And when the devil had thrown him in the midst, he came out of him, and hurt him not.

³⁶ And they were all amazed, and spake among themselves, saying, What a word *is* this! for with authority and power he commandeth the unclean spirits, and they come out.

³⁷ And the fame of him went out into every place of the country round about.

Jesus Heals Many People

*A*nd he arose out of the synagogue, and entered into Simon's house. And Simon's wife's mother was taken with a great fever; and they besought him for her.

³⁹ And he stood over her, and rebuked the fever; and it left her: and immediately she arose and ministered unto them.

⁴⁰ Now when the sun was setting, all they that had any sick with divers diseases brought them unto him; and he laid his hands on every one of them, and healed them.

⁴¹ And devils also came out of many, crying out, and saying, Thou art Christ the Son of God. And he rebuking *them* suffered them not to speak: for they knew that he was Christ.

⁴² And when it was day, he departed and went into a desert place: and the people sought him, and came unto him, and stayed him, that he should not depart from them.

⁴³ And he said unto them, I must preach the kingdom of God to other cities also: for therefore am I sent.

⁴⁴ And he preached in the synagogues of Galilee.

Jesus' First Disciples

5 And it came to pass, that, as the people pressed upon him to hear the word of God, he stood by the lake of Gennesaret,

² and saw two ships standing by the lake: but the fishermen were gone out of them, and were washing *their* nets.

³ And he entered into one of the ships, which was Simon's, and prayed him that he would thrust out a little from the land. And he sat down, and taught the people out of the ship.

⁴ Now when he had left speaking, he said unto Simon, Launch out into the deep, and let down your nets for a draught.

⁵ And Simon answering said unto him, Master, we have toiled all the night, and have taken nothing: nevertheless at thy word I will let down the net.

6 And when they had this done, they inclosed a great multitude of fishes: and their net brake.

7 And they beckoned unto *their* partners, which were in the other ship, that they should come and help them. And they came, and filled both the ships, so that they began to sink.

8 When Simon Peter saw *it*, he fell down at Jesus' knees, saying, Depart from me; for I am a sinful man, O Lord.

9 For he was astonished, and all that were with him, at the draught of the fishes which they had taken:

10 and so *was* also James, and John, the sons of Zebedee, which were partners with Simon. And Jesus said unto Simon, Fear not; from henceforth thou shalt catch men.

11 And when they had brought their ships to land, they forsook all, and followed him.

OLD TESTAMENT READING

*A*nd Elisha sent a messenger unto him, saying, Go and wash in Jordan seven times, and thy flesh shall come again to thee, and thou shalt be clean.

11 But Naaman was wroth, and went away.

13 And his servants came near, and spake unto him, and said, My father, *if* the prophet had bid thee *do some* great thing, wouldest thou not have done *it*? how much rather then, when he saith to thee, Wash, and be clean?

14 Then went he down, and dipped himself seven times in Jordan, according to the saying of the man of God: and his flesh came again like unto the flesh of a little child, and he was clean.

2 Kings 5:10–11a, 13–14

INSIGHTS

*T*rust and obey, for there's no other way
   To be happy in Jesus, but to trust and obey."

All too often we glibly sing the words of this familiar Christian hymn without giving them much thought. These important words convey exactly what the Bible teaches. The secret of spiritual happiness and blessing is simply trusting and obeying the Lord. . . . The divine method for happiness and blessing is full trust in God and complete obedience to His Word. Lack of faith and partial obedience not only result in unhappiness and loss of blessing; they bring serious consequences in the life of the believer. . . .

. . . Can we say without reservation that we simply trust and obey, or must we confess that we selfishly bargain with God? . . .

. . . God does not expect us to question or change or compromise His commands; He expects us to simply trust Him and obey Him. That's the way to find spiritual blessing and happiness.

David Reid

PAUSE FOR REFLECTION

*D*id Naaman and Simon expect God to work the way he did? Do you think anything less than total obedience will accomplish God's work and blessing in your life?

FRIDAY

*Jesus Often Slipped Away
to Be Alone and Pray*

Luke 5:12–35

Jesus Heals a Leper

*A*nd it came to pass, when he was in a certain city, behold a man full of leprosy: who seeing Jesus fell on *his* face, and besought him, saying, Lord, if thou wilt, thou canst make me clean.

[13] And he put forth *his* hand, and touched him, saying, I will: be thou clean. And immediately the leprosy departed from him.

[14] And he charged him to tell no man: But go, and show thyself to the priest, and offer for thy cleansing, according as Moses commanded, for a testimony unto them.

[15] But so much the more went there a fame abroad of him: and great multitudes came together to hear, and to be healed by him of their infirmities.

[16] And he withdrew himself into the wilderness, and prayed.

Jesus Heals a Palsied Man

*A*nd it came to pass on a certain day, as he was teaching, that there were Pharisees and doctors of the law sitting by, which were come out of every town of Galilee, and Judea, and Jerusalem: and the power of the Lord was *present* to heal them.

[18] And, behold, men brought in a bed a man which was taken with a palsy: and they sought *means* to bring him in, and to lay *him* before him.

[19] And when they could not find by what *way* they might bring him in because of the multitude, they went upon the housetop, and let him down through the tiling with *his* couch into the midst before Jesus.

[20] And when he saw their faith, he said unto him, Man, thy sins are forgiven thee.

[21] And the scribes and the Pharisees began to reason, saying, Who is this which speaketh blasphemies? Who can forgive sins, but God alone?

[22] But when Jesus perceived their thoughts, he answering said unto them, What reason ye in your hearts?

[23] Whether is easier, to say, Thy sins be forgiven thee; or to say, Rise up and walk?

[24] But that ye may know that the Son of man hath power upon earth to forgive sins, (he said unto the sick of the palsy,) I say unto thee, Arise, and take up thy couch, and go into thine house.

[25] And immediately he rose up before them, and took up that whereon he lay, and departed to his own house, glorifying God.

[26] And they were all amazed, and they glorified God, and were filled with fear, saying, We have seen strange things today.

Levi Follows Jesus

*A*nd after these things he went forth, and saw a publican, named Levi, sitting at the receipt of custom: and he said unto him, Follow me.

[28] And he left all, rose up, and followed him.

[29] And Levi made him a great feast in his own house: and there was a great company of publicans and of others that sat down with them.

³⁰ But their scribes and Pharisees murmured against his disciples, saying, Why do ye eat and drink with publicans and sinners?

³¹ And Jesus answering said unto them, They that are whole need not a physician; but they that are sick.

³² I came not to call the righteous, but sinners to repentance.

Jesus Answers a Question

*A*nd they said unto him, Why do the disciples of John fast often, and make prayers, and likewise *the disciples* of the Pharisees; but thine eat and drink?

³⁴ And he said unto them, Can ye make the children of the bridechamber fast, while the bridegroom is with them?

³⁵ But the days will come, when the bridegroom shall be taken away from them, and then shall they fast in those days.

OLD TESTAMENT READING

I cried with *my* whole heart; hear me, O LORD: I will keep thy statutes.

¹⁴⁶ I cried unto thee; save me, and I shall keep thy testimonies.

¹⁴⁷ I prevented the dawning of the morning, and cried: I hoped in thy word.

¹⁴⁸ Mine eyes prevent the *night* watches, that I might meditate in thy word.

¹⁴⁹ Hear my voice according unto thy loving-kindness: O LORD, quicken me according to thy judgment.

¹⁵⁰ They draw nigh that follow after mischief: they are far from thy law.

¹⁵¹ Thou *art* near, O LORD; and all thy commandments *are* truth.

Psalm 119:145–151

INSIGHTS

*J*esus needed solitude simply because he was human—the only fully human person who has ever lived. He sought solitude. . . .

He went apart to cure his loneliness. He needed the silence of eternity as a thirsting man in the desert needs water. And he essentially needed the silence of eternity which was interpreted by love. For he who was love incarnate had his own needs to love and be loved. His deepest need, and likewise ours, could be met only by God. Ultimately no human being, no matter how close or dear, can fully satisfy our need for love. Those who imagine they can end up devouring one another.

Jesus longed for time apart to bask and sunbathe in his Father's love, to soak in it and repose in it. No matter how drained he felt, it seems that this deep, silent communion refreshed him more than a good night's sleep. . . .

. . . Human love and friendship indeed enrich our lives and partly meet this need—but not entirely, for at the core of our being is . . . a lovelonging for God which will only be met by converting our loneliness into deep solitude, by fleeing the sweets and cordials that may give temporary satisfaction, and finding the real thing in him.

Margaret Magdalen

PAUSE FOR REFLECTION

*I*t seems as if the psalmist thrived on his time with God, doesn't it? What is in your heart and on your lips when you slip away from life's demands?

WEEKEND

God Cares for Those Who Trust Him, but Will Judge the Wicked

Luke 5:36—6:23

*A*nd he spake also a parable unto them; No man putteth a piece of a new garment upon an old; if otherwise, then both the new maketh a rent, and the piece that was *taken* out of the new agreeth not with the old.

[37] And no man putteth new wine into old bottles; else the new wine will burst the bottles, and be spilled, and the bottles shall perish.

[38] But new wine must be put into new bottles; and both are preserved.

[39] No man also having drunk old *wine* straightway desireth new: for he saith, The old is better.

Jesus Is Lord over the Sabbath

6 And it came to pass on the second sabbath after the first, that he went through the corn fields; and his disciples plucked the ears of corn, and did eat, rubbing *them* in *their* hands.

[2] And certain of the Pharisees said unto them, Why do ye that which is not lawful to do on the sabbath days?

[3] And Jesus answering them said, Have ye not read so much as this, what David did, when himself was ahungered, and they which were with him;

[4] how he went into the house of God, and did take and eat the showbread, and gave also to them that were with him; which it is not lawful to eat but for the priests alone?

[5] And he said unto them, That the Son of man is Lord also of the sabbath.

Jesus Heals a Man's Hand

*A*nd it came to pass also on another sabbath, that he entered into the synagogue and taught: and there was a man whose right hand was withered.

[7] And the scribes and Pharisees watched him, whether he would heal on the sabbath day; that they might find an accusation against him.

[8] But he knew their thoughts, and said to the man which had the withered hand, Rise up, and stand forth in the midst. And he arose and stood forth.

[9] Then said Jesus unto them, I will ask you one thing; Is it lawful on the sabbath days to do good, or to do evil? to save life, or to destroy *it*?

[10] And looking round about upon them all, he said unto the man, Stretch forth thy hand. And he did so: and his hand was restored whole as the other.

[11] And they were filled with madness; and communed one with another what they might do to Jesus.

Jesus Chooses His Apostles

*A*nd it came to pass in those days, that he went out into a mountain to pray, and continued all night in prayer to God.

[13] And when it was day, he called *unto him* his disciples: and of them he chose twelve, whom also he named apostles;

[14] Simon, (whom he also named Peter,) and Andrew his brother, James and John, Philip and Bartholomew,

[15] Matthew and Thomas, James the

son of Alpheus, and Simon called Zelotes,

¹⁶ and Judas *the brother* of James, and Judas Iscariot, which also was the traitor.

Jesus Teaches and Heals

*A*nd he came down with them, and stood in the plain, and the company of his disciples, and a great multitude of people out of all Judea and Jerusalem, and from the sea coast of Tyre and Sidon, which came to hear him, and to be healed of their diseases;

¹⁸ and they that were vexed with unclean spirits: and they were healed.

¹⁹ And the whole multitude sought to touch him: for there went virtue out of him, and healed *them* all.

²⁰ And he lifted up his eyes on his disciples, and said, Blessed *be ye* poor: for yours is the kingdom of God.

²¹ Blessed *are ye* that hunger now: for ye shall be filled. Blessed *are ye* that weep now: for ye shall laugh.

²² Blessed are ye, when men shall hate you, and when they shall separate you *from their company*, and shall reproach *you*, and cast out your name as evil, for the Son of man's sake.

²³ Rejoice ye in that day, and leap for joy: for, behold, your reward *is* great in heaven: for in the like manner did their fathers unto the prophets.

OLD TESTAMENT READING

*F*or yet a little while, and the wicked *shall* not *be*; yea, thou shalt diligently consider his place, and it *shall* not *be*.

¹¹ But the meek shall inherit the earth; and shall delight themselves in the abundance of peace.

¹² The wicked plotteth against the just, and gnasheth upon him with his teeth.

¹³ The Lord shall laugh at him: for he seeth that his day is coming.

Psalm 37:10–13

INSIGHTS

*T*he representations of the Bible with regard to the final doom of the wicked are exceedingly striking. . . . A spiritual telescope is put into our hands; we are permitted to point it towards the glorious city "whose builder and Maker is God"; we may survey its inner sanctuary, where the worshipping hosts praise God without ceasing. We see their flowing robes of white—the palms of victory in their hands—the beaming joy of their faces—the manifestations of ineffable bliss in their souls. . . .

Then we have the other side. The veil is lifted, and you come to the very verge of hell to see what is there. Whereas on the one hand all was glorious, on the other all is fearful, and full of horrors.

There is a bottomless pit. A deathless soul is cast therein; it sinks and sinks and sinks, going down that awful pit which knows no bottom, weeping and wailing as it descends, and you hear its groans as they echo and re-echo from the sides of that dread cavern of woe!

Charles Finney

PAUSE FOR REFLECTION

*S*tudy the contrasting images of reward and suffering on earth and in heaven. Thank God that he sees all and cares for those who love him.

MONDAY

Do Good to All—Show Mercy, as God Shows Mercy

Luke 6:24–45

*B*ut woe unto you that are rich! for ye have received your consolation.
²⁵ Woe unto you that are full! for ye shall hunger. Woe unto you that laugh now! for ye shall mourn and weep.
²⁶ Woe unto you, when all men shall speak well of you! for so did their fathers to the false prophets.

Love Your Enemies

*B*ut I say unto you which hear, Love your enemies, do good to them which hate you,
²⁸ bless them that curse you, and pray for them which despitefully use you.
²⁹ And unto him that smiteth thee on the *one* cheek offer also the other; and him that taketh away thy cloak forbid not *to take thy* coat also.
³⁰ Give to every man that asketh of thee; and of him that taketh away thy goods ask *them* not again.
³¹ And as ye would that men should do to you, do ye also to them likewise.
³² For if ye love them which love you, what thank have ye? for sinners also love those that love them.
³³ And if ye do good to them which do good to you, what thank have ye? for sinners also do even the same.
³⁴ And if ye lend *to them* of whom ye hope to receive, what thank have ye? for sinners also lend to sinners, to receive as much again.

³⁵ But love ye your enemies, and do good, and lend, hoping for nothing again; and your reward shall be great, and ye shall be the children of the Highest: for he is kind unto the unthankful and to the evil.
³⁶ Be ye therefore merciful, as your Father also is merciful.

Look at Yourselves

*J*udge not, and ye shall not be judged: condemn not, and ye shall not be condemned: forgive, and ye shall be forgiven:
³⁸ give, and it shall be given unto you; good measure, pressed down, and shaken together, and running over, shall men give into your bosom. For with the same measure that ye mete withal it shall be measured to you again.
³⁹ And he spake a parable unto them; Can the blind lead the blind? shall they not both fall into the ditch?
⁴⁰ The disciple is not above his master: but every one that is perfect shall be as his master.
⁴¹ And why beholdest thou the mote that is in thy brother's eye, but perceivest not the beam that is in thine own eye?
⁴² Either how canst thou say to thy brother, Brother, let me pull out the mote that is in thine eye, when thou thyself beholdest not the beam that is in thine own eye? Thou hypocrite, cast out first the beam out of thine own eye, and then shalt thou see clearly to pull out the mote that is in thy brother's eye.

Two Kinds of Fruit

*F*or a good tree bringeth not forth corrupt fruit; neither doth a cor-

rupt tree bring forth good fruit.
⁴⁴ For every tree is known by his own fruit. For of thorns men do not gather figs, nor of a bramble bush gather they grapes.
⁴⁵ A good man out of the good treasure of his heart bringeth forth that which is good; and an evil man out of the evil treasure of his heart bringeth forth that which is evil: for of the abundance of the heart his mouth speaketh.

OLD TESTAMENT READING

*B*ut it displeased Jonah exceedingly, and he was very angry.
² And he prayed unto the LORD, and said, I pray thee, O LORD, *was* not this my saying, when I was yet in my country? Therefore I fled before unto Tarshish: for I knew that thou *art* a gracious God, and merciful, slow to anger, and of great kindness, and repentest thee of the evil.

Jonah 4:1–2

INSIGHTS

*M*ercy is concern for people in need. It is ministry to the miserable. Offering help for those who hurt . . .

Those special servants of God who extend mercy to the miserable often do so with much encouragement because they identify with the sorrowing—they "get inside their skin." Rather than watching from a distance or keeping the needy safely at arm's length, they get in touch, involved, and offer assistance that alleviates some of the pain.

A large group of the collegians in our church in Fullerton, California, pile into our bus one weekend a month and travel together—not to a mountain resort or the beach for fun-n-games, but to a garbage dump in Tijuana, Mexico, where hundreds of poverty-stricken Mexican families live. Our young adults, under the encouraging leadership of Kenneth Kemp (one of our pastoral staff team members), bring apples and other foodstuff plus money they have collected to share with those in that miserable existence. . . .

What are they doing? They are showing mercy . . . a ministry to others that is born out of the womb of identification. . . .

And what do they get in return? What does Christ promise? ". . . they shall receive mercy." Those who remain detached, distant, and disinterested in others will receive like treatment. But God promises that those who reach out and demonstrate mercy will, in turn, receive it. . . .

That is exactly what Jesus, our Savior, did for us when He came to earth. By becoming human. He got right inside our skin, literally. That made it possible for Him to see life through our eyes, feel the sting of our pain, and identify with the anguish of human need. He understands.

Charles Swindoll

ACTION POINT

*W*ho is our model for mercy? Are any of his instructions in mercy difficult for you to practice? Pray that God will continue to reveal his mercy to you and enable you to be merciful—to those who suffer as well as to those who hate you.

TUESDAY
Build Your Life on a Solid Foundation

Luke 6:46—7:23

Two Kinds of People

*A*nd why call ye me, Lord, Lord, and do not the things which I say? [47] Whosoever cometh to me, and heareth my sayings, and doeth them, I will show you to whom he is like:

[48] he is like a man which built a house, and digged deep, and laid the foundation on a rock: and when the flood arose, the stream beat vehemently upon that house, and could not shake it; for it was founded upon a rock.

[49] But he that heareth, and doeth not, is like a man that without a foundation built a house upon the earth; against which the stream did beat vehemently, and immediately it fell; and the ruin of that house was great.

Jesus Heals a Soldier's Servant

7 Now when he had ended all his sayings in the audience of the people, he entered into Capernaum. [2] And a certain centurion's servant, who was dear unto him, was sick, and ready to die.

[3] And when he heard of Jesus, he sent unto him the elders of the Jews, beseeching him that he would come and heal his servant.

[4] And when they came to Jesus, they besought him instantly, saying, That he was worthy for whom he should do this:

[5] for he loveth our nation, and he hath built us a synagogue.

[6] Then Jesus went with them. And when he was now not far from the house, the centurion sent friends to him, saying unto him, Lord, trouble not thyself; for I am not worthy that thou shouldest enter under my roof:

[7] wherefore neither thought I myself worthy to come unto thee: but say in a word, and my servant shall be healed.

[8] For I also am a man set under authority, having under me soldiers, and I say unto one, Go, and he goeth; and to another, Come, and he cometh; and to my servant, Do this, and he doeth *it*.

[9] When Jesus heard these things, he marveled at him, and turned him about, and said unto the people that followed him, I say unto you, I have not found so great faith, no, not in Israel.

[10] And they that were sent, returning to the house, found the servant whole that had been sick.

Jesus Brings a Man Back to Life

*A*nd it came to pass the day after, that he went into a city called Nain; and many of his disciples went with him, and much people.

[12] Now when he came nigh to the gate of the city, behold, there was a dead man carried out, the only son of his mother, and she was a widow: and much people of the city was with her. [13] And when the Lord saw her, he had compassion on her, and said unto her, Weep not.

[14] And he came and touched the bier: and they that bare *him* stood still. And he said, Young man, I say unto thee, Arise.

¹⁵ And he that was dead sat up, and began to speak. And he delivered him to his mother.

¹⁶ And there came a fear on all: and they glorified God, saying, That a great prophet is risen up among us; and, That God hath visited his people.

¹⁷ And this rumor of him went forth throughout all Judea, and throughout all the region round about.

John Asks a Question

And the disciples of John showed him of all these things.

¹⁹ And John calling *unto him* two of his disciples sent *them* to Jesus, saying, Art thou he that should come? or look we for another?

²⁰ When the men were come unto him, they said, John Baptist hath sent us unto thee, saying, Art thou he that should come? or look we for another?

²¹ And in that same hour he cured many of *their* infirmities and plagues, and of evil spirits; and unto many *that were* blind he gave sight.

²² Then Jesus answering said unto them, Go your way, and tell John what things ye have seen and heard; how that the blind see, the lame walk, the lepers are cleansed, the deaf hear, the dead are raised, to the poor the gospel is preached.

²³ And blessed is *he*, whosoever shall not be offended in me.

OLD TESTAMENT READING

The LORD liveth; and blessed *be* my Rock; and let the God of my salvation be exalted.

Psalm 18:46

INSIGHTS

Suppose it were possible for a man never to have seen any season but summer. Then suppose that this man was called upon to advise in the erection of a building. You can imagine his procedure; everything is to be light, because he never heard a high wind. Waterpipes may be exposed, for he never felt the severity of frost. The most flimsy roof will be sufficient, for he knows nothing of the great rains of winter and spring.

Tell such a man that the winds will become stormy, that the rivers will be chilled into ice, that his windows will be blinded with snow, and that floods will beat upon his roof. If he is a wise man, he will say, "I must not build for one season, but for all seasons. I must not build for fine days, but for days that will be tempestuous. I must, as far as possible, prepare for the most inclement and trying weather." That is simple common sense.

Why be less sensible in building a character than in building a house? We build our bricks for severity as well as for sunshine, so why build our character with less care? . . .

As he would be infinitely foolish who would build his house without thinking of the natural forces that will try its strength, so is he cursed with insanity who builds his character without thinking of the fire with which God will try every man's work.

Joseph Parker

ACTION POINT

On what are you building your life? What can strengthen your foundation?

161

WEDNESDAY

Be Sorry for Your Sin

Luke 7:24-50

*A*nd when the messengers of John were departed, he began to speak unto the people concerning John, What went ye out into the wilderness for to see? A reed shaken with the wind?

[25] But what went ye out for to see? A man clothed in soft raiment? Behold, they which are gorgeously apparelled, and live delicately, are in kings' courts.

[26] But what went ye out for to see? A prophet? Yea, I say unto you, and much more than a prophet.

[27] This is *he*, of whom it is written, Behold, I send my messenger before thy face, which shall prepare thy way before thee.

[28] For I say unto you, Among those that are born of women there is not a greater prophet than John the Baptist: but he that is least in the kingdom of God is greater than he.

[29] And all the people that heard *him*, and the publicans, justified God, being baptized with the baptism of John.

[30] But the Pharisees and lawyers rejected the counsel of God against themselves, being not baptized of him.

[31] And the Lord said, Whereunto then shall I liken the men of this generation? and to what are they like?

[32] They are like unto children sitting in the marketplace, and calling one to another, and saying, We have piped unto you, and ye have not danced; we have mourned to you, and ye have not wept.

[33] For John the Baptist came neither eating bread nor drinking wine; and ye say, He hath a devil.

[34] The Son of man is come eating and drinking; and ye say, Behold a gluttonous man, and a winebibber, a friend of publicans and sinners!

[35] But wisdom is justified of all her children.

A Woman Washes Jesus' Feet

*A*nd one of the Pharisees desired him that he would eat with him. And he went into the Pharisee's house, and sat down to meat.

[37] And, behold, a woman in the city, which was a sinner, when she knew that *Jesus* sat at meat in the Pharisee's house, brought an alabaster box of ointment,

[38] and stood at his feet behind *him* weeping, and began to wash his feet with tears, and did wipe *them* with the hairs of her head, and kissed his feet, and anointed *them* with the ointment.

[39] Now when the Pharisee which had bidden him saw *it*, he spake within himself, saying, This man, if he were a prophet, would have known who and what manner of woman *this is* that toucheth him: for she is a sinner.

[40] And Jesus answering said unto him, Simon, I have somewhat to say unto thee. And he saith, Master, say on.

[41] There was a certain creditor which had two debtors: the one owed five hundred pence, and the other fifty.

[42] And when they had nothing to pay, he frankly forgave them both. Tell me therefore, which of them will love him most?

[43] Simon answered and said, I sup-

pose that *he*, to whom he forgave most. And he said unto him, Thou hast rightly judged.

⁴⁴ And he turned to the woman, and said unto Simon, Seest thou this woman? I entered into thine house, thou gavest me no water for my feet: but she hath washed my feet with tears, and wiped *them* with the hairs of her head.

⁴⁵ Thou gavest me no kiss: but this woman since the time I came in, hath not ceased to kiss my feet.

⁴⁶ My head with oil thou didst not anoint: but this woman hath anointed my feet with ointment.

⁴⁷ Wherefore I say unto thee, Her sins, which are many, are forgiven; for she loved much: but to whom little is forgiven, *the same* loveth little.

⁴⁸ And he said unto her, Thy sins are forgiven.

⁴⁹ And they that sat at meat with him began to say within themselves, Who is this that forgiveth sins also?

⁵⁰ And he said to the woman, Thy faith hath saved thee; go in peace.

OLD TESTAMENT READING

*F*or thou hast said, My doctrine *is* pure, and I am clean in thine eyes. ⁵ But oh that God would speak, and open his lips against thee; ⁶ and that he would show thee the secrets of wisdom, that *they are* double to that which is! Know therefore that God exacteth of thee *less* than thine iniquity *deserveth*.

Job 11:4–6

INSIGHTS

*B*efore I can become wise, I must first realize that I am foolish. Before I can receive power, I must first confess that I am powerless. I must lament my sins before I can rejoice in a Savior. Mourning, in God's sequence, always comes before exultation. Blessed are those who mourn their unworthiness, their helplessness, and their inadequacy.

Isaiah, the mighty prophet of God, knew by experience that one must bow the knee in mourning before one can lift the voice in jubilation. When his sin appeared ugly and venomous in the bright light of God's holiness, he said: "Woe is me! for I am undone; because I am a man of unclean lips: for mine eyes have seen the King, the LORD of hosts" (Isaiah 6:5).

We cannot be satisfied with our goodness after beholding the holiness of God. But our mourning over our unworthiness and sinfulness should be of short duration, for God has said: "I, even I, am he that blotteth out thy transgressions for mine own sake, and will not remember thy sins" (Isaiah 43:25). . . .

In God's economy, a person must go down into the valley of grief before he or she can scale the heights of spiritual glory. One must become tired and weary of living without Christ before he or she can seek and find His fellowship. One must come to the end of "self" before one can really begin to live.

Billy Graham

ACTION POINT

*A*re you ever tempted to brush your sins off as being of little consequence? Pray that you will truly mourn the burden of your sin and love God deeply because of his great forgiveness.

THURSDAY

Jesus Understands the Hearts of Spiritually Closed People

Luke 8:1–21

The Group with Jesus

8 And it came to pass afterward, that he went throughout every city and village, preaching and showing the glad tidings of the kingdom of God: and the twelve *were* with him,

² and certain women, which had been healed of evil spirits and infirmities, Mary called Magdalene, out of whom went seven devils,

³ and Joanna the wife of Chuza Herod's steward, and Susanna, and many others, which ministered unto him of their substance.

A Parable About Planting Seed

*A*nd when much people were gathered together, and were come to him out of every city, he spake by a parable:

⁵ A sower went out to sow his seed: and as he sowed, some fell by the way side; and it was trodden down, and the fowls of the air devoured it.

⁶ And some fell upon a rock; and as soon as it was sprung up, it withered away, because it lacked moisture.

⁷ And some fell among thorns; and the thorns sprang up with it, and choked it.

⁸ And other fell on good ground, and sprang up, and bare fruit a hundredfold. And when he had said these things, he cried, He that hath ears to hear, let him hear.

⁹ And his disciples asked him, saying, What might this parable be?

¹⁰ And he said, Unto you it is given to know the mysteries of the kingdom of God: but to others in parables; that seeing they might not see, and hearing they might not understand.

¹¹ Now the parable is this: The seed is the word of God.

¹² Those by the way side are they that hear; then cometh the devil, and taketh away the word out of their hearts, lest they should believe and be saved.

¹³ They on the rock *are they,* which, when they hear, receive the word with joy; and these have no root, which for a while believe, and in time of temptation fall away.

¹⁴ And that which fell among thorns are they, which, when they have heard, go forth, and are choked with cares and riches and pleasures of *this* life, and bring no fruit to perfection.

¹⁵ But that on the good ground are they, which in an honest and good heart, having heard the word, keep *it,* and bring forth fruit with patience.

Use What You Have

*N*o man, when he hath lighted a candle, covereth it with a vessel, or putteth *it* under a bed; but setteth *it* on a candlestick, that they which enter in may see the light.

¹⁷ For nothing is secret, that shall not be made manifest; neither *any thing* hid, that shall not be known and come abroad.

¹⁸ Take heed therefore how ye hear: for whosoever hath, to him shall be given; and whosoever hath not, from him shall be taken even that which he seemeth to have.

Jesus' True Family

*T*hen came to him his mother and his brethren, and could not come at him for the press.

²⁰ And it was told him *by certain* which said, Thy mother and thy brethren stand without, desiring to see thee.

²¹ And he answered and said unto them, My mother and my brethren are these which hear the word of God, and do it.

OLD TESTAMENT READING

*G*ive ear, O my people, *to* my law: incline your ears to the words of my mouth.

² I will open my mouth in a parable: I will utter dark sayings of old:

³ which we have heard and known, and our fathers have told us.

⁴ We will not hide *them* from their children, showing to the generation to come the praises of the LORD, and his strength, and his wonderful works that he hath done.

Psalm 78:1–4

INSIGHTS

*N*ot all of Christ's parables are explained. In fact, most are not. But this one is. . . .

The first type of soil represents the hard heart. . . . What is it that makes the human heart hard? Sin hardens the heart, and the heart that is hardened sins even more.

. . . . That type of person is described in the first chapter of Romans. He or she begins by suppressing the truth about God that may be known from nature (vv. 18–20), plunges inevitably into spiritual ignorance and moral degradation (vv. 21–31), and eventually comes not only to practice the sins of the heathen but to approve them as well (v. 32). Here we see both halves of the circle; sin leads to a rejection of God and God's truth, and the rejection of God's truth leads to even greater sin. What is it that leads such a person to reject the truth of God in the first place? According to Paul, it is a determined opposition to the nature of God Himself, which the apostle describes as human "godlessness and wickedness" (Rom. 1:18).

So rather than repent of sin and turn for mercy to a God who is altogether sovereign, holy, knowing, and unchangeable, men and women suppress what knowledge they have and refuse to seek out that additional knowledge that could be the salvation of their souls. . . .

. . . When Jesus came preaching the kingdom of God, He came preaching God's right to rule over the minds and hearts of all people. But that is precisely what the people involved did not want. . . .

So it is also today. That is probably the greatest reason for the rejection of the gospel of God's grace in Jesus Christ.

James Boice

APPLICATION

*W*hy do you think Jesus twice warns his hearers to listen to his teaching carefully? What message do you think Jesus wants you to hear? What difference do his words make in your heart and life?

FRIDAY

God Meets Us in Our Suffering

Luke 8:22–48

Jesus Calms a Storm

Now it came to pass on a certain day, that he went into a ship with his disciples: and he said unto them, Let us go over unto the other side of the lake. And they launched forth.

²³ But as they sailed he fell asleep: and there came down a storm of wind on the lake; and they were filled *with water,* and were in jeopardy.

²⁴ And they came to him, and awoke him, saying, Master, Master, we perish. Then he arose, and rebuked the wind and the raging of the water: and they ceased, and there was a calm.

²⁵ And he said unto them, Where is your faith? And they being afraid wondered, saying one to another, What manner of man is this! for he commandeth even the winds and water, and they obey him.

A Man with Demons Inside Him

And they arrived at the country of the Gadarenes, which is over against Galilee.

²⁷ And when he went forth to land, there met him out of the city a certain man, which had devils long time, and ware no clothes, neither abode in *any* house, but in the tombs.

²⁸ When he saw Jesus, he cried out, and fell down before him, and with a loud voice said, What have I to do with thee, Jesus, *thou* Son of God most high? I beseech thee, torment me not.

²⁹ (For he had commanded the unclean spirit to come out of the man. For oftentimes it had caught him: and he was kept bound with chains and in fetters; and he brake the bands, and was driven of the devil into the wilderness.)

³⁰ And Jesus asked him, saying, What is thy name? And he said, Legion: because many devils were entered into him.

³¹ And they besought him that he would not command them to go out into the deep.

³² And there was there a herd of many swine feeding on the mountain: and they besought him that he would suffer them to enter into them. And he suffered them.

³³ Then went the devils out of the man, and entered into the swine: and the herd ran violently down a steep place into the lake, and were choked.

³⁴ When they that fed *them* saw what was done, they fled, and went and told *it* in the city and in the country.

³⁵ Then they went out to see what was done; and came to Jesus, and found the man, out of whom the devils were departed, sitting at the feet of Jesus, clothed, and in his right mind: and they were afraid.

³⁶ They also which saw *it* told them by what means he that was possessed of the devils was healed.

³⁷ Then the whole multitude of the country of the Gadarenes round about besought him to depart from them; for they were taken with great fear: and he went up into the ship, and returned back again.

³⁸ Now the man out of whom the devils were departed besought him that

he might be with him: but Jesus sent him away, saying,

39 Return to thine own house, and show how great things God hath done unto thee. And he went his way, and published throughout the whole city how great things Jesus had done unto him

Jesus Raises a Dead Girl and Heals a Sick Woman.

And it came to pass, that, when Jesus was returned, the people *gladly* received him: for they were all waiting for him.

41 And, behold, there came a man named Jairus, and he was a ruler of the synagogue; and he fell down at Jesus' feet, and besought him that he would come into his house:

42 for he had one only daughter, about twelve years of age, and she lay a dying. But as he went the people thronged him.

43 And a woman having an issue of blood twelve years, which had spent all her living upon physicians, neither could be healed of any,

44 came behind *him*, and touched the border of his garment: and immediately her issue of blood stanched.

45 And Jesus said, Who touched me? When all denied, Peter and they that were with him said, Master, the multitude throng thee and press *thee*, and sayest thou, Who touched me?

46 And Jesus said, Somebody hath touched me: for I perceive that virtue is gone out of me.

47 And when the woman saw that she was not hid, she came trembling, and falling down before him, she declared unto him before all the people for what cause she had touched him and how she was healed immediately.

48 And he said unto her, Daughter, be of good comfort: thy faith hath made thee whole; go in peace.

OLD TESTAMENT READING

The LORD also will be a refuge for the oppressed, a refuge in times of trouble.

Psalm 9:9

INSIGHTS

The image Jesus left with the world, the cross, . . . is proof that God cares about our suffering and pain. He died of it. . . .

. . . Jesus, who had said He could call down angels at any moment and rescue Himself from the horror, chose not to—because of us. For God so loved us, that He sent His only Son to die for us. . . .

Jesus' followers are not insulated from the tragedies of this world, just as He was not. God has never promised that tornados will skip our houses on the way to our pagan neighbors'. Microbes do not flee from Christian bodies. Rather, Peter could say to suffering Christians, "This suffering is all part of the work God has given you. Christ, who suffered for you, is your example. Follow in his steps" (1 Peter 2:21 LB).

Philip Yancey

PAUSE FOR REFLECTION

How much does Jesus care about your suffering? Thank him that he took our greatest suffering upon himself on the cross.

WEEKEND

God Is in Control

Luke 8:49—9:17

*W*hile he yet spake, there cometh one from the ruler of the synagogue's *house*, saying to him, Thy daughter is dead; trouble not the Master.

⁵⁰ But when Jesus heard *it*, he answered him, saying, Fear not: believe only, and she shall be made whole.

⁵¹ And when he came into the house, he suffered no man to go in, save Peter, and James, and John, and the father and the mother of the maiden.

⁵² And all wept, and bewailed her: but he said, Weep not; she is not dead, but sleepeth.

⁵³ And they laughed him to scorn, knowing that she was dead.

⁵⁴ And he put them all out, and took her by the hand, and called, saying, Maid, arise.

⁵⁵ And her spirit came again, and she arose straightway: and he commanded to give her meat.

⁵⁶ And her parents were astonished: but he charged them that they should tell no man what was done.

Jesus Sends Out the Apostles

9 Then he called his twelve disciples together, and gave them power and authority over all devils, and to cure diseases.

² And he sent them to preach the kingdom of God, and to heal the sick.

³ And he said unto them, Take nothing for *your* journey, neither staves, nor scrip, neither bread, neither money; neither have two coats apiece.

⁴ And whatsoever house ye enter into, there abide, and thence depart.

⁵ And whosoever will not receive you, when ye go out of that city, shake off the very dust from your feet for a testimony against them.

⁶ And they departed, and went through the towns, preaching the gospel, and healing every where.

Herod Is Perplexed About Jesus

*N*ow Herod the tetrarch heard of all that was done by him: and he was perplexed, because that it was said of some, that John was risen from the dead;

⁸ and of some, that Elijah had appeared; and of others, that one of the old prophets was risen again.

⁹ And Herod said, John have I beheaded; but who is this, of whom I hear such things? And he desired to see him.

More than Five Thousand Fed

*A*nd the apostles, when they were returned, told him all that they had done. And he took them, and went aside privately into a desert place belonging to the city called Bethsaida.

¹¹ And the people, when they knew *it*, followed him: and he received them, and spake unto them of the kingdom of God, and healed them that had need of healing.

¹² And when the day began to wear away, then came the twelve, and said unto him, Send the multitude away, that they may go into the towns and country round about, and lodge, and get victuals: for we are here in a desert place.

¹³ But he said unto them, Give ye them to eat. And they said, We have no more but five loaves and two fishes; except we should go and buy meat for all this people.

¹⁴ For they were about five thousand men. And he said to his disciples, Make them sit down by fifties in a company.

¹⁵ And they did so, and made them all sit down.

¹⁶ Then he took the five loaves and the two fishes, and looking up to heaven, he blessed them, and brake, and gave to the disciples to set before the multitude.

¹⁷ And they did eat, and were all filled: and there was taken up of fragments that remained to them twelve baskets.

OLD TESTAMENT READING

*B*ut ask now the beasts, and they shall teach thee; and the fowls of the air, and they shall tell thee:

⁸ or speak to the earth, and it shall teach thee; and the fishes of the sea shall declare unto thee.

⁹ Who knoweth not in all these that the hand of the LORD hath wrought this?

¹⁰ in whose hand *is* the soul of every living thing, and the breath of all mankind.

Job 12:7–10

INSIGHTS

*N*o two days were ever exactly the same on my bit of beach. Part of its great appeal lay in the ever-changing appearance of its shoreline.

The subtle play of sunlight and shadow on the cliff faces altered their contours. Some mornings the rugged rocks seemed softened by the muted shades of the rising sun. They glowed warm, golden, wrapped in sunshine and serenity.

Other days the same rock buttresses stood gray and forbidding in the fog and mist that swirled in off the sea. The shoreline looked almost black, dark with dampness, soaked with sea spray.

Always, always, always the ocean is at work on the land. Summer and winter, spring and autumn the changing tides rise and ebb, shaping the character of the coast. Their force is utterly relentless—their power immeasurable—their titanic thrust untamed.

Great mysteries surround the majestic, awesome action of the tides. With incredible precision they move billions of tons of water from surface to surface upon the sea. They are the reflection of gigantic energy within the cosmos that knows no rest, that never slumbers, that never sleeps.

In the same overshadowing way, our Father watches over His children, quietly overseeing the events of their lives that they might accomplish His purposes for Him.

W. Phillip Keller

ACTION POINT

*W*hat do these readings show that God controls? Is there anything more for him to control? What experience in your life or image from nature reminds you that God is in control? Think of it often, and praise God for his great sovereignty!

MONDAY

God Is a Patient Teacher

Luke 9:18–43a

Jesus Is the Christ

*A*nd it came to pass, as he was alone praying, his disciples were with him; and he asked them, saying, Whom say the people that I am? ¹⁹ They answering said, John the Baptist; but some *say*, Elijah; and others *say*, that one of the old prophets is risen again.

²⁰ He said unto them, But whom say ye that I am? Peter answering said, The Christ of God.

²¹ And he straitly charged them, and commanded *them* to tell no man that thing;

²² saying, The Son of man must suffer many things, and be rejected of the elders and chief priests and scribes, and be slain, and be raised the third day.

²³ And he said to *them* all, If any *man* will come after me, let him deny himself, and take up his cross daily, and follow me.

²⁴ For whosoever will save his life shall lose it: but whosoever will lose his life for my sake, the same shall save it.

²⁵ For what is a man advantaged, if he gain the whole world, and lose himself, or be cast away?

²⁶ For whosoever shall be ashamed of me and of my words, of him shall the Son of man be ashamed, when he shall come in his own glory, and *in his* Father's, and of the holy angels.

²⁷ But I tell you of a truth, there be some standing here, which shall not taste of death, till they see the kingdom of God.

Jesus Talks with Moses and Elijah

*A*nd it came to pass about an eight days after these sayings, he took Peter and John and James, and went up into a mountain to pray.

²⁹ And as he prayed, the fashion of his countenance was altered, and his raiment *was* white *and* glistering.

³⁰ And, behold, there talked with him two men, which were Moses and Elijah:

³¹ who appeared in glory, and spake of his decease which he should accomplish at Jerusalem.

³² But Peter and they that were with him were heavy with sleep: and when they were awake, they saw his glory, and the two men that stood with him.

³³ And it came to pass, as they departed from him, Peter said unto Jesus, Master, it is good for us to be here: and let us make three tabernacles; one for thee, and one for Moses, and one for Elijah: not knowing what he said.

³⁴ While he thus spake, there came a cloud, and overshadowed them: and they feared as they entered into the cloud.

³⁵ And there came a voice out of the cloud, saying, This is my beloved Son: hear him.

³⁶ And when the voice was past, Jesus was found alone. And they kept *it* close, and told no man in those days any of those things which they had seen.

³⁷ And it came to pass, that on the next day, when they were come

down from the hill, much people met him.

Jesus Heals a Boy

*A*nd, behold, a man of the company cried out, saying, Master, I beseech thee, look upon my son; for he is mine only child.

³⁹ And, lo, a spirit taketh him, and he suddenly crieth out; and it teareth him that he foameth again, and bruising him, hardly departeth from him.

⁴⁰ And I besought thy disciples to cast him out; and they could not.

⁴¹ And Jesus answering said, O faithless and perverse generation, how long shall I be with you, and suffer you? Bring thy son hither.

⁴² And as he was yet a coming, the devil threw him down, and tare *him*. And Jesus rebuked the unclean spirit, and healed the child, and delivered him again to his father.

⁴³ And they were all amazed at the mighty power of God.

OLD TESTAMENT READING

*Y*et many years didst thou forbear them, and testifiedst against them by thy Spirit in thy prophets: yet would they not give ear: therefore gavest thou them into the hand of the people of the lands.

³¹ Nevertheless for thy great mercies' sake thou didst not utterly consume them, nor forsake them; for thou *art* a gracious and merciful God.

Nehemiah 9:30–31

INSIGHTS

*I*n Judaism it was the custom for the pupil to select the rabbi of his choice and attach himself to him for instruction. Thus Paul sat "at the feet of Gamaliel" (Acts 22:3, KJV). But here it was Jesus and not the disciples who took the initiative. "When day came, He called His disciples to Him; and chose twelve of them" (Luke 6:13). . . . He called them personally and bound them to Him with bonds of affection that stood the test of time. Thus He chose to invest His life and channel it into that little group of men. . . .

. . . They were not theologians or political leaders—just ordinary men who became extraordinary under the molding hand of the Master Potter. That makes His selection of them the more wonderful. . . .

Their imperfections were painfully apparent, but those did not debar them from His fellowship and friendship. If God required perfection before He admitted us into the circle of His fellowship, who would qualify? Quirks of temperament did not disqualify them, or Peter with his volatile nature would not have been counted in. Nor would James and John with their selfish ambition and callous racism. Thomas's disbelief would have placed him outside the circle. But Jesus welcomed them all into the circle of His love and intimacy.

J. Oswald Sanders

PAUSE FOR REFLECTION

*C*hronicle your own spiritual journey in a way similar to Nehemiah's account of God's dealings with the children of Israel (9:19–31). In what ways has God stood beside you as a patient, wise, and ever-merciful teacher? Thank him for claiming you as his own.

TUESDAY

God Seeks Those Who Follow Him Faithfully

Luke 9:43b—10:7

Jesus Talks About His Death

*B*ut while they wondered every one at all things which Jesus did, he said unto his disciples,
⁴⁴ Let these sayings sink down into your ears: for the Son of man shall be delivered into the hands of men.
⁴⁵ But they understood not this saying, and it was hid from them, that they perceived it not: and they feared to ask him of that saying.

Who Is the Greatest?

*T*hen there arose a reasoning among them, which of them should be greatest.
⁴⁷ And Jesus, perceiving the thought of their heart, took a child, and set him by him,
⁴⁸ and said unto them, Whosoever shall receive this child in my name receiveth me; and whosoever shall receive me receiveth him that sent me: for he that is least among you all, the same shall be great.

Anyone Not Against Us Is for Us

*A*nd John answered and said, Master, we saw one casting out devils in thy name; and we forbad him, because he followeth not with us.
⁵⁰ And Jesus said unto him, Forbid *him* not: for he that is not against us is for us.

A Town Rejects Jesus

*A*nd it came to pass, when the time was come that he should be received up, he stedfastly set his face to go to Jerusalem,
⁵² and sent messengers before his face: and they went, and entered into a village of the Samaritans, to make ready for him.
⁵³ And they did not receive him, because his face was as though he would go to Jerusalem.
⁵⁴ And when his disciples James and John saw *this,* they said, Lord, wilt thou that we command fire to come down from heaven, and consume them, even as Elijah did?
⁵⁵ But he turned, and rebuked them, and said, Ye know not what manner of spirit ye are of.
⁵⁶ For the Son of man is not come to destroy men's lives, but to save *them.* And they went to another village.

Following Jesus

*A*nd it came to pass, that, as they went in the way, a certain *man* said unto him, Lord, I will follow thee whithersoever thou goest.
⁵⁸ And Jesus said unto him, Foxes have holes, and birds of the air *have* nests; but the Son of man hath not where to lay *his* head.
⁵⁹ And he said unto another, Follow me. But he said, Lord, suffer me first to go and bury my father.
⁶⁰ Jesus said unto him, Let the dead bury their dead: but go thou and preach the kingdom of God.
⁶¹ And another also said, Lord, I will follow thee; but let me first go bid them farewell, which are at home at my house.

172

62 And Jesus said unto him, No man, having put his hand to the plow, and looking back, is fit for the kingdom of God.

Jesus Sends Out the Seventy

10 After these things the Lord appointed other seventy also, and sent them two and two before his face into every city and place, whither he himself would come.

2 Therefore said he unto them, The harvest truly *is* great, but the laborers *are* few: pray ye therefore the Lord of the harvest, that he would send forth laborers into his harvest.

3 Go your ways: behold, I send you forth as lambs among wolves.

4 Carry neither purse, nor scrip, nor shoes: and salute no man by the way.

5 And into whatsoever house ye enter, first say, Peace *be* to this house.

6 And if the son of peace be there, your peace shall rest upon it: if not, it shall turn to you again.

7 And in the same house remain, eating and drinking such things as they give: for the laborer is worthy of his hire. Go not from house to house.

OLD TESTAMENT READING

*A*nd at that time Hanani the seer came to Asa king of Judah, and said unto him, Because thou hast relied on the king of Syria, and not relied on the LORD thy God, therefore is the host of the king of Syria escaped out of thine hand.

8 Were not the Ethiopians and the Lubim a huge host, with very many chariots and horsemen? yet, because thou didst rely on the LORD, he delivered them into thine hand.

9 For the eyes of the LORD run to and fro throughout the whole earth, to show himself strong in the behalf of *them* whose heart *is* perfect toward him.

2 Chronicles 16:7–9a

INSIGHTS

When you begin to pray, your life can take on all kinds of perils and problems that you never had before. Think about it. As far as we know, Abraham was living a comfortable, trouble-free life until he began to pray. It was through prayer that he heard God's message to leave home, move out, hit the road for an unknown destination, and start a journey of indeterminate length. His life became exceedingly difficult and dangerous. . . .

Prayer was the launching pad for Moses as well. He was quietly tending sheep in the Midian hills, leading a settled life with his wife and sons and his father-in-law. Things changed when he started to pray. It started dramatically enough at a burning bush, where he heard God speak to him and entrust him with an impossible task—that of leading the Israelites out of Egypt. From one perspective, that was the last really comfortable day of Moses' life. . . .

That is the peril of prayer. . . . As we begin to talk to God and hear him speak to us, life may never be the same.

Bruce Larson

APPLICATION

*I*s God calling you, through your prayers, to break out into new territory, to follow him more faithfully?

WEDNESDAY

God Gives His Wisdom and Power to His Servants

Luke 10:8–29

*A*nd into whatsoever city ye enter, and they receive you, eat such things as are set before you:

9 and heal the sick that are therein, and say unto them, The kingdom of God is come nigh unto you.

10 But into whatsoever city ye enter, and they receive you not, go your ways out into the streets of the same, and say,

11 Even the very dust of your city, which cleaveth on us, we do wipe off against you: notwithstanding, be ye sure of this, that the kingdom of God is come nigh unto you.

12 But I say unto you, that it shall be more tolerable in that day for Sodom, than for that city.

Jesus Warns Unbelievers

*W*oe unto thee, Chorazin! woe unto thee, Bethsaida! for if the mighty works had been done in Tyre and Sidon, which have been done in you, they had a great while ago repented, sitting in sackcloth and ashes.

14 But it shall be more tolerable for Tyre and Sidon at the judgment, than for you.

15 And thou, Capernaum, which art exalted to heaven, shalt be thrust down to hell.

16 He that heareth you heareth me; and he that despiseth you despiseth me; and he that despiseth me despiseth him that sent me.

Satan Falls

*A*nd the seventy returned again with joy, saying, Lord, even the devils are subject unto us through thy name.

18 And he said unto them, I beheld Satan as lightning fall from heaven.

19 Behold, I give unto you power to tread on serpents and scorpions, and over all the power of the enemy; and nothing shall by any means hurt you.

20 Notwithstanding in this rejoice not, that the spirits are subject unto you; but rather rejoice, because your names are written in heaven.

Jesus Prays to the Father

*I*n that hour Jesus rejoiced in spirit, and said, I thank thee, O Father, Lord of heaven and earth, that thou hast hid these things from the wise and prudent, and hast revealed them unto babes: even so, Father; for so it seemed good in thy sight.

22 All things are delivered to me of my Father: and no man knoweth who the Son is, but the Father; and who the Father is, but the Son, and *he* to whom the Son will reveal *him*.

23 And he turned him unto *his* disciples, and said privately, Blessed *are* the eyes which see the things that ye see:

24 for I tell you, that many prophets and kings have desired to see those things which ye see, and have not seen *them*; and to hear those things which ye hear, and have not heard *them*.

Who Is My Neighbor?

*A*nd, behold, a certain lawyer stood

up, and tempted him, saying, Master, what shall I do to inherit eternal life?
²⁶ He said unto him, What is written in the law? how readest thou?
²⁷ And he answering said, Thou shalt love the Lord thy God with all thy heart, and with all thy soul, and with all thy strength, and with all thy mind; and thy neighbor as thyself.
²⁸ And he said unto him, Thou hast answered right: this do, and thou shalt live.
²⁹ But he, willing to justify himself, said unto Jesus, And who is my neighbor?

OLD TESTAMENT READING

And God gave Solomon wisdom and understanding exceeding much, and largeness of heart, even as the sand that *is* on the seashore.
³⁰ And Solomon's wisdom excelled the wisdom of all the children of the east country, and all the wisdom of Egypt.
³¹ For he was wiser than all men; then Ethan the Ezrahite, and Heman, and Chalcol, and Darda, the sons of Mahol: and his fame was in all nations round about.
³² And he spake three thousand proverbs: and his songs were a thousand and five.
³³ And he spake of trees, from the cedar tree that *is* in Lebanon even unto the hyssop that springeth out of the wall: he spake also of beasts, and of fowl, and of creeping things, and of fishes.
³⁴ And there came of all people to hear the wisdom of Solomon, from all kings of the earth, which had heard of his wisdom.

1 Kings 4:29–34

INSIGHTS

Too many Christians do not believe Christ's promise that He would endue the Church with spiritual power; they doubt that His promise is to every believer. Consequently, they have no faith to lay hold of Christ's power. If His promise does not belong to all, how can they know to whom it does belong? Of course, with this limited understanding they cannot lay hold of the promise by faith.

Another lack in Christians is persistence in waiting upon God for that which He has promised to us in the Scriptures. People give up before they have prevailed, and hence, the enduement of spiritual power is not received.

Of great concern also is the extent to which the Church has practically lost sight of the necessity of the enduement of spiritual power. Much is said about our dependence upon the Holy Spirit by almost everybody, but how little is this dependence realized. . . . I mourn to be obliged to say that the ranks of the ministry seem to be filling up with those who do not possess spiritual power. May the Lord have mercy upon us! Will this last remark be thought uncharitable? If so, let the current state of the Church and her success in evangelism be heard on this subject. Surely, something is wrong.

Charles Finney

APPLICATION

What is the source of the believer's wisdom and power? Is spiritual power evident in your life? Pray that God's spirit will be alive in you.

THURSDAY

It Is Good to
Show Kindness to Others

Luke 10:30—11:13

*A*nd Jesus answering said, A certain *man* went down from Jerusalem to Jericho, and fell among thieves, which stripped him of his raiment, and wounded *him*, and departed, leaving *him* half dead.

31 And by chance there came down a certain priest that way: and when he saw him, he passed by on the other side.

32 And likewise a Levite, when he was at the place, came and looked *on him*, and passed by on the other side.

33 But a certain Samaritan, as he journeyed, came where he was; and when he saw him, he had compassion *on him*,

34 and went to *him*, and bound up his wounds, pouring in oil and wine, and set him on his own beast, and brought him to an inn, and took care of him.

35 And on the morrow when he departed, he took out two pence, and gave *them* to the host, and said unto him, Take care of him; and whatsoever thou spendest more, when I come again, I will repay thee.

36 Which now of these three, thinkest thou, was neighbor unto him that fell among the thieves?

37 And he said, He that showed mercy on him. Then said Jesus unto him, Go, and do thou likewise.

Mary and Martha

*N*ow it came to pass, as they went, that he entered into a certain village:

and a certain woman named Martha received him into her house.

39 And she had a sister called Mary, which also sat at Jesus' feet, and heard his word.

40 But Martha was cumbered about much serving, and came to him, and said, Lord, dost thou not care that my sister hath left me to serve alone? bid her therefore that she help me.

41 And Jesus answered and said unto her, Martha, Martha, thou art careful and troubled about many things:

42 but one thing is needful: and Mary hath chosen that good part, which shall not be taken away from her.

Jesus Teaches About Prayer

11 And it came to pass, that, as he was praying in a certain place, when he ceased, one of his disciples said unto him, Lord, teach us to pray, as John also taught his disciples.

2 And he said unto them, When ye pray, say, Our Father which art in heaven, Hallowed be thy name. Thy kingdom come. Thy will be done, as in heaven, so in earth.

3 Give us day by day our daily bread.

4 And forgive us our sins; for we also forgive every one that is indebted to us. And lead us not into temptation; but deliver us from evil.

Continue to Ask

*A*nd he said unto them, Which of you shall have a friend, and shall go unto him at midnight, and say unto him, Friend, lend me three loaves;

6 for a friend of mine in his journey is come to me, and I have nothing to set before him?

7 And he from within shall answer and

say, Trouble me not: the door is now shut, and my children are with me in bed; I cannot rise and give thee.

⁸ I say unto you, Though he will not rise and give him, because he is his friend, yet because of his importunity he will rise and give him as many as he needeth.

⁹ And I say unto you, Ask, and it shall be given you; seek, and ye shall find; knock, and it shall be opened unto you.

¹⁰ For every one that asketh receiveth; and he that seeketh findeth; and to him that knocketh it shall be opened.

¹¹ If a son shall ask bread of any of you that is a father, will he give him a stone? or if *he ask* a fish, will he for a fish give him a serpent?

¹² Or if he shall ask an egg, will he offer him a scorpion?

¹³ If ye then, being evil, know how to give good gifts unto your children: how much more shall *your* heavenly Father give the Holy Spirit to them that ask him?

OLD TESTAMENT READING

*W*ithhold not good from them to whom it is due, when it is in the power of thine hand to do *it*.

²⁸ Say not unto thy neighbor, Go, and come again, and tomorrow I will give; when thou hast it by thee.

Proverbs 3:27–28

INSIGHTS

*K*indness is a sincere desire for the happiness of others; goodness is the activity calculated to advance that happiness. . . .

. . . The New Testament has much to say about the kindness of God. The first mention is in Luke 6:

Jesus says that God "is kind to the ungrateful and wicked." Next we find that God's kindness leads sinners toward repentance (Romans 2:4). In Ephesians 2:7, in the context of our utter lostness and sin, Paul speaks of the incomparable riches of God's grace, expressed in his kindness to us in Christ Jesus. . . .

What lesson can we draw from these accounts of the kindness of God? He is kind to all men—the ungrateful, the wicked, the utterly lost and hopeless, the rebellious—without distinction. . . .

Our natural inclination is to show kindness only to those for whom we have some natural affinity—family, friends, likable neighbors. But God shows kindness to those who are most despicable—the ungrateful and wicked. Have you ever tried to be kind to someone who was ungrateful? Unless God's grace was working in your heart in a significant way, your reaction to his ingratitude may well have been, "I'll never do anything for him again!" But God doesn't turn his back on the ungrateful. . . .

We need to develop a kind disposition, to be sensitive to others and truly desire their happiness. But sensitivity alone is not enough: the grace of goodness impels us to take action to meet those needs.

Jerry Bridges

ACTION POINT

*T*hink about contemporary parallels to the story of the good Samaritan. Diligently pray that you will express God's kindness even when it is inconvenient or unpleasant.

FRIDAY

Focus Your Eyes on the Things of God

Luke 11:14–36

Jesus' Power Is from God

*A*nd he was casting out a devil, and it was dumb. And it came to pass, when the devil was gone out, the dumb spake; and the people wondered.

15 But some of them said, He casteth out devils through Beelzebub the chief of the devils.

16 And others, tempting *him*, sought of him a sign from heaven.

17 But he, knowing their thoughts, said unto them, Every kingdom divided against itself is brought to desolation; and a house *divided* against a house falleth.

18 If Satan also be divided against himself, how shall his kingdom stand? because ye say that I cast out devils through Beelzebub.

19 And if I by Beelzebub cast out devils, by whom do your sons cast *them* out? therefore shall they be your judges.

20 But if I with the finger of God cast out devils, no doubt the kingdom of God is come upon you.

21 When a strong man armed keepeth his palace, his goods are in peace:

22 But when a stronger than he shall come upon him, and overcome him, he taketh from him all his armor wherein he trusted, and divideth his spoils.

23 He that is not with me is against me: and he that gathereth not with me scattereth.

The Empty Person

*W*hen the unclean spirit is gone out of a man, he walketh through dry places, seeking rest; and finding none, he saith, I will return unto my house whence I came out.

25 And when he cometh, he findeth *it* swept and garnished.

26 Then goeth he, and taketh *to him* seven other spirits more wicked than himself; and they enter in, and dwell there: and the last *state* of that man is worse than the first.

People Who Are Truly Blessed

*A*nd it came to pass, as he spake these things, a certain woman of the company lifted up her voice, and said unto him, Blessed *is* the womb that bare thee, and the paps which thou hast sucked.

28 But he said, Yea rather, blessed *are* they that hear the word of God, and keep it.

The People Want a Sign

*A*nd when the people were gathered thick together, he began to say, This is an evil generation: they seek a sign; and there shall no sign be given it, but the sign of Jonah the prophet.

30 For as Jonah was a sign unto the Ninevites, so shall also the Son of man be to this generation.

31 The queen of the south shall rise up in the judgment with the men of this generation, and condemn them: for she came from the utmost parts of the earth to hear the wisdom of Solomon; and, behold, a greater than Solomon *is* here.

32 The men of Nineveh shall rise up

in the judgment with this generation, and shall condemn it: for they repented at the preaching of Jonah; and, behold, a greater than Jonah *is* here.

Be a Light for the World

*N*o man, when he hath lighted a candle, putteth *it* in a secret place, neither under a bushel, but on a candlestick, that they which come in may see the light.

³⁴ The light of the body is the eye: therefore when thine eye is single, thy whole body also is full of light; but when *thine eye* is evil, thy body also *is* full of darkness.

³⁵ Take heed therefore, that the light which is in thee be not darkness.

³⁶ If thy whole body therefore *be* full of light, having no part dark, the whole shall be full of light, as when the bright shining of a candle doth give thee light.

OLD TESTAMENT READING

*L*et thine eyes look right on, and let thine eyelids look straight before thee.

²⁶ Ponder the path of thy feet, and let all thy ways be established.

²⁷ Turn not to the right hand nor to the left: remove thy foot from evil.

Proverbs 4:25–27

INSIGHTS

*T*he nature of the Christian life is Christ's life taking hold upon all the inner life of a man, changing, dominating, pulsating. It is seen therefore, and I do not think we can be too careful in emphasizing this, that Christian life is neither human imitation of Christ, nor correct intellec-

tual positions concerning Christ. Neither is it a cult, or a system of thought. I may attempt to imitate Christ sincerely through long years, and yet never be a Christian. I may hold absolutely correct intellectual views concerning Christ as a person, and His power, and yet never be a Christian. It is possible for me to admire Him, and attempt with all the power of my life to imitate Him, and yet never realize Him. It is quite possible for a person to believe most sincerely in His Deity, and in the fact of His atoning work, and moreover, in the necessity for regeneration, and yet never be submitted to His Lordship, never to have personal share in the work of His atonement, never to be born again.

Nothing short of the coming into life of the individual of Christ Himself constitutes a Christian. If Jesus Christ is external to your life there will be times when the world will not see Him and hear Him, and will not know you belong to Him. But if Christ be in you, living, reigning there absolutely, and you are obeying Him, there never will be a moment when the truth will not be evident. You cannot hide Christ if once He comes within. If the light is there, it simply must shine.

G. Campbell Morgan

APPLICATION

*W*hat happens when a person focuses his or her eyes on the good things of God? Is your body filled with the light of Christ? What practical reminder will help you keep your eyes focused on God?

WEEKEND
Trust God; Don't Fear People

Luke 11:37—12:7

Jesus Accuses the Pharisees

*A*nd as he spake, a certain Pharisee besought him to dine with him: and he went in, and sat down to meat. [38] And when the Pharisee saw *it*, he marveled that he had not first washed before dinner. [39] And the Lord said unto him, Now do ye Pharisees make clean the outside of the cup and the platter; but your inward part is full of ravening and wickedness. [40] *Ye* fools, did not he that made that which is without, make that which is within also? [41] But rather give alms of such things as ye have; and, behold, all things are clean unto you. [42] But woe unto you, Pharisees! for ye tithe mint and rue and all manner of herbs, and pass over judgment and the love of God: these ought ye to have done, and not to leave the other undone. [43] Woe unto you, Pharisees! for ye love the uppermost seats in the synagogues, and greetings in the markets. [44] Woe unto you, scribes and Pharisees, hypocrites! for ye are as graves which appear not, and the men that walk over *them* are not aware *of them*.

Jesus Talks to Experts on the Law

*T*hen answered one of the lawyers, and said unto him, Master, thus saying thou reproachest us also.

[46] And he said, Woe unto you also, *ye* lawyers! for ye lade men with burdens grievous to be borne, and ye yourselves touch not the burdens with one of your fingers. [47] Woe unto you! for ye build the sepulchres of the prophets, and your fathers killed them. [48] Truly ye bear witness that ye allow the deeds of your fathers: for they indeed killed them, and ye build their sepulchres. [49] Therefore also said the wisdom of God, I will send them prophets and apostles, and *some* of them they shall slay and persecute: [50] that the blood of all the prophets, which was shed from the foundation of the world, may be required of this generation; [51] from the blood of Abel unto the blood of Zechariah, which perished between the altar and the temple: verily I say unto you, It shall be required of this generation. [52] Woe unto you, lawyers! for ye have taken away the key of knowledge: ye entered not in yourselves, and them that were entering in ye hindered. [53] And as he said these things unto them, the scribes and the Pharisees began to urge him vehemently, and to provoke him to speak of many things: [54] laying wait for him, and seeking to catch something out of his mouth, that they might accuse him.

Don't Be Like the Pharisees

12 In the mean time, when there were gathered together an innumerable multitude of people, insomuch that they trode one upon another, he began to say unto his disciples first of all, Beware ye of the leaven of the Pharisees, which is hypocrisy.

² For there is nothing covered, that shall not be revealed; neither hid, that shall not be known.

³ Therefore whatsoever ye have spoken in darkness shall be heard in the light; and that which ye have spoken in the ear in closets shall be proclaimed upon the housetops.

⁴ And I say unto you my friends, Be not afraid of them that kill the body, and after that have no more that they can do.

⁵ But I will forewarn you whom ye shall fear: Fear him, which after he hath killed hath power to cast into hell; yea, I say unto you, Fear him.

⁶ Are not five sparrows sold for two farthings, and not one of them is forgotten before God?

⁷ But even the very hairs of your head are all numbered. Fear not therefore: ye are of more value than many sparrows.

OLD TESTAMENT READING

I, *even*, I *am* he that comforteth you: who art thou, that thou shouldest be afraid of a man *that* shall die, and of the son of man *which* shall be made *as* grass;

¹³ and forgettest the LORD thy maker, that hath stretched forth the heavens, and laid the foundations of the earth.

Isaiah 51:12–13a

INSIGHTS

*M*any of us have lost the fear of the Lord. We have forgotten our deep awe for the character of God, His holiness, His eternality, His sovereignty over all the affairs of men. We let Him get smaller. We let our impression of ourselves get bigger. We see ourselves as larger in intellect and capabilities, as more technologically advanced and more scientific. As we prosper, we don't need God as we once did.

What is the fear of the Lord? And how can we get it into our lives? The fear of the Lord is to love what God loves and to hate what God hates. The fear of the Lord is both positive and negative. . . .

The positive is to love what God loves—wisdom. God loves wisdom. The fear of the Lord is to love wisdom. "My son, if you accept my words and store up my commands within you, turning your ear to wisdom and applying your heart to understanding . . . then you will understand the fear of the Lord and find the knowledge of God. For the Lord gives wisdom." (Proverbs 2:1–2, 5–6). . . .

The negative is to hate what God hates—evil. God hates evil. "To fear the Lord is to hate evil." (Proverbs 8:13). "Through the fear of the Lord a man avoids evil" (Proverbs 16:6). . . .

The person gripped by godly fear cannot tolerate evil because God does not tolerate evil. He hates evil with the intensity that God hates evil, or at least he tries to. He is a reformer, not a recluse.

Patrick Morley

PAUSE FOR REFLECTION

*W*hat kind of fear of God did Jesus tell the Pharisees and teachers of the law they should have? Describe the two kinds of fear that those who trust the Lord should have.

MONDAY

Where Is Your Treasure?

Luke 12:8–34

Don't Be Ashamed of Jesus

*A*lso I say unto you, Whosoever shall confess me before men, him shall the Son of man also confess before the angels of God:

⁹ but he that denieth me before men shall be denied before the angels of God.

¹⁰ And whosoever shall speak a word against the Son of man, it shall be forgiven him: but unto him that blasphemeth against the Holy Ghost it shall not be forgiven.

¹¹ And when they bring you unto the synagogues, and *unto* magistrates, and powers, take ye no thought how or what thing ye shall answer, or what ye shall say:

¹² for the Holy Ghost shall teach you in the same hour what ye ought to say.

Don't Be Greedy

*A*nd one of the company said unto him, Master, speak to my brother, that he divide the inheritance with me.

¹⁴ And he said unto him, Man, who made me a judge or a divider over you?

¹⁵ And he said unto them, Take heed, and beware of covetousness: for a man's life consisteth not in the abundance of the things which he possesseth.

¹⁶ And he spake a parable unto them, saying, The ground of a certain rich man brought forth plentifully:

¹⁷ and he thought within himself, saying, What shall I do, because I have no room where to bestow my fruits?

¹⁸ And he said, This will I do: I will pull down my barns, and build greater; and there will I bestow all my fruits and my goods.

¹⁹ And I will say to my soul, Soul, thou hast much goods laid up for many years; take thine ease, eat, drink, *and* be merry.

²⁰ But God said unto him, *Thou* fool, this night thy soul shall be required of thee: then whose shall those things be, which thou hast provided?

²¹ So *is* he that layeth up treasure for himself, and is not rich toward God.

Don't Worry

*A*nd he said unto his disciples, Therefore I say unto you, Take no thought for your life, what ye shall eat; neither for the body, what ye shall put on.

²³ The life is more than meat, and the body *is more* than raiment.

²⁴ Consider the ravens: for they neither sow nor reap; which neither have storehouse nor barn; and God feedeth them: how much more are ye better than the fowls?

²⁵ And which of you with taking thought can add to his stature one cubit?

²⁶ If ye then be not able to do that thing which is least, why take ye thought for the rest?

²⁷ Consider the lilies how they grow: they toil not, they spin not; and yet I say unto you, that Solomon in all his glory was not arrayed like one of these.

²⁸ If then God so clothe the grass, which is today in the field, and tomorrow is cast into the oven; how

much more *will he clothe* you, O ye of little faith? ²⁹ And seek not ye what ye shall eat, or what ye shall drink, neither be ye of doubtful mind. ³⁰ For all these things do the nations of the world seek after: and your Father knoweth that ye have need of these things. ³¹ But rather seek ye the kingdom of God; and all these things shall be added unto you.

Don't Trust in Money

*F*ear not, little flock; for it is your Father's good pleasure to give you the kingdom. ³³ Sell that ye have, and give alms; provide yourselves bags which wax not old, a treasure in the heavens that faileth not, where no thief approacheth, neither moth corrupteth. ³⁴ For where your treasure is, there will your heart be also.

OLD TESTAMENT READING

*H*e that loveth silver shall not be satisfied with silver; nor he that loveth abundance with increase: this *is* also vanity. ¹¹ When goods increase, they are increased that eat them: and what good *is there* to the owners thereof, saving the beholding *of them* with their eyes?

Ecclesiastes 5:10–11

INSIGHTS

*C*onstantly the Bible deals decisively with the inner spirit of slavery that an idolatrous attachment to wealth brings. "If riches increase, set not your heart on them," counsels the psalmist (Ps. 62:10). . . .

. . . Jesus . . . saw the grip that wealth can have on a person. He knew that "where your treasure is, there will your heart be also," which is precisely why he commanded his followers: "Do not lay up for yourselves treasures on earth" (Matt. 6:21, 19). He is not saying that the heart should or should not be where the treasure is. He is stating the plain fact that wherever you find the treasure, you will find the heart.

He exhorted the rich young ruler not just to have an inner attitude of detachment from his possessions, but literally to get rid of his possessions if he wanted the kingdom of God (Matt. 19:16–22). . . . He told the parable of the rich farmer whose life centered in hoarding—we would call him prudent; Jesus called him a fool (Luke 12:16–21). He states that if we really want the kingdom of God we must, like a merchant in search of fine pearls, be willing to sell everything we have to get it (Matt. 13:45, 46). He calls all who would follow him to a joyful life of carefree unconcern for possessions: "Give to every one who begs from you; and of him who takes away your goods do not ask them again" (Luke 6:30).

Richard Foster

PAUSE FOR REFLECTION

*W*hat things does God say are important in life? What causes people to be greedy? What necessities are we to trust God to provide? Why is it important for those who follow Christ to guard against greed?

TUESDAY

Live a Godly Life While You Wait for Christ's Return

Luke 12:35–56

Always Be Ready

*L*et your loins be girded about, and *your* lights burning;

36 and ye yourselves like unto men that wait for their lord, when he will return from the wedding; that when he cometh and knocketh, they may open unto him immediately.

37 Blessed *are* those servants, whom the lord when he cometh shall find watching: verily I say unto you, that he shall gird himself, and make them to sit down to meat, and will come forth and serve them.

38 And if he shall come in the second watch, or come in the third watch, and find *them* so, blessed are those servants.

39 And this know, that if the goodman of the house had known what hour the thief would come, he would have watched, and not have suffered his house to be broken through.

40 Be ye therefore ready also: for the Son of man cometh at an hour when ye think not.

Who Is the Faithful Servant?

*T*hen Peter said unto him, Lord, speakest thou this parable unto us, or even to all?

42 And the Lord said, Who then is that faithful and wise steward, whom his lord shall make ruler over his household, to give *them their* portion of meat in due season?

43 Blessed *is* that servant, whom his lord when he cometh shall find so doing.

44 Of a truth I say unto you, that he will make him ruler over all that he hath.

45 But and if that servant say in his heart, My lord delayeth his coming; and shall begin to beat the menservants and maidens, and to eat and drink, and to be drunken;

46 the lord of that servant will come in a day when he looketh not for *him*, and at an hour when he is not aware, and will cut him in sunder, and will appoint him his portion with the unbelievers.

47 And that servant, which knew his lord's will, and prepared not *himself,* neither did according to his will, shall be beaten with many *stripes.*

48 But he that knew not, and did commit things worthy of stripes, shall be beaten with few *stripes.* For unto whomsoever much is given, of him shall be much required; and to whom men have committed much, of him they will ask the more.

Jesus Causes Division

I am come to send fire on the earth; and what will I, if it be already kindled?

50 But I have a baptism to be baptized with; and how am I straitened till it be accomplished!

51 Suppose ye that I am come to give peace on earth? I tell you, Nay; but rather division:

52 for from henceforth there shall be five in one house divided, three against two, and two against three.

53 The father shall be divided against the son, and the son against the father; the mother against the daughter,

and the daughter against the mother; the mother-in-law against her daughter-in-law, and the daughter-in-law against her mother-in-law.

Understanding the Times

*A*nd he said also to the people, When ye see a cloud rise out of the west, straightway ye say, There cometh a shower; and so it is.
⁵⁵ And when *ye see* the south wind blow, ye say, There will be heat; and it cometh to pass.
⁵⁶ *Ye* hypocrites, ye can discern the face of the sky and of the earth; but how is it that ye do not discern this time?

OLD TESTAMENT READING

*T*he earth *is* the LORD's, and the fulness thereof; the world, and they that dwell therein.
² For he hath founded it upon the seas, and established it upon the floods.
³ Who shall ascend into the hill of the LORD? Or who shall stand in his holy place?
⁴ He that hath clean hands, and a pure heart; who hath not lifted up his soul unto vanity, nor sworn deceitfully.
⁵ He shall receive the blessing from the LORD, and righteousness from the God of his salvation.
⁶ This *is* the generation of them that seek him, that seek thy face, O Jacob. Selah.

Psalm 24:1–6

INSIGHTS

*T*he last message the risen Christ gave his people was the promise of his soon return. Couple this with Paul's admonition to the Thessalonian Christians and you get a good rule for life: Live both expectantly and patiently, and you will be fulfilling the Lord's will until he returns.

What are some of the blessings awaiting the believer when Jesus Christ comes back? First of all, the faithful ones can confidently expect to be rewarded for their faithfulness. . . .

There is also a clear-cut promise of reward to the obedient Christian. . . .

But in addition to waiting expectantly, we are also admonished to wait patiently, to "occupy 'til he comes." And while we are waiting, we are to be yielded to the "love of God" operative in our lives. If the love of God flows through us, we will find ourselves sharing that love with those around us, for God is love, and that love is bigger than its container, the Christian, so it must overflow. Those around us long for love, for our world is full of hate, Satan's legacy since the Garden of Eden episode. Let us as Christians share God's love as we await the return of his Son from heaven.

Al Bryant

PAUSE FOR REFLECTION

*W*hat warnings does Jesus give to servants who are not ready for his return? What does he promise to those who are ready? What must your life be like in order to obey Jesus' words to be dressed and ready for service?

WEDNESDAY

Produce Good Fruit
or Be Destroyed

Luke 12:57—13:21

Settle Your Problems

*Y*ea, and why even of yourselves judge ye not what is right?
58 When thou goest with thine adversary to the magistrate, *as thou art* in the way, give diligence that thou mayest be delivered from him; lest he hale thee to the judge, and the judge deliver thee to the officer, and the officer cast thee into prison.
59 I tell thee, thou shalt not depart thence, till thou hast paid the very last mite.

Repent

13 There were present at that season some that told him of the Galileans, whose blood Pilate had mingled with their sacrifices.
2 And Jesus answering said unto them, Suppose ye that these Galileans were sinners above all the Galileans, because they suffered such things?
3 I tell you, Nay: but, except ye repent, ye shall all likewise perish.
4 Or those eighteen, upon whom the tower in Siloam fell, and slew them, think ye that they were sinners above all men that dwelt in Jerusalem?
5 I tell you, Nay: but, except ye repent, ye shall all likewise perish.

The Useless Tree

*H*e spake also this parable; A certain *man* had a fig tree planted in his vineyard; and he came and sought fruit thereon, and found none.
7 Then said he unto the dresser of his vineyard, Behold, these three years I come seeking fruit on this fig tree, and find none: cut it down; why cumbereth it the ground?
8 And he answering said unto him, Lord, let it alone this year also, till I shall dig about it, and dung *it*:
9 and if it bear fruit, *well*: and if not, *then* after that thou shalt cut it down.

Jesus Heals on the Sabbath

*A*nd he was teaching in one of the synagogues on the sabbath.
11 And, behold, there was a woman which had a spirit of infirmity eighteen years, and was bowed together, and could in no wise lift up *herself*.
12 And when Jesus saw her, he called *her to him*, and said unto her, Woman, thou art loosed from thine infirmity.
13 And he laid *his* hands on her: and immediately she was made straight, and glorified God.
14 And the ruler of the synagogue answered with indignation, because that Jesus had healed on the sabbath day, and said unto the people, There are six days in which men ought to work: in them therefore come and be healed, and not on the sabbath day.
15 The Lord then answered him, and said, *Thou* hypocrite, doth not each one of you on the sabbath loose his ox or *his* ass from the stall, and lead *him* away to watering?
16 And ought not this woman, being a daughter of Abraham, whom Satan hath bound, lo, these eighteen years, be loosed from this bond on the sabbath day?

¹⁷And when he had said these things, all his adversaries were ashamed: and all the people rejoiced for all the glorious things that were done by him.

Mustard Seed and Yeast

*T*hen said he, Unto what is the kingdom of God like? and whereunto shall I resemble it?

¹⁹It is like a grain of mustard seed, which a man took, and cast into his garden; and it grew, and waxed a great tree; and the fowls of the air lodged in the branches of it.

²⁰And again he said, Whereunto shall I liken the kingdom of God?

²¹It is like leaven, which a woman took and hid in three measures of meal, till the whole was leavened.

OLD TESTAMENT READING

*F*or the vineyard of the LORD of hosts *is* the house of Israel, and the men of Judah his pleasant plant: and he looked for judgment, but behold oppression; for righteousness, but behold a cry.

¹⁵And the mean man shall be brought down, and the mighty man shall be humbled, and the eyes of the lofty shall be humbled:

¹⁶but the LORD of hosts shall be exalted in judgment and God that is holy shall be sanctified in righteousness.

Isaiah 5:7,15–16

INSIGHTS

*W*e all know what fruit is. The produce of the branch, by which men are refreshed and nourished. The fruit is not for the branch, but for those who come to carry it away. As soon as the fruit is ripe, the branch gives it off, to commence afresh its work of beneficence, and anew prepare its fruit for another season. A fruit-bearing tree lives not for itself, but wholly for those to whom its fruit brings refreshment and life. And so the branch exists only and entirely for the sake of the fruit. To make glad the heart of the husbandman is its object, its safety, and its glory.

Beautiful image of the believer, abiding in Christ! He not only grows in strength, the union with the vine becoming ever surer and firmer, he also bears fruit, yea, much fruit. He has the power to offer that to others of which they can eat and live. Amid all who surround him he becomes like a tree of life, of which they can taste and be refreshed. He is in his circle a centre of life and of blessing, and that simply because he abides in Christ, and receives from Him the Spirit and the life of which he can impart to others. Learn thus, if you would bless others, to abide in Christ, and that if you do abide, you shall surely bless.

Andrew Murray

APPLICATION

*W*hat result did Christ's healing work have on the people? Does he expect anything less from those who follow him? What does he do to nurture his people so they will bear good fruit? What does he promise if they don't? Are you bearing the fruit Christ has prepared you to bear?

THURSDAY
Pride Leads to Dishonor

Luke 13:22—14:14

The Narrow Gate

*A*nd he went through the cities and villages, teaching, and journeying toward Jerusalem.

²³ Then said one unto him, Lord, are there few that be saved? And he said unto them,

²⁴ Strive to enter in at the strait gate: for many, I say unto you, will seek to enter in, and shall not be able.

²⁵ When once the master of the house is risen up, and hath shut to the door, and ye begin to stand without, and to knock at the door, saying, Lord, Lord, open unto us; and he shall answer and say unto you, I know you not whence ye are:

²⁶ then shall ye begin to say, We have eaten and drunk in thy presence, and thou hast taught in our streets.

²⁷ But he shall say, I tell you, I know you not whence ye are; depart from me, all ye workers of iniquity.

²⁸ There shall be weeping and gnashing of teeth, when ye shall see Abraham, and Isaac, and Jacob, and all the prophets, in the kingdom of God, and you *yourselves* thrust out.

²⁹ And they shall come from the east, and *from* the west, and from the north, and *from* the south, and shall sit down in the kingdom of God.

³⁰ And, behold, there are last which shall be first; and there are first which shall be last.

Jesus Will Die in Jerusalem

*T*he same day there came certain of the Pharisees, saying unto him, Get thee out, and depart hence; for Herod will kill thee.

³² And he said unto them, Go ye, and tell that fox, Behold, I cast out devils, and I do cures today and tomorrow, and the third *day* I shall be perfected.

³³ Nevertheless I must walk today, and tomorrow, and the *day* following: for it cannot be that a prophet perish out of Jerusalem.

³⁴ O Jerusalem, Jerusalem, which killest the prophets, and stonest them that are sent unto thee; how often would I have gathered thy children together, as a hen *doth gather* her brood under *her* wings, and ye would not!

³⁵ Behold, your house is left unto you desolate: and verily I say unto you, Ye shall not see me, until *the time* come when ye shall say, Blessed *is* he that cometh in the name of the Lord.

Healing on the Sabbath

14 And it came to pass, as he went into the house of one of the chief Pharisees to eat bread on the sabbath day, that they watched him.

² And, behold, there was a certain man before him which had the dropsy.

³ And Jesus answering spake unto the lawyers and Pharisees, saying, Is it lawful to heal on the sabbath day?

⁴ And they held their peace. And he took *him*, and healed him, and let him go;

⁵ and answered them, saying, Which of you shall have an ass or an ox

fallen into a pit, and will not straight-way pull him out on the sabbath day? ⁶And they could not answer him again to these things.

Be Humble

*A*nd he put forth a parable to those which were bidden, when he marked how they chose out the chief rooms; saying unto them, ⁸When thou art bidden of any *man* to a wedding, sit not down in the high-est room; lest a more honorable man than thou be bidden of him; ⁹and he that bade thee and him come and say to thee, Give this man place; and thou begin with shame to take the lowest room. ¹⁰But when thou art bidden, go and sit down in the lowest room; that when he that bade thee cometh, he may say unto thee, Friend, go up higher: then shalt thou have worship in the presence of them that sit at meat with thee. ¹¹For whosoever exalteth himself shall be abased; and he that hum-bleth himself shall be exalted.

You Will Be Blessed

*T*hen said he also to him that bade him, When thou makest a dinner or a supper, call not thy friends, nor thy brethren, neither thy kinsmen, nor *thy* rich neighbors; lest they also bid thee again, and a recompense be made thee. ¹³But when thou makest a feast, call the poor, the maimed, the lame, the blind: ¹⁴and thou shalt be blessed; for they cannot recompense thee: for thou shalt be recompensed at the resur-rection of the just.

OLD TESTAMENT READING

*S*urely he scorneth the scorners: but he giveth grace unto the lowly.

Proverbs 3:34

INSIGHTS

*G*od does not denigrate pride in its positive sense. The Bible has a hun-dred ways to illustrate the quiet feel-ing of competence that lies behind one's ability to do what he knows he has to do and can do. The apostle Paul's ministry was grounded on the assurance that Christ would help him finish what he had started. If that is what is meant by pride, we should certainly cultivate it and thank God for it. . . .

Pride in the dictionary sense of conceited and overbearing behavior . . . brings out the worst in antiso-cial relationships. . . . All of the major transgressions to inflict woe upon the human race—fear, greed, avarice, cruelty, lust, unbelief—can be traced to runaway pride. . . .

As to whether or not our pride is sin, the answer ultimately rests with each of us. The Christian knows the condition of his own heart. He mea-sures it by the Word of God. Is he at peace? Is his conscience clear? Is he filled with the Spirit? . . . Then his personal life should reflect the mod-est, open, worshipful, loving stance of a humble creature of God who has been in the presence of his Creator.

Sherwood Wirt

PAUSE FOR REFLECTION

*W*hy does God so detest pride? Why is humility necessary in the lives of those who belong to God?

FRIDAY

Count the Cost
of Serving Christ

Luke 14:15—15:10

A Parable About a Banquet

*A*nd when one of them that sat at meat with him heard these things, he said unto him, Blessed *is* he that shall eat bread in the kingdom of God.

¹⁶ Then said he unto him, A certain man made a great supper, and bade many:

¹⁷ and sent his servant at supper time to say to them that were bidden, Come; for all things are now ready.

¹⁸ And they all with one *consent* began to make excuse. The first said unto him, I have bought a piece of ground, and I must needs go and see it: I pray thee have me excused.

¹⁹ And another said, I have bought five yoke of oxen, and I go to prove them: I pray thee have me excused.

²⁰ And another said, I have married a wife, and therefore I cannot come.

²¹ So that servant came, and showed his lord these things. Then the master of the house being angry said to his servant, Go out quickly into the streets and lanes of the city, and bring in hither the poor, and the maimed, and the halt, and the blind.

²² And the servant said, Lord, it is done as thou hast commanded, and yet there is room.

²³ And the lord said unto the servant, Go out into the highways and hedges, and compel *them* to come in, that my house may be filled.

²⁴ For I say unto you, That none of those men which were bidden shall taste of my supper.

The Cost of Being Jesus' Disciple

*A*nd there went great multitudes with him: and he turned, and said unto them,

²⁶ If any *man* come to me, and hate not his father, and mother, and wife, and children, and brethren, and sisters, yea, and his own life also, he cannot be my disciple.

²⁷ And whosoever doth not bear his cross, and come after me, cannot be my disciple.

²⁸ For which of you, intending to build a tower, sitteth not down first, and counteth the cost, whether he have *sufficient* to finish *it*?

²⁹ Lest haply, after he hath laid the foundation, and is not able to finish *it*, all that behold *it* begin to mock him,

³⁰ saying, This man began to build, and was not able to finish.

³¹ Or what king, going to make war against another king, sitteth not down first, and consulteth whether he be able with ten thousand to meet him that cometh against him with twenty thousand?

³² Or else, while the other is yet a great way off, he sendeth an ambassage, and desireth conditions of peace.

³³ So likewise, whosoever he be of you that forsaketh not all that he hath, he cannot be my disciple.

Don't Lose Your Influence

*S*alt *is* good: but if the salt have lost his savor, wherewith shall it be seasoned?

³⁵ It is neither fit for the land, nor yet for the dunghill; *but* men cast it out. He that hath ears to hear, let him hear.

A Lost Sheep, a Lost Coin

15 Then drew near unto him all the publicans and sinners for to hear him.

[2] And the Pharisees and scribes murmured, saying, This man receiveth sinners, and eateth with them.

[3] And he spake this parable unto them, saying,

[4] What man of you, having a hundred sheep, if he lose one of them, doth not leave the ninety and nine in the wilderness, and go after that which is lost, until he find it?

[5] And when he hath found *it*, he layeth *it* on his shoulders, rejoicing.

[6] And when he cometh home, he calleth together *his* friends and neighbors, saying unto them, Rejoice with me; for I have found my sheep which was lost.

[7] I say unto you, that likewise joy shall be in heaven over one sinner that repenteth, more than over ninety and nine just persons, which need no repentance.

[8] Either what woman having ten pieces of silver, if she lose one piece, doth not light a candle, and sweep the house, and seek diligently till she find *it*?

[9] And when she hath found it, she calleth *her* friends and *her* neighbors together, saying, Rejoice with me; for I have found the piece which I had lost.

[10] Likewise, I say unto you, there is joy in the presence of the angels of God over one sinner that repenteth.

ful to answer thee in this matter.

[17] If it be *so*, our God whom we serve is able to deliver us from the burning fiery furnace, and he will deliver *us* out of thine hand, O king.

[18] But if not, be it known unto thee, O king, that we will not serve thy gods, nor worship the golden image which thou hast set up.

Daniel 3:16–18

INSIGHTS

The Christian faith brings its own "blood, sweat and tears" to those who would follow Jesus Christ. Christ calls us to discipleship. When we come to Him, He takes away one set of burdens—the burden of sin, the burden of guilt, the burden of separation from God, the burden of hopelessness. But He also calls upon us to "Take my yoke upon you and learn from me" (Matthew 11:29). It is not a yoke that is too heavy for us to bear, for Christ bears it with us: "For my yoke is easy and my burden is light" (Matthew 11:30). Nevertheless, Christ calls us to follow Him, regardless of the cost, and He has never promised that our path will always be smooth. . . .

But in the midst of the suffering, trials and temptations, He will provide His peace, joy and fellowship. . . . In the midst of every situation of life He can give an inner calm and strength that you could never imagine apart from Him.

Billy Graham

OLD TESTAMENT READING

Shadrach, Meshach and Abednego, answered and said to the king, O Nebuchadnezzar, we *are* not care-

APPLICATION

What might it cost you to serve Christ? Are you willing to pay that price?

WEEKEND

*God Welcomes All
Who Come to Him*

Luke 15:11—16:8

The Son Who Left Home

And he said, A certain man had two sons:

[12] and the younger of them said to *his* father, Father, give me the portion of goods that falleth *to me*. And he divided unto them *his* living.

[13] And not many days after the younger son gathered all together, and took his journey into a far country, and there wasted his substance with riotous living.

[14] And when he had spent all, there arose a mighty famine in that land; and he began to be in want.

[15] And he went and joined himself to a citizen of that country; and he sent him into his fields to feed swine.

[16] And he would fain have filled his belly with the husks that the swine did eat: and no man gave unto him.

[17] And when he came to himself, he said, How many hired servants of my father's have bread enough and to spare, and I perish with hunger!

[18] I will arise and go to my father, and will say unto him, Father, I have sinned against heaven, and before thee,

[19] and am no more worthy to be called thy son: make me as one of thy hired servants.

[20] And he arose, and came to his father. But when he was yet a great way off, his father saw him, and had compassion, and ran, and fell on his neck, and kissed him.

[21] And the son said unto him, Father, I have sinned against heaven, and in thy sight, and am no more worthy to be called thy son.

[22] But the father said to his servants, Bring forth the best robe, and put *it* on him; and put a ring on his hand, and shoes on *his* feet:

[23] and bring hither the fatted calf, and kill *it*; and let us eat, and be merry:

[24] for this my son was dead, and is alive again; he was lost, and is found. And they began to be merry.

[25] Now his elder son was in the field: and as he came and drew nigh to the house, he heard musick and dancing.

[26] And he called one of the servants, and asked what these things meant.

[27] And he said unto him, Thy brother is come; and thy father hath killed the fatted calf, because he hath received him safe and sound.

[28] And he was angry, and would not go in: therefore came his father out, and intreated him.

[29] And he answering said to *his* father, Lo, these many years do I serve thee, neither transgressed I at any time thy commandment; and yet thou never gavest me a kid, that I might make merry with my friends:

[30] but as soon as this thy son was come, which hath devoured thy living with harlots, thou hast killed for him the fatted calf.

[31] And he said unto him, Son, thou art ever with me, and all that I have is thine.

[32] It was meet that we should make merry, and be glad: for this thy brother was dead, and is alive again; and was lost, and is found.

True Wealth

16 And he said also unto his disciples, There was a certain rich man, which had a steward; and the same was accused unto him that he had wasted his goods.

2 And he called him, and said unto him, How is it that I hear this of thee? give an account of thy stewardship; for thou mayest be no longer steward.

3 Then the steward said within himself, What shall I do? for my lord taketh away from me the stewardship: I cannot dig; to beg I am ashamed.

4 I am resolved what to do, that, when I am put out of the stewardship, they may receive me into their houses.

5 So he called every one of his lord's debtors *unto him*, and said unto the first, How much owest thou unto my lord?

6 And he said, A hundred measures of oil. And he said unto him, Take thy bill, and sit down quickly, and write fifty.

7 Then said he to another, And how much owest thou? And he said, A hundred measures of wheat. And he said unto him, Take thy bill, and write fourscore.

8 And the lord commended the unjust steward, because he had done wisely: for the children of this world are in their generation wiser than the children of light.

OLD TESTAMENT READING

*I*f the wicked restore the pledge, give again that he had robbed, walk in the statutes of life, without committing iniquity; he shall surely live, he shall not die.

Ezekiel 33:15

INSIGHTS

*R*epentance is a rather dramatic word. It refers to the act of traveling in one direction and then suddenly changing to go the opposite way. Both John the Baptizer and Jesus used repentance as the centerpoint of their teaching because they were talking to a generation of people whose personal worlds were terribly broken. . . .

Repentance is activated, first, in the act of confession: the candid acknowledgment before God, and perhaps to others, that one has sinned and is in need of forgiveness. Both by example and by teaching, the Scriptures place a high priority on confessing, for in so doing, one actually reveals the secrets of the heart. And until the heart is voluntarily opened up, the process of rebuilding a broken world cannot begin. . . .

. . . Restoration looks to the damage done in a broken-world experience and asks how it can be repaired. . . . Forgiveness must be requested and granted, and that requires people to come together and offer mercy and grace to one another. These are not simple or easy things to give. . . .

But restoration is one of the unique acts of the Christian community. In the final analysis, it cannot be demanded or even earned by the broken-world person; it must be freely given as God once freely gave grace to whoever wished to receive it.

Gordon MacDonald

PAUSE FOR REFLECTION

*W*hat does God promise to those who confess and reject their sins? Is repentance a one-time or ongoing action? How freely do you extend mercy to restore repentant sinners?

MONDAY

God Knows Our Hearts

Luke 16:9—17:4

*A*nd I say unto you, Make to yourselves friends of the mammon of unrighteousness; that, when ye fail, they may receive you into everlasting habitations.

[10] He that is faithful in that which is least is faithful also in much: and he that is unjust in the least is unjust also in much.

[11] If therefore ye have not been faithful in the unrighteous mammon, who will commit to your trust the true *riches*?

[12] And if ye have not been faithful in that which is another man's, who shall give you that which is your own?

[13] No servant can serve two masters: for either he will hate the one, and love the other; or else he will hold to the one, and despise the other. Ye cannot serve God and mammon.

God's Law Cannot Be Changed

*A*nd the Pharisees also, who were covetous, heard all these things: and they derided him.

[15] And he said unto them, Ye are they which justify yourselves before men; but God knoweth your hearts: for that which is highly esteemed among men is abomination in the sight of God.

[16] The law and the prophets *were* until John: since that time the kingdom of God is preached, and every man presseth into it.

[17] And it is easier for heaven and earth to pass, than one tittle of the law to fail.

Divorce and Remarriage

*W*hosoever putteth away his wife, and marrieth another, committeth adultery: and whosoever marrieth her that is put away from *her* husband committeth adultery.

The Rich Man and Lazarus

*T*here was a certain rich man, which was clothed in purple and fine linen, and fared sumptuously every day:

[20] and there was a certain beggar named Lazarus, which was laid at his gate, full of sores,

[21] and desiring to be fed with the crumbs which fell from the rich man's table: moreover the dogs came and licked his sores.

[22] And it came to pass, that the beggar died, and was carried by the angels into Abraham's bosom: the rich man also died, and was buried;

[23] and in hell he lift up his eyes, being in torments, and seeth Abraham afar off, and Lazarus in his bosom.

[24] And he cried and said, Father Abraham, have mercy on me, and send Lazarus, that he may dip the tip of his finger in water, and cool my tongue; for I am tormented in this flame.

[25] But Abraham said, Son, remember that thou in thy lifetime receivedst thy good things, and likewise Lazarus evil things: but now he is comforted, and thou art tormented.

[26] And beside all this, between us and you there is a great gulf fixed: so that they which would pass from hence to you cannot; neither can they pass

to us, that *would come* from thence.
²⁷ Then he said, I pray thee therefore, father, that thou wouldest send him to my father's house:

²⁸ for I have five brethren; that he may testify unto them, lest they also come into this place of torment.

²⁹ Abraham saith unto him, They have Moses and the prophets; let them hear them.

³⁰ And he said, Nay, father Abraham: but if one went unto them from the dead, they will repent.

³¹ And he said unto him, If they hear not Moses and the prophets, neither will they be persuaded, though one rose from the dead.

Sin and Forgiveness

17 Then said he unto the disciples, It is impossible but that offenses will come: but woe *unto him*, through whom they come!

² It were better for him that a millstone were hanged about his neck, and he cast into the sea, than that he should offend one of these little ones.

³ Take heed to yourselves: If thy brother trespass against thee, rebuke him; and if he repent, forgive him.

⁴ And if he trespass against thee seven times in a day, and seven times in a day turn again to thee, saying, I repent; thou shalt forgive him

OLD TESTAMENT READING

Search me, O God, and know my heart: try me, and know my thoughts:
²⁴ and see if *there be any* wicked way in me, and lead me in the way everlasting.

Psalm 139:23–24

INSIGHTS

Making good judgments in this world is sometimes a hit-and-miss proposition. Often we fail. In baseball, a hitter is constantly trying to guess what the pitcher will throw next. In football, a defensive coach tries to predict where the offense will run next. Basketball coaches continually try to outmaneuver each other. Sometimes they are right, and sometimes they are wrong. We fail because we seldom have all the facts. We have no idea what the other person is thinking. . . . We don't know all the facts, we don't know the future, and sometimes we don't even react properly when we do know! But with God, life is not a guessing game. . . . God knows everything about us. He knows our thoughts before we think them (Psalm 139:1–6). No one can escape His sight (Psalm 139:7–12). He even judges the thoughts and intentions of our hearts (Hebrews 4:12–13). God's judgment is always perfect, because He knows all the facts. Those who think they are getting away with something may escape our notice, but they will never escape the notice of God. The eyes of the Lord are in every place, watching the evil and the good (Proverbs 15:3). Take comfort, righteous ones, for goodness will be vindicated and evil will be punished!

Elliot Johnson / Al Schierbaum

ACTION POINT

Pray that God's knowledge of you will lead you closer to him. Take comfort that he not only knows you, but loves you!

TUESDAY

*When God's Judgment Comes,
There Will Be No
Turning Back*

Luke 17:5–37

Faith Like a Mustard Seed

*A*nd the apostles said unto the Lord, Increase our faith.

6 And the Lord said, If ye had faith as a grain of mustard seed, ye might say unto this sycamine tree, Be thou plucked up by the root, and be thou planted in the sea; and it should obey you.

Be Good Servants

*B*ut which of you, having a servant plowing or feeding cattle, will say unto him by and by, when he is come from the field, Go and sit down to meat?

8 and will not rather say unto him, Make ready wherewith I may sup, and gird thyself, and serve me, till I have eaten and drunken; and afterward thou shalt eat and drink?

9 Doth he thank that servant because he did the things that were commanded him? I trow not.

10 So likewise ye, when ye shall have done all those things which are commanded you, say, We are unprofitable servants: we have done that which was our duty to do.

Be Thankful

*A*nd it came to pass, as he went to Jerusalem, that he passed through the midst of Samaria and Galilee.

12 And as he entered into a certain village, there met him ten men that were lepers, which stood afar off:

13 and they lifted up *their* voices, and said, Jesus, Master, have mercy on us.

14 And when he saw *them*, he said unto them, Go show yourselves unto the priests. And it came to pass, that, as they went, they were cleansed.

15 And one of them, when he saw that he was healed, turned back, and with a loud voice glorified God,

16 and fell down on *his* face at his feet, giving him thanks: and he was a Samaritan.

17 And Jesus answering said, Were there not ten cleansed? but where *are* the nine?

18 There are not found that returned to give glory to God, save this stranger.

19 And he said unto him, Arise, go thy way: thy faith hath made thee whole.

God's Kingdom Is Within You

*A*nd when he was demanded of the Pharisees, when the kingdom of God should come, he answered them and said, The kingdom of God cometh not with observation:

21 neither shall they say, Lo here! or, lo there! for, behold, the kingdom of God is within you.

22 And he said unto the disciples, The days will come, when ye shall desire to see one of the days of the Son of man, and ye shall not see *it*.

23 And they shall say to you, See here; or, see there: go not after *them,* nor follow *them.*

24 For as the lightning, that lighteneth out of the one *part* under heaven, shineth unto the other *part* under heaven; so shall also the Son of man be in his day.

When Jesus Comes Again

*B*ut first must he suffer many things, and be rejected of this generation.

²⁶ And as it was in the days of Noah, so shall it be also in the days of the Son of man.

²⁷ They did eat, they drank, they married wives, they were given in marriage, until the day that Noah entered into the ark, and the flood came, and destroyed them all.

²⁸ Likewise also as it was in the days of Lot; they did eat, they drank, they bought, they sold, they planted, they builded;

²⁹ but the same day that Lot went out of Sodom it rained fire and brimstone from heaven, and destroyed *them* all.

³⁰ Even thus shall it be in the day when the Son of man is revealed.

³¹ In that day, he which shall be upon the housetop, and his stuff in the house, let him not come down to take it away: and he that is in the field, let him likewise not return back.

³² Remember Lot's wife.

³³ Whosoever shall seek to save his life shall lose it; and whosoever shall lose his life shall preserve it.

³⁴ I tell you, in that night there shall be two *men* in one bed; the one shall be taken, and the other shall be left.

³⁵ Two *women* shall be grinding together; the one shall be taken, and the other left.

³⁶ Two *men* shall be in the field; the one shall be taken, and the other left.

³⁷ And they answered and said unto him, Where, Lord? And he said unto them, Wheresoever the body *is*, thither will the eagles be gathered together.

OLD TESTAMENT READING

*A*nd the men said unto Lot, Hast thou here any besides? son-in-law, and thy sons, and thy daughters, and whatsoever thou hast in the city, bring *them* out of this place:

¹³ for we will destroy this place, because the cry of them is waxen great before the face of the LORD; and the LORD hath sent us to destroy it.

Genesis 19:12–13

INSIGHTS

*I*n John's vision . . . you will get a feeling for the absolute horror of this final judgment for those who do not believe. Picture it. Carefully the Lamb opens the sixth seal (Revelation 6:12–17). Suddenly, chaos grips the universe. An earthquake shakes the entire world, no Richter scale could measure its fury. There is a complete eclipse of the sun. . . .

The world is trembling with terror. The great cities collapse. John sees kings, princes, generals; the rich, the mighty, slave and free—every human being left on the earth running to escape the horror of God's final judgment. They flee to mountain caves. They cower behind rocks and boulders. But there is no escape. . . .

There will be a day of reckoning when God closes His books on time and judges every creature, living and dead.

Billy Graham

APPLICATION

*H*ow does Jesus' warning about his coming judgment affect your everyday life?

WEDNESDAY

*Trust in God,
Not in Pride or Riches*

Luke 18:1–25

God Will Avenge His People

18 And he spake a parable unto them *to this end*, that men ought always to pray, and not to faint; [2] saying, There was in a city a judge, which feared not God, neither regarded man:

[3] and there was a widow in that city; and she came unto him, saying, Avenge me of mine adversary.

[4] And he would not for a while: but afterward he said within himself, Though I fear not God, nor regard man;

[5] yet because this widow troubleth me, I will avenge her, lest by her continual coming she weary me.

[6] And the Lord said, Hear what the unjust judge saith.

[7] And shall not God avenge his own elect, which cry day and night unto him, though he bear long with them?

[8] I tell you that he will avenge them speedily. Nevertheless, when the Son of man cometh, shall he find faith on the earth?

The Pharisee and the Publican

And he spake this parable unto certain which trusted in themselves that they were righteous, and despised others:

[10] Two men went up into the temple to pray; the one a Pharisee, and the other a publican.

[11] The Pharisee stood and prayed thus with himself, God, I thank thee, that I am not as other men *are*, extortioners, unjust, adulterers, or even as this publican.

[12] I fast twice in the week, I give tithes of all that I possess.

[13] And the publican, standing afar off, would not lift up so much as *his* eyes unto heaven, but smote upon his breast, saying, God be merciful to me a sinner.

[14] I tell you, this man went down to his house justified *rather* than the other: for every one that exalteth himself shall be abased; and he that humbleth himself shall be exalted.

Who Will Enter God's Kingdom?

And they brought unto him also infants, that he would touch them: but when *his* disciples saw *it*, they rebuked them.

[16] But Jesus called them *unto him*, and said, Suffer little children to come unto me, and forbid them not: for of such is the kingdom of God.

[17] Verily I say unto you, Whosoever shall not receive the kingdom of God as a little child shall in no wise enter therein.

A Rich Man's Question

And a certain ruler asked him, saying, Good Master, what shall I do to inherit eternal life?

[19] And Jesus said unto him, Why callest thou me good? none *is* good, save one, *that is*, God.

[20] Thou knowest the commandments, Do not commit adultery, Do not kill, Do not steal, Do not bear false witness, Honor thy father and thy mother.

[21] And he said, All these have I kept from my youth up.

²² Now when Jesus heard these things, he said unto him, Yet lackest thou one thing: sell all that thou hast, and distribute unto the poor, and thou shalt have treasure in heaven: and come, follow me.

²³ And when he heard this, he was very sorrowful: for he was very rich.

²⁴ And when Jesus saw that he was very sorrowful, he said, How hardly shall they that have riches enter into the kingdom of God!

²⁵ For it is easier for a camel to go through a needle's eye, than for a rich man to enter into the kingdom of God.

OLD TESTAMENT READING

*T*hus saith the LORD, Let not the wise *man* glory in his wisdom, neither let the mighty *man* glory in his might, let not the rich *man* glory in his riches:

²⁴ but let him that glorieth glory in this, that he understandeth and knoweth me, that I *am* the LORD which exercise loving-kindness, judgment, and righteousness, in the earth: for in these things I delight, saith the LORD.

Jeremiah 9:23–24

INSIGHTS

*T*o receive what we have as a gift from God is the first inner attitude of simplicity. We work but we know that it is not our work that gives us what we have. We live by grace even when it comes to "daily bread." We are dependent upon God for the simplest elements of life: air, water, sun. What we have is not the result of our labor, but of the gracious care of God. When we are tempted to think that what we own is the result of our personal efforts, it takes only a little drought or a small accident to show us once again how utterly dependent we are for everything.

To know that it is God's business, and not ours, to care for what we have is the second inner attitude of simplicity. God is able to protect what we possess. We can trust him. . . . Obviously, these matters are not restricted to possessions but include such things as our reputation and our employment. Simplicity means the freedom to trust God for these (and all) things.

To have our goods available to others marks the third inner attitude of simplicity. If our goods are not available to the community when it is clearly right and good, then they are stolen goods. . . . We cling to our possessions rather than sharing them because we are anxious about tomorrow. But if we truly believe that God is who Jesus says he is, then we do not need to be afraid. When we come to see God as the almighty Creator and our loving Father, we can share because we know that he will care for us. . . .

When we are seeking first the kingdom of God, these three attitudes will characterize our lives. Taken together they define what Jesus means by "do not be anxious." They comprise the inner reality of Christian simplicity.

Richard Foster

APPLICATION

*W*hat great risk do we face when our hearts are focused on our abilities, goodness, strength, or riches? What is the next step for you to take in trusting God?

THURSDAY

When God Changes
Our Hearts,
Our Actions Change, Too

Luke 18:26—19:10

Who Can Be Saved?

*A*nd they that heard *it* said, Who then can be saved?

²⁷ And he said, The things which are impossible with men are possible with God.

²⁸ Then Peter said, Lo, we have left all, and followed thee.

²⁹ And he said unto them, Verily I say unto you, There is no man that hath left house, or parents, or brethren, or wife, or children, for the kingdom of God's sake,

³⁰ who shall not receive manifold more in this present time, and in the world to come life everlasting.

Jesus Will Rise
from the Dead

*T*hen he took *unto him* the twelve, and said unto them, Behold, we go up to Jerusalem, and all things that are written by the prophets concerning the Son of man shall be accomplished.

³² For he shall be delivered unto the Gentiles, and shall be mocked, and spitefully entreated, and spitted on:

³³ and they shall scourge *him*, and put him to death: and the third day he shall rise again.

³⁴ And they understood none of these things: and this saying was hid from them, neither knew they the things which were spoken.

Jesus Heals a Blind Man

*A*nd it came to pass, that as he was come nigh unto Jericho, a certain blind man sat by the way side begging:

³⁶ and hearing the multitude pass by, he asked what it meant.

³⁷ And they told him, that Jesus of Nazareth passeth by.

³⁸ And he cried, saying, Jesus, *thou* Son of David, have mercy on me.

³⁹ And they which went before rebuked him, that he should hold his peace: but he cried so much the more, *Thou* Son of David, have mercy on me.

⁴⁰ And Jesus stood, and commanded him to be brought unto him: and when he was come near, he asked him,

⁴¹ saying, What wilt thou that I shall do unto thee? And he said, Lord, that I may receive my sight.

⁴² And Jesus said unto him, Receive thy sight: thy faith hath saved thee.

⁴³ And immediately he received his sight, and followed him, glorifying God: and all the people, when they saw *it*, gave praise unto God.

Zaccheus Meets Jesus

19 And *Jesus* entered and passed through Jericho.

² And, behold, *there was* a man named Zaccheus, which was the chief among the publicans, and he was rich.

³ And he sought to see Jesus who he was; and could not for the press, because he was little of stature.

⁴ And he ran before, and climbed up into a sycamore tree to see him; for he was to pass that *way*.

⁵ And when Jesus came to the place, he looked up, and saw him, and said unto him, Zaccheus, make haste,

and come down; for today I must abide at thy house.

⁶ And he made haste, and came down, and received him joyfully.

⁷ And when they saw *it*, they all murmured, saying, That he was gone to be guest with a man that is a sinner.

⁸ And Zaccheus stood, and said unto the Lord; Behold, Lord, the half of my goods I give to the poor; and if I have taken any thing from any man by false accusation, I restore *him* fourfold.

⁹ And Jesus said unto him, This day is salvation come to this house, forsomuch as he also is a son of Abraham.

¹⁰ For the Son of man is come to seek and to save that which was lost.

OLD TESTAMENT READING

*A*nd Jonah began to enter into the city a day's journey, and he cried, and said, Yet forty days, and Nineveh shall be overthrown.

⁵ So the people of Nineveh believed God, and proclaimed a fast, and put on sackcloth, from the greatest of them even to the least of them.

¹⁰ And God saw their works, that they turned from their evil way; and God repented of the evil, that he had said that he would do unto them; and he did *it* not.

Jonah 3:4–5, 10

INSIGHTS

*T*rue repentance occurs when we begin to see sin from God's point of view—when we see the way our sin has broken his heart. Perhaps the idea that God's heart can be broken by our sin is new to you. In Genesis 6:5–6 we are told, "Then the LORD saw that the wickedness of man was great on the earth, and that every intent of the thoughts of his heart was only evil continually. And the LORD was sorry that he had made man on the earth, and he was grieved in his heart" (NASB). God was so disappointed with what he saw that there was a grief or sorrow in his heart.

Jesus also was brokenhearted as he wept over Jerusalem. "O Jerusalem, Jerusalem, you who kill the prophets and stone those sent to you, how often I have longed to gather your children together, as a hen gathers her chicks under her wings, but you were not willing!" (Lk 13:34). God's heart aches over our sin. It alienates us from him and from our fellow believers.

If we want to have victory over sin and turn our lives wholeheartedly over to God, then we must see our sin from God's perspective. No sermon on hell can ever change a person's heart like seeing the grief sin has brought to the heart of the One who created us. We must ask God to show us what our sin does to him. As we do this and begin to understand his great love for us, despite how much we have hurt and grieved his heart, turning away from that sin is the natural thing to do. This is the test of our sincerity and of the level of our desperation to be right with God.

Floyd McClung

ACTION POINT

*D*o you think the people mentioned in these passages recognized that their sin grieved God? What in your life grieves God? Will you turn away from it—today?

FRIDAY

God Will Reward the Righteous and Punish Those Who Don't Serve Him

Luke 19:11–40

A Parable About Three Servants

*A*nd as they heard these things, he added and spake a parable, because he was nigh to Jerusalem, and because they thought that the kingdom of God should immediately appear.

¹² He said therefore, A certain nobleman went into a far country to receive for himself a kingdom, and to return.

¹³ And he called his ten servants, and delivered them ten pounds, and said unto them, Occupy till I come.

¹⁴ But his citizens hated him, and sent a message after him, saying, We will not have this *man* to reign over us.

¹⁵ And it came to pass, that when he was returned, having received the kingdom, then he commanded these servants to be called unto him, to whom he had given the money, that he might know how much every man had gained by trading.

¹⁶ Then came the first, saying, Lord, thy pound hath gained ten pounds.

¹⁷ And he said unto him, Well, thou good servant: because thou hast been faithful in a very little, have thou authority over ten cities.

¹⁸ And the second came, saying, Lord, thy pound hath gained five pounds.

¹⁹ And he said likewise to him, Be thou also over five cities.

²⁰ And another came, saying, Lord, behold, *here is* thy pound, which I have kept laid up in a napkin:

²¹ for I feared thee, because thou art an austere man: thou takest up that thou layedst not down, and reapest that thou didst not sow.

²² And he saith unto him, Out of thine own mouth will I judge thee, *thou* wicked servant. Thou knewest that I was an austere man, taking up that I laid not down, and reaping that I did not sow:

²³ wherefore then gavest not thou my money into the bank, that at my coming I might have required mine own with usury?

²⁴ And he said unto them that stood by, Take from him the pound, and give *it* to him that hath ten pounds.

²⁵ (And they said unto him, Lord, he hath ten pounds.)

²⁶ For I say unto you, That unto every one which hath shall be given; and from him that hath not, even that he hath shall be taken away from him.

²⁷ But those mine enemies, which would not that I should reign over them, bring hither, and slay *them* before me.

Jesus Enters Jerusalem as a King

*A*nd when he had thus spoken, he went before, ascending up to Jerusalem.

²⁹ And it came to pass, when he was come nigh to Bethphage and Bethany, at the mount called *the mount* of Olives, he sent two of his disciples,

³⁰ Saying, Go ye into the village over against *you*; in the which at your entering ye shall find a colt tied, whereon yet never man sat: loose him, and bring *him hither*.

³¹ And if any man ask you, Why do ye loose *him*? thus shall ye say unto him, Because the Lord hath need of him.

32 And they that were sent went their way, and found even as he had said unto them.

33 And as they were loosing the colt, the owners thereof said unto them, Why loose ye the colt?

34 And they said, The Lord hath need of him.

35 And they brought him to Jesus: and they cast their garments upon the colt, and they set Jesus thereon.

36 And as he went, they spread their clothes in the way.

37 And when he was come nigh, even now at the descent of the mount of Olives, the whole multitude of the disciples began to rejoice and praise God with a loud voice for all the mighty works that they had seen;

38 saying, Blessed *be* the King that cometh in the name of the Lord: peace in heaven, and glory in the highest.

39 And some of the Pharisees from among the multitude said unto him, Master, rebuke thy disciples.

40 And he answered and said unto them, I tell you that, if these should hold their peace, the stones would immediately cry out.

OLD TESTAMENT READING

A man shall be satisfied with good by the fruit of *his* mouth: and the recompense of a man's hands shall be rendered unto him.

Proverbs 12:14

*S*ay ye to the righteous, that it shall *be* well *with him*: for they shall eat the fruit of their doings.

11 Woe unto the wicked! *it shall be* ill with *him*: for the reward of his hands shall be given him.

Isaiah 3:10–11

INSIGHTS

*H*ow does free forgiveness and justification by faith square with judgment according to works? The answer seems to be as follows. First, the gift of justification certainly shields believers from being condemned and banished from God's presence as sinners. This appears from the vision of judgment in Revelation 20:11–15, where alongside 'the books' recording each man's work 'the book of life' is opened, and those whose names are written there are not 'cast into the lake of fire' as the rest of men are. But, second, the gift of justification does not at all shield believers from being assessed as Christians, and from forfeiting good which others will enjoy if it turns out that as Christians they have been slack, mischievous and destructive. This appears from Paul's warning to the Corinthians to be careful what life-style they build on Christ, the one foundation. 'If any man builds upon this foundation . . . If any man's work abide . . . he shall receive a reward. If any man's work shall be burned, he shall suffer loss: but he himself shall be saved; yet so as by fire' (1 Corinthians 3:12–15). 'Reward' and 'loss' signify an enriched or impoverished relationship with God, though in what ways it is beyond our present power to know.*

J. I. Packer

APPLICATION

*W*hat do you think God expects his servants to do while they wait for his return? How can you be a better servant?*

WEEKEND

God Punishes Sin

Luke 19:41—20:19

Jesus Weeps for Jerusalem

*A*nd when he was come near, he beheld the city, and wept over it,

[42] saying, If thou hadst known, even thou, at least in this thy day, the things *which belong* unto thy peace! but now they are hid from thine eyes.

[43] For the days shall come upon thee, that thine enemies shall cast a trench about thee, and compass thee round, and keep thee in on every side,

[44] and shall lay thee even with the ground, and thy children within thee; and they shall not leave in thee one stone upon another; because thou knewest not the time of thy visitation.

Jesus Goes to the Temple

*A*nd he went into the temple, and began to cast out them that sold therein, and them that bought;

[46] saying unto them, It is written, My house is the house of prayer; but ye have made it a den of thieves.

[47] And he taught daily in the temple. But the chief priests and the scribes and the chief of the people sought to destroy him,

[48] and could not find what they might do: for all the people were very attentive to hear him.

Jewish Leaders Question Jesus

20 And it came to pass, *that* on one of those days, as he taught the people in the temple, and preached the gospel, the chief priests and the scribes came upon *him* with the elders,

[2] and spake unto him, saying, Tell us, by what authority doest thou these things? or who is he that gave thee this authority?

[3] And he answered and said unto them, I will also ask you one thing; and answer me:

[4] The baptism of John, was it from heaven, or of men?

[5] And they reasoned with themselves, saying, If we shall say, From heaven; he will say, Why then believed ye him not?

[6] But and if we say, Of men; all the people will stone us: for they be persuaded that John was a prophet.

[7] And they answered, that they could not tell whence *it was*.

[8] And Jesus said unto them, Neither tell I you by what authority I do these things.

A Parable About God's Son

*T*hen began he to speak to the people this parable; A certain man planted a vineyard, and let it forth to husbandmen, and went into a far country for a long time.

[10] And at the season he sent a servant to the husbandmen, that they should give him of the fruit of the vineyard: but the husbandmen beat him, and sent *him* away empty.

[11] And again he sent another servant: and they beat him also, and entreated *him* shamefully, and sent *him* away empty.

[12] And again he sent a third: and they wounded him also, and cast *him* out.

[13] Then said the lord of the vineyard, What shall I do? I will send my be-

loved son: it may be they will reverence *him* when they see him.

¹⁴ But when the husbandmen saw him, they reasoned among themselves, saying, This is the heir: come, let us kill him, that the inheritance may be ours.

¹⁵ So they cast him out of the vineyard, and killed *him*. What therefore shall the lord of the vineyard do unto them?

¹⁶ He shall come and destroy these husbandmen, and shall give the vineyard to others. And when they heard *it*, they said, God forbid.

¹⁷ And he beheld them, and said, What is this then that is written, The stone which the builders rejected, the same is become the head of the corner?

¹⁸ Whosoever shall fall upon that stone shall be broken; but on whomsoever it shall fall, it will grind him to powder.

¹⁹ And the chief priests and the scribes the same hour sought to lay hands on him; and they feared the people: for they perceived that he had spoken this parable against them.

OLD TESTAMENT READING

*H*ear the word of the LORD, ye rulers of Sodom; give ear unto the law of our God, ye people of Gomorrah. ¹⁵ᵇ Yea, when ye make many prayers, I will not hear: your hands are full of blood. ¹⁶ Wash ye, make you clean; put away the evil of your doings from before mine eyes; cease to do evil.

Isaiah 1:10, 15b–16

INSIGHTS

*J*esus did not come to change Israel's politics, He came to change men's hearts. When He rode into Jerusalem, Jesus presented Himself as a humble king, not a violent conqueror. Led by the spiritually blind rulers, the nation rejected Him and said, "We have no king but Caesar!"

What were the consequences of this rebellion? In a few years, Jerusalem was reduced to shambles by the Roman armies and the temple was destroyed. The Jewish nation was dispersed across the face of the earth to wander "many days, without a king, and without a prince" (Hosea 3:4).

But there is a much wider application. When the Lord returns, he will have to punish those who will not bow before Him and submit to His will. . . .

Sad to say, most of the people in our world want nothing to do with Jesus Christ. "There is none that understandeth, there is none that seeketh after God" (Rom. 3:11). But God is seeking after men! "For the Son of man is come to seek and to save that which was lost." . . .

When the Lord returns, it will mean reward for the faithful, loss of reward for the unfaithful, and terrible judgment for the unbelieving, rebellious people who rejected Him. . . (2 Thes. 1:8–9).

Warren Wiersbe

APPLICATION

*J*erusalem is identified in Scripture as God's holy city. For what reasons did Jesus weep over it? In a broader sense, what does this scene reveal about how Jesus views sin? Does Jesus weep or rejoice over the condition of your heart?

MONDAY

Jesus Warns Against False Religious Leaders

Luke 20:20–47

To Pay Tribute or Not?

*A*nd they watched *him*, and sent forth spies, which should feign themselves just men, that they might take hold of his words, that so they might deliver him unto the power and authority of the governor. [21] And they asked him, saying, Master, we know that thou sayest and teachest rightly, neither acceptest thou the person *of any*, but teachest the way of God truly: [22] Is it lawful for us to give tribute unto Caesar, or no? [23] But he perceived their craftiness, and said unto them, Why tempt ye me? [24] Show me a penny. Whose image and superscription hath it? They answered and said, Caesar's. [25] And he said unto them, Render therefore unto Caesar the things which be Caesar's, and unto God the things which be God's. [26] And they could not take hold of his words before the people: and they marveled at his answer, and held their peace.

Some Sadducees Try to Trick Jesus

*T*hen came to *him* certain of the Sadducees, which deny that there is any resurrection; and they asked him, [28] saying, Master, Moses wrote unto us, If any man's brother die, having a wife, and he die without children, that his brother should take his wife, and raise up seed unto his brother. [29] There were therefore seven brethren: and the first took a wife, and died without children. [30] And the second took her to wife, and he died childless. [31] And the third took her; and in like manner the seven also: and they left no children, and died. [32] Last of all the woman died also. [33] Therefore in the resurrection whose wife of them is she? for seven had her to wife. [34] And Jesus answering said unto them, The children of this world marry, and are given in marriage: [35] but they which shall be accounted worthy to obtain that world, and the resurrection from the dead, neither marry, nor are given in marriage: [36] neither can they die any more: for they are equal unto the angels; and are the children of God, being the children of the resurrection. [37] Now that the dead are raised, even Moses showed at the bush, when he calleth the Lord the God of Abraham, and the God of Isaac, and the God of Jacob. [38] For he is not a God of the dead, but of the living: for all live unto him. [39] Then certain of the scribes answering said, Master, thou hast well said. [40] And after that they durst not ask him any *question at all*.

Is the Christ the Son of David?

*A*nd he said unto them, How say they that Christ is David's son? [42] And David himself saith in the book of Psalms, The Lord said unto my Lord, Sit thou on my right hand,

43 Till I make thine enemies thy footstool.

44 David therefore calleth him Lord, how is he then his son?

Jesus Accuses the Scribes

Then in the audience of all the people he said unto his disciples,

46 Beware of the scribes, which desire to walk in long robes, and love greetings in the markets, and the highest seats in the synagogues, and the chief rooms at feasts;

47 which devour widows' houses, and for a show make long prayers: the same shall receive greater damnation.

OLD TESTAMENT READING

Woe to them that devise iniquity, and work evil upon their beds! when the morning is light, they practise it, because it is in the power of their hand.

2 And they covet fields, and take *them* by violence; and houses, and take *them* away: so they oppress a man and his house, even a man and his heritage.

3 Therefore thus saith the LORD; Behold, against this family do I devise an evil, from which ye shall not remove your necks; neither shall ye go haughtily: for this time *is* evil.

Micah 2:1–3

INSIGHTS

Not long ago a discerning man said that his minister preaches against sin, but he does not tell what sin is. He preaches against sin in general, but never against any particular sin. He denounces it in the

aggregate, but never meddles with it in detail as it exists among his people. . . .

Do you see the importance of praying continually for a quick and tender and powerful conscience? Do you see the importance of great watchfulness lest we should abuse and seduce our conscience by indulgence in sin? Do you see the great importance of faithful dealings with the consciences all around you, so as to keep your own and their consciences fully awake and as quick and sensitive as the apple of the eye? . . .

It is impossible for me to understand how some could really be in love with the law of God, earnestly and honestly engaged in supporting it in all the length and breadth of its claims, and yet indulge in so many forms of violating it with so little compunction or misgiving. Is there not, my beloved brethren, some delusion in this?

Charles Finney

ACTION POINT

What are the leaders of God's people responsible to do? What does God promise to spiritual leaders who plan wickedness? Pray that God will open your eyes and protect you from the blinding influence of false spiritual leaders.

TUESDAY

*God Gives His People
Words to Say*

Luke 21:1–28

True Giving

21 And he looked up, and saw the rich men casting their gifts into the treasury.

² And he saw also a certain poor widow casting in thither two mites.

³ And he said, Of a truth I say unto you, that this poor widow hath cast in more than they all:

⁴ for all these have of their abundance cast in unto the offerings of God: but she of her penury hath cast in all the living that she had.

The Temple Will Be Destroyed

*A*nd as some spake of the temple, how it was adorned with goodly stones and gifts, he said,

⁶ *As for* these things which ye behold, the days will come, in the which there shall not be left one stone upon another, that shall not be thrown down.

⁷ And they asked him, saying, Master, but when shall these things be? and what sign *will there be* when these things shall come to pass?

⁸ And he said, Take heed that ye be not deceived: for many shall come in my name, saying, I am *Christ*; and the time draweth near: go ye not therefore after them.

⁹ But when ye shall hear of wars and commotions, be not terrified: for these things must first come to pass; but the end *is* not by and by.

¹⁰ Then said he unto them, Nation shall rise against nation, and kingdom against kingdom:

¹¹ and great earthquakes shall be in divers places, and famines, and pestilences; and fearful sights and great signs shall there be from heaven.

¹² But before all these, they shall lay their hands on you, and persecute you, delivering *you* up to the synagogues, and into prisons, being brought before kings and rulers for my name's sake.

¹³ And it shall turn to you for a testimony.

¹⁴ Settle *it* therefore in your hearts, not to meditate before what ye shall answer:

¹⁵ for I will give you a mouth and wisdom, which all your adversaries shall not be able to gainsay nor resist.

¹⁶ And ye shall be betrayed both by parents, and brethren, and kinsfolks, and friends; and *some* of you shall they cause to be put to death.

¹⁷ And ye shall be hated of all *men* for my name's sake.

¹⁸ But there shall not a hair of your head perish.

¹⁹ In your patience possess ye your souls.

Jerusalem Will Be Destroyed

*A*nd when ye shall see Jerusalem compassed with armies, then know that the desolation thereof is nigh.

²¹ Then let them which are in Judea flee to the mountains; and let them which are in the midst of it depart out; and let not them that are in the countries enter thereinto.

²² For these be the days of vengeance, that all things which are written may be fulfilled.

²³ But woe unto them that are with

child, and to them that give suck, in those days! for there shall be great distress in the land, and wrath upon this people.

²⁴ And they shall fall by the edge of the sword, and shall be led away captive into all nations: and Jerusalem shall be trodden down of the Gentiles, until the times of the Gentiles be fulfilled.

Don't Fear

*A*nd there shall be signs in the sun, and in the moon, and in the stars; and upon the earth distress of nations, with perplexity; the sea and the waves roaring;

²⁶ men's hearts failing them for fear, and for looking after those things which are coming on the earth: for the powers of heaven shall be shaken.

²⁷ And then shall they see the Son of man coming in a cloud with power and great glory.

²⁸ And when these things begin to come to pass, then look up, and lift up your heads; for your redemption draweth nigh.

OLD TESTAMENT READING

*A*nd Moses said unto the LORD, O my Lord, I *am* not eloquent, neither heretofore, nor since thou hast spoken unto thy servant; but I *am* slow of speech, and of a slow tongue.

¹¹ And the LORD said unto him, Who hath made man's mouth? or who maketh the dumb, or deaf, or the seeing, or the blind? have not I the LORD?

¹⁴ And the anger of the LORD was kindled against Moses, and he said, *Is* not Aaron the Levite thy brother? I know that he can speak well. And

also, behold, he cometh forth to meet thee: and when he seeth thee, he will be glad in his heart.

¹⁵ And thou shalt speak unto him, and put words in his mouth: and I will be with thy mouth, and with his mouth, and will teach you what ye shall do.

Exodus 4:10–11, 14–15

INSIGHTS

*T*here may be times when you are concerned about sharing your faith in Christ with someone or when you are challenged in your faith by other people. Rely upon the fact that God is the source of your thoughts and words at those times. Dr. Lloyd Ogilvie says:

Our only task is to open our minds in calm expectation of wisdom beyond our own capacity. We were never meant to be adequate on our own. It is when we think we are adequate that we get into trouble. A Christian is not one who works for the Lord but one in whom and through whom the Lord works. We are not to speak for God but to yield our tongues to express the thoughts the Lord has implanted.

H. Norman Wright

ACTION POINT

*W*hat did God promise to do for both Moses and Aaron? Have you ever been worried about what to say? Pray for a willing spirit that God can use.

WEDNESDAY

Focus Your Eyes on God;
Be Ready for His Coming

Luke 21:29—22:20

Jesus' Words Will Live Forever

*A*nd he spake to them a parable; Behold the fig tree, and all the trees; [30] when they now shoot forth, ye see and know of your own selves that summer is now nigh at hand. [31] So likewise ye, when ye see these things come to pass, know ye that the kingdom of God is nigh at hand. [32] Verily I say unto you, This generation shall not pass away, till all be fulfilled. [33] Heaven and earth shall pass away; but my words shall not pass away.

Watch and Pray

*A*nd take heed to yourselves, lest at any time your hearts be overcharged with surfeiting, and drunkenness, and cares of this life, and so that day come upon you unawares. [35] For as a snare shall it come on all them that dwell on the face of the whole earth. [36] Watch ye therefore, and pray always, that ye may be accounted worthy to escape all these things that shall come to pass, and to stand before the Son of man. [37] And in the day time he was teaching in the temple; and at night he went out, and abode in the mount that is called *the mount* of Olives. [38] And all the people came early in the morning to him in the temple, for to hear him.

Judas Becomes an Enemy of Jesus

22 Now the feast of unleavened bread drew nigh, which is called the Passover. [2] And the chief priests and scribes sought how they might kill him; for they feared the people. [3] Then entered Satan into Judas surnamed Iscariot, being of the number of the twelve. [4] And he went his way, and communed with the chief priests and captains, how he might betray him unto them. [5] And they were glad, and covenanted to give him money. [6] And he promised, and sought opportunity to betray him unto them in the absence of the multitude.

Jesus Eats the Passover Meal

*T*hen came the day of unleavened bread, when the passover must be killed. [8] And he sent Peter and John, saying, Go and prepare us the passover, that we may eat. [9] And they said unto him, Where wilt thou that we prepare? [10] And he said unto them, Behold, when ye are entered into the city, there shall a man meet you, bearing a pitcher of water; follow him into the house where he entereth in. [11] And ye shall say unto the goodman of the house, The Master saith unto thee, Where is the guestchamber, where I shall eat the passover with my disciples? [12] And he shall show you a large upper room furnished: there make ready. [13] And they went, and found as he had said unto them: and they made ready the passover.

The Lord's Supper

*A*nd when the hour was come, he sat down, and the twelve apostles with him.

¹⁵ And he said unto them, With desire I have desired to eat this passover with you before I suffer:

¹⁶ for I say unto you, I will not any more eat thereof, until it be fulfilled in the kingdom of God.

¹⁷ And he took the cup, and gave thanks, and said, Take this, and divide *it* among yourselves:

¹⁸ for I say unto you, I will not drink of the fruit of the vine, until the kingdom of God shall come.

¹⁹ And he took bread, and gave thanks, and brake *it*, and gave unto them, saying, This is my body which is given for you: this do in remembrance of me.

²⁰ Likewise also the cup after supper, saying, This cup *is* the new testament in my blood, which is shed for you.

OLD TESTAMENT READING

*T*hou art my portion, O LORD: I have said that I would keep thy words.

⁵⁸ I entreated thy favor with *my* whole heart: be merciful unto me according to thy word.

⁵⁹ I thought on my ways, and turned my feet unto thy testimonies.

⁶⁰ I made haste, and delayed not to keep thy commandments.

Psalm 119:57–60

INSIGHTS

*T*he coming of God's Son is the real hope of the believers. . . . The early Christians constantly looked forward to it. The Church in its first love waited for its Lord. How often too Jesus Himself and His apostles admonished us to wait for His coming and to hasten to meet Him! The return of the Lord is not a theme with which certain specialists occupy themselves, but it is the great theme of Scripture and it must also become ours. We are all deeply aware of the fact that our congregations need a spiritual renewal. "How can this take place?" I asked a missionary. "When the hope of the Lord's return becomes living in our congregations," he answered. . . .

. . . John says, "Everyone that hath this hope set on him purifieth himself even as he is pure." He that does not have this hope, does not cleanse himself. Those who are really waiting need not be exhorted to cleanse themselves; they do it without outward prompting. They do not need to be urged to press forward, to deny themselves, to humble themselves; they just naturally strive to be like the Lamb. . . .

Hitherto many of us have been like the brother who once said: "For many years I have known that I was converted, but I did not know for what purpose. I have long known that I was sealed with the Holy Spirit, but not to what end. But I understood it when I Thess. 1:9–10 and Eph. 4:30 became clear to me: we are converted to serve the true and living God, and to wait for His Son from Heaven."

G. Steinberger

ACTION POINT

*W*hy is it important to be ready for Jesus' return? What must we do to be ready? Will you pray daily to be ready?

THURSDAY

*Jesus Sought the Will
of the Father*

Luke 22:21–53

Who Will Betray Jesus?

*B*ut, behold, the hand of him that betrayeth me *is* with me on the table. ²² And truly the Son of man goeth, as it was determined: but woe unto that man by whom he is betrayed! ²³ And they began to inquire among themselves, which of them it was that should do this thing.

Be Like a Servant

*A*nd there was also a strife among them, which of them should be accounted the greatest. ²⁵ And he said unto them, The kings of the Gentiles exercise lordship over them; and they that exercise authority upon them are called benefactors. ²⁶ But ye *shall* not *be* so: but he that is greatest among you, let him be as the younger; and he that is chief, as he that doth serve. ²⁷ For whether *is* greater, he that sitteth at meat, or he that serveth? *is* not he that sitteth at meat? but I am among you as he that serveth. ²⁸ Ye are they which have continued with me in my temptations. ²⁹ And I appoint unto you a kingdom, as my Father hath appointed unto me; ³⁰ that ye may eat and drink at my table in my kingdom, and sit on thrones judging the twelve tribes of Israel.

Don't Lose Your Faith!

*A*nd the Lord said, Simon, Simon, behold, Satan hath desired *to have* you, that he may sift *you* as wheat: ³² but I have prayed for thee, that thy faith fail not: and when thou art converted, strengthen thy brethren. ³³ And he said unto him, Lord, I am ready to go with thee, both into prison, and to death. ³⁴ And he said, I tell thee, Peter, the cock shall not crow this day, before that thou shalt thrice deny that thou knowest me.

Be Ready for Trouble

*A*nd he said unto them, When I sent you without purse, and scrip, and shoes, lacked ye any thing? And they said, Nothing. ³⁶ Then said he unto them, But now, he that hath a purse, let him take *it*, and likewise *his* scrip: and he that hath no sword, let him sell his garment, and buy one. ³⁷ For I say unto you, that this that is written must yet be accomplished in me, And he was reckoned among the transgressors: for the things concerning me have an end. ³⁸ And they said, Lord, behold, here *are* two swords. And he said unto them, It is enough.

Jesus Prays Alone

*A*nd he came out, and went, as he was wont, to the mount of Olives; and his disciples also followed him. ⁴⁰ And when he was at the place, he said unto them, Pray that ye enter not into temptation. ⁴¹ And he was withdrawn from them about a stone's cast, and kneeled down, and prayed,

⁴²saying, Father, if thou be willing, remove this cup from me: nevertheless, not my will, but thine, be done.

⁴³And there appeared an angel unto him from heaven, strengthening him.

⁴⁴And being in an agony he prayed more earnestly: and his sweat was as it were great drops of blood falling down to the ground.

⁴⁵And when he rose up from prayer, and was come to his disciples, he found them sleeping for sorrow,

⁴⁶and said unto them, Why sleep ye? rise and pray, lest ye enter into temptation.

Jesus Is Arrested

*A*nd while he yet spake, behold a multitude, and he that was called Judas, one of the twelve, went before them, and drew near unto Jesus to kiss him.

⁴⁸But Jesus said unto him, Judas, betrayest thou the Son of man with a kiss?

⁴⁹When they which were about him saw what would follow, they said unto him, Lord, shall we smite with the sword?

⁵⁰And one of them smote the servant of the high priest, and cut off his right ear.

⁵¹And Jesus answered and said, Suffer ye thus far. And he touched his ear, and healed him.

⁵²Then Jesus said unto the chief priests, and captains of the temple, and the elders, which were come to him, Be ye come out, as against a thief, with swords and staves?

⁵³When I was daily with you in the temple, ye stretched forth no hands against me: but this is your hour, and the power of darkness.

OLD TESTAMENT READING

*D*eliver me, O LORD, from mine enemies: I flee unto thee to hide me.

¹⁰Teach me to do thy will; for thou art my God: thy spirit *is* good; lead me into the land of uprightness.

Psalm 143:9–10

INSIGHTS

I seek at the beginning to get my heart in such a state that it has no will of its own in regard to a given matter. . . . When one is truly in this state, it is usually but a little way to the knowledge of what His will is.

Having done this, . . . I seek the will of the Spirit of God through, or in connection with, the Word of God. . . . If the Holy Spirit guides us at all, He will do it according to the Scriptures and never contrary to them.

Next I take into account providential circumstances. These often plainly indicate God's will in connection with His Word and Spirit.

I ask God in prayer to reveal His will to me aright.

Thus through prayer to God, the study of the Word, and reflection, I come to a deliberate judgment according to the best of my ability and knowledge; and if my mind is thus at peace, and continues so after two or three more petitions, I proceed accordingly.

George Müller

PAUSE FOR REFLECTION

*W*hat did Jesus do to know God's will? What do you do to discover God's will?

FRIDAY

Deceit Leads to Great Pain

Luke 22:54—23:12

Peter Denies Jesus

*T*hen took they him, and led *him,* and brought him into the high priest's house. And Peter followed afar off.

⁵⁵ And when they had kindled a fire in the midst of the hall, and were set down together, Peter sat down among them.

⁵⁶ But a certain maid beheld him as he sat by the fire, and earnestly looked upon him, and said, This man was also with him.

⁵⁷ And he denied him, saying, Woman, I know him not.

⁵⁸ And after a little while another saw him, and said, Thou art also of them. And Peter said, Man, I am not.

⁵⁹ And about the space of one hour after another confidently affirmed, saying, Of a truth this *fellow* also was with him; for he is a Galilean.

⁶⁰ And Peter said, Man, I know not what thou sayest. And immediately, while he yet spake, the cock crew.

⁶¹ And the Lord turned, and looked upon Peter. And Peter remembered the word of the Lord, how he had said unto him, Before the cock crow, thou shalt deny me thrice.

⁶² And Peter went out, and wept bitterly.

The People Mock Jesus

*A*nd the men that held Jesus mocked him, and smote *him.*

⁶⁴ And when they had blindfolded him, they struck him on the face, and asked him, saying, Prophesy, who is it that smote thee?

⁶⁵ And many other things blasphemously spake they against him.

Jesus Before the Council

*A*nd as soon as it was day, the elders of the people and the chief priests and the scribes came together, and led him into their council, saying,

⁶⁷ Art thou the Christ? tell us. And he said unto them, If I tell you, ye will not believe:

⁶⁸ and if I also ask *you,* ye will not answer me, nor let *me* go.

⁶⁹ Hereafter shall the Son of man sit on the right hand of the power of God.

⁷⁰ Then said they all, Art thou then the Son of God? And he said unto them, Ye say that I am.

⁷¹ And they said, What need we any further witness? for we ourselves have heard of his own mouth.

Pilate Questions Jesus

23 And the whole multitude of them arose, and led him unto Pilate.

² And they began to accuse him, saying, We found this *fellow* perverting the nation, and forbidding to give tribute to Caesar, saying that he himself is Christ a King.

³ And Pilate asked him, saying, Art thou the King of the Jews? And he answered him and said, Thou sayest *it.*

⁴ Then said Pilate to the chief priests and *to* the people, I find no fault in this man.

⁵ And they were the more fierce, saying, He stirreth up the people, teach-

ing throughout all Jewry, beginning from Galilee to this place.

Pilate Sends Jesus to Herod

*W*hen Pilate heard of Galilee, he asked whether the man were a Galilean.

⁷And as soon as he knew that he belonged unto Herod's jurisdiction, he sent him to Herod, who himself also was at Jerusalem at that time.

⁸And when Herod saw Jesus, he was exceeding glad: for he was desirous to see him of a long *season*, because he had heard many things of him; and he hoped to have seen some miracle done by him.

⁹Then he questioned with him in many words; but he answered him nothing.

¹⁰And the chief priests and scribes stood and vehemently accused him.

¹¹And Herod with his men of war set him at nought, and mocked *him*, and arrayed him in a gorgeous robe, and sent him again to Pilate.

¹²And the same day Pilate and Herod were made friends together; for before they were at enmity between themselves.

OLD TESTAMENT READING

*A*nd he said, Thy brother came with subtilty, and hath taken away thy blessing.

³⁶And he said, Is not he rightly named Jacob? for he hath supplanted me these two times: he took away my birthright; and, behold, now he hath taken away my blessing. And he said, Hast thou not reserved a blessing for me?

³⁷And Isaac answered and said unto Esau, Behold, I have made him thy lord, and all his brethren have I given to him for servants; and with corn and wine have I sustained him: and what shall I do now unto thee, my son?

⁴¹And Esau hated Jacob because of the blessing wherewith his father blessed him: and Esau said in his heart, The days of mourning for my father are at hand; then will I slay my brother Jacob.

Genesis 27:35–37, 41

INSIGHTS

*T*ruth is personal—it is a special part of any close human relationship. Trust is a by-product of truth, and personal relationships are built upon trust. I trust people who demonstrate that they are truthful. I do not trust people who show themselves to be habitual liars. . . .

. . . It is painful for anybody to invest his heart in a lie. A broken truth often means a broken heart.

This is the problem with lies. We do invest our hearts in the promises people make and the stories they tell us. When the promises are not kept and the stories prove to be false, we are hurt. We are disillusioned. We sometimes grow bitter. Trust is a fragile commodity and is as precious as it is delicate. Deep levels of trust take years to develop. Yet, such trust can be smashed to pieces in seconds.
R. C. Sproul

PAUSE FOR REFLECTION

*H*ow did deceit in Isaac's family change the family relationships? When Peter lied about knowing Jesus, how did he feel? How did his relationship with Jesus change?

WEEKEND

*God Always Welcomes
Repentant Sinners*

Luke 23:13–43

Jesus Must Die

And Pilate, when he had called together the chief priests and the rulers and the people,

¹⁴ said unto them, Ye have brought this man unto me, as one that perverteth the people; and, behold, I, having examined *him* before you, have found no fault in this man touching those things whereof ye accuse him:

¹⁵ no, nor yet Herod: for I sent you to him; and, lo, nothing worthy of death is done unto him.

¹⁶ I will therefore chastise him, and release *him*.

¹⁷ (For of necessity he must release one unto them at the feast.)

¹⁸ And they cried out all at once, saying, Away with this *man*, and release unto us Barabbas:

¹⁹ (who for a certain sedition made in the city, and for murder, was cast into prison.)

²⁰ Pilate therefore, willing to release Jesus, spake again to them.

²¹ But they cried, saying, Crucify *him*, crucify him.

²² And he said unto them the third time, Why, what evil hath he done? I have found no cause of death in him: I will therefore chastise him, and let *him* go.

²³ And they were instant with loud voices, requiring that he might be crucified: and the voices of them and of the chief priests prevailed.

²⁴ And Pilate gave sentence that it should be as they required.

²⁵ And he released unto them him that for sedition and murder was cast into prison, whom they had desired; but he delivered Jesus to their will.

Jesus Is Crucified

And as they led him away, they laid hold upon one Simon, a Cyrenian, coming out of the country, and on him they laid the cross, that he might bear *it* after Jesus.

²⁷ And there followed him a great company of people, and of women, which also bewailed and lamented him.

²⁸ But Jesus turning unto them said, Daughters of Jerusalem, weep not for me, but weep for yourselves, and for your children.

²⁹ For, behold, the days are coming, in the which they shall say, Blessed *are* the barren, and the wombs that never bare, and the paps which never gave suck.

³⁰ Then shall they begin to say to the mountains, Fall on us; and to the hills, Cover us.

³¹ For if they do these things in a green tree, what shall be done in the dry?

³² And there were also two other, malefactors, led with him to be put to death.

³³ And when they were come to the place, which is called Calvary, there they crucified him, and the malefactors, one on the right hand, and the other on the left.

³⁴ Then said Jesus, Father, forgive them; for they know not what they do. And they parted his raiment, and cast lots.

35 And the people stood beholding. And the rulers also with them derided *him*, saying, He saved others; let him save himself, if he be Christ, the chosen of God.

36 And the soldiers also mocked him, coming to him, and offering him vinegar,

37 and saying, If thou be the king of the Jews, save thyself.

38 And a superscription also was written over him in letters of Greek, and Latin, and Hebrew, THIS IS THE KING OF THE JEWS.

39 And one of the malefactors which were hanged railed on him, saying, If thou be Christ, save thyself and us.

40 But the other answering rebuked him, saying, Dost not thou fear God, seeing thou art in the same condemnation?

41 And we indeed justly; for we receive the due reward of our deeds: but this man hath done nothing amiss.

42 And he said unto Jesus, Lord, remember me when thou comest into thy kingdom.

43 And Jesus said unto him, Verily I say unto thee, Today shalt thou be with me in paradise.

OLD TESTAMENT READING

*F*or thus saith the Lord GOD, the Holy One of Israel; In returning and rest shall ye be saved; in quietness and in confidence shall be your strength: and ye would not.

18 And therefore will the LORD wait, that he may be gracious unto you, and therefore will he be exalted, that he may have mercy upon you: for the LORD *is* a God of judgment: blessed *are* all they that wait for him.

Isaiah 30:15, 18

INSIGHTS

*T*he prisoners in the Montinlupa Prison who gathered for a large assembly were astonished to see a woman in her seventies make her way up the steps of the platform to address them. What would an old woman have to say to them? . . .

. . . The speaker was Corrie ten Boom. . . .

After the war was over, the two Dutchmen who had betrayed her family were taken into custody and put on trial. . . . "My sister Nollie," Corrie told her audience, "heard of the trial of these two men who told the Gestapo about us, and she wrote a letter to both of them. . . . She told them that we had forgiven them and that we could do this because of Jesus, who is in our hearts."

Both men responded. One wrote: "I have received Jesus as my Savior. When you can give such ability to forgive to people like Corrie ten Boom and her sister, then there is hope for me. . . ." The other letter gave an opposite viewpoint: " . . . The only thing I regret is that I have not been able to kill more of your kind." Corrie went on to challenge the prisoners that every one of them—even as those criminals who had been on the cross—could accept or reject Christ and his forgiveness.

Ruth Tucker

APPLICATION

*H*ow much evil will God forgive? Will you accept or reject Jesus' forgiveness?

MONDAY

The Resurrected Christ
Saves His People

Luke 23:44—24:12

Jesus Dies

*A*nd it was about the sixth hour, and there was a darkness over all the earth until the ninth hour.

⁴⁵ And the sun was darkened, and the veil of the temple was rent in the midst.

⁴⁶ And when Jesus had cried with a loud voice, he said, Father, into thy hands I commend my spirit: and having said thus, he gave up the ghost.

⁴⁷ Now when the centurion saw what was done, he glorified God, saying, Certainly this was a righteous man.

⁴⁸ And all the people that came together to that sight, beholding the things which were done, smote their breasts, and returned.

⁴⁹ And all his acquaintance, and the women that followed him from Galilee, stood afar off, beholding these things.

Joseph Takes Jesus' Body

*A*nd, behold, *there was* a man named Joseph, a counselor; *and he was* a good man, and a just:

⁵¹ (the same had not consented to the counsel and deed of them:) *he was* of Arimathea, a city of the Jews: who also himself waited for the kingdom of God.

⁵² This *man* went unto Pilate, and begged the body of Jesus.

⁵³ And he took it down, and wrapped it in linen, and laid it in a sepulchre that was hewn in stone, wherein never man before was laid.

⁵⁴ And that day was the preparation, and the sabbath drew on.

⁵⁵ And the women also, which came with him from Galilee, followed after, and beheld the sepulchre, and how his body was laid.

⁵⁶ And they returned, and prepared spices and ointments; and rested the sabbath day according to the commandment.

Jesus Rises from the Dead

24 Now upon the first *day* of the week, very early in the morning, they came unto the sepulchre, bringing the spices which they had prepared, and certain *others* with them.

² And they found the stone rolled away from the sepulchre.

³ And they entered in, and found not the body of the Lord Jesus.

⁴ And it came to pass, as they were much perplexed thereabout, behold, two men stood by them in shining garments:

⁵ and as they were afraid, and bowed down *their* faces to the earth, they said unto them, Why seek ye the living among the dead?

⁶ He is not here, but is risen: remember how he spake unto you when he was yet in Galilee,

⁷ saying, The Son of man must be delivered into the hands of sinful men, and be crucified, and the third day rise again.

⁸ And they remembered his words,

⁹ and returned from the sepulchre, and told all these things unto the eleven, and to all the rest.

¹⁰ It was Mary Magdalene, and Joanna, and Mary *the mother* of

James, and other *women that were with them,* which told these things unto the apostles.

[11] And their words seemed to them as idle tales, and they believed them not.

[12] Then arose Peter, and ran unto the sepulchre; and stooping down, he beheld the linen clothes laid by themselves, and departed, wondering in himself at that which was come to pass.

OLD TESTAMENT READING

*B*ehold my servant, whom I uphold; mine elect, *in whom* my soul delighteth; I have put my Spirit upon him: he shall bring forth judgment to the Gentiles.

[2] He shall not cry, nor lift up, nor cause his voice to be heard in the street.

[3] A bruised reed shall he not break, and the smoking flax shall he not quench: he shall bring forth judgment unto truth.

[4] He shall not fail nor be discouraged, till he have set judgment in the earth: and the isles shall wait for his law.

[6] I the LORD have called thee in righteousness, and will hold thine hand, and will keep thee, and give thee for a covenant of the people, for a light of the Gentiles.

Isaiah 42:1-4, 6

INSIGHTS

*N*ever underestimate the power of a seed.

God didn't. When his kingdom was ravaged and his people had forgotten his name, he planted his seed. When the soil of the human heart had grown crusty, he planted his seed. When religion had become a ritual and the temple a trading post, he planted his seed.

Want to see a miracle? Watch him as he places the seed of his own self in the fertile womb of a Jewish girl.

Up it grew, "like a tender green shoot, sprouting from a root in dry and sterile ground." The seed spent a lifetime pushing back the stones that tried to keep it underground. The seed made a ministry out of shoving away the rocks that cluttered his father's soil.

The stones of legalism that burdened backs.

The stones of oppression that broke bones.

The stones of prejudice that fenced out the needy.

But it was the final stone that proved to be the supreme test of the seed. The stone of death—rolled by humans and sealed by Satan in front of the tomb. For a moment it appeared the seed would be stuck in the earth. For a moment, it looked like this rock was too big to be budged.

But then, somewhere in the heart of the earth, the seed of God stirred, shoved, and sprouted. The ground trembled, and the rock of the tomb tumbled. And the flower of Easter blossomed.

Never underestimate the power of a seed.

Max Lucado

PAUSE FOR REFLECTION

*W*hat warnings did Jesus' followers have that he would die and rise again? Do you take time alone to ponder Christ's awesome salvation?

TUESDAY

Jesus Sends His Witnesses to All Nations

Luke 24:13–53

Jesus on the Road to Emmaus

And, behold, two of them went that same day to a village called Emmaus, which was from Jerusalem *about* threescore furlongs.

14 And they talked together of all these things which had happened.

15 And it came to pass, that, while they communed *together* and reasoned, Jesus himself drew near, and went with them.

16 But their eyes were holden that they should not know him.

17 And he said unto them, What manner of communications *are* these that ye have one to another, as ye walk, and are sad?

18 And the one of them, whose name was Cleopas, answering said unto him, Art thou only a stranger in Jerusalem, and hast not known the things which are come to pass there in these days?

19 And he said unto them, What things? And they said unto him, Concerning Jesus of Nazareth, which was a prophet mighty in deed and word before God and all the people:

20 and how the chief priests and our rulers delivered him to be condemned to death, and have crucified him.

21 But we trusted that it had been he which should have redeemed Israel: and beside all this, today is the third day since these things were done.

22 Yea, and certain women also of our company made us astonished, which were early at the sepulchre;

23 and when they found not his body, they came, saying, that they had also seen a vision of angels, which said that he was alive.

24 And certain of them which were with us went to the sepulchre, and found *it* even so as the women had said: but him they saw not.

25 Then he said unto them, O fools, and slow of heart to believe all that the prophets have spoken:

26 ought not Christ to have suffered these things, and to enter into his glory?

27 And beginning at Moses and all the prophets, he expounded unto them in all the Scriptures the things concerning himself.

28 And they drew nigh unto the village, whither they went: and he made as though he would have gone further.

29 But they constrained him, saying, Abide with us; for it is toward evening, and the day is far spent. And he went in to tarry with them.

30 And it came to pass, as he sat at meat with them, he took bread, and blessed *it*, and brake, and gave to them.

31 And their eyes were opened, and they knew him; and he vanished out of their sight.

32 And they said one to another, Did not our heart burn within us, while he talked with us by the way, and while he opened to us the Scriptures?

33 And they rose up the same hour, and returned to Jerusalem, and found the eleven gathered together, and them that were with them,

34 saying, The Lord is risen indeed, and hath appeared to Simon.

35 And they told what things *were done* in the way, and how he was

known of them in breaking of bread.

Jesus Appears to His Disciples

*A*nd as they thus spake, Jesus himself stood in the midst of them, and saith unto them, Peace *be* unto you. ³⁷ But they were terrified and affrighted, and supposed that they had seen a spirit.

³⁸ And he said unto them, Why are ye troubled? and why do thoughts arise in your hearts?

³⁹ Behold my hands and my feet, that it is I myself: handle me, and see; for a spirit hath not flesh and bones, as ye see me have.

⁴⁰ And when he had thus spoken, he showed them *his* hands and *his* feet.

⁴¹ And while they yet believed not for joy, and wondered, he said unto them, Have ye here any meat?

⁴² And they gave him a piece of a broiled fish, and of a honeycomb.

⁴³ And he took *it*, and did eat before them.

⁴⁴ And he said unto them, These *are* the words which I spake unto you, while I was yet with you, that all things must be fulfilled, which were written in the law of Moses, and *in* the prophets, and *in* the psalms, concerning me.

⁴⁵ Then opened he their understanding, that they might understand the Scriptures,

⁴⁶ and said unto them, Thus it is written, and thus it behooved Christ to suffer, and to rise from the dead the third day:

⁴⁷ and that repentance and remission of sins should be preached in his name among all nations, beginning at Jerusalem.

⁴⁸ And ye are witnesses of these things.

⁴⁹ And, behold, I send the promise of my Father upon you: but tarry ye in the city of Jerusalem, until ye be endued with power from on high.

Jesus Goes Back to Heaven

*A*nd he led them out as far as to Bethany, and he lifted up his hands, and blessed them.

⁵¹ And it came to pass, while he blessed them, he was parted from them, and carried up into heaven.

⁵² And they worshipped him, and returned to Jerusalem with great joy:

⁵³ and were continually in the temple, praising and blessing God. Amen.

OLD TESTAMENT READING

O Jerusalem, that bringest good tidings, lift up thy voice with strength; lift *it* up, be not afraid; say unto the cities of Judah, Behold your God!

Isaiah 40:9

INSIGHTS

*E*veryone has the great responsibility to win as many people as possible to Christ. This is the great privilege and the great duty of all disciples of Christ. . . .

Many believers suppose it belongs only to those who are called to preach the gospel as a life work. They fail to realize that all are called to preach the gospel, that the whole life of every believer is to be a proclamation of the glad tidings.

Charles Finney

ACTION POINT

*W*rite the message of salvation Jesus wants you to proclaim.

WEDNESDAY

*Christis: The True Light
of the World*

John 1:1–28

Christ Comes to the World

1 In the beginning was the Word, and the Word was with God, and the Word was God.

2 The same was in the beginning with God.

3 All things were made by him; and without him was not any thing made that was made.

4 In him was life; and the life was the light of men.

5 And the light shineth in darkness; and the darkness comprehended it not.

6 There was a man sent from God, whose name *was* John.

7 The same came for a witness, to bear witness of the Light, that all *men* through him might believe.

8 He was not that Light, but *was sent* to bear witness of that Light.

9 *That* was the true Light, which lighteth every man that cometh into the world.

10 He was in the world, and the world was made by him, and the world knew him not.

11 He came unto his own, and his own received him not.

12 But as many as received him, to them gave he power to become the sons of God, *even* to them that believe on his name:

13 which were born, not of blood, nor of the will of the flesh, nor of the will of man, but of God.

14 And the Word was made flesh, and dwelt among us, (and we beheld his glory, the glory as of the only begotten of the Father,) full of grace and truth.

15 John bare witness of him, and cried, saying, This was he of whom I spake, He that cometh after me is preferred before me; for he was before me.

16 And of his fulness have all we received, and grace for grace.

17 For the law was given by Moses, *but* grace and truth came by Jesus Christ.

18 No man hath seen God at any time; the only begotten Son, which is in the bosom of the Father, he hath declared *him*.

John Tells People About Jesus

And this is the record of John, when the Jews sent priests and Levites from Jerusalem to ask him, Who art thou?

20 And he confessed, and denied not; but confessed, I am not the Christ.

21 And they asked him, What then? Art thou Elijah? And he saith, I am not. Art thou that Prophet? And he answered, No.

22 Then said they unto him, Who art thou? that we may give an answer to them that sent us. What sayest thou of thyself?

23 He said, I *am* the voice of one crying in the wilderness, Make straight the way of the Lord, as said the prophet Isaiah.

24 And they which were sent were of the Pharisees.

25 And they asked him, and said unto him, Why baptizest thou then, if thou be not that Christ, nor Elijah, neither that Prophet?

26 John answered them, saying, I baptize with water: but there stand-

eth one among you, whom ye know not;

²⁷ he it is, who coming after me is preferred before me, whose shoe latchet I am not worthy to unloose.

²⁸ These things were done in Bethabara beyond Jordan, where John was baptizing.

OLD TESTAMENT READING

*T*he people that walked in darkness have seen a great light: they that dwell in the land of the shadow of death, upon them hath the light shined.

⁶ For unto us a child is born, unto us a son is given: and the government shall be upon his shoulder: and his name shall be called Wonderful, Counselor, The mighty God, The everlasting Father, The Prince of Peace.

Isaiah 9:2, 6

INSIGHTS

Thanks to the great mercy and marvel of the Incarnation, the cosmic scene is resolved into a human drama. God reaches down to relate himself to man, and man reaches up to relate himself to God. Time looks into eternity and eternity into time, making now always and always now. Everything is transformed by this sublime drama of the Incarnation, God's special parable for fallen man in a fallen world. The way opens before us that was charted in the birth, ministry, death, and resurrection of Jesus Christ, a way that successive generations of believers have striven to follow. They have derived therefrom the moral, spiritual, and intellectual creativity out of which has come everything truly great in our art, our literature, our music. . . .

. . . Whatever may happen, however seemingly inimical to it may be the world's going and those who preside over the world's affairs, the truth of the Incarnation remains intact and inviolate. . . .

. . . Christ shows what life really is, and what our true destiny is. We escape from the cave. We emerge from the darkness and instead of shadows we have all around us the glory of God's creation. Instead of darkness we have light; instead of despair, hope; instead of time and the clocks ticking inexorably on, eternity, which never began and never ends and yet is sublimely now. . . . By identifying ourselves with Christ, by absorbing ourselves in his teaching, by living out the drama of his life with him, including especially the passion, that powerhouse of love and creativity—by living with, by, and in him, we can be reborn to become new men and women in a new world.

Malcolm Muggeridge

PAUSE FOR REFLECTION

In what ways would you say Christ's coming to earth enlightened the world? What did Christ's coming reveal? What difference does being reborn of God—becoming one of his children—make in your life?

THURSDAY

Jesus Comes as the Lamb of God

John 1:29–51

*T*he next day John seeth Jesus coming unto him, and saith, Behold the Lamb of God, which taketh away the sin of the world!

[30] This is he of whom I said, After me cometh a man which is preferred before me; for he was before me.

[31] And I knew him not: but that he should be made manifest to Israel, therefore am I come baptizing with water.

[32] And John bare record, saying, I saw the Spirit descending from heaven like a dove, and it abode upon him.

[33] And I knew him not: but he that sent me to baptize with water, the same said unto me, Upon whom thou shalt see the Spirit descending, and remaining on him, the same is he which baptizeth with the Holy Ghost.

[34] And I saw, and bare record that this is the Son of God.

The First Disciples of Jesus

*A*gain the next day after, John stood, and two of his disciples;

[36] and looking upon Jesus as he walked, he saith, Behold the Lamb of God!

[37] And the two disciples heard him speak, and they followed Jesus.

[38] Then Jesus turned, and saw them following, and saith unto them, What seek ye? They said unto him, Rabbi, (which is to say, being interpreted, Master,) where dwellest thou?

[39] He saith unto them, Come and see. They came and saw where he dwelt, and abode with him that day: for it was about the tenth hour.

[40] One of the two which heard John *speak*, and followed him, was Andrew, Simon Peter's brother.

[41] He first findeth his own brother Simon, and saith unto him, We have found the Messias, which is, being interpreted, the Christ.

[42] And he brought him to Jesus. And when Jesus beheld him, he said, Thou art Simon the son of Jona: thou shalt be called Cephas, which is by interpretation, A stone.

[43] The day following Jesus would go forth into Galilee, and findeth Philip, and saith unto him, Follow me.

[44] Now Philip was of Bethsaida, the city of Andrew and Peter.

[45] Philip findeth Nathanael, and saith unto him, We have found him, of whom Moses in the law, and the prophets, did write, Jesus of Nazareth, the son of Joseph.

[46] And Nathanael said unto him, Can there any good thing come out of Nazareth? Philip saith unto him, Come and see.

[47] Jesus saw Nathanael coming to him, and saith of him, Behold an Israelite indeed, in whom is no guile!

[48] Nathanael saith unto him, Whence knowest thou me? Jesus answered and said unto him, Before that Philip called thee, when thou wast under the fig tree, I saw thee.

[49] Nathanael answered and saith unto him, Rabbi, thou art the Son of God; thou art the King of Israel.

[50] Jesus answered and said unto

him, Because I said unto thee, I saw thee under the fig tree, believest thou? thou shalt see greater things than these.

⁵¹ And he saith unto him, Verily, verily, I say unto you, Hereafter ye shall see heaven open, and the angels of God ascending and descending upon the Son of man.

OLD TESTAMENT READING

*A*ll we like sheep have gone astray; we have turned every one to his own way; and the LORD hath laid on him the iniquity of us all.

⁷ He was oppressed, and he was afflicted, yet he opened not his mouth: he is brought as a lamb to the slaughter, and as a sheep before her shearers is dumb, so he openeth not his mouth.

⁸ He was taken from prison and from judgment: and who shall declare his generation? for he was cut off out of the land of the living: for the transgression of my people was he stricken.

Isaiah 53:6–8

INSIGHTS

*I*t was never meant
to burst from the body
so fiercely, to pour
unchannelled from
the five wounds
and the unbandaged brow,
drowning the dark wood,
staining the stones
and the gravel below,
clotting in the air
dark with God's absence.

It was created for
a closed system—

the unbroken
rhythms of human blood
binding the body
of God, circulating
hot, brilliant,
saline, without
interruption
between heart, lungs
and all cells.

But because he
was once emptied
I am each day refilled;
my spirit-arteries
pulse with the vital red
of love; poured out,
it is his life
that now pumps through
my own heart's core.
He bled, and died, and I
have been transfused.

Luci Shaw

PAUSE FOR REFLECTION

*W*hat an awesome thing to be saved by the Lamb of God! How well do you know the Lamb of God? As certainly as John, Andrew, and Philip did? Or are you a bit skeptical, as Nathanael was? Reread the Isaiah passage and pray for a renewed knowledge of the Lamb of God—in your mind and in your heart.

F R I D A Y

Jesus Shows His Love
for God's Temple and
His Hatred of Sin

John 2:1–25

The Marriage at Cana

2 And the third day there was a marriage in Cana of Galilee; and the mother of Jesus was there:

[2] and both Jesus was called, and his disciples, to the marriage.

[3] And when they wanted wine, the mother of Jesus saith unto him, They have no wine.

[4] Jesus saith unto her, Woman, what have I to do with thee? mine hour is not yet come.

[5] His mother saith unto the servants, Whatsoever he saith unto you, do *it*.

[6] And there were set there six waterpots of stone, after the manner of the purifying of the Jews, containing two or three firkins apiece.

[7] Jesus saith unto them, Fill the waterpots with water. And they filled them up to the brim.

[8] And he saith unto them, Draw out now, and bear unto the governor of the feast. And they bare *it*.

[9] When the ruler of the feast had tasted the water that was made wine, and knew not whence it was, (but the servants which drew the water knew,) the governor of the feast called the bridegroom,

[10] and saith unto him, Every man at the beginning doth set forth good wine; and when men have well drunk, then that which is worse: *but* thou hast kept the good wine until now.

[11] This beginning of miracles did Jesus in Cana of Galilee, and manifested forth his glory; and his disciples believed on him.

Jesus in the Temple

*A*fter this he went down to Capernaum, he, and his mother, and his brethren, and his disciples; and they continued there not many days.

[13] And the Jews' passover was at hand, and Jesus went up to Jerusalem,

[14] and found in the temple those that sold oxen and sheep and doves, and the changers of money sitting:

[15] and when he had made a scourge of small cords, he drove them all out of the temple, and the sheep, and the oxen; and poured out the changers' money, and overthrew the tables;

[16] and said unto them that sold doves, Take these things hence; make not my Father's house an house of merchandise.

[17] And his disciples remembered that it was written, The zeal of thine house hath eaten me up.

[18] Then answered the Jews and said unto him, What sign showest thou unto us, seeing that thou doest these things?

[19] Jesus answered and said unto them, Destroy this temple, and in three days I will raise it up.

[20] Then said the Jews, Forty and six years was this temple in building, and wilt thou rear it up in three days?

[21] But he spake of the temple of his body.

[22] When therefore he was risen from the dead, his disciples remembered that he had said this unto them; and they believed the Scripture, and the word which Jesus had said.

226

²³ Now when he was in Jerusalem at the passover, in the feast *day*, many believed in his name, when they saw the miracles which he did. ²⁴ But Jesus did not commit himself unto them, because he knew all *men*, ²⁵ and needed not that any should testify of man: for he knew what was in man.

OLD TESTAMENT READING

*M*ine eyes *shall be* upon the faithful of the land, that they may dwell with me: he that walketh in a perfect way, he shall serve me. ⁷ He that worketh deceit shall not dwell within my house: he that telleth lies shall not tarry in my sight. ⁸ I will early destroy all the wicked of the land; that I may cut off all wicked doers from the city of the LORD.

Psalm 101:6–8

INSIGHTS

*I*n Cana Jesus manifested His power as the Creator. Now He came to manifest His authority as the Messiah, the Son of God. Not only did He drive the sheep and oxen out of the temple, but He whipped the merchants out of the place. These Jews knew that He was right. The law and their consciences were witnesses against them. Christ was filled with righteous indignation in His zeal for His Father's house.

Christ cleansed the temple by crying, "Make not my Father's house an house of merchandise." Mark that He calls the temple "My Father's house." Christ was claiming a unique relationship with the Living God. . . .

When Christ drove the merchandisers out of the temple, they experienced something of the terror of the Lord. In the future men will cry to the mountains and rocks to hide them "from the face of him that sitteth on the throne, and from the wrath of the Lamb: For the great day of his wrath is come; and who shall be able to stand?" (Revelation 6:16–17).

Sometimes we forget that He is a righteous God and that every one of us must one day stand in His presence and give an account to Him. "It is a fearful thing to fall into the hands of the living God" (Hebrews 10:31). . . .

. . . Christ cleansed the temple when men sinned and made it unclean. Similarly, the Lord has a right to cleanse us when we sin. It is much better for us to willingly confess our sins so that He may forgive and cleanse us. And He is willing and ready to do just that. How wonderful it is to know that the blood of Jesus Christ, God's Son, cleanseth us from all sin (1 John 1:7).

John G. Mitchell

ACTION POINT

*W*hat was revealed by the Jews' demand that Jesus prove he had the right to cleanse God's temple? In what ways do you demand that Jesus prove his right to purge the sin from your heart (which is also his temple)? Ask for his forgiveness.

WEEKEND

*God's Love Caused Him
to Send Salvation
Through His Son*

John 3:1–30

Nicodemus Comes to Jesus

3 There was a man of the Pharisees, named Nicodemus, a ruler of the Jews:

2 the same came to Jesus by night, and said unto him, Rabbi, we know that thou art a teacher come from God: for no man can do these miracles that thou doest, except God be with him.

3 Jesus answered and said unto him, Verily, verily, I say unto thee, Except a man be born again, he cannot see the kingdom of God.

4 Nicodemus saith unto him, How can a man be born when he is old? can he enter the second time into his mother's womb, and be born?

5 Jesus answered, Verily, verily, I say unto thee, Except a man be born of water and *of* the Spirit, he cannot enter into the kingdom of God.

6 That which is born of the flesh is flesh; and that which is born of the Spirit is spirit.

7 Marvel not that I said unto thee, Ye must be born again.

8 The wind bloweth where it listeth, and thou hearest the sound thereof, but canst not tell whence it cometh, and whither it goeth: so is every one that is born of the Spirit.

9 Nicodemus answered and said unto him, How can these things be?

10 Jesus answered and said unto him, Art thou a master of Israel, and knowest not these things?

11 Verily, verily, I say unto thee, We speak that we do know, and testify that we have seen; and ye receive not our witness.

12 If I have told you earthly things, and ye believe not, how shall ye believe, if I tell you *of* heavenly things?

13 And no man hath ascended up to heaven, but he that came down from heaven, *even* the Son of man which is in heaven.

14 And as Moses lifted up the serpent in the wilderness, even so must the Son of man be lifted up:

15 that whosoever believeth in him should not perish, but have eternal life.

16 For God so loved the world, that he gave his only begotten Son, that whosoever believeth in him should not perish, but have everlasting life.

17 For God sent not his Son into the world to condemn the world; but that the world through him might be saved.

18 He that believeth on him is not condemned: but he that believeth not is condemned already, because he hath not believed in the name of the only begotten Son of God.

19 And this is the condemnation, that light is come into the world, and men loved darkness rather than light, because their deeds were evil.

20 For every one that doeth evil hateth the light, neither cometh to the light, lest his deeds should be reproved.

21 But he that doeth truth cometh to the light, that his deeds may be made manifest, that they are wrought in God.

Jesus and John the Baptist

*A*fter these things came Jesus and

his disciples into the land of Judea; and there he tarried with them, and baptized.

²³ And John also was baptizing in Aenon near to Salim, because there was much water there: and they came, and were baptized.

²⁴ For John was not yet cast into prison.

²⁵ Then there arose a question between *some* of John's disciples and the Jews about purifying.

²⁶ And they came unto John, and said unto him, Rabbi, he that was with thee beyond Jordan, to whom thou barest witness, behold, the same baptizeth, and all *men* come to him.

²⁷ John answered and said, A man can receive nothing, except it be given him from heaven.

²⁸ Ye yourselves bear me witness, that I said, I am not the Christ, but that I am sent before him.

²⁹ He that hath the bride is the bridegroom: but the friend of the bridegroom, which standeth and heareth him, rejoiceth greatly because of the bridegroom's voice: this my joy therefore is fulfilled.

³⁰ He must increase, but I *must* decrease.

OLD TESTAMENT READING

*A*nd the LORD saw *it*, and it displeased him that *there was* no judgment.

¹⁶ And he saw that *there was* no man, and wondered that *there was* no intercessor: therefore his arm brought salvation unto him; and his righteousness, it sustained him.

¹⁷ For he put on righteousness as a breastplate, and a helmet of salvation upon his head; and he put on the garments of vengeance *for* clothing, and was clad with zeal as a cloak.

Isaiah 59:15b–17

INSIGHTS

*G*od loves us, not only as a host of human beings who are living on the earth at this time, but as individuals whom He knows by name. He has a personal interest in each one. He has a perfect plan for every detail in the life of each individual. He is not willing that any should perish, but wants all mankind to be saved and come to the knowledge of the truth (1 Timothy 2:4).

The greatest and most profound expression of God's love for us is in the death of Christ on the cross. Men rejected the Lord Jesus Christ as God's Son, falsely accused Him, condemned Him to death, beat Him, crowned Him with thorns, spit on Him, made sport of Him, crucified Him with thieves, and ridiculed Him. While they were doing this, He forgave them and paid the penalty of their sin by dying for them.

This speaks most powerfully of the extent of God's unchanging, everlasting love. There is no greater expression of love than for a man to lay down his life for his friends.

Lucille Sollenberger

ACTION POINT

*W*hat motivated God to use his own power, to send his own son, to save us? Why do some reject God's salvation? Reread Isaiah 59:15b–17 and as you do, ask God for his forgiveness of your wrongs and praise him for offering himself to save you.

MONDAY

Jesus Gives Living Water

John 3:31—4:26

The One Who Comes from Heaven

*H*e that cometh from above is above all: he that is of the earth is earthly, and speaketh of the earth: he that cometh from heaven is above all.

³² And what he hath seen and heard, that he testifieth; and no man receiveth his testimony.

³³ He that hath received his testimony hath set to his seal that God is true.

³⁴ For he whom God hath sent speaketh the words of God: for God giveth not the Spirit by measure *unto him*.

³⁵ The Father loveth the Son, and hath given all things into his hand.

³⁶ He that believeth on the Son hath everlasting life: and he that believeth not the Son shall not see life; but the wrath of God abideth on him.

Jesus and a Samaritan Woman

4 When therefore the Lord knew how the Pharisees had heard that Jesus made and baptized more disciples than John,

² (though Jesus himself baptized not, but his disciples,)

³ he left Judea, and departed again into Galilee.

⁴ And he must needs go through Samaria.

⁵ Then cometh he to a city of Samaria, which is called Sychar, near to the parcel of ground that Jacob gave to his son Joseph.

⁶ Now Jacob's well was there. Jesus therefore, being wearied with *his* journey, sat thus on the well: *and* it was about the sixth hour.

⁷ There cometh a woman of Samaria to draw water: Jesus saith unto her, Give me to drink.

⁸ (For his disciples were gone away unto the city to buy meat.)

⁹ Then saith the woman of Samaria unto him, How is it that thou, being a Jew, askest drink of me, which am a woman of Samaria? for the Jews have no dealings with the Samaritans.

¹⁰ Jesus answered and said unto her, If thou knewest the gift of God, and who it is that saith to thee, Give me to drink; thou wouldest have asked of him, and he would have given thee living water.

¹¹ The woman saith unto him, Sir, thou hast nothing to draw with, and the well is deep: from whence then hast thou that living water?

¹² Art thou greater than our father Jacob, which gave us the well, and drank thereof himself, and his children, and his cattle?

¹³ Jesus answered and said unto her, Whosoever drinketh of this water shall thirst again:

¹⁴ but whosoever drinketh of the water that I shall give him shall never thirst; but the water that I shall give him shall be in him a well of water springing up into everlasting life.

¹⁵ The woman saith unto him, Sir, give me this water, that I thirst not, neither come hither to draw.

¹⁶ Jesus saith unto her, Go, call thy husband, and come hither.

¹⁷ The woman answered and said, I have no husband. Jesus said unto her, Thou hast well said, I have no husband:

¹⁸ for thou hast had five husbands; and he whom thou now hast is not thy

husband: in that saidst thou truly.

¹⁹ The woman saith unto him, Sir, I perceive that thou art a prophet.

²⁰ Our fathers worshipped in this mountain; and ye say, that in Jerusalem is the place where men ought to worship.

²¹ Jesus saith unto her, Woman, believe me, the hour cometh, when ye shall neither in this mountain, nor yet at Jerusalem, worship the Father.

²² Ye worship ye know not what: we know what we worship; for salvation is of the Jews.

²³ But the hour cometh, and now is, when the true worshippers shall worship the Father in spirit and in truth: for the Father seeketh such to worship him.

²⁴ God *is* a Spirit: and they that worship him must worship *him* in spirit and in truth.

²⁵ The woman saith unto him, I know that Messiah cometh, which is called Christ: when he is come, he will tell us all things.

²⁶ Jesus saith unto her, I that speak unto thee am *he.*

OLD TESTAMENT READING

*B*e astonished, O ye heavens, at this, and be horribly afraid, be ye very desolate, saith the LORD.

¹³ For my people have committed two evils; they have forsaken me the fountain of living waters, *and* hewed them out cisterns, broken cisterns, that can hold no water.

¹⁸ And now what hast thou to do in the way of Egypt, to drink the waters of Sihor? or what hast thou to do in the way of Assyria, to drink the waters of the river?

¹⁹ Thine own wickedness shall correct thee, and thy backslidings shall reprove thee: know therefore and see that *it is* an evil *thing* and bitter, that thou hast forsaken the LORD thy God, and that my fear *is* not in thee, saith the Lord GOD of hosts.

Jeremiah 2:12-13,18-19

INSIGHTS

*T*he flow of life surging and pulsing through me to refresh this weary old world must be from God Himself. It must be the continuous outpouring of His Presence by His Spirit which touches and transforms all around me. Any person naive enough, arrogant enough, stupid enough to believe that it is his or her own charm, charisma, or capabilities that change and enliven others, lives in utter self-delusion.

One of the terrible tragedies of human behavior is for people to turn to other human beings in an effort to find sustenance for their spirits. They are always deluded, ever disappointed. Our spirits can only find life in the Living Spirit of the Living Lord. Our eternal quest for life-giving water can only be quenched by the eternal life of God Himself coming to us through the hidden springs of His own person who indwells those who are open channels for His life.

W. Phillip Keller

PAUSE FOR REFLECTION

*W*hat do those who drink of Jesus' living water receive? How does one receive living water? What happens to everyone who rejects God's living water? What is the source of your sustenance?

TUESDAY

*When People Believe,
God Does Great Things*

John 4:27–54

*A*nd upon this came his disciples, and marveled that he talked with the woman: yet no man said, What seekest thou? or, Why talkest thou with her?

²⁸ The woman then left her waterpot, and went her way into the city, and saith to the men,

²⁹ Come, see a man, which told me all things that ever I did: is not this the Christ?

³⁰ Then they went out of the city, and came unto him.

³¹ In the mean while his disciples prayed him, saying, Master, eat.

³² But he said unto them, I have meat to eat that ye know not of.

³³ Therefore said the disciples one to another, Hath any man brought him *ought* to eat?

³⁴ Jesus saith unto them, My meat is to do the will of him that sent me, and to finish his work.

³⁵ Say not ye, There are yet four months, and *then* cometh harvest? behold, I say unto you, Lift up your eyes, and look on the fields; for they are white already to harvest.

³⁶ And he that reapeth receiveth wages, and gathereth fruit unto life eternal: that both he that soweth and he that reapeth may rejoice together.

³⁷ And herein is that saying true, One soweth, and another reapeth.

³⁸ I sent you to reap that whereupon ye bestowed no labor: other men labored, and ye are entered into their labors.

³⁹ And many of the Samaritans of that city believed on him for the saying of the woman, which testified, He told me all that ever I did.

⁴⁰ So when the Samaritans were come unto him, they besought him that he would tarry with them: and he abode there two days.

⁴¹ And many more believed because of his own word;

⁴² and said unto the woman, Now we believe, not because of thy saying: for we have heard *him* ourselves, and know that this is indeed the Christ, the Saviour of the world.

Jesus Heals a Nobleman's Son

*N*ow after two days he departed thence, and went into Galilee.

⁴⁴ For Jesus himself testified, that a prophet hath no honor in his own country.

⁴⁵ Then when he was come into Galilee, the Galileans received him, having seen all the things that he did at Jerusalem at the feast: for they also went unto the feast.

⁴⁶ So Jesus came again into Cana of Galilee, where he made the water wine. And there was a certain nobleman, whose son was sick at Capernaum.

⁴⁷ When he heard that Jesus was come out of Judea into Galilee, he went unto him, and besought him that he would come down, and heal his son: for he was at the point of death.

⁴⁸ Then said Jesus unto him, Except ye see signs and wonders, ye will not believe.

⁴⁹ The nobleman saith unto him, Sir, come down ere my child die.

⁵⁰ Jesus saith unto him, Go thy way; thy son liveth. And the man believed the word that Jesus had spoken unto him, and he went his way.

⁵¹ And as he was now going down, his servants met him, and told *him,* saying, Thy son liveth.

⁵² Then enquired he of them the hour when he began to amend. And they said unto him, Yesterday at the seventh hour the fever left him.

⁵³ So the father knew that *it was* at the same hour, in the which Jesus said unto him, Thy son liveth: and himself believed, and his whole house.

⁵⁴ This *is* again the second miracle *that* Jesus did, when he was come out of Judea into Galilee.

OLD TESTAMENT READING

*A*nd they rose early in the morning, and went forth into the wilderness of Tekoa: and as they went forth, Jehoshaphat stood and said, Hear me, O Judah, and ye inhabitants of Jerusalem; Believe in the LORD your God, so shall ye be established; believe his prophets, so shall ye prosper.

²¹ And when he had consulted with the people, he appointed singers unto the LORD, and that should praise the beauty of holiness, as they went out before the army, and to say, Praise the LORD; for his mercy *endureth* for ever.

²² And when they began to sing and to praise, the LORD set ambushments against the children of Ammon, Moab, and mount Seir, which were come against Judah; and they were smitten.

2 Chronicles 20:20-22

INSIGHTS

*A*s Joshua 3 opens, the Israelites are camped on the bank of the Jordan River. . . . They are in sight of the Promised Land, Canaan, but they have an enormous problem: a river is right in their path, and there's no convenient way around it. To make matters worse, it is flood season, and any usual fording places are impassable. The waters are deep and turbulent and menacing.

God could easily make the river subside right before their eyes. He could throw a wide bridge across it. But he doesn't. Instead, he gives Joshua some strange orders. . .

. . . Joshua commands the priests to pick up the ark and go stand in the river. . . .

In spite of the problems, the priests had faith enough to obey, and this is what happened: "As soon as the priests who carried the ark reached the Jordan and their feet touched the water's edge, the water from upstream stopped flowing. . . . The priests who carried the ark of the covenant of the LORD stood firm on dry ground in the middle of the Jordan, while all Israel passed by until the whole nation had completed the crossing on dry ground" (Josh 3:15–17).

God didn't give the priests absolute proof or even overwhelming evidence that the waters would part. He did nothing until they put their feet in the water, taking the first step of commitment and obedience. Only then did he stop the flow of the river. In the same way, mountain-moving faith will be given to us as we step out and follow the Lord's direction.

Bill Hybels

PAUSE FOR REFLECTION

*W*ho ever heard of a flooding river that stopped instantly? An adulterous woman bringing others to Christ? For what do you believe God?

WEDNESDAY

God Gives Eternal Life to Those Who Believe

John 5:1–29

Jesus Heals a Man at a Pool

5 After this there was a feast of the Jews; and Jesus went up to Jerusalem.

2 Now there is at Jerusalem by the sheep *market* a pool, which is called in the Hebrew tongue Bethesda, having five porches.

3 In these lay a great multitude of impotent folk, of blind, halt, withered, waiting for the moving of the water.

4 For an angel went down at a certain season into the pool, and troubled the water: whosoever then first after the troubling of the water stepped in was made whole of whatsoever disease he had.

5 And a certain man was there, which had an infirmity thirty and eight years.

6 When Jesus saw him lie, and knew that he had been now a long time *in that case*, he saith unto him, Wilt thou be made whole?

7 The impotent man answered him, Sir, I have no man, when the water is troubled, to put me into the pool: but while I am coming, another steppeth down before me.

8 Jesus saith unto him, Rise, take up thy bed, and walk.

9 And immediately the man was made whole, and took up his bed, and walked: and on the same day was the sabbath.

10 The Jews therefore said unto him that was cured, It is the sabbath day: it is not lawful for thee to carry *thy* bed.

11 He answered them, He that made me whole, the same said unto me, Take up thy bed, and walk.

12 Then asked they him, What man is that which said unto thee, Take up thy bed, and walk?

13 And he that was healed wist not who it was: for Jesus had conveyed himself away, a multitude being in *that* place.

14 Afterward Jesus findeth him in the temple, and said unto him, Behold, thou art made whole: sin no more, lest a worse thing come unto thee.

15 The man departed, and told the Jews that it was Jesus, which had made him whole.

16 And therefore did the Jews persecute Jesus, and sought to slay him, because he had done these things on the sabbath day.

17 But Jesus answered them, My Father worketh hitherto, and I work.

18 Therefore the Jews sought the more to kill him, because he not only had broken the sabbath, but said also that God was his Father, making himself equal with God.

Jesus Has God's Authority

*T*hen answered Jesus and said unto them, Verily, verily, I say unto you, The Son can do nothing of himself, but what he seeth the Father do: for what things soever he doeth, these also doeth the Son likewise.

20 For the Father loveth the Son, and showeth him all things that himself doeth: and he will show him greater works than these, that ye may marvel.

21 For as the Father raiseth up the dead, and quickeneth *them*; even so the Son quickeneth whom he will.

22 For the Father judgeth no man, but hath committed all judgment unto the Son:

²³ that all *men* should honor the Son, even as they honor the Father. He that honoreth not the Son honoreth not the Father which hath sent him.

²⁴ Verily, verily, I say unto you, He that heareth my word, and believeth on him that sent me, hath everlasting life, and shall not come into condemnation; but is passed from death unto life.

²⁵ Verily, verily, I say unto you, The hour is coming, and now is, when the dead shall hear the voice of the Son of God: and they that hear shall live.

²⁶ For as the Father hath life in himself; so hath he given to the Son to have life in himself;

²⁷ and hath given him authority to execute judgment also, because he is the Son of man.

²⁸ Marvel not at this: for the hour is coming, in the which all that are in the graves shall hear his voice,

²⁹ and shall come forth; they that have done good, unto the resurrection of life; and they that have done evil, unto the resurrection of damnation.

OLD TESTAMENT READING

*E*vil shall slay the wicked: and they that hate the righteous shall be desolate.

²² The LORD redeemeth the soul of his servants: and none of them that trust in him shall be desolate.

Psalm 34:21-22

*T*he LORD *is* my light and my salvation; whom shall I fear? The LORD *is* the strength of my life; of whom shall I be afraid?

Psalm 27:1

INSIGHTS

*T*he New Testament teaching is not that everyone has eternal life, but that those who come to God through Jesus Christ are given eternal life as a gift. Many passages contain this teaching; it is not found in only one or two texts. The new birth, being "born of the Spirit," is to have the life of God given to us. Not all are born of the Spirit. The Scripture rejects the idea that everybody has a spark of deity within. In fact, the Bible says that man, in his natural condition, is "dead to God" and that rebirth, an action of the Holy Spirit, is required to plant the life of God.

That "the gift of God is eternal life" doesn't mean that our lives just go on and on and on. It means that we share in the divine nature of God, which is itself eternal. It is His life, then, that is lived in our bodies. That's what's meant by eternal life. We don't begin eternal life when we die; we begin it while we still live. Eternity begins with belief in Christ. . . .

. . . Eternal life comes to those who believe in the Son of Man, who has been lifted up on the cross—that act of obedience to the Father, His death, that brought salvation to all who believe in Him. It belongs to those who will share in the resurrection victory of Jesus Christ over death.

Terry Fullam

APPLICATION

*I*n the Old Testament, God is clearly recognized as the source and giver of life. What claims does Jesus make regarding his ability to give eternal life? Have you accepted Jesus' daring offer of eternal life?

THURSDAY

People Choose Whether or Not to Believe in Christ

John 5:30—6:15

Jesus Is God's Son

I can of mine own self do nothing: as I hear, I judge: and my judgment is just; because I seek not mine own will, but the will of the Father which hath sent me.

[31] If I bear witness of myself, my witness is not true.

[32] There is another that beareth witness of me; and I know that the witness which he witnesseth of me is true.

[33] Ye sent unto John, and he bare witness unto the truth.

[34] But I receive not testimony from man: but these things I say, that ye might be saved.

[35] He was a burning and a shining light: and ye were willing for a season to rejoice in his light.

[36] But I have greater witness than *that* of John: for the works which the Father hath given me to finish, the same works that I do, bear witness of me, that the Father hath sent me.

[37] And the Father himself, which hath sent me, hath borne witness of me. Ye have neither heard his voice at any time, nor seen his shape.

[38] And ye have not his word abiding in you: for whom he hath sent, him ye believe not.

[39] Search the Scriptures; for in them ye think ye have eternal life: and they are they which testify of me.

[40] And ye will not come to me, that ye might have life.

[41] I receive not honor from men.

[42] But I know you, that ye have not the love of God in you.

[43] I am come in my Father's name, and ye receive me not: if another shall come in his own name, him ye will receive.

[44] How can ye believe, which receive honor one of another, and seek not the honor that *cometh* from God only?

[45] Do not think that I will accuse you to the Father: there is *one* that accuseth you, *even* Moses, in whom ye trust.

[46] For had ye believed Moses, ye would have believed me: for he wrote of me.

[47] But if ye believe not his writings, how shall ye believe my words?

More than Five Thousand Fed

6 After these things Jesus went over the sea of Galilee, which is *the sea* of Tiberias.

[2] And a great multitude followed him, because they saw his miracles which he did on them that were diseased.

[3] And Jesus went up into a mountain, and there he sat with his disciples.

[4] And the passover, a feast of the Jews, was nigh.

[5] When Jesus then lifted up *his* eyes, and saw a great company come unto him, he saith unto Philip, Whence shall we buy bread, that these may eat?

[6] And this he said to prove him: for he himself knew what he would do.

[7] Philip answered him, Two hundred pennyworth of bread is not sufficient for them, that every one of them may take a little.

[8] One of his disciples, Andrew, Simon Peter's brother, saith unto him,

[9] There is a lad here, which hath five barley loaves, and two small fishes:

but what are they among so many? ¹⁰ And Jesus said, Make the men sit down. Now there was much grass in the place. So the men sat down, in number about five thousand.

¹¹ And Jesus took the loaves; and when he had given thanks, he distributed to the disciples, and the disciples to them that were set down; and likewise of the fishes as much as they would.

¹² When they were filled, he said unto his disciples, Gather up the fragments that remain, that nothing be lost.

¹³ Therefore they gathered *them* together, and filled twelve baskets with the fragments of the five barley loaves, which remained over and above unto them that had eaten.

¹⁴ Then those men, when they had seen the miracle that Jesus did, said, This is of a truth that Prophet that should come into the world.

¹⁵ When Jesus therefore perceived that they would come and take him by force, to make him a king, he departed again into a mountain himself alone.

OLD TESTAMENT READING

*T*he sceptre shall not depart from Judah, nor a lawgiver from between his feet, until Shiloh come; and unto him *shall* the gathering of the people *be.*

Genesis 49:10

INSIGHTS

*W*hat God did makes sense. It makes sense that Jesus would be our sacrifice because a sacrifice was needed to justify man's presence before God. It makes sense that God would use the Old Law to tutor Israel on their need for grace. It makes sense that Jesus would be our High Priest. What God did makes sense. It can be taught, charted, and put in books on systematic theology.

However, why God did it is absolutely absurd. When one leaves the method and examines the motive, the carefully stacked blocks of logic begin to tumble. That type of love isn't logical; it can't be neatly outlined in a sermon or explained in a term paper. . . .

Even after generations of people had spit in his face, he still loved them. After a nation of chosen ones had stripped him naked and ripped his incarnated flesh, he still died for them. And even today, after billions have chosen to prostitute themselves before pimps of power, fame, and wealth, he still waits for them.

It is inexplicable. It doesn't have a drop of logic nor a thread of rationality. . . .

Bloodstained royalty. A God with tears. A creator with a heart. God became earth's mockery to save his children.

How absurd to think that such nobility would go to such poverty to share such a treasure with such thankless souls.

But he did.

In fact, the only thing more absurd than the gift is our stubborn unwillingness to receive it.

Max Lucado

APPLICATION

*W*hat evidence from his life and from the Scriptures proves that Jesus was who he said he was? Why didn't most Jews believe Jesus? Do you believe and trust him?

FRIDAY

Believe in the God of Miracles

John 6:16–40

Jesus Walks on the Water

*A*nd when even was *now* come, his disciples went down unto the sea,

[17] and entered into a ship, and went over the sea toward Capernaum. And it was now dark, and Jesus was not come to them.

[18] And the sea arose by reason of a great wind that blew.

[19] So when they had rowed about five and twenty or thirty furlongs, they see Jesus walking on the sea, and drawing nigh unto the ship: and they were afraid.

[20] But he saith unto them, It is I; be not afraid.

[21] Then they willingly received him into the ship: and immediately the ship was at the land whither they went.

The People Seek Jesus

*T*he day following, when the people, which stood on the other side of the sea, saw that there was none other boat there, save that one whereinto his disciples were entered, and that Jesus went not with his disciples into the boat, but *that* his disciples were gone away alone;

[23] (howbeit there came other boats from Tiberias nigh unto the place where they did eat bread, after that the Lord had given thanks:)

[24] when the people therefore saw that Jesus was not there, neither his disciples, they also took shipping, and came to Capernaum, seeking for Jesus.

Jesus, the Bread of Life

*A*nd when they had found him on the other side of the sea, they said unto him, Rabbi, when camest thou hither?

[26] Jesus answered them and said, Verily, verily, I say unto you, Ye seek me, not because ye saw the miracles, but because ye did eat of the loaves, and were filled.

[27] Labor not for the meat which perisheth, but for that meat which endureth unto everlasting life, which the Son of man shall give unto you: for him hath God the Father sealed.

[28] Then said they unto him, What shall we do, that we might work the works of God?

[29] Jesus answered and said unto them, This is the work of God, that ye believe on him whom he hath sent.

[30] They said therefore unto him, What sign showest thou then, that we may see, and believe thee? what dost thou work?

[31] Our fathers did eat manna in the desert; as it is written, He gave them bread from heaven to eat.

[32] Then Jesus said unto them, Verily, verily, I say unto you, Moses gave you not that bread from heaven; but my Father giveth you the true bread from heaven.

[33] For the bread of God is he which cometh down from heaven, and giveth life unto the world.

[34] Then said they unto him, Lord, evermore give us this bread.

[35] And Jesus said unto them, I am the bread of life: he that cometh to me shall never hunger; and he that believeth on me shall never thirst.

[36] But I said unto you, That ye also

have seen me, and believe not.

37 All that the Father giveth me shall come to me; and him that cometh to me I will in no wise cast out.

38 For I came down from heaven, not to do mine own will, but the will of him that sent me.

39 And this is the Father's will which hath sent me, that of all which he hath given me I should lose nothing, but should raise it up again at the last day.

40 And this is the will of him that sent me, that every one which seeth the Son, and believeth on him, may have everlasting life: and I will raise him up at the last day.

OLD TESTAMENT READING

*G*ive thanks unto the LORD, call upon his name, make known his deeds among the people.

9 Sing unto him, sing psalms unto him, talk ye of all his wondrous works.

10 Glory ye in his holy name: let the heart of them rejoice that seek the LORD.

11 Seek the LORD and his strength, seek his face continually.

12 Remember his marvelous works that he hath done, his wonders, and the judgments of his mouth.

1 Chronicles 16:8-12

INSIGHTS

*M*om, I need new shoes," Nicky announced as he burst through the door after school. "Miss Bell says it's dangerous to run in gym with my toe sticking out."

I looked down at my son's blue tennies. Hadn't I just bought them last month? But the protruding toe, a slit along the side, and tattered laces told me he'd had them longer. "You're right,

Nicky. It's time for some new tennies, but you'll have to wait until our next paycheck. . . ."

"But, Mother," Nicky protested, "I can't wear these shoes for gym anymore. Miss Bell said!"

I launched into an elaborate discourse on budgeting principles. "So you see, Nicky," I concluded, "that's how Mommy and Daddy spend money. Tennis shoes are not in the budget this time; next time they will be."

"Then I'll pray about my shoes," Nicky announced. "I'll tell God I need the money by tomorrow." . . .

. . . When he left for school the next morning, new tennis shoes were still uppermost on his mind. "Can we buy my shoes tonight? You'll get the money today, because I prayed about it."

"We'll see, Nicky," I replied as I kissed him good-bye. There wasn't time to explain just then.

But the need to explain didn't come; Nicky's answer came instead. "This is long overdue . . . sorry for the oversight," said the note I received in the mail that afternoon. The enclosed check, payment for an article I'd written long ago and forgotten, was more than enough to pay for Nicky's new shoes.

After school, Nicky's blue eyes danced. "See, Mom I told you it would come. Now can we buy my shoes?"

Today Nicky wears new blue-and-gold tennis shoes—poignant reminders of a child's simple trust and of my need to continually relearn what faith is all about.

Ruth Senter

ACTION POINT

*W*hat is your psalm of praise to God? Praise him with joy!

WEEKEND

When Difficulties Come,
Some Want to Reject God

John 6:41–71

*T*he Jews then murmured at him, because he said, I am the bread which came down from heaven.

42 And they said, Is not this Jesus, the son of Joseph, whose father and mother we know? how is it then that he saith, I came down from heaven?

43 Jesus therefore answered and said unto them, Murmur not among yourselves.

44 No man can come to me, except the Father which hath sent me draw him: and I will raise him up at the last day.

45 It is written in the prophets, And they shall be all taught of God. Every man therefore that hath heard, and hath learned of the Father, cometh unto me.

46 Not that any man hath seen the Father, save he which is of God, he hath seen the Father.

47 Verily, verily, I say unto you, He that believeth on me hath everlasting life.

48 I am that bread of life.

49 Your fathers did eat manna in the wilderness, and are dead.

50 This is the bread which cometh down from heaven, that a man may eat thereof, and not die.

51 I am the living bread which came down from heaven: if any man eat of this bread, he shall live for ever: and the bread that I will give is my flesh, which I will give for the life of the world.

52 The Jews therefore strove among themselves, saying, How can this man give us *his* flesh to eat?

53 Then Jesus said unto them, Verily, verily, I say unto you, Except ye eat the flesh of the Son of man, and drink his blood, ye have no life in you.

54 Whoso eateth my flesh, and drinketh my blood, hath eternal life; and I will raise him up at the last day.

55 For my flesh is meat indeed, and my blood is drink indeed.

56 He that eateth my flesh, and drinketh my blood, dwelleth in me, and I in him.

57 As the living Father hath sent me, and I live by the Father; so he that eateth me, even he shall live by me.

58 This is that bread which came down from heaven: not as your fathers did eat manna, and are dead: he that eateth of this bread shall live for ever.

59 These things said he in the synagogue, as he taught in Capernaum.

The Words of Eternal Life

*M*any therefore of his disciples, when they had heard *this*, said, This is a hard saying; who can hear it?

61 When Jesus knew in himself that his disciples murmured at it, he said unto them, Doth this offend you?

62 *What* and if ye shall see the Son of man ascend up where he was before?

63 It is the spirit that quickeneth; the flesh profiteth nothing: the words that I speak unto you, *they* are spirit, and *they* are life.

64 But there are some of you that believe not. For Jesus knew from the beginning who they were that believed not, and who should betray him.

65 And he said, Therefore said I unto you, that no man can come unto me, except it were given unto him of my Father.

66 From that *time* many of his disciples

went back, and walked no more with him.

⁶⁷ Then said Jesus unto the twelve, Will ye also go away?

⁶⁸ Then Simon Peter answered him, Lord, to whom shall we go? thou hast the words of eternal life.

⁶⁹ And we believe and are sure that thou art that Christ, the Son of the living God.

⁷⁰ Jesus answered them, Have not I chosen you twelve, and one of you is a devil?

⁷¹ He spake of Judas Iscariot *the son* of Simon: for he it was that should betray him, being one of the twelve.

OLD TESTAMENT READING

*A*nd all the congregation lifted up their voice, and cried; and the people wept that night.

² And all the children of Israel murmured against Moses and against Aaron: and the whole congregation said unto them, Would God that we had died in the land of Egypt! or would God we had died in this wilderness!

³ And wherefore hath the LORD brought us unto this land, to fall by the sword, that our wives and our children should be a prey? were it not better for us to return into Egypt?

⁴ And they said one to another, Let us make a captain, and let us return into Egypt.

Numbers 14:1-4

INSIGHTS

*A*s God's children, through having accepted Christ's work for us, accusations are definitely always off limits. As we stand before the Creator of the universe, the all-wise, perfectly holy, mighty God, who made us in

His image, who upholds the universe, who understands all things, who has shown His compassion in providing a way for us to come to Him through the Messiah, the Lamb . . . how dare we shake our fist in His face? How dare we question God and say, "Why did you do this to me?" . . .

. . . We can be angry at a person when we are caught in the awful results of cause-and-effect history following the Fall, or following attacks of Satan, or following human choices of one kind or another—but that person is never God. We may not understand our tragic situation. We may not feel we can face life after a terrible shock. We may not feel that we know how to cope in the midst of a war, or avalanche, or earthquake, or famine. But it is always off limits to blame God. We are not to run away from God, shaking our fist at Him and screaming. We are to run to Him when we are shaking with grief or trembling with fear.

He is our refuge and strength; a very present help in trouble. Our help is to come from Him as we run into the shelter of His arms, away from the noise of the battle, or the storm. He has promised us comfort, and we need to climb on His lap as a weeping, hurt child, not to kick at Him.

Edith Schaeffer

PAUSE FOR REFLECTION

*W*hat difficulties or lack of understanding in life have tempted you to turn away from God? Did you reject or run toward God? What gives you confidence that Jesus is the "Holy One from God," the one on whom you can believe, the one you can run to for shelter?

M O N D A Y

The World Hates Those Who Expose Evil

John 7:1–31

Jesus' Brothers Don't Believe

7 After these things Jesus walked in Galilee: for he would not walk in Jewry, because the Jews sought to kill him.

2 Now the Jews' feast of tabernacles was at hand.

3 His brethren therefore said unto him, Depart hence, and go into Judea, that thy disciples also may see the works that thou doest.

4 For *there is* no man *that* doeth any thing in secret, and he himself seeketh to be known openly. If thou do these things, show thyself to the world.

5 For neither did his brethren believe in him.

6 Then Jesus said unto them, My time is not yet come: but your time is always ready.

7 The world cannot hate you; but me it hateth, because I testify of it, that the works thereof are evil.

8 Go ye up unto this feast; I go not up yet unto this feast; for my time is not yet full come.

9 When he had said these words unto them, he abode *still* in Galilee.

10 But when his brethren were gone up, then went he also up unto the feast, not openly, but as it were in secret.

11 Then the Jews sought him at the feast, and said, Where is he?

12 And there was much murmuring among the people concerning him: for some said, He is a good man: others said, Nay; but he deceiveth the people.

13 Howbeit no man spake openly of him for fear of the Jews.

Jesus Teaches at the Feast

Now about the midst of the feast Jesus went up into the temple, and taught.

15 And the Jews marveled, saying, How knoweth this man letters, having never learned?

16 Jesus answered them, and said, My doctrine is not mine, but his that sent me.

17 If any man will do his will, he shall know of the doctrine, whether it be of God, or *whether* I speak of myself.

18 He that speaketh of himself seeketh his own glory: but he that seeketh his glory that sent him, the same is true, and no unrighteousness is in him.

19 Did not Moses give you the law, and *yet* none of you keepeth the law? Why go ye about to kill me?

20 The people answered and said, Thou hast a devil: who goeth about to kill thee?

21 Jesus answered and said unto them, I have done one work, and ye all marvel.

22 Moses therefore gave unto you circumcision; (not because it is of Moses, but of the fathers;) and ye on the sabbath day circumcise a man.

23 If a man on the sabbath day receive circumcision, that the law of Moses should not be broken; are ye angry at me, because I have made a man every whit whole on the sabbath day?

24 Judge not according to the appearance, but judge righteous judgment.

Is Jesus the Christ?

Then said some of them of Jerusalem, Is not this he, whom they seek to kill?

²⁶ But, lo, he speaketh boldly, and they say nothing unto him. Do the rulers know indeed that this is the very Christ?

²⁷ Howbeit we know this man whence he is: but when Christ cometh, no man knoweth whence he is.

²⁸ Then cried Jesus in the temple as he taught, saying, Ye both know me, and ye know whence I am: and I am not come of myself, but he that sent me is true, whom ye know not.

²⁹ But I know him; for I am from him, and he hath sent me.

³⁰ Then they sought to take him: but no man laid hands on him, because his hour was not yet come.

³¹ And many of the people believed on him, and said, When Christ cometh, will he do more miracles than these which this *man* hath done?

OLD TESTAMENT READING

*A*nd Jehoshaphat said, *Is there* not here a prophet of the LORD besides, that we might inquire of him?

⁸ And the king of Israel said unto Jehoshaphat, *There is* yet one man, Micaiah the son of Imlah, by whom we may inquire of the LORD.

1 Kings 22:7-8a

INSIGHTS

A few years ago one of the leading golfers on the professional tour was invited to play in a foursome with Gerald Ford, then president of the United States, Jack Nicklaus, and Billy Graham. . . .

After the round of golf was finished, one of the other pros came up to the golfer and asked, "Hey, what was it like playing with the president and with Billy Graham?"

The pro unleashed a torrent of cursing, and in a disgusted manner said, "I don't need Billy Graham stuffing religion down my throat." With that he turned on his heel and stormed off, heading for the practice tee. . . .

Astonishing. Billy Graham had said not a word about God, Jesus, or religion, yet the pro had stormed away after the game accusing Billy of trying to ram religion down his throat. How can we explain this? It's really not difficult. Billy Graham didn't have to say a word; he didn't have to give a single sideward glance to make the pro feel uncomfortable. Billy Graham is so identified with religion, so associated with the things of God, that his very presence is enough to smother the wicked man who flees when no man pursues. . . .

. . . The greater the holiness the greater the human hostility toward it. It seems insane. No man was ever more loving than Jesus Christ. Yet even His love provoked men to anger. His love was a perfect love, a transcendent and holy love, but His very love brought trauma to people. This kind of love is so majestic we can't stand it.

R. C. Sproul

PAUSE FOR REFLECTION

*F*or what reasons did the leaders of the Jews hate Jesus? Was their hatred for righteousness anything new? Is your life holy enough to incur the wrath of the unrighteous?

TUESDAY
Everyone Has Sinned

John 7:32—8:11

The Leaders Try to Arrest Jesus

*T*he Pharisees heard that the people murmured such things concerning him; and the Pharisees and the chief priests sent officers to take him.

33 Then said Jesus unto them, Yet a little while am I with you, and *then* I go unto him that sent me.

34 Ye shall seek me, and shall not find *me*: and where I am, *thither* ye cannot come.

35 Then said the Jews among themselves, Whither will he go, that we shall not find him? will he go unto the dispersed among the Gentiles, and teach the Gentiles?

36 What *manner of* saying is this that he said, Ye shall seek me, and shall not find *me*: and where I am, *thither* ye cannot come?

Jesus Talks About the Spirit

*I*n the last day, that great *day* of the feast, Jesus stood and cried, saying, If any man thirst, let him come unto me, and drink.

38 He that believeth on me, as the Scripture hath said, out of his belly shall flow rivers of living water.

39 (But this spake he of the Spirit, which they that believe on him should receive: for the Holy Ghost was not yet *given*; because that Jesus was not yet glorified.)

The People Argue About Jesus

*M*any of the people therefore, when they heard this saying, said, Of a truth this is the Prophet.

41 Others said, This is the Christ. But some said, Shall Christ come out of Galilee?

42 Hath not the Scripture said, That Christ cometh of the seed of David, and out of the town of Bethlehem, where David was?

43 So there was a division among the people because of him.

44 And some of them would have taken him; but no man laid hands on him.

Some Leaders Won't Believe

*T*hen came the officers to the chief priests and Pharisees; and they said unto them, Why have ye not brought him?

46 The officers answered, Never man spake like this man.

47 Then answered them the Pharisees, Are ye also deceived?

48 Have any of the rulers or of the Pharisees believed on him?

49 But this people who knoweth not the law are cursed.

50 Nicodemus saith unto them, (he that came to Jesus by night, being one of them,)

51 Doth our law judge *any* man, before it hear him, and know what he doeth?

52 They answered and said unto him, Art thou also of Galilee? Search, and look: for out of Galilee ariseth no prophet.

53 And every man went unto his own house.

The Woman Caught in Adultery

8 Jesus went unto the mount of Olives.
2 And early in the morning he

came again into the temple, and all the people came unto him; and he sat down, and taught them.

³ And the scribes and Pharisees brought unto him a woman taken in adultery; and when they had set her in the midst,

⁴ they say unto him, Master, this woman was taken in adultery, in the very act.

⁵ Now Moses in the law commanded us, that such should be stoned: but what sayest thou?

⁶ This they said, tempting him, that they might have to accuse him. But Jesus stooped down, and with *his* finger wrote on the ground, *as though he heard them not.*

⁷ So when they continued asking him, he lifted up himself, and said unto them, He that is without sin among you, let him first cast a stone at her.

⁸ And again he stooped down, and wrote on the ground.

⁹ And they which heard *it*, being convicted by *their own* conscience, went out one by one, beginning at the eldest, *even* unto the last: and Jesus was left alone, and the woman standing in the midst.

¹⁰ When Jesus had lifted up himself, and saw none but the woman, he said unto her, Woman, where are those thine accusers? hath no man condemned thee?

¹¹ She said, No man, Lord. And Jesus said unto her, Neither do I condemn thee: go, and sin no more.

OLD TESTAMENT READING

*W*ho can say, I have made my heart clean, I am pure from my sin?

Proverbs 20:9

INSIGHTS

*T*he same sin that Adam introduced has polluted the entire human race. No one is immune to the sin disease. And no human accomplishment can erase the internal stain that separates us from God. Because Adam sinned, all have sinned. This leads to one conclusion: We all need help. We need forgiveness. We need a Savior.

So . . . how do we get out of this mess? . . .

So then as through one transgression there resulted condemnation to all men, even so through one act of righteousness there resulted justification of life to all men. For as through the one man's disobedience the many were made sinners, even so through the obedience of the One the many will be made righteous. (Rom. 5:18–19)

"You're telling me, Chuck, that by simply believing in Jesus Christ I can have eternal life with God, my sins forgiven, a destiny secure in heaven, all of this and much more without my working for that?" Yes, that is precisely what Scripture teaches. I remind you, it is called grace. . . . Salvation is offered by divine grace, not by human works.

Charles Swindoll

PAUSE FOR REFLECTION

*L*ist the ways Scripture readings show that every person has sinned. What did Jesus say to the woman caught in adultery? Is it different than what he says to you? How have you responded?

WEDNESDAY

*Jesus' Relationship
with His Father*

John 8:12–41

Jesus Is the Light of the World

*T*hen spake Jesus again unto them, saying, I am the light of the world: he that followeth me shall not walk in darkness, but shall have the light of life.

[13] The Pharisees therefore said unto him, Thou bearest record of thyself; thy record is not true.

[14] Jesus answered and said unto them, Though I bear record of myself, *yet* my record is true: for I know whence I came, and whither I go; but ye cannot tell whence I come, and whither I go.

[15] Ye judge after the flesh; I judge no man.

[16] And yet if I judge, my judgment is true: for I am not alone, but I and the Father that sent me.

[17] It is also written in your law, that the testimony of two men is true.

[18] I am one that bear witness of myself, and the Father that sent me beareth witness of me.

[19] Then said they unto him, Where is thy Father? Jesus answered, Ye neither know me, nor my Father: if ye had known me, ye should have known my Father also.

[20] These words spake Jesus in the treasury, as he taught in the temple: and no man laid hands on him; for his hour was not yet come.

The People Misunderstand Jesus

*T*hen said Jesus again unto them,

I go my way, and ye shall seek me, and shall die in your sins: whither I go, ye cannot come.

[22] Then said the Jews, Will he kill himself? because he saith, Whither I go, ye cannot come.

[23] And he said unto them, Ye are from beneath; I am from above: ye are of this world; I am not of this world.

[24] I said therefore unto you, that ye shall die in your sins: for if ye believe not that I am *he*, ye shall die in your sins.

[25] Then said they unto him, Who art thou? And Jesus saith unto them, Even *the same* that I said unto you from the beginning.

[26] I have many things to say and to judge of you: but he that sent me is true; and I speak to the world those things which I have heard of him.

[27] They understood not that he spake to them of the Father.

[28] Then said Jesus unto them, When ye have lifted up the Son of man, then shall ye know that I am *he*, and *that* I do nothing of myself; but as my Father hath taught me, I speak these things.

[29] And he that sent me is with me: the Father hath not left me alone; for I do always those things that please him.

[30] As he spake these words, many believed on him.

Freedom from Sin

*T*hen said Jesus to those Jews which believed on him, If ye continue in my word, then are ye my disciples indeed;

[32] and ye shall know the truth, and the truth shall make you free.

[33] They answered him, We be Abraham's seed, and were never in bondage to any man: how sayest

thou, Ye shall be made free?

³⁴ Jesus answered them, Verily, verily, I say unto you, Whosoever committeth sin is the servant of sin.

³⁵ And the servant abideth not in the house for ever: *but* the Son abideth ever.

³⁶ If the Son therefore shall make you free, ye shall be free indeed.

³⁷ I know that ye are Abraham's seed; but ye seek to kill me, because my word hath no place in you.

³⁸ I speak that which I have seen with my Father: and ye do that which ye have seen with your father.

³⁹ They answered and said unto him, Abraham is our father. Jesus saith unto them, If ye were Abraham's children, ye would do the works of Abraham.

⁴⁰ But now ye seek to kill me, a man that hath told you the truth, which I have heard of God: this did not Abraham.

⁴¹ Ye do the deeds of your father. Then said they to him, We be not born of fornication; we have one Father, *even* God.

OLD TESTAMENT READING

*B*e wise now therefore, O ye kings: be instructed, ye judges of the earth.

¹¹ Serve the LORD with fear, and rejoice with trembling.

¹² Kiss the Son, lest he be angry, and ye perish *from* the way, when his wrath is kindled but a little. Blessed *are* all they that put their trust in him.

Psalm 2:10-12

INSIGHTS

*T*hink first of the origin of that life of Christ in the Father. They were

ONE—one in life and one in love. In this His abiding in the Father had its root. Though dwelling here on earth, He knew that He was one with the Father; that the Father's life was in Him, and His love on Him. . . .

. . . The Son is not afraid of losing aught by giving up all to the Father, for He knows that the Father loves Him, and can have no interest apart from that of the beloved Son. He knows that as complete as is the dependence on His part is the communication on the part of the Father of all He possesses. Hence when He had said, "The Son can do nothing of Himself, except he see the Father do it," He adds at once, "Whatsoever things the Father doeth, them also doeth the Son likewise: for the Father loveth the Son, and showeth Him all things that Himself doeth." . . .

. . . Christ was the revelation of the Father on earth. He could not be this if there were not the most perfect unity, the most complete communication of all the Father had to the Son. He could be it because the Father loved Him, and He abode in that love.

Andrew Murray

PAUSE FOR REFLECTION

*H*ow many different ways in this passage did Jesus tell the people he was the Son of God? How does God say the people of earth are to treat his son? What convinced you that Jesus is God's son?

THURSDAY

What Does It Mean to Honor God?

John 8:42—9:12

*J*esus said unto them, If God were your Father, ye would love me: for I proceeded forth and came from God; neither came I of myself, but he sent me.

⁴³ Why do ye not understand my speech? *even* because ye cannot hear my word.

⁴⁴ Ye are of *your* father the devil, and the lusts of your father ye will do: he was a murderer from the beginning, and abode not in the truth, because there is no truth in him. When he speaketh a lie, he speaketh of his own: for he is a liar, and the father of it.

⁴⁵ And because I tell *you* the truth, ye believe me not.

⁴⁶ Which of you convinceth me of sin? And if I say the truth, why do ye not believe me?

⁴⁷ He that is of God heareth God's words: ye therefore hear *them* not, because ye are not of God.

Jesus Is Greater than Abraham

*T*hen answered the Jews, and said unto him, Say we not well that thou art a Samaritan, and hast a devil?

⁴⁹ Jesus answered, I have not a devil; but I honor my Father, and ye do dishonor me.

⁵⁰ And I seek not mine own glory: there is one that seeketh and judgeth.

⁵¹ Verily, verily, I say unto you, If a man keep my saying, he shall never see death.

⁵² Then said the Jews unto him, Now we know that thou hast a devil. Abraham is dead, and the prophets; and thou sayest, If a man keep my saying, he shall never taste of death.

⁵³ Art thou greater than our father Abraham, which is dead? and the prophets are dead: whom makest thou thyself?

⁵⁴ Jesus answered, If I honor myself, my honor is nothing: it is my Father that honoreth me; of whom ye say, that he is your God:

⁵⁵ yet ye have not known him; but I know him: and if I should say, I know him not, I shall be a liar like unto you: but I know him, and keep his saying.

⁵⁶ Your father Abraham rejoiced to see my day: and he saw *it*, and was glad.

⁵⁷ Then said the Jews unto him, Thou art not yet fifty years old, and hast thou seen Abraham?

⁵⁸ Jesus said unto them, Verily, verily, I say unto you, Before Abraham was, I am.

⁵⁹ Then took they up stones to cast at him: but Jesus hid himself, and went out of the temple, going through the midst of them, and so passed by.

Jesus Heals a Man Born Blind

9 And as *Jesus* passed by, he saw a man which was blind from *his* birth.

² And his disciples asked him, saying, Master, who did sin, this man, or his parents, that he was born blind?

³ Jesus answered, Neither hath this man sinned, nor his parents: but that the works of God should be made manifest in him.

⁴ I must work the works of him that sent me, while it is day: the night cometh, when no man can work.

⁵ As long as I am in the world, I am the light of the world.

6 When he had thus spoken, he spat on the ground, and made clay of the spittle, and he anointed the eyes of the blind man with the clay,

7 and said unto him, Go, wash in the pool of Siloam, (which is by interpretation, Sent.) He went his way therefore, and washed, and came seeing.

8 The neighbors therefore, and they which before had seen him that he was blind, said, Is not this he that sat and begged?

9 Some said, This is he: others *said*, He is like him: *but* he said, I am *he*.

10 Therefore said they unto him, How were thine eyes opened?

11 He answered and said, A man that is called Jesus made clay, and anointed mine eyes, and said unto me, Go to the pool of Siloam, and wash: and I went and washed, and I received sight.

12 Then said they unto him, Where is he? He said, I know not.

OLD TESTAMENT READING

*A*nd the LORD spake unto Moses, saying,

11 Phinehas, the son of Eleazar, the son of Aaron the priest, hath turned my wrath away from the children of Israel, while he was zealous for my sake among them, that I consumed not the children of Israel in my jealousy.

12 Wherefore say, Behold, I give unto him my covenant of peace.

Numbers 25:10-12

INSIGHTS

Jesus glorified God by giving himself for the work of His redeeming love. God's glory is His holiness, and God's holiness is His redeeming love—love that triumphs over sin by conquering the sin and rescuing the sinner. Jesus not only told of the Father being the righteous One, whose condemnation must rest on sin, and the loving One, who saves everyone who turns from his sin, but He gave himself to be a sacrifice to that righteousness, a servant to that love, even unto death. It was not only in acts of obedience or words of confession that He glorified God, but in giving himself to magnify the holiness of God, to vindicate at once His law and His love by His atonement. He gave himself, His whole life and being, to show how the Father loved, how the Father must condemn the sin, and yet would save the sinner. He counted nothing too great a sacrifice. He lived and died only that the glory of the Father, the glory of His holiness, of His redeeming love, might break through the dark veil of sin and flesh, and shine into the hearts of the children. . . .

If we want to know the way, let us again study Jesus. He obeyed the Father. Let simple obedience mark our whole life. Let humble, childlike waiting for direction, a Christlike dependence on the Father's showing us His way, be our daily attitude. Let everything be done to the Lord, according to His will, for His glory, in direct relationship to himself. Let God's glory shine out in the holiness of our life.

Andrew Murray

ACTION POINT

*W*hat brings honor to God? How did Jesus honor God? How do you think God wants you to honor him? Are you willing to honor him with a holy life?

F R I D A Y

*Jesus Opens the Eyes
of Those Who Believe*

John 9:13–41

Pharisees Question the Healing

*T*hey brought to the Pharisees him that aforetime was blind.

¹⁴ And it was the sabbath day when Jesus made the clay, and opened his eyes.

¹⁵ Then again the Pharisees also asked him how he had received his sight. He said unto them, He put clay upon mine eyes, and I washed, and do see.

¹⁶ Therefore said some of the Pharisees, This man is not of God, because he keepeth not the sabbath day. Others said, How can a man that is a sinner do such miracles? And there was a division among them.

¹⁷ They say unto the blind man again, What sayest thou of him, that he hath opened thine eyes? He said, He is a prophet.

¹⁸ But the Jews did not believe concerning him, that he had been blind, and received his sight, until they called the parents of him that had received his sight.

¹⁹ And they asked them, saying, Is this your son, who ye say was born blind? how then doth he now see?

²⁰ His parents answered them and said, We know that this is our son, and that he was born blind:

²¹ but by what means he now seeth, we know not; or who hath opened his eyes, we know not: he is of age; ask him: he shall speak for himself.

²² These *words* spake his parents, because they feared the Jews: for the Jews had agreed already, that if any man did confess that he was Christ, he should be put out of the synagogue.

²³ Therefore said his parents, He is of age; ask him.

²⁴ Then again called they the man that was blind, and said unto him, Give God the praise: we know that this man is a sinner.

²⁵ He answered and said, Whether he be a sinner *or no*, I know not: one thing I know, that, whereas I was blind, now I see.

²⁶ Then said they to him again, What did he to thee? how opened he thine eyes?

²⁷ He answered them, I have told you already, and ye did not hear: wherefore would ye hear *it* again? will ye also be his disciples?

²⁸ Then they reviled him, and said, Thou art his disciple; but we are Moses' disciples.

²⁹ We know that God spake unto Moses: *as for* this *fellow*, we know not from whence he is.

³⁰ The man answered and said unto them, Why herein is a marvelous thing, that ye know not from whence he is, and *yet* he hath opened mine eyes.

³¹ Now we know that God heareth not sinners: but if any man be a worshipper of God, and doeth his will, him he heareth.

³² Since the world began was it not heard that any man opened the eyes of one that was born blind.

³³ If this man were not of God, he could do nothing.

³⁴ They answered and said unto him, Thou wast altogether born in sins, and dost thou teach us? And they cast him out.

Spiritual Blindness

*J*esus heard that they had cast him out; and when he had found him, he said unto him, Dost thou believe on the Son of God?

³⁶ He answered and said, Who is he, Lord, that I might believe on him?

³⁷ And Jesus said unto him, Thou hast both seen him, and it is he that talketh with thee.

³⁸ And he said, Lord, I believe. And he worshipped him.

³⁹ And Jesus said, For judgment I am come into this world, that they which see not might see; and that they which see might be made blind.

⁴⁰ And *some* of the Pharisees which were with him heard these words, and said unto him, Are we blind also?

⁴¹ Jesus said unto them, If ye were blind, ye should have no sin: but now ye say, We see; therefore your sin remaineth.

OLD TESTAMENT READING

*D*eal bountifully with thy servant, *that* I may live, and keep thy word.

¹⁸ Open thou mine eyes, that I may behold wondrous things out of thy law.

¹⁹ I *am* a stranger in the earth: hide not thy commandments from me.

²⁰ My soul breaketh for the longing *that it hath* unto thy judgments at all times.

²¹ Thou hast rebuked the proud *that are* cursed, which do err from thy commandments.

²² Remove from me reproach and contempt; for I have kept thy testimonies.

²³ Princes also did sit *and* speak against me: *but* thy servant did meditate in thy statutes.

²⁴ Thy testimonies also *are* my delight *and* my counselors.

Psalm 119:17-24

INSIGHTS

*T*he Lord loves to do things differently. At least four times He opened blind eyes, and He does it a different way each time, depending on the personality and the circumstances.

The Lord deals with each of us, not en masse, but as individuals. Each of us is a special object of the grace and care and faithfulness of God. If you were the only one on the face of the earth, He would still take care of you. This is demonstrated here. He made clay and put it on the man's eyes. And this calls for two things from the man: faith and obedience. The moment he obeyed, he had deliverance. Deliverance comes from obedience.

. . . To follow Him means not to walk in darkness. Here is a man who has never seen the light of day, or seen a tree or a flower, or seen his mother. He has never seen anything. He has always lived in the dark. How glad I am the Savior is the light of the world and can come into any darkened heart that wants to know God. The moment your heart is open to Him, the light shines in.

John G. Mitchell

APPLICATION

*W*hat words of faith and wisdom did the blind man speak to the Jewish leaders? Why do you think Jesus looked for him after he was thrown out of the temple? Pray that you will see how much Jesus wants you to believe and trust him.

WEEKEND

*Jesus Is Our
Caring Shepherd*

John 10:1–33

The Shepherd and His Sheep

10 Verily, verily, I say unto you, He that entereth not by the door into the sheepfold, but climbeth up some other way, the same is a thief and a robber.

² But he that entereth in by the door is the shepherd of the sheep.

³ To him the porter openeth; and the sheep hear his voice: and he calleth his own sheep by name, and leadeth them out.

⁴ And when he putteth forth his own sheep, he goeth before them, and the sheep follow him: for they know his voice.

⁵ And a stranger will they not follow, but will flee from him; for they know not the voice of strangers.

⁶ This parable spake Jesus unto them; but they understood not what things they were which he spake unto them.

Jesus Is the Good Shepherd

*T*hen said Jesus unto them again, Verily, verily, I say unto you, I am the door of the sheep.

⁸ All that ever came before me are thieves and robbers: but the sheep did not hear them.

⁹ I am the door: by me if any man enter in, he shall be saved, and shall go in and out, and find pasture.

¹⁰ The thief cometh not, but for to steal, and to kill, and to destroy; I am come that they might have life, and that they might have *it* more abundantly.

¹¹ I am the good shepherd: the good shepherd giveth his life for the sheep.

¹² But he that is a hireling, and not the shepherd, whose own the sheep are not, seeth the wolf coming, and leaveth the sheep, and fleeth; and the wolf catcheth them, and scattereth the sheep.

¹³ The hireling fleeth, because he is a hireling, and careth not for the sheep.

¹⁴ I am the good shepherd, and know my *sheep*, and am known of mine.

¹⁵ As the Father knoweth me, even so know I the Father: and I lay down my life for the sheep.

¹⁶ And other sheep I have, which are not of this fold: them also I must bring, and they shall hear my voice; and there shall be one fold, *and* one shepherd.

¹⁷ Therefore doth my Father love me, because I lay down my life, that I might take it again.

¹⁸ No man taketh it from me, but I lay it down of myself. I have power to lay it down, and I have power to take it again. This commandment have I received of my Father.

¹⁹ There was a division therefore again among the Jews for these sayings.

²⁰ And many of them said, He hath a devil, and is mad; why hear ye him?

²¹ Others said, These are not the words of him that hath a devil. Can a devil open the eyes of the blind?

Jesus Is Rejected

*A*nd it was at Jerusalem the feast of the dedication, and it was winter.

²³ And Jesus walked in the temple in Solomon's porch.

²⁴ Then came the Jews round about him, and said unto him, How long

dost thou make us to doubt? If thou be the Christ, tell us plainly.

25 Jesus answered them, I told you, and ye believed not: the works that I do in my Father's name, they bear witness of me.

26 But ye believe not, because ye are not of my sheep, as I said unto you.

27 My sheep hear my voice, and I know them, and they follow me:

28 and I give unto them eternal life; and they shall never perish, neither shall any *man* pluck them out of my hand.

29 My Father, which gave *them* me, is greater than all; and no *man* is able to pluck *them* out of my Father's hand.

30 I and *my* Father are one.

31 Then the Jews took up stones again to stone him.

32 Jesus answered them, Many good works have I showed you from my Father; for which of those works do ye stone me?

33 The Jews answered him, saying, For a good work we stone thee not; but for blasphemy; and because that thou, being a man, makest thyself God.

OLD TESTAMENT READING

*H*e shall feed his flock like a shepherd: he shall gather the lambs with his arm, and carry *them* in his bosom, *and* shall gently lead those that are with young.

Isaiah 40:11

INSIGHTS

*D*o you need guidance as to your path? Look unto Jesus; it is always possible to discern His form, though partially veiled in mist; and when it is lost, be sure to stand still until He comes back. . . .

Sometimes He guides us to the rest of the green pastures, and the quiet of the still waters. In other words, we are left through happy months and years to fulfil the ordinary commonplaces of life, content to fill a little space, and receiving great increments of spiritual force for future service. At other times, we are guided from the lowland pastures up into the hills. The way is sunny, above us the precipitous cliffs, beneath the dark turbid stream; but this is well; we would not always be lying in the pastures or walking softly by the waters. It is good to climb the heights with their far view and bracing air.

In the late afternoon the Shepherd may lead his flock back into the valleys, through the dark woods, where the branches meet overhead and the wild beast lurks in ambush, but we know that in one hand He has the rod or club, with which to belabour anything that may attack; and in the other the crook to drag us out of the hole. He would not lead us into the dark valley which He had not explored, and whose perils He was not prepared to overcome. Darkness, sorrow, or death do not prove that we have missed His guidance, or have taken the wrong path, but rather that He accounts us able to bear the trial by faith in Himself.

F. B. Meyer

PAUSE FOR REFLECTION

*W*hat does Jesus promise to give his sheep who follow him? Study the qualities of the good shepherd that Jesus describes and think about the ways Jesus has been your shepherd.

MONDAY

*Trust in God to Protect
and Care for You*

John 10:34—11:27

*J*esus answered them, Is it not written in your law, I said, Ye are gods?

[35] If he called them gods, unto whom the word of God came, and the Scripture cannot be broken;

[36] say ye of him, whom the Father hath sanctified, and sent into the world, Thou blasphemest; because I said, I am the Son of God?

[37] If I do not the works of my Father, believe me not.

[38] But if I do, though ye believe not me, believe the works; that ye may know, and believe, that the Father *is* in me, and I in him.

[39] Therefore they sought again to take him; but he escaped out of their hand,

[40] and went away again beyond Jordan into the place where John at first baptized; and there he abode.

[41] And many resorted unto him and said, John did no miracle: but all things that John spake of this man were true.

[42] And many believed on him there.

The Death of Lazarus

11 Now a certain *man* was sick, *named* Lazarus, of Bethany, the town of Mary and her sister Martha.

[2] (It was *that* Mary which anointed the Lord with ointment, and wiped his feet with her hair, whose brother Lazarus was sick.)

[3] Therefore his sisters sent unto him, saying, Lord, behold, he whom thou lovest is sick.

[4] When Jesus heard *that*, he said, This sickness is not unto death, but for the glory of God, that the Son of God might be glorified thereby.

[5] Now Jesus loved Martha, and her sister, and Lazarus.

[6] When he had heard therefore that he was sick, he abode two days still in the same place where he was.

[7] Then after that saith he to *his* disciples, Let us go into Judea again.

[8] *His* disciples say unto him, Master, the Jews of late sought to stone thee; and goest thou thither again?

[9] Jesus answered, Are there not twelve hours in the day? If any man walk in the day, he stumbleth not, because he seeth the light of this world.

[10] But if a man walk in the night, he stumbleth, because there is no light in him.

[11] These things said he: and after that he saith unto them, Our friend Lazarus sleepeth; but I go, that I may awake him out of sleep.

[12] Then said his disciples, Lord, if he sleep, he shall do well.

[13] Howbeit Jesus spake of his death: but they thought that he had spoken of taking of rest in sleep.

[14] Then said Jesus unto them plainly, Lazarus is dead.

[15] And I am glad for your sakes that I was not there, to the intent ye may believe; nevertheless let us go unto him.

[16] Then said Thomas, which is called Didymus, unto his fellow disciples, Let us also go, that we may die with him.

Jesus in Bethany

*T*hen when Jesus came, he found that he had *lain* in the grave four days already.

[18] Now Bethany was nigh unto Jerusalem, about fifteen furlongs off:

¹⁹ and many of the Jews came to Martha and Mary, to comfort them concerning their brother.

²⁰ Then Martha, as soon as she heard that Jesus was coming, went and met him: but Mary sat *still* in the house.

²¹ Then said Martha unto Jesus, Lord, if thou hadst been here, my brother had not died.

²² But I know, that even now, whatsoever thou wilt ask of God, God will give *it* thee.

²³ Jesus saith unto her, Thy brother shall rise again.

²⁴ Martha saith unto him, I know that he shall rise again in the resurrection at the last day.

²⁵ Jesus said unto her, I am the resurrection, and the life: he that believeth in me, though he were dead, yet shall he live:

²⁶ and whosoever liveth and believeth in me shall never die. Believest thou this?

²⁷ She saith unto him, Yea, Lord: I believe that thou art the Christ, the Son of God, which should come into the world.

OLD TESTAMENT READING

I waited patiently for the Lord; and he inclined unto me, and heard my cry.

² He brought me up also out of a horrible pit, out of the miry clay, and set my feet upon a rock, *and* established my goings.

³ And he hath put a new song in my mouth, *even* praise unto our God: many shall see *it*, and fear, and shall trust in the Lord.

Psalm 40:1-3

INSIGHTS

A pair of scientists and botanists were exploring in the Alps for some special kinds of flowers. One day they spied through their field glass a flower of rare beauty. But it was in a ravine with perpendicular cliffs on both sides. Someone must be lowered over the cliff to get it.

A native boy was watching. They said to him, "We will give you five pounds if you will let us lower you into the valley to get the flower." The boy looked into the valley and said, "Just a moment. I'll be back." He soon returned with a man. "I'll go over the cliff," he said, "and get the flower for you if this man holds the rope. He's my dad." Have we learned to trust the Lord as this little boy did his father?

Sometimes we find ourselves putting our confidence in man and what we think he can do for us. But man can let us down. Man can disappoint us. Not so the Lord. Needs may be pressing in but we can look up, trusting an all-wise, all-loving God to do all for our good and His glory.

We can trust the rope of our circumstances to Him. Man may become weary and let the rope drop; or he may be distracted or become impatient. But God never wearies of holding the rope. We can confidently leave it in His strong hand.

Millie Stamm

PAUSE FOR REFLECTION

How long had Lazarus been dead before Jesus reached out and saved him? Doesn't that stretch your ability to trust in his protection? Can you, like the psalmist, confidently praise God for his protection?

TUESDAY

God Honors Our Faith

John 11:28–57

Jesus Weeps

*A*nd when she had so said, she went her way, and called Mary her sister secretly, saying, The Master is come, and calleth for thee.

²⁹ As soon as she heard *that*, she arose quickly, and came unto him.

³⁰ Now Jesus was not yet come into the town, but was in that place where Martha met him.

³¹ The Jews then which were with her in the house, and comforted her, when they saw Mary, that she rose up hastily and went out, followed her, saying, She goeth unto the grave to weep there.

³² Then when Mary was come where Jesus was, and saw him, she fell down at his feet, saying unto him, Lord, if thou hadst been here, my brother had not died.

³³ When Jesus therefore saw her weeping, and the Jews also weeping which came with her, he groaned in the spirit, and was troubled,

³⁴ and said, Where have ye laid him? They said unto him, Lord, come and see.

³⁵ Jesus wept.

³⁶ Then said the Jews, Behold how he loved him!

³⁷ And some of them said, Could not this man, which opened the eyes of the blind, have caused that even this man should not have died?

Jesus Raises Lazarus

*J*esus therefore again groaning in himself cometh to the grave. It was a cave, and a stone lay upon it.

³⁹ Jesus said, Take ye away the stone. Martha, the sister of him that was dead, saith unto him, Lord, by this time he stinketh: for he hath been *dead* four days.

⁴⁰ Jesus saith unto her, Said I not unto thee, that, if thou wouldest believe, thou shouldest see the glory of God?

⁴¹ Then they took away the stone *from the place* where the dead was laid. And Jesus lifted up *his* eyes, and said, Father, I thank thee that thou hast heard me.

⁴² And I knew that thou hearest me always: but because of the people which stand by I said *it,* that they may believe that thou hast sent me.

⁴³ And when he thus had spoken, he cried with a loud voice, Lazarus, come forth.

⁴⁴ And he that was dead came forth, bound hand and foot with grave clothes; and his face was bound about with a napkin. Jesus saith unto them, Loose him, and let him go.

The Plan to Kill Jesus

*T*hen many of the Jews which came to Mary, and had seen the things which Jesus did, believed on him.

⁴⁶ But some of them went their ways to the Pharisees, and told them what things Jesus had done.

⁴⁷ Then gathered the chief priests and the Pharisees a council, and said, What do we? for this man doeth many miracles.

⁴⁸ If we let him thus alone, all *men* will believe on him; and the Romans shall come and take away both our place and nation.

⁴⁹ And one of them, *named* Caiaphas, being the high priest that same year, said unto them, Ye know nothing at all,

⁵⁰ nor consider that it is expedient for us, that one man should die for the people, and that the whole nation perish not.

⁵¹ And this spake he not of himself: but being high priest that year, he prophesied that Jesus should die for that the nation;

⁵² and not for that nation only, but that also he should gather together in one the children of God that were scattered abroad.

⁵³ Then from that day forth they took counsel together for to put him to death.

⁵⁴ Jesus therefore walked no more openly among the Jews; but went thence unto a country near to the wilderness, into a city called Ephraim, and there continued with his disciples.

⁵⁵ And the Jews' passover was nigh at hand: and many went out of the country up to Jerusalem before the passover, to purify themselves.

⁵⁶ Then sought they for Jesus, and spake among themselves, as they stood in the temple, What think ye, that he will not come to the feast?

⁵⁷ Now both the chief priests and the Pharisees had given a commandment, that, if any man knew where he were, he should show it, that they might take him.

OLD TESTAMENT READING

And he stretched himself upon the child three times, and cried unto the LORD, and said, O LORD my God, I pray thee, let this child's soul come into him again.

²² And the LORD heard the voice of Elijah; and the soul of the child came into him again, and he revived.

²⁴ And the woman said to Elijah, Now by this I know that thou art a man
of God, and that the word of the LORD in thy mouth is truth.

1 Kings 17:21–22, 24

INSIGHTS

Faith is man's response to God's initiative. . . .

To realize that faith is your response to something God does or says, will take pressure off you and enable you to adopt a more constructive attitude to it. Do not look inside yourself and ask, "How much faith do I have?" Look to God and ask, "What is he saying to me? What would he have me do?" When Jesus praised the great faith of different men and women in the Gospels, he was not praising a mystical inner state. He was usually commenting on a concrete action by which someone responded to him. . . .

How much faith did Martha need to get Lazarus back from the dead? Precious little (Jn. 11:38–40). If we are to go by mystical inner states, every evidence points to Martha having no faith at all. No, what she needed (and what she had) was enough faith to give orders for the tombstone to be moved, in spite of the doubts she felt. And Lazarus was raised from the dead.

John White

PAUSE FOR REFLECTION

Did Mary and Martha believe Jesus had come to raise Lazarus from the dead? Is your faith in Jesus enough for him to accomplish his purposes?

WEDNESDAY

*Evil People Have Always
Conspired Against the
Righteous and Innocent*

John 12:1–26

Jesus with Friends in Bethany

12 Then Jesus six days before the passover came to Bethany, where Lazarus was which had been dead, whom he raised from the dead.

[2] There they made him a supper; and Martha served: but Lazarus was one of them that sat at the table with him.

[3] Then took Mary a pound of ointment of spikenard, very costly, and anointed the feet of Jesus, and wiped his feet with her hair: and the house was filled with the odor of the ointment.

[4] Then saith one of his disciples, Judas Iscariot, Simon's *son*, which should betray him,

[5] Why was not this ointment sold for three hundred pence, and given to the poor?

[6] This he said, not that he cared for the poor; but because he was a thief, and had the bag, and bare what was put therein.

[7] Then said Jesus, Let her alone: against the day of my burying hath she kept this.

[8] For the poor always ye have with you; but me ye have not always.

The Plot Against Lazarus

*M*uch people of the Jews therefore knew that he was there: and they came not for Jesus' sake only, but that they might see Lazarus also, whom he had raised from the dead.

[10] But the chief priests consulted that they might put Lazarus also to death;

[11] Because that by reason of him many of the Jews went away, and believed on Jesus.

Jesus Enters Jerusalem

*O*n the next day much people that were come to the feast, when they heard that Jesus was coming to Jerusalem,

[13] took branches of palm trees, and went forth to meet him, and cried, Hosanna: Blessed *is* the King of Israel that cometh in the name of the Lord.

[14] And Jesus, when he had found a young ass, sat thereon; as it is written,

[15] Fear not, daughter of Zion: behold, thy King cometh, sitting on an ass's colt.

[16] These things understood not his disciples at the first: but when Jesus was glorified, then remembered they that these things were written of him, and *that* they had done these things unto him.

People Tell About Jesus

*T*he people therefore that was with him when he called Lazarus out of his grave, and raised him from the dead, bare record.

[18] For this cause the people also met him, for that they heard that he had done this miracle.

[19] The Pharisees therefore said among themselves, Perceive ye how ye prevail nothing? behold, the world is gone after him.

Jesus Talks About His Death

*A*nd there were certain Greeks

among them that came up to worship at the feast:

²¹ the same came therefore to Philip, which was of Bethsaida of Galilee, and desired him, saying, Sir, we would see Jesus.

²² Philip cometh and telleth Andrew: and again Andrew and Philip tell Jesus.

²³ And Jesus answered them, saying, The hour is come, that the Son of man should be glorified.

²⁴ Verily, verily, I say unto you, Except a corn of wheat fall into the ground and die, it abideth alone: but if it die, it bringeth forth much fruit.

²⁵ He that loveth his life shall lose it; and he that hateth his life in this world shall keep it unto life eternal.

²⁶ If any man serve me, let him follow me; and where I am, there shall also my servant be: if any man serve me, him will *my* Father honor.

OLD TESTAMENT READING

*A*rise, O Lᴏʀᴅ; O God, lift up thine hand: forget not the humble.

¹³ Wherefore doth the wicked contemn God? he hath said in his heart, Thou wilt not require *it.*

¹⁴ Thou hast seen *it*; for thou beholdest mischief and spite, to requite *it* with thy hand: the poor committeth himself unto thee; thou art the helper of the fatherless.

¹⁵ Break thou the arm of the wicked and the evil *man*: seek out his wickedness *till* thou find none.

Psalm 10:12–15

INSIGHTS

*C*harles Haddon Spurgeon remains one of the most colorful and gifted preachers in the history of the church. . . . The new Tabernacle was filled to overflowing every Lord's Day as people came miles by horse and buggy to hear the gifted man handle the Word of God. They were challenged, encouraged, exhorted, fed, and built up in the Christian faith. He was truly a phenomenon. As a result, he became the object of great criticism by the press, by other pastors, by influential people in London, and by petty parishioners. . . .

I am told that his wife, seeing the results of those verbal blows on her husband, decided to assist him in getting back on his feet and regaining his powerful stature in the pulpit. She found in her Bible Matthew 5:10–12—and she printed in beautiful old English the words of this passage on a large sheet of paper. Then she tacked that sheet to the ceiling of their bedroom, directly above Charles' side of the bed! . . .

. . . Servants, that statement will help us call a halt to the next pity party we are tempted to throw for ourselves. We are not alone. It has been going on for centuries.

Charles Swindoll

PAUSE FOR REFLECTION

*W*hy did the religious leaders of the day hate Jesus and Lazarus? From whom does persecution come in your life? What portion of Scripture encourages and comforts you during such times?

THURSDAY

Some Who See God's Work Still Do Not Believe

John 12:27—13:5

*N*ow is my soul troubled; and what shall I say? Father, save me from this hour: but for this cause came I unto this hour.

28 Father, glorify thy name. Then came there a voice from heaven, *saying*, I have both glorified *it*, and will glorify *it* again.

29 The people therefore that stood by, and heard *it,* said that it thundered: others said, An angel spake to him.

30 Jesus answered and said, This voice came not because of me, but for your sakes.

31 Now is the judgment of this world: now shall the prince of this world be cast out.

32 And I, if I be lifted up from the earth, will draw all *men* unto me.

33 This he said, signifying what death he should die.

34 The people answered him, We have heard out of the law that Christ abideth for ever: and how sayest thou, The Son of man must be lifted up? who is this Son of man?

35 Then Jesus said unto them, Yet a little while is the light with you. Walk while ye have the light, lest darkness come upon you: for he that walketh in darkness knoweth not whither he goeth.

36 While ye have light, believe in the light, that ye may be the children of light. These things spake Jesus, and departed, and did hide himself from them.

Some Won't Believe in Jesus

*B*ut though he had done so many miracles before them, yet they believed not on him:

38 that the saying of Isaiah the prophet might be fulfilled, which he spake, Lord, who hath believed our report? and to whom hath the arm of the Lord been revealed?

39 Therefore they could not believe, because that Isaiah said again,

40 He hath blinded their eyes, and hardened their heart; that they should not see with *their* eyes, nor understand with *their* heart, and be converted, and I should heal them.

41 These things said Isaiah, when he saw his glory, and spake of him.

42 Nevertheless among the chief rulers also many believed on him; but because of the Pharisees they did not confess *him*, lest they should be put out of the synagogue:

43 for they loved the praise of men more than the praise of God.

44 Jesus cried and said, He that believeth on me, believeth not on me, but on him that sent me.

45 And he that seeth me seeth him that sent me.

46 I am come a light into the world, that whosoever believeth on me should not abide in darkness.

47 And if any man hear my words, and believe not, I judge him not: for I came not to judge the world, but to save the world.

48 He that rejecteth me, and receiveth not my words, hath one that judgeth him: the word that I have spoken, the same shall judge him in the last day.

49 For I have not spoken of myself; but the Father which sent me, he gave me a commandment, what I should say, and what I should speak.

⁵⁰ And I know that his commandment is life everlasting: whatsoever I speak therefore, even as the Father said unto me, so I speak.

Jesus Washes His Disciples' Feet

13 Now before the feast of the passover, when Jesus knew that his hour was come that he should depart out of this world unto the Father, having loved his own which were in the world, he loved them unto the end. ² And supper being ended, the devil having now put into the heart of Judas Iscariot, Simon's *son*, to betray him; ³ Jesus knowing that the Father had given all things into his hands, and that he was come from God, and went to God; ⁴ he riseth from supper, and laid aside his garments; and took a towel, and girded himself. ⁵ After that he poureth water into a basin, and began to wash the disciples' feet, and to wipe *them* with the towel wherewith he was girded.

OLD TESTAMENT READING

*T*hen Moses heard the people weep throughout their families, every man in the door of his tent: and the anger of the LORD was kindled greatly; Moses also was displeased. ¹¹ And Moses said unto the LORD, Wherefore hast thou afflicted thy servant? and wherefore have I not found favor in thy sight, that thou layest the burden of all this people upon me? ¹³ᵇ For they weep unto me, saying, Give us flesh, that we may eat. ¹⁴ I am not able to bear all this people alone, because *it is* too heavy for me. ¹⁵ And if thou deal thus with me, kill me, I pray thee, out of hand, if I have found favor in thy sight; and let me not see my wretchedness. ²¹ And Moses said, The people, among whom I *am, are* six hundred thousand footmen; and thou hast said, I will give them flesh, that they may eat a whole month. ²² Shall the flocks and the herds be slain for them, to suffice them? or shall all the fish of the sea be gathered together for them, to suffice them? ²³ And the LORD said unto Moses, Is the LORD's hand waxed short? thou shalt see now whether my word shall come to pass unto thee or not.

Numbers 11:10–11, 13b–15, 21–23

INSIGHTS

*T*he late Dr. Heugh, of Glasgow, a short time before he breathed his last, said, "There is nothing I feel more than the criminality of not trusting Christ without doubt— without doubt. Oh, to think what Christ is, what he did, and whom he did it for, and then not to believe him, not to trust him! There is no wickedness like the wickedness of unbelief!"

Charles Spurgeon

PAUSE FOR REFLECTION

*D*oes it surprise you that Moses, even after all the miracles he had seen (and been a part of), still struggled with unbelief? Why is it important for us to believe Jesus? In what ways do you find it difficult to trust and believe Jesus? What "miracles" have you seen that ought to strengthen your belief?

FRIDAY

Jesus Gives a New Commandment to His People

John 13:6–35

*T*hen cometh he to Simon Peter: and Peter saith unto him, Lord, dost thou wash my feet?

[7] Jesus answered and said unto him, What I do thou knowest not now; but thou shalt know hereafter.

[8] Peter saith unto him, Thou shalt never wash my feet. Jesus answered him, If I wash thee not, thou hast no part with me.

[9] Simon Peter saith unto him, Lord, not my feet only, but also *my* hands and *my* head.

[10] Jesus saith to him, He that is washed needeth not save to wash *his* feet, but is clean every whit: and ye are clean, but not all.

[11] For he knew who should betray him; therefore said he, Ye are not all clean.

[12] So after he had washed their feet, and had taken his garments, and was set down again, he said unto them, Know ye what I have done to you?

[13] Ye call me Master and Lord: and ye say well; for *so* I am.

[14] If I then, *your* Lord and Master, have washed your feet; ye also ought to wash one another's feet.

[15] For I have given you an example, that ye should do as I have done to you.

[16] Verily, verily, I say unto you, The servant is not greater than his lord; neither he that is sent greater than he that sent him.

[17] If ye know these things, happy are ye if ye do them.

[18] I speak not of you all: I know whom I have chosen: but that the Scripture may be fulfilled, He that eateth bread with me hath lifted up his heel against me.

[19] Now I tell you before it come, that, when it is come to pass, ye may believe that I am *he*.

[20] Verily, verily, I say unto you, He that receiveth whomsoever I send receiveth me; and he that receiveth me receiveth him that sent me.

Jesus Talks About His Death

*W*hen Jesus had thus said, he was troubled in spirit, and testified, and said, Verily, verily, I say unto you, that one of you shall betray me.

[22] Then the disciples looked one on another, doubting of whom he spake.

[23] Now there was leaning on Jesus' bosom one of his disciples, whom Jesus loved.

[24] Simon Peter therefore beckoned to him, that he should ask who it should be of whom he spake.

[25] He then lying on Jesus' breast saith unto him, Lord, who is it?

[26] Jesus answered, He it is, to whom I shall give a sop, when I have dipped *it*. And when he had dipped the sop, he gave *it* to Judas Iscariot, *the son* of Simon.

[27] And after the sop Satan entered into him. Then said Jesus unto him, That thou doest, do quickly.

[28] Now no man at the table knew for what intent he spake this unto him.

[29] For some *of them* thought, because Judas had the bag, that Jesus had said unto him, Buy *those things* that we have need of against the feast; or, that he should give something to the poor.

[30] He then, having received the sop went immediately out; and it was night.

[31] Therefore, when he was gone out,

Jesus said, Now is the Son of man glorified, and God is glorified in him.

³² If God be glorified in him, God shall also glorify him in himself, and shall straightway glorify him.

³³ Little children, yet a little while I am with you. Ye shall seek me; and as I said unto the Jews, Whither I go, ye cannot come; so now I say to you.

³⁴ A new commandment I give unto you, That ye love one another; as I have loved you, that ye also love one another.

³⁵ By this shall all *men* know that ye are my disciples, if ye have love one to another.

OLD TESTAMENT READING

*T*hou shalt have no other gods before me.

⁵ Thou shalt not bow down thyself to them, nor serve them.

⁷ Thou shalt not take the name of the LORD thy God in vain.

⁸ Remember the sabbath day, to keep it holy.

¹² Honor thy father and thy mother.

¹³ Thou shalt not kill.

¹⁴ Thou shalt not commit adultery.

¹⁵ Thou shalt not steal.

¹⁶ Thou shalt not bear false witness against thy neighbor.

¹⁷ Thou shalt not covet thy neighbor's house.

Exodus 20:3, 5a, 7a, 8, 12a, 13–17a

---

in amazement and said of the believers, "How they love one another!"

Within a few years following this command to love one another, the gospel had spread like a prairie fire throughout the known world. The miracle of God's love, His supernatural agape, had captivated multitudes throughout the decadent, wicked Roman Empire.

Tragically, today one seldom hears "How they love one another!" about Christians. Instead there is far too much suspicion, jealousy, criticism and conflict between Christians, churches and denominations. The unbelieving world often laughs at our publicized conflicts.

But those individuals who do demonstrate this supernatural love are usually warmly received by non-believers as well as believers. The churches that obey our Lord's command to "love one another" usually are filled to overflowing and are making a great impact for good and for the glory of God. They represent a highly desirable alternative to secular society.

How does one love supernaturally? By faith. God's Word commands us to love (John 13:34, 35). God's Word promises that He will enable us to do what He commands us to do (1 John 5:14, 15).

Bill Bright

INSIGHTS

*W*ith the resurrection of the Lord Jesus and the day of Pentecost came a breath of heavenly love. Those who received Jesus, the incarnation of love, into their lives and who chose to obey His command began to love one another. The pagan world looked on

APPLICATION

*A*s Jesus prepared to leave his disciples, what one command did he give them? Why do you think this command differs from those given at Mount Sinai? How can you more fully follow this command in your life today?

WEEKEND

*Our Obedience Demonstrates
Our Love for God*

John 13:36—14:26

Peter Will Deny Jesus

Simon Peter said unto him, Lord, whither goest thou? Jesus answered him, Whither I go, thou canst not follow me now; but thou shalt follow me afterwards.

³⁷ Peter said unto him, Lord, why cannot I follow thee now? I will lay down my life for thy sake.

³⁸ Jesus answered him, Wilt thou lay down thy life for my sake? Verily, verily, I say unto thee, The cock shall not crow, till thou hast denied me thrice.

Jesus Comforts His Disciples

14 Let not your heart be troubled: ye believe in God, believe also in me.

² In my Father's house are many mansions: if *it were* not *so*, I would have told you. I go to prepare a place for you.

³ And if I go and prepare a place for you, I will come again, and receive you unto myself; that where I am, *there* ye may be also.

⁴ And whither I go ye know, and the way ye know.

⁵ Thomas saith unto him, Lord, we know not whither thou goest; and how can we know the way?

⁶ Jesus saith unto him, I am the way, the truth, and the life; no man cometh unto the Father, but by me.

⁷ If ye had known me, ye should have known my Father also: and from henceforth ye know him, and have seen him.

⁸ Philip saith unto him, Lord, shew us the Father, and it sufficeth us.

⁹ Jesus saith unto him, Have I been so long time with you, and yet hast thou not known me, Philip? he that hath seen me hath seen the Father; and how sayest thou *then*, Show us the Father?

¹⁰ Believest thou not that I am in the Father, and the Father in me? the words that I speak unto you I speak not of myself: but the Father that dwelleth in me, he doeth the works.

¹¹ Believe me that I *am* in the Father, and the Father in me: or else believe me for the very works' sake.

¹² Verily, verily, I say unto you, He that believeth on me, the works that I do shall he do also; and greater *works* than these shall he do; because I go unto my Father.

¹³ And whatsoever ye shall ask in my name, that will I do, that the Father may be glorified in the Son.

¹⁴ If ye shall ask any thing in my name, I will do *it*.

The Promise of the Holy Spirit

If ye love me, keep my commandments.

¹⁶ And I will pray the Father, and he shall give you another Comforter, that he may abide with you for ever;

¹⁷ *even* the Spirit of truth; whom the world cannot receive, because it seeth him not, neither knoweth him: but ye know him; for he dwelleth with you, and shall be in you.

¹⁸ I will not leave you comfortless: I will come to you.

¹⁹ Yet a little while, and the world seeth me no more; but ye see me: because I live, ye shall live also.

²⁰ At that day ye shall know that I *am* in my Father, and ye in me, and I in you.

²¹ He that hath my commandments, and keepeth them, he it is that loveth me: and he that loveth me shall be loved of my Father, and I will love him, and will manifest myself to him.

²² Judas saith unto him, not Iscariot, Lord, how is it that thou wilt manifest thyself unto us, and not unto the world?

²³ Jesus answered and said unto him, If a man love me, he will keep my words: and my Father will love him, and we will come unto him, and make our abode with him.

²⁴ He that loveth me not keepeth not my sayings: and the word which ye hear is not mine, but the Father's which sent me.

²⁵ These things have I spoken unto you, being *yet* present with you.

²⁶ But the Comforter, *which is* the Holy Ghost, whom the Father will send in my name, he shall teach you all things, and bring all things to your remembrance, whatsoever I have said unto you.

OLD TESTAMENT READING

*A*nd it shall come to pass, if ye shall hearken diligently unto my commandments which I command you this day, to love the LORD your God, and to serve him with all your heart and with all your soul,

¹⁴ that I will give *you* the rain of your land in his due season, the first rain and the latter rain, that thou mayest gather in thy corn, and thy wine, and thine oil.

Deuteronomy 11:13–14

INSIGHTS

*T*he Master has revealed Himself to you, and is calling for your complete surrender, and you shrink and hesitate. A measure of surrender you are willing to make, and think indeed it is fit and proper that you should. But an utter abandonment, without any reserves, seems to you too much to be asked for. You are afraid of it. It involves too much, you think, and is too great a risk. . . .

. . . *Your Lord says, "He that hath my commandments, and keepeth them, he it is that loveth me; and he that loveth me shall be loved of my Father, and I will love him, and will manifest myself to him. . . ."*

He loves you with more than the love of friendship. . . . He has given you all, and He asks for all in return. The slightest reserve will grieve Him to the heart. He spared not Himself, and how can you spare yourself? . . .

Oh, be generous in your self-surrender! Meet His measureless devotion for you with a measureless devotion to Him. . . . Whatever there is of you, let Him have it all. Give up forever everything that is separate from Him. . . .

. . . *The perfect happiness of perfect obedience will dawn upon your soul, and you will begin to know something of what Jesus meant when He said, "I delight to do thy will, O my God."*

Hannah Whitall Smith

PAUSE FOR REFLECTION

*W*hy do you obey God? Out of obligation? Because it is the "right" thing to do? God wants us to obey him simply because we love him! Pray for such a love-filled heart that obedience will be a delight.

MONDAY

Serving God Brings Joy

John 14:27—15:27

*P*eace I leave with you, my peace I give unto you: not as the world giveth, give I unto you. Let not your heart be troubled, neither let it be afraid.

28 Ye have heard how I said unto you, I go away, and come *again* unto you. If ye loved me, ye would rejoice, because I said, I go unto the Father: for my Father is greater than I.

29 And now I have told you before it come to pass, that, when it is come to pass, ye might believe.

30 Hereafter I will not talk much with you: for the prince of this world cometh, and hath nothing in me.

31 But that the world may know that I love the Father; and as the Father gave me commandment, even so I do. Arise, let us go hence.

Jesus Is Like a Vine

15 I am the true vine, and my Father is the husbandman.

2 Every branch in me that beareth not fruit he taketh away: and every *branch* that beareth fruit, he purgeth it, that it may bring forth more fruit.

3 Now ye are clean through the word which I have spoken unto you.

4 Abide in me, and I in you. As the branch cannot bear fruit of itself, except it abide in the vine; no more can ye, except ye abide in me.

5 I am the vine, ye *are* the branches. He that abideth in me, and I in him, the same bringeth forth much fruit; for without me ye can do nothing.

6 If a man abide not in me, he is cast forth as a branch, and is withered; and men gather them, and cast *them* into the fire, and they are burned.

7 If ye abide in me, and my words abide in you, ye shall ask what ye will, and it shall be done unto you.

8 Herein is my Father glorified, that ye bear much fruit; so shall ye be my disciples.

9 As the Father hath loved me, so have I loved you: continue ye in my love.

10 If ye keep my commandments, ye shall abide in my love; even as I have kept my Father's commandments, and abide in his love.

11 These things have I spoken unto you, that my joy might remain in you, and *that* your joy might be full.

12 This is my commandment, That ye love one another, as I have loved you.

13 Greater love hath no man than this, that a man lay down his life for his friends.

14 Ye are my friends, if ye do whatsoever I command you.

15 Henceforth I call you not servants; for the servant knoweth not what his lord doeth: but I have called you friends; for all things that I have heard of my Father I have made known unto you.

16 Ye have not chosen me, but I have chosen you, and ordained you, that ye should go and bring forth fruit, and *that* your fruit should remain; that whatsoever ye shall ask of the Father in my name, he may give it you.

17 These things I command you, that ye love one another.

Jesus Warns His Disciples

*I*f the world hate you, ye know that it hated me before *it hated* you.

19 If ye were of the world, the world would love his own; but because ye

are not of the world, but I have chosen you out of the world, therefore the world hateth you.

20 Remember the word that I said unto you, The servant is not greater than his lord. If they have persecuted me, they will also persecute you; if they have kept my saying, they will keep yours also.

21 But all these things will they do unto you for my name's sake, because they know not him that sent me.

22 If I had not come and spoken unto them, they had not had sin; but now they have no cloak for their sin.

23 He that hateth me hateth my Father also.

24 If I had not done among them the works which none other man did, they had not had sin: but now have they both seen and hated both me and my Father.

25 But *this cometh to pass*, that the word might be fulfilled that is written in their law, They hated me without a cause.

26 But when the Comforter is come, whom I will send unto you from the Father, *even* the Spirit of truth, which proceedeth from the Father, he shall testify of me:

27 and ye also shall bear witness, because ye have been with me from the beginning.

OLD TESTAMENT READING

Create in me a clean heart, O God; and renew a right spirit within me.

11 Cast me not away from thy presence; and take not thy Holy Spirit from me.

12 Restore unto me the joy of thy salvation; and uphold me *with thy* free Spirit.

13 *Then* will I teach transgressors thy ways; and sinners shall be converted unto thee.

Psalm 51:10–13

INSIGHTS

If anyone asks the question, "How can I be a happy Christian?" our Lord's answer is very simple: . . . "You cannot have My joy without My life. Abide in Me, and let Me abide in you, and My joy will be in you." . . .

. . . There is no joy like love. There is no joy but love. Christ had just spoken of the Father's love and His own abiding in it, and of His having loved us with that same love. His joy is nothing but the joy of love, of being loved and of loving. It was the joy of receiving His Father's love and abiding in it, and then the joy of passing on that love and pouring it out on sinners. It is this joy He wants us to share: the joy of being loved of the Father and of Him; the joy of in our turn loving and living for those around us. . . .

. . . How sad that we should so need to be reminded that as God alone is the fountain of all joy, "God our exceeding joy," the only way to be perfectly happy is to have as much of God, as much of His will and fellowship, as possible! Religion is meant to be in everyday life a thing of unspeakable joy.

Andrew Murray

PAUSE FOR REFLECTION

How does the peace that Jesus promises (John 14:27) differ from the world's peace? What does Jesus say about the relationship between love, joy, and obedience to God?

TUESDAY

God Cares for Those Who Serve Him

John 16:1–28

16 These things have I spoken unto you, that ye should not be offended.

2 They shall put you out of the synagogues: yea, the time cometh, that whosoever killeth you will think that he doeth God service.

3 And these things will they do unto you, because they have not known the Father, nor me.

4 But these things have I told you, that when the time shall come, ye may remember that I told you of them. And these things I said not unto you at the beginning, because I was with you.

The Work of the Holy Spirit

*B*ut now I go my way to him that sent me; and none of you asketh me, Whither goest thou?

6 But because I have said these things unto you, sorrow hath filled your heart.

7 Nevertheless I tell you the truth; It is expedient for you that I go away: for if I go not away, the Comforter will not come unto you; but if I depart, I will send him unto you.

8 And when he is come, he will reprove the world of sin, and of righteousness, and of judgment:

9 of sin, because they believe not on me;

10 of righteousness, because I go to my Father, and ye see me no more;

11 of judgment, because the prince of this world is judged.

12 I have yet many things to say unto you, but ye cannot bear them now.

13 Howbeit when he, the Spirit of truth, is come, he will guide you into all truth: for he shall not speak of himself; but whatsoever he shall hear, *that* shall he speak: and he will show you things to come.

14 He shall glorify me: for he shall receive of mine, and shall show *it* unto you.

15 All things that the Father hath are mine: therefore said I, that he shall take of mine, and shall show *it* unto you.

Sorrow Will Become Joy

A little while, and ye shall not see me: and again, a little while, and ye shall see me, because I go to the Father.

17 Then said *some* of his disciples among themselves, What is this that he saith unto us, A little while, and ye shall not see me: and again, a little while, and ye shall see me: and, Because I go to the Father?

18 They said therefore, What is this that he saith, A little while? we cannot tell what he saith.

19 Now Jesus knew that they were desirous to ask him, and said unto them, Do ye inquire among yourselves of that I said, A little while, and ye shall not see me: and again, a little while, and ye shall see me?

20 Verily, verily, I say unto you, That ye shall weep and lament, but the world shall rejoice; and ye shall be sorrowful, but your sorrow shall be turned into joy.

21 A woman when she is in travail hath sorrow, because her hour is come: but as soon as she is delivered of the child, she remembereth no more the

anguish, for joy that a man is born into the world.

22 And ye now therefore have sorrow: but I will see you again, and your heart shall rejoice, and your joy no man taketh from you.

23 And in that day ye shall ask me nothing. Verily, verily, I say unto you, Whatsoever ye shall ask the Father in my name, he will give *it* you.

24 Hitherto have ye asked nothing in my name: ask, and ye shall receive, that your joy may be full.

Victory over the World

These things have I spoken unto you in proverbs: but the time cometh, when I shall no more speak unto you in proverbs, but I shall show you plainly of the Father.

26 At that day ye shall ask in my name: and I say not unto you, that I will pray the Father for you:

27 for the Father himself loveth you, because ye have loved me, and have believed that I came out from God.

28 I came forth from the Father, and am come into the world: again, I leave the world, and go to the Father.

OLD TESTAMENT READING

Trust in the LORD, and do good; *so* shalt thou dwell in the land, and verily thou shalt be fed.

4 Delight thyself also in the LORD; and he shall give thee the desires of thine heart.

5 Commit thy way unto the LORD; trust also in him; and he shall bring *it* to pass.

6 And he shall bring forth thy righteousness as the light, and thy judgment as the noonday.

Psalm 37:3–6

INSIGHTS

You walk your daughter down the aisle. "When did she grow up?"

You wake up in an emergency room to the beeping of a machine and find wires suction-cupped to your chest.

Be the event pleasant or painful, the result is the same. Reality breaks through the papier-mâché mask and screams at you like a Marine drill sergeant. "You are getting old! You are going to die! You can't be someone you are not!". . .

Jesus does his best work at such moments. Just when the truth about life sinks in, his truth starts to surface. He takes us by the hand and dares us not to sweep the facts under the rug but to confront them with him at our side.

Aging? A necessary process to pass on to a better world.

Death? Merely a brief passage, a tunnel.

Self? Designed and created for a purpose, purchased by God himself.

There, was that so bad? . . .

The next time you find yourself alone in a dark alley facing the undeniables of life, don't cover them with a blanket, or ignore them with a nervous grin. Don't turn up the TV and pretend they aren't there. Instead, stand still, whisper his name, and listen. He is nearer than you think.

Max Lucado

PAUSE FOR REFLECTION

Who did Jesus promise to send to his followers? What would he do for them? How is he comforting you today?

WEDNESDAY

God Protects Those Who Follow Him

John 16:29—17:19

*H*is disciples said unto him, Lo, now speakest thou plainly, and speakest no proverb.

³⁰ Now are we sure that thou knowest all things, and needest not that any man should ask thee: by this we believe that thou camest forth from God.

³¹ Jesus answered them, Do ye now believe?

³² Behold, the hour cometh, yea, is now come, that ye shall be scattered, every man to his own, and shall leave me alone: and yet I am not alone, because the Father is with me.

³³ These things I have spoken unto you, that in me ye might have peace. In the world ye shall have tribulation: but be of good cheer; I have overcome the world.

Jesus Prays for His Disciples

17 These words spake Jesus, and lifted up his eyes to heaven, and said, Father, the hour is come; glorify thy Son, that thy Son also may glorify thee:

² as thou hast given him power over all flesh, that he should give eternal life to as many as thou hast given him.

³ And this is life eternal, that they might know thee the only true God, and Jesus Christ, whom thou hast sent.

⁴ I have glorified thee on the earth: I have finished the work which thou gavest me to do.

⁵ And now, O Father, glorify thou me with thine own self with the glory which I had with thee before the world was.

⁶ I have manifested thy name unto the men which thou gavest me out of the world: thine they were, and thou gavest them me; and they have kept thy word.

⁷ Now they have known that all things whatsoever thou hast given me are of thee.

⁸ For I have given unto them the words which thou gavest me; and they have received *them*, and have known surely that I came out from thee, and they have believed that thou didst send me.

⁹ I pray for them: I pray not for the world, but for them which thou hast given me; for they are thine.

¹⁰ And all mine are thine, and thine are mine; and I am glorified in them.

¹¹ And now I am no more in the world, but these are in the world, and I come to thee. Holy Father, keep through thine own name those whom thou hast given me, that they may be one, as we *are*.

¹² While I was with them in the world, I kept them in thy name: those that thou gavest me I have kept, and none of them is lost, but the son of perdition; that the Scripture might be fulfilled.

¹³ And now come I to thee; and these things I speak in the world, that they might have my joy fulfilled in themselves.

¹⁴ I have given them thy word; and the world hath hated them, because they are not of the world, even as I am not of the world.

¹⁵ I pray not that thou shouldest take them out of the world, but that thou shouldest keep them from the evil.

16 They are not of the world, even as I am not of the world.

17 Sanctify them through thy truth: thy word is truth.

18 As thou hast sent me into the world, even so have I also sent them into the world.

19 And for their sakes I sanctify myself, that they also might be sanctified through the truth.

OLD TESTAMENT READING

*H*e that dwelleth in the secret place of the Most High shall abide under the shadow of the Almighty.

2 I will say of the LORD, *He is* my refuge and my fortress: my God; in him will I trust.

3 Surely he shall deliver thee from the snare of the fowler, *and* from the noisome pestilence.

4 He shall cover thee with his feathers, and under his wings shalt thou trust: his truth *shall be thy* shield and buckler.

5 Thou shalt not be afraid for the terror by night; *nor* for the arrow *that* flieth by day;

6 *nor* for the pestilence *that* walketh in darkness; *nor* for the destruction *that* wasteth at noonday.

7 A thousand shall fall at thy side, and ten thousand at thy right hand; *but* it shall not come nigh thee.

8 Only with thine eyes shalt thou behold and see the reward of the wicked.

Psalm 91:1–8

INSIGHTS

*S*omeone has said that Psalm 91 is an expanded commentary on the great cry of the apostle Paul: "If God is for us, who can be against us?"

(Rom. 8:31). What is the message of the Psalm? . . .

. . . God promises us shelter, covering, and comprehensive protection based on His very nature. Those who claim the promise and dwell in the shelter of the Most High will rest in the shadow of the Almighty. God offers us security, says the psalmist, by providing secret shelter. . . .

. . . Almighty God is saying, in effect, "When you dwell in My most secret place, I promise to be your divine host with the sacred responsibility of covering and caring for you." When we deposit our trust in Him, then He guarantees He will give us His sheltering protection against all that harms us—until our duty is done and our race is finished in His service.

We will still go through trials. That is part of life. But . . . if we are "dwelling" in communion with God, if we are accepting the shelter only He can give, then we will be safe until our work for the Lord is over, until our time on this earth is done. . . .

Our security does not rest in our weak, feeble, timid, fragile, finite humanity—not for a moment. Our security is in clinging to a God who takes care of those who take the conscious step of faith to believe.

Joel Gregory

PAUSE FOR REFLECTION

*W*hat kind of protection did Jesus want for his followers? As you read Jesus' prayer, do you feel his personal love and care for you? Thank him.

THURSDAY

The Unity of All Believers

John 17:20—18:18

*N*either pray I for these alone, but for them also which shall believe on me through their word;

²¹ that they all may be one; as thou, Father, *art* in me, and I in thee, that they also may be one in us: that the world may believe that thou hast sent me.

²² And the glory which thou gavest me I have given them; that they may be one, even as we are one:

²³ I in them, and thou in me, that they may be made perfect in one; and that the world may know that thou hast sent me, and hast loved them, as thou hast loved me.

²⁴ Father, I will that they also, whom thou hast given me, be with me where I am; that they may behold my glory, which thou hast given me: for thou lovedst me before the foundation of the world.

²⁵ O righteous Father, the world hath not known thee: but I have known thee, and these have known that thou hast sent me.

²⁶ And I have declared unto them thy name, and will declare *it*; that the love wherewith thou hast loved me may be in them, and I in them.

Jesus Is Arrested

18 When Jesus had spoken these words, he went forth with his disciples over the brook Cedron, where was a garden, into the which he entered, and his disciples.

² And Judas also, which betrayed him, knew the place: for Jesus ofttimes resorted thither with his disciples.

³ Judas then, having received a band *of men* and officers from the chief priests and Pharisees, cometh thither with lanterns and torches and weapons.

⁴ Jesus therefore, knowing all things that should come upon him, went forth, and said unto them, Whom seek ye?

⁵ They answered him, Jesus of Nazareth. Jesus saith unto them, I am *he*. And Judas also, which betrayed him, stood with them.

⁶ As soon then as he had said unto them, I am *he*, they went backward, and fell to the ground.

⁷ Then asked he them again, Whom seek ye? And they said, Jesus of Nazareth.

⁸ Jesus answered, I have told you that I am *he*: if therefore ye seek me, let these go their way:

⁹ that the saying might be fulfilled, which he spake, Of them which thou gavest me have I lost none.

¹⁰ Then Simon Peter having a sword drew it, and smote the high priest's servant, and cut off his right ear. The servant's name was Malchus.

¹¹ Then said Jesus unto Peter, Put up thy sword into the sheath: the cup which my Father hath given me, shall I not drink it?

Jesus Is Brought Before Annas

*T*hen the band and the captain and officers of the Jews took Jesus, and bound him,

¹³ and led him away to Annas first; for he was father-in-law to Caiaphas, which was the high priest that same year.

¹⁴ Now Caiaphas was he, which gave

counsel to the Jews, that it was expedient that one man should die for the people.

Peter Denies Jesus

*A*nd Simon Peter followed Jesus, and *so did* another disciple: that disciple was known unto the high priest, and went in with Jesus into the palace of the high priest.
[16] But Peter stood at the door without. Then went out that other disciple, which was known unto the high priest, and spake unto her that kept the door, and brought in Peter.
[17] Then saith the damsel that kept the door unto Peter, Art not thou also *one* of this man's disciples? He saith, I am not.
[18] And the servants and officers stood there, who had made a fire of coals: for it was cold; and they warmed themselves: and Peter stood with them, and warmed himself.

OLD TESTAMENT READING

*B*ehold, how good and how pleasant *it is* for brethren to dwell together in unity!
[2] *It is* like the precious ointment upon the head, that ran down upon the beard, *even* Aaron's beard: that went down to the skirts of his garments;
[3] as the dew of Hermon, *and as the dew* that descended upon the mountains of Zion: for there the LORD commanded the blessing, *even* life for evermore.

Psalm 133:1–3

INSIGHTS

*O*ur God is a God of unity. It is against His nature to work in the midst of division. That is why in His high priestly prayer (John 17) Jesus repeatedly prayed that "they may be one, just as We are one." . . .

God's insistence on unity is why so much of the New Testament gives instruction for maintaining the unity of the church. For example, 1 Corinthians 14:40 instructs the church to do all things properly and in order. Ephesians 4:3 exhorts believers to be "diligent to preserve the unity of the Spirit in the bond of peace." . . .

Satan recognizes the power of God's people. He knows that we are the only ones in the world who can keep him from messing up God's plan. So he is desperate to stop us. That is why the church is always under attack from Satan. He wants to get choir folks fighting each other. He wants to get church leaders fighting each other. He wants to get members fighting each other. He wants husbands and wives to be fighting each other. If he succeeds, God's people become ineffective.

As God's people, we must overcome disunity before we can fight any other battles. When we see disunity, we should not join Satan's side and keep it going. We should stop, recognize the source, and act under God's authority to restore our unity so He can continue His work through us.

Anthony Evans

ACTION POINT

*I*n what ways does disunity limit God's work through your life? Prayerfully read Psalm 133 and begin working for the unity that is such a precious blessing to God.

FRIDAY

God Is Truth

John 18:19—19:3

The High Priest Questions Jesus

*T*he high priest then asked Jesus of his disciples, and of his doctrine.
²⁰ Jesus answered him, I spake openly to the world; I ever taught in the synagogue, and in the temple, whither the Jews always resort; and in secret have I said nothing.
²¹ Why askest thou me? ask them which heard me, what I have said unto them: behold, they know what I said.
²² And when he had thus spoken, one of the officers which stood by struck Jesus with the palm of his hand, saying, Answerest thou the high priest so?
²³ Jesus answered him, If I have spoken evil, bear witness of the evil: but if well, why smitest thou me?
²⁴ Now Annas had sent him bound unto Caiaphas the high priest.

Peter Again Denies He Knows Jesus

*A*nd Simon Peter stood and warmed himself. They said therefore unto him, Art not thou also *one* of his disciples? He denied *it*, and said, I am not.
²⁶ One of the servants of the high priest, being *his* kinsman whose ear Peter cut off, saith, Did not I see thee in the garden with him?
²⁷ Peter then denied again; and immediately the cock crew.

Jesus Is Brought Before Pilate

*T*hen led they Jesus from Caiaphas unto the hall of judgment: and it was early; and they themselves went not into the judgment hall, lest they should be defiled; but that they might eat the passover.
²⁹ Pilate then went out unto them, and said, What accusation bring ye against this man?
³⁰ They answered and said unto him, If he were not a malefactor, we would not have delivered him up unto thee.
³¹ Then said Pilate unto them, Take ye him, and judge him according to your law. The Jews therefore said unto him, It is not lawful for us to put any man to death:
³² that the saying of Jesus might be fulfilled, which he spake, signifying what death he should die.
³³ Then Pilate entered into the judgment hall again, and called Jesus, and said unto him, Art thou the King of the Jews?
³⁴ Jesus answered him, Sayest thou this thing of thyself, or did others tell it thee of me?
³⁵ Pilate answered, Am I a Jew? Thine own nation and the chief priests have delivered thee unto me: what hast thou done?
³⁶ Jesus answered, My kingdom is not of this world: if my kingdom were of this world, then would my servants fight, that I should not be delivered to the Jews: but now is my kingdom not from hence.
³⁷ Pilate therefore said unto him, Art thou a king then? Jesus answered, Thou sayest that I am a king. To this end was I born, and for this cause came I into the world, that I should bear witness unto the truth. Every

one that is of the truth heareth my voice.

38 Pilate saith unto him, What is truth? And when he had said this, he went out again unto the Jews, and saith unto them, I find in him no fault *at all*.

39 But ye have a custom, that I should release unto you one at the passover: will ye therefore that I release unto you the King of the Jews?

40 Then cried they all again, saying, Not this man, but Barabbas. Now Barabbas was a robber.

19 Then Pilate therefore took Jesus, and scourged *him*.

2 And the soldiers platted a crown of thorns, and put *it* on his head, and they put on him a purple robe,

3 and said, Hail, King of the Jews! and they smote him with their hands.

OLD TESTAMENT READING

O praise the LORD, all ye nations: praise him, all ye people.

2 For his merciful kindness is great toward us: and the truth of the LORD *endureth* for ever. Praise ye the LORD.
Psalm 117:1–2

*R*ighteous *art* thou, O LORD, and upright *are* thy judgments.

138 Thy testimonies *that* thou hast commanded *are* righteous and very faithful.

139 My zeal hath consumed me, because mine enemies have forgotten thy words.

140 Thy word *is* very pure: therefore thy servant loveth it.

141 I *am* small and despised: *yet* do not I forget thy precepts.

142 Thy righteousness *is* an everlasting righteousness, and thy law *is* the truth.
Psalm 119:137–142

INSIGHTS

What is truth? I have often wondered how Pilate asked this question. What was his tone of voice? What kind of expression did he have on his face? Was the question raised in jest? Was it cynical? Was Pilate pensive for a moment? We don't really know. If Pilate was momentarily concerned for truth, his mood soon gave way to a spirit of expediency. If he cared about knowing the truth, he certainly didn't care much about doing the truth. . . .

To declare that Jesus was without fault and then minutes later to turn Him over to a barbarous mob was to slaughter the truth. Pilate judged the Truth. He sentenced the Truth. He scourged the Truth. He mocked the Truth. He crucified the Truth.

The irony is that at the very moment he asked his question "What is truth?" he was staring at the pure incarnation of Truth. The One who is the Truth had just said to him, "Everyone who is of the truth hears My voice."

Pilate missed that voice. The words bounced off his ears. He was not "of the truth."

R. C. Sproul

APPLICATION

How ironic that Pilate was so close to the God of truth, yet failed to understand truth. What claims to truth does God make? Does he make his truth available to people? How? Pray that you will draw close to God and trust his truth.

WEEKEND

All Power on Earth Is Given by God

John 19:4–27

*P*ilate therefore went forth again, and saith unto them, Behold, I bring him forth to you, that ye may know that I find no fault in him.

[5] Then came Jesus forth, wearing the crown of thorns, and the purple robe. And *Pilate* saith unto them, Behold the man!

[6] When the chief priests therefore and officers saw him, they cried out, saying, Crucify *him*, crucify *him*. Pilate saith unto them, Take ye him, and crucify *him*: for I find no fault in him.

[7] The Jews answered him, We have a law, and by our law he ought to die, because he made himself the Son of God.

[8] When Pilate therefore heard that saying, he was the more afraid;

[9] and went again into the judgment hall, and saith unto Jesus, Whence art thou? But Jesus gave him no answer.

[10] Then saith Pilate unto him, Speakest thou not unto me? knowest thou not that I have power to crucify thee, and have power to release thee?

[11] Jesus answered, Thou couldest have no power *at all* against me, except it were given thee from above: therefore he that delivered me unto thee hath the greater sin.

[12] And from thenceforth Pilate sought to release him: but the Jews cried out, saying, If thou let this man go, thou art not Caesar's friend: whosoever maketh himself a king speaketh against Caesar.

[13] When Pilate therefore heard that saying, he brought Jesus forth, and sat down in the judgment seat in a place that is called the Pavement, but in the Hebrew, Gabbatha.

[14] And it was the preparation of the passover, and about the sixth hour: and he saith unto the Jews, Behold your King!

[15] But they cried out, Away with *him*, away with *him*, crucify him. Pilate saith unto them, Shall I crucify your King? The chief priests answered, We have no king but Caesar.

[16] Then delivered he him therefore unto them to be crucified. And they took Jesus, and led *him* away.

Jesus Is Crucified

*A*nd he bearing his cross went forth into a place called *the place* of a skull, which is called in the Hebrew Golgotha:

[18] where they crucified him, and two others with him, on either side one, and Jesus in the midst.

[19] And Pilate wrote a title, and put *it* on the cross. And the writing was, JESUS OF NAZARETH THE KING OF THE JEWS.

[20] This title then read many of the Jews; for the place where Jesus was crucified was nigh to the city: and it was written in Hebrew, *and* Greek, *and* Latin.

[21] Then said the chief priests of the Jews to Pilate, Write not, The King of the Jews; but that he said, I am King of the Jews.

[22] Pilate answered, What I have written I have written.

[23] Then the soldiers, when they had crucified Jesus, took his garments, and made four parts, to every soldier a part; and also *his* coat: now the coat

was without seam, woven from the top throughout.

[24] They said therefore among themselves, Let us not rend it, but cast lots for it, whose it shall be: that the Scripture might be fulfilled, which saith, They parted my raiment among them, and for my vesture they did cast lots. These things therefore the soldiers did.

[25] Now there stood by the cross of Jesus his mother, and his mother's sister, Mary the *wife* of Cleophas, and Mary Magdalene.

[26] When Jesus therefore saw his mother, and the disciple standing by, whom he loved, he saith unto his mother, Woman, behold thy son!

[27] Then saith he to the disciple, Behold thy mother! And from that hour that disciple took her unto his own *home.*

OLD TESTAMENT READING

*A*nd command them to say unto their masters, Thus saith the LORD of hosts, the God of Israel; Thus shall ye say unto your masters;

[5] I have made the earth, the man and the beast that *are* upon the ground, by my great power and by my outstretched arm, and have given it unto whom it seemed meet unto me.

[6] And now have I given all these lands into the hand of Nebuchadnezzar the king of Babylon, my servant; and the beasts of the field have I given him also to serve him.

[7] And all nations shall serve him, and his son, and his son's son, until the very time of his land come: and then many nations and great kings shall serve themselves of him.

Jeremiah 27:4–7

INSIGHTS

*O*ur sovereign Lord . . . exerts control over His entire universe from beginning to end! His sovereignty means that He either causes or He allows all things to happen that do happen. He is absolutely independent, subject to no one, and influenced by no one. Despite the suffering, violence, and filth of this world, God remains in control—whether or not we acknowledge him. Before time began, God was in control. He has ruled over all creation ever since He created heaven and earth. . . .

The Israelites must have wondered whether God was in control, as they spent four hundred years of bondage in Egypt. Driven day after day by cruel taskmasters, they surely asked, "If there is a God, where is He?" . . . They probably reasoned that either there is no God, or that God did not have the power to stop the madness. But what happened? The sovereign God who controls every circumstance led Israel out of Egypt with mighty demonstrations of His power! Israel never forgot His deliverance. The entire world was shaken! Nations trembled at the prospect of confronting God's people.

Elliot Johnson
Al Schierbaum

PAUSE FOR REFLECTION

*W*ho holds the only real power there is? Why does God give power to certain people for a time? What happens to those who think their power is their own? Submit your heart to his power today!

MONDAY

Rejoice! Jesus Has Risen

John 19:28—20:9

Jesus Dies

After this, Jesus knowing that all things were now accomplished, that the Scripture might be fulfilled, saith, I thirst.

29 Now there was set a vessel full of vinegar: and they filled a sponge with vinegar, and put *it* upon hyssop, and put *it* to his mouth.

30 When Jesus therefore had received the vinegar, he said, It is finished: and he bowed his head, and gave up the ghost.

31 The Jews therefore, because it was the preparation, that the bodies should not remain upon the cross on the sabbath day, (for that sabbath day was a high day,) besought Pilate that their legs might be broken, and *that* they might be taken away.

32 Then came the soldiers, and brake the legs of the first, and of the other which was crucified with him.

33 But when they came to Jesus, and saw that he was dead already, they brake not his legs:

34 but one of the soldiers with a spear pierced his side, and forthwith came there out blood and water.

35 And he that saw *it* bare record, and his record is true; and he knoweth that he saith true, that ye might believe.

36 For these things were done, that the Scripture should be fulfilled, A bone of him shall not be broken.

37 And again another Scripture saith, They shall look on him whom they pierced.

Jesus Is Buried

And after this Joseph of Arimathea, being a disciple of Jesus, but secretly for fear of the Jews, besought Pilate that he might take away the body of Jesus: and Pilate gave *him* leave. He came therefore, and took the body of Jesus.

39 And there came also Nicodemus, which at the first came to Jesus by night, and brought a mixture of myrrh and aloes, about an hundred pound *weight*.

40 Then took they the body of Jesus, and wound it in linen clothes with the spices, as the manner of the Jews is to bury.

41 Now in the place where he was crucified there was a garden; and in the garden a new sepulchre, wherein was never man yet laid.

42 There laid they Jesus therefore because of the Jews' preparation *day*; for the sepulchre was nigh at hand.

Jesus' Tomb Is Empty

20 The first *day* of the week cometh Mary Magdalene early, when it was yet dark, unto the sepulchre, and seeth the stone taken away from the sepulchre.

2 Then she runneth, and cometh to Simon Peter, and to the other disciple, whom Jesus loved, and saith unto them, They have taken away the Lord out of the sepulchre, and we know not where they have laid him.

3 Peter therefore went forth, and that other disciple, and came to the sepulchre.

4 So they ran both together: and the

other disciple did outrun Peter, and came first to the sepulchre.

5 And he stooping down, *and looking in*, saw the linen clothes lying; yet went he not in.

6 Then cometh Simon Peter following him, and went into the sepulchre, and seeth the linen clothes lie,

7 and the napkin, that was about his head, not lying with the linen clothes, but wrapped together in a place by itself.

8 Then went in also that other disciple, which came first to the sepulchre, and he saw, and believed.

9 For as yet they knew not the Scripture, that he must rise again from the dead.

OLD TESTAMENT READING

O clap your hands, all ye people; shout unto God with the voice of triumph.

2 For the LORD most high *is* terrible; *he is* a great King over all the earth.

3 He shall subdue the people under us, and the nations under our feet.

4 He shall choose our inheritance for us, the excellency of Jacob whom he loved. Selah.

5 God is gone up with a shout, the LORD with the sound of a trumpet.

6 Sing praises to God, sing praises: sing praises unto our King, sing praises.

7 For God *is* the King of all the earth: sing ye praises with understanding.

8 God reigneth over the heathen: God sitteth upon the throne of his holiness.

9 The princes of the people are gathered together, *even* the people of the God of Abraham: for the shields of the earth *belong* unto God: he is greatly exalted.

Psalm 47:1–9

F or I know *that* my Redeemer liveth, and *that* he shall stand at the latter *day* upon the earth:

26 and *though* after my skin *worms* destroy this *body*, yet in my flesh shall I see God:

27 whom I shall see for myself, and mine eyes shall behold, and not another; *though* my reins be consumed within me.

Job 19:25–27

INSIGHTS

C hrist is risen:
The world below lies desolate.
Christ is risen:
The spirits of evil are fallen.
Christ is risen:
The angels of God are rejoicing.
Christ is risen:
The tombs of the dead are empty.
Christ is risen indeed from the dead,
The first of the sleepers.
Glory and power are his forever and ever.
Amen.

Hippolytus of Rome

ACTION POINT

W hen Mary revealed the stunning news that Jesus was no longer in the tomb, the disciples took off running to see it for themselves! Does the realization that Jesus is truly alive set your heart racing? Ask God to renew your excitement and joy in Jesus' resurrection.

TUESDAY

*Thomas Wasn't Alone
in His Unbelief*

John 20:10—21:3

Jesus Appears to Mary Magdalene

*T*hen the disciples went away again unto their own home.

[11] But Mary stood without at the sepulchre weeping: and as she wept, she stooped down, *and looked* into the sepulchre,

[12] and seeth two angels in white sitting, the one at the head, and the other at the feet, where the body of Jesus had lain.

[13] And they say unto her, Woman, why weepest thou? She saith unto them, Because they have taken away my Lord, and I know not where they have laid him.

[14] And when she had thus said, she turned herself back, and saw Jesus standing, and knew not that it was Jesus.

[15] Jesus saith unto her, Woman, why weepest thou? whom seekest thou? She, supposing him to be the gardener, saith unto him, Sir, if thou have borne him hence, tell me where thou hast laid him, and I will take him away.

[16] Jesus saith unto her, Mary. She turned herself, and saith unto him, Rabboni; which is to say, Master.

[17] Jesus saith unto her, Touch me not; for I am not yet ascended to my Father: but go to my brethren, and say unto them, I ascend unto my Father, and your Father; and *to* my God, and your God.

[18] Mary Magdalene came and told the disciples that she had seen the Lord, and *that* he had spoken these things unto her.

Jesus Appears to His Disciples

*T*hen the same day at evening, being the first *day* of the week, when the doors were shut where the disciples were assembled for fear of the Jews, came Jesus and stood in the midst, and saith unto them, Peace *be* unto you.

[20] And when he had so said, he showed unto them *his* hands and his side. Then were the disciples glad, when they saw the Lord.

[21] Then said Jesus to them again, Peace *be* unto you: as *my* Father hath sent me, even so send I you.

[22] And when he had said this, he breathed on *them*, and saith unto them, Receive ye the Holy Ghost:

[23] whosesoever sins ye remit, they are remitted unto them; *and* whosesoever *sins* ye retain, they are retained.

Jesus Appears to Thomas

*B*ut Thomas, one of the twelve, called Didymus, was not with them when Jesus came.

[25] The other disciples therefore said unto him, We have seen the Lord. But he said unto them, Except I shall see in his hands the print of the nails, and put my finger into the print of the nails, and thrust my hand into his side, I will not believe.

[26] And after eight days again his disciples were within, and Thomas with them: *then* came Jesus, the doors being shut, and stood in the midst, and said, Peace *be* unto you.

[27] Then saith he to Thomas, Reach

hither thy finger, and behold my hands; and reach hither thy hand, and thrust *it* into my side; and be not faithless, but believing.

²⁸ And Thomas answered and said unto him, My Lord and my God.

²⁹ Jesus saith unto him, Thomas, because thou hast seen me, thou hast believed: blessed *are* they that have not seen, and *yet* have believed.

Why John Wrote This Book

*A*nd many other signs truly did Jesus in the presence of his disciples, which are not written in this book:

³¹ but these are written, that ye might believe that Jesus is the Christ, the Son of God; and that believing ye might have life through his name.

Jesus Appears to Seven Disciples

21 After these things Jesus showed himself again to the disciples at the sea of Tiberias; and on this wise showed he *himself.*

² There were together Simon Peter, and Thomas called Didymus, and Nathanael of Cana in Galilee, and the *sons* of Zebedee, and two other of his disciples.

³ Simon Peter saith unto them, I go a fishing. They say unto him, We also go with thee. They went forth, and entered into a ship immediately; and that night they caught nothing.

*A*nd Gideon said unto God, If thou wilt save Israel by mine hand, as thou hast said,

³⁷ behold, I will put a fleece of wool in the floor; *and* if the dew be on the fleece only, and *it be* dry upon all the earth *besides*, then shall I know that thou wilt save Israel by mine hand, as thou hast said.

³⁸ And it was so: for he rose up early on the morrow, and thrust the fleece together, and wringed the dew out of the fleece, a bowlful of water.

³⁹ And Gideon said unto God, Let not thine anger be hot against me, and I will speak but this once: let me prove, I pray thee, but this once with the fleece; let it now be dry only upon the fleece, and upon all the ground let there be dew.

⁴⁰ And God did so that night: for it was dry upon the fleece only, and there was dew on all the ground.

Judges 6:36-40

---

*G*ive your whole being to God without holding back and without doubting. He will prove himself to you, and work in you that which is pleasing in His sight through Jesus Christ. . . . However weak you feel, only be willing, and he who has worked to will, will work to do by His power. . . .

. . . So come with every temptation you feel in yourself, every memory of unwillingness, unwatchfulness, unfaithfulness, and all that causes your unceasing self-condemnation. Put your powerlessness in God's almighty power.

Andrew Murray

---

*H*ow does God treat those who doubt? Do you struggle with unbelief? Ask God to prove himself to you.

WEDNESDAY

God's People Need
a Shepherd

John 21:4–25

*B*ut when the morning was now come, Jesus stood on the shore: but the disciples knew not that it was Jesus.

⁵ Then Jesus saith unto them, Children, have ye any meat? They answered him, No.

⁶ And he said unto them, Cast the net on the right side of the ship, and ye shall find. They cast therefore, and now they were not able to draw it for the multitude of fishes.

⁷ Therefore that disciple whom Jesus loved saith unto Peter, It is the Lord. Now when Simon Peter heard that it was the Lord, he girt *his* fisher's coat *unto him*, (for he was naked,) and did cast himself into the sea.

⁸ And the other disciples came in a little ship, (for they were not far from land, but as it were two hundred cubits,) dragging the net with fishes.

⁹ As soon then as they were come to land, they saw a fire of coals there, and fish laid thereon, and bread.

¹⁰ Jesus saith unto them, Bring of the fish which ye have now caught.

¹¹ Simon Peter went up, and drew the net to land full of great fishes, a hundred and fifty and three: and for all there were so many, yet was not the net broken.

¹² Jesus saith unto them, Come *and* dine. And none of the disciples durst ask him, Who art thou? knowing that it was the Lord.

¹³ Jesus then cometh, and taketh bread, and giveth them, and fish likewise.

¹⁴ This is now the third time that Jesus showed himself to his disciples, after that he was risen from the dead.

Jesus Talks to Peter

*S*o when they had dined, Jesus saith to Simon Peter, Simon, *son* of Jona, lovest thou me more than these? He saith unto him, Yea, Lord; thou knowest that I love thee. He saith unto him, Feed my lambs.

¹⁶ He saith to him again the second time, Simon, *son* of Jona, lovest thou me? He saith unto him, Yea, Lord; thou knowest that I love thee. He saith unto him, Feed my sheep.

¹⁷ He saith unto him the third time, Simon, *son* of Jona, lovest thou me? Peter was grieved because he said unto him the third time, Lovest thou me? And he said unto him, Lord, thou knowest all things; thou knowest that I love thee. Jesus saith unto him, Feed my sheep.

¹⁸ Verily, verily, I say unto thee, When thou wast young, thou girdedst thyself, and walkedst whither thou wouldest: but when thou shalt be old, thou shalt stretch forth thy hands, and another shall gird thee, and carry *thee* whither thou wouldest not.

¹⁹ This spake he, signifying by what death he should glorify God. And when he had spoken this, he saith unto him, Follow me.

²⁰ Then Peter, turning about, seeth the disciple whom Jesus loved following; which also leaned on his breast at supper, and said, Lord, which is he that betrayeth thee?

²¹ Peter seeing him saith to Jesus, Lord, and what *shall* this man *do*?

²² Jesus saith unto him, If I will that

he tarry till I come, what *is that* to thee? follow thou me.

²³ Then went this saying abroad among the brethren, that that disciple should not die: yet Jesus said not unto him, He shall not die; but, If I will that he tarry till I come, what *is that* to thee?

²⁴ This is the disciple which testifieth of these things, and wrote these things: and we know that his testimony is true.

²⁵ And there are also many other things which Jesus did, the which, if they should be written every one, I suppose that even the world itself could not contain the books that should be written. Amen.

OLD TESTAMENT READING

*A*nd Moses spake unto the LORD, saying,

¹⁶ Let the LORD, the God of the spirits of all flesh, set a man over the congregation,

¹⁷ which may go out before them, and which may go in before them, and which may lead them out, and which may bring them in; that the congregation of the LORD be not as sheep which have no shepherd.

Numbers 27:15–17

*T*hus shall they know that I the LORD their God *am* with them, and *that* they, *even* the house of Israel, *are* my people, saith the Lord GOD.

³¹ And ye my flock, the flock of my pasture, *are* men, *and* I *am* your God, saith the Lord GOD.

Ezekiel 34:30–31

INSIGHTS

*T*he shepherd is at the very center of the life of the sheep. He provides for their every need, satisfying them completely.

Sheep will not lie down if they have cause to be fearful. They are easily frightened. However, as soon as the shepherd appears and moves in the midst of the restless flock, they become quiet.

. . . Our Good Shepherd appears, saying, "Fear THOU not; for I am with thee" (Isa. 41:10). His presence in the midst of our need removes fear and gives rest.

Sheep will not lie down if they are hungry. The shepherd searches for the best pasture land available for his sheep. Our Good Shepherd knows we need to be well nourished for inner satisfaction. He provides nourishment for us from the green pastures of His Word. Nourished by it, we can lie down in quiet contentment.

Occasionally He has to MAKE us lie down. It may take illness, loneliness, heartache, or sorrow to accomplish this.

Not only does the shepherd lead his sheep in the green meadows of nourishment and rest, but beside the still waters. We are refreshed at the waters of quietness. . . .

Our Good Shepherd loves to see His sheep contented and relaxed, refreshed and satisfied with Him.

Millie Stamm

PAUSE FOR REFLECTION

*W*hy is it important that God's people be led by a shepherd? How will a good shepherd lead the Lord's sheep? What relationship do you see between loving Jesus and caring for his sheep?

THURSDAY

*Tell All the Nations
that Jesus Will Return!*

Acts 1:1–26

Luke Writes Another Book

1 The former treatise have I made, O Theophilus, of all that Jesus began both to do and teach,

[2] until the day in which he was taken up, after that he through the Holy Ghost had given commandments unto the apostles whom he had chosen:

[3] to whom also he showed himself alive after his passion by many infallible proofs, being seen of them forty days, and speaking of the things pertaining to the kingdom of God:

[4] and, being assembled together with *them*, commanded them that they should not depart from Jerusalem, but wait for the promise of the Father, which, *saith he*, ye have heard of me.

[5] For John truly baptized with water; but ye shall be baptized with the Holy Ghost not many days hence.

Jesus Is Taken Up Into Heaven

When they therefore were come together, they asked of him, saying, Lord, wilt thou at this time restore again the kingdom to Israel?

[7] And he said unto them, It is not for you to know the times or the seasons, which the Father hath put in his own power.

[8] But ye shall receive power, after that the Holy Ghost is come upon you: and ye shall be witnesses unto me both in Jerusalem, and in all Judea, and in Samaria, and unto the uttermost part of the earth.

[9] And when he had spoken these things, while they beheld, he was taken up; and a cloud received him out of their sight.

[10] And while they looked steadfastly toward heaven as he went up, behold, two men stood by them in white apparel;

[11] which also said, Ye men of Galilee, why stand ye gazing up into heaven? this same Jesus, which is taken up from you into heaven, shall so come in like manner as ye have seen him go into heaven.

A New Apostle Is Chosen

Then returned they unto Jerusalem from the mount called Olivet, which is from Jerusalem a sabbath day's journey.

[13] And when they were come in, they went up into an upper room, where abode both Peter, and James, and John, and Andrew, Philip, and Thomas, Bartholomew, and Matthew, James *the son* of Alphaeus, and Simon Zelotes, and Judas *the brother* of James.

[14] These all continued with one accord in prayer and supplication, with the women, and Mary the mother of Jesus, and with his brethren.

[15] And in those days Peter stood up in the midst of the disciples, and said, (the number of names together were about a hundred and twenty,)

[16] Men *and* brethren, this Scripture must needs have been fulfilled, which the Holy Ghost by the mouth of David spake before concerning Judas, which was guide to them that took Jesus.

[17] For he was numbered with us, and had obtained part of this ministry.

18 Now this man purchased a field with the reward of iniquity; and falling headlong, he burst asunder in the midst, and all his bowels gushed out. 19 And it was known unto all the dwellers at Jerusalem; insomuch as that field is called in their proper tongue, Aceldama, that is to say, The field of blood.
20 For it is written in the book of Psalms, Let his habitation be desolate, and let no man dwell therein: and His bishopric let another take.
21 Wherefore of these men which have companied with us all the time that the Lord Jesus went in and out among us, 22 beginning from the baptism of John, unto that same day that he was taken up from us, must one be ordained to be a witness with us of his resurrection.
23 And they appointed two, Joseph called Barsabas, who was surnamed Justus, and Matthias.
24 And they prayed, and said, Thou, Lord, which knowest the hearts of all *men*, show whether of these two thou hast chosen,
25 That he may take part of this ministry and apostleship, from which Judas by transgression fell, that he might go to his own place.
26 And they gave forth their lots; and the lot fell upon Matthias; and he was numbered with the eleven apostles.

OLD TESTAMENT READING

*L*et the field be joyful, and all that *is* therein: then shall all the trees of the wood rejoice
13 before the LORD: for he cometh, for he cometh to judge the earth: he shall judge the world with righteousness, and the people with his truth.

Psalm 96:12–13

INSIGHTS

*A*ll *true Christians believe that Jesus Christ is coming again. They may differ in their views of when certain promised events will occur, but they all agree that He is returning as He promised. Furthermore, all Christians agree that this faith in future glory ought to motivate the church. . . .*

Because we do not know the day or the hour of our Lord's return, we must constantly be ready. The believer who starts to neglect the "blessed hope" (Titus 2:13) will gradually develop a cold heart, a worldly attitude, and an unfaithful life (Luke 12:35–48). . . .

Not only should this expectant attitude make a difference in our conduct, but it should also make a difference in our witness. . . .

Since this is the day of salvation, we must be diligent to do all we can to win the lost. . . . We must understand what the Bible teaches about God's program for this present age, and we must be motivated by a love for the lost (2 Cor. 5:14) and a desire to be pleasing to Him when He returns.

Warren Wiersbe

ACTION POINT

*W*hat *were Jesus' last words to his apostles? After he went up into heaven, what did God's messengers promise them? Praise God that his people still take his message into every part of the world!*

285

FRIDAY

God's Spirit Fills His People

Acts 2:1–28

The Coming of the Holy Spirit

2 And when the day of Pentecost was fully come, they were all with one accord in one place.

² And suddenly there came a sound from heaven as of a rushing mighty wind, and it filled all the house where they were sitting.

³ And there appeared unto them cloven tongues like as of fire, and it sat upon each of them.

⁴ And they were all filled with the Holy Ghost, and began to speak with other tongues, as the Spirit gave them utterance.

⁵ And there were dwelling at Jerusalem Jews, devout men, out of every nation under heaven.

⁶ Now when this was noised abroad, the multitude came together, and were confounded, because that every man heard them speak in his own language.

⁷ And they were all amazed and marveled, saying one to another, Behold, are not all these which speak Galileans?

⁸ And how hear we every man in our own tongue, wherein we were born?

⁹ Parthians, and Medes, and Elamites, and the dwellers in Mesopotamia, and in Judea, and Cappadocia, in Pontus, and Asia,

¹⁰ Phrygia, and Pamphylia, in Egypt, and in the parts of Libya about Cyrene, and strangers of Rome, Jews and proselytes,

¹¹ Cretes and Arabians, we do hear them speak in our tongues the wonderful works of God.

¹² And they were all amazed, and were in doubt, saying one to another, What meaneth this?

¹³ Others mocking said, These men are full of new wine.

Peter Speaks to the People

*B*ut Peter, standing up with the eleven, lifted up his voice, and said unto them, Ye men of Judea, and all *ye* that dwell at Jerusalem, be this known unto you, and hearken to my words:

¹⁵ for these are not drunken, as ye suppose, seeing it is *but* the third hour of the day.

¹⁶ But this is that which was spoken by the prophet Joel;

¹⁷ And it shall come to pass in the last days, saith God, I will pour out of my Spirit upon all flesh: and your sons and your daughters shall prophesy, and your young men shall see visions, and your old men shall dream dreams:

¹⁸ and on my servants and on my handmaidens I will pour out in those days of my Spirit; and they shall prophesy:

¹⁹ And I will show wonders in heaven above, and signs in the earth beneath; blood, and fire, and vapor of smoke:

²⁰ the sun shall be turned into darkness, and the moon into blood, before that great and notable day of the Lord come:

²¹ and it shall come to pass, *that* whosoever shall call on the name of the Lord shall be saved.

²² Ye men of Israel, hear these words; Jesus of Nazareth, a man approved of God among you by miracles and

wonders and signs, which God did by him in the midst of you, as ye yourselves also know:

²³ him, being delivered by the determinate counsel and foreknowledge of God, ye have taken, and by wicked hands have crucified and slain:

²⁴ whom God hath raised up, having loosed the pains of death: because it was not possible that he should be holden of it.

²⁵ For David speaketh concerning him, I foresaw the Lord always before my face; for he is on my right hand, that I should not be moved:

²⁶ therefore did my heart rejoice, and my tongue was glad; moreover also my flesh shall rest in hope:

²⁷ because thou wilt not leave my soul in hell, neither wilt thou suffer thine Holy One to see corruption.

²⁸ Thou hast made known to me the ways of life; thou shalt make me full of joy with thy countenance.

OLD TESTAMENT READING

*Y*et now hear, O Jacob my servant; and Israel, whom I have chosen:

² thus saith the LORD that made thee, and formed thee from the womb, *which* will help thee; Fear not, O Jacob, my servant; and thou, Jeshurun, whom I have chosen.

³ For I will pour water upon him that is thirsty, and floods upon the dry ground: I will pour my Spirit upon thy seed, and my blessing upon thine offspring.

Isaiah 44:1–3

INSIGHTS

*O*ne day while I was sailing, the wind went down and the sea became calm and flat. There was nothing to do but sit in irons and wait for the wind. "Irons" is a sailing term for a windless time of drifting. While waiting for the wind, I drifted past another sailboat that was floating aimlessly. The people on board the craft waved and made a flat of the hand gesture of complaint about the lack of wind. One man stood by the sails and blew on them.

I thought about that for a long time afterward. How like many Christians and far too many churches. Human breath blowing on the sails—no wonder we make so little progress!

The Spirit of God in Hebrew is ruach, meaning "breath" and "wind." At Pentecost the power of the Holy Spirit was like a mighty wind. The Spirit filled the disciples and got them moving again. What we need is a mighty wind—a fresh, bracing wind of a new Pentecost. . . .

. . . So stop blowing your own breath into the sails of your life or your church. Ask for a fresh wind to fill the sails. Without the Holy Spirit, we'll drift in irons and be lost at sea. . . .

Lloyd Ogilvie

ACTION POINT

*W*hat did God's Spirit enable the believers to do? For what purpose? Has your life been renewed by God's Spirit? Pray that God's Spirit will fill you, direct you, and enable you to complete God's work in your life!

WEEKEND

*Change Your Hearts,
and God Will Forgive*

Acts 2:29—3:10

Men *and* brethren, let me freely speak unto you of the patriarch David, that he is both dead and buried, and his sepulchre is with us unto this day.

30 Therefore being a prophet, and knowing that God had sworn with an oath to him, that of the fruit of his loins, according to the flesh, he would raise up Christ to sit on his throne;

31 he seeing this before spake of the resurrection of Christ, that his soul was not left in hell, neither his flesh did see corruption.

32 This Jesus hath God raised up, whereof we all are witnesses.

33 Therefore being by the right hand of God exalted, and having received of the Father the promise of the Holy Ghost, he hath shed forth this, which ye now see and hear.

34 For David is not ascended into the heavens: but he saith himself, The LORD said unto my Lord, Sit thou on my right hand,

35 until I make thy foes thy footstool.

36 Therefore let all the house of Israel know assuredly, that God hath made that same Jesus, whom ye have crucified, both Lord and Christ.

37 Now when they heard *this*, they were pricked in their heart, and said unto Peter and to the rest of the apostles, Men *and* brethren, what shall we do?

38 Then Peter said unto them, Repent, and be baptized every one of you in the name of Jesus Christ for the remission of sins, and ye shall receive the gift of the Holy Ghost.

39 For the promise is unto you, and to your children, and to all that are afar off, *even* as many as the Lord our God shall call.

40 And with many other words did he testify and exhort, saying, Save yourselves from this untoward generation.

41 Then they that gladly received his word were baptized: and the same day there were added *unto them* about three thousand souls.

42 And they continued steadfastly in the apostles' doctrine and fellowship, and in breaking of bread, and in prayers.

The Believers Share

And fear came upon every soul: and many wonders and signs were done by the apostles.

44 And all that believed were together, and had all things common;

45 and sold their possessions and goods, and parted them to all *men*, as every man had need.

46 And they, continuing daily with one accord in the temple, and breaking bread from house to house, did eat their meat with gladness and singleness of heart,

47 praising God, and having favor with all the people. And the Lord added to the church daily such as should be saved.

Peter Heals a Lame Man

3 Now Peter and John went up together into the temple at the hour of prayer, *being* the ninth *hour*.

2 And a certain man lame from his mother's womb was carried, whom

they laid daily at the gate of the temple which is called Beautiful, to ask alms of them that entered into the temple;

³ who, seeing Peter and John about to go into the temple asked an alms.

⁴ And Peter, fastening his eyes upon him with John, said, Look on us.

⁵ And he gave heed unto them, expecting to receive something of them.

⁶ Then Peter said, Silver and gold have I none; but such as I have give I thee: In the name of Jesus Christ of Nazareth rise up and walk.

⁷ And he took him by the right hand, and lifted *him* up: and immediately his feet and ankle bones received strength.

⁸ And he leaping up stood, and walked, and entered with them into the temple, walking, and leaping, and praising God.

⁹ And all the people saw him walking and praising God:

¹⁰ and they knew that it was he which sat for alms at the Beautiful gate of the temple: and they were filled with wonder and amazement at that which had happened unto him.

OLD TESTAMENT READING

*C*ome, and let us return unto the LORD: for he hath torn, and he will heal us; he hath smitten, and he will bind us up.

² After two days will he revive us: in the third day he will raise us up, and we shall live in his sight.

³ Then shall we know, *if* we follow on to know the LORD: his going forth is prepared as the morning; and he shall come unto us as the rain, as the latter *and* former rain unto the earth.

Hosea 6:1–3

INSIGHTS

*A*re you running on empty because of sin in your life that you think is well hidden? God sees and knows all about it. He wants you to face it, name it, confess it, turn from it, and, where you can, put things right. Self-flagellation will not make any lasting difference. Listen to David: "You do not delight in sacrifice, or I would bring it; you do not take pleasure in burnt offerings. The sacrifices of God are a broken spirit; a broken and contrite heart, O God, you will not despise" (Ps. 51:16–17).

God looks for brokenness of spirit—for a contrite, humble heart that, quickened by the Holy Spirit, teaches us to regard our sin as He does. We learn to pray, in the words of the old hymn:

Throw light into the darkened cells,
Where passion reigns within;
Quicken my conscience till it feels
The loathsomeness of sin.

And when we have seen our sin for what it is and rejected it, God will help us to have the right spirit in our hearts. Then we will be able to add:

Thus prostrate I shall learn of Thee,
What now I feebly prove,
That God alone in Christ can be
Unutterable love.

Jill Briscoe

ACTION POINT

*H*ow did Peter's audience respond when they learned the truth about Christ? Do your sins make you sick at heart?

MONDAY

Jesus Is the Only Way to Salvation

Acts 3:11—4:12

Peter Speaks to the People

*A*nd as the lame man which was healed held Peter and John, all the people ran together unto them in the porch that is called Solomon's, greatly wondering.

¹² And when Peter saw *it*, he answered unto the people, Ye men of Israel, why marvel ye at this? or why look ye so earnestly on us, as though by our own power or holiness we had made this man to walk?

¹³ The God of Abraham, and of Isaac, and of Jacob, the God of our fathers, hath glorified his Son Jesus; whom ye delivered up, and denied him in the presence of Pilate, when he was determined to let *him* go.

¹⁴ But ye denied the Holy One and the Just, and desired a murderer to be granted unto you;

¹⁵ and killed the Prince of life, whom God hath raised from the dead; whereof we are witnesses.

¹⁶ And his name, through faith in his name, hath made this man strong, whom ye see and know: yea, the faith which is by him hath given him this perfect soundness in the presence of you all.

¹⁷ And now, brethren, I wot that through ignorance ye did *it*, as *did* also your rulers.

¹⁸ But those things, which God before had showed by the mouth of all his prophets, that Christ should suffer, he hath so fulfilled.

¹⁹ Repent ye therefore, and be converted, that your sins may be blotted out, when the times of refreshing shall come from the presence of the Lord;

²⁰ and he shall send Jesus Christ, which before was preached unto you:

²¹ whom the heaven must receive until the times of restitution of all things, which God hath spoken by the mouth of all his holy prophets since the world began.

²² For Moses truly said unto the fathers, A Prophet shall the Lord your God raise up unto you of your brethren, like unto me; him shall ye hear in all things whatsoever he shall say unto you.

²³ And it shall come to pass, *that* every soul, which will not hear that Prophet, shall be destroyed from among the people.

²⁴ Yea, and all the prophets from Samuel and those that follow after, as many as have spoken, have likewise foretold of these days.

²⁵ Ye are the children of the prophets, and of the covenant which God made with our fathers, saying unto Abraham, And in thy seed shall all the kindreds of the earth be blessed.

²⁶ Unto you first God, having raised up his Son Jesus, sent him to bless you, in turning away every one of you from his iniquities.

Peter and John at the Council

4 And as they spake unto the people, the priests, and the captain of the temple, and the Sadducees, came upon them,

² being grieved that they taught the people, and preached through Jesus the resurrection from the dead.

³ And they laid hands on them, and put *them* in hold unto the next day: for it was now eventide.

⁴ Howbeit many of them which heard the word believed; and the number of the men was about five thousand.

⁵ And it came to pass on the morrow, that their rulers, and elders, and scribes,

⁶ and Annas the high priest, and Caiaphas, and John, and Alexander, and as many as were of the kindred of the high priest, were gathered together at Jerusalem.

⁷ And when they had set them in the midst, they asked, By what power, or by what name, have ye done this?

⁸ Then Peter, filled with the Holy Ghost, said unto them, Ye rulers of the people, and elders of Israel,

⁹ if we this day be examined of the good deed done to the impotent man, by what means he is made whole;

¹⁰ be it known unto you all, and to all the people of Israel, that by the name of Jesus Christ of Nazareth, whom ye crucified, whom God raised from the dead, *even* by him doth this man stand here before you whole.

¹¹ This is the stone which was set at nought of you builders, which is become the head of the corner.

¹² Neither is there salvation in any other: for there is none other name under heaven given among men, whereby we must be saved.

OLD TESTAMENT READING

*T*herefore thus saith the Lord GOD, Behold, I lay in Zion for a foundation a stone, a tried stone, a precious corner *stone*, a sure foundation: he that believeth shall not make haste.

¹⁷ Judgment also will I lay to the line,

and righteousness to the plummet: and the hail shall sweep away the refuge of lies, and the waters shall overflow the hiding place.

Isaiah 28:16–17

INSIGHTS

I am the way and the truth and the life. No one comes to the Father except through me" (John 14:6). . . .

. . . Jesus did not merely show the way to God; He said, "I am the way." He did not claim merely to know the truth; He said, "I am the truth." He did not merely point to the abundant life; He said, "I am the life." Therefore, within Christianity if there is no Christ, there is no way to God, no truth about God, and no vitality.

How could Jesus make such claims? If He was only a man, His claims are preposterous. But if He is who He said He is, and if He did what He said He would do, His claims make sense. Jesus claimed to be God and to have come to earth to die for our own sin. We deserve to die for our own sin, but Jesus died in our place. He who was sinless accepted the guilt of our sin and died for us. No one else could do it, but He could and did. Thus, He literally became the door by which sinful men and women can approach the Father.

James Boice

APPLICATION

*W*ho is the rock on whom God's salvation is built? What is the way of salvation? Why does no other way of salvation exist? Have you followed God's way of salvation?

TUESDAY

Christ's Witnesses Have Nothing to Fear

Acts 4:13–37

*N*ow when they saw the boldness of Peter and John, and perceived that they were unlearned and ignorant men, they marveled; and they took knowledge of them, that they had been with Jesus.

¹⁴ And beholding the man which was healed standing with them, they could say nothing against it.

¹⁵ But when they had commanded them to go aside out of the council, they conferred among themselves,

¹⁶ saying, What shall we do to these men? for that indeed a notable miracle hath been done by them *is* manifest to all them that dwell in Jerusalem; and we cannot deny *it*.

¹⁷ But that it spread no further among the people, let us straitly threaten them, that they speak henceforth to no man in this name.

¹⁸ And they called them, and commanded them not to speak at all nor teach in the name of Jesus.

¹⁹ But Peter and John answered and said unto them, Whether it be right in the sight of God to hearken unto you more than unto God, judge ye.

²⁰ For we cannot but speak the things which we have seen and heard.

²¹ So when they had further threatened them, they let them go, finding nothing how they might punish them, because of the people: for all *men* glorified God for that which was done.

²² For the man was above forty years old, on whom this miracle of healing was showed.

The Believers Pray

*A*nd being let go, they went to their own company, and reported all that the chief priests and elders had said unto them.

²⁴ And when they heard that, they lifted up their voice to God with one accord, and said, Lord, thou *art* God, which hast made heaven, and earth, and the sea, and all that in them is;

²⁵ who by the mouth of thy servant David hast said, Why did the heathen rage, and the people imagine vain things?

²⁶ The kings of the earth stood up, and the rulers were gathered together against the Lord, and against his Christ.

²⁷ For of a truth against thy holy child Jesus, whom thou hast anointed, both Herod, and Pontius Pilate, with the Gentiles, and the people of Israel, were gathered together,

²⁸ for to do whatsoever thy hand and thy counsel determined before to be done.

²⁹ And now, Lord, behold their threatenings: and grant unto thy servants, that with all boldness they may speak thy word,

³⁰ by stretching forth thine hand to heal; and that signs and wonders may be done by the name of thy holy child Jesus.

³¹ And when they had prayed, the place was shaken where they were assembled together; and they were all filled with the Holy Ghost, and they spake the word of God with boldness.

The Believers Share

*A*nd the multitude of them that believed were of one heart and of one soul: neither said any *of them* that ought of the things which he possessed was his own; but they had all things common.

³³ And with great power gave the apostles witness of the resurrection of the Lord Jesus: and great grace was upon them all.

³⁴ Neither was there any among them that lacked: for as many as were possessors of lands or houses sold them, and brought the prices of the things that were sold,

³⁵ and laid *them* down at the apostles' feet: and distribution was made unto every man according as he had need.

³⁶ And Joses, who by the apostles was surnamed Barnabas, (which is, being interpreted, The son of consolation,) a Levite, *and* of the country of Cyprus,

³⁷ having land, sold *it*, and brought the money, and laid *it* at the apostles' feet.

OLD TESTAMENT READING

*S*ince thou wast precious in my sight, thou hast been honorable, and I have loved thee: therefore will I give men for thee, and people for thy life.

⁵ Fear not; for I *am* with thee: I will bring thy seed from the east, and gather thee from the west:

⁶ I will say to the north, Give up; and to the south, Keep not back: bring my sons from far, and my daughters from the ends of the earth;

⁷ *even* every one that is called by my name: for I have created him for my glory, I have formed him; yea, I have made him.

Isaiah 43:4-7

INSIGHTS

*I*f we are Christians, we have all been delivered to be deliverers! The Word of God commands us to tell people they are in bondage to sin and that God would love to set them free from that taskmaster. . . .

Sometimes this is disappointing work. The people we go to may not want us to deliver them. Moses knew that particular scenario (Exod. 2:13–14). Or it can even be dangerous work. We may not be in danger of losing our life . . . but we may be in danger of losing our popularity, our friends, or in some extreme cases, even our job. Yes, a delivering work can be a disappointing work and even a dangerous work. But it is above all, a directed work, and that's what helps. To have a sense of God's direction when we are disappointed or in danger is a huge boost to our morale. The inner thrill that God has invited us to cooperate with Him takes the worry out of the work. People work is His work, and He will show us what to do, and even how to do it.

Jill Briscoe

PAUSE FOR REFLECTION

*N*otice how the recitation of one's spiritual heritage served as encouragement to be God's fearless witness. How does your spiritual heritage encourage you to bravely proclaim God's truth?

WEDNESDAY
Give to God What Is His

Acts 5:1–26

Ananias and Sapphira Die

5 But a certain man named Ananias, with Sapphira his wife, sold a possession,

2 and kept back *part* of the price, his wife also being privy *to it*, and brought a certain part, and laid *it* at the apostles' feet.

3 But Peter said, Ananias, why hath Satan filled thine heart to lie to the Holy Ghost, and to keep back *part* of the price of the land?

4 While it remained, was it not thine own? and after it was sold, was it not in thine own power? why hast thou conceived this thing in thine heart? thou hast not lied unto men, but unto God.

5 And Ananias hearing these words fell down, and gave up the ghost: and great fear came on all them that heard these things.

6 And the young men arose, wound him up, and carried *him* out, and buried *him*.

7 And it was about the space of three hours after, when his wife, not knowing what was done, came in.

8 And Peter answered unto her, Tell me whether ye sold the land for so much? And she said, Yea, for so much.

9 Then Peter said unto her, How is it that ye have agreed together to tempt the Spirit of the Lord? behold, the feet of them which have buried thy husband *are* at the door, and shall carry thee out.

10 Then fell she down straightway at his feet, and yielded up the ghost: and the young men came in, and found her dead, and, carrying *her* forth, buried *her* by her husband.

11 And great fear came upon all the church, and upon as many as heard these things.

The Apostles Heal Many

And by the hands of the apostles were many signs and wonders wrought among the people; (and they were all with one accord in Solomon's porch.

13 And of the rest durst no man join himself to them: but the people magnified them.

14 And believers were the more added to the Lord, multitudes both of men and women;)

15 insomuch that they brought forth the sick into the streets, and laid *them* on beds and couches, that at the least the shadow of Peter passing by might overshadow some of them.

16 There came also a multitude *out* of the cities round about unto Jerusalem, bringing sick folks, and them which were vexed with unclean spirits: and they were healed every one.

Leaders Try to Stop the Apostles

Then the high priest rose up, and all they that were with him, (which is the sect of the Sadducees,) and were filled with indignation,

18 and laid their hands on the apostles, and put them in the common prison.

19 But the angel of the Lord by night opened the prison doors, and brought them forth, and said,

20 Go, stand and speak in the temple to the people all the words of this life.

²¹ And when they heard *that*, they entered into the temple early in the morning, and taught. But the high priest came, and they that were with him, and called the council together, and all the senate of the children of Israel, and sent to the prison to have them brought.

²² But when the officers came, and found them not in the prison, they returned, and told,

²³ saying, The prison truly found we shut with all safety, and the keepers standing without before the doors: but when we had opened, we found no man within.

²⁴ Now when the high priest and the captain of the temple and the chief priests heard these things, they doubted of them whereunto this would grow.

²⁵ Then came one and told them, saying, Behold, the men whom ye put in prison are standing in the temple, and teaching the people.

²⁶ Then went the captain with the officers, and brought them without violence: for they feared the people, lest they should have been stoned.

OLD TESTAMENT READING

*A*nd Achan answered Joshua, and said, Indeed I have sinned against the LORD God of Israel, and thus and thus have I done:

²¹ When I saw among the spoils a goodly Babylonish garment, and two hundred shekels of silver, and a wedge of gold of fifty shekels weight, then I coveted them, and took them; and, behold, they *are* hid in the earth in the midst of my tent, and the silver under it.

²⁵ And Joshua said, Why hast thou troubled us? the LORD shall trouble thee this day. And all Israel stoned him with stones, and burned them with fire, after they had stoned them with stones.

Joshua 7:20-21, 25

INSIGHTS

A farmer was explaining to a minister, "Well, if I'd get enough, I'd give half to the Lord."

"If you had two thousand acres of oil wells," asked the preacher, "would you give revenues from one thousand acres to the Lord?"

"Why, sure," the farmer gloated. "Anyone could live off a thousand acres of oil."

"If you had two hogs, would you give one to the Lord?" queried the minister.

At that, the farmer complained, "That's not fair. You know I have two pigs!"

We don't suddenly, someday, have an abundance of time and money to give. We begin with the little pieces. We are in training now, learning bit by bit to manage money, power, time, relationships and temptation. Then maybe someday we will find ourselves competent to manage life on a grander scale.

Lynn Anderson

PAUSE FOR REFLECTION

What was Ananias and Sapphira's sin against God? Achan's sin? Are you waiting to acquire enough to satisfy yourself before you give to God? What do you have now that you give to him?

THURSDAY

God's Will
Can't Be Thwarted

Acts 5:27—6:7

And when they had brought them, they set *them* before the council: and the high priest asked them,

28 saying, Did not we straitly command you that ye should not teach in this name? and, behold, ye have filled Jerusalem with your doctrine, and intend to bring this man's blood upon us.

29 Then Peter and the *other* apostles answered and said, We ought to obey God rather than men.

30 The God of our fathers raised up Jesus, whom ye slew and hanged on a tree.

31 Him hath God exalted with his right hand *to be* a Prince and a Saviour, for to give repentance to Israel, and forgiveness of sins.

32 And we are his witnesses of these things; and *so is* also the Holy Ghost, whom God hath given to them that obey him.

33 When they heard *that*, they were cut *to the heart*, and took counsel to slay them.

34 Then stood there up one in the council, a Pharisee, named Gamaliel, a doctor of the law, had in reputation among all the people, and commanded to put the apostles forth a little space;

35 and said unto them, Ye men of Israel, take heed to yourselves what ye intend to do as touching these men.

36 For before these days rose up Theudas, boasting himself to be somebody; to whom a number of men, about four hundred, joined themselves: who was slain; and all, as many as obeyed him, were scattered, and brought to nought.

37 After this man rose up Judas of Galilee in the days of the taxing, and drew away much people after him: he also perished; and all, *even* as many as obeyed him, were dispersed.

38 And now I say unto you, Refrain from these men, and let them alone: for if this counsel or this work be of men, it will come to nought:

39 but if it be of God, ye cannot overthrow it; lest haply ye be found even to fight against God.

40 And to him they agreed: and when they had called the apostles, and beaten *them*, they commanded that they should not speak in the name of Jesus, and let them go.

41 And they departed from the presence of the council, rejoicing that they were counted worthy to suffer shame for his name.

42 And daily in the temple, and in every house, they ceased not to teach and preach Jesus Christ.

Seven Servants Are Chosen

6 And in those days, when the number of the disciples was multiplied, there arose a murmuring of the Grecians against the Hebrews, because their widows were neglected in the daily ministration.

2 Then the twelve called the multitude of the disciples *unto them*, and said, It is not reason that we should leave the word of God, and serve tables.

3 Wherefore, brethren, look ye out among you seven men of honest report, full of the Holy Ghost and wisdom, whom we may appoint over this business.

⁴ But we will give ourselves continually to prayer, and to the ministry of the word.

⁵ And the saying pleased the whole multitude: and they chose Stephen, a man full of faith and of the Holy Ghost, and Philip, and Prochorus, and Nicanor, and Timon, and Parmenas, and Nicolas a proselyte of Antioch;

⁶ whom they set before the apostles: and when they had prayed, they laid *their* hands on them.

⁷ And the word of God increased; and the number of the disciples multiplied in Jerusalem greatly; and a great company of the priests were obedient to the faith.

OLD TESTAMENT READING

*R*emember this, and show yourselves men: bring *it* again to mind, O ye transgressors.

⁹ Remember the former things of old: for I *am* God, and *there is* none else; *I am* God, and *there is* none like me,

¹⁰ declaring the end from the beginning, and from ancient times *the things* that are not *yet* done, saying, My counsel shall stand, and I will do all my pleasure:

¹¹ calling a ravenous bird from the east, the man that executeth my counsel from a far country: yea, I have spoken *it*, I will also bring it to pass; I have purposed *it*, I will also do it.

Isaiah 46:8-11

INSIGHTS

*T*he Lord's thoughts are all working toward "an expected end." . . . God is working with a motive. All things are working together for one object: the good of those who love God. We see only the beginning; God sees the end from the beginning. He knows every letter of the Book of Providence; He sees not only what He is doing, but what will come of what He is doing.

As to our present pain and grief, God sees not these things exclusively, but He sees the future joy and usefulness which will come of them. He regards not only the tearing up of the soil with the plow, but the clothing of that soil with the golden harvest. He sees the after consequences of affliction, and He accounts those painful incidents to be blessed which lead up to so much of happiness. Let us comfort ourselves with this. . . .

You have never seen the Great Artist's masterpiece; you have seen the rough marble, you have marked the chippings that fall on the ground; you have felt the edge of His chisel, you know the weight of His hammer, and you are full of the memory of these things; but oh, could you see that glorious image as it will be when He has put the finishing stroke to it, you would then understand the chisel, and the hammer, and the Worker better than you now do!

Charles Spurgeon

APPLICATION

*D*id Gamaliel speak to the Jews with true wisdom? What do you learn about God's sovereign will in these readings? Pray to remember that God is working toward "an expected end" and to understand that what happens in your life is part of his work.

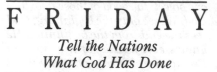

FRIDAY
Tell the Nations
What God Has Done

Acts 6:8—7:16

Stephen Is Accused

*A*nd Stephen, full of faith and power, did great wonders and miracles among the people.

⁹ Then there arose certain of the synagogue, which is called *the synagogue* of the Libertines, and Cyrenians, and Alexandrians, and of them of Cilicia and of Asia, disputing with Stephen.

¹⁰ And they were not able to resist the wisdom and the spirit by which he spake.

¹¹ Then they suborned men, which said, We have heard him speak blasphemous words against Moses, and *against* God.

¹² And they stirred up the people, and the elders, and the scribes, and came upon *him*, and caught him, and brought *him* to the council,

¹³ and set up false witnesses, which said, This man ceaseth not to speak blasphemous words against this holy place, and the law:

¹⁴ for we have heard him say, that this Jesus of Nazareth shall destroy this place, and shall change the customs which Moses delivered us.

¹⁵ And all that sat in the council, looking steadfastly on him, saw his face as it had been the face of an angel.

Stephen's Speech

7 Then said the high priest, Are these things so?

² And he said, Men, brethren, and fathers, hearken; The God of glory appeared unto our father Abraham, when he was in Mesopotamia, before he dwelt in Haran,

³ and said unto him, Get thee out of thy country, and from thy kindred, and come into the land which I shall show thee.

⁴ Then came he out of the land of the Chaldeans, and dwelt in Haran: and from thence, when his father was dead, he removed him into this land, wherein ye now dwell.

⁵ And he gave him none inheritance in it, no, not *so much as* to set his foot on: yet he promised that he would give it to him for a possession, and to his seed after him, when *as yet* he had no child.

⁶ And God spake on this wise, That his seed should sojourn in a strange land; and that they should bring them into bondage, and entreat *them* evil four hundred years.

⁷ And the nation to whom they shall be in bondage will I judge, said God: and after that shall they come forth, and serve me in this place.

⁸ And he gave him the covenant of circumcision: and so *Abraham* begat Isaac, and circumcised him the eighth day; and Isaac *begat* Jacob; and Jacob *begat* the twelve patriarchs.

⁹ And the patriarchs, moved with envy, sold Joseph into Egypt: but God was with him,

¹⁰ and delivered him out of all his afflictions, and gave him favor and wisdom in the sight of Pharaoh king of Egypt; and he made him governor over Egypt and all his house.

¹¹ Now there came a dearth over all the land of Egypt and Canaan, and great affliction: and our fathers found no sustenance.

¹²But when Jacob heard that there was corn in Egypt, he sent out our fathers first.

¹³And at the second *time* Joseph was made known to his brethren; and Joseph's kindred was made known unto Pharaoh.

¹⁴Then sent Joseph, and called his father Jacob to *him*, and all his kindred, threescore and fifteen souls.

¹⁵So Jacob went down into Egypt, and died, he, and our fathers,

¹⁶and were carried over into Shechem, and laid in the sepulchre that Abraham bought for a sum of money of the sons of Hamor *the father* of Shechem.

OLD TESTAMENT READING

O give thanks unto the LORD; call upon his name: make known his deeds among the people.

²Sing unto him, sing psalms unto him: talk ye of all his wondrous works.

³Glory ye in his holy name: let the heart of them rejoice that seek the LORD.

⁴Seek the LORD, and his strength: seek his face evermore.

Psalm 105:1-4

INSIGHTS

What appears to be foolish in the eyes of society is often that which is most effective in the work of the kingdom. The ignorant, the uneducated, the despised of the world are sometimes God's choicest servants. So it was with Sophie "the scrubwoman" Lichtenfels, "whose sermons rose not from an exalted podium or pulpit but from callused hands and knees and with the rhythm of a lowly washtub and scrub brush." . . .

. . . Her testimony was simple.

"God called me to scrub and preach. I was born a preacher, but since I was poor I had to work. My work is good and I can be trusted, so they want me. But if they have me, they must hear me preach. No preach, no work. I scrub as unto the Lord and I preach to all in the house. When I am out of work I tell my father. He is the best employment office. You don't have to pay or wait. . . .

"Sometimes we pray so foolish. For 12 years I prayed the Lord make me a foreign missionary. One day I prayed like that and my Father said, 'Stop Sophie. Where were you born?' 'In Germany,' I replied. 'And where are you now?' 'In America.' 'Well, aren't you already a foreign missionary?' Then He said to me, 'Who lives on the floor above you?' 'A family of Swedes.' 'And above them?' 'Some Swiss.' . . .

"'Yes, and in back are Italians, and a block away Chinese. You have never spoken to them about My Son. Do you think I'll send you a thousand miles away when you've got foreigners, even heathen all around you?'"

Ruth Tucker

PAUSE FOR REFLECTION

Stephen was a powerful witness for God among Jews from many nations. What message did both Stephen and the psalmist have to share? What message has God given you to share to the "nations" around you?

WEEKEND

*God Is Faithful
to His People*

Acts 7:17–42a

*B*ut when the time of the promise drew nigh, which God had sworn to Abraham, the people grew and multiplied in Egypt,

¹⁸ till another king arose, which knew not Joseph.

¹⁹ The same dealt subtiley with our kindred, and evil entreated our fathers, so that they cast out their young children, to the end they might not live.

²⁰ In which time Moses was born, and was exceeding fair, and nourished up in his father's house three months:

²¹ and when he was cast out, Pharaoh's daughter took him up, and nourished him for her own son.

²² And Moses was learned in all the wisdom of the Egyptians, and was mighty in words and in deeds.

²³ And when he was full forty years old, it came into his heart to visit his brethren the children of Israel.

²⁴ And seeing one *of them* suffer wrong, he defended *him*, and avenged him that was oppressed, and smote the Egyptian:

²⁵ for he supposed his brethren would have understood how that God by his hand would deliver them; but they understood not.

²⁶ And the next day he showed himself unto them as they strove, and would have set them at one again, saying, Sirs, ye are brethren; why do ye wrong one to another?

²⁷ But he that did his neighbor wrong thrust him away, saying, Who made thee a ruler and a judge over us?

²⁸ Wilt thou kill me, as thou didst the Egyptian yesterday?

²⁹ Then fled Moses at this saying, and was a stranger in the land of Midian, where he begat two sons.

³⁰ And when forty years were expired, there appeared to him in the wilderness of mount Sinai an angel of the Lord in a flame of fire in a bush.

³¹ When Moses saw *it*, he wondered at the sight: and as he drew near to behold *it*, the voice of the Lord came unto him,

³² *saying,* I *am* the God of thy fathers, the God of Abraham and the God of Isaac, and the God of Jacob. Then Moses trembled, and durst not behold.

³³ Then said the Lord to him, Put off thy shoes from thy feet: for the place where thou standest is holy ground.

³⁴ I have seen, I have seen the affliction of my people which is in Egypt, and I have heard their groaning, and am come down to deliver them. And now come, I will send thee into Egypt.

³⁵ This Moses whom they refused, saying, Who made thee a ruler and a judge? the same did God send *to be* a ruler and a deliverer by the hand of the angel which appeared to him in the bush.

³⁶ He brought them out, after that he had showed wonders and signs in the land of Egypt, and in the Red sea, and in the wilderness forty years.

³⁷ This is that Moses, which said unto the children of Israel, A Prophet shall the Lord your God raise up unto you of your brethren, like unto me; him shall ye hear.

³⁸ This is he, that was in the church in the wilderness with the angel which

spake to him in the mount Sinai, and *with* our fathers: who received the lively oracles to give unto us:

³⁹ to whom our fathers would not obey, but thrust *him* from them, and in their hearts turned back again into Egypt,

⁴⁰ saying unto Aaron, Make us gods to go before us: for *as for* this Moses, which brought us out of the land of Egypt, we wot not what is become of him.

⁴¹ And they made a calf in those days, and offered sacrifice unto the idol, and rejoiced in the works of their own hands.

⁴² Then God turned, and gave them up to worship the host of heaven.

OLD TESTAMENT READING

*H*e brought them forth also with silver and gold: and *there was* not one feeble *person* among their tribes.

³⁸ Egypt was glad when they departed: for the fear of them fell upon them.

³⁹ He spread a cloud for a covering; and fire to give light in the night.

⁴⁰ *The people* asked, and he brought quails, and satisfied them with the bread of heaven.

⁴¹ He opened the rock, and the waters gushed out; they ran in the dry places *like* a river.

⁴² For he remembered his holy promise, *and* Abraham his servant.

⁴³ And he brought forth his people with joy, *and* his chosen with gladness.

Psalm 105:37–43

INSIGHTS

*G*reat is Thy faithfulness, O God my Father,

There is no shadow of turning with Thee;
Thou changest not, Thy compassions they fail not;
As Thou hast been Thou forever wilt be.

Summer and winter, and springtime and harvest,
Sun, moon and stars in their courses above
Join with all nature in manifold witness
To Thy great faithfulness, mercy and love.

Pardon for sin and a peace that endureth,
Thy own dear presence to cheer and to guide;
Strength for today and bright hope for tomorrow,
Blessings all mine, with ten thousand beside!

Great is Thy faithfulness! Great is Thy faithfulness!
Morning by morning new mercies I see;
All I have needed Thy hand hath provided.
Great is Thy faithfulness, Lord, unto me!

Thomas O. Chisholm

ACTION POINT

*F*rom what trials did God, in his faithfulness, deliver the people of Israel? List as many as you can. When you doubt his faithfulness in your life, reread your list and believe that God is and always will be faithful!

MONDAY

Some Refuse to Hear
God's Messengers

Acts 7:42b—8:1

As it is written in the book of the prophets, O ye house of Israel, have ye offered to me slain beasts and sacrifices *by the space* of forty years in the wilderness?

43 Yea, ye took up the tabernacle of Moloch, and the star of your god Remphan, figures which ye made to worship them: and I will carry you away beyond Babylon.

44 Our fathers had the tabernacle of witness in the wilderness, as he had appointed, speaking unto Moses, that he should make it according to the fashion that he had seen.

45 Which also our fathers that came after brought in with Joshua into the possession of the Gentiles, whom God drave out before the face of our fathers, unto the days of David;

46 who found favor before God, and desired to find a tabernacle for the God of Jacob.

47 But Solomon built him a house.

48 Howbeit the Most High dwelleth not in temples made with hands; as saith the prophet,

49 Heaven *is* my throne, and earth *is* my footstool: what house will ye build me? saith the Lord: or what *is* the place of my rest?

50 Hath not my hand made all these things?

51 Ye stiffnecked and uncircumcised in heart and ears, ye do always resist the Holy Ghost: as your fathers *did*, so *do* ye.

52 Which of the prophets have not your fathers persecuted? and they have slain them which shewed before of the coming of the Just One; of whom ye have been now the betrayers and murderers:

53 who have received the law by the disposition of angels, and have not kept *it*.

Stephen Is Killed

When they heard these things, they were cut to the heart, and they gnashed on him with *their* teeth.

55 But he, being full of the Holy Ghost, looked up steadfastly into heaven, and saw the glory of God, and Jesus standing on the right hand of God,

56 and said, Behold, I see the heavens opened, and the Son of man standing on the right hand of God.

57 Then they cried out with a loud voice, and stopped their ears, and ran upon him with one accord,

58 and cast *him* out of the city, and stoned *him*: and the witnesses laid down their clothes at a young man's feet, whose name was Saul.

59 And they stoned Stephen, calling upon *God*, and saying, Lord Jesus, receive my spirit.

60 And he kneeled down, and cried with a loud voice, Lord, lay not this sin to their charge. And when he had said this, he fell asleep.

The Believers Are Persecuted

8 And Saul was consenting unto his death. And at that time there was a great persecution against the church which was at Jerusalem; and they were all scattered abroad throughout the regions of Judea and Samaria, except the apostles.

*A*nd they left the house of the LORD God of their fathers, and served groves and idols: and wrath came upon Judah and Jerusalem for this their trespass.

¹⁹ Yet he sent prophets to them, to bring them again unto the LORD; and they testified against them: but they would not give ear.

²⁰ And the Spirit of God came upon Zechariah the son of Jehoiada the priest, which stood above the people, and said unto them, Thus saith God, Why transgress ye the commandments of the LORD, that ye cannot prosper? because ye have forsaken the LORD, he hath also forsaken you. ²¹ And they conspired against him, and stoned him with stones at the commandment of the king in the court of the house of the LORD.

2 Chronicles 24:18–21

INSIGHTS

*I*n his remarkable and eloquent sermon, Stephen revealed his accurate grasp of Jewish history and its relevance to the new faith he had embraced. He turned the tables on his attackers and charged them with being the guilty ones. He refuted their charges in a closely reasoned, eloquent speech that reviewed their history from the time of Abraham onward. From it he demonstrated that the presence of the eternal God cannot be localized and confined to an earthly temple, be it ever so magnificent.

He cited God's presence with Joseph even when he was in Egypt. He reminded them that as a nation they had persistently rejected and resisted the messengers of God. They had envied and mistreated Joseph, whom God had sent as their preserver. They had rebelled against Moses and rejected his message. They had stoned the prophets and abused the functions of the Temple. They boasted of the angelic mediation of the Law, yet they failed to keep it. . . .

When Stephen delivered his final, blistering denunciation, he did it with his eyes open. He knew what the inevitable reaction of those bigoted men would be when he told them that they were stiff-necked, uncircumcised in heart, and murderers and betrayers of the Righteous One (Acts 7:51–52).

J. Oswald Sanders

PAUSE FOR REFLECTION

*W*as Stephen's martyrdom a unique event in Jewish history? Why did the religious leaders kill him? Why did they kill those who had preceded him? Is your heart in any way hardened to God's message today?

TUESDAY

There Is No Room for Jealousy in God's Kingdom

Acts 8:2–25

*A*nd devout men carried Stephen *to his burial*, and made great lamentation over him.

³ As for Saul, he made havoc of the church, entering into every house, and haling men and women committed *them* to prison.

⁴ Therefore they that were scattered abroad went every where preaching the word.

Philip Preaches in Samaria

*T*hen Philip went down to the city of Samaria, and preached Christ unto them.

⁶ And the people with one accord gave heed unto those things which Philip spake, hearing and seeing the miracles which he did.

⁷ For unclean spirits, crying with loud voice, came out of many that were possessed *with them*: and many taken with palsies, and that were lame, were healed.

⁸ And there was great joy in that city.

⁹ But there was a certain man, called Simon, which beforetime in the same city used sorcery, and bewitched the people of Samaria, giving out that himself was some great one:

¹⁰ to whom they all gave heed, from the least to the greatest, saying, This man is the great power of God.

¹¹ And to him they had regard, because that of long time he had bewitched them with sorceries.

¹² But when they believed Philip preaching the things concerning the kingdom of God, and the name of Jesus Christ, they were baptized, both men and women.

¹³ Then Simon himself believed also: and when he was baptized, he continued with Philip, and wondered, beholding the miracles and signs which were done.

¹⁴ Now when the apostles which were at Jerusalem heard that Samaria had received the word of God, they sent unto them Peter and John:

¹⁵ who, when they were come down, prayed for them, that they might receive the Holy Ghost:

¹⁶ (for as yet he was fallen upon none of them: only they were baptized in the name of the Lord Jesus.)

¹⁷ Then laid they *their* hands on them, and they received the Holy Ghost.

¹⁸ And when Simon saw that through laying on of the apostles' hands the Holy Ghost was given, he offered them money,

¹⁹ saying, Give me also this power, that on whomsoever I lay hands, he may receive the Holy Ghost.

²⁰ But Peter said unto him, Thy money perish with thee, because thou hast thought that the gift of God may be purchased with money.

²¹ Thou hast neither part nor lot in this matter: for thy heart is not right in the sight of God.

²² Repent therefore of this thy wickedness, and pray God, if perhaps the thought of thine heart may be forgiven thee.

²³ For I perceive that thou art in the gall of bitterness, and *in* the bond of iniquity.

²⁴ Then answered Simon, and said,

Pray ye to the Lord for me, that none of these things which ye have spoken come upon me.

²⁵ And they, when they had testified and preached the word of the Lord, returned to Jerusalem, and preached the gospel in many villages of the Samaritans.

OLD TESTAMENT READING

*N*ow Korah, the son of Izhar, the son of Kohath, the son of Levi, and Dathan and Abiram, the sons of Eliab, and On, the son of Peleth, sons of Reuben, took *men*:

³ and they gathered themselves together against Moses and against Aaron, and said unto them, *Ye take* too much upon you, seeing all the congregation *are* holy, every one of them, and the LORD *is* among them: wherefore then lift ye up yourselves above the congregation of the LORD?

⁸ And Moses said unto Korah, Hear, I pray you, ye sons of Levi:

⁹ *seemeth it but* a small thing unto you, that the God of Israel hath separated you from the congregation of Israel, to bring you near to himself to do the service of the tabernacle of the LORD, and to stand before the congregation to minister unto them?

²⁸ And Moses said, Hereby ye shall know that the LORD hath sent me to do all these works; for *I have* not *done them* of mine own mind.

²⁹ If these men die the common death of all men, or if they be visited after the visitation of all men; *then* the LORD hath not sent me.

³⁰ But if the LORD make a new thing, and the earth open her mouth, and swallow them up, with all that *appertain* unto them, and they go down quick into the pit; then ye shall understand that these men have provoked the LORD.

Numbers 16:1, 3, 8–9, 28–30

INSIGHTS

*D*elight yourself in the spiritual
    victories of others:
    Delight in all triumphs
    in Christ Jesus.
Rejoice when another's success
    is greater than yours:
    Be glad when another receives
    what you need.
Remain at peace when another
    receives the attention
    you think you deserve.
You must not strive:
You must war against
    all jealousy and contention.

Say today:
    I will not be jealous.
    I will not contend.
    I will not strive.
    I will rejoice at another's victories.
    I will delight in the success of others.
    I will not think others less worthy
    or less important than I.
    I will not see my work as more
    important than someone else's.
    I will pray for those who are my
    competitors.
    I will rejoice in my relationship
    with the Lord.

And so it will be.

Marie Chapian

ACTION POINT

*G*od considers jealousy of his chosen servants to be an insult to him, not to his servants. For what sins of jealousy do you need to ask God's forgiveness?

WEDNESDAY

God's Word Brings Joy
to Those Who Understand It

Acts 8:26—9:9

Philip Teaches an Ethiopian

*A*nd the angel of the Lord spake unto Philip, saying, Arise, and go toward the south, unto the way that goeth down from Jerusalem unto Gaza, which is desert.

27 And he arose and went: and, behold, a man of Ethiopia, a eunuch of great authority under Candace queen of the Ethiopians, who had the charge of all her treasure, and had come to Jerusalem for to worship,

28 was returning, and sitting in his chariot read Isaiah the prophet.

29 Then the Spirit said unto Philip, Go near, and join thyself to this chariot.

30 And Philip ran thither to *him*, and heard him read the prophet Isaiah, and said, Understandest thou what thou readest?

31 And he said, How can I, except some man should guide me? And he desired Philip that he would come up and sit with him.

32 The place of the Scripture which he read was this, He was led as a sheep to the slaughter; and like a lamb dumb before his shearer, so opened he not his mouth:

33 in his humiliation his judgment was taken away: and who shall declare his generation? for his life is taken from the earth.

34 And the eunuch answered Philip, and said, I pray thee, of whom speaketh the prophet this? of himself, or of some other man?

35 Then Philip opened his mouth, and began at the same Scripture, and preached unto him Jesus.

36 And as they went on *their* way, they came unto a certain water: and the eunuch said, See, *here is* water; what doth hinder me to be baptized?

37 And Philip said, If thou believest with all thine heart, thou mayest. And he answered and said, I believe that Jesus Christ is the Son of God.

38 And he commanded the chariot to stand still: and they went down both into the water, both Philip and the eunuch; and he baptized him.

39 And when they were come up out of the water, the Spirit of the Lord caught away Philip, that the eunuch saw him no more: and he went on his way rejoicing.

40 But Philip was found at Azotus: and passing through he preached in all the cities, till he came to Caesarea.

Saul Is Converted

9 And Saul, yet breathing out threatenings and slaughter against the disciples of the Lord, went unto the high priest,

2 and desired of him letters to Damascus to the synagogues, that if he found any of this way, whether they were men or women, he might bring them bound unto Jerusalem.

3 And as he journeyed, he came near Damascus: and suddenly there shined round about him a light from heaven:

4 and he fell to the earth, and heard a voice saying unto him, Saul, Saul, why persecutest thou me?

5 And he said, Who art thou, Lord? And the Lord said, I am Jesus whom thou persecutest: *it is* hard for thee to kick against the pricks.

⁶And he trembling and astonished said, Lord, what wilt thou have me to do? And the Lord *said* unto him, Arise, and go into the city, and it shall be told thee what thou must do. ⁷And the men which journeyed with him stood speechless, hearing a voice, but seeing no man.

⁸And Saul arose from the earth; and when his eyes were opened, he saw no man: but they led him by the hand, and brought *him* into Damascus.

⁹And he was three days without sight, and neither did eat nor drink.

OLD TESTAMENT READING

*A*lso Jeshua, and Bani, and Sherebiah, Jamin, Akkub, Shabbethai, Hodijah, Maaseiah, Kelita, Azariah, Jozabad, Hanan, Pelaiah, and the Levites, caused the people to understand the law: and the people *stood* in their place.

⁸So they read in the book in the law of God distinctly, and gave the sense, and caused *them* to understand the reading.

⁹And Nehemiah, which *is* the Tirshatha, and Ezra the priest the scribe, and the Levites that taught the people, said unto all the people, This day *is* holy unto the LORD your God; mourn not, nor weep. For all the people wept, when they heard the words of the law.

¹⁰Then he said unto them, Go your way, eat the fat, and drink the sweet, and send portions unto them for whom nothing is prepared: for *this* day *is* holy unto our Lord: neither be ye sorry; for the joy of the LORD is your strength.

¹¹So the Levites stilled all the people, saying, Hold your peace, for the day *is* holy; neither be ye grieved.

¹²And all the people went their way to eat, and to drink, and to send portions, and to make great mirth, because they had understood the words that were declared unto them.

Nehemiah 8:7–12

INSIGHTS

*T*he Word of God is a constant and continuing source of joy for the Christian. I don't think I've ever met a joyless Christian who was regularly employed in searching the Scriptures. The result of such searching is to see beyond the words the One who inspired them. Of all the habits the Christian can cultivate, this is one of the most blessed and profitable. Some books are exhausting and exhaustible. The Bible is the only Book that rewards the student with increasing insight as he allows the Word of God to flow through and cleanse him. Indeed, it is the only Book that can cleanse and purify the life of its reader. Other books can inform, but only the Scripture can transform, infill, and inspire.

Al Bryant

ACTION POINT

*W*hy were the Israelites saddened when they first heard the Lord's teachings? What enabled them to be joyous? What brought great joy to the Ethiopian officer? Who has helped you understand God's Word? Thank God for that person and pray that you will experience the joy of living by God's Word.

THURSDAY

"I Am Here, Lord"

Acts 9:10–35

*A*nd there was a certain disciple at Damascus, named Ananias; and to him said the Lord in a vision, Ananias. And he said, Behold, I *am here*, Lord. [11] And the Lord *said* unto him, Arise, and go into the street which is called Straight, and inquire in the house of Judas for *one* called Saul, of Tarsus: for, behold, he prayeth,

[12] and hath seen in a vision a man named Ananias coming in, and putting *his* hand on him, that he might receive his sight.

[13] Then Ananias answered, Lord, I have heard by many of this man, how much evil he hath done to thy saints at Jerusalem:

[14] and here he hath authority from the chief priests to bind all that call on thy name.

[15] But the Lord said unto him, Go thy way: for he is a chosen vessel unto me, to bear my name before the Gentiles, and kings, and the children of Israel:

[16] for I will show him how great things he must suffer for my name's sake.

[17] And Ananias went his way, and entered into the house; and putting his hands on him said, Brother Saul, the Lord, *even* Jesus, that appeared unto thee in the way as thou camest, hath sent me, that thou mightest receive thy sight, and be filled with the Holy Ghost.

[18] And immediately there fell from his eyes as it had been scales: and he received sight forthwith, and arose, and was baptized.

[19] And when he had received meat, he was strengthened. Then was Saul certain days with the disciples which were at Damascus.

Saul Preaches in Damascus

*A*nd straightway he preached Christ in the synagogues, that he is the Son of God.

[21] But all that heard *him* were amazed, and said; Is not this he that destroyed them which called on this name in Jerusalem, and came hither for that intent, that he might bring them bound unto the chief priests?

[22] But Saul increased the more in strength, and confounded the Jews which dwelt at Damascus, proving that this is very Christ.

[23] And after that many days were fulfilled, the Jews took counsel to kill him:

[24] but their laying wait was known of Saul. And they watched the gates day and night to kill him.

[25] Then the disciples took him by night, and let *him* down by the wall in a basket.

Saul Preaches in Jerusalem

*A*nd when Saul was come to Jerusalem, he assayed to join himself to the disciples: but they were all afraid of him, and believed not that he was a disciple.

[27] But Barnabas took him, and brought *him* to the apostles, and declared unto them how he had seen the Lord in the way, and that he had spoken to him, and how he had preached boldly at Damascus in the name of Jesus.

[28] And he was with them coming in and going out at Jerusalem.

[29] And he spake boldly in the name of

the Lord Jesus, and disputed against the Grecians: but they went about to slay him.

³⁰ *Which* when the brethren knew, they brought him down to Caesarea, and sent him forth to Tarsus.

³¹ Then had the churches rest throughout all Judea and Galilee and Samaria, and were edified; and walking in the fear of the Lord, and in the comfort of the Holy Ghost, were multiplied.

Peter Heals Aeneas

*A*nd it came to pass, as Peter passed throughout all *quarters*, he came down also to the saints which dwelt at Lydda.

³³ And there he found a certain man named Aeneas, which had kept his bed eight years, and was sick of the palsy.

³⁴ And Peter said unto him, Aeneas, Jesus Christ maketh thee whole: arise, and make thy bed. And he arose immediately.

³⁵ And all that dwelt at Lydda and Sharon saw him, and turned to the Lord.

OLD TESTAMENT READING

*A*nd the Lᴏʀᴅ said, Arise, anoint him: for this *is* he.

¹³ Then Samuel took the horn of oil, and anointed him in the midst of his brethren: and the Spirit of the Lᴏʀᴅ came upon David from that day forward. So Samuel rose up, and went to Ramah.

1 Samuel 16:12c–13

INSIGHTS

*B*lessed and happy are they who have a sweet faith in Jesus, intertwined with deep affection for Him, for this is a restful confidence. These lovers of Jesus are charmed with His character and delighted with His mission; they are carried away by the loving-kindness that He has manifested, and therefore they cannot help trusting Him because they so much admire, revere, and love Him. . . .

. . . We love Him and He loves us, and therefore we put ourselves into His hands, accept whatever He prescribes, and do whatever He bids. We feel that nothing can be wrongly ordered while He is the Director of our affairs, for He loves us too well to let us perish or suffer a single needless pang.

Faith is the root of obedience, and this may be clearly seen in the affairs of life. When a captain trusts a pilot to steer his vessel into port, he manages the vessel according to his direction. When a traveler trusts a guide to conduct him over a difficult pass, he follows the track which his guide points out. When a patient believes in a physician, he carefully follows his prescriptions and directions. Faith which refuses to obey the commands of the Saviour is a mere pretence and will never save the soul.

Charles Spurgeon

APPLICATION

*W*hat kind of faith is needed to earnestly say the words, "Here I am, Lord"? Is your faith sufficient to do anything your Savior may ask? What objections to complete obedience must you overcome?

FRIDAY

God Hears and Answers Our Prayers

Acts 9:36—10:23a

Peter Heals Tabitha

*N*ow there was at Joppa a certain disciple named Tabitha, which by interpretation is called Dorcas: this woman was full of good works and almsdeeds which she did.

37 And it came to pass in those days, that she was sick, and died: whom when they had washed, they laid *her* in an upper chamber.

38 And forasmuch as Lydda was nigh to Joppa, and the disciples had heard that Peter was there, they sent unto him two men, desiring *him* that he would not delay to come to them.

39 Then Peter arose and went with them. When he was come, they brought him into the upper chamber: and all the widows stood by him weeping, and showing the coats and garments which Dorcas made, while she was with them.

40 But Peter put them all forth, and kneeled down, and prayed; and turning *him* to the body said, Tabitha, arise. And she opened her eyes: and when she saw Peter, she sat up.

41 And he gave her *his* hand, and lifted her up, and when he had called the saints and widows, he presented her alive.

42 And it was known throughout all Joppa; and many believed in the Lord.

43 And it came to pass, that he tarried many days in Joppa with one Simon a tanner.

Peter Teaches Cornelius

10 There was a certain man in Caesarea called Cornelius, a centurion of the band called the Italian *band,*

2 *a* devout *man,* and one that feared God with all his house, which gave much alms to the people, and prayed to God always.

3 He saw in a vision evidently, about the ninth hour of the day, an angel of God coming in to him, and saying unto him, Cornelius.

4 And when he looked on him, he was afraid, and said, What is it, Lord? And he said unto him, Thy prayers and thine alms are come up for a memorial before God.

5 And now send men to Joppa, and call for *one* Simon, whose surname is Peter:

6 he lodgeth with one Simon a tanner, whose house is by the sea side: he shall tell thee what thou oughtest to do.

7 And when the angel which spake unto Cornelius was departed, he called two of his household servants, and a devout soldier of them that waited on him continually;

8 and when he had declared all *these* things unto them, he sent them to Joppa.

9 On the morrow, as they went on their journey, and drew nigh unto the city, Peter went up upon the housetop to pray about the sixth hour:

10 and he became very hungry, and would have eaten: but while they made ready, he fell into a trance,

11 and saw heaven opened, and a certain vessel descending unto him, as it had been a great sheet knit at the four corners, and let down to the earth:

¹²wherein were all manner of fourfooted beasts of the earth, and wild beasts, and creeping things, and fowls of the air.

¹³And there came a voice to him, Rise, Peter; kill, and eat.

¹⁴But Peter said, Not so, Lord; for I have never eaten any thing that is common or unclean.

¹⁵And the voice *spake* unto him again the second time, What God hath cleansed, *that* call not thou common.

¹⁶This was done thrice: and the vessel was received up again into heaven.

¹⁷Now while Peter doubted in himself what this vision which he had seen should mean, behold, the men which were sent from Cornelius had made inquiry for Simon's house, and stood before the gate,

¹⁸and called, and asked whether Simon, which was surnamed Peter, were lodged there.

¹⁹While Peter thought on the vision, the Spirit said unto him, Behold, three men seek thee.

²⁰Arise therefore, and get thee down, and go with them, doubting nothing: for I have sent them.

²¹Then Peter went down to the men which were sent unto him from Cornelius; and said, Behold, I am he whom ye seek: what *is* the cause wherefore ye are come?

²²And they said, Cornelius the centurion, a just man, and one that feareth God, and of good report among all the nation of the Jews, was warned from God by a holy angel to send for thee into his house, and to hear words of thee.

²³Then called he them in, and lodged *them*.

*A*nd it came to pass, when Solomon had finished the building of the house of the LORD, and the king's house, and all Solomon's desire which he was pleased to do,

²that the LORD appeared to Solomon the second time, as he had appeared unto him at Gibeon.

³And the LORD said unto him, I have heard thy prayer and thy supplication, that thou hast made before me: I have hallowed this house, which thou hast built, to put my name there for ever; and mine eyes and mine heart shall be there perpetually.

1 Kings 9:1–3

*P*rayer, *like everything else in the Christian life, is for God's glory and for our benefit, in that order. Everything that God does, everything that God allows and ordains, is in the supreme sense for His glory. It is also true that while God seeks His own glory supremely, man benefits when God is glorified. We pray to glorify God, but also to receive the benefits of prayer from His hand. . . .*

. . . Prayer is discourse with the personal God Himself. . . . He says, "Come. Speak to Me. Make your requests known to Me." And so, we come in order to know Him and to be known by Him.

R. C. Sproul

*T*ake these Scriptures to heart. *Pray as if God is the ultimate reality in your life. Then listen. His response will come!*

WEEKEND

God Forgives All
Who Come to Him

Acts 10:23b–48

And on the morrow Peter went away with them, and certain brethren from Joppa accompanied him.

²⁴ And the morrow after they entered into Caesarea. And Cornelius waited for them, and had called together his kinsmen and near friends.

²⁵ And as Peter was coming in, Cornelius met him, and fell down at his feet, and worshipped *him*.

²⁶ But Peter took him up, saying, Stand up; I myself also am a man.

²⁷ And as he talked with him, he went in, and found many that were come together.

²⁸ And he said unto them, Ye know how that it is an unlawful thing for a man that is a Jew to keep company, or come unto one of another nation; but God hath showed me that I should not call any man common or unclean.

²⁹ Therefore came I *unto you* without gainsaying, as soon as I was sent for: I ask therefore for what intent ye have sent for me?

³⁰ And Cornelius said, Four days ago I was fasting until this hour; and at the ninth hour I prayed in my house, and, behold, a man stood before me in bright clothing,

³¹ and said, Cornelius, thy prayer is heard, and thine alms are had in remembrance in the sight of God.

³² Send therefore to Joppa, and call hither Simon, whose surname is Peter; he is lodged in the house of *one* Simon a tanner by the sea side: who,

when he cometh, shall speak unto thee.

³³ Immediately therefore I sent to thee; and thou hast well done that thou art come. Now therefore are we all here present before God, to hear all things that are commanded thee of God.

³⁴ Then Peter opened *his* mouth, and said, Of a truth I perceive that God is no respecter of persons:

³⁵ but in every nation he that feareth him, and worketh righteousness, is accepted with him.

³⁶ The word which *God* sent unto the children of Israel, preaching peace by Jesus Christ: (he is Lord of all:)

³⁷ that word, *I say*, ye know, which was published throughout all Judea, and began from Galilee, after the baptism which John preached;

³⁸ how God anointed Jesus of Nazareth with the Holy Ghost and with power: who went about doing good, and healing all that were oppressed of the devil; for God was with him.

³⁹ And we are witnesses of all things which he did both in the land of the Jews, and in Jerusalem; whom they slew and hanged on a tree:

⁴⁰ him God raised up the third day, and showed him openly;

⁴¹ not to all the people, but unto witnesses chosen before of God, *even* to us, who did eat and drink with him after he rose from the dead.

⁴² And he commanded us to preach unto the people, and to testify that it is he which was ordained of God *to be* the Judge of quick and dead.

⁴³ To him give all the prophets witness, that through his name whosoever believeth in him shall receive remission of sins.

⁴⁴ While Peter yet spake these words,

the Holy Ghost fell on all them which heard the word.

⁴⁵ And they of the circumcision which believed were astonished, as many as came with Peter, because that on the Gentiles also was poured out the gift of the Holy Ghost.

⁴⁶ For they heard them speak with tongues, and magnify God. Then answered Peter,

⁴⁷ Can any man forbid water, that these should not be baptized, which have received the Holy Ghost as well as we?

⁴⁸ And he commanded them to be baptized in the name of the Lord. Then prayed they him to tarry certain days.

OLD TESTAMENT READING

*C*ome now, and let us reason together, saith the LORD: though your sins be as scarlet, they shall be as white as snow; though they be red like crimson, they shall be as wool. ¹⁹ If ye be willing and obedient, ye shall eat good of the land: ²⁰ but if ye refuse and rebel, ye shall be devoured with the sword: for the mouth of the LORD hath spoken *it*.

Isaiah 1:18–20

INSIGHTS

*T*he usual notion of what Jesus did on the cross runs something like this: people were so bad and so mean and God was so angry with them that he could not forgive them unless somebody big enough took the rap for the whole lot of them.

Nothing could be further from the truth. Love, not anger, brought Jesus to the cross. Golgotha came as a result of God's great desire to forgive,

not his reluctance. Jesus knew that by his vicarious suffering he could actually absorb all the evil of humanity and so heal it, forgive it, redeem it. . . .

Having accomplished this greatest of all his works, Jesus then took refreshment. "It is finished," he announced. That is, this great work of redemption was completed. He could feel the last dregs of the misery of humankind flow through him and into the care of the Father. The last twinges of evil, hostility, anger, and fear drained out of him, and he was able to turn again into the light of God's presence. . . .

This redemptive process is a great mystery hidden in the heart of God. But I know that it is true. I know this not only because the Bible says it is true, but because I have seen its effects in the lives of many people, including myself. It is the ground upon which we can know that confession and forgiveness are realities that transform us. Without the cross the Discipline of confession would be only psychologically therapeutic. But it is so much more. It involves an objective change in our relationship with God and a subjective change in us. It is a means of healing and transforming the inner spirit.

Richard Foster

PAUSE FOR REFLECTION

*P*eter was one of Jesus' closest disciples, yet we see here that he discovers a new, wonderful, and unexpected truth about God's forgiveness. What is it?

MONDAY

God's People Are to Care for One Another

Acts 11:1–30

Peter Returns to Jerusalem

11 And the apostles and brethren that were in Judea heard that the Gentiles had also received the word of God.

2 And when Peter was come up to Jerusalem, they that were of the circumcision contended with him,

3 saying, Thou wentest in to men uncircumcised, and didst eat with them.

4 But Peter rehearsed *the matter* from the beginning, and expounded *it* by order unto them, saying,

5 I was in the city of Joppa praying: and in a trance I saw a vision, a certain vessel descend, as it had been a great sheet, let down from heaven by four corners; and it came even to me:

6 upon the which when I had fastened mine eyes, I considered, and saw fourfooted beasts of the earth, and wild beasts, and creeping things, and fowls of the air.

7 And I heard a voice saying unto me, Arise, Peter; slay and eat.

8 But I said, Not so, Lord: for nothing common or unclean hath at any time entered into my mouth.

9 But the voice answered me again from heaven, What God hath cleansed, *that* call not thou common.

10 And this was done three times: and all were drawn up again into heaven.

11 And, behold, immediately there were three men already come unto the house where I was, sent from Caesarea unto me.

12 And the Spirit bade me go with them, nothing doubting. Moreover these six brethren accompanied me, and we entered into the man's house:

13 and he showed us how he had seen an angel in his house, which stood and said unto him, Send men to Joppa, and call for Simon, whose surname is Peter;

14 who shall tell thee words, whereby thou and all thy house shall be saved.

15 And as I began to speak, the Holy Ghost fell on them, as on us at the beginning.

16 Then remembered I the word of the Lord, how that he said, John indeed baptized with water; but ye shall be baptized with the Holy Ghost.

17 Forasmuch then as God gave them the like gift as *he did* unto us, who believed on the Lord Jesus Christ, what was I, that I could withstand God?

18 When they heard these things, they held their peace, and glorified God, saying, Then hath God also to the Gentiles granted repentance unto life.

The Gospel Comes to Antioch

*N*ow they which were scattered abroad upon the persecution that arose about Stephen traveled as far as Phoenicia, and Cyprus, and Antioch, preaching the word to none but unto the Jews only.

20 And some of them were men of Cyprus and Cyrene, which, when they were come to Antioch, spake unto the Grecians, preaching the Lord Jesus.

21 And the hand of the Lord was with

them: and a great number believed, and turned unto the Lord.

²² Then tidings of these things came unto the ears of the church which was in Jerusalem: and they sent forth Barnabas, that he should go as far as Antioch.

²³ Who, when he came, and had seen the grace of God, was glad, and exhorted them all, that with purpose of heart they would cleave unto the Lord.

²⁴ For he was a good man, and full of the Holy Ghost and of faith: and much people was added unto the Lord.

²⁵ Then departed Barnabas to Tarsus, for to seek Saul:

²⁶ and when he had found him, he brought him unto Antioch. And it came to pass, that a whole year they assembled themselves with the church, and taught much people. And the disciples were called Christians first in Antioch.

²⁷ And in these days came prophets from Jerusalem unto Antioch.

²⁸ And there stood up one of them named Agabus, and signified by the Spirit that there should be great dearth throughout all the world: which came to pass in the days of Claudius Caesar.

²⁹ Then the disciples, every man according to his ability, determined to send relief unto the brethren which dwelt in Judea:

³⁰ which also they did, and sent it to the elders by the hands of Barnabas and Saul.

OLD TESTAMENT READING

*H*e that hath a bountiful eye shall be blessed; for he giveth of his bread to the poor.

Proverbs 22:9

INSIGHTS

*S*omeone has said, "We have no permission from Jesus to be selective in our compassion." It is our natural tendency, however, to choose whom we will reach out to. Perhaps this was the problem of the priest and the Levite in the parable of the good Samaritan. In any event, we know it is often our problem. Jesus mingled with all men, the rich and the poor, the socially acceptable and the backward and undesirable. This willingness to enter into others' lives is costly. . . .

Our God wants to dislodge us from our comfortable, smug existence, to move us to mingle with our needy brothers, to stir us to touch those we might otherwise shun. A poet, whose name is lost in history, expresses the challenge well: "Love has a hem to her garment that trails in the very dust; it can reach the stains of the streets and lanes, and because it can, it must." This is clearly the brand of compassion Jesus exemplified, and it is the kind of loving outreach he calls us to in our modern world. . . .

True compassion is an expression of the life of our Lord Jesus Christ. It is always ready to give, and always willing to sacrifice.

William Fletcher

ACTION POINT

*W*hen has God shaken up your view of how you are to live for him or to care for others? Does your view of Christian compassion need some adjustment? Pray for a heart that will gladly give and sacrifice for Jesus' sake.

TUESDAY

God Intervenes to Save His People

Acts 12:1–25

The Church Is Persecuted

12 Now about that time Herod the king stretched forth *his* hands to vex certain of the church.

² And he killed James the brother of John with the sword.

³ And because he saw it pleased the Jews, he proceeded further to take Peter also. (Then were the days of unleavened bread.)

⁴ And when he had apprehended him, he put *him* in prison, and delivered *him* to four quaternions of soldiers to keep him; intending after Easter to bring him forth to the people.

⁵ Peter therefore was kept in prison: but prayer was made without ceasing of the church unto God for him.

Peter Freed from Jail

*A*nd when Herod would have brought him forth, the same night Peter was sleeping between two soldiers, bound with two chains: and the keepers before the door kept the prison.

⁷ And, behold, the angel of the Lord came upon *him*, and a light shined in the prison: and he smote Peter on the side, and raised him up, saying, Arise up quickly. And his chains fell off from *his* hands.

⁸ And the angel said unto him, Gird thyself, and bind on thy sandals. And so he did. And he saith unto him, Cast thy garment about thee, and follow me.

⁹ And he went out, and followed him; and wist not that it was true which was done by the angel; but thought he saw a vision.

¹⁰ When they were past the first and the second ward, they came unto the iron gate that leadeth unto the city; which opened to them of his own accord: and they went out, and passed on through one street; and forthwith the angel departed from him.

¹¹ And when Peter was come to himself, he said, Now I know of a surety, that the Lord hath sent his angel, and hath delivered me out of the hand of Herod, and *from* all the expectation of the people of the Jews.

¹² And when he had considered *the thing*, he came to the house of Mary the mother of John, whose surname was Mark; where many were gathered together praying.

¹³ And as Peter knocked at the door of the gate, a damsel came to hearken, named Rhoda.

¹⁴ And when she knew Peter's voice, she opened not the gate for gladness, but ran in, and told how Peter stood before the gate.

¹⁵ And they said unto her, Thou art mad. But she constantly affirmed that it was even so. Then said they, It is his angel.

¹⁶ But Peter continued knocking: and when they had opened *the door*, and saw him, they were astonished.

¹⁷ But he, beckoning unto them with the hand to hold their peace, declared unto them how the Lord had brought him out of the prison. And he said, Go show these things unto James, and to the brethren. And he departed, and went into another place.

¹⁸ Now as soon as it was day, there was no small stir among the soldiers, what was become of Peter.

The Death of Herod Agrippa

*A*nd when Herod had sought for him, and found him not, he examined the keepers, and commanded that *they* should be put to death. And he went down from Judea to Caesarea, and *there* abode.

20 And Herod was highly displeased with them of Tyre and Sidon: but they came with one accord to him, and, having made Blastus the king's chamberlain their friend, desired peace; because their country was nourished by the king's *country.*

21 And upon a set day Herod, arrayed in royal apparel, sat upon his throne, and made an oration unto them.

22 And the people gave a shout, *saying, It is* the voice of a god, and not of a man.

23 And immediately the angel of the Lord smote him, because he gave not God the glory: and he was eaten of worms, and gave up the ghost.

24 But the word of God grew and multiplied.

25 And Barnabas and Saul returned from Jerusalem, when they had fulfilled *their* ministry, and took with them John, whose surname was Mark.

OLD TESTAMENT READING

*B*ut the children of Israel walked upon dry *land* in the midst of the sea; and the waters *were* a wall unto them on their right hand, and on their left.

30 Thus the LORD saved Israel that day out of the hand of the Egyptians; and Israel saw the Egyptians dead upon the seashore.

31 And Israel saw that great work which the LORD did upon the Egyptians: and the people feared the LORD, and believed the LORD, and his servant Moses.

Exodus 14:29–31

INSIGHTS

*I*nterestingly, the Book of Daniel opens with a story of the Babylonian invasion of Judah. In the invasion the Babylonians were totally successful and a number of the children of Israel were deported into captivity, including Daniel and his three friends. . . . These young men understood that they were not in Babylon by chance. God had put them there. . . .

God knew what kind of persecution His children were facing and what He would have to do to deliver them out of it. . . . The fiery furnace, the intensity of the heat, and the anger of Nebuchadnezzar were all human efforts to thwart the will of God. But He overcame them all! At the moment of His children's greatest need, He sent His Son to deliver them from the fire. In so doing, God gives us a beautiful picture of His working in our lives. He does not always choose to keep us from the fire, but often brings about our deliverance while we are in the fire itself.

If God could deliver these young men from a fiery furnace, it should seem evident He can deliver us from whatever trouble we find ourselves in.

Richard Lee

PAUSE FOR REFLECTION

*H*ow did God's miraculous deliverance in each of these instances build faith? What result does his intervention bring about in your life?

WEDNESDAY

*God's Miracles Can Lead
Us Toward Faith*

Acts 13:1–25

Barnabas and Saul Are Chosen

13 Now there were in the church that was at Antioch certain prophets and teachers; as Barnabas, and Simeon that was called Niger, and Lucius of Cyrene, and Manaen, which had been brought up with Herod the tetrarch, and Saul.

2 As they ministered to the Lord, and fasted, the Holy Ghost said, Separate me Barnabas and Saul for the work whereunto I have called them.

3 And when they had fasted and prayed, and laid *their* hands on them, they sent *them* away.

Barnabas and Saul in Cyprus

So they, being sent forth by the Holy Ghost, departed unto Seleucia; and from thence they sailed to Cyprus.

5 And when they were at Salamis, they preached the word of God in the synagogues of the Jews: and they had also John to *their* minister.

6 And when they had gone through the isle unto Paphos, they found a certain sorcerer, a false prophet, a Jew, whose name *was* Bar-jesus:

7 which was with the deputy of the country, Sergius Paulus, a prudent man; who called for Barnabas and Saul, and desired to hear the word of God.

8 But Elymas the sorcerer (for so is his name by interpretation) withstood them, seeking to turn away the deputy from the faith.

9 Then Saul, (who also *is called* Paul,) filled with the Holy Ghost, set his eyes on him,

10 and said, O full of all subtilty and all mischief, *thou* child of the devil, *thou* enemy of all righteousness, wilt thou not cease to pervert the right ways of the Lord?

11 And now, behold, the hand of the Lord *is* upon thee, and thou shalt be blind, not seeing the sun for a season. And immediately there fell on him a mist and a darkness; and he went about seeking some to lead him by the hand.

12 Then the deputy, when he saw what was done, believed, being astonished at the doctrine of the Lord.

Paul and Barnabas Leave Cyprus

Now when Paul and his company loosed from Paphos, they came to Perga in Pamphylia: and John departing from them returned to Jerusalem.

14 But when they departed from Perga, they came to Antioch in Pisidia, and went into the synagogue on the sabbath day, and sat down.

15 And after the reading of the law and the prophets, the rulers of the synagogue sent unto them, saying, *Ye* men *and* brethren, if ye have any word of exhortation for the people, say on.

16 Then Paul stood up, and beckoning with *his* hand said, Men of Israel, and ye that fear God, give audience.

17 The God of this people of Israel chose our fathers, and exalted the people when they dwelt as strangers in the land of Egypt, and with a high arm brought he them out of it.

18 And about the time of forty years suffered he their manners in the wilderness.

¹⁹ And when he had destroyed seven nations in the land of Canaan, he divided their land to them by lot.

²⁰ And after that he gave *unto them* judges about the space of four hundred and fifty years, until Samuel the prophet.

²¹ And afterward they desired a king: and God gave unto them Saul the son of Kish, a man of the tribe of Benjamin, by the space of forty years.

²² And when he had removed him, he raised up unto them David to be their king; to whom also he gave testimony, and said, I have found David the *son* of Jesse, a man after mine own heart, which shall fulfil all my will.

²³ Of this man's seed hath God according to *his* promise, raised unto Israel a Saviour, Jesus:

²⁴ when John had first preached before his coming the baptism of repentance to all the people of Israel.

²⁵ And as John fulfilled his course, he said, Whom think ye that I am? I am not *he*. But, behold, there cometh one after me, whose shoes of *his* feet I am not worthy to loose.

OLD TESTAMENT READING

*O*ur fathers understood not thy wonders in Egypt; they remembered not the multitude of thy mercies; but provoked *him* at the sea, *even* at the Red sea.

⁸ Nevertheless he saved them for his name's sake, that he might make his mighty power to be known.

Psalm 106:7–8

*A*nd Moses and Aaron went and gathered together all the elders of the children of Israel:

³⁰ and Aaron spake all the words which the Lord had spoken unto Moses, and did the signs in the sight of the people.

³¹ And the people believed: and when they heard that the Lord had visited the children of Israel, and that he had looked upon their affliction, then they bowed their heads and worshipped.

Exodus 4:29–31

INSIGHTS

*G*od, who made the visible heaven and earth, does not disdain to work visible miracles in heaven or earth. . . .

He restored to the blind those eyes which death was sure some time to close; He raised Lazarus from the dead, who was to die again. And whatever He did for the health of bodies, He did it not to the end that they should exist for evermore; whereas at the last He will give eternal health even to the body itself. But because those things which were not seen were not believed, by means of those temporal things which were seen He built up faith in those things which were not seen. Let no one therefore say that our Lord Jesus Christ doeth not those things now, and on this account prefer the former to the present ages of the Church. . . . The Lord did those things to invite us to the faith.

St. Augustine

PAUSE FOR REFLECTION

*I*n each of these Scripture readings, what did the miracles reveal about God? What was the result? In what way has God revealed himself to you? How have you responded?

THURSDAY

*Those Who Believe
Are Happy*

Acts 13:26–52

*M*en *and* brethren, children of the stock of Abraham, and whosoever among you feareth God, to you is the word of this salvation sent.

27 For they that dwell at Jerusalem, and their rulers, because they knew him not, nor yet the voices of the prophets which are read every sabbath day, they have fulfilled *them* in condemning *him*.

28 And though they found no cause of death *in him*, yet desired they Pilate that he should be slain.

29 And when they had fulfilled all that was written of him, they took *him* down from the tree, and laid *him* in a sepulchre.

30 But God raised him from the dead:

31 and he was seen many days of them which came up with him from Galilee to Jerusalem, who are his witnesses unto the people.

32 And we declare unto you glad tidings, how that the promise which was made unto the fathers,

33 God hath fulfilled the same unto us their children, in that he hath raised up Jesus again; as it is also written in the second psalm, Thou art my Son, this day have I begotten thee.

34 And as concerning that he raised him up from the dead, *now* no more to return to corruption, he said on this wise, I will give you the sure mercies of David.

35 Wherefore he saith also in another *psalm*, Thou shalt not suffer thine Holy One to see corruption.

36 For David, after he had served his own generation by the will of God, fell on sleep, and was laid unto his fathers, and saw corruption:

37 but he, whom God raised again, saw no corruption.

38 Be it known unto you therefore, men *and* brethren, that through this man is preached unto you the forgiveness of sins:

39 and by him all that believe are justified from all things, from which ye could not be justified by the law of Moses.

40 Beware therefore, lest that come upon you, which is spoken of in the prophets;

41 Behold, ye despisers, and wonder, and perish: for I work a work in your days, a work which ye shall in no wise believe, though a man declare it unto you.

42 And when the Jews were gone out of the synagogue, the Gentiles besought that these words might be preached to them the next sabbath.

43 Now when the congregation was broken up, many of the Jews and religious proselytes followed Paul and Barnabas: who, speaking to them, persuaded them to continue in the grace of God.

44 And the next sabbath day came almost the whole city together to hear the word of God.

45 But when the Jews saw the multitudes, they were filled with envy, and spake against those things which were spoken by Paul, contradicting and blaspheming.

46 Then Paul and Barnabas waxed bold, and said, It was necessary that the word of God should first have been spoken to you: but seeing ye put it from you, and judge yourselves

unworthy of everlasting life, lo, we turn to the Gentiles.

⁴⁷ For so hath the Lord commanded us, *saying*, I have set thee to be a light of the Gentiles, that thou shouldest be for salvation unto the ends of the earth.

⁴⁸ And when the Gentiles heard this, they were glad, and glorified the word of the Lord: and as many as were ordained to eternal life believed.

⁴⁹ And the word of the Lord was published throughout all the region.

⁵⁰ But the Jews stirred up the devout and honorable women, and the chief men of the city, and raised persecution against Paul and Barnabas, and expelled them out of their coasts.

⁵¹ But they shook off the dust of their feet against them, and came unto Iconium.

⁵² And the disciples were filled with joy, and with the Holy Ghost.

OLD TESTAMENT READING

*T*hy words were found, and I did eat them; and thy word was unto me the joy and rejoicing of mine heart: for I am called by thy name, O LORD God of hosts.

Jeremiah 15:16

INSIGHTS

I'm convinced that enjoyment is the ultimate stage of knowledge. When we set out to learn the basic truths of an intellectual discipline, we are confounded by all we don't know. Little by little, we become more secure in ideas and theories. Then one day, we suddenly realize that we have captured the subject and know how to use our knowledge. . . .

. . . Enjoyment of our faith grows in the same way. In the beginning, God seems distant and aloof. Biblical and theological terms are like a foreign language. Our prayers are strained and shallow. . . . And then, with the touch of the Father's hand, we discover how much He loves us and wants us to know Him personally. Secondary theories about Him are replaced by an intimate relationship with Him. None of our awe and adoration is lost as we begin to enjoy Him. . . .

Enjoying God is really a vital expression of glorifying Him. The glory of God is the manifestation and revelation of all that He is as Creator, Sustainer, Redeemer, and Lord of all. We glorify Him when we worship Him for His lovingkindness, goodness, and mercifulness. Our worship becomes intimate when we joyfully experience God's nature and attributes. From that joy springs our desire to glorify Him by serving Him. Our faithful obedience becomes an enjoyable response.

Lloyd Ogilvie

PAUSE FOR REFLECTION

*H*ow did the people respond when Paul and Barnabas spoke God's Word in Antioch? In what ways does the Lord make you happy? How has your happiness grown as you have come to know him better?

FRIDAY

*Seek God's Guidance
When Making Decisions*

Acts 14:1–28

Paul and Barnabas in Iconium

14 And it came to pass in Iconium, that they went both together into the synagogue of the Jews, and so spake, that a great multitude both of the Jews and also of the Greeks believed.

² But the unbelieving Jews stirred up the Gentiles, and made their minds evil affected against the brethren.

³ Long time therefore abode they speaking boldly in the Lord, which gave testimony unto the word of his grace, and granted signs and wonders to be done by their hands.

⁴ But the multitude of the city was divided: and part held with the Jews, and part with the apostles.

⁵ And when there was an assault made both of the Gentiles, and also of the Jews with their rulers, to use *them* despitefully, and to stone them,

⁶ they were ware of *it*, and fled unto Lystra and Derbe, cities of Lycaonia, and unto the region that lieth round about:

⁷ and there they preached the gospel.

Paul in Lystra and Derbe

*A*nd there sat a certain man at Lystra, impotent in his feet, being a cripple from his mother's womb, who never had walked:

⁹ the same heard Paul speak: who steadfastly beholding him, and perceiving that he had faith to be healed,

¹⁰ said with a loud voice, Stand upright on thy feet. And he leaped and walked.

¹¹ And when the people saw what Paul had done, they lifted up their voices, saying in the speech of Lycaonia, The gods are come down to us in the likeness of men.

¹² And they called Barnabas, Jupiter; and Paul, Mercurius, because he was the chief speaker.

¹³ Then the priest of Jupiter, which was before their city, brought oxen and garlands unto the gates, and would have done sacrifice with the people.

¹⁴ *Which* when the apostles, Barnabas and Paul, heard *of*, they rent their clothes, and ran in among the people, crying out,

¹⁵ and saying, Sirs, why do ye these things? We also are men of like passions with you, and preach unto you that ye should turn from these vanities unto the living God, which made heaven, and earth, and the sea, and all things that are therein:

¹⁶ who in times past suffered all nations to walk in their own ways.

¹⁷ Nevertheless he left not himself without witness, in that he did good, and gave us rain from heaven, and fruitful seasons, filling our hearts with food and gladness.

¹⁸ And with these sayings scarce restrained they the people, that they had not done sacrifice unto them.

¹⁹ And there came thither *certain* Jews from Antioch and Iconium, who persuaded the people, and, having stoned Paul, drew *him* out of the city, supposing he had been dead.

²⁰ Howbeit, as the disciples stood round about him, he rose up, and

came into the city: and the next day he departed with Barnabas to Derbe.

The Return to Antioch in Syria

And when they had preached the gospel to that city, and had taught many, they returned again to Lystra, and *to* Iconium, and Antioch, ²² confirming the souls of the disciples, *and* exhorting them to continue in the faith, and that we must through much tribulation enter into the kingdom of God.

²³ And when they had ordained them elders in every church, and had prayed with fasting, they commended them to the Lord, on whom they believed.

²⁴ And after they had passed throughout Pisidia, they came to Pamphylia. ²⁵ And when they had preached the word in Perga, they went down into Attalia:

²⁶ and thence sailed to Antioch, from whence they had been recommended to the grace of God for the work which they fulfilled.

²⁷ And when they were come, and had gathered the church together, they rehearsed all that God had done with them, and how he had opened the door of faith unto the Gentiles.

²⁸ And there they abode long time with the disciples.

OLD TESTAMENT READING

Trust in the LORD with all thine heart; and lean not unto thine own understanding.

⁶ In all thy ways acknowledge him, and he shall direct thy paths.

⁷ Be not wise in thine own eyes: fear the LORD, and depart from evil.

Proverbs 3:5–7

INSIGHTS

When I was in my late teens I had life all figured out . . . . Now I realize how uncertain this world is, how limited my own experience is, how deceptive the evil one is, how easily I can be duped. I desperately need a guide though the maze of options every day. Don't you?

I need a guide who knows me, who understands me and has my best interests in mind. The best guide would understand my personality, my temperament, my gifts and abilities, my likes and dislikes. Wouldn't it be something to have a guide who takes all that into consideration as He charts a path for your life?

Such a guide exists, friend. God reaches out to you and says, in effect, "Take My hand. You matter to Me. I am trustworthy. I know you. I understand you. I know what will fulfill you. I created you." . . .

. . . He wants to guide your life. Will you let Him? Will you read and heed the Word? Will you be yielded and listen to and trust the leadings of the Holy Spirit? Will you submit your plans to others for their input? When you do, you'll find that life can truly be an adventure.

Bill Hybels

APPLICATION

Why do you think Paul and Barnabas especially sought God's guidance in choosing elders for the churches? For what decisions do you seek God's guidance? Should you be seeking his wisdom more?

WEEKEND

*God Accepts Anyone
Who Comes to Him*

Acts 15:1–21

The Council at Jerusalem

15 And certain men which came down from Judea taught the brethren, *and said*, Except ye be circumcised after the manner of Moses, ye cannot be saved.

² When therefore Paul and Barnabas had no small dissension and disputation with them, they determined that Paul and Barnabas, and certain other of them, should go up to Jerusalem unto the apostles and elders about this question.

³ And being brought on their way by the church, they passed through Phoenicia and Samaria, declaring the conversion of the Gentiles: and they caused great joy unto all the brethren.

⁴ And when they were come to Jerusalem, they were received of the church, and *of* the apostles and elders, and they declared all things that God had done with them.

⁵ But there rose up certain of the sect of the Pharisees which believed, saying, That it was needful to circumcise them, and to command *them* to keep the law of Moses.

⁶ And the apostles and elders came together for to consider of this matter.

⁷ And when there had been much disputing, Peter rose up, and said unto them, Men *and* brethren, ye know how that a good while ago God made choice among us, that the Gentiles by my mouth should hear the word of the gospel, and believe.

⁸ And God, which knoweth the hearts, bare them witness, giving them the Holy Ghost, even as *he did* unto us;

⁹ and put no difference between us and them, purifying their hearts by faith.

¹⁰ Now therefore why tempt ye God, to put a yoke upon the neck of the disciples, which neither our fathers nor we were able to bear?

¹¹ But we believe that through the grace of the Lord Jesus Christ we shall be saved, even as they.

¹² Then all the multitude kept silence, and gave audience to Barnabas and Paul, declaring what miracles and wonders God had wrought among the Gentiles by them.

¹³ And after they had held their peace, James answered, saying, Men *and* brethren, hearken unto me:

¹⁴ Simeon hath declared how God at the first did visit the Gentiles, to take out of them a people for his name.

¹⁵ And to this agree the words of the prophets; as it is written,

¹⁶ After this I will return, and will build again the tabernacle of David, which is fallen down; and I will build again the ruins thereof, and I will set it up:

¹⁷ that the residue of men might seek after the Lord, and all the Gentiles, upon whom my name is called, saith the Lord, who doeth all these things.

¹⁸ Known unto God are all his works from the beginning of the world.

¹⁹ Wherefore my sentence is, that we trouble not them, which from among the Gentiles are turned to God:

²⁰ but that we write unto them, that they abstain from pollutions of idols, and *from* fornication, and *from* things strangled, and *from* blood.

²¹ For Moses of old time hath in every city them that preach him, being read in the synagogues every sabbath day.

---

*G*od be merciful unto us, and bless us; *and* cause his face to shine upon us; Selah.
² that thy way may be known upon the earth, thy saving health among all nations.
³ Let the people praise thee, O God; let all the people praise thee.
⁴ O let the nations be glad and sing for joy: for thou shalt judge the people righteously, and govern the nations upon earth. Selah.
⁵ Let the people praise thee, O God; let all the people praise thee.

Psalm 67:1–5

*L*ook unto me, and be ye saved, all the ends of the earth: for I *am* God, and *there is* none else.

Isaiah 45:22

---

*T*he Law came and in bold letters etched by the finger of God it read, "This is holiness! Honor My Name by keeping My Law!" But the fact is, nobody could keep it, which explains the statement in Romans 5:20 that says "sin increased." The Law arouses sin but never arrests it. So how can the tailspin stop? What hope is there? The answer is found in the same verse: ". . . but where sin increased, grace abounded all the more." . . .

Let me amplify the scriptural statement even more. Where sin overflowed, grace flooded in. Where sin measurably increased, grace immeasurably increased. Where sin was finite, grace was infinite. Where sin was colossal, grace was super-colossal. Where sin abounds, grace superabounds. The sin identified by the Law in no way stopped the flow of the grace of God. Jesus' death on the cross was the sufficient payment for sin, putting grace into action that was not simply adequate but abundant. . . .

. . . God, in grace, offers you the free gift of forgiveness. All you can do is take it. Once you take it, you will be given the power to give up, to put on, to take off, to quit, to start—whatever. But don't confuse the issue of salvation. It is yours strictly on the basis of God's free gift. In spite of all the stuff you may hear to the contrary, the emphasis is not on what we do for God; instead, it is on what God has done for us.

Charles Swindoll

---

*T*o whom was the law of Moses given? Why? What evidence in the Old and New Testaments reveals that God offers salvation through Jesus Christ to all people—Jew and Gentile?

MONDAY
The Value of Encouragement

Acts 15:22—16:10

Letter to Gentile Believers

*T*hen pleased it the apostles and elders, with the whole church, to send chosen men of their own company to Antioch with Paul and Barnabas; *namely*, Judas surnamed Barsabas, and Silas, chief men among the brethren:

23 and they wrote *letters* by them after this manner; The apostles and elders and brethren *send* greeting unto the brethren which are of the Gentiles in Antioch and Syria and Cilicia:

24 Forasmuch as we have heard, that certain which went out from us have troubled you with words, subverting your souls, saying, *Ye must* be circumcised, and keep the law; to whom we gave no *such* commandment:

25 it seemed good unto us, being assembled with one accord, to send chosen men unto you with our beloved Barnabas and Paul,

26 men that have hazarded their lives for the name of our Lord Jesus Christ.

27 We have sent therefore Judas and Silas, who shall also tell *you* the same things by mouth.

28 For it seemed good to the Holy Ghost, and to us, to lay upon you no greater burden than these necessary things;

29 that ye abstain from meats offered to idols, and from blood, and from things strangled, and from fornica-tion: from which if ye keep yourselves, ye shall do well. Fare ye well.

30 So when they were dismissed, they came to Antioch: and when they had gathered the multitude together, they delivered the epistle:

31 *which* when they had read, they rejoiced for the consolation.

32 And Judas and Silas, being prophets also themselves, exhorted the brethren with many words, and confirmed *them*.

33 And after they had tarried *there* a space, they were let go in peace from the brethren unto the apostles.

34 Notwithstanding it pleased Silas to abide there still.

35 Paul also and Barnabas continued in Antioch, teaching and preaching the word of the Lord, with many others also.

Paul and Barnabas Part

*A*nd some days after, Paul said unto Barnabas, Let us go again and visit our brethren in every city where we have preached the word of the Lord, *and see* how they do.

37 And Barnabas determined to take with them John, whose surname was Mark.

38 But Paul thought not good to take him with them, who departed from them from Pamphylia, and went not with them to the work.

39 And the contention was so sharp between them, that they departed asunder one from the other: and so Barnabas took Mark, and sailed unto Cyprus;

40 and Paul chose Silas, and departed, being recommended by the brethren unto the grace of God.

41 And he went through Syria and Cilicia, confirming the churches.

Timothy Goes with Paul

16 Then came he to Derbe and Lystra: and, behold, a certain disciple was there, named Timothy, the son of a certain woman, which was a Jewess, and believed; but his father *was* a Greek:

² which was well reported of by the brethren that were at Lystra and Iconium.

³ Him would Paul have to go forth with him; and took and circumcised him because of the Jews which were in those quarters: for they knew all that his father was a Greek.

⁴ And as they went through the cities, they delivered them the decrees for to keep, that were ordained of the apostles and elders which were at Jerusalem.

⁵ And so were the churches established in the faith, and increased in number daily.

Paul Is Called Out of Asia

N ow when they had gone throughout Phrygia and the region of Galatia, and were forbidden of the Holy Ghost to preach the word in Asia,

⁷ after they were come to Mysia, they assayed to go into Bithynia: but the Spirit suffered them not.

⁸ And they passing by Mysia came down to Troas.

⁹ And a vision appeared to Paul in the night; There stood a man of Macedonia, and prayed him, saying, Come over into Macedonia, and help us.

¹⁰ And after he had seen the vision, immediately we endeavored to go into Macedonia, assuredly gathering that the Lord had called us for to preach the gospel unto them.

A word fitly spoken *is like* apples of gold in pictures of silver.

Proverbs 25:11

INSIGHTS

I was rushing around trying to get dinner ready for my husband and houseguests. . . .

. . . Just as I began last-minute preparations, the doorbell rang. I ran to answer it. A friend had stopped by to drop off a folder of information for my husband.

"How are you, Doris?"

I began to tell her that I was a little tired and frazzled around the edges, when I noticed she wasn't listening. Before I could finish my response, she said, "That's good. It's nice to see you." And with that she left.

I walked slowly back to my kitchen, feeling lonely and deflated. My friend had let me down when I could have used just a word of encouragement, maybe even a quick prayer. . . .

And then I heard the words: Doris, you've done this to people, too. Let this be a lesson to you. Listen to those I send across your path. Give them at least five minutes, even if you are in a hurry. Stop and pray with them.

Doris Greig

APPLICATION

W hat kind of encouragement is offered in each of these examples? How do they help you know how to encourage others?

TUESDAY

"Come into My House"

Acts 16:11–34

Lydia Becomes a Christian

*T*herefore loosing from Troas, we came with a straight course to Samothracia, and the next *day* to Neapolis;

[12] and from thence to Philippi, which is the chief city of that part of Macedonia, *and* a colony: and we were in that city abiding certain days.

[13] And on the sabbath we went out of the city by a river side, where prayer was wont to be made; and we sat down, and spake unto the women which resorted *thither.*

[14] And a certain woman named Lydia, a seller of purple, of the city of Thyatira, which worshipped God, heard *us*: whose heart the Lord opened, that she attended unto the things which were spoken of Paul.

[15] And when she was baptized, and her household, she besought *us*, saying, If ye have judged me to be faithful to the Lord, come into my house, and abide *there.* And she constrained us.

Paul and Silas in Prison

*A*nd it came to pass, as we went to prayer, a certain damsel possessed with a spirit of divination met us, which brought her masters much gain by soothsaying:

[17] the same followed Paul and us, and cried, saying, These men are the servants of the most high God, which show unto us the way of salvation.

[18] And this did she many days. But Paul, being grieved, turned and said to the spirit, I command thee in the name of Jesus Christ to come out of her. And he came out the same hour.

[19] And when her masters saw that the hope of their gains was gone, they caught Paul and Silas, and drew *them* into the market place unto the rulers,

[20] and brought them to the magistrates, saying, These men, being Jews, do exceedingly trouble our city,

[21] and teach customs, which are not lawful for us to receive, neither to observe, being Romans.

[22] And the multitude rose up together against them; and the magistrates rent off their clothes, and commanded to beat *them.*

[23] And when they had laid many stripes upon them, they cast *them* into prison, charging the jailer to keep them safely:

[24] who, having received such a charge, thrust them into the inner prison, and made their feet fast in the stocks.

[25] And at midnight Paul and Silas prayed, and sang praises unto God: and the prisoners heard them.

[26] And suddenly there was a great earthquake, so that the foundations of the prison were shaken: and immediately all the doors were opened, and every one's bands were loosed.

[27] And the keeper of the prison awaking out of his sleep, and seeing the prison doors open, he drew out his sword, and would have killed himself, supposing that the prisoners had been fled.

[28] But Paul cried with a loud voice, saying, Do thyself no harm: for we are all here.

[29] Then he called for a light, and sprang in, and came trembling, and

fell down before Paul and Silas,

30 and brought them out, and said, Sirs, what must I do to be saved?

31 And they said, Believe on the Lord Jesus Christ, and thou shalt be saved, and thy house.

32 And they spake unto him the word of the Lord, and to all that were in his house.

33 And he took them the same hour of the night, and washed *their* stripes; and was baptized, he and all his, straightway.

34 And when he had brought them into his house, he set meat before them, and rejoiced, believing in God with all his house.

OLD TESTAMENT READING

*A*nd it fell on a day, that Elisha passed to Shunem, where *was* a great woman; and she constrained him to eat bread. And *so* it was, *that,* as oft as he passed by, he turned in thither to eat bread.

9 And she said unto her husband, Behold now, I perceive that this *is* an holy man of God, which passeth by us continually.

10 Let us make a little chamber, I pray thee, on the wall; and let us set for him there a bed, and a table, and a stool, and a candlestick: and it shall be, when he cometh to us, that he shall turn in thither.

2 Kings 4:8–10

INSIGHTS

THERE IS ROOM

*Y*ou know how it happened, Lord:
*She said, "May I live with you
Just a little while?*

*I have no place to go.
I'm lonely
And afraid."
I hastily glanced at the small
  room.
I thought of other rooms
Smaller and extremely crowded.
I said, "You see my small house.
There is really no room.
But I have room in my heart
For caring
For praying
I'll make phone calls—
There must be a family some-
  where . . ."
That was this morning, Lord.
All day long
I prayed
I called
I waited . . .
Then You accomplished
What I cannot explain.
Through the hours
You pushed back the walls—
Until suddenly, tonight
There is room for her in my house
As well as in my heart
You are indeed a Master Builder!*

Ruth Calkin

ACTION POINT

*W*hat do you find particularly interesting about these examples of hospitality? What do you think it means to express Christian hospitality to people today? Pray about how God wants you to use your home to serve him.

WEDNESDAY

*It's Important to Know
God's Powerful Word*

Acts 16:35—17:15

*A*nd when it was day, the magistrates sent the sergeants, saying, Let those men go.

36 And the keeper of the prison told this saying to Paul, The magistrates have sent to let you go: now therefore depart, and go in peace.

37 But Paul said unto them, They have beaten us openly uncondemned, being Romans, and have cast *us* into prison; and now do they thrust us out privily? nay verily; but let them come themselves and fetch us out.

38 And the sergeants told these words unto the magistrates: and they feared, when they heard that they were Romans.

39 And they came and besought them, and brought *them* out, and desired *them* to depart out of the city.

40 And they went out of the prison, and entered into *the house* of Lydia: and when they had seen the brethren, they comforted them, and departed.

Paul and Silas in Thessalonica

17 Now when they had passed through Amphipolis and Apollonia, they came to Thessalonica, where was a synagogue of the Jews:

2 and Paul, as his manner was, went in unto them, and three sabbath days reasoned with them out of the Scriptures,

3 opening and alleging, that Christ must needs have suffered, and risen again from the dead; and that this Jesus, whom I preach unto you, is Christ.

4 And some of them believed, and consorted with Paul and Silas; and of the devout Greeks a great multitude, and of the chief women not a few.

5 But the Jews which believed not, moved with envy, took unto them certain lewd fellows of the baser sort, and gathered a company, and set all the city on an uproar, and assaulted the house of Jason, and sought to bring them out to the people.

6 And when they found them not, they drew Jason and certain brethren unto the rulers of the city, crying, These that have turned the world upside down are come hither also;

7 whom Jason hath received: and these all do contrary to the decrees of Caesar, saying that there is another king, *one* Jesus.

8 And they troubled the people and the rulers of the city, when they heard these things.

9 And when they had taken security of Jason, and of the other, they let them go.

Paul and Silas Go to Beroea

*A*nd the brethren immediately sent away Paul and Silas by night unto Beroea: who coming *thither* went into the synagogue of the Jews.

11 These were more noble than those in Thessalonica, in that they received the word with all readiness of mind, and searched the Scriptures daily, whether those things were so.

¹²Therefore many of them believed; also of honorable women which were Greeks, and of men, not a few. ¹³But when the Jews of Thessalonica had knowledge that the word of God was preached of Paul at Beroea, they came thither also, and stirred up the people.

¹⁴And then immediately the brethren sent away Paul to go as it were to the sea: but Silas and Timothy abode there still.

¹⁵And they that conducted Paul brought him unto Athens: and receiving a commandment unto Silas and Timothy for to come to him with all speed, they departed.

OLD TESTAMENT READING

*F*or as the rain cometh down, and the snow from heaven, and returneth not thither, but watereth the earth, and maketh it bring forth and bud, that it may give seed to the sower, and bread to the eater:

¹¹so shall my word be that goeth forth out of my mouth: it shall not return unto me void, but it shall accomplish that which I please, and it shall prosper *in the thing* whereto I sent it.

Isaiah 55:10–11

*T*hy word *is* a lamp unto my feet, and a light unto my path.

¹⁰⁶I have sworn, and I will perform *it*, that I will keep thy righteous judgments.

¹⁰⁷I am afflicted very much: quicken me, O LORD, according unto thy word.

¹⁰⁸Accept, I beseech thee, the freewill offerings of my mouth, O LORD, and teach me thy judgments.

Psalm 119:105–108

INSIGHTS

I never pretend to make but one book my study. I read them occasionally, but have little time or inclination to read other books much while I have so much to learn of my Bible. I find it like a deep mine, the more I work it, the richer it grows. We must read that more than any or all other books. We must pause and pray over it, verse after verse, and compare part with part, dwell on it, digest it, and get it into our minds, till we feel that the Spirit of God has filled us with the spirit of holiness.

Will you do it? Will you lay your hearts open to God, and not give him rest, till he has filled you with divine knowledge? Will you search the scriptures? I have often been asked by young converts, and young men preparing for the ministry, what they should read. Read the Bible. I would give the same answer five hundred times. Over and above all other things, study the Bible.

Charles Finney

ACTION POINT

*W*hat was unusual about the Jews in Beroea? Is it, then, surprising that many of them believed? What does God say about his word in Isaiah? How much do you treasure and seek after God's Word? Will you begin today to search after it more diligently?

THURSDAY

*Paul Tells Others
About the True God*

Acts 17:16—18:4

Paul Preaches in Athens

*N*ow while Paul waited for them at Athens, his spirit was stirred in him, when he saw the city wholly given to idolatry.

[17] Therefore disputed he in the synagogue with the Jews, and with the devout persons, and in the market daily with them that met with him.

[18] Then certain philosophers of the Epicureans, and of the Stoics, encountered him. And some said, What will this babbler say? other some, He seemeth to be a setter forth of strange gods: because he preached unto them Jesus, and the resurrection.

[19] And they took him, and brought him unto Areopagus, saying, May we know what this new doctrine, whereof thou speakest, *is*?

[20] For thou bringest certain strange things to our ears: we would know therefore what these things mean.

[21] (For all the Athenians, and strangers which were there, spent their time in nothing else, but either to tell, or to hear some new thing.)

[22] Then Paul stood in the midst of Mars' hill, and said, *Ye* men of Athens, I perceive that in all things ye are too superstitious.

[23] For as I passed by, and beheld your devotions, I found an altar with this inscription, To the Unknown God. Whom therefore ye ignorantly worship, him declare I unto you.

[24] God that made the world and all things therein, seeing that he is Lord of heaven and earth, dwelleth not in temples made with hands;

[25] neither is worshipped with men's hands, as though he needed any thing, seeing he giveth to all life, and breath, and all things;

[26] and hath made of one blood all nations of men for to dwell on all the face of the earth, and hath determined the times before appointed, and the bounds of their habitation;

[27] that they should seek the Lord, if haply they might feel after him, and find him, though he be not far from every one of us:

[28] for in him we live, and move, and have our being; as certain also of your own poets have said, For we are also his offspring.

[29] Forasmuch then as we are the offspring of God, we ought not to think that the Godhead is like unto gold, or silver, or stone, graven by art and man's device.

[30] And the times of this ignorance God winked at; but now commandeth all men every where to repent:

[31] because he hath appointed a day, in the which he will judge the world in righteousness by *that* man whom he hath ordained; *whereof* he hath given assurance unto all *men*, in that he hath raised him from the dead.

[32] And when they heard of the resurrection of the dead, some mocked: and others said, We will hear thee again of this *matter*.

[33] So Paul departed from among them.

[34] Howbeit certain men clave unto him, and believed: among the which *was* Dionysius the Areopagite, and a woman named Damaris, and others with them.

Paul in Corinth

18 After these things Paul departed from Athens, and came to Corinth;

2 and found a certain Jew named Aquila, born in Pontus, lately come from Italy, with his wife Priscilla, (because that Claudius had commanded all Jews to depart from Rome,) and came unto them.

3 And because he was of the same craft, he abode with them, and wrought: (for by their occupation they were tentmakers.)

4 And he reasoned in the synagogue every sabbath, and persuaded the Jews and the Greeks.

OLD TESTAMENT READING

*T*hese *are* the generations of the heavens and of the earth when they were created, in the day that the Lord God made the earth and the heavens,

5 and every plant of the field before it was in the earth, and every herb of the field before it grew: for the Lord God had not caused it to rain upon the earth, and *there was* not a man to till the ground.

6 But there went up a mist from the earth, and watered the whole face of the ground.

7 And the Lord God formed man *of* the dust of the ground, and breathed into his nostrils the breath of life; and man became a living soul.

Genesis 2:4–7

INSIGHTS

I WILL WORSHIP

*G*od, you are with me
and you can help me;

You were with me when I was
taken,
and you are with me now.
You strengthen me.

The God I serve is everywhere—
in heaven and earth and the
sea,
but he is above them all,
for all live in him:
All were created by him,
and by him only do they remain.

I will worship only the true God;
you will I carry in my heart;
No one on earth shall be able to
separate me from you.
Quirinus of Siscia

MY COMFORT

*J*esus Christ is my comfort.
It is you who created us all.
There is only you, one God,
Father, Son, and Holy Spirit,
to whom homage and praise
are due.
Januarius of Cordova

PAUSE FOR REFLECTION

*I*n order to help them understand the Good News, what did Paul tell the philosophers and important people of Athens about the true God? What knowledge of God helps you to understand, trust, and worship him?

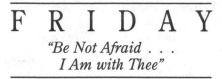

FRIDAY

"Be Not Afraid . . . I Am with Thee"

Acts 18:5–28

*A*nd when Silas and Timothy were come from Macedonia, Paul was pressed in the spirit, and testified to the Jews *that* Jesus *was* Christ.

⁶ And when they opposed themselves, and blasphemed, he shook *his* raiment, and said unto them, Your blood *be* upon your own heads; I *am* clean: from henceforth I will go unto the Gentiles.

⁷ And he departed thence, and entered into a certain *man's* house, named Justus, *one* that worshipped God, whose house joined hard to the synagogue.

⁸ And Crispus, the chief ruler of the synagogue, believed on the Lord with all his house; and many of the Corinthians hearing believed, and were baptized.

⁹ Then spake the Lord to Paul in the night by a vision, Be not afraid, but speak, and hold not thy peace:

¹⁰ for I am with thee, and no man shall set on thee to hurt thee: for I have much people in this city.

¹¹ And he continued *there* a year and six months, teaching the word of God among them.

Paul Is Brought Before Gallio

*A*nd when Gallio was the deputy of Achaia, the Jews made insurrection with one accord against Paul, and brought him to the judgment seat,

¹³ Saying, This *fellow* persuadeth men to worship God contrary to the law.

¹⁴ And when Paul was now about to open *his* mouth, Gallio said unto the Jews, If it were a matter of wrong or wicked lewdness, O *ye* Jews, reason would that I should bear with you:

¹⁵ but if it be a question of words and names, and *of* your law, look ye *to it*; for I will be no judge of such *matters*.

¹⁶ And he drave them from the judgment seat.

¹⁷ Then all the Greeks took Sosthenes, the chief ruler of the synagogue, and beat *him* before the judgment seat. And Gallio cared for none of those things.

Paul Returns to Antioch

*A*nd Paul *after* this tarried *there* yet a good while, and then took his leave of the brethren, and sailed thence into Syria, and with him Priscilla and Aquila; having shorn *his* head in Cenchreae: for he had a vow.

¹⁹ And he came to Ephesus, and left them there: but he himself entered into the synagogue, and reasoned with the Jews.

²⁰ When they desired *him* to tarry longer time with them, he consented not;

²¹ but bade them farewell, saying, I must by all means keep this feast that cometh in Jerusalem: but I will return again unto you, if God will. And he sailed from Ephesus.

²² And when he had landed at Caesarea, and gone up, and saluted the church, he went down to Antioch.

²³ And after he had spent some time

there, he departed, and went over *all* the country of Galatia and Phrygia in order, strengthening all the disciples.

Apollos in Ephesus and Corinth

*A*nd a certain Jew named Apollos, born at Alexandria, an eloquent man, *and* mighty in the Scriptures, came to Ephesus.
²⁵ This man was instructed in the way of the Lord; and being fervent in the spirit, he spake and taught diligently the things of the Lord, knowing only the baptism of John.
²⁶ And he began to speak boldly in the synagogue: whom when Aquila and Priscilla had heard, they took him unto *them*, and expounded unto him the way of God more perfectly.
²⁷ And when he was disposed to pass into Achaia, the brethren wrote, exhorting the disciples to receive him: who, when he was come, helped them much which had believed through grace:
²⁸ for he mightily convinced the Jews, *and that* publicly, showing by the Scriptures that Jesus was Christ.

OLD TESTAMENT READING

*T*he LORD *is* thy keeper: the LORD *is* thy shade upon thy right hand.
⁶ The sun shall not smite thee by day, nor the moon by night.
⁷ The LORD shall preserve thee from all evil: he shall preserve thy soul.
⁸ The LORD shall preserve thy going out and thy coming in from this time forth, and even for evermore.

Psalm 121:5–8

*A*nd, behold, I *am* with thee, and will keep thee in all *places* whither thou goest, and will bring thee again into this land; for I will not leave thee, until I have done *that* which I have spoken to thee of.

Genesis 28:15

INSIGHTS

*H*ow tenderly God soothes our fears! How sweetly He says, . . . "Fear thou not; for I am with thee: be not dismayed; for I am thy God: . . . I will uphold thee with the right hand of my righteousness" (Isaiah 41:10). And yet again, still with tender thoughtfulness, "I the Lord thy God will hold thy right hand, saying unto thee, Fear not; I will help thee" (Isaiah 41:13). He does not say it only once, but He keeps holding our right hand and repeating such promises.

The blessed Lord condensed it all into one single message of eternal comfort spoken to the disciples on the Sea of Galilee, It is I; be not afraid. He is the antidote to fear; He is the remedy for trouble; He is the substance and the sum of deliverance. We should, therefore, rise above fear. Let us keep our eyes fastened upon Him; let us abide continually in Him; let us be content with Him.

Let us cling closely to Him.

A. B. Simpson

ACTION POINT

*W*hat encouragement from the Lord have you received in times of fear? Which of the readings assures you that God is with you? Pray that you will always cling to God and feel the blessing of his presence!

WEEKEND

*True Repentance Involves
Abandoning Sinful Practices*

Acts 19:1–22

Paul in Ephesus

19 And it came to pass, that, while Apollos was at Corinth, Paul having passed through the upper coasts came to Ephesus: and finding certain disciples,

² he said unto them, Have ye received the Holy Ghost since ye believed? And they said unto him, We have not so much as heard whether there be any Holy Ghost.

³ And he said unto them, Unto what then were ye baptized? And they said, Unto John's baptism.

⁴ Then said Paul, John verily baptized with the baptism of repentance, saying unto the people, that they should believe on him which should come after him, that is, on Christ Jesus.

⁵ When they heard *this*, they were baptized in the name of the Lord Jesus.

⁶ And when Paul had laid *his* hands upon them, the Holy Ghost came on them; and they spake with tongues, and prophesied.

⁷ And all the men were about twelve.

⁸ And he went into the synagogue, and spake boldly for the space of three months, disputing and persuading the things concerning the kingdom of God.

⁹ But when divers were hardened, and believed not, but spake evil of that way before the multitude, he departed from them, and separated the disciples, disputing daily in the school of one Tyrannus.

¹⁰ And this continued by the space of two years; so that all they which dwelt in Asia heard the word of the Lord Jesus, both Jews and Greeks.

The Sons of Sceva

And God wrought special miracles by the hands of Paul:

¹² so that from his body were brought unto the sick handkerchiefs or aprons, and the diseases departed from them, and the evil spirits went out of them.

¹³ Then certain of the vagabond Jews, exorcists, took upon them to call over them which had evil spirits the name of the Lord Jesus, saying, We adjure you by Jesus whom Paul preacheth.

¹⁴ And there were seven sons of *one* Sceva, a Jew, *and* chief of the priests, which did so.

¹⁵ And the evil spirit answered and said, Jesus I know, and Paul I know; but who are ye?

¹⁶ And the man in whom the evil spirit was leaped on them, and overcame them, and prevailed against them, so that they fled out of that house naked and wounded.

¹⁷ And this was known to all the Jews and Greeks also dwelling at Ephesus; and fear fell on them all, and the name of the Lord Jesus was magnified.

¹⁸ And many that believed came, and confessed, and shewed their deeds.

¹⁹ Many of them also which used curious arts brought their books together, and burned them before all *men*: and they counted the price of them, and found *it* fifty thousand *pieces* of silver.

²⁰ So mightily grew the word of God and prevailed.

²¹ After these things were ended, Paul purposed in the spirit, when he had passed through Macedonia and

Achaia, to go to Jerusalem, saying, After I have been there, I must also see Rome.

²² So he sent into Macedonia two of them that ministered unto him, Timothy and Erastus; but he himself stayed in Asia for a season.

OLD TESTAMENT READING

*A*nd Jehoiada made a covenant between the LORD and the king and the people, that they should be the LORD'S people; between the king also and the people.

¹⁸ And all the people of the land went into the house of Baal, and brake it down; his altars and his images brake they in pieces thoroughly, and slew Mattan the priest of Baal before the altars. And the priest appointed officers over the house of the LORD.

2 Kings 11:17–18

INSIGHTS

*W*hen I was a boy, each Saturday my father would make a list of chores for me to do before I could go and play. When he came home in the evening, he would take the list and—walking with me beside him—check how each job had been done. Sometimes he would point out a hidden, unswept corner that I had missed or find a small, untrimmed area of the yard that I had overlooked. When he did so, I would take a brush or clippers right then and finish the job properly. And you can be sure that, the next week, I would remember to carefully check those places I'd missed.

In checking on my work, my father was not being unkind or critical of what I'd done. He was helping me learn to do a job right the first time. And when I did, he would always encourage me and say, "That's good work, son."

That's how we should be with the Lord. We need to learn to be quick to take care of everything we see on the Father's "list" in his Word and then be open and ready for him to point out the things we have overlooked or neglected. We must offer daily confession, both for known sins that blot a day's activities and for sins we overlooked.

When we do these things, we know that through the blood of Christ we have instant and complete forgiveness: "If we confess our sins to him, he can be depended on to forgive us and to cleanse us from every wrong" (1 John 1:9).

"Hidden corners" do slip by unnoticed, and there are many believers caught up in sinful habits that at first they don't even recognize as sin. We might find, as we open to the Lord, that he begins to confront and adjust a pattern of our relationships, an aspect of our daily activities or entertainment, or some continued practice from childhood. We need to bring all aspects of our lives, regardless of what the world says is right or acceptable, under the searching eyes of the Lord.

Jack Hayford

APPLICATION

*W*hat happens when God's people turn away from sin and truly seek to obey him? These readings show that God's people must continually put away their hidden sins and follow God more diligently. What sins in your life need to be put away?

MONDAY

God Can Defeat Those Who Stir Up Trouble for His People

Acts 19:23—20:6

Trouble in Ephesus

*A*nd the same time there arose no small stir about that way.

[24] For a certain *man* named Demetrius, a silversmith, which made silver shrines for Diana, brought no small gain unto the craftsmen;

[25] whom he called together with the workmen of like occupation, and said, Sirs, ye know that by this craft we have our wealth.

[26] Moreover ye see and hear, that not alone at Ephesus, but almost throughout all Asia, this Paul hath persuaded and turned away much people, saying that they be no gods, which are made with hands:

[27] so that not only this our craft is in danger to be set at nought; but also that the temple of the great goddess Diana should be despised, and her magnificence should be destroyed, whom all Asia and the world worshippeth.

[28] And when they heard *these sayings*, they were full of wrath, and cried out, saying, Great *is* Diana of the Ephesians.

[29] And the whole city was filled with confusion: and having caught Gaius and Aristarchus, men of Macedonia, Paul's companions in travel, they rushed with one accord into the theatre.

[30] And when Paul would have entered in unto the people, the disciples suffered him not.

[31] And certain of the chief of Asia, which were his friends, sent unto him, desiring *him* that he would not adventure himself into the theatre.

[32] Some therefore cried one thing, and some another: for the assembly was confused; and the more part knew not wherefore they were come together.

[33] And they drew Alexander out of the multitude, the Jews putting him forward. And Alexander beckoned with the hand, and would have made his defense unto the people.

[34] But when they knew that he was a Jew, all with one voice about the space of two hours cried out, Great *is* Diana of the Ephesians.

[35] And when the townclerk had appeased the people, he said, *Ye* men of Ephesus, what man is there that knoweth not how that the city of the Ephesians is a worshipper of the great goddess Diana, and of the *image* which fell down from Jupiter?

[36] Seeing then that these things cannot be spoken against, ye ought to be quiet, and to do nothing rashly.

[37] For ye have brought hither these men, which are neither robbers of churches, nor yet blasphemers of your goddess.

[38] Wherefore if Demetrius, and the craftsmen which are with him, have a matter against any man, the law is open, and there are deputies: let them implead one another.

[39] But if ye inquire any thing concerning other matters, it shall be determined in a lawful assembly.

[40] For we are in danger to be called in question for this day's uproar, there being no cause whereby we may give an account of this concourse.

⁴¹ And when he had thus spoken, he dismissed the assembly.

Paul in Macedonia and Greece

20 And after the uproar was ceased, Paul called unto *him* the disciples, and embraced *them*, and departed for to go into Macedonia.

² and when he had gone over those parts, and had given them much exhortation, he came into Greece,

³ and *there* abode three months. And when the Jews laid wait for him, as he was about to sail into Syria, he purposed to return through Macedonia.

⁴ And there accompanied him into Asia Sopater of Beroea; and of the Thessalonians, Aristarchus and Secundus; and Gaius of Derbe, and Timothy; and of Asia, Tychicus and Trophimus.

⁵ These going before tarried for us at Troas.

⁶ And we sailed away from Philippi after the days of unleavened bread, and came unto them to Troas in five days; where we abode seven days.

OLD TESTAMENT READING

*I*f *it had* not *been* the LORD who was on our side, when men rose up against us:

³ then they had swallowed us up quick, when their wrath was kindled against us.

⁶ Blessed *be* the LORD, who hath not given us *as* a prey to their teeth.

⁷ Our soul is escaped as a bird out of the snare of the fowlers: the snare is broken, and we are escaped.

⁸ Our help is in the name of the LORD, who made heaven and earth.

Psalm 124:2–3, 6–8

INSIGHTS

A mighty fortress is our God,
A bulwark never failing;
Our helper He amid the flood
Of mortal ills prevailing.
For still our ancient foe
Doth seek to work us woe—
His craft and pow'r are great,
And, armed with cruel hate,
On earth is not his equal.

Did we in our own strength con-
fide,
Our striving would be losing,
Were not the right man on our
side,
The man of God's own choosing.
Dost ask who that may be?
Christ Jesus, it is He—
Lord Sabaoth His name,
From age to age the same,
And He must win the battle.

And tho this world, with devils
filled,
Should threaten to undo us,
We will not fear, for God hath
willed
His truth to triumph thru us.
The prince of darkness grim,
We tremble not for him—
His rage we can endure,
For lo, his doom is sure:
One little word shall fell him.

Martin Luther

PAUSE FOR REFLECTION

What motivated Demetrius to start the trouble in Ephesus? For what other reasons do people cause trouble for God's people? What comfort and strength do you find in Psalm 124 and Luther's famous hymn?

TUESDAY

Serving God Is Most Important . . . Even If We Risk Our Lives

Acts 20:7–38

Paul's Last Visit to Troas

*A*nd upon the first *day* of the week, when the disciples came together to break bread, Paul preached unto them, ready to depart on the morrow; and continued his speech until midnight.

[8] And there were many lights in the upper chamber, where they were gathered together.

[9] And there sat in a window a certain young man named Eutychus, being fallen into a deep sleep: and as Paul was long preaching, he sunk down with sleep, and fell down from the third loft, and was taken up dead.

[10] And Paul went down, and fell on him, and embracing *him* said, Trouble not yourselves; for his life is in him.

[11] When he therefore was come up again, and had broken bread, and eaten, and talked a long while, even till break of day, so he departed.

[12] And they brought the young man alive, and were not a little comforted.

[13] And we went before to ship, and sailed unto Assos, there intending to take in Paul: for so had he appointed, minding himself to go afoot.

[14] And when he met with us at Assos, we took him in, and came to Mitylene.

[15] And we sailed thence, and came the next *day* over against Chios; and the next *day* we arrived at Samos,

and tarried at Trogyllium; and the next *day* we came to Miletus.

[16] For Paul had determined to sail by Ephesus, because he would not spend the time in Asia: for he hasted, if it were possible for him, to be at Jerusalem the day of Pentecost.

The Elders from Ephesus

*A*nd from Miletus he sent to Ephesus, and called the elders of the church.

[18] And when they were come to him, he said unto them, Ye know, from the first day that I came into Asia, after what manner I have been with you at all seasons,

[19] serving the Lord with all humility of mind, and with many tears, and temptations, which befell me by the lying in wait of the Jews:

[20] *and* how I kept back nothing that was profitable *unto you*, but have showed you, and have taught you publicly, and from house to house,

[21] testifying both to the Jews, and also to the Greeks, repentance toward God, and faith toward our Lord Jesus Christ.

[22] And now, behold, I go bound in the spirit unto Jerusalem, not knowing the things that shall befall me there:

[23] save that the Holy Ghost witnesseth in every city, saying that bonds and afflictions abide me.

[24] But none of these things move me, neither count I my life dear unto myself, so that I might finish my course with joy, and the ministry, which I have received of the Lord Jesus, to testify the gospel of the grace of God.

[25] And now, behold, I know that ye all, among whom I have gone preaching the kingdom of God, shall see my face no more.

²⁶ Wherefore I take you to record this day, that I *am* pure from the blood of all *men*.

²⁷ For I have not shunned to declare unto you all the counsel of God.

²⁸ Take heed therefore unto yourselves, and to all the flock, over the which the Holy Ghost hath made you overseers, to feed the church of God, which he hath purchased with his own blood.

²⁹ For I know this, that after my departing shall grievous wolves enter in among you, not sparing the flock.

³⁰ Also of your own selves shall men arise, speaking perverse things, to draw away disciples after them.

³¹ Therefore watch, and remember, that by the space of three years I ceased not to warn every one night and day with tears.

³² And now, brethren, I commend you to God, and to the word of his grace, which is able to build you up, and to give you an inheritance among all them which are sanctified.

³³ I have coveted no man's silver, or gold, or apparel.

³⁴ Yea, ye yourselves know, that these hands have ministered unto my necessities, and to them that were with me.

³⁵ I have showed you all things, how that so laboring ye ought to support the weak, and to remember the words of the Lord Jesus, how he said, It is more blessed to give than to receive.

³⁶ And when he had thus spoken, he kneeled down, and prayed with them all.

³⁷ And they all wept sore, and fell on Paul's neck, and kissed him,

³⁸ sorrowing most of all for the words which he spake, that they should see his face no more. And they accompanied him unto the ship.

OLD TESTAMENT READING

*A*nd behold, the word of the LORD *came* to him, and he said unto him, What doest thou here, Elijah?

¹⁰ And he said, I have been very jealous for the LORD God of hosts: for the children of Israel have forsaken thy covenant, thrown down thine altars, and slain thy prophets with the sword; and I, *even* I only, am left; and they seek my life, to take it away.

1 Kings 19:9b-10

INSIGHTS

*D*avid Brainerd, early missionary to the Indians of the United States, was so consumed with a passion for the glory of Christ in the salvation of souls that he claimed: "I cared not how or where I lived, or what hardships I endured, so that I could but gain souls for Christ."

Our Lord was gripped by a master ambition that integrated the whole of His life. It can be summarized in a single sentence: "I have come to do your will, O God" (Hebrews 10:7). When at life's end He offered His wonderful high-priestly prayer, He was able to report the complete achievement of this ambition: "I have brought you glory on earth by completing the work you gave me to do" (John 17:4).

J. Oswald Sanders

PAUSE FOR REFLECTION

*W*hat was Paul's most important goal in life? What sustains a person who makes such a commitment?

WEDNESDAY

God Requires
Uncompromising Faithfulness

Acts 21:1–25

Paul Goes to Jerusalem

21 And it came to pass, that after we were gotten from them, and had launched, we came with a straight course unto Coos, and the *day* following unto Rhodes, and from thence unto Patara:

2 and finding a ship sailing over unto Phoenicia, we went aboard, and set forth.

3 Now when we had discovered Cyprus, we left it on the left hand, and sailed into Syria, and landed at Tyre: for there the ship was to unlade her burden.

4 And finding disciples, we tarried there seven days: who said to Paul through the Spirit, that he should not go up to Jerusalem.

5 And when we had accomplished those days, we departed and went our way; and they all brought us on our way, with wives and children, till *we were* out of the city: and we kneeled down on the shore, and prayed.

6 And when we had taken our leave one of another, we took ship; and they returned home again.

7 And when we had finished *our* course from Tyre, we came to Ptolemais, and saluted the brethren, and abode with them one day.

8 And the next *day* we that were of Paul's company departed, and came unto Caesarea; and we entered into the house of Philip the evangelist, which was *one* of the seven; and abode with him.

9 And the same man had four daughters, virgins, which did prophesy.

10 And as we tarried *there* many days, there came down from Judea a certain prophet, named Agabus.

11 And when he was come unto us, he took Paul's girdle, and bound his own hands and feet, and said, Thus saith the Holy Ghost, So shall the Jews at Jerusalem bind the man that owneth this girdle, and shall deliver *him* into the hands of the Gentiles.

12 And when we heard these things, both we, and they of that place, besought him not to go up to Jerusalem.

13 Then Paul answered, What mean ye to weep and to break mine heart? for I am ready not to be bound only, but also to die at Jerusalem for the name of the Lord Jesus.

14 And when he would not be persuaded, we ceased, saying, The will of the Lord be done.

15 And after those days we took up our carriages, and went up to Jerusalem.

16 There went with us also *certain* of the disciples of Caesarea, and brought with them one Mnason of Cyprus, an old disciple, with whom we should lodge.

Paul Visits James

*A*nd when we were come to Jerusalem, the brethren received us gladly.

18 And the *day* following Paul went in with us unto James; and all the elders were present.

19 And when he had saluted them, he declared particularly what things God had wrought among the Gentiles by his ministry.

²⁰ And when they heard *it*, they glorified the Lord, and said unto him, Thou seest, brother, how many thousands of Jews there are which believe; and they are all zealous of the law:

²¹ and they are informed of thee, that thou teachest all the Jews which are among the Gentiles to forsake Moses, saying that they ought not to circumcise *their* children, neither to walk after the customs.

²² What is it therefore? the multitude must needs come together: for they will hear that thou art come.

²³ Do therefore this that we say to thee: We have four men which have a vow on them;

²⁴ them take, and purify thyself with them, and be at charges with them, that they may shave *their* heads: and all may know that those things, whereof they were informed concerning thee, are nothing; but *that* thou thyself also walkest orderly, and keepest the law.

²⁵ As touching the Gentiles which believe, we have written *and* concluded that they observe no such thing, save only that they keep themselves from *things* offered to idols, and from blood, and from strangled, and from fornication.

OLD TESTAMENT READING

*A*nd the Lord said unto Moses, Go, get thee down; for thy people, which thou broughtest out of the land of Egypt, have corrupted *themselves*.

²⁶ Then Moses stood in the gate of the camp, and said, Who *is* on the Lord's side? *let him come* unto me. And all the sons of Levi gathered themselves together unto him.

²⁷ And he said unto them, Thus saith the Lord God of Israel, Put every man his sword by his side, *and* go in and out from gate to gate throughout the camp, and slay every man his brother, and every man his companion, and every man his neighbor.

²⁹ For Moses had said, Consecrate yourselves today to the Lord, even every man upon his son, and upon his brother; that he may bestow upon you a blessing this day.

Exodus 32:7, 26–27, 29

INSIGHTS

*P*ray God to send a few men with "grit" in them; men, who when they know a thing to be right, will not turn away, or turn aside, or stop; men who will persevere all the more because there are difficulties to meet or foes to encounter; who stand all the more true to their Master because they are opposed; who, the more they are thrust into the fire, the hotter they become; who, just like the bow, the further the string is drawn the more powerfully it sends forth its arrows, and so the more they are trodden upon, the more mighty will they become in the cause of truth against error.

Charles Spurgeon

PAUSE FOR REFLECTION

*A*re you so convinced of the reality of God in your life that you would risk your life to serve him?

THURSDAY

Proclaim God's Truth Boldly

Acts 21:26—22:5

*T*hen Paul took the men, and the next day purifying himself with them entered into the temple, to signify the accomplishment of the days of purification, until that an offering should be offered for every one of them.

²⁷ And when the seven days were almost ended, the Jews which were of Asia, when they saw him in the temple, stirred up all the people, and laid hands on him,

²⁸ crying out, Men of Israel, help: This is the man, that teacheth all *men* every where against the people, and the law, and this place: and further brought Greeks also into the temple, and hath polluted this holy place.

²⁹ (For they had seen before with him in the city Trophimus an Ephesian, whom they supposed that Paul had brought into the temple.)

³⁰ And all the city was moved, and the people ran together: and they took Paul, and drew him out of the temple: and forthwith the doors were shut.

³¹ And as they went about to kill him, tidings came unto the chief captain of the band, that all Jerusalem was in an uproar.

³² who immediately took soldiers and centurions, and ran down unto them: and when they saw the chief captain and the soldiers, they left beating of Paul.

³³ Then the chief captain came near, and took him, and commanded *him* to be bound with two chains; and demanded who he was, and what he had done.

³⁴ And some cried one thing, some another, among the multitude: and when he could not know the certainty for the tumult, he commanded him to be carried into the castle.

³⁵ And when he came upon the stairs, so it was, that he was borne of the soldiers for the violence of the people.

³⁶ For the multitude of the people followed after, crying, Away with him.

³⁷ And as Paul was to be led into the castle, he said unto the chief captain, May I speak unto thee? Who said, Canst thou speak Greek?

³⁸ Art not thou that Egyptian, which before these days madest an uproar, and leddest out into the wilderness four thousand men that were murderers?

³⁹ But Paul said, I am a man *which am* a Jew of Tarsus, *a city* in Cilicia, a citizen of no mean city: and, I beseech thee, suffer me to speak unto the people.

⁴⁰ And when he had given him license, Paul stood on the stairs, and beckoned with the hand unto the people. And when there was made a great silence, he spake unto *them* in the Hebrew tongue, saying,

Paul Speaks to the People

22 Men, brethren, and fathers, hear ye my defense *which I make* now unto you.

² (And when they heard that he spake in the Hebrew tongue to them, they kept the more silence: and he saith,)

³ I am verily a man *which am* a Jew, born in Tarsus, *a city* in Cilicia, yet brought up in this city at the feet of Gamaliel, *and* taught according to the perfect manner of the law of the fathers, and was zealous toward God, as ye all are this day.

⁴ And I persecuted this way unto the death, binding and delivering into prisons both men and women.

⁵ As also the high priest doth bear me witness, and all the estate of the elders: from whom also I received letters unto the brethren, and went to Damascus, to bring them which were there bound unto Jerusalem, for to be punished.

OLD TESTAMENT READING

*A*nd he said unto me, Son of man, I send thee to the children of Israel, to a rebellious nation that hath rebelled against me: they and their fathers have transgressed against me, *even* unto this very day.

⁴ For *they are* impudent children and stiffhearted. I do send thee unto them; and thou shalt say unto them, Thus saith the Lord GOD.

⁵ And they, whether they will hear, or whether they will forbear, (for they *are* a rebellious house,) yet shall know that there hath been a prophet among them.

⁶ And thou, son of man, be not afraid of them, neither be afraid of their words, though briers and thorns *be* with thee, and thou dost dwell among scorpions: be not afraid of their words, nor be dismayed at their looks, though they *be* a rebellious house.

Ezekiel 2:3–6

INSIGHTS

*J*ohan is young, tall, blond, and Dutch. . . . Gifted and handsome, Johan could have carved out a comfortable youth ministry in his native Netherlands—or most anywhere in the world, for that matter.

Comfort, however, isn't one of Johan's major goals. He chose to take the gospel of Christ to the bedouins and nomads near Israel's desolate Sinai desert. A forgotten people in one of the most desolate corners of the world.

Johan works by an oasis near the sea, attracting travelers and bedouins by offering hot meals, clothing, and first aid. . . .

From the bedouins, Johan learned it is considered worse than murder if you know of a water source and yet neglect to tell your fellow man.

Few of us will ever live in a wilderness like the one where young Johan has pitched his tent. Not many among us will ever proclaim salvation to desert nomads. But all around us, no matter where we reside or work, there are thirsty men and women. The neighbor down the street, the man at the service station, the boy who carries our groceries, the secretary who types and files, or even the distant aunt who occasionally comes by for visits.

If these people don't know Christ, they're going to die of thirst. . . .

Do you know the Source of living water? If you do, please don't withhold a drink from somebody who is thirsty.

It's not just a matter of hospitality. It's a matter of life and death.

Joni Eareckson Tada

APPLICATION

*W*hy did Paul and Ezekiel speak God's Word, even at great personal risk? To whom is God leading you to share Christ? Will you take the risk?

FRIDAY

*God Has Plans for
Those He Has Chosen*

Acts 22:6–29

*A*nd it came to pass, that, as I made my journey, and was come nigh unto Damascus about noon, suddenly there shone from heaven a great light round about me.

⁷ And I fell unto the ground, and heard a voice saying unto me, Saul, Saul, why persecutest thou me?

⁸ And I answered, Who art thou, Lord? And he said unto me, I am Jesus of Nazareth, whom thou persecutest.

⁹ And they that were with me saw indeed the light, and were afraid; but they heard not the voice of him that spake to me.

¹⁰ And I said, What shall I do, Lord? And the Lord said unto me, Arise, and go into Damascus; and there it shall be told thee of all things which are appointed for thee to do.

¹¹ And when I could not see for the glory of that light, being led by the hand of them that were with me, I came into Damascus.

¹² And one Ananias, a devout man according to the law, having a good report of all the Jews which dwelt *there*,
¹³ came unto me, and stood, and said unto me, Brother Saul, receive thy sight. And the same hour I looked up upon him.

¹⁴ And he said, The God of our fathers hath chosen thee, that thou shouldest know his will, and see that Just One, and shouldest hear the voice of his mouth.

¹⁵ For thou shalt be his witness unto all men of what thou hast seen and heard.

¹⁶ And now why tarriest thou? arise, and be baptized, and wash away thy sins, calling on the name of the Lord.

¹⁷ And it came to pass, that, when I was come again to Jerusalem, even while I prayed in the temple, I was in a trance;

¹⁸ and saw him saying unto me, Make haste, and get thee quickly out of Jerusalem: for they will not receive thy testimony concerning me.

¹⁹ And I said, Lord, they know that I imprisoned and beat in every synagogue them that believed on thee:

²⁰ and when the blood of thy martyr Stephen was shed, I also was standing by, and consenting unto his death, and kept the raiment of them that slew him.

²¹ And he said unto me, Depart: for I will send thee far hence unto the Gentiles.

²² And they gave him audience unto this word, and *then* lifted up their voices, and said, Away with such a *fellow* from the earth: for it is not fit that he should live.

²³ And as they cried out, and cast off *their* clothes, and threw dust into the air,

²⁴ the chief captain commanded him to be brought into the castle, and bade that he should be examined by scourging; that he might know wherefore they cried so against him.

²⁵ And as they bound him with thongs, Paul said unto the centurion that stood by, Is it lawful for you to scourge a man that is a Roman, and uncondemned?

²⁶ When the centurion heard *that*, he went and told the chief captain, saying, Take heed what thou doest; for this man is a Roman.

²⁷ Then the chief captain came, and said unto him, Tell me, art thou a Roman? He said, Yea.

²⁸ And the chief captain answered, With a great sum obtained I this freedom. And Paul said, But I was *free-born*.

²⁹ Then straightway they departed from him which should have examined him: and the chief captain also was afraid, after he knew that he was a Roman, and because he had bound him.

OLD TESTAMENT READING

*L*et all the earth fear the LORD: let all the inhabitants of the world stand in awe of him.

⁹ For he spake, and it was *done*; he commanded, and it stood fast.

¹⁰ The LORD bringeth the counsel of the heathen to nought: he maketh the devices of the people of none effect.

¹¹ The counsel of the LORD standeth for ever, the thoughts of his heart to all generations.

¹² Blessed *is* the nation whose God *is* the LORD; *and* the people *whom* he hath chosen for his own inheritance.

Psalm 33:8–12

A man's heart deviseth his way: but the LORD directeth his steps.

Proverbs 16:9

INSIGHTS

*G*od is at work in all the kaleidoscoping family transitions: not only in the high points but in the endings, beginnings, detours, dead ends, and in-between times. His powerful tools are not just the promotions and graduations but the failures and firings and losses and sicknesses and shocks and periods of boredom. In them all He's silently, busily, unceasingly encouraging, punishing, shaping. . . .

. . . And during all His working—all God's silent activity in the disappointments, surprises, delights, irritations—transformations are taking place. . . .

Do you feel as if nothing is happening . . . ?

I guess so does a lobster, encased in that ridiculous armor. As he grows it even gets crowded inside. But he sheds it fourteen times during his first year of life. Each shedding takes ten days, and each time in the period between shells—when he's naked, exposed, vulnerable—he grows about seven percent.

You feel stifled, unfulfilled? You don't know when you'll break out into change?

Wait for God.

Wait on God.

Wait with God.

Life is not fixed. Let it happen; don't rush it. "It is God who works in you to will and to act according to his good purpose. Do everything without complaining or arguing" (Phil. 2:13, 14). Keep your eyes fixed on Him, live in obedience as you see it, and then just be there.

Anne Ortlund

APPLICATION

*I*magine yourself as Paul. How would you have taken the news that God had very different plans than what you had chosen? Pray that you will trust God's plans and obey them as they are revealed to you.

WEEKEND

Be Brave; God Stands by His Own

Acts 22:30—23:22

Paul Speaks to Jewish Leaders

*O*n the morrow, because he would have known the certainty wherefore he was accused of the Jews, he loosed him from *his* bands, and commanded the chief priests and all their council to appear, and brought Paul down, and set him before them.

23 And Paul, earnestly beholding the council, said, Men *and* brethren, I have lived in all good conscience before God until this day.

2 And the high priest Ananias commanded them that stood by him to smite him on the mouth.

3 Then said Paul unto him, God shall smite thee, *thou* whited wall: for sittest thou to judge me after the law, and commandest me to be smitten contrary to the law?

4 And they that stood by said, Revilest thou God's high priest?

5 Then said Paul, I wist not, brethren, that he was the high priest: for it is written, Thou shalt not speak evil of the ruler of thy people.

6 But when Paul perceived that the one part were Sadducees, and the other Pharisees, he cried out in the council, Men *and* brethren, I am a Pharisee, the son of a Pharisee: of the hope and resurrection of the dead I am called in question.

7 And when he had so said, there arose a dissension between the Pharisees and the Sadducees: and the multitude was divided.

8 For the Sadducees say that there is no resurrection, neither angel, nor spirit: but the Pharisees confess both.

9 And there arose a great cry: and the scribes *that were* of the Pharisees' part arose, and strove, saying, We find no evil in this man: but if a spirit or an angel hath spoken to him, let us not fight against God.

10 And when there arose a great dissension, the chief captain, fearing lest Paul should have been pulled in pieces of them, commanded the soldiers to go down, and to take him by force from among them, and to bring *him* into the castle.

11 And the night following the Lord stood by him, and said, Be of good cheer, Paul: for as thou hast testified of me in Jerusalem, so must thou bear witness also at Rome.

12 And when it was day, certain of the Jews banded together, and bound themselves under a curse, saying that they would neither eat nor drink till they had killed Paul.

13 And they were more than forty which had made this conspiracy.

14 And they came to the chief priests and elders, and said, We have bound ourselves under a great curse, that we will eat nothing until we have slain Paul.

15 Now therefore ye with the council signify to the chief captain that he bring him down unto you tomorrow, as though ye would inquire something more perfectly concerning him: and we, or ever he come near, are ready to kill him.

16 And when Paul's sister's son heard of their lying in wait, he went and entered into the castle, and told Paul.

17 Then Paul called one of the centurions unto *him*, and said, Bring this young man unto the chief captain: for

he hath a certain thing to tell him.

[18] So he took him, and brought *him* to the chief captain, and said, Paul the prisoner called me unto *him*, and prayed me to bring this young man unto thee, who hath something to say unto thee.

[19] Then the chief captain took him by the hand, and went *with him* aside privately, and asked *him*, What is that thou hast to tell me?

[20] And he said, The Jews have agreed to desire thee that thou wouldest bring down Paul tomorrow into the council, as though they would inquire somewhat of him more perfectly.

[21] But do not thou yield unto them: for there lie in wait for him of them more than forty men, which have bound themselves with an oath, that they will neither eat nor drink till they have killed him: and now are they ready, looking for a promise from thee.

[22] So the chief captain *then* let the young man depart, and charged *him*, *See thou* tell no man that thou hast showed these things to me.

OLD TESTAMENT READING

*U*nto thee, O God, do we give thanks, *unto thee* do we give thanks: for *that* thy name is near thy wondrous works declare.

[9] But I will declare for ever. I will sing praises to the God of Jacob.

[10] All the horns of the wicked also will I cut off; *but* the horns of the righteous shall be exalted.

Psalm 75:1, 9–10

INSIGHTS

*N*ow on whom dost thou trust?" (2 Kings 18:20). Such was the challenge which the blatant Assyrian

field-marshal, Rab-shakeh, flung at the beleagured king Hezekiah, more than two-and-a-half millenniums ago. Little did he guess that before many more sunrises 185,000 of his proud army would be corpses, cut down by an invisible scythe of the Almighty! Hezekiah did not reply to Rab-shakeh, but despite the hopeless-looking circumstances his heart was fixed, trusting in Jehovah (18:5). This was his secret of victory.

Even so today, the first mark of the true Christian is reliance on Jehovah-Jesus. We rely on Him exclusively as the vicarious Sinbearer through whom we have the salvation of our souls.

But we are to rely on Him continually as our victorious Champion through whom we have victory in our daily life. . . . So long as we rely on Him we have victory. Temper, fear, lust, pride, envy, grudging, moodiness, impatience, despondency, worry; over all such we gain victory as we really rely on Jesus.

Again, we are to rely on Him as our vigilant Provider, who "supplies all our need" (Phil. 4:19; Ps. 34:22). He does not always employ ravens to feed His Elijahs, but by one means or another He sustains them if they really rely on Him.

J. Sydlow Baxter

ACTION POINT

*I*n what ways has the Lord stood next to you and encouraged you to be brave for his sake? For what in your life do you need confidence that he is standing with you? Pray for his protection. Trust him. He will supply the victory!

MONDAY

God Wants His People to Do What Is Right

Acts 23:23—24:16

Paul Is Sent to Caesarea

*A*nd he called unto *him* two centurions, saying, Make ready two hundred soldiers to go to Caesarea, and horsemen threescore and ten, and spearmen two hundred, at the third hour of the night;

²⁴ and provide *them* beasts, that they may set Paul on, and bring *him* safe unto Felix the governor.

²⁵ And he wrote a letter after this manner:

²⁶ Claudius Lysias unto the most excellent governor Felix *sendeth* greeting.

²⁷ This man was taken of the Jews, and should have been killed of them: then came I with an army, and rescued him, having understood that he was a Roman.

²⁸ And when I would have known the cause wherefore they accused him, I brought him forth into their council:

²⁹ whom I perceived to be accused of questions of their law, but to have nothing laid to his charge worthy of death or of bonds.

³⁰ And when it was told me how that the Jews laid wait for the man, I sent straightway to thee, and gave commandment to his accusers also to say before thee what *they had* against him. Farewell.

³¹ Then the soldiers, as it was commanded them, took Paul, and brought *him* by night to Antipatris.

³² On the morrow they left the horsemen to go with him, and returned to the castle:

³³ who, when they came to Caesarea, and delivered the epistle to the governor, presented Paul also before him.

³⁴ And when the governor had read *the letter*, he asked of what province he was. And when he understood that *he was* of Cilicia;

³⁵ I will hear thee, said he, when thine accusers are also come. And he commanded him to be kept in Herod's judgment hall.

Paul Is Accused

24 And after five days Ananias the high priest descended with the elders, and *with* a certain orator *named* Tertullus, who informed the governor against Paul.

² And when he was called forth, Tertullus began to accuse *him*, saying, Seeing that by thee we enjoy great quietness, and that very worthy deeds are done unto this nation by thy providence,

³ we accept *it* always, and in all places, most noble Felix, with all thankfulness.

⁴ Notwithstanding, that I be not further tedious unto thee, I pray thee that thou wouldest hear us of thy clemency a few words.

⁵ For we have found this man *a* pestilent *fellow*, and a mover of sedition among all the Jews throughout the world, and a ringleader of the sect of the Nazarenes:

⁶ who also hath gone about to profane the temple: whom we took, and would have judged according to our law.

⁷ But the chief captain Lysias came *upon us*, and with great violence took *him* away out of our hands,

⁸commanding his accusers to come unto thee: by examining of whom thyself mayest take knowledge of all these things, whereof we accuse him.

⁹And the Jews also assented, saying that these things were so.

¹⁰Then Paul, after that the governor had beckoned unto him to speak, answered, Forasmuch as I know that thou hast been of many years a judge unto this nation, I do the more cheerfully answer for myself:

¹¹because that thou mayest understand, that there are yet but twelve days since I went up to Jerusalem for to worship.

¹²And they neither found me in the temple disputing with any man, neither raising up the people, neither in the synagogues, nor in the city:

¹³neither can they prove the things whereof they now accuse me.

¹⁴But this I confess unto thee, that after the way which they call heresy, so worship I the God of my fathers, believing all things which are written in the law and in the prophets:

¹⁵and have hope toward God, which they themselves also allow, that there shall be a resurrection of the dead, both of the just and unjust.

¹⁶And herein do I exercise myself, to have always a conscience void of offense toward God, and *toward* men.

OLD TESTAMENT READING

*A*nd in every work that he began in the service of the house of God, and in the law, and in the commandments, to seek his God, he did *it* with all his heart, and prospered.

2 Chronicles 31:21

INSIGHTS

*F*aithfully pleasing God is an activity, not just a nice set of beliefs. It must be a way of life.

. . . Twenty years ago, people were asking the question: Does God exist? Today that question has changed to: What difference does He make? The answer for too many people is: Not much. Even for many people who have an enormous amount of Bible knowledge, God makes little difference in how they actually live their lives.

. . . If Christ doesn't make any difference in my ethics and values at my job; if He doesn't affect my speech and attitudes toward coworkers; . . . if He makes absolutely no difference in the way I live and work, then pray tell, what difference does He make?! What's the point of playing a religious game that is all talk and no action?

I take the matter of obedience as an action quite seriously. I challenge you to do the same. Whenever you're exposed to Scripture, ask yourself: How can I apply this to my life? What practical thing can I do to embed this truth in my attitude, character, and behavior? Where does it need to make a difference? That's a commitment to life-change.

Doug Sherman
William Hendricks

ACTION POINT

*W*hy did Paul try to do what was right before God and men? Pray that you will give yourself fully to obeying God's commands!

TUESDAY

The Unrighteous Fear God's Judgment

Acts 24:17—25:12

Now after many years I came to bring alms to my nation, and offerings.

18 Whereupon certain Jews from Asia found me purified in the temple, neither with multitude, nor with tumult.

19 Who ought to have been here before thee, and object, if they had ought against me.

20 Or else let these same *here* say, if they have found any evil doing in me, while I stood before the council,

21 except it be for this one voice, that I cried standing among them, Touching the resurrection of the dead I am called in question by you this day.

22 And when Felix heard these things, having more perfect knowledge of *that* way, he deferred them, and said, When Lysias the chief captain shall come down, I will know the uttermost of your matter.

23 And he commanded a centurion to keep Paul, and to let *him* have liberty, and that he should forbid none of his acquaintance to minister or come unto him.

Paul Speaks to Felix and His Wife

And after certain days, when Felix came with his wife Drusilla, which was a Jewess, he sent for Paul, and heard him concerning the faith in Christ.

25 And as he reasoned of righteousness, temperance, and judgment to come, Felix trembled, and answered, Go thy way for this time; when I have a convenient season, I will call for thee.

26 He hoped also that money should have been given him of Paul, that he might loose him: wherefore he sent for him the oftener, and communed with him.

27 But after two years Porcius Festus came into Felix' room: and Felix, willing to show the Jews a pleasure, left Paul bound.

Paul Asks to See Caesar

25 Now when Festus was come into the province, after three days he ascended from Caesarea to Jerusalem.

2 Then the high priest and the chief of the Jews informed him against Paul, and besought him,

3 and desired favor against him, that he would send for him to Jerusalem, laying wait in the way to kill him.

4 But Festus answered, that Paul should be kept at Caesarea, and that he himself would depart shortly *thither.*

5 Let them therefore, said he, which among you are able, go down with *me*, and accuse this man, if there be any wickedness in him.

6 And when he had tarried among them more than ten days, he went down unto Caesarea; and the next day sitting on the judgment seat commanded Paul to be brought.

7 And when he was come, the Jews which came down from Jerusalem stood round about, and laid many and grievous complaints against Paul, which they could not prove.

8 While he answered for himself, Neither against the law of the Jews, neither against the temple, nor yet

against Caesar, have I offended any thing at all.

⁹ But Festus, willing to do the Jews a pleasure, answered Paul, and said, Wilt thou go up to Jerusalem, and there be judged of these things before me?

¹⁰ Then said Paul, I stand at Caesar's judgment seat, where I ought to be judged: to the Jews have I done no wrong, as thou very well knowest.

¹¹ For if I be an offender, or have committed any thing worthy of death, I refuse not to die: but if there be none of these things whereof these accuse me, no man may deliver me unto them. I appeal unto Caesar.

¹² Then Festus, when he had conferred with the council, answered, Hast thou appealed unto Caesar? unto Caesar shalt thou go.

OLD TESTAMENT READING

*A*nd the eyes of them both were opened, and they knew that they *were* naked; and they sewed fig leaves together, and made themselves aprons.

⁸ And they heard the voice of the LORD God walking in the garden in the cool of the day: and Adam and his wife hid themselves from the presence of the LORD God amongst the trees of the garden.

⁹ And the LORD God called unto Adam, and said unto him, Where *art* thou?

¹⁰ And he said, I heard thy voice in the garden, and I was afraid, because I *was* naked; and I hid myself.

Genesis 3:7–10

INSIGHTS

If our fathers emphasized God's "awful purity" at the expense of His

love, we have emphasized His love at the expense of His "awful purity." We delight in these days to say, "Gentle, gentle, gentle, is the God and Father." We have almost forgotten that cherubim and seraphim, with veiled faces, continually cry, "Holy, holy, holy is the Lord of Hosts."

In our absorption in the thought of God as Father, we have almost lost sight of the fact that He is the Holy Sovereign, ruling the world in righteousness. The result has been that to a large extent we have lost the sense of religious awe, of reverence, and of godly fear. . . .

To believe that an Almighty God is on the throne, working out His own holy and perfect and acceptable righteousness—is there not enough in that to fill the hearts of sinful men with "godly fear"? . . .

The Puritan's religion was a serious religion. He was afraid of God—afraid of Him in a worthy sense. He conceived of God as with him and about him always, and he was afraid of sinning against His holiness.

And is there not enough in the mere realization of the fact that a Holy God sits upon the throne, a God who is actively and unceasingly asserting His holiness—is there not enough in that one fact to make us, who are so prone to sin, serious and fearful?

John Jones

ACTION POINT

*H*ow do you respond to God's insistence on purity and his declarations of coming judgment? Pray that God will convince you of his holiness and your need for him!

WEDNESDAY

The Testimony of
a Blameless Life

Acts 25:13—26:8

Paul Before King Agrippa

*A*nd after certain days king Agrippa and Bernice came unto Caesarea to salute Festus.

14 And when they had been there many days, Festus declared Paul's cause unto the king, saying, There is a certain man left in bonds by Felix:

15 about whom, when I was at Jerusalem, the chief priests and the elders of the Jews informed *me*, desiring *to have* judgment against him.

16 To whom I answered, It is not the manner of the Romans to deliver any man to die, before that he which is accused have the accusers face to face, and have license to answer for himself concerning the crime laid against him.

17 Therefore, when they were come hither, without any delay on the morrow I sat on the judgment seat, and commanded the man to be brought forth.

18 Against whom when the accusers stood up, they brought none accusation of such things as I supposed:

19 but had certain questions against him of their own superstition, and of one Jesus, which was dead, whom Paul affirmed to be alive.

20 And because I doubted of such manner of questions, I asked *him* whether he would go to Jerusalem, and there be judged of these matters.

21 But when Paul had appealed to be reserved unto the hearing of Augustus, I commanded him to be kept till I might send him to Caesar.

22 Then Agrippa said unto Festus, I would also hear the man myself. Tomorrow, said he, thou shalt hear him.

23 And on the morrow, when Agrippa was come, and Bernice, with great pomp, and was entered into the place of hearing, with the chief captains, and principal men of the city, at Festus' commandment Paul was brought forth.

24 And Festus said, King Agrippa, and all men which are here present with us, ye see this man, about whom all the multitude of the Jews have dealt with me, both at Jerusalem, and *also* here, crying that he ought not to live any longer.

25 But when I found that he had committed nothing worthy of death, and that he himself hath appealed to Augustus, I have determined to send him.

26 Of whom I have no certain thing to write unto my lord. Wherefore I have brought him forth before you, and specially before thee, O king Agrippa, that, after examination had, I might have somewhat to write.

27 For it seemeth to me unreasonable to send a prisoner, and not withal to signify the crimes *laid* against him.

Paul Defends Himself

26 Then Agrippa said unto Paul, Thou art permitted to speak for thyself. Then Paul stretched forth the hand, and answered for himself:

2 I think myself happy, king Agrippa, because I shall answer for myself this day before thee touching all the

things whereof I am accused of the Jews:

³ especially *because I know* thee to be expert in all customs and questions which are among the Jews: wherefore I beseech thee to hear me patiently.

⁴ My manner of life from my youth, which was at the first among mine own nation at Jerusalem, know all the Jews;

⁵ which knew me from the beginning, if they would testify, that after the most straitest sect of our religion I lived a Pharisee.

⁶ And now I stand and am judged for the hope of the promise made of God unto our fathers:

⁷ unto which *promise* our twelve tribes, instantly serving *God* day and night, hope to come. For which hope's sake, king Agrippa, I am accused of the Jews.

⁸ Why should it be thought a thing incredible with you, that God should raise the dead?

OLD TESTAMENT READING

*T*he LORD rewarded me according to my righteousness; according to the cleanness of my hands hath he recompensed me.

²² For I have kept the ways of the LORD, and have not wickedly departed from my God.

²³ For all his judgments *were* before me: and *as for* his statutes, I did not depart from them.

²⁴ I was also upright before him, and have kept myself from mine iniquity.

²⁵ Therefore the LORD hath recompensed me according to my righteousness; according to my cleanness in his eyesight.

2 Samuel 22:21–25

INSIGHTS

*W*e must show nonbelievers what it looks like to be at peace with ourselves, and to truly love other people. The best means of creating an interest in Christ and the Christian way of life is to so thoroughly live and enjoy it that others will want to know how they, too, can have it.

. . . Most Americans believe that you cannot tell a born-again Christian from nonbelievers because there is no difference in the way they live. The only distinction, people say, is that Christians are more religious, more fanatical or more closed-minded. There is no widespread sense that the religious experience of Christians has changed the fabric of our thinking or the nature of our life-styles (other than requiring regular participation in church activities).

To convince a hardened and cynical world that we are not just different, but better off for those differences, we must allow them to see how our struggles in life have been altered for the better as a result of our relationship with Christ.

George Barna

APPLICATION

*H*ow might Paul's testimony to King Agrippa have been different if he hadn't been so careful to live in a way that honored God? Is living in a way that pleases God most important to you? Pray that your life will make a positive difference in the world around you!

THURSDAY

Called to Be God's Witnesses

Acts 26:9–32

I verily thought with myself, that I ought to do many things contrary to the name of Jesus of Nazareth.

¹⁰ Which thing I also did in Jerusalem: and many of the saints did I shut up in prison, having received authority from the chief priests; and when they were put to death, I gave my voice against *them*.

¹¹ And I punished them oft in every synagogue, and compelled *them* to blaspheme; and being exceedingly mad against them, I persecuted *them* even unto strange cities.

¹² Whereupon as I went to Damascus with authority and commission from the chief priests,

¹³ at midday, O king, I saw in the way a light from heaven, above the brightness of the sun, shining round about me and them which journeyed with me.

¹⁴ And when we were all fallen to the earth, I heard a voice speaking unto me, and saying in the Hebrew tongue, Saul, Saul, why persecutest thou me? *it is* hard for thee to kick against the pricks.

¹⁵ And I said, Who art thou, Lord? And he said, I am Jesus whom thou persecutest.

¹⁶ But rise, and stand upon thy feet: for I have appeared unto thee for this purpose, to make thee a minister and a witness both of these things which thou hast seen, and of those things in the which I will appear unto thee;

¹⁷ delivering thee from the people, and *from* the Gentiles, unto whom now I send thee,

¹⁸ to open their eyes, *and* to turn *them* from darkness to light, and *from* the power of Satan unto God, that they may receive forgiveness of sins, and inheritance among them which are sanctified by faith that is in me.

¹⁹ Whereupon, O king Agrippa, I was not disobedient unto the heavenly vision:

²⁰ but showed first unto them of Damascus, and at Jerusalem, and throughout all the coasts of Judea, and *then* to the Gentiles, that they should repent and turn to God, and do works meet for repentance.

²¹ For these causes the Jews caught me in the temple, and went about to kill *me*.

²² Having therefore obtained help of God, I continue unto this day, witnessing both to small and great, saying none other things than those which the prophets and Moses did say should come:

²³ that Christ should suffer, *and* that he should be the first that should rise from the dead, and should show light unto the people, and to the Gentiles.

Paul Tries to Persuade Agrippa

*A*nd as he thus spake for himself, Festus said with a loud voice, Paul, thou art beside thyself; much learning doth make thee mad.

²⁵ But he said, I am not mad, most noble Festus; but speak forth the words of truth and soberness.

²⁶ For the king knoweth of these things, before whom also I speak freely: for I am persuaded that none of these things are hidden from him; for this thing was not done in a corner.

²⁷ King Agrippa, believest thou the prophets? I know that thou believest. ²⁸ Then Agrippa said unto Paul, Almost thou persuadest me to be a Christian.

²⁹ And Paul said, I would to God, that not only thou, but also all that hear me this day, were both almost, and altogether such as I am, except these bonds.

³⁰ And when he had thus spoken, the king rose up, and the governor, and Bernice, and they that sat with them:

³¹ and when they were gone aside, they talked between themselves, saying, This man doeth nothing worthy of death or of bonds.

³² Then said Agrippa unto Festus, This man might have been set at liberty, if he had not appealed unto Caesar.

OLD TESTAMENT READING

God Chose the Nation of Israel to Be His Witness

*W*ho *is* like unto thee, O LORD, among the gods? Who *is* like thee, glorious in holiness, fearful *in* praises, doing wonders?

¹² Thou stretchedst out thy right hand, the earth swallowed them.

¹³ Thou in thy mercy hast led forth the people *which* thou hast redeemed: thou hast guided *them* in thy strength unto thy holy habitation.

¹⁴ The people shall hear, *and* be afraid.

Exodus 15:11–14a

INSIGHTS

*T*he best instrument for evangelism is the ordinary church member bearing witness to a vital faith. It always has been; it always will be. . . .

There is a high probability that if you are a Christian, it is because a member of the church invited you and then some of the people of the church loved you into making a decision for Christ. Generally, people are led into a personal relationship with Christ because there have been church members who cared enough to talk to them and love them into the Kingdom. . . .

. . . Our lifestyle as Christians should be a testimony to the validity of our message, but if we had to be spiritually perfect in order to witness for Christ, no one would qualify. . . . According to Paul, we must share the gospel while we are still in the process of changing into truly Christianized people. He wanted us to know that if we wait until we are the kind of people we ought to be before witnessing, we will never get the evangelistic job done. As imperfect people who are heirs to the grace of God, we are called to invite people to join us as we strive together to become more and more like Christ.

Tony Campolo

APPLICATION

*H*ave you ever felt unworthy to be God's witness? Despite your feelings, how is God making his name known through you? Pray to be a diligent and faithful witness!

FRIDAY

We Can Trust God to Keep His Promises

Acts 27:1–26

Paul Sails for Rome

27 And when it was determined that we should sail into Italy, they delivered Paul and certain other prisoners unto *one* named Julius, a centurion of Augustus' band.

² And entering into a ship of Adramyttium, we launched, meaning to sail by the coasts of Asia; *one* Aristarchus, a Macedonian of Thessalonica, being with us.

³ And the next *day* we touched at Sidon. And Julius courteously entreated Paul, and gave *him* liberty to go unto his friends to refresh himself.

⁴ And when we had launched from thence, we sailed under Cyprus, because the winds were contrary.

⁵ And when we had sailed over the sea of Cilicia and Pamphylia, we came to Myra, *a city* of Lycia.

⁶ And there the centurion found a ship of Alexandria sailing into Italy; and he put us therein.

⁷ And when we had sailed slowly many days, and scarce were come over against Cnidus, the wind not suffering us, we sailed under Crete, over against Salmone;

⁸ and, hardly passing it, came unto a place which is called The fair havens; nigh whereunto was the city *of* Lasea.

⁹ Now when much time was spent, and when sailing was now dangerous, because the fast was now already past, Paul admonished *them*,

¹⁰ and said unto them, Sirs, I perceive that this voyage will be with hurt and much damage, not only of the lading and ship, but also of our lives.

¹¹ Nevertheless the centurion believed the master and the owner of the ship, more than those things which were spoken by Paul.

¹² And because the haven was not commodious to winter in, the more part advised to depart thence also, if by any means they might attain to Phoenix, *and there* to winter; *which is* a haven of Crete, and lieth toward the south west and north west.

The Storm

And when the south wind blew softly, supposing that they had obtained *their* purpose, loosing *thence*, they sailed close by Crete.

¹⁴ But not long after there arose against it a tempestuous wind, called Euroclydon.

¹⁵ And when the ship was caught, and could not bear up into the wind, we let *her* drive.

¹⁶ And running under a certain island which is called Clauda, we had much work to come by the boat:

¹⁷ which when they had taken up, they used helps, undergirding the ship; and, fearing lest they should fall into the quicksands, strake sail, and so were driven.

¹⁸ And we being exceedingly tossed with a tempest, the next *day* they lightened the ship;

¹⁹ and the third *day* we cast out with our own hands the tackling of the ship.

²⁰ And when neither sun nor stars in many days appeared, and no small tempest lay on *us*, all hope that we

should be saved was then taken away. ²¹ But after long abstinence, Paul stood forth in the midst of them, and said, Sirs, ye should have hearkened unto me, and not have loosed from Crete, and to have gained this harm and loss.

²² And now I exhort you to be of good cheer: for there shall be no loss of *any man's* life among you, but of the ship.

²³ For there stood by me this night the angel of God, whose I am, and whom I serve,

²⁴ saying, Fear not, Paul; thou must be brought before Caesar: and, lo, God hath given thee all them that sail with thee.

²⁵ Wherefore, sirs, be of good cheer: for I believe God, that it shall be even as it was told me.

²⁶ Howbeit we must be cast upon a certain island.

OLD TESTAMENT READING

*B*e strong and of a good courage: for unto this people shalt thou divide for an inheritance the land, which I sware unto their fathers to give them. ⁷ Only be thou strong and very courageous, that thou mayest observe to do according to all the law, which Moses my servant commanded thee: turn not from it *to* the right hand or *to* the left, that thou mayest prosper whithersoever thou goest.

Joshua 1:6–7

INSIGHTS

*T*he story of Jericho's conquest is a fine example of the completed promises of God. . . .

. . . On the seventh circuit of the seventh day the people shouted and the walls of Jericho fell down flat. The army of Israel entered the city unhindered and utterly destroyed all that was in the city, with one notable exception—the household of Rahab. Because they obeyed the Lord explicitly, the people saw two great promises of the Lord performed on the same day. The city of Jericho, the strongest outpost of the Canaanite defenses, had been utterly destroyed as God had promised. Likewise Rahab and her household had been spared destruction, as God had promised.

But there is one final promise of God that can be seen in the conquest of Jericho. . . . To show that God means business when He makes a promise, Joshua imprecated a solemn curse on anyone who would rebuild the now-destroyed Jericho. This curse was literally fulfilled in the fate of Heil, the Bethelite, who rebuilt Jericho in the reign of Ahab (about 925 B.C.). Heil's firstborn son, Abiram, died as he was laying the foundation for the rebuilding of Jericho. Also his youngest son, Segub, died while he was setting up the gates of the city (1 Kings 16:34). What God promises, God performs.

Whether the promise is for salvation, as in the case of Rahab, or for destruction, as in the case of Heil, the promises of God must never be taken lightly. Whatever God promises, God performs. You can count on it.

Woodrow Kroll

PAUSE FOR REFLECTION

*H*ow did Paul and Joshua respond to God's promises? When faced with great challenges, how well do you trust God's promises?

WEEKEND

God Saves His Own
to Accomplish His Purposes

Acts 27:27—28:10

*B*ut when the fourteenth night was come, as we were driven up and down in Adria, about midnight the shipmen deemed that they drew near to some country;

28 and sounded, and found *it* twenty fathoms: and when they had gone a little further, they sounded again, and found *it* fifteen fathoms.

29 Then fearing lest we should have fallen upon rocks, they cast four anchors out of the stern, and wished for the day.

30 And as the shipmen were about to flee out of the ship, when they had let down the boat into the sea, under color as though they would have cast anchors out of the foreship,

31 Paul said to the centurion and to the soldiers, Except these abide in the ship, ye cannot be saved.

32 Then the soldiers cut off the ropes of the boat, and let her fall off.

33 And while the day was coming on, Paul besought *them* all to take meat, saying, This day is the fourteenth day that ye have tarried and continued fasting, having taken nothing.

34 Wherefore I pray you to take *some* meat; for this is for your health: for there shall not a hair fall from the head of any of you.

35 And when he had thus spoken, he took bread, and gave thanks to God in presence of them all; and when he had broken *it*, he began to eat.

36 Then were they all of good cheer, and they also took *some* meat.

37 And we were in all in the ship two hundred threescore and sixteen souls.

38 And when they had eaten enough, they lightened the ship, and cast out the wheat into the sea.

The Ship Is Destroyed

*A*nd when it was day, they knew not the land: but they discovered a certain creek with a shore, into the which they were minded, if it were possible, to thrust in the ship.

40 And when they had taken up the anchors, they committed *themselves* unto the sea, and loosed the rudder bands, and hoised up the mainsail to the wind, and made toward shore.

41 And falling into a place where two seas met, they ran the ship aground; and the forepart stuck fast, and remained unmoveable, but the hinder part was broken with the violence of the waves.

42 And the soldiers' counsel was to kill the prisoners, lest any of them should swim out, and escape.

43 But the centurion, willing to save Paul, kept them from *their* purpose; and commanded that they which could swim should cast *themselves* first *into the sea*, and get to land:

44 and the rest, some on boards, and some on *broken pieces* of the ship. And so it came to pass, that they escaped all safe to land.

Paul on the Island of Melita

28 And when they were escaped, then they knew that the island was called Melita.

2 And the barbarous people showed us no little kindness: for they kindled a fire, and received us every one,

because of the present rain, and because of the cold.

³ And when Paul had gathered a bundle of sticks, and laid *them* on the fire, there came a viper out of the heat, and fastened on his hand. ⁴ And when the barbarians saw the *venomous* beast hang on his hand, they said among themselves, No doubt this man is a murderer, whom, though he hath escaped the sea, yet vengeance suffereth not to live. ⁵ And he shook off the beast into the fire, and felt no harm. ⁶ Howbeit they looked when he should have swollen, or fallen down dead suddenly: but after they had looked a great while, and saw no harm come to him, they changed their minds, and said that he was a god. ⁷ In the same quarters were possessions of the chief man of the island, whose name was Publius; who received us, and lodged us three days courteously. ⁸ And it came to pass, that the father of Publius lay sick of a fever and of a bloody flux: to whom Paul entered in, and prayed, and laid his hands on him, and healed him. ⁹ So when this was done, others also, which had diseases in the island, came, and were healed: ¹⁰ who also honored us with many honors; and when we departed, they laded *us* with such things as were necessary.

OLD TESTAMENT READING

So they took up Jonah, and cast him forth into the sea: and the sea ceased from her raging.

¹⁶ Then the men feared the LORD exceedingly, and offered a sacrifice unto the LORD, and made vows.

Jonah 1:15–16

INSIGHTS

Mary and Martha did not understand why Jesus waited until after Lazarus died before He came to them (John 11:21). The disciples did not understand why Jesus took them through Samaria, or why He waited at the well rather than go with them to buy food (John 4:8). . . . Today, we understand the reason for these things because we can see the end result.

After Jesus had raised Lazarus from the dead, Mary and Martha understood how the sickness and death of their brother had brought glory to God (John 11:43–45).

By the time they left Samaria, the disciples realized why they had to go through Samaria. A whole city, which otherwise would have been closed to them, heard the gospel and believed in Christ, all because Jesus talked to a woman while he waited at the well (John 4:39–41).

When difficulties come, we can know they have a purpose. . . . If we are in right relationship with God, we may not understand at the time, but we can know He will make all that happens to us work out for our good and His glory.

Lucille Sollenberger

ACTION POINT

Notice how God used each of these adventures at sea to bring glory to himself. Pray for faithful confidence in God's perfect plan, even when you face difficult situations.

MONDAY

*God's People Welcome All
Who Visit Them*

Acts 28:11–31

Paul Goes to Rome

*A*nd after three months we departed in a ship of Alexandria, which had wintered in the isle, whose sign was Castor and Pollux.

¹² And landing at Syracuse, we tarried *there* three days.

¹³ And from thence we fetched a compass, and came to Rhegium: and after one day the south wind blew, and we came the next day to Puteoli:

¹⁴ where we found brethren, and were desired to tarry with them seven days: and so we went toward Rome.

¹⁵ And from thence, when the brethren heard of us, they came to meet us as far as Appi-i forum, and The three taverns: whom when Paul saw, he thanked God, and took courage.

Paul in Rome

*A*nd when we came to Rome, the centurion delivered the prisoners to the captain of the guard: but Paul was suffered to dwell by himself with a soldier that kept him.

¹⁷ And it came to pass, that after three days Paul called the chief of the Jews together: and when they were come together, he said unto them, Men *and* brethren, though I have committed nothing against the people, or customs of our fathers, yet was I delivered prisoner from Jerusalem into the hands of the Romans:

¹⁸ who, when they had examined me, would have let *me* go, because there was no cause of death in me.

¹⁹ But when the Jews spake against *it*, I was constrained to appeal unto Caesar; not that I had ought to accuse my nation of.

²⁰ For this cause therefore have I called for you, to see *you,* and to speak with *you*: because that for the hope of Israel I am bound with this chain.

²¹ And they said unto him, We neither received letters out of Judea concerning thee, neither any of the brethren that came showed or spake any harm of thee.

²² But we desire to hear of thee what thou thinkest: for as concerning this sect, we know that every where it is spoken against.

²³ And when they had appointed him a day, there came many to him into *his* lodging; to whom he expounded and testified the kingdom of God, persuading them concerning Jesus, both out of the law of Moses, and *out of* the prophets, from morning till evening.

²⁴ And some believed the things which were spoken, and some believed not.

²⁵ And when they agreed not among themselves, they departed, after that Paul had spoken one word, Well spake the Holy Ghost by Isaiah the prophet unto our fathers,

²⁶ saying, Go unto this people, and say, Hearing ye shall hear, and shall not understand; and seeing ye shall see, and not perceive:

²⁷ for the heart of this people is waxed gross, and their ears are dull of hearing, and their eyes have they closed; lest they should see with *their* eyes, and hear with *their* ears,

and understand with *their* heart, and should be converted, and I should heal them.

[28] Be it known therefore unto you, that the salvation of God is sent unto the Gentiles, and *that* they will hear it.

[29] And when he had said these words, the Jews departed, and had great reasoning among themselves.

[30] And Paul dwelt two whole years in his own hired house, and received all that came in unto him,

[31] preaching the kingdom of God, and teaching those things which concern the Lord Jesus Christ, with all confidence, no man forbidding him.

OLD TESTAMENT READING

*A*nd the damsel ran, and told *them of* her mother's house these things.
[29] And Rebekah had a brother, and his name *was* Laban: and Laban ran out unto the man, unto the well.
[30b] He came unto the man; and, behold, he stood by the camels at the well.
[31] And he said, Come in, thou blessed of the LORD; wherefore standest thou without? for I have prepared the house, and room for the camels.
[32] And the man came into the house.

Genesis 24:28, 29, 30b–32a

INSIGHTS

*R*ecently I finally got around to inviting a couple from our home church over for Sunday lunch. Sandy and Mike are young college graduates with promising careers and an adorable new baby. They are busy people and had not yet gotten involved in our church. I was ashamed to discover that although they'd been members of our church

for nearly three years, ours was the first personal invitation they had received from anyone in our congregation. . . .

. . . In addition to providing examples of hospitality, Scripture gives us specific instructions to practice this kind of loving care for others. In his letters to Timothy and Titus, Paul listed it as a necessary qualification of an elder of the church. He combined encouragement and hospitality as important Christian traits in Titus 1:8–9. . . .

Paul's instructions in Romans 12:9–13 emphasize that this ministry of love in action belongs not just to elders, but should be a trademark of all believers. . . .

The emphasis in our practice of hospitality should be on how we give of ourselves to minister to others— not on how we perform to entertain others. The Bible commands us to carry out this ministry; it does not set up requirements for housing or meals. We do not need a large, beautifully decorated, immaculately tidy house in order to invite others into our home. "Breaking bread" with others does not require serving filet mignon or lobster tails. The issue is not spending money, but spending our time—not giving things, but giving ourselves. . . .

. . . Focus on people, not preparations. In the Lord's hands, a few loaves and fishes go a long way.

Rachael Crabb

PAUSE FOR REFLECTION

*D*o you think Paul, a prisoner, offered his guests luxurious accommodations? What do you think are the biblical standards for hospitality?

TUESDAY

All of Creation
Tells Us About God

Romans 1:1–27

1 Paul, a servant of Jesus Christ, called *to be* an apostle, separated unto the gospel of God,

2 (which he had promised afore by his prophets in the holy scriptures,)

3 concerning his Son Jesus Christ our Lord, which was made of the seed of David according to the flesh;

4 And declared *to be* the Son of God with power, according to the spirit of holiness, by the resurrection from the dead:

5 by whom we have received grace and apostleship, for obedience to the faith among all nations, for his name:

6 among whom are ye also the called of Jesus Christ:

7 To all that be in Rome, beloved of God, called *to be* saints: Grace to you and peace from God our Father, and the Lord Jesus Christ.

A Prayer of Thanks

*F*irst, I thank my God through Jesus Christ for you all, that your faith is spoken of throughout the whole world.

9 For God is my witness, whom I serve with my spirit in the gospel of his Son, that without ceasing I make mention of you always in my prayers;

10 making request, if by any means now at length I might have a prosperous journey by the will of God to come unto you.

11 For I long to see you, that I may impart unto you some spiritual gift, to the end ye may be established;

12 that is, that I may be comforted together with you by the mutual faith both of you and me.

13 Now I would not have you ignorant, brethren, that oftentimes I purposed to come unto you, (but was let hitherto,) that I might have some fruit among you also, even as among other Gentiles.

14 I am debtor both to the Greeks, and to the Barbarians; both to the wise, and to the unwise.

15 So, as much as in me is, I am ready to preach the gospel to you that are at Rome also.

16 For I am not ashamed of the gospel of Christ: for it is the power of God unto salvation to every one that believeth; to the Jew first, and also to the Greek.

17 For therein is the righteousness of God revealed from faith to faith: as it is written, The just shall live by faith.

All People Have Sinned

*F*or the wrath of God is revealed from heaven against all ungodliness and unrighteousness of men, who hold the truth in unrighteousness;

19 because that which may be known of God is manifest in them; for God hath showed *it* unto them.

20 For the invisible things of him from the creation of the world are clearly seen, being understood by the things that are made, *even* his eternal power and Godhead; so that they are without excuse:

21 because that, when they knew God, they glorified *him* not as God, neither were thankful; but became

vain in their imaginations, and their foolish heart was darkened.

22 Professing themselves to be wise, they became fools,

23 And changed the glory of the uncorruptible God into an image made like to corruptible man, and to birds, and fourfooted beasts, and creeping things.

24 Wherefore God also gave them up to uncleanness, through the lusts of their own hearts, to dishonor their own bodies between themselves:

25 who changed the truth of God into a lie, and worshipped and served the creature more than the Creator, who is blessed for ever. Amen.

26 For this cause God gave them up unto vile affections: for even their women did change the natural use into that which is against nature:

27 and likewise also the men, leaving the natural use of the woman, burned in their lust one toward another; men with men working that which is unseemly, and receiving in themselves that recompense of their error which was meet.

OLD TESTAMENT READING

*T*he heavens declare the glory of God; and the firmament showeth his handiwork.

2 Day unto day uttereth speech, and night unto night showeth knowledge.

3 *There is* no speech nor language, *where* their voice is not heard.

4 Their line is gone out through all the earth, and their words to the end of the world.

Psalm 19:1–4a

INSIGHTS

*T*his is my Father's world,

And to my listening ears
All nature sings, and round me rings
The music of the spheres.
This is my Father's world:
I rest me in the thought
Of rocks and trees, of skies and seas—
His hand the wonders wrought.

This is my Father's world,
The birds their carols raise,
The morning light, the lily white,
Declare their Maker's praise.
This is my Father's world:
He shines in all that's fair;
In the rustling grass I hear Him pass,
He speaks to me everywhere.

This is my Father's world,
O let me ne'er forget
That though the wrong seems oft so strong,
God is the Ruler yet.
This is my Father's world:
The battle is not done;
Jesus who died shall be satisfied,
And earth and heav'n be one.

Maltbie Babcock

PAUSE FOR REFLECTION

*A*ccording to Paul, what excuses do people have for not knowing God? What testifies to God's glory and goodness? Describe the ways in which God's creation has influenced your beliefs about God.

WEDNESDAY

*People Do What They Want,
but God Holds Them
Accountable*

Romans 1:28—2:16

And even as they did not like to retain God in *their* knowledge, God gave them over to a reprobate mind, to do those things which are not convenient;

29 being filled with all unrighteousness, fornication, wickedness, covetousness, maliciousness; full of envy, murder, debate, deceit, malignity; whisperers,

30 backbiters, haters of God, despiteful, proud, boasters, inventors of evil things, disobedient to parents,

31 without understanding, covenantbreakers, without natural affection, implacable, unmerciful:

32 who knowing the judgment of God, that they which commit such things are worthy of death, not only do the same, but have pleasure in them that do them.

You People Also Are Sinful

2 Therefore thou art inexcusable, O man, whosoever thou art that judgest: for wherein thou judgest another, thou condemnest thyself; for thou that judgest doest the same things.

2 But we are sure that the judgment of God is according to truth against them which commit such things.

3 And thinkest thou this, O man, that judgest them which do such things, and doest the same, that thou shalt escape the judgment of God?

4 Or despisest thou the riches of his goodness and forbearance and longsuffering; not knowing that the goodness of God leadeth thee to repentance?

5 but after thy hardness and impenitent heart, treasurest up unto thyself wrath against the day of wrath and revelation of the righteous judgment of God;

6 who will render to every man according to his deeds:

7 to them who by patient continuance in well doing seek for glory and honor and immortality, eternal life:

8 but unto them that are contentious, and do not obey the truth, but obey unrighteousness, indignation and wrath,

9 tribulation and anguish, upon every soul of man that doeth evil; of the Jew first, and also of the Gentile;

10 but glory, honor, and peace, to every man that worketh good, to the Jew first, and also to the Gentile:

11 for there is no respect of persons with God.

12 For as many as have sinned without law shall also perish without law; and as many as have sinned in the law shall be judged by the law;

13 (for not the hearers of the law *are* just before God, but the doers of the law shall be justified.

14 For when the Gentiles, which have not the law, do by nature the things contained in the law, these, having not the law, are a law unto themselves:

15 which show the work of the law written in their hearts, their conscience also bearing witness, and *their* thoughts the mean while accusing or else excusing one another;)

16 in the day when God shall judge

the secrets of men by Jesus Christ according to my gospel.

*T*he way of the wicked *is* an abomination unto the LORD: but he loveth him that followeth after righteousness.

[10] Correction *is* grievous unto him that forsaketh the way: *and* he that hateth reproof shall die.

[11] Hell and destruction *are* before the LORD: how much more then the hearts of the children of men?

Proverbs 15:9–11

*T*he Bible's proclamation of God's work as Judge is part of its witness to His character. It confirms what is said elsewhere of His moral perfection, His righteousness and justice, His wisdom, omniscience, and omnipotence. It shows us also that the heart of the justice which expresses God's nature is retribution, the rendering to men what they have deserved; for this is the essence of the judge's task. To reward good with good, and evil with evil, is natural to God. So, when the New Testament speaks of the final judgment, it always represents it in terms of retribution. God will judge all men, it says, 'according to their works' (Matthew 16:27; Revelation 20:12f.). Paul amplifies. 'God . . . will render to every man according to his deeds: to them who by patient continuance in well doing seek for glory and honour and immortality, eternal life; but unto them that are contentious, and do not obey the truth, but obey unrighteousness, in-dignation and wrath; tribulation and anguish, upon every soul of man that doeth evil . . . but glory, honor, and peace, to every man that worketh good . . . for there is no respect of persons throughout: Christians, as well as non-Christians, will receive 'according to their works'. . . .*

Thus retribution appears as a natural and predetermined expression of the divine character. God has resolved to be every man's Judge, rewarding every man according to his works. Retribution is the inescapable moral law of creation; God will see that each man sooner or later receives what he deserves—if not here, then hereafter.

J. I. Packer

*W*hat do people do when God gives them freedom to do as they please? What does God, in his kindness, wait for people to do? What will God, the Judge of the earth, do when people refuse to repent and live in obedience to him?*

THURSDAY

*God Wants Us to Change Our
Hearts and Lives*

<hr>

Romans 2:17—3:18

The Jews and the Law

*B*ehold, thou art called a Jew, and restest in the law, and makest thy boast of God,

18 and knowest *his* will, and approvest the things that are more excellent, being instructed out of the law;

19 and art confident that thou thyself art a guide of the blind, a light of them which are in darkness,

20 an instructor of the foolish, a teacher of babes, which hast the form of knowledge and of the truth in the law.

21 Thou therefore which teachest another, teachest thou not thyself? thou that preachest a man should not steal, dost thou steal?

22 thou that sayest a man should not commit adultery, dost thou commit adultery? thou that abhorrest idols, dost thou commit sacrilege?

23 thou that makest thy boast of the law, through breaking the law dishonorest thou God?

24 For the name of God is blasphemed among the Gentiles through you, as it is written.

25 For circumcision verily profiteth, if thou keep the law: but if thou be a breaker of the law, thy circumcision is made uncircumcision.

26 Therefore if the uncircumcision keep the righteousness of the law, shall not his uncircumcision be counted for circumcision?

27 And shall not uncircumcision which is by nature, if it fulfil the law, judge thee, who by the letter and circumcision dost transgress the law?

28 For he is not a Jew, which is one outwardly; neither is *that* circumcision, which is outward in the flesh:

29 but he *is* a Jew, which is one inwardly; and circumcision *is that* of the heart, in the spirit, *and* not in the letter; whose praise *is* not of men, but of God.

3 What advantage then hath the Jew? or what profit *is there* of circumcision?

2 Much every way: chiefly, because that unto them were committed the oracles of God.

3 For what if some did not believe? shall their unbelief make the faith of God without effect?

4 God forbid: yea, let God be true, but every man a liar; as it is written, That thou mightest be justified in thy sayings, and mightest overcome when thou art judged.

5 But if our unrighteousness commend the righteousness of God, what shall we say? *Is* God unrighteous who taketh vengeance? (I speak as a man)

6 God forbid: for then how shall God judge the world?

7 For if the truth of God hath more abounded through my lie unto his glory; why yet am I also judged as a sinner?

8 and not *rather,* (as we be slanderously reported, and as some affirm that we say,) Let us do evil, that good may come? whose damnation is just.

All People Are Sinful

*W*hat then? are we better *than they?* No, in no wise: for we have before proved both Jews and Gentiles, that they are all under sin;

¹⁰ as it is written, There is none righteous, no, not one:

¹¹ there is none that understandeth, there is none that seeketh after God.

¹² They are all gone out of the way, they are together become unprofitable; there is none that doeth good, no, not one.

¹³ Their throat *is* an open sepulchre; with their tongues they have used deceit; the poison of asps *is* under their lips:

¹⁴ whose mouth *is* full of cursing and bitterness:

¹⁵ their feet *are* swift to shed blood:

¹⁶ destruction and misery *are* in their ways:

¹⁷ and the way of peace have they not known:

¹⁸ there is no fear of God before their eyes.

OLD TESTAMENT READING

*T*hus saith the LORD of hosts, the God of Israel, Amend your ways and your doings, and I will cause you to dwell in this place.

⁶ *if* ye oppress not the stranger, the fatherless, and the widow, and shed not innocent blood in this place, neither walk after other gods to your hurt;

⁷ then I will cause you to dwell in this place, in the land that I gave to your fathers, for ever and ever.

Jeremiah 7:3, 6–7

INSIGHTS

*E*verywhere Jesus went He proclaimed the twofold message of repentance and faith in God (Mark 1:15). The faith He proclaimed was not mere mental assent, but the kind of faith that produces change in people's lives. There is no such thing as biblical faith that does not produce obedience. . . .

It is important to note that the Bible identifies both a true and a false repentance. Second Corinthians 7:10 says, "Godly grief produces a repentance that leads to salvation and brings no regret, but worldly grief produces death." Godly grief is true repentance, and true repentance is more than contrition. A person may be sorrowful over his sins yet unrepentant because he is sorrowing for the wrong reasons. Instead of sorrowing because his sins have hurt and disappointed God, he may just feel bad because his sins have been personally painful, stressful, or costly, or because his sins have been found out. If there is no change in character, there has been no true repentance. . . .

The results of false repentance are seen everywhere in the church. Hearts are unbroken. Sin is covered up. . . . And many professing Christians do not walk in the light with God and one another. The fruit of true repentance is a change of mind, heart, and behavior.

Floyd McClung

PAUSE FOR REFLECTION

*W*hat value does God place on outward signs of obedience to his law? What does circumcision represent? How does God want those who are called "his people" to live?

FRIDAY

Faith in God Is Our Salvation

Romans 3:19—4:12

*N*ow we know that what things soever the law saith, it saith to them who are under the law: that every mouth may be stopped, and all the world may become guilty before God.

²⁰ Therefore by the deeds of the law there shall no flesh be justified in his sight: for by the law is the knowledge of sin.

How God Justifies People

*B*ut now the righteousness of God without the law is manifested, being witnessed by the law and the prophets;

²² even the righteousness of God *which is* by faith of Jesus Christ unto all and upon all them that believe; for there is no difference:

²³ for all have sinned, and come short of the glory of God;

²⁴ being justified freely by his grace through the redemption that is in Christ Jesus:

²⁵ whom God hath set forth *to be* a propitiation through faith in his blood, to declare his righteousness for the remission of sins that are past, through the forbearance of God;

²⁶ to declare, *I say,* at this time his righteousness: that he might be just, and the justifier of him which believeth in Jesus.

²⁷ Where is boasting then? It is excluded. By what law? of works?

Nay; but by the law of faith.

²⁸ Therefore we conclude that a man is justified by faith without the deeds of the law.

²⁹ *Is he* the God of the Jews only? *is he* not also of the Gentiles? Yes, of the Gentiles also:

³⁰ seeing *it is* one God, which shall justify the circumcision by faith, and uncircumcision through faith.

³¹ Do we then make void the law through faith? God forbid: yea, we establish the law.

The Example of Abraham

4 What shall we say then that Abraham our father, as pertaining to the flesh, hath found?

² For if Abraham were justified by works, he hath *whereof* to glory; but not before God.

³ For what saith the scripture? Abraham believed God, and it was counted unto him for righteousness.

⁴ Now to him that worketh is the reward not reckoned of grace, but of debt.

⁵ But to him that worketh not, but believeth on him that justifieth the ungodly, his faith is counted for righteousness.

⁶ Even as David also describeth the blessedness of the man, unto whom God imputeth righteousness without works,

⁷ *saying,* Blessed *are* they whose iniquities are forgiven, and whose sins are covered.

⁸ Blessed *is* the man to whom the Lord will not impute sin.

⁹ *Cometh* this blessedness then upon the circumcision *only,* or upon the uncircumcision also? for we say that faith was reckoned to Abraham for righteousness.

10 How was it then reckoned? when he was in circumcision, or in uncircumcision? Not in circumcision, but in uncircumcision.

11 And he received the sign of circumcision, a seal of the righteousness of the faith which *he had yet* being uncircumcised: that he might be the father of all them that believe, though they be not circumcised; that righteousness might be imputed unto them also:

12 and the father of circumcision to them who are not of the circumcision only, but who also walk in the steps of that faith of our father Abraham, which *he had* being *yet* uncircumcised.

OLD TESTAMENT READING

*M*any sorrows *shall be* to the wicked: but he that trusteth in the LORD, mercy shall compass him about.

11 Be glad in the LORD, and rejoice, ye righteous: and shout for joy, all *ye that are* upright in heart.

Psalm 32:10–11

INSIGHTS

*F*aith is believing that Christ is what He is said to be and that He will do what He has promised to do, and then to expect this of Him. The Scriptures speak of Jesus Christ as being God in human flesh, as being perfect in His character, as being made a sin offering on our behalf, as bearing our sins in His own body on the tree. . . . The sacred records further tell us that He "rose again" (1 Co 15:4) from the dead, that He "ever liveth to make intercession for us" (Heb 7:25), that He has gone up into glory and has taken possession of heaven on the behalf of His people, and that he will shortly come again "to judge the . . . world with righteousness, and the peoples with equity" (Ps 98:9, ASV). . . .

. . . Jesus is what He is said to be. Jesus will do what He says He will do. Therefore, we must each trust Him, saying, "He will be to me what He says He is, and He will do to me what He has promised to do. I leave myself in the hands of Him who is appointed to save, that he may save me. I rest upon His promise that He will do even as He has said." This is saving faith, and he that has it has everlasting life. Whatever his dangers and difficulties, whatever his darkness and depression, whatever his infirmities and sins, he that believes thus on Christ Jesus is not condemned, and shall never come into condemnation.

Charles Spurgeon

PAUSE FOR REFLECTION

*H*ow are people justified in God's sight? Who can be justified? How did God enable us to be justified? How does God bless those who trust him? Have you received that blessing?

WEEKEND

God Has Great Love for Us

Romans 4:13—5:11

God Keeps His Promise

*F*or the promise, that he should be the heir of the world, *was* not to Abraham, or to his seed, through the law, but through the righteousness of faith.

14 For if they which are of the law *be* heirs, faith is made void, and the promise made of none effect:

15 because the law worketh wrath: for where no law is, *there is* no transgression.

16 Therefore *it is* of faith, that *it might be* by grace; to the end the promise might be sure to all the seed; not to that only which is of the law, but to that also which is of the faith of Abraham; who is the father of us all,

17 (as it is written, I have made thee a father of many nations,) before him whom he believed, *even* God, who quickeneth the dead, and calleth those things which be not as though they were.

18 who against hope believed in hope, that he might become the father of many nations, according to that which was spoken, So shall thy seed be.

19 And being not weak in faith, he considered not his own body now dead, when he was about a hundred years old, neither yet the deadness of Sarah's womb:

20 he staggered not at the promise of God through unbelief; but was strong in faith, giving glory to God;

21 and being fully persuaded, that what he had promised, he was able also to perform.

22 And therefore it was imputed to him for righteousness.

23 Now it was not written for his sake alone, that it was imputed to him;

24 but for us also, to whom it shall be imputed, if we believe on him that raised up Jesus our Lord from the dead;

25 who was delivered for our offences, and was raised again for our justification.

Peace with God

5 Therefore being justified by faith, we have peace with God through our Lord Jesus Christ:

2 by whom also we have access by faith into this grace wherein we stand, and rejoice in hope of the glory of God.

3 And not only *so*, but we glory in tribulations also; knowing that tribulation worketh patience;

4 and patience, experience; and experience, hope:

5 and hope maketh not ashamed; because the love of God is shed abroad in our hearts by the Holy Ghost which is given unto us.

6 For when we were yet without strength, in due time Christ died for the ungodly.

7 For scarcely for a righteous man will one die: yet peradventure for a good man some would even dare to die.

8 But God commendeth his love toward us, in that, while we were yet sinners, Christ died for us.

9 Much more then, being now justified by his blood, we shall be saved from wrath through him.

10 For if, when we were enemies, we were reconciled to God by the death

of his Son; much more, being reconciled, we shall be saved by his life. [11] And not only so, but we also joy in God through our Lord Jesus Christ, by whom we have now received the atonement.

---

*B*ut as for me, my prayer *is* unto thee, O LORD, *in* an acceptable time: O God, in the multitude of thy mercy hear me, in the truth of thy salvation.

Psalm 69:13

I will mention the loving-kindnesses of the LORD, *and* the praises of the LORD, according to all that the LORD hath bestowed on us, and the great goodness toward the house of Israel, which he hath bestowed on them according to his mercies, and according to the multitude of his loving-kindnesses. [8] For he said, Surely they *are* my people, children *that* will not lie: so he was their Saviour. [9] In all their affliction he was afflicted, and the angel of his presence saved them: in his love and in his pity he redeemed them; and he bare them, and carried them all the days of old.

Isaiah 63:7–9

---

*M*ay God through His Holy Spirit teach you to cherish the unfathomable mystery of His love. Jesus said, "None is good save one, even God." The glory of God in heaven is that everything He wills and does is good. . . .

The God who wills only good is a God of love. He does not seek His own. He does not live for himself. He pours out His love upon all living creatures. . . .

Love "seeketh not her own." Love finds happiness in giving to others. Love sacrifices wholly for others. Therefore, God offered himself to us in the person of His Son. And the Son offered himself upon the cross to bring love to us and to win our hearts. The everlasting love with which the Father loves the Son is the same love with which the Son loves us. This same love of the Father, Jesus Christ has poured into our hearts through the Holy Spirit. God desires that our whole life be permeated with this love's vital power. . . .

. . . Love is the power of the Godhead: in the Father, Son, and Holy Spirit. All who are members of the body of Christ possess the love of God, and this love streams forth from them to take the whole world within its compass.

Andrew Murray

---

*H*ow has God shown his love for the world? When we place our faith in his love, what are the results? Write your own psalm of thanksgiving, praising God for his gift of love.

MONDAY

Christ Frees Us from the Power of Sin

Romans 5:12—6:14

Adam and Christ Compared

*W*herefore, as by one man sin entered into the world, and death by sin; and so death passed upon all men, for that all have sinned:

[13] for until the law sin was in the world: but sin is not imputed when there is no law.

[14] Nevertheless death reigned from Adam to Moses, even over them that had not sinned after the similitude of Adam's transgression, who is the figure of him that was to come.

[15] But not as the offense, so also *is* the free gift: For if through the offense of one many be dead, much more the grace of God, and the gift by grace, *which is* by one man, Jesus Christ, hath abounded unto many.

[16] And not as *it was* by one that sinned, so *is* the gift: for the judgment *was* by one to condemnation, but the free gift *is* of many offences unto justification.

[17] For if by one man's offense death reigned by one; much more they which receive abundance of grace and of the gift of righteousness shall reign in life by one, Jesus Christ.)

[18] Therefore, as by the offense of one *judgment came* upon all men to condemnation; even so by the righteousness of one *the free gift came* upon all men unto justification of life.

[19] For as by one man's disobedience many were made sinners, so by the obedience of one shall many be made righteous.

[20] Moreover the law entered, that the offense might abound. But where sin abounded, grace did much more abound:

[21] that as sin hath reigned unto death, even so might grace reign through righteousness unto eternal life by Jesus Christ our Lord.

Dead to Sin but Alive in Christ

6 What shall we say then? Shall we continue in sin, that grace may abound?

[2] God forbid. How shall we, that are dead to sin, live any longer therein?

[3] Know ye not, that so many of us as were baptized into Jesus Christ were baptized into his death?

[4] Therefore we are buried with him by baptism into death: that like as Christ was raised up from the dead by the glory of the Father, even so we also should walk in newness of life.

[5] For if we have been planted together in the likeness of his death, we shall be also *in the likeness* of *his* resurrection:

[6] knowing this, that our old man is crucified with *him*, that the body of sin might be destroyed, that henceforth we should not serve sin.

[7] For he that is dead is freed from sin.

[8] Now if we be dead with Christ, we believe that we shall also live with him:

[9] knowing that Christ being raised from the dead dieth no more; death hath no more dominion over him.

[10] For in that he died, he died unto sin once: but in that he liveth, he liveth unto God.

[11] Likewise reckon ye also yourselves

to be dead indeed unto sin, but alive unto God through Jesus Christ our Lord.

¹² Let not sin therefore reign in your mortal body, that ye should obey it in the lusts thereof.

¹³ Neither yield ye your members *as* instruments of unrighteousness unto sin: but yield yourselves unto God, as those that are alive from the dead, and your members *as* instruments of righteousness unto God.

¹⁴ For sin shall not have dominion over you: for ye are not under the law, but under grace.

OLD TESTAMENT READING

*N*ow therefore go to, speak to the men of Judah, and to the inhabitants of Jerusalem, saying, Thus saith the LORD; Behold, I frame evil against you, and devise a device against you: return ye now every one from his evil way, and make your ways and your doings good.

¹² And they said, There is no hope: but we will walk after our own devices, and we will every one do the imagination of his evil heart.

Jeremiah 18:11–12

INSIGHTS

*I*f we would know what Christ wants to be to us, we must first of all know Him as our Saviour from sin. When the angel came down from heaven to proclaim that He was to be born into the world, you remember he gave His name, "He shall be called Jesus, for he shall save his people from their sins." HAVE WE BEEN DELIVERED FROM SIN? He did not come to save us in our sins, but from our sins. . . .

Let us look at Him as He hangs upon the Cross, and see how He has put away sin. He was manifested that He might take away our sins. . . .

But Christ is not only a Saviour. I might save a man from drowning and rescue him from an untimely grave; but I might probably not be able to do any more for him. Christ is something more than a Saviour. When the children of Israel were placed behind the blood, that blood was their salvation; but they would still have heard the crack of the slave-driver's whip, if they had not been delivered from the Egyptian yoke of bondage: then it was that God delivered them from the hand of the King of Egypt. I have little sympathy with the idea that God comes down to save us, and then leaves us in prison, the slaves of our besetting sins. No; He has come to deliver us, and to give us victory over our evil tempers, our passions, and our lusts. Are you a professed Christian, but one who is a slave to some besetting sin? If you want to get victory over that temper or that lust, go on to know Christ more intimately. He brings deliverance for the past, the present, and the future.

D. L. Moody

APPLICATION

*I*n your own words, describe what the burden of sin does to people. How have you been enslaved to sin? Does your life give evidence that you are no longer a slave to sin? What can you do so that God will truly be your master?

TUESDAY
God's People Belong to Him

Romans 6:15—7:13

Servants of Righteousness

*W*hat then? shall we sin, because we are not under the law, but under grace? God forbid.

¹⁶ Know ye not, that to whom ye yield yourselves servants to obey, his servants ye are to whom ye obey; whether of sin unto death, or of obedience unto righteousness?

¹⁷ But God be thanked, that ye were the servants of sin, but ye have obeyed from the heart that form of doctrine which was delivered you.

¹⁸ Being then made free from sin, ye became the servants of righteousness.

¹⁹ I speak after the manner of men because of the infirmity of your flesh: for as ye have yielded your members servants to uncleanness and to iniquity unto iniquity; even so now yield your members servants to righteousness unto holiness.

²⁰ For when ye were the servants of sin, ye were free from righteousness.

²¹ What fruit had ye then in those things whereof ye are now ashamed? for the end of those things *is* death.

²² But now being made free from sin, and become servants to God, ye have your fruit unto holiness, and the end everlasting life.

²³ For the wages of sin *is* death; but the gift of God *is* eternal life through Jesus Christ our Lord.

An Example from Marriage

7 Know ye not, brethren, (for I speak to them that know the law,) how that the law hath dominion over a man as long as he liveth?

² For the woman which hath an husband is bound by the law to *her* husband so long as he liveth; but if the husband be dead, she is loosed from the law of *her* husband.

³ So then if, while *her* husband liveth, she be married to another man, she shall be called an adulteress: but if her husband be dead, she is free from that law; so that she is no adulteress, though she be married to another man.

⁴ Wherefore, my brethren, ye also are become dead to the law by the body of Christ; that ye should be married to another, *even* to him who is raised from the dead, that we should bring forth fruit unto God.

⁵ For when we were in the flesh, the motions of sins, which were by the law, did work in our members to bring forth fruit unto death.

⁶ But now we are delivered from the law, that being dead wherein we were held; that we should serve in newness of spirit, and not *in* the oldness of the letter.

Our Fight Against Sin

*W*hat shall we say then? *Is* the law sin? God forbid. Nay, I had not known sin, but by the law: for I had not known lust, except the law had said, Thou shalt not covet.

⁸ But sin, taking occasion by the commandment, wrought in me all manner of concupiscence. For without the law sin *was* dead.

⁹ For I was alive without the law

once: but when the commandment came, sin revived, and I died.

[10] And the commandment, which *was ordained* to life, I found to be unto death.

[11] For sin, taking occasion by the commandment, deceived me, and by it slew *me.*

[12] Wherefore the law *is* holy, and the commandment holy, and just, and good.

[13] Was then that which is good made death unto me? God forbid. But sin, that it might appear sin, working death in me by that which is good; that sin by the commandment might become exceeding sinful.

OLD TESTAMENT READING

*F*or thou *art* a holy people unto the LORD thy God: the LORD thy God hath chosen thee to be a special people unto himself, above all people that *are* upon the face of the earth.

[7] The LORD did not set his love upon you, nor choose you, because ye were more in number than any people; for ye *were* the fewest of all people:

[8] but because the LORD loved you, and because he would keep the oath which he had sworn unto your fathers, hath the LORD brought you out with a mighty hand, and redeemed you out of the house of bondmen, from the hand of Pharaoh king of Egypt.

Deuteronomy 7:6–8

INSIGHTS

*W*e are chosen to be holy. This is what the word "saint" means. In Greek, the word is hagios, meaning holy, set apart, and belonging to God. It does not mean the spiritual elitism of a "Holy Joe" or the aloof smugness of a "Perfect Pat." Rather, it indicates ownership. God says to us, "You belong to Me!"

When Paul addressed the saints, he was not writing to church leaders or to spiritually advanced people. Rather, Paul wrote to all of God's people who stood equally with him as those chosen, called, and cherished.

We, then, can also enjoy our status as loved and forgiven people.

This is a lofty thought, but what does it mean practically? Nothing less than that all we are and have belongs to God. This means our minds, emotions, will and bodies belong to God. We expand God's reign in our lives to include the people, the possessions, and the plans of our lives. And we don't stop here. Our list grows to include the memories that shape our present and the values that etch our future. In addition, we must be sure to include our work world where we spend most of our days. We must also remember that our money is holy, too.

Choosing to be chosen means accepting Christ's lordship over our total lives. This requires our committed surrender to Him.

Lloyd Ogilvie

APPLICATION

*D*escribe as fully as you can what it means to be a servant to sin. Describe what it means to be a servant of God. What difference does belonging to God make in a person's life? In your life? Have you surrendered to him as your Lord?

WEDNESDAY

*We Must Choose Either to
Follow Sin or Serve God*

Romans 7:14—8:17

The War Within Us

*F*or we know that the law is spiritual: but I am carnal, sold under sin.
[15] For that which I do I allow not: for what I would, that do I not; but what I hate, that do I.
[16] If then I do that which I would not, I consent unto the law that *it is* good.
[17] Now then it is no more I that do it, but sin that dwelleth in me.
[18] For I know that in me (that is, in my flesh,) dwelleth no good thing: for to will is present with me; but *how* to perform that which is good I find not.
[19] For the good that I would I do not: but the evil which I would not, that I do.
[20] Now if I do that I would not, it is no more I that do it, but sin that dwelleth in me.
[21] I find then a law, that, when I would do good, evil is present with me.
[22] For I delight in the law of God after the inward man:
[23] but I see another law in my members, warring against the law of my mind, and bringing me into captivity to the law of sin which is in my members.
[24] O wretched man that I am! who shall deliver me from the body of this death?
[25] I thank God through Jesus Christ our Lord. So then with the mind I myself serve the law of God; but with the flesh the law of sin.

Be Ruled by the Spirit

8 *There is* therefore now no condemnation to them which are in Christ Jesus, who walk not after the flesh, but after the Spirit.
[2] For the law of the Spirit of life in Christ Jesus hath made me free from the law of sin and death.
[3] For what the law could not do, in that it was weak through the flesh, God sending his own Son in the likeness of sinful flesh, and for sin, condemned sin in the flesh:
[4] that the righteousness of the law might be fulfilled in us, who walk not after the flesh, but after the Spirit.
[5] For they that are after the flesh do mind the things of the flesh; but they that are after the Spirit the things of the Spirit.
[6] For to be carnally minded *is* death; but to be spiritually minded *is* life and peace.
[7] Because the carnal mind *is* enmity against God: for it is not subject to the law of God, neither indeed can be.
[8] So then they that are in the flesh cannot please God.
[9] But ye are not in the flesh, but in the Spirit, if so be that the Spirit of God dwell in you. Now if any man have not the Spirit of Christ, he is none of his.
[10] And if Christ *be* in you, the body *is* dead because of sin; but the Spirit *is* life because of righteousness.
[11] But if the Spirit of him that raised up Jesus from the dead dwell in you, he that raised up Christ from the dead shall also quicken your mortal bodies by his Spirit that dwelleth in you.
[12] Therefore, brethren, we are debtors, not to the flesh, to live after the flesh.

¹³ For if ye live after the flesh, ye shall die: but if ye through the Spirit do mortify the deeds of the body, ye shall live.

¹⁴ For as many as are led by the Spirit of God, they are the sons of God.

¹⁵ For ye have not received the spirit of bondage again to fear; but ye have received the Spirit of adoption, whereby we cry, Abba, Father.

¹⁶ The Spirit itself beareth witness with our spirit, that we are the children of God:

¹⁷ and if children, then heirs; heirs of God, and joint-heirs with Christ, if so be that we suffer with *him*, that we may be also glorified together.

OLD TESTAMENT READING

*N*ow therefore fear the LORD, and serve him in sincerity and in truth; and put away the gods which your fathers served on the other side of the flood, and in Egypt; and serve ye the LORD.

¹⁵ And if it seem evil unto you to serve the LORD, choose you this day whom ye will serve; whether the gods which your fathers served that *were* on the other side of the flood, or the gods of the Amorites, in whose land ye dwell: but as for me and my house, we will serve the LORD.

Joshua 24:14–15

INSIGHTS

*T*he Bible does not leave us floundering as to what is right and what is wrong in the basic areas of life. We do have an absolute base for choosing. The choices are not so vague that we need to be frightened that we are choosing the wrong thing. . . .

. . . Through Joshua God challenged the Israelites to choose among "the gods . . . on the other side of the River, or the gods of the Amorites," or the Lord. Elijah presented the choice on Mount Carmel, and made the difference very vivid. Choice continues to be important time after time for each of us, but there are crisis moments in each of our lives when we are tempted to make a tremendously wrong choice. . . .

What are your choices? Whom are your choices for? Not just for yourself. Choose now whom you will serve, and that choice is going to affect the next generation, and the next generation, and the next. Choice never affects one single person alone. It goes on and on and the effect goes out into geography and history. You are a part of history and your choices become a part of history.

Edith Schaeffer

ACTION POINT

*I*n what ways are you aware of your life struggle between choosing God or the way of sin? Pray that you will see clearly the choices you must make and that you will unfailingly obey God's way of life.

THURSDAY

Nothing Can Separate Us from God's Love

Romans 8:18–39

Our Future Glory

*F*or I reckon that the sufferings of this present time *are* not worthy to *be compared* with the glory which shall be revealed in us.

¹⁹ For the earnest expectation of the creature waiteth for the manifestation of the sons of God.

²⁰ For the creature was made subject to vanity, not willingly, but by reason of him who hath subjected *the same* in hope;

²¹ because the creature itself also shall be delivered from the bondage of corruption into the glorious liberty of the children of God.

²² For we know that the whole creation groaneth and travaileth in pain together until now.

²³ And not only *they*, but ourselves also, which have the firstfruits of the Spirit, even we ourselves groan within ourselves, waiting for the adoption, *to wit*, the redemption of our body.

²⁴ For we are saved by hope: but hope that is seen is not hope: for what a man seeth, why doth he yet hope for?

²⁵ But if we hope for that we see not, *then* do we with patience wait for *it*.

²⁶ Likewise the Spirit also helpeth our infirmities: for we know not what we should pray for as we ought: but the Spirit itself maketh intercession for us with groanings which cannot be uttered.

²⁷ And he that searcheth the hearts knoweth what *is* the mind of the Spirit, because he maketh intercession for the saints according to *the will of* God.

²⁸ And we know that all things work together for good to them that love God, to them who are the called according to *his* purpose.

²⁹ For whom he did foreknow, he also did predestinate *to be* conformed to the image of his Son, that he might be the firstborn among many brethren.

³⁰ Moreover whom he did predestinate, them he also called: and whom he called, them he also justified: and whom he justified, them he also glorified.

God's Love in Christ Jesus

*W*hat shall we then say to these things? If God *be* for us, who *can be* against us?

³² He that spared not his own Son, but delivered him up for us all, how shall he not with him also freely give us all things?

³³ Who shall lay any thing to the charge of God's elect? *It is* God that justifieth.

³⁴ Who *is* he that condemneth? *It is* Christ that died, yea rather, that is risen again, who is even at the right hand of God, who also maketh intercession for us.

³⁵ Who shall separate us from the love of Christ? *shall* tribulation, or distress, or persecution, or famine, or nakedness, or peril, or sword?

³⁶ As it is written, For thy sake we are killed all the day long; we are accounted as sheep for the slaughter.

³⁷ Nay, in all these things we are

more than conquerors through him that loved us.

[38] For I am persuaded, that neither death, nor life, nor angels, nor principalities, nor powers, nor things present, nor things to come,

[39] Nor height, nor depth, nor any other creature, shall be able to separate us from the love of God, which is in Christ Jesus our Lord.

OLD TESTAMENT READING

*A*nd the LORD saw it, and it displeased him that *there was* no judgment.

[16] And he saw that *there was* no man, and wondered that *there was* no intercessor: therefore his arm brought salvation unto him; and his righteousness, it sustained him.

[17] For he put on righteousness as a breastplate, and a helmet of salvation upon his head; and he put on the garments of vengeance *for* clothing, and was clad with zeal as a cloak.

[21] As for me, this *is* my covenant with them, saith the LORD; My Spirit that *is* upon thee, and my words which I have put in thy mouth, shall not depart out of thy mouth, nor out of the mouth of thy seed, nor out of the mouth of thy seed's seed, saith the LORD, from henceforth and for ever.

Isaiah 59:15b–17, 21

INSIGHTS

*I*n the very nature of things we soon discover in life that in order to be loved either in a physical or filial dimension we must show ourselves lovable. Somehow we have to demonstrate to others that we are worth loving. We have to prove that we are worthy of their love. And, sad to say, in most cases, the moment we fail to do this we discover that we are being cut off. . . .

Now, amazing as it may sound, and incredible as it may seem, there is none of this in the love of God. The simple truth is that His love for me does not in any way depend on my worthiness of it. In other words, I do not have to merit His love. I do not, so to speak, have to earn His love.

Scripture repeats this theme again and again. For example, in that most poignant of all the stories told by Jesus, the account of the prodigal son, we see clearly portrayed for us what the love of God is like. . . .

No doubt the dear old man had died a thousand deaths after his son's departure. . . .

Yet his attitude of devotion, affection, and utter selflessness never altered. It mattered not what happened to himself as long as his son could be restored and redeemed and remade. His care and concern for this one's welfare never abated.

This is the love of God.

Phillip Keller

ACTION POINT

*L*ist the things (as many as you want) that, powerful and dreadful as they may be, cannot separate us from the love of God. Thank God that his love for you is greater than every one of those things!

F R I D A Y

Is God Unfair?

Romans 9:1–29

God and the Jewish People

9 I say the truth in Christ, I lie not, my conscience also bearing me witness in the Holy Ghost,

² that I have great heaviness and continual sorrow in my heart.

³ For I could wish that myself were accursed from Christ for my brethren, my kinsmen according to the flesh:

⁴ who are Israelites; to whom *pertaineth* the adoption, and the glory, and the covenants, and the giving of the law, and the service *of God,* and the promises;

⁵ whose *are* the fathers, and of whom as concerning the flesh Christ *came,* who is over all, God blessed for ever. Amen.

⁶ Not as though the word of God hath taken none effect. For they *are* not all Israel, which are of Israel:

⁷ neither, because they are the seed of Abraham, *are they* all children: but, In Isaac shall thy seed be called.

⁸ That is, They which are the children of the flesh, these *are* not the children of God: but the children of the promise are counted for the seed.

⁹ For this *is* the word of promise, At this time will I come, and Sarah shall have a son.

¹⁰ And not only *this*; but when Rebecca also had conceived by one, *even* by our father Isaac;

¹¹ (for *the children* being not yet born, neither having done any good or evil,

that the purpose of God according to election might stand, not of works, but of him that calleth;)

¹² it was said unto her, The elder shall serve the younger.

¹³ As it is written, Jacob have I loved, but Esau have I hated.

¹⁴ What shall we say then? *Is there* unrighteousness with God? God forbid.

¹⁵ For he saith to Moses, I will have mercy on whom I will have mercy, and I will have compassion on whom I will have compassion.

¹⁶ So then *it is* not of him that willeth, nor of him that runneth, but of God that showeth mercy.

¹⁷ For the scripture saith unto Pharaoh, Even for this same purpose have I raised thee up, that I might shew my power in thee, and that my name might be declared throughout all the earth.

¹⁸ Therefore hath he mercy on whom he will *have mercy,* and whom he will he hardeneth.

¹⁹ Thou wilt say then unto me, Why doth he yet find fault? For who hath resisted his will?

²⁰ Nay but, O man, who art thou that repliest against God? Shall the thing formed say to him that formed *it,* Why hast thou made me thus?

²¹ Hath not the potter power over the clay, of the same lump to make one vessel unto honor, and another unto dishonor?

²² *What* if God, willing to show his wrath, and to make his power known, endured with much longsuffering the vessels of wrath fitted to destruction:

²³ and that he might make known the riches of his glory on the vessels of mercy, which he had afore prepared unto glory,

24 even us, whom he hath called, not of the Jews only, but also of the Gentiles?

25 As he saith also in Hosea, I will call them my people, which were not my people; and her beloved, which was not beloved.

26 And it shall come to pass, *that* in the place where it was said unto them, Ye *are* not my people; there shall they be called the children of the living God.

27 Isaiah also crieth concerning Israel, Though the number of the children of Israel be as the sand of the sea, a remnant shall be saved:

28 for he will finish the work, and cut it short in righteousness: because a short work will the Lord make upon the earth.

29 And as Isaiah said before, Except the Lord of Sabaoth had left us a seed, we had been as Sodom, and been made like unto Gomorrah.

OLD TESTAMENT READING

*S*hall the clay say to him that fashioneth it, What makest thou? or thy work, He hath no hands?

Isaiah 45:9c

INSIGHTS

*C*hild, don't try to understand Me. Just love Me. Just let Me love you. You don't have to understand Me to open yourself to My love.

You're right—I do ride the wild winds into town sometimes. I do appear in forms you have never seen, sound notes you have never heard. This makes you wonder if I get My signals crossed, if I take you south in order to get you north. I seem to have plopped you down, reasonable creature that you are, into an unreasonable world. You do not understand all this because I am God and you are you.

May I remind you how different we really are? You are human; I am divine. You are finite; I am infinite. You need love; I delight in love but do not need it. You need to be understood; I am above the need to be understood. You cannot understand; I understand perfectly. You are of time; I am of eternity. You are of reason; I am above reason. You are blown by the wind; I blow the wind.

Ruth Senter

ACTION POINT

*A*re you comfortable with the fact that God is the potter and you are the clay? Pray for the humility to accept God's love for you in the way that he gives it.

WEEKEND

*Salvation Comes to
Those Who Believe*

Romans 9:30—10:21

*W*hat shall we say then? That the Gentiles, which followed not after righteousness, have attained to righteousness, even the righteousness which is of faith.

³¹ But Israel, which followed after the law of righteousness, hath not attained to the law of righteousness.

³² Wherefore? Because *they sought it* not by faith, but as it were by the works of the law. For they stumbled at that stumblingstone;

³³ as it is written, Behold, I lay in Zion a stumblingstone and rock of offense: and whosoever believeth on him shall not be ashamed.

10 Brethren, my heart's desire and prayer to God for Israel is, that they might be saved.

² For I bear them record that they have a zeal of God, but not according to knowledge.

³ For they being ignorant of God's righteousness, and going about to establish their own righteousness, have not submitted themselves unto the righteousness of God.

⁴ For Christ *is* the end of the law for righteousness to every one that believeth.

⁵ For Moses describeth the righteousness which is of the law, That the man which doeth those things shall live by them.

⁶ But the righteousness which is of faith speaketh on this wise, Say not in thine heart, Who shall ascend into heaven? (that is, to bring Christ down *from above*:)

⁷ or, Who shall descend into the deep? (that is, to bring up Christ again from the dead.)

⁸ But what saith it? The word is nigh thee, *even* in thy mouth, and in thy heart: that is, the word of faith, which we preach;

⁹ that if thou shalt confess with thy mouth the Lord Jesus, and shalt believe in thine heart that God hath raised him from the dead, thou shalt be saved.

¹⁰ For with the heart man believeth unto righteousness; and with the mouth confession is made unto salvation.

¹¹ For the scripture saith, Whosoever believeth on him shall not be ashamed.

¹² For there is no difference between the Jew and the Greek: for the same Lord over all is rich unto all that call upon him.

¹³ For whosoever shall call upon the name of the Lord shall be saved.

¹⁴ How then shall they call on him in whom they have not believed? and how shall they believe in him of whom they have not heard? and how shall they hear without a preacher?

¹⁵ and how shall they preach, except they be sent? as it is written, How beautiful are the feet of them that preach the gospel of peace, and bring glad tidings of good things!

¹⁶ But they have not all obeyed the gospel. For Isaiah saith, Lord, who hath believed our report?

¹⁷ So then faith *cometh* by hearing, and hearing by the word of God.

¹⁸ But I say, Have they not heard? Yes verily, Their sound went into all the earth, and their words unto the ends of the world.

¹⁹ But I say, Did not Israel know? First Moses saith, I will provoke you to jealousy by *them that are* no people, *and* by a foolish nation I will anger you.

²⁰ But Isaiah is very bold, and saith, I was found of them that sought me not; I was made manifest unto them that asked not after me.

²¹ But to Israel he saith, All day long I have stretched forth my hands unto a disobedient and gainsaying people.

OLD TESTAMENT READING

Those Who Obey the Law Will Live

*A*nd the LORD spake unto Moses, saying,

² Speak unto the children of Israel, and say unto them, I *am* the LORD your God.

³ After the doings of the land of Egypt, wherein ye dwelt, shall ye not do: and after the doings of the land of Canaan, whither I bring you, shall ye not do: neither shall ye walk in their ordinances.

⁴ Ye shall do my judgments, and keep mine ordinances, to walk therein: I *am* the LORD your God.

⁵ Ye shall therefore keep my statutes, and my judgments: which if a man do, he shall live in them: I *am* the LORD.

Leviticus 18:1–5

INSIGHTS

*I*t's not through wisdom that people come to the knowledge of God and their absolute equality before Him. It's not through endless arguments of fine points of theology that they will find a humble heart. The door-

way into the kingdom is so low down that one must bend in humility to get through. I've never known a single person who has been convinced of the kingdom of God through head knowledge—a person just can't think his or her way into the kingdom of God. Nor can anyone come into the kingdom of God based on a religious experience. It is knowledge of and faith in Christ that enables the equality of life in the kingdom to be real. "For Jews request a sign, and Greeks seek after wisdom; but we preach Christ crucified, to the Jews a stumbling block and to the Greeks foolishness, but to those who are called, both Jews and Greeks, Christ the power of God and the wisdom of God" (1 Cor 1:22–25).

Terry Fullam

PAUSE FOR REFLECTION

*C*an a person successfully follow God in his or her own way (Romans 10:1–4)? What is the way of salvation? To whom does God offer it?

MONDAY

*God's Mercy and Kindness
Are Great*

Romans 11:1–21

God Shows Mercy to All People

11 I say then, Hath God cast away his people? God forbid. For I also am an Israelite, of the seed of Abraham, *of* the tribe of Benjamin. [2] God hath not cast away his people which he foreknew. Wot ye not what the scripture saith of Elijah? how he maketh intercession to God against Israel, saying,

[3] Lord, they have killed thy prophets, and digged down thine altars; and I am left alone, and they seek my life. [4] But what saith the answer of God unto him? I have reserved to myself seven thousand men, who have not bowed the knee to *the image* of Baal. [5] Even so then at this present time also there is a remnant according to the election of grace. [6] And if by grace, then *is it* no more of works: otherwise grace is no more grace. But if *it be* of works, then is it no more grace: otherwise work is no more work. [7] What then? Israel hath not obtained that which he seeketh for; but the election hath obtained it, and the rest were blinded [8] (according as it is written, God hath given them the spirit of slumber, eyes that they should not see, and ears that they should not hear;) unto this day. [9] And David saith, Let their table be made a snare, and a trap, and a stumbling block, and a recompence unto them:

[10] let their eyes be darkened, that they may not see, and bow down their back alway. [11] I say then, Have they stumbled that they should fall? God forbid: but *rather* through their fall salvation *is come* unto the Gentiles, for to provoke them to jealousy. [12] Now if the fall of them *be* the riches of the world, and the diminishing of them the riches of the Gentiles; how much more their fulness?

[13] For I speak to you Gentiles, inasmuch as I am the apostle of the Gentiles, I magnify mine office: [14] if by any means I may provoke to emulation *them which are* my flesh, and might save some of them. [15] For if the casting away of them *be* the reconciling of the world, what *shall* the receiving of *them be*, but life from the dead? [16] For if the firstfruit *be* holy, the lump *is* also *holy*: and if the root *be* holy, so *are* the branches. [17] And if some of the branches be broken off, and thou, being a wild olive tree, wert graffed in among them, and with them partakest of the root and fatness of the olive tree; [18] boast not against the branches. But if thou boast, thou bearest not the root, but the root thee. [19] Thou wilt say then, The branches were broken off, that I might be graffed in. [20] Well; because of unbelief they were broken off, and thou standest by faith. Be not highminded, but fear: [21] for if God spared not the natural branches, *take heed* lest he also spare not thee.

OLD TESTAMENT READING

*B*ut if the wicked will turn from all

his sins that he hath committed, and keep all my statutes, and do that which is lawful and right, he shall surely live, he shall not die.

²² All his transgressions that he hath committed, they shall not be mentioned unto him: in his righteousness that he hath done he shall live.

²³ Have I any pleasure at all that the wicked should die? saith the Lord GOD: *and* not that he should return from his ways, and live?

Ezekiel 18:21–23

I N S I G H T S

*K*indness is invariably associated with mercy. It is impossible to be kind without being merciful. Likewise to be merciful is to be kind. It implies that there is a deep and genuine concern for another. This concern is one of compassion and mercy. . . .

Throughout the Scriptures the great theme of God's unrelenting kindness throbs like a powerful heartbeat. . . .

The kindness of God has drawn me to Him with bonds of love stronger than steel. The mercy of my Lord has endeared me to Him with enormous gratitude and thanksgiving. . . .

It is the kindness of God, expressed in Christ and revealed to us by His Spirit that supplies my salvation. His kindness makes provision for my pardon from sins and selfishness at the cost of His own laid down life. It is His kindness that forgives my faults and accepts me into His family as His dearly beloved child. His kindness enables me to stand acquitted of my wrongdoing, justified freely in His pres-

ence. God's kindness removes my guilt and I am at one with Him and others in peace. It is the kindness of God that enables Him to share Himself with me in the inner sanctuary of my spirit, soul, and body. His kindness enables me to be re-made, refashioned, re-formed gently into His likeness. His kindness gives enormous meaning and dignity to this life and endless delight in the life yet to come.

It is the constant, enduring, unchanging kindness of God that gives me every reason to rejoice and revel in life . . . all of life . . . this one and the next.

W. Phillip Keller

P A U S E   F O R   R E F L E C T I O N

*I*s there anyone to whom God doesn't want to offer his forgiveness? In what ways has God shown his forgiveness and mercy to the Jews? To Gentiles? Describe how God's unfailing kindness has touched your heart.

TUESDAY

*God Wants Our Lives to Be
a Sacrifice of Obedience*

Romans 11:22—12:8

*B*ehold therefore the goodness and severity of God: on them which fell, severity; but toward thee, goodness, if thou continue in *his* goodness: otherwise thou also shalt be cut off.

23 And they also, if they abide not still in unbelief, shall be graffed in: for God is able to graff them in again.

24 For if thou wert cut out of the olive tree which is wild by nature, and wert graffed contrary to nature into a good olive tree; how much more shall these, which be the natural *branches*, be graffed into their own olive tree?

25 For I would not, brethren, that ye should be ignorant of this mystery, lest ye should be wise in your own conceits, that blindness in part is happened to Israel, until the fulness of the Gentiles be come in.

26 And so all Israel shall be saved: as it is written, There shall come out of Zion the Deliverer, and shall turn away ungodliness from Jacob:

27 for this *is* my covenant unto them, when I shall take away their sins.

28 As concerning the gospel, *they are* enemies for your sakes: but as touching the election, *they are* beloved for the fathers' sakes.

29 for the gifts and calling of God *are* without repentance.

30 For as ye in times past have not believed God, yet have now obtained mercy through their unbelief:

31 even so have these also now not believed, that through your mercy they also may obtain mercy.

32 For God hath concluded them all in unbelief, that he might have mercy upon all.

Praise to God

O the depth of the riches both of the wisdom and knowledge of God! how unsearchable *are* his judgments, and his ways past finding out!

34 For who hath known the mind of the Lord? or who hath been his counsellor?

35 Or who hath first given to him, and it shall be recompensed unto him again?

36 For of him, and through him, and to him, *are* all things: to whom *be* glory for ever. Amen.

Be Living Sacrifices

12 I beseech you therefore, brethren, by the mercies of God, that ye present your bodies a living sacrifice, holy, acceptable unto God, *which is* your reasonable service.

2 And be not conformed to this world: but be ye transformed by the renewing of your mind, that ye may prove what *is* that good, and acceptable, and perfect, will of God.

3 For I say, through the grace given unto me, to every man that is among you, not to think *of himself* more highly than he ought to think; but to think soberly, according as God hath dealt to every man the measure of faith.

4 For as we have many members in one body, and all members have not the same office:

5 so we, *being* many, are one body in

Christ, and every one members one of another.

[6] Having then gifts differing according to the grace that is given to us, whether prophecy, *let us prophesy* according to the proportion of faith; [7] or ministry, *let us wait* on *our* ministering; or he that teacheth, on teaching;

[8] or he that exhorteth, on exhortation: he that giveth, *let him do it* with simplicity; he that ruleth, with diligence; he that sheweth mercy, with cheerfulness.

OLD TESTAMENT READING

*A*nd Samuel said, Hath the LORD as great delight in burnt offerings and sacrifices, as in obeying the voice of the LORD? Behold, to obey *is* better than sacrifice, *and* to hearken than the fat of rams.

1 Samuel 15:22

INSIGHTS

*M*en would understand; they do not care to obey. They try to understand where it is impossible they could understand except by obeying. They would search into the work of the Lord instead of doing their part in it—thus making it impossible for the Lord to go on with his work, and for themselves to become capable of seeing and understanding what he does. Instead of immediately obeying the Lord of life, the one condition upon which he can help them, and in itself the beginning of their deliverance, they set themselves to question their unenlightened intellects as to his plans for their deliverance—and not merely how he means to carry it out, but whether he is able

to carry it out. They would bind their Samson until they have scanned his limbs and muscles. They delay in setting their foot on the stair that alone can lead them to the house of wisdom until they shall have determined the material and mode of its construction.

For the sake of knowing, they postpone that which alone can enable them to know, and substitute for the true understanding that lies beyond, a false persuasion that they already understand. They will not accept, that is, act upon, their highest privilege, that of obeying the Son of God.

It is on them that do his will that the day dawns. To them the Daystar rises in their hearts. Obedience is the soul of knowledge.

George MacDonald

ACTION POINT

*I*n what ways is your life an offering to God? In what ways are you tempted to fall short of full obedience? Pray that your deepest desire will be to give yourself fully as a living sacrifice to God.

389

WEDNESDAY

Owe Nothing but Love

Romans 12:9—13:14

*L*et love be without dissimulation. Abhor that which is evil; cleave to that which is good.

[10] *Be* kindly affectioned one to another with brotherly love; in honor preferring one another;

[11] not slothful in business; fervent in spirit; serving the Lord;

[12] rejoicing in hope; patient in tribulation; continuing instant in prayer;

[13] distributing to the necessity of saints; given to hospitality.

[14] Bless them which persecute you: bless, and curse not.

[15] Rejoice with them that do rejoice, and weep with them that weep.

[16] *Be* of the same mind one toward another. Mind not high things, but condescend to men of low estate. Be not wise in your own conceits.

[17] Recompense to no man evil for evil. Provide things honest in the sight of all men.

[18] If it be possible, as much as lieth in you, live peaceably with all men.

[19] Dearly beloved, avenge not yourselves, but *rather* give place unto wrath: for it is written, Vengeance *is* mine; I will repay, saith the Lord.

[20] Therefore if thine enemy hunger, feed him; if he thirst, give him drink: for in so doing thou shalt heap coals of fire on his head.

[21] Be not overcome of evil, but overcome evil with good.

Christians Should Obey the Law

13 Let every soul be subject unto the higher powers. For there is no power but of God: the powers that be are ordained of God.

[2] Whosoever therefore resisteth the power, resisteth the ordinance of God: and they that resist shall receive to themselves damnation.

[3] for rulers are not a terror to good works, but to the evil. Wilt thou then not be afraid of the power? do that which is good, and thou shalt have praise of the same:

[4] for he is the minister of God to thee for good. But if thou do that which is evil, be afraid; for he beareth not the sword in vain: for he is the minister of God, a revenger to *execute* wrath upon him that doeth evil.

[5] Wherefore *ye* must needs be subject, not only for wrath, but also for conscience' sake.

[6] For for this cause pay ye tribute also: for they are God's ministers, attending continually upon this very thing.

[7] Render therefore to all their dues: tribute to whom tribute *is due*; custom to whom custom; fear to whom fear; honor to whom honor.

Loving Others

*O*we no man any thing, but to love one another: for he that loveth another hath fulfilled the law.

[9] For this, Thou shalt not commit adultery, Thou shalt not kill, Thou shalt not steal, Thou shalt not bear false witness, Thou shalt not covet; and if *there be* any other commandment, it is briefly comprehended in this saying, namely, Thou shalt love thy neighbor as thyself.

[10] Love worketh no ill to his neighbor: therefore love *is* the fulfilling of the law.

[11] And that, knowing the time, that now *it is* high time to awake out of

sleep: for now *is* our salvation nearer than when we believed.

¹² The night is far spent, the day is at hand: let us therefore cast off the works of darkness, and let us put on the armor of light.

¹³ Let us walk honestly, as in the day; not in rioting and drunkenness, not in chambering and wantonness, not in strife and envying:

¹⁴ but put ye on the Lord Jesus Christ, and make not provision for the flesh, to *fulfil* the lusts *thereof.*

OLD TESTAMENT READING

*T*he wicked borroweth, and payeth not again: but the righteous showeth mercy, and giveth.

²⁶ *He is* ever merciful, and lendeth; and his seed *is* blessed.

Psalm 37:21, 26

INSIGHTS

*T*he context of this passage does . . . set up a principle that says, "If I owe anyone anything, I am not free to give love to that person." Anyone who has borrowed money from another person, and especially another Christian, realizes the wall that immediately goes up from being in a debtor / lender relationship. Debtors and lenders are not really free to love one another. This verse suggests principles for both sides. Lending to another Christian needs to be considered very, very seriously before it is done. On the other side, before you borrow from anyone for anything, consider the ramifications of being in bondage to that person. Are you, in fact, free to love that person? . . .

. . . The reality is that whenever you have borrowed from anyone, you are a servant to that person. . . .

. . . "Why is so much written about debt in God's Word?" I believe there are three reasons. First of all, debt is extremely deceptive. As we said earlier, getting into debt is easy—getting out is next to impossible. Second, debt creates bondage, and if that bondage is to the world system, we are no longer free to be the witnesses in this world that God has called us to be. Third, debt is almost blasphemous when we use it and deny God an opportunity to work. . . .

. . . Being in debt is never the real problem; it is only symptomatic of the real problem, which is usually greed, self-indulgence, impatience, fear, poor self-image, lack of self-discipline, and perhaps others. So, if you find yourself in debt, your first question is not, "How do I get out of debt?" Ask first of all, "Why am I in this situation?" and answer that question. Then getting out of debt will become much easier.

Ron Blue

PAUSE FOR REFLECTION

*W*hat is Jesus' greatest commandment? Examine the relationships between love, debt, ministry, and giving in your life. How do your lifestyle choices hinder your obedience to Christ's commandment to love one another?

THURSDAY

*Live in a Way
that Pleases God;
He Will Judge Our Actions*

Romans 14:1—15:3

Do Not Judge Other People

14 Him that is weak in the faith receive ye, *but* not to doubtful disputations.

2 For one believeth that he may eat all things: another, who is weak, eateth herbs.

3 Let not him that eateth despise him that eateth not; and let not him which eateth not judge him that eateth: for God hath received him.

4 Who art thou that judgest another man's servant? to his own master he standeth or falleth. Yea, he shall be holden up: for God is able to make him stand.

5 One man esteemeth one day above another: another esteemeth every day *alike.* Let every man be fully persuaded in his own mind.

6 He that regardeth the day, regardeth *it* unto the Lord; and he that regardeth not the day, to the Lord he doth not regard *it.* He that eateth, eateth to the Lord, for he giveth God thanks; and he that eateth not, to the Lord he eateth not, and giveth God thanks.

7 For none of us liveth to himself, and no man dieth to himself.

8 For whether we live, we live unto the Lord; and whether we die, we die unto the Lord: whether we live therefore, or die, we are the Lord's.

9 For to this end Christ both died, and rose, and revived, that he might be Lord both of the dead and living.

10 But why dost thou judge thy brother? or why dost thou set at nought thy brother? for we shall all stand before the judgment seat of Christ.

11 For it is written, as I live, saith the Lord, every knee shall bow to me, and every tongue shall confess to God.

12 So then every one of us shall give account of himself to God.

Do Not Cause Others to Sin

*L*et us not therefore judge one another any more: but judge this rather, that no man put a stumbling block or an occasion to fall in *his* brother's way.

14 I know, and am persuaded by the Lord Jesus, that *there is* nothing unclean of itself: but to him that esteemeth any thing to be unclean, to him *it is* unclean.

15 But if thy brother be grieved with *thy* meat, now walkest thou not charitably. Destroy not him with thy meat, for whom Christ died.

16 Let not then your good be evil spoken of:

17 for the kingdom of God is not meat and drink; but righteousness, and peace, and joy in the Holy Ghost.

18 For he that in these things serveth Christ *is* acceptable to God, and approved of men.

19 Let us therefore follow after the things which make for peace, and things wherewith one may edify another.

20 For meat destroy not the work of God. All things indeed *are* pure; but *it is* evil for that man who eateth with offense.

²¹ *It is* good neither to eat flesh, nor to drink wine, nor *any thing* whereby thy brother stumbleth, or is offended, or is made weak.

²² Hast thou faith? have *it* to thyself before God. Happy *is* he that condemneth not himself in that thing which he alloweth.

²³ And he that doubteth is damned if he eat, because *he eateth* not of faith: for whatsoever *is* not of faith is sin.

15 We then that are strong ought to bear the infirmities of the weak, and not to please ourselves.

² Let every one of us please *his* neighbor for *his* good to edification.

³ For even Christ pleased not himself; but, as it is written, The reproaches of them that reproached thee fell on me.

OLD TESTAMENT READING

A man shall be satisfied with good by the fruit of *his* mouth: and the recompense of a man's hands shall be rendered unto him.

Proverbs 12:14

*L*et us hear the conclusion of the whole matter: Fear God, and keep his commandments: for this *is* the whole *duty* of man.

¹⁴ For God shall bring every work into judgment, with every secret thing, whether *it be* good, or whether *it be* evil.

Ecclesiastes 12:13–14

I will say to the north, Give up; and to the south, Keep not back: bring my sons from far, and my daughters from the ends of the earth;

⁷ *even* every one that is called by my name: for I have created him for my glory, I have formed him; yea, I have made him.

Isaiah 43:6–7

INSIGHTS

*W*hen we please God, we have peace. We're not trying to juggle a dozen different things in order to please everyone around us. Instead, we have a single purpose—to please God.

When we try to please ourselves or others, however, things get out of balance. Far too many of us have become overly involved in various causes and have lost our perspective. Our priorities no longer are established by God, but by all the voices—many of which are sincere and good—clamoring around us. We have forgotten that our purpose is to please God.

But as spiritually renewed Christians who aim to please God, we can walk with security and confidence. We no longer view life and its problems with the short-sighted limitations of a merely human perspective. Instead, we view life with the long-term assurance that comes only from God's eternal perspective.

Luis Palau

PAUSE FOR REFLECTION

*F*or whom do believers live and die? How does that affect our lifestyle? What is our guideline for living in a way that pleases God? Who exemplifies such a lifestyle? How are we to treat those whose faith is weak? Why?

FRIDAY

God Is the Source of Our Hope and Joy

Romans 15:4–29

*F*or whatsoever things were written aforetime were written for our learning, that we through patience and comfort of the scriptures might have hope.

[5] Now the God of patience and consolation grant you to be likeminded one toward another according to Christ Jesus:

[6] that ye may with one mind *and* one mouth glorify God, even the Father of our Lord Jesus Christ.

[7] Wherefore receive ye one another, as Christ also received us, to the glory of God.

[8] Now I say that Jesus Christ was a minister of the circumcision for the truth of God, to confirm the promises *made* unto the fathers:

[9] and that the Gentiles might glorify God for *his* mercy; as it is written, For this cause I will confess to thee among the Gentiles, and sing unto thy name.

[10] And again he saith, Rejoice, ye Gentiles, with his people.

[11] And again, Praise the Lord, all ye Gentiles; and laud him, all ye people.

[12] And again, Isaiah saith, There shall be a root of Jesse, and he that shall rise to reign over the Gentiles; in him shall the Gentiles trust.

[13] Now the God of hope fill you with all joy and peace in believing, that ye may abound in hope, through the power of the Holy Ghost.

Paul Talks About His Work

*A*nd I myself also am persuaded of you, my brethren, that ye also are full of goodness, filled with all knowledge, able also to admonish one another.

[15] Nevertheless, brethren, I have written the more boldly unto you in some sort, as putting you in mind, because of the grace that is given to me of God,

[16] that I should be the minister of Jesus Christ to the Gentiles, ministering the gospel of God, that the offering up of the Gentiles might be acceptable, being sanctified by the Holy Ghost.

[17] I have therefore whereof I may glory through Jesus Christ in those things which pertain to God.

[18] For I will not dare to speak of any of those things which Christ hath not wrought by me, to make the Gentiles obedient, by word and deed,

[19] through mighty signs and wonders, by the power of the Spirit of God; so that from Jerusalem, and round about unto Illyricum, I have fully preached the gospel of Christ.

[20] Yea, so have I strived to preach the gospel, not where Christ was named, lest I should build upon another man's foundation:

[21] but as it is written, To whom he was not spoken of, they shall see: and they that have not heard shall understand.

Paul's Plan to Visit Rome

*F*or which cause also I have been much hindered from coming to you.

[23] But now having no more place in these parts, and having a great

394

desire these many years to come unto you;

²⁴ whensoever I take my journey into Spain, I will come to you: for I trust to see you in my journey, and to be brought on my way thitherward by you, if first I be somewhat filled with your *company.*

²⁵ But now I go unto Jerusalem to minister unto the saints.

²⁶ For it hath pleased them of Macedonia and Achaia to make a certain contribution for the poor saints which are at Jerusalem.

²⁷ It hath pleased them verily; and their debtors they are. For if the Gentiles have been made partakers of their spiritual things, their duty is also to minister unto them in carnal things.

²⁸ When therefore I have performed this, and have sealed to them this fruit, I will come by you into Spain.

²⁹ And I am sure that, when I come unto you, I shall come in the fulness of the blessing of the gospel of Christ.

OLD TESTAMENT READING

*O*ur soul waiteth for the LORD: he *is* our help and our shield.

²¹ For our heart shall rejoice in him, because we have trusted in his holy name.

²² Let thy mercy, O LORD, be upon us, according as we hope in thee.

Psalm 33:20–22

INSIGHTS

*A*s Jesus was entering into the last days of his life on earth, he prayed for his disciples and for all disciples to come. His petitions were for union with the Father, joy, protection, and usefulness. The sequence of those petitions is significant (John 17:11–17).

Friendship with Christ is the first priority and is basic for the qualities that follow. Out of that intimate, love relationship, joy is a logical consequence. Jesus knew, as he prayed for his disciples, that if they did indeed come into fellowship with him and exhibit the kind of full-fledged joy that he gives, there would be opposition from the world, and so he prayed not that his disciples would be protected from the world or taken out of it into a kind of insulated, holy huddle, but that they would be protected from anything that would destroy that union and joy. Then, out of that dynamic partnership, usefulness would naturally flow.

Many of us, brought up in the work ethic of our churches, have tried to get the union by our works. We have tried to exhibit joy we didn't have or have hoped to earn joy by working hard. While joy comes through giving myself away, I become burned out unless that joy and my service flow from friendship with Christ. . . .

. . . The more I know Him, the more I experience that deep inner well of joy that is not dependent on external circumstances. This joy is present even in the midst of suffering and sorrow; it is a motivating power even in discouragement and dismay.

Jeanie Miley

ACTION POINT

*W*hom does God fill with hope and joy? Why is God worthy of our trust and hope? Thank him. Rejoice in his unfailing love!

WEEKEND

Watch Out for False Prophets

Romans 15:30—16:27

*N*ow I beseech you, brethren, for the Lord Jesus Christ's sake, and for the love of the Spirit, that ye strive together with me in *your* prayers to God for me;

[31] that I may be delivered from them that do not believe in Judea; and that my service which *I have* for Jerusalem may be accepted of the saints;

[32] that I may come unto you with joy by the will of God, and may with you be refreshed.

[33] Now the God of peace *be* with you all. Amen.

Greetings to the Christians

16 I commend unto you Phoebe our sister, which is a servant of the church which is at Cenchrea:

[2] that ye receive her in the Lord, as becometh saints, and that ye assist her in whatsoever business she hath need of you: for she hath been a succorer of many, and of myself also.

[3] Greet Priscilla and Aquila my helpers in Christ Jesus:

[4] who have for my life laid down their own necks: unto whom not only I give thanks, but also all the churches of the Gentiles.

[5] Likewise *greet* the church that is in their house. Salute my wellbeloved Epenetus, who is the firstfruits of Achaia unto Christ.

[6] Greet Mary, who bestowed much labor on us.

[7] Salute Andronicus and Junia, my kinsmen, and my fellowprisoners, who are of note among the apostles, who also were in Christ before me.

[8] Greet Amplias my beloved in the Lord.

[9] Salute Urbane, our helper in Christ, and Stachys my beloved.

[10] Salute Apelles approved in Christ. Salute them which are of Aristobulus' *household.*

[11] Salute Herodion my kinsman. Greet them that be of the *household* of Narcissus, which are in the Lord.

[12] Salute Tryphaena and Tryphosa, who labor in the Lord. Salute the beloved Persis, which labored much in the Lord.

[13] Salute Rufus chosen in the Lord, and his mother and mine.

[14] Salute Asyncritus, Phlegon, Hermas, Patrobas, Hermes, and the brethren which are with them.

[15] Salute Philologus, and Julia, Nereus, and his sister, and Olympas, and all the saints which are with them.

[16] Salute one another with a holy kiss. The churches of Christ salute you.

[17] Now I beseech you, brethren, mark them which cause divisions and offenses contrary to the doctrine which ye have learned; and avoid them.

[18] For they that are such serve not our Lord Jesus Christ, but their own belly; and by good words and fair speeches deceive the hearts of the simple.

[19] For your obedience is come abroad unto all *men.* I am glad therefore on your behalf: but yet I would have you wise unto that which is good, and simple concerning evil.

[20] And the God of peace shall bruise Satan under your feet shortly. The grace of our Lord Jesus Christ *be* with you. Amen.

[21] Timothy my workfellow, and Lucius, and Jason, and Sosipater, my kinsmen, salute you.

[22] I Tertius, who wrote *this* epistle, salute you in the Lord.

[23] Gaius mine host, and of the whole church, saluteth you. Erastus the chamberlain of the city saluteth you, and Quartus a brother.

[24] The grace of our Lord Jesus Christ *be* with you all. Amen.

[25] Now to him that is of power to stablish you according to my gospel, and the preaching of Jesus Christ, according to the revelation of the mystery, which was kept secret since the world began,

[26] but now is made manifest, and by the Scriptures of the prophets, according to the commandment of the everlasting God, made known to all nations for the obedience of faith:

[27] To God only wise, *be* glory through Jesus Christ for ever. Amen.

OLD   TESTAMENT   READING

*T*hus saith the Lord GOD; Woe unto the foolish prophets, that follow their own spirit, and have seen nothing!

[7] Have ye not seen a vain vision, and have ye not spoken a lying divination, whereas ye say, The LORD saith *it*; albeit I have not spoken?

Ezekiel 13:3, 7

INSIGHTS

*F*or the last sixty or so years professors and teachers in centers of theological training have had Satan's special attention, and so successful has he been that modernism has thoroughly penetrated the church. His ministers—yes, the devil's ministers, for he has many in the ministry!—are masquerading as ministers of truth and righteousness.

. . . Modern heresies and criticism are pitted against the infallible Word, the infallible Christ, the fact of sin, the redemptive works of the cross, the witness of the Holy Spirit. Knowing how completely the deity and death of Christ destroyed his works, Satan, through religious teachers, has been attacking the virgin birth, the sinlessness, the efficacious death, and the resurrection of our blessed Lord. . . .

By modernism, Satan has succeeded in robbing the church of her power in the world. With a humanized Christ, a mutilated Bible, and a glorified self, modernism is bankrupt. Nothing can damn evangelism like modernism, and Satan knows that—hence his untiring efforts to create an ever-increasing army of false teachers. . . . Let us pray for spiritual perception, whereby we can detect, and that immediately, the subtle error in a good deal we hear from some of the pulpits of our land.

Herbert Lockyer

APPLICATION

*H*ow seriously does God want his people to view the problem of false prophets? How can we guard against their deception?

MONDAY

God's Wisdom Defies Human Wisdom

---

1 Corinthians 1:1–25

1 Paul, called *to be* an apostle of Jesus Christ through the will of God, and Sosthenes *our* brother,

2 Unto the church of God which is at Corinth, to them that are sanctified in Christ Jesus, called *to be* saints, with all that in every place call upon the name of Jesus Christ our Lord, both theirs and ours:

3 Grace *be* unto you, and peace, from God our Father, and *from* the Lord Jesus Christ.

Paul Gives Thanks to God

I thank my God always on your behalf, for the grace of God which is given you by Jesus Christ;

5 that in every thing ye are enriched by him, in all utterance, and *in* all knowledge;

6 even as the testimony of Christ was confirmed in you:

7 so that ye come behind in no gift; waiting for the coming of our Lord Jesus Christ:

8 who shall also confirm you unto the end, *that ye may be* blameless in the day of our Lord Jesus Christ.

9 God *is* faithful, by whom ye were called unto the fellowship of his Son Jesus Christ our Lord.

Divisions in the Church

*N*ow I beseech you, brethren, by the name of our Lord Jesus Christ, that ye all speak the same thing, and *that* there be no divisions among you; but *that* ye be perfectly joined together in the same mind and in the same judgment.

11 For it hath been declared unto me of you, my brethren, by them *which are of the house* of Chloe, that there are contentions among you.

12 Now this I say, that every one of you saith, I am of Paul; and I of Apollos; and I of Cephas; and I of Christ.

13 Is Christ divided? was Paul crucified for you? or were ye baptized in the name of Paul?

14 I thank God that I baptized none of you, but Crispus and Gaius;

15 lest any should say that I had baptized in mine own name.

16 And I baptized also the household of Stephanas: besides, I know not whether I baptized any other.

17 For Christ sent me not to baptize, but to preach the gospel: not with wisdom of words, lest the cross of Christ should be made of none effect.

Christ Is God's Power and Wisdom

*F*or the preaching of the cross is to them that perish, foolishness; but unto us which are saved, it is the power of God.

19 For it is written, I will destroy the wisdom of the wise, and will bring to nothing the understanding of the prudent.

20 Where *is* the wise? where *is* the scribe? where *is* the disputer of this world? hath not God made foolish the wisdom of this world?

21 For after that in the wisdom of God the world by wisdom knew not God, it pleased God by the foolishness of preaching to save them that believe.

22 For the Jews require a sign, and the Greeks seek after wisdom:

23 but we preach Christ crucified, unto the Jews a stumblingblock, and unto the Greeks foolishness;

24 but unto them which are called, both Jews and Greeks, Christ the power of God, and the wisdom of God.

25 Because the foolishness of God is wiser than men; and the weakness of God is stronger than men.

OLD TESTAMENT READING

I am the Lord that maketh all *things*: that stretcheth forth the heavens alone; that spreadeth abroad the earth by myself;

25 that frustrateth the tokens of the liars, and maketh diviners mad; that turneth wise *men* backward, and maketh their knowledge foolish;

26 that confirmeth the word of his servant, and performeth the counsel of his messengers.

Isaiah 44:24b–26a

INSIGHTS

The Jews sought after wonders, but the Greeks sought after wisdom. The Greeks were known for their great philosophers and their knowledge. They had come to the point where they literally deified wisdom. They were worshiping at the shrine of science and knowledge. Does that sound familiar today in the twentieth century?

We have people today who say, "If you can't put it into the test tube or in a mathematical equation, we will not believe it." But you can't put the Cross in a crucible, and you can't put faith in a formula. The great

philosopher, Pascal, said, "The heart has its reasons that reason knows nothing of." . . .

. . . God is too wise to let man come to know Him by his own wisdom. Man cannot solve his problems because he will not recognize their source, which is sin. Furthermore, he will not recognize the solution, which is salvation. God is so wise that He is not going to let man come to Him by his own wisdom.

As a matter of fact, we are told in 1 Corinthians 3:19 that "the wisdom of this world is foolishness with God." Think about it, a world full of wisdom is just a thimble full of foolishness to God. The Prophet Jeremiah said, "The wise men are ashamed. They are dismayed and taken. Behold they have rejected the Word of the Lord; so what wisdom do they have?" (Jer. 8:9). . . .

. . . If a person is going to come to God, he or she will have to come as a little child (Matt. 18:3).

James Merritt

PAUSE FOR REFLECTION

Why do you think Paul says, "For Christ sent me . . . to preach the gospel: not with wisdom of words, lest the cross of Christ should be made of none effect"? Do you agree that worldly wisdom would nullify the cross? Why? Why do you think that God, the source of all wisdom, turns the world's wisdom into foolishness?

TUESDAY

God Is the Source of Wisdom

1 Corinthians 1:26–2:16

*F*or ye see your calling, brethren, how that not many wise men after the flesh, not many mighty, not many noble, *are called:*

27 but God hath chosen the foolish things of the world to confound the wise; and God hath chosen the weak things of the world to confound the things which are mighty;

28 and base things of the world, and things which are despised, hath God chosen, *yea*, and things which are not, to bring to nought things that are:

29 that no flesh should glory in his presence.

30 But of him are ye in Christ Jesus, who of God is made unto us wisdom, and righteousness, and sanctification, and redemption:

31 that, according as it is written, He that glorieth, let him glory in the Lord.

The Message of Christ's Death

2 And I, brethren, when I came to you, came not with excellency of speech or of wisdom, declaring unto you the testimony of God.

2 For I determined not to know any thing among you, save Jesus Christ, and him crucified.

3 And I was with you in weakness, and in fear, and in much trembling.

4 And my speech and my preaching *was* not with enticing words of man's wisdom, but in demonstration of the Spirit and of power:

5 that your faith should not stand in the wisdom of men, but in the power of God.

God's Wisdom

*H*owbeit we speak wisdom among them that are perfect: yet not the wisdom of this world, nor of the princes of this world, that come to nought:

7 but we speak the wisdom of God in a mystery, *even* the hidden *wisdom*, which God ordained before the world unto our glory;

8 which none of the princes of this world knew: for had they known *it*, they would not have crucified the Lord of glory.

9 But as it is written, Eye hath not seen, nor ear heard, neither have entered into the heart of man, the things which God hath prepared for them that love him.

10 But God hath revealed *them* unto us by his Spirit: for the Spirit searcheth all things, yea, the deep things of God.

11 For what man knoweth the things of a man, save the spirit of man which is in him? even so the things of God knoweth no man, but the Spirit of God.

12 Now we have received, not the spirit of the world, but the spirit which is of God; that we might know the things that are freely given to us of God.

13 Which things also we speak, not in the words which man's wisdom teacheth, but which the Holy Ghost teacheth; comparing spiritual things with spiritual.

14 But the natural man receiveth not the things of the Spirit of God: for they are foolishness unto him: nei-

ther can he know *them*, because they are spiritually discerned.

¹⁵ But he that is spiritual judgeth all things, yet he himself is judged of no man.

¹⁶ For who hath known the mind of the Lord, that he may instruct him? But we have the mind of Christ.

OLD TESTAMENT READING

*W*hence then cometh wisdom? And where *is* the place of understanding?

²¹ seeing it is hid from the eyes of all living, and kept close from the fowls of the air.

²² Destruction and death say, We have heard the fame thereof with our ears.

²³ God understandeth the way thereof, and he knoweth the place thereof.

²⁴ For he looketh to the ends of the earth, *and* seeth under the whole heaven;

²⁵ to make the weight for the winds; and he weigheth the waters by measure.

²⁶ When he made a decree for the rain, and a way for the lightning of the thunder;

²⁷ then did he see it, and declare it; he prepared it, yea, and searched it out.

²⁸ And unto man he said, Behold, the fear of the Lord, that *is* wisdom; and to depart from evil *is* understanding.

Job 28:20–28

INSIGHTS

*M*en are always seeking for greater wisdom, but they usually bypass the Ultimate Source of wisdom. The Scriptures clearly point this direc-

tion. They reveal, "The fear of the Lord is the beginning of wisdom, and the knowledge of the Holy One is understanding" (Prov. 9:10). But what has man done with this tremendous resource at his fingertips? Ignored it! "For even though they knew God, they did not honor Him as God, or give thanks; but they became futile in their speculations, and their foolish heart was darkened. Professing to be wise, they became fools" (Rom. 1:21–22).*

Since God's wisdom resides in His Word, it is imperative to know what He has revealed, but even many Christians ignore a regular time reading and studying the Scriptures. Therefore, many of their decisions are foolish, because they've not consulted the Ultimate Source of wisdom.

Rick Yohn

APPLICATION

*H*ow does Scripture define wisdom? How does a person gain wisdom? Does God need educated and wise teachers to communicate his message? What kind of person does God use? Are you willing to be that kind of person? How will you gain God's wisdom?*

WEDNESDAY

Christ Is the Cornerstone of Our Faith, so Our Works Must Stand His Test

1 Corinthians 3:1—4:5

Following People Is Wrong

3 And I, brethren, could not speak unto you as unto spiritual, but as unto carnal, *even* as unto babes in Christ.

2 I have fed you with milk, and not with meat: for hitherto ye were not able *to bear it*, neither yet now are ye able.

3 For ye are yet carnal: for whereas *there is* among you envying, and strife, and divisions, are ye not carnal, and walk as men?

4 For while one saith, I am of Paul; and another, *I am* of Apollos; are ye not carnal?

5 Who then is Paul, and who *is* Apollos, but ministers by whom ye believed, even as the Lord gave to every man?

6 I have planted, Apollos watered; but God gave the increase.

7 So then neither is he that planteth any thing, neither he that watereth; but God that giveth the increase.

8 Now he that planteth and he that watereth are one: and every man shall receive his own reward according to his own labor.

9 For we are laborers together with God: ye are God's husbandry, *ye are* God's building.

10 According to the grace of God which is given unto me, as a wise masterbuilder, I have laid the foundation, and another buildeth thereon. But let every man take heed how he buildeth thereupon.

11 For other foundation can no man lay than that is laid, which is Jesus Christ.

12 Now if any man build upon this foundation gold, silver, precious stones, wood, hay, stubble;

13 every man's work shall be made manifest: for the day shall declare it, because it shall be revealed by fire; and the fire shall try every man's work of what sort it is.

14 If any man's work abide which he hath built thereupon, he shall receive a reward.

15 If any man's work shall be burned, he shall suffer loss: but he himself shall be saved; yet so as by fire.

16 Know ye not that ye are the temple of God, and *that* the Spirit of God dwelleth in you?

17 If any man defile the temple of God, him shall God destroy; for the temple of God is holy, which *temple* ye are.

18 Let no man deceive himself. If any man among you seemeth to be wise in this world, let him become a fool, that he may be wise.

19 For the wisdom of this world is foolishness with God: For it is written, He taketh the wise in their own craftiness.

20 And again, The Lord knoweth the thoughts of the wise, that they are vain.

21 Therefore let no man glory in men: For all things are yours;

22 Whether Paul, or Apollos, or Cephas, or the world, or life, or death, or things present, or things to come; all are yours;

23 and ye are Christ's; and Christ *is* God's.

Apostles Are Stewards of Christ

4 Let a man so account of us, as of the ministers of Christ, and stewards of the mysteries of God.

2 Moreover it is required in stewards, that a man be found faithful.

3 But with me it is a very small thing that I should be judged of you, or of man's judgment: yea, I judge not mine own self.

4 For I know nothing by myself; yet am I not hereby justified: but he that judgeth me is the Lord.

5 Therefore judge nothing before the time, until the Lord come, who both will bring to light the hidden things of darkness, and will make manifest the counsels of the hearts: and then shall every man have praise of God.

OLD TESTAMENT READING

And it shall come to pass, *that* in all the land, saith the LORD, two parts therein shall be cut off *and* die; but the third shall be left therein.

9 And I will bring the third part through the fire, and will refine them as silver is refined, and will try them as gold is tried: they shall call on my name, and I will hear them: I will say, It *is* my people: and they shall say, The LORD *is* my God.

Zechariah 13:8–9

The stone *which* the builders refused is become the head *stone* of the corner.

Psalm 118:22

INSIGHTS

What does it mean to build your house on the rock or to dig deeply and lay a foundation? . . . It is a

matter of building on Jesus Himself. . . . *To practice His words means . . . to believe that He is who He says He is and to turn from sin to faith in Him as the way of salvation. . . .*

Isaiah writes, "This is what the Sovereign LORD says: 'See I lay a stone in Zion, a tested stone, a precious cornerstone for a sure foundation'" (Isa. 28:16). Paul declares, "You are . . . built on the foundation of the apostles and prophets, with Christ Jesus himself as the chief cornerstone" (Eph 2:19–20). . . . That is the true sense of Christ's teaching: "If you want a life that will last for eternity, build on Me." We sing:

*My hope is built on nothing less
Than Jesus' blood and righteousness;
I dare not trust the sweetest frame,
But wholly lean on Jesus' name.*

*On Christ, the solid rock, I stand;
All other ground is sinking sand. . . .*

. . . A life built on Jesus and His teachings will stand—it will stand in the trials and testings of this life, and it will stand in eternity. . . .

. . . Jesus says that although rains will fall, floods will rise, and winds will blow, the life that is constructed on Him will survive the blast and last forever.

James Boice

ACTION POINT

Who will test our works? Why? On what foundation are you building your life's work?

THURSDAY

God Will Not Tolerate Sin Among His People

1 Corinthians 4:6—5:8

*A*nd these things, brethren, I have in a figure transferred to myself and to Apollos for your sakes; that ye might learn in us not to think *of men* above that which is written, that no one of you be puffed up for one against another.

7 For who maketh thee to differ *from another?* and what hast thou that thou didst not receive? now if thou didst receive *it*, why dost thou glory, as if thou hadst not received *it?*

8 Now ye are full, now ye are rich, ye have reigned as kings without us: and I would to God ye did reign, that we also might reign with you.

9 For I think that God hath set forth us the apostles last, as it were appointed to death: for we are made a spectacle unto the world, and to angels, and to men.

10 We *are* fools for Christ's sake, but ye *are* wise in Christ; we *are* weak, but ye *are* strong; ye *are* honorable, but we *are* despised.

11 Even unto this present hour we both hunger, and thirst, and are naked, and are buffeted, and have no certain dwellingplace;

12 and labor, working with our own hands: being reviled, we bless; being persecuted, we suffer it:

13 being defamed, we entreat: we are made as the filth of the world, *and are* the offscouring of all things unto this day.

14 I write not these things to shame you, but as my beloved sons I warn *you*.

15 For though ye have ten thousand instructors in Christ, yet *have ye* not many fathers: for in Christ Jesus I have begotten you through the gospel.

16 Wherefore I beseech you, be ye followers of me.

17 For this cause have I sent unto you Timothy, who is my beloved son, and faithful in the Lord, who shall bring you into remembrance of my ways which be in Christ, as I teach every where in every church.

18 Now some are puffed up, as though I would not come to you.

19 But I will come to you shortly, if the Lord will, and will know, not the speech of them which are puffed up, but the power.

20 For the kingdom of God *is* not in word, but in power.

21 What will ye? shall I come unto you with a rod, or in love, and *in* the spirit of meekness?

Wickedness in the Church

5 It is reported commonly *that there is* fornication among you, and such fornication as is not so much as named among the Gentiles, that one should have his father's wife.

2 And ye are puffed up, and have not rather mourned, that he that hath done this deed might be taken away from among you.

3 For I verily, as absent in body, but present in spirit, have judged already, as though I were present, *concerning* him that hath so done this deed,

4 in the name of our Lord Jesus Christ, when ye are gathered together, and my spirit, with the power of our Lord Jesus Christ,

⁵ to deliver such a one unto Satan for the destruction of the flesh, that the spirit may be saved in the day of the Lord Jesus.

⁶ Your glorying *is* not good. Know ye not that a little leaven leaveneth the whole lump?

⁷ Purge out therefore the old leaven, that ye may be a new lump, as ye are unleavened. For even Christ our passover is sacrificed for us:

⁸ therefore let us keep the feast, not with old leaven, neither with the leaven of malice and wickedness; but with the unleavened *bread* of sincerity and truth.

OLD TESTAMENT READING

*I*f there be found among you, within any of thy gates which the LORD thy God giveth thee, man or woman, that hath wrought wickedness in the sight of the LORD thy God, in transgressing his covenant,

⁴ and it be told thee, and thou hast heard *of it*, and inquired diligently, and, behold, *it be* true, *and* the thing certain, *that* such abomination is wrought in Israel:

⁵ then shalt thou bring forth that man or that woman, which have committed that wicked thing, unto thy gates, *even* that man or that woman, and shalt stone them with stones, till they die.

¹² And the man that will do presumptuously, and will not hearken unto the priest that standeth to minister there before the LORD thy God, or unto the judge, even that man shall die: and thou shalt put away the evil from Israel.

¹³ And all the people shall hear, and fear, and do no more presumptuously.
Deuteronomy 17:2, 4–5, 12–13

INSIGHTS

*C*an a Christian get away with sin? Some people seem to think so. However, a closer look points to another answer. God is always opposed to sin. He is never deceived and cannot be outwitted. He may allow sin to continue for a time, but there will be a day of accountability.

Nothing leads to evil quite as much as the idea that this world is all there is. Those who commit violent crimes and who harm the innocent have usually first convinced themselves that there will never be a day of judgment. Even the motorist speeding down the highway has convinced himself he will not receive a speeding ticket.

However, Jesus says that people who believe they will never be found out are wrong: "There is nothing covered up that will not be revealed, and hidden that will not be known" (Luke 12:2). . . .

. . . God totally opposes sin. Take a favorable attitude toward sin and God must take an unfavorable attitude toward you. No Christian can entertain sin and get away with it. . . .

God will not allow sin in the lives of His children to go unchecked.
George Sweeting
Donald Sweeting

APPLICATION

*W*hy does God tell his people to punish the sinners among them? What was Paul's response to sin in the Corinthian church? What is your response to sin? How might your response be more pleasing to God?

FRIDAY

*Honor God with Your Body;
Keep Yourself from Sexual Sin*

1 Corinthians 5:9—6:20

I wrote unto you in an epistle not to company with fornicators:

¹⁰ yet not altogether with the fornicators of this world, or with the covetous, or extortioners, or with idolaters; for then must ye needs go out of the world.

¹¹ But now I have written unto you not to keep company, if any man that is called a brother be a fornicator, or covetous, or an idolater, or a railer, or a drunkard, or a extortioner; with such a one, no, not to eat.

¹² For what have I to do to judge them also that are without? do not ye judge them that are within?

¹³ But them that are without God judgeth. Therefore put away from among yourselves that wicked person.

Judging Problems Among Christians

6 Dare any of you, having a matter against another, go to law before the unjust, and not before the saints?

² Do ye not know that the saints shall judge the world? and if the world shall be judged by you, are ye unworthy to judge the smallest matters?

³ Know ye not that we shall judge angels? how much more things that pertain to this life?

⁴ If then ye have judgments of things pertaining to this life, set them to judge who are least esteemed in the church.

⁵ I speak to your shame. Is it so, that there is not a wise man among you? no, not one that shall be able to judge between his brethren?

⁶ but brother goeth to law with brother, and that before the unbelievers.

⁷ Now therefore there is utterly a fault among you, because ye go to law one with another. Why do ye not rather take wrong? why do ye not rather *suffer yourselves* to be defrauded?

⁸ Nay, ye do wrong, and defraud, and that *your* brethren.

⁹ Know ye not that the unrighteous shall not inherit the kingdom of God? Be not deceived: neither fornicators, nor idolaters, nor adulterers, nor effeminate, nor abusers of themselves with mankind,

¹⁰ nor thieves, nor covetous, nor drunkards, nor revilers, nor extortioners, shall inherit the kingdom of God.

¹¹ And such were some of you: but ye are washed, but ye are sanctified, but ye are justified in the name of the Lord Jesus, and by the Spirit of our God.

Use Your Bodies for God's Glory

*A*ll things are lawful unto me, but all things are not expedient: all things are lawful for me, but I will not be brought under the power of any.

¹³ Meats for the belly, and the belly for meats: but God shall destroy both it and them. Now the body *is* not for fornication, but for the Lord; and the Lord for the body.

¹⁴ And God hath both raised up the Lord, and will also raise up us by his own power.

¹⁵ Know ye not that your bodies are the members of Christ? shall I then take the members of Christ, and make *them* the members of a harlot? God forbid.
¹⁶ What! know ye not that he which is joined to a harlot is one body? for two, saith he, shall be one flesh.
¹⁷ But he that is joined unto the Lord is one spirit.
¹⁸ Flee fornication. Every sin that a man doeth is without the body; but he that committeth fornication sinneth against his own body.
¹⁹ What! know ye not that your body is the temple of the Holy Ghost *which is* in you, which ye have of God, and ye are not your own?
²⁰ For ye are bought with a price: therefore glorify God in your body, and in your spirit, which are God's.

OLD TESTAMENT READING

*C*an a man take fire in his bosom, and his clothes not be burned?
²⁸ Can one go upon hot coals, and his feet not be burned?
²⁹ So he that goeth in to his neighbor's wife; whosoever toucheth her shall not be innocent.

Proverbs 6:27–29

INSIGHTS

*I*t's often said that people "fall" into immorality. The expression is as revealing as it is faulty and dangerous. The very term fall betrays a victim mentality. It sounds as if we were walking down a street and someone tripped us or kicked our feet out from under us. It implies that moral collapse comes out of nowhere, that there is little or noth-

ing we could have done to prevent what happened.

We do not fall into immorality. We walk into it. Indeed, sometimes we run headlong into it. We must realize from the beginning that immorality is a choice. It is not something that happens to people. . . .

Sexual sin never comes out of the clear blue sky. It is often the result of a long process in which a mind susceptible to sin is granted unguarded exposure to immoral input. "Sow a thought, reap an action. Sow an action, reap a habit. Sow a habit, reap a character. Sow a character, reap a destiny." Our thoughts are the fabric with which we weave our character and destiny. We must actively fight off thoughts of impurity. But the key to doing this is not simply saying "I will not lust, I will not lust"—that often has the same effect as saying, "I will not think of purple elephants." We must cultivate our hearts and minds with what is godly and pure. These better thoughts will displace others (Phil 4:8).

Randy Alcorn

PAUSE FOR REFLECTION

*W*hat does Paul say about judging the lifestyles of other Christians? What sins, in addition to sexual sins, does Paul take a hard line against? Why are we to run away from sin? What are the penalties for continuing in sin?

WEEKEND

*Marriage Is a Gift from God
Not to Be Taken Lightly*

1 Corinthians 7:1–24

About Marriage

7 Now concerning the things whereof ye wrote unto me: *It is* good for a man not to touch a woman.
² Nevertheless, *to avoid* fornication, let every man have his own wife, and let every woman have her own husband.
³ Let the husband render unto the wife due benevolence: and likewise also the wife unto the husband.
⁴ The wife hath not power of her own body, but the husband: and likewise also the husband hath not power of his own body, but the wife.
⁵ Defraud ye not one the other, except *it be* with consent for a time, that ye may give yourselves to fasting and prayer; and come together again, that Satan tempt you not for your incontinency.
⁶ But I speak this by permission, *and* not of commandment.
⁷ For I would that all men were even as I myself. But every man hath his proper gift of God, one after this manner, and another after that.
⁸ I say therefore to the unmarried and widows, It is good for them if they abide even as I.
⁹ But if they cannot contain, let them marry: for it is better to marry than to burn.
¹⁰ And unto the married I command, *yet* not I, but the Lord, Let not the wife depart from *her* husband:
¹¹ but and if she depart, let her remain unmarried, or be reconciled to *her* husband: and let not the husband put away *his* wife.
¹² But to the rest speak I, not the Lord: If any brother hath a wife that believeth not, and she be pleased to dwell with him, let him not put her away.
¹³ And the woman which hath a husband that believeth not, and if he be pleased to dwell with her, let her not leave him.
¹⁴ For the unbelieving husband is sanctified by the wife, and the unbelieving wife is sanctified by the husband: else were your children unclean; but now are they holy.
¹⁵ But if the unbelieving depart, let him depart. A brother or a sister is not under bondage in such *cases:* but God hath called us to peace.
¹⁶ For what knowest thou, O wife, whether thou shalt save *thy* husband? or how knowest thou, O man, whether thou shalt save *thy* wife?

Live as God Called You

B ut as God hath distributed to every man, as the Lord hath called every one, so let him walk. And so ordain I in all churches.
¹⁸ Is any man called being circumcised? let him not become uncircumcised. Is any called in uncircumcision? let him not be circumcised.
¹⁹ Circumcision is nothing, and uncircumcision is nothing, but the keeping of the commandments of God.
²⁰ Let every man abide in the same calling wherein he was called.
²¹ Art thou called *being* a servant? care not for it: but if thou mayest be made free, use *it* rather.
²² For he that is called in the Lord,

being a servant, is the Lord's free-man: likewise also he that is called, *being* free, is Christ's servant.

²³ Ye are bought with a price; be not ye the servants of men.

²⁴ Brethren, let every man, wherein he is called, therein abide with God.

OLD TESTAMENT READING

*A*nd did not he make one? Yet had he the residue of the Spirit. And wherefore one? That he might seek a godly seed. Therefore take heed to your spirit, and let none deal treacherously against the wife of his youth.

¹⁶ For the LORD, the God of Israel, saith that he hateth putting away: for *one* covereth violence with his garment, saith the LORD of hosts: therefore take heed to your spirit, that ye deal not treacherously.

Malachi 2:15–16

INSIGHTS

If Paul is writing anything . . . , he is writing this, "When you marry, you marry for life." He has permanence in mind.

- *The wife should not leave her husband (v. 10).*
- *The husband should not leave his wife (v. 11).*
- *Let him not send her away (v. 12).*
- *Let her not send him away (v. 13).*

To write it once would be sufficient. Twice would be extremely and unmistakably clear. Three times would be more than enough. But four times? The man means business!

Years ago Cynthia and I took the ugly word divorce out of our dia-logues. We agreed we would not even store it in the arsenal of our argument vocabulary. No matter how heated our disagreements may be, we'd not threaten each other with that term. It does something to a marriage when you can count on your partner to stick around and hammer out your differences with each other instead of walking away from them.

What does it take to stick it out . . . to be permanently committed to each other? I repeat, it takes grace! It takes an enormous amount of grace to negotiate through the mine field of disagreements. It takes grace to forgive and go on. Grace to hang tough even though the same mistake is made over and over or the same sin committed again and again. A marriage well-oiled by grace is durable, longlasting—protected against the wear and tear of friction.

Charles Swindoll

APPLICATION

*W*hat do you learn about the seriousness of marriage from these Scripture readings? What adjustments need to be made in your thinking toward marriage? Will you make them?

MONDAY

To Marry or Not to Marry?

1 Corinthians 7:25—8:8

Questions About Getting Married

Now concerning virgins I have no commandment of the Lord: yet I give my judgment, as one that hath obtained mercy of the Lord to be faithful.

²⁶ I suppose therefore that this is good for the present distress, *I say*, that *it is* good for a man so to be.

²⁷ Art thou bound unto a wife? seek not to be loosed. Art thou loosed from a wife? seek not a wife.

²⁸ But and if thou marry, thou hast not sinned; and if a virgin marry, she hath not sinned. Nevertheless such shall have trouble in the flesh: but I spare you.

²⁹ But this I say, brethren, the time *is* short: it remaineth, that both they that have wives be as though they had none;

³⁰ and they that weep, as though they wept not; and they that rejoice, as though they rejoiced not; and they that buy, as though they possessed not;

³¹ and they that use this world, as not abusing *it*: for the fashion of this world passeth away.

³² But I would have you without carefulness. He that is unmarried careth for the things that belong to the Lord, how he may please the Lord:

³³ but he that is married careth for the things that are of the world, how he may please *his* wife.

³⁴ There is difference *also* between a wife and a virgin. The unmarried woman careth for the things of the Lord, that she may be holy both in body and in spirit: but she that is married careth for the things of the world, how she may please *her* husband.

³⁵ And this I speak for your own profit; not that I may cast a snare upon you, but for that which is comely, and that ye may attend upon the Lord without distraction.

³⁶ But if any man think that he behaveth himself uncomely toward his virgin, if she pass the flower of *her age,* and need so require, let him do what he will, he sinneth not: let them marry.

³⁷ Nevertheless he that standeth steadfast in his heart, having no necessity, but hath power over his own will, and hath so decreed in his heart that he will keep his virgin, doeth well.

³⁸ So then he that giveth *her* in marriage doeth well; but he that giveth *her* not in marriage doeth better.

³⁹ The wife is bound by the law as long as her husband liveth; but if her husband be dead, she is at liberty to be married to whom she will; only in the Lord.

⁴⁰ But she is happier if she so abide, after my judgment: and I think also that I have the Spirit of God.

About Food Offered to Idols

8 Now as touching things offered unto idols, we know that we all have knowledge. Knowledge puffeth up, but charity edifieth.

² And if any man think that he knoweth anything, he knoweth nothing yet as he ought to know.

³ But if any man love God, the same is known of him.

⁴ As concerning therefore the eating of those things that are offered in sacrifice unto idols, we know that an idol *is* nothing in the world, and that *there is* none other God but one.

⁵ For though there be that are called gods, whether in heaven or in earth, (as there be gods many, and lords many,)

⁶ but to us *there is but* one God, the Father, of whom *are* all things, and we in him; and one Lord Jesus Christ, by whom *are* all things, and we by him.

⁷ Howbeit *there is* not in every man that knowledge: for some with conscience of the idol unto this hour eat *it* as a thing offered unto an idol; and their conscience being weak is defiled.

⁸ But meat commendeth us not to God: for neither, if we eat, are we the better; neither, if we eat not, are we the worse.

OLD TESTAMENT READING

God Calls Jeremiah for Special Service

*T*hen the word of the LORD came unto me, saying,

⁵ Before I formed thee in the belly I knew thee; and before thou camest forth out of the womb I sanctified thee, *and* I ordained thee a prophet unto the nations.

⁶ Then said I, Ah, Lord GOD! behold, I cannot speak: for I *am* a child.

⁷ But the LORD said unto me, Say not, I *am* a child: for thou shalt go to all that I shall send thee, and whatsoever I command thee thou shalt speak.

⁸ Be not afraid of their faces: for I *am* with thee to deliver thee, saith the LORD.

⁹ Then the LORD put forth his hand, and touched my mouth. And the LORD said unto me, Behold, I have put my words in thy mouth.

Jeremiah 1:4–9

INSIGHTS

*S*ome have a special call of God to a single life, as both Jesus and Paul taught. This was a genuine contribution. . . .

Jesus declared that there were those who were single "for the sake of the kingdom of heaven" (Matt. 19:12). And Paul builds on this foundation by suggesting that the unmarried can focus their energies toward the work of God in a way that the married simply cannot (1 Cor. 7:32–35).

Some have railed at Paul for urging people to seriously consider the single life, but the truth is that his words are filled with practical wisdom. He was not against marriage—in fact his great contribution to Christian sexual theology is the way he compares the sexual union in marriage to the union of Christ and his Church. But Paul did insist that we count the cost.

Richard Foster

APPLICATION

*W*hat does a person's marital status have to do with his or her spiritual service? What is more important than whether a person is married or single? Pray that you will be true to God's calling for you.

TUESDAY

Don't Do Anything to Cause Someone to Sin

1 Corinthians 8:9—9:18

*B*ut take heed lest by any means this liberty of yours become a stumblingblock to them that are weak.

10 For if any man see thee which hast knowledge sit at meat in the idol's temple, shall not the conscience of him which is weak be emboldened to eat those things which are offered to idols;

11 And through thy knowledge shall the weak brother perish, for whom Christ died?

12 But when ye sin so against the brethren, and wound their weak conscience, ye sin against Christ.

13 Wherefore, if meat make my brother to offend, I will eat no flesh while the world standeth, lest I make my brother to offend.

Paul Is like the Other Apostles

9 Am I not an apostle? am I not free? have I not seen Jesus Christ our Lord? are not ye my work in the Lord?

2 If I be not an apostle unto others, yet doubtless I am to you: for the seal of mine apostleship are ye in the Lord.

3 Mine answer to them that do examine me is this:

4 Have we not power to eat and to drink?

5 Have we not power to lead about a sister, a wife, as well as other apostles, and *as* the brethren of the Lord, and Cephas?

6 Or I only and Barnabas, have not we power to forbear working?

7 Who goeth a warfare any time at his own charges? who planteth a vineyard, and eateth not of the fruit thereof? or who feedeth a flock, and eateth not of the milk of the flock?

8 Say I these things as a man? or saith not the law the same also?

9 For it is written in the law of Moses, Thou shalt not muzzle the mouth of the ox that treadeth out the corn. Doth God take care for oxen?

10 or saith he *it* altogether for our sakes? For our sakes, no doubt, *this* is written: that he that ploweth should plow in hope; and that he that thresheth in hope should be partaker of his hope.

11 If we have sown unto you spiritual things, *is it* a great thing if we shall reap your carnal things?

12 If others be partakers of *this* power over you, *are* not we rather? Nevertheless we have not used this power; but suffer all things, lest we should hinder the gospel of Christ.

13 Do ye not know that they which minister about holy things live *of the things* of the temple? and they which wait at the altar are partakers with the altar?

14 Even so hath the Lord ordained that they which preach the gospel should live of the gospel.

15 But I have used none of these things: neither have I written these things, that it should be so done unto me: for *it were* better for me to die, than that any man should make my glorying void.

16 For though I preach the gospel, I have nothing to glory of: for necessity is laid upon me; yea, woe is unto me, if I preach not the gospel!

17 For if I do this thing willingly, I have a reward: but if against my will, a dispensation *of the gospel* is committed unto me.
18 What is my reward then? *Verily* that, when I preach the gospel, I may make the gospel of Christ without charge, that I abuse not my power in the gospel.

OLD TESTAMENT READING

*A*nd I raised up of your sons for prophets, and of your young men for Nazarites. *Is it* not even thus, O ye children of Israel? saith the LORD.
12 But ye gave the Nazarites wine to drink; and commanded the prophets, saying, Prophesy not.
13 Behold, I am pressed under you, as a cart is pressed *that is* full of sheaves.
14 Therefore the flight shall perish from the swift, and the strong shall not strengthen his force, neither shall the mighty deliver himself.

Amos 2:11–14

INSIGHTS

*F*ew would question the assertion that we should renounce the wrong things in our lives. It is self-evident that such things mar our lives, spoil our enjoyment of life, and limit our usefulness to God and man. But not everyone is equally convinced that in the interest of the gospel the disciple of Christ may need to renounce some things that are perfectly right and legitimate. . . .

Four times in 1 Corinthians 9 Paul asserts his rights in the gospel. Three times he claims that he has refrained from exercising these rights in the higher interests of spreading the gospel. He affirms that he is ready to forgo any right he may have, and forsake any privilege, out of love for Christ and in the interests of the progress of the gospel. . . .

Oswald Chambers had some trenchant words to say in this connection: "If we are willing to give up only wrong things for Jesus, never let us talk about being in love with Him. Anyone will give up wrong things if he knows how, but are we prepared to give up the best we have for Jesus Christ? The only right a Christian has is the right to give up his rights. If we are to be the best for God, there must be victory in the realm of legitimate desire as well as in the realm of unlawful indulgence.". . .

. . . The disciple must choose his priorities very carefully, even in things that are right in themselves. If we are aiming at the heights of Christian experience, there will always come the challenge to voluntary renunciation of some rights.

J. Oswald Sanders

APPLICATION

*D*efine Christian liberty in your own words. What is the objective of Christian freedom? What legitimate freedoms did Paul sacrifice for the sake of the Gospel? How much freedom will you sacrifice for the cause of Christ?

WEDNESDAY

Stand Firm
Against Temptation

1 Corinthians 9:19—10:22

*F*or though I be free from all *men*, yet have I made myself servant unto all, that I might gain the more.

20 And unto the Jews I became as a Jew, that I might gain the Jews; to them that are under the law, as under the law, that I might gain them that are under the law;

21 to them that are without law, as without law, (being not without law to God, but under the law to Christ,) that I might gain them that are without law.

22 To the weak became I as weak, that I might gain the weak: I am made all things to all *men*, that I might by all means save some.

23 And this I do for the gospel's sake, that I might be partaker thereof with *you*.

24 Know ye not that they which run in a race run all, but one receiveth the prize? So run, that ye may obtain.

25 And every man that striveth for the mastery is temperate in all things. Now they *do it* to obtain a corruptible crown; but we an incorruptible.

26 I therefore so run, not as uncertainly; so fight I, not as one that beateth the air:

27 But I keep under my body, and bring *it* into subjection: lest that by any means, when I have preached to others, I myself should be a castaway.

Warnings from Israel's Past

10 Moreover, brethren, I would not that ye should be ignorant, how that all our fathers were under the cloud, and all passed through the sea;

2 and were all baptized unto Moses in the cloud and in the sea;

3 and did all eat the same spiritual meat;

4 and did all drink the same spiritual drink: for they drank of that spiritual Rock that followed them: and that Rock was Christ.

5 But with many of them God was not well pleased: for they were overthrown in the wilderness.

6 Now these things were our examples, to the intent we should not lust after evil things, as they also lusted.

7 Neither be ye idolaters, as *were* some of them; as it is written, The people sat down to eat and drink, and rose up to play.

8 Neither let us commit fornication, as some of them committed, and fell in one day three and twenty thousand.

9 Neither let us tempt Christ, as some of them also tempted, and were destroyed of serpents.

10 Neither murmur ye, as some of them also murmured, and were destroyed of the destroyer.

11 Now all these things happened unto them for ensamples: and they are written for our admonition, upon whom the ends of the world are come.

12 Wherefore let him that thinketh he standeth take heed lest he fall.

13 There hath no temptation taken you but such as is common to man: but God *is* faithful, who will not suffer you to be tempted above that ye are able; but will with the temptation also make a way to escape, that ye may be able to bear *it*.

¹⁴ Wherefore, my dearly beloved, flee from idolatry.

¹⁵ I speak as to wise men; judge ye what I say.

¹⁶ The cup of blessing which we bless, is it not the communion of the blood of Christ? The bread which we break, is it not the communion of the body of Christ?

¹⁷ For we *being* many are one bread, *and* one body: for we are all partakers of that one bread.

¹⁸ Behold Israel after the flesh: are not they which eat of the sacrifices partakers of the altar?

¹⁹ What say I then? that the idol is any thing, or that which is offered in sacrifice to idols is any thing?

²⁰ But I *say*, that the things which the Gentiles sacrifice, they sacrifice to devils, and not to God: and I would not that ye should have fellowship with devils.

²¹ Ye cannot drink the cup of the Lord, and the cup of devils: ye cannot be partakers of the Lord's table, and of the table of devils.

²² Do we provoke the Lord to jealousy? are we stronger than he?

OLD TESTAMENT READING

*A*nd the LORD said unto Satan, Hast thou considered my servant Job, that *there is* none like him in the earth, a perfect and an upright man, one that feareth God, and escheweth evil? and still he holdeth fast his integrity, although thou movedst me against him, to destroy him without cause.

⁴ And Satan answered the LORD, and said, Skin for skin, yea, all that a man hath will he give for his life.

⁵ But put forth thine hand now, and touch his bone and his flesh, and he will curse thee to thy face.

⁶ And the LORD said unto Satan, Behold, he *is* in thine hand; but save his life.

⁷ So went Satan forth from the presence of the LORD, and smote Job with sore boils from the sole of his foot unto his crown.

⁹ Then said his wife unto him, Dost thou, still retain thine integrity? curse God, and die.

¹⁰ But he said unto her, Thou speakest as one of the foolish women speaketh. What? shall we receive good at the hand of God, and shall we not receive evil? In all this did not Job sin with his lips.

Job 2:3–7, 9–10

INSIGHTS

I have often heard my husband tell our teenagers, "Temptation is not only an opportunity to do the wrong thing, but an opportunity to do the right!" Although we usually consider temptation in negative terms, God allows us to be tempted in order to provide us with a chance to be obedient. If we are to learn to say no, and we are certainly supposed to say no sometimes to some things, then circumstances become life's workshop to that end. Saying no when you want to say yes strengthens you, produces endurance, and builds character—Christian character.

Jill Briscoe

APPLICATION

*W*hat did Paul mean when he said he made his body a servant? What does the example of the Israelites in the desert warn us against? How seriously do you take that warning?

THURSDAY

*Everything We Do
Should Honor God*

---

1 Corinthians 10:23—11:22

How to Use Christian Freedom

*A*ll things are lawful for me, but all things are not expedient: all things are lawful for me, but all things edify not.

²⁴ Let no man seek his own, but every man another's *wealth*.

²⁵ Whatsoever is sold in the shambles, *that* eat, asking no question for conscience' sake:

²⁶ for the earth is the Lord's, and the fulness thereof.

²⁷ If any of them that believe not bid you *to a feast*, and ye be disposed to go; whatsoever is set before you, eat, asking no question for conscience' sake.

²⁸ But if any man say unto you, This is offered in sacrifice unto idols, eat not for his sake that showed it, and for conscience' sake: for the earth is the Lord's, and the fulness thereof:

²⁹ conscience, I say, not thine own, but of the other: for why is my liberty judged of another *man's* conscience?

³⁰ For if I by grace be a partaker, why am I evil spoken of for that for which I give thanks?

³¹ Whether therefore ye eat, or drink, or whatsoever ye do, do all to the glory of God.

³² Give none offense, neither to the Jews, nor to the Gentiles, nor to the church of God:

³³ even as I please all *men* in all *things,* not seeking mine own profit, but the *profit* of many, that they may be saved.

Being Under Authority

11 Be ye followers of me, even as I also *am* of Christ.

² Now I praise you, brethren, that ye remember me in all things, and keep the ordinances, as I delivered *them* to you.

³ But I would have you know, that the head of every man is Christ; and the head of the woman *is* the man; and the head of Christ *is* God.

⁴ Every man praying or prophesying, having *his* head covered, dishonoreth his head.

⁵ But every woman that prayeth or prophesieth with *her* head uncovered dishonoreth her head: for that is even all one as if she were shaven.

⁶ For if the woman be not covered, let her also be shorn: but if it be a shame for a woman to be shorn or shaven, let her be covered.

⁷ For a man indeed ought not to cover *his* head, forasmuch as he is the image and glory of God: but the woman is the glory of the man.

⁸ For the man is not of the woman; but the woman of the man.

⁹ Neither was the man created for the woman; but the woman for the man.

¹⁰ For this cause ought the woman to have power on *her* head because of the angels.

¹¹ Nevertheless neither is the man without the woman, neither the woman without the man, in the Lord.

¹² For as the woman *is* of the man, even so *is* the man also by the woman; but all things of god.

¹³ Judge in yourselves: is it comely that a woman pray unto God uncovered?

14 Doth not even nature itself teach you, that, if a man have long hair, it is a shame unto him? 15 But if a woman have long hair, it is a glory to her: for *her* hair is given her for a covering. 16 But if any man seem to be contentious, we have no such custom, neither the churches of God.

The Lord's Supper

*N*ow in this that I declare *unto you* I praise *you* not, that ye come together not for the better, but for the worse. 18 For first of all, when ye come together in the church, I hear that there be divisions among you; and I partly believe it. 19 For there must be also heresies among you, that they which are approved may be made manifest among you. 20 When ye come together therefore into one place, *this* is not to eat the Lord's supper. 21 For in eating every one taketh before *other* his own supper: and one is hungry, and another is drunken. 22 What! have ye not houses to eat and to drink in? or despise ye the church of God, and shame them that have not? What shall I say to you? shall I praise you in this? I praise *you* not.

OLD TESTAMENT READING

Eli's Sons Refuse to Honor God

*N*ow the sons of Eli *were* sons of Beli-al; they knew not the LORD. 30 Wherefore the LORD God of Israel saith, I said indeed *that* thy house, and the house of thy father, should walk before me for ever: but now the LORD saith, Be it far from me; for them that honor me I will honor, and they that despise me shall be lightly esteemed. 31 Behold, the days come, that I will cut off thine arm, and the arm of thy father's house, that there shall not be an old man in thine house.

1 Samuel 2:12, 30–31

INSIGHTS

*E*verything created was through Christ and His power, and furthermore, it was created for His honor. That includes everyday things today. You have a good job? It's to be enjoyed for Him. You have a nice salary? It's to be enjoyed and invested for Him. You have good health? It is for Him. You have a family? The family members are for Him. You're planning a move? It's to be for Him. You're thinking about a career change? It needs to be for Him. That is true because He's the ruler of our kingdom. He is Lord. And that's not simply the title of a chorus Christians sing; it's a statement of faith. He has the right to take charge of our decisions so that He might be honored through them. Every day I live I must address that. Again, it is a matter of priorities. . . .

. . . Those who are really committed to excellence give Him top priority.

Charles Swindoll

APPLICATION

*I*n what practical ways can you obey Christ's commandments to honor God and love one another in your daily life?

FRIDAY

The Holy Spirit Gives Gifts

1 Corinthians 11:23—12:13

*F*or I have received of the Lord that which also I delivered unto you, That the Lord Jesus, the *same* night in which he was betrayed, took bread: ²⁴ and when he had given thanks, he brake *it*, and said, Take, eat: this is my body, which is broken for you: this do in remembrance of me.

²⁵ After the same manner also *he took* the cup, when he had supped, saying, This cup is the new testament in my blood: this do ye, as oft as ye drink *it*, in remembrance of me.

²⁶ For as often as ye eat this bread, and drink this cup, ye do show the Lord's death till he come.

²⁷ Wherefore whosoever shall eat this bread, and drink *this* cup of the Lord, unworthily, shall be guilty of the body and blood of the Lord.

²⁸ But let a man examine himself, and so let him eat of *that* bread, and drink of *that* cup.

²⁹ For he that eateth and drinketh unworthily, eateth and drinketh damnation to himself, not discerning the Lord's body.

³⁰ For this cause many *are* weak and sickly among you, and many sleep.

³¹ For if we would judge ourselves, we should not be judged.

³² But when we are judged, we are chastened of the Lord, that we should not be condemned with the world.

³³ Wherefore, my brethren, when ye come together to eat, tarry one for another.

³⁴ And if any man hunger, let him eat at home; that ye come not together unto condemnation. And the rest will I set in order when I come.

Gifts from the Holy Spirit

12 Now concerning spiritual *gifts*, brethren, I would not have you ignorant.

² Ye know that ye were Gentiles, carried away unto these dumb idols, even as ye were led.

³ Wherefore I give you to understand, that no man speaking by the Spirit of God calleth Jesus accursed: and *that* no man can say that Jesus is the Lord, but by the Holy Ghost.

⁴ Now there are diversities of gifts, but the same Spirit.

⁵ And there are differences of administrations, but the same Lord.

⁶ And there are diversities of operations, but it is the same God which worketh all in all.

⁷ But the manifestation of the Spirit is given to every man to profit withal.

⁸ For to one is given by the Spirit the word of wisdom; to another the word of knowledge by the same Spirit;

⁹ to another faith by the same Spirit; to another the gifts of healing by the same Spirit;

¹⁰ to another the working of miracles; to another prophecy; to another discerning of spirits; to another *divers* kinds of tongues; to another the interpretation of tongues:

¹¹ but all these worketh that one and the selfsame Spirit, dividing to every man severally as he will.

The Body of Christ

*F*or as the body is one, and hath many members, and all the members of that one body, being many, are one body: so also *is* Christ.

¹³ For by one Spirit are we all baptized into one body, whether *we be* Jews or Gentiles, whether *we be* bond or free; and have been all made to drink into one Spirit.

OLD   TESTAMENT   READING

Gift of Speaking with Knowledge

*A*nd Joshua the son of Nun was full of the spirit of wisdom; for Moses had laid his hands upon him: and the children of Israel hearkened unto him, and did as the LORD commanded Moses.

Deuteronomy 34:9

Gift of Artistry

*A*nd the LORD spake unto Moses, saying,

² See, I have called by name Bezaleel the son of Uri, the son of Hur, of the tribe of Judah:

³ and I have filled him with the spirit of God, in wisdom, and in understanding, and in knowledge, and in all manner of workmanship,

⁴ to devise cunning works, to work in gold, and in silver, and in brass,

⁵ and in cutting of stones, to set *them*, and in carving of timber, to work in all manner of workmanship.

⁶ And I, behold, I have given with him Aholiab, the son of Ahisamach, of the tribe of Dan: and in the hearts of all that are wise-hearted I have put wisdom, that they may make all that I have commanded thee;

⁷ the tabernacle of the congregation, and the ark of the testimony, and the mercy seat that *is* thereupon, and all the furniture of the tabernacle.

Exodus 31:1–7

INSIGHTS

*I*t may take another Christian to pinpoint for us a particular talent we have. For instance, in the course of speaking at a meeting, I started, "I'm a one-talent person." . . . The meeting was scarcely over when a young woman dashed up to me and said, "That's not true what you said tonight. . . . I know about your writing and other things you do, but the best part is that you're good at sitting by the fire and being a friend."

It's evident, then, that we can be using a talent even when we do not recognize that we possess it. . . .

Perhaps we wish we could have had some choice as to which gift or ability would be ours. Maybe we would gladly trade ours off for something that has more appeal for us. But our all-wise God has apportioned His gifts as He wills, and one day He will require from each of us an accounting of our use of those gifts. . . .

If you and I really want to be used by our Lord, it will pay us to ferret out what our particular ability is, then get busy putting it to use.

Jeanette Lockerbie

PAUSE   FOR   REFLECTION

*H*ow are the gifts that the Spirit gives to different individuals intended to work together (1 Cor. 12:1–13)? What do the Scriptures reveal to you about the purpose of spiritual gifts?

WEEKEND

The Great Gift of Love

1 Corinthians 12:14—13:13

*F*or the body is not one member, but many.

15 If the foot shall say, Because I am not the hand, I am not of the body; is it therefore not of the body?

16 And if the ear shall say, Because I am not the eye, I am not of the body; is it therefore not of the body?

17 If the whole body *were* an eye, where *were* the hearing? If the whole *were* hearing, where *were* the smelling?

18 But now hath God set the members every one of them in the body, as it hath pleased him.

19 And if they were all one member, where *were* the body?

20 But now *are they* many members, yet but one body.

21 And the eye cannot say unto the hand, I have no need of thee: nor again the head to the feet, I have no need of you.

22 Nay, much more those members of the body, which seem to be more feeble, are necessary:

23 And those *members* of the body, which we think to be less honorable, upon these we bestow more abundant honor; and our uncomely *parts* have more abundant comeliness.

24 For our comely *parts* have no need: but God hath tempered the body together, having given more abundant honor to that *part* which lacked:

25 that there should be no schism in the body; but *that* the members should have the same care one for another.

26 And whether one member suffer, all the members suffer with it; or one member be honored, all the members rejoice with it.

27 Now ye are the body of Christ, and members in particular.

28 And God hath set some in the church, first apostles, secondarily prophets, thirdly teachers, after that miracles, then gifts of healings, helps, governments, diversities of tongues.

29 *Are* all apostles? *are* all prophets? *are* all teachers? *are* all workers of miracles?

30 have all the gifts of healing? do all speak with tongues? do all interpret?

31 But covet earnestly the best gifts: and yet show I unto you a more excellent way.

Love Is the Greatest Gift

13 Though I speak with the tongues of men and of angels, and have not charity, I am become *as* sounding brass, or a tinkling cymbal.

2 And though I have *the gift* of prophecy, and understand all mysteries, and all knowledge; and though I have all faith, so that I could remove mountains, and have not charity, I am nothing.

3 And though I bestow all my goods to feed *the poor*, and though I give my body to be burned, and have not charity, it profiteth me nothing.

4 Charity suffereth long, *and* is kind; charity envieth not; charity vaunteth not itself, is not puffed up,

5 doth not behave itself unseemly, seeketh not her own, is not easily provoked, thinketh no evil;

6 rejoiceth not in iniquity, but rejoiceth in the truth;

⁷ beareth all things, believeth all things, hopeth all things, endureth all things.

⁸ Charity never faileth: but whether *there be* prophecies, they shall fail; whether *there be* tongues, they shall cease; whether *there be* knowledge, it shall vanish away.

⁹ For we know in part, and we prophesy in part.

¹⁰ But when that which is perfect is come, then that which is in part shall be done away.

¹¹ When I was a child, I spake as a child, I understood as a child, I thought as a child: but when I became a man, I put away childish things.

¹² For now we see through a glass, darkly; but then face to face: now I know in part; but then shall I know even as also I am known.

¹³ And now abideth faith, hope, charity, these three; but the greatest of these *is* charity.

OLD TESTAMENT READING

Boaz Shows Love to Ruth

*A*nd Boaz said unto her, At mealtime come thou hither, and eat of the bread, and dip thy morsel in the vinegar. And she sat beside the reapers: and he reached her parched *corn*, and she did eat, and was sufficed, and left.

¹⁵ And when she was risen up to glean, Boaz commanded his young men, saying, Let her glean even among the sheaves, and reproach her not:

¹⁶ and let fall also *some* of the handfuls of purpose for her, and leave *them*, that she may glean *them*, and rebuke her not.

Ruth 2:14–16

INSIGHTS

*J*esus never wrote a book, yet the nature of his love was indelibly impressed upon the minds of his followers. . . . His very life clearly defined love for them. . . .

• *Jesus was concerned about their families, homes, and health.*

• *Jesus was willing to take time for people in need even though he was engaged in a busy ministry.*

• *Jesus provided faithful support in the spiritual battle by intercessory prayer.*

• *Jesus extended complete forgiveness, even when it seemed undeserved.*

• *Jesus humbly served his followers, exemplified in his washing their feet.*

• *Jesus ultimately gave himself in his death on Calvary's cross.*

In all of these acts of compassion, Jesus modeled a practical brand of love. His was a love that ministered to his disciples' pressing needs. Calvary, of course, tied it all together: The cross dealt finally with their sins and opened the way for them to experience all the blessings of God. . . .

So it is with us. If we are to love our brothers and sisters as Jesus commanded, we must learn to express a practical love for the whole person. It must be the kind of love our Master has shown to us.

William Fletcher

APPLICATION

*W*hat examples of Christian love have you experienced? What example of Jesus' love do you want to put into practice in your life?

MONDAY

*Desire Spiritual Gifts
that Strengthen the Church*

1 Corinthians 14:1–25

Desire Spiritual Gifts

14 Follow after charity, and desire spiritual *gifts*, but rather that ye may prophesy.

2 For he that speaketh in an *unknown* tongue speaketh not unto men, but unto God: for no man understandeth *him*; howbeit in the spirit he speaketh mysteries.

3 But he that prophesieth speaketh unto men *to* edification, and exhortation, and comfort.

4 He that speaketh in an *unknown* tongue edifieth himself; but he that prophesieth edifieth the church.

5 I would that ye all spake with tongues, but rather that ye prophesied: for greater *is* he that prophesieth than he that speaketh with tongues, except he interpret, that the church may receive edifying.

6 Now, brethren, if I come unto you speaking with tongues, what shall I profit you, except I shall speak to you either by revelation, or by knowledge, or by prophesying, or by doctrine?

7 And even things without life giving sound, whether pipe or harp, except they give a distinction in the sounds, how shall it be known what is piped or harped?

8 For if the trumpet give an uncertain sound, who shall prepare himself to the battle?

9 So likewise ye, except ye utter by the tongue words easy to be understood, how shall it be known what is spoken? for ye shall speak into the air.

10 There are, it may be, so many kinds of voices in the world, and none of them *is* without signification.

11 Therefore if I know not the meaning of the voice, I shall be unto him that speaketh a barbarian, and he that speaketh *shall be* a barbarian unto me.

12 Even so ye, forasmuch as ye are zealous of spiritual *gifts*, seek that ye may excel to the edifying of the church.

13 Wherefore let him that speaketh in an *unknown* tongue pray that he may interpret.

14 For if I pray in an *unknown* tongue, my spirit prayeth, but my understanding is unfruitful.

15 What is it then? I will pray with the spirit, and I will pray with the understanding also: I will sing with the spirit, and I will sing with the understanding also.

16 Else when thou shalt bless with the spirit, how shall he that occupieth the room of the unlearned say Amen at thy giving of thanks, seeing he understandeth not what thou sayest?

17 For thou verily givest thanks well, but the other is not edified.

18 I thank my God, I speak with tongues more than ye all:

19 yet in the church I had rather speak five words with my understanding, that *by my voice* I might teach others also, than ten thousand words in an *unknown* tongue.

20 Brethren, be not children in understanding: howbeit in malice be ye children, but in understanding be men.

21 In the law it is written, With *men of* other tongues and other lips will I speak unto this people; and yet for

all that will they not hear me, saith the Lord.

²² Wherefore tongues are for a sign, not to them that believe, but to them that believe not: but prophesying *serveth* not for them that believe not, but for them which believe.

²³ If therefore the whole church be come together into one place, and all speak with tongues, and there come in *those that are* unlearned, or unbelievers, will they not say that ye are mad?

²⁴ But if all prophesy, and there come in one that believeth not, or *one* unlearned, he is convinced of all, he is judged of all:

²⁵ and thus are the secrets of his heart made manifest; and so falling down on *his* face he will worship God, and report that God is in you of a truth.

OLD TESTAMENT READING

*M*oreover the altar that *was* at Bethel, *and* the high place which Jeroboam the son of Nebat, who made Israel to sin, had made, both that altar and the high place he brake down, and burned the high place, *and* stamped *it* small to powder, and burned the grove.

¹⁶ And as Josiah turned himself, he spied the sepulchres that *were* there in the mount, and sent, and took the bones out of the sepulchres, and burned *them* upon the altar, and polluted it, according to the word of the LORD which the man of God proclaimed, who proclaimed these words.

2 Kings 23:15–16

INSIGHTS

*T*he gifts of the Spirit . . . come to us from the Holy Spirit. He chooses who gets which gifts, and He dispenses them at His good pleasure. While we are held accountable for the use of any gifts He gives us, we have no responsibility for gifts we have not been given. Nor are we to covet what someone else has or be envious of that person. We may wish to have certain gifts and even ask for them, but if it is not the will of the Holy Spirit, we will not get what we ask for. And if we are dissatisfied because the Holy Spirit does not give us the gifts we want, we sin. . . .

Paul says that the purpose of these spiritual gifts is, "for the equipping of the saints for the work of service, to the building up of the body of Christ" (Eph. 4:12). In other words, God has given each of us a task to do, and supernatural gifts to equip us for it. . . .

In 1 Corinthians 12:7, the apostle Paul says the gifts are given "for the common good" so we are not to use them selfishly. Instead, we are to use them to help each other. . . .

God has also designed the gifts to help "unite" the body of Christ. . . .

Thus the gifts of the Spirit should never divide the body of Christ; they should unify it.

Billy Graham

APPLICATION

*W*hat is the purpose of spiritual gifts? What is the difference between prophesying and speaking in tongues? Why do you desire spiritual gifts? Pray that you will use your gift to God's glory.

TUESDAY

The Essentials
of Christian Faith

1 Corinthians 14:26—15:11

Meetings To Edify the Church

*H*ow is it then, brethren? when ye come together, every one of you hath a psalm, hath a doctrine, hath a tongue, hath a revelation, hath an interpretation. Let all things be done unto edifying.

²⁷ If any man speak in an *unknown* tongue, *let it be* by two, or at the most *by* three, and *that* by course; and let one interpret.

²⁸ But if there be no interpreter, let him keep silence in the church; and let him speak to himself, and to God.

²⁹ Let the prophets speak two or three, and let the other judge.

³⁰ If *any thing* be revealed to another that sitteth by, let the first hold his peace.

³¹ For ye may all prophesy one by one, that all may learn, and all may be comforted.

³² And the spirits of the prophets are subject to the prophets.

³³ For God is not *the author* of confusion, but of peace, as in all churches of the saints.

³⁴ Let your women keep silence in the churches: for it is not permitted unto them to speak; but *they are commanded* to be under obedience, as also saith the law.

³⁵ And if they will learn any thing, let them ask their husbands at home: for it is a shame for women to speak in the church.

³⁶ What! came the word of God out from you? or came it unto you only?

³⁷ If any man think himself to be a prophet, or spiritual, let him acknowledge that the things that I write unto you are the commandments of the Lord.

³⁸ But if any man be ignorant, let him be ignorant.

³⁹ Wherefore, brethren, covet to prophesy, and forbid not to speak with tongues.

⁴⁰ Let all things be done decently and in order.

The Gospel of Christ

15 Moreover, brethren, I declare unto you the gospel which I preached unto you, which also ye have received, and wherein ye stand; ² by which also ye are saved, if ye keep in memory what I preached unto you, unless ye have believed in vain.

³ For I delivered unto you first of all that which I also received, how that Christ died for our sins according to the Scriptures;

⁴ and that he was buried, and that he rose again the third day according to the Scriptures:

⁵ and that he was seen of Cephas, then of the twelve:

⁶ after that, he was seen of above five hundred brethren at once; of whom the greater part remain unto this present, but some are fallen asleep.

⁷ After that, he was seen of James; then of all the apostles.

⁸ And last of all he was seen of me also, as of one born out of due time.

⁹ For I am the least of the apostles, that am not meet to be called an apostle, because I persecuted the church of God.

[10] But by the grace of God I am what I am: and his grace which *was bestowed* upon me was not in vain; but I labored more abundantly than they all: yet not I, but the grace of God which was with me.

[11] Therefore whether *it were* I or they, so we preach, and so ye believed.

OLD TESTAMENT READING

*F*or he was cut off out of the land of the living: for the transgression of my people was he stricken. [9] And he made his grave with the wicked, and with the rich in his death; because he had done no violence, neither *was any* deceit in his mouth.

Isaiah 53:8b–9

*G*od is gone up with a shout, the LORD with the sound of a trumpet. [6] Sing praises to God, sing praises: sing praises unto our King, sing praises. [7] For God *is* the King of all the earth: sing ye praises with understanding. [8] God reigneth over the heathen: God sitteth upon the throne of his holiness.

Psalm 47:5–8

INSIGHTS

*I*n the guise of a man, Jesus the Christ, was born, lived, grew up, worked, was crucified, and rose from the grave among us, He ascended back to His splendor among us.

In all of this, though subject to the strains and stresses of our human society, he never sinned. His was a perfect performance. His was a life without a single stain. His was the "perfect doing" and "perfect dying" required to redeem all men for all time from all their wrongs and sins and stains. . . .

It was in my stead He did all this: He paid the penalty for all my wrongs. He bled and suffered and died for me. He took my sins to set me free. It was to satisfy His own righteousness that He became my substitute. He did this to impute to me His own wondrous righteousness.

This is a titanic transaction of eternal dimensions. God, very God, in Christ takes my sins and gives me His goodness . . . His own righteousness.

Nothing else can satisfy my searching spirit. I look away from myself to see the splendor of His supreme self-sacrifice for my salvation. I see that He has made me whole. He has enfolded and filled me with His righteousness. He has accepted me as His own son. He is my living Lord and Savior. He is my Father!

My spirit leaps for joy, where before it was sunk with sin and despair. His Spirit bears witness with my spirit that I am now His son. In overwhelming appreciation and gratitude, I look up and my spirit cries, "Abba Father!"

W. Phillip Keller

APPLICATION

*W*hat are the essential elements of the Christian faith? How fully was the gospel foretold in the Old Testament? Why must we continue believing the gospel? Pray that your faith will continue strong!

WEDNESDAY

God's People Will Be Raised to Life Again

---

1 Corinthians 15:12–44a

We Will Be Raised from the Dead

*N*ow if Christ be preached that he rose from the dead, how say some among you that there is no resurrection of the dead?

13 But if there be no resurrection of the dead, then is Christ not risen:

14 and if Christ be not risen, then *is* our preaching vain, and your faith *is* also vain.

15 Yea, and we are found false witnesses of God; because we have testified of God that he raised up Christ: whom he raised not up, if so be that the dead rise not.

16 For if the dead rise not, then is not Christ raised:

17 And if Christ be not raised, your faith *is* vain; ye are yet in your sins.

18 Then they also which are fallen asleep in Christ are perished.

19 If in this life only we have hope in Christ, we are of all men most miserable.

20 But now is Christ risen from the dead, *and* become the firstfruits of them that slept.

21 For since by man *came* death, by man *came* also the resurrection of the dead.

22 For as in Adam all die, even so in Christ shall all be made alive.

23 But every man in his own order: Christ the firstfruits; afterward they that are Christ's at his coming.

24 Then *cometh* the end, when he shall have delivered up the kingdom to God, even the Father; when he shall have put down all rule, and all authority and power.

25 For he must reign, till he hath put all enemies under his feet.

26 The last enemy *that* shall be destroyed *is* death.

27 For he hath put all things under his feet. But when he saith, All things are put under *him, it is* manifest that he is excepted, which did put all things under him.

28 And when all things shall be subdued unto him, then shall the Son also himself be subject unto him that put all things under him, that God may be all in all.

29 Else what shall they do which are baptized for the dead, if the dead rise not at all? why are they then baptized for the dead?

30 and why stand we in jeopardy every hour?

31 I protest by your rejoicing which I have in Christ Jesus our Lord, I die daily.

32 If after the manner of men I have fought with beasts at Ephesus, what advantageth it me, if the dead rise not? let us eat and drink; for to morrow we die.

33 Be not deceived: evil communications corrupt good manners.

34 Awake to righteousness, and sin not; for some have not the knowledge of God: I speak *this* to your shame.

What Kind of Body Will We Have?

*B*ut some *man* will say, How are the dead raised up? and with what body do they come?

36 *Thou* fool, that which thou sowest is not quickened, except it die:

37 and that which thou sowest, thou

sowest not that body that shall be, but bare grain, it may chance of wheat, or of some other *grain*:
38 but God giveth it a body as it hath pleased him, and to every seed his own body.
39 All flesh is not the same flesh: but *there is* one *kind of* flesh of men, another flesh of beasts, another of fishes, *and* another of birds.
40 *There are* also celestial bodies, and bodies terrestrial: but the glory of the celestial *is* one, and the *glory* of the terrestrial *is* another.
41 *There is* one glory of the sun, and another glory of the moon, and another glory of the stars: for *one* star differeth from *another* star in glory.
42 So also *is* the resurrection of the dead. It is sown in corruption, it is raised in incorruption:
43 it is sown in dishonor, it is raised in glory: it is sown in weakness, it is raised in power:
44 it is sown a natural body, it is raised a spiritual body.

OLD TESTAMENT READING

*A*nd many of them that sleep in the dust of the earth shall awake, some to everlasting life, and some to shame *and* everlasting contempt.
3 And they that be wise shall shine as the brightness of the firmament; and they that turn many to righteousness, as the stars for ever and ever.

Daniel 12:2–3

INSIGHTS

*O*ften when we are racked with pain and unable to think or worship, we feel that this indeed is "the body of our humiliation," and when we are tempted by the passions which rise from the flesh we do not think the word "vile" at all too vigorous a translation. Our bodies humble us; and that is about the best thing they do for us. Oh, that we were duly lowly, because our bodies ally us with animals and even link us with the dust!

But our Savior, the Lord Jesus, shall change all this. We shall be fashioned like His own body of glory. This will take place in all who believe in Jesus. By faith their souls have been transformed, and their bodies will undergo such a renewal as shall fit them for their regenerated spirits. How soon this grand transformation will happen we cannot tell; but the thought of it should help us to bear the trials of today and all the woes of the flesh. In a little while we shall be as Jesus now is. No more aching brows, no more swollen limbs, no more dim eyes, no more fainting hearts. The old man shall be no more a bundle of infirmities, nor the sick man a mass of agony. "Like unto his glorious body" [Phil. 3:21]. What an expression! Even our flesh shall rest in hope of such a resurrection!

Charles Spurgeon

PAUSE FOR REFLECTION

*W*hat is the significance and what are the results of Christ's resurrection? What will all those who rise up in Christ be given? What about the resurrection gives you the greatest hope?

THURSDAY

*Be Prepared for Opposition
as You Serve God*

1 Corinthians 15:44b—16:24

*T*here is a natural body, and there is a spiritual body.

⁴⁵ And so it is written, The first man Adam was made a living soul; the last Adam *was made* a quickening spirit.

⁴⁶ Howbeit that *was* not first which is spiritual, but that which is natural; and afterward that which is spiritual.

⁴⁷ The first man *is* of the earth, earthy: the second man *is* the Lord from heaven.

⁴⁸ As *is* the earthy, such *are* they also that are earthy: and as *is* the heavenly, such *are* they also that are heavenly.

⁴⁹ And as we have borne the image of the earthy, we shall also bear the image of the heavenly.

⁵⁰ Now this I say, brethren, that flesh and blood cannot inherit the kingdom of God; neither doth corruption inherit incorruption.

⁵¹ Behold, I show you a mystery; We shall not all sleep, but we shall all be changed,

⁵² in a moment, in the twinkling of an eye, at the last trump: for the trumpet shall sound, and the dead shall be raised incorruptible, and we shall be changed.

⁵³ For this corruptible must put on incorruption, and this mortal *must* put on immortality.

⁵⁴ So when this corruptible shall have put on incorruption, and this mortal shall have put on immortality, then shall be brought to pass the saying that is written, Death is swallowed up in victory.

⁵⁵ O death, where *is* thy sting? O grave, where *is* thy victory?

⁵⁶ The sting of death *is* sin; and the strength of sin *is* the law.

⁵⁷ But thanks *be* to God, which giveth us the victory through our Lord Jesus Christ.

⁵⁸ Therefore, my beloved brethren, be ye steadfast, unmovable, always abounding in the work of the Lord, forasmuch as ye know that your labor is not in vain in the Lord.

Collection for the Saints

16 Now concerning the collection for the saints, as I have given order to the churches of Galatia, even so do ye.

² Upon the first *day* of the week let every one of you lay by him in store, as *God* hath prospered him, that there be no gatherings when I come.

³ And when I come, whomsoever ye shall approve by *your* letters, them will I send to bring your liberality unto Jerusalem.

⁴ And if it be meet that I go also, they shall go with me.

Paul's Plans

*N*ow I will come unto you, when I shall pass through Macedonia: for I do pass through Macedonia.

⁶ And it may be that I will abide, yea, and winter with you, that ye may bring me on my journey whithersoever I go.

⁷ For I will not see you now by the way; but I trust to tarry a while with you, if the Lord permit.

⁸ But I will tarry at Ephesus until Pentecost.

⁹ For a great door and effectual is opened unto me, and *there are* many adversaries.

¹⁰ Now if Timothy come, see that he may be with you without fear: for he worketh the work of the Lord, as I also *do*.

¹¹ Let no man therefore despise him: but conduct him forth in peace, that he may come unto me: for I look for him with the brethren.

¹² As touching *our* brother Apollos, I greatly desired him to come unto you with the brethren: but his will was not at all to come at this time; but he will come when he shall have convenient time.

Paul Ends His Letter

*W*atch ye, stand fast in the faith, quit you like men, be strong.

¹⁴ Let all your things be done with charity.

¹⁵ I beseech you, brethren, (ye know the house of Stephanas, that it is the firstfruits of Achaia, and *that* they have addicted themselves to the ministry of the saints,)

¹⁶ that ye submit yourselves unto such, and to every one that helpeth with *us,* and laboreth.

¹⁷ I am glad of the coming of Stephanas and Fortunatus and Achaicus: for that which was lacking on your part they have supplied.

¹⁸ For they have refreshed my spirit and yours: therefore acknowledge ye them that are such.

¹⁹ The churches of Asia salute you. Aquila and Priscilla salute you much in the Lord, with the church that is in their house.

²⁰ All the brethren greet you. Greet ye one another with a holy kiss.

²¹ The salutation of *me* Paul with mine own hand.

²² If any man love not the Lord Jesus Christ, let him be Anathema, Maranatha.

²³ The grace of our Lord Jesus Christ *be* with you.

²⁴ My love *be* with you all in Christ Jesus. Amen.

OLD TESTAMENT READING

*P*lead *my cause*, O LORD, with them that strive with me: fight against them that fight against me.

⁷ For without cause have they hid for me their net *in* a pit, *which* without cause they have digged for my soul.

Psalm 35:1, 7

INSIGHTS

*F*or many years as a struggling young Christian I was led to believe that if I was just good enough, and kind enough, and loving enough, the whole of the world would be bound to hug me to its heart. Unfortunately and unhappily one learns in time that simply is not so. It is one of the sobering shocks that comes to us as mature Christians.

If God, very God, who was all perfection, suffered such abuse at the hands of His adversaries when He was here among us as the Man Christ Jesus, how can we expect less? . . .

W. Phillip Keller

APPLICATION

*W*hy did Paul plan to stay in Ephesus? What was taking place that he was so excited about?

FRIDAY

When Troubles Come,
Trust in the God
Who Comforts Us

2 Corinthians 1:1–17

Paul Answers His Accusers

1 Paul, an apostle of Jesus Christ by the will of God, and Timothy *our* brother, unto the church of God which is at Corinth, with all the saints which are in all Achaia:
2 Grace *be* to you, and peace, from God our Father, and *from* the Lord Jesus Christ.

Paul Gives Thanks to God

*B*lessed *be* God, even the Father of our Lord Jesus Christ, the Father of mercies, and the God of all comfort;
4 who comforteth us in all our tribulation, that we may be able to comfort them which are in any trouble, by the comfort wherewith we ourselves are comforted of God.
5 For as the sufferings of Christ abound in us, so our consolation also aboundeth by Christ.
6 And whether we be afflicted, *it is* for your consolation and salvation, which is effectual in the enduring of the same sufferings which we also suffer: or whether we be comforted, *it is* for your consolation and salvation.
7 And our hope of you is stedfast, knowing, that as ye are partakers of the sufferings, so *shall ye be* also of the consolation.
8 For we would not, brethren, have you ignorant of our trouble which came to us in Asia, that we were pressed out of measure, above strength, insomuch that we despaired even of life:
9 but we had the sentence of death in ourselves, that we should not trust in ourselves, but in God which raiseth the dead:
10 who delivered us from so great a death, and doth deliver: in whom we trust that he will yet deliver *us;*
11 ye also helping together by prayer for us, that for the gift *bestowed* upon us by the means of many persons thanks may be given by many on our behalf.

The Change in Paul's Plans

*F*or our rejoicing is this, the testimony of our conscience, that in simplicity and godly sincerity, not with fleshly wisdom, but by the grace of God, we have had our conversation in the world, and more abundantly to you-ward.
13 For we write none other things unto you, than what ye read and acknowledge; and I trust ye shall acknowledge even to the end;
14 as also ye have acknowledged us in part, that we are your rejoicing, even as ye also *are* ours in the day of the Lord Jesus.
15 And in this confidence I was minded to come unto you before, that ye might have a second benefit;
16 and to pass by you into Macedonia, and to come again out of Macedonia unto you, and of you to be brought on my way toward Judea.
17 When I therefore was thus minded, did I use lightness? or the things that I purpose, do I purpose according to the flesh, that with me there should be yea, yea, and nay, nay?

*B*e merciful unto me, O God: for man would swallow me up; he fighting daily oppresseth me.

² Mine enemies would daily swallow *me* up: for *they be* many that fight against me, O thou Most High.

³ What time I am afraid, I will trust in thee.

⁴ In God I will praise his word, in God I have put my trust; I will not fear what flesh can do unto me.

Psalm 56:1–4

*T*he earth, O Lᴏʀᴅ, is full of thy mercy: teach me thy statutes.

⁶⁵ Thou hast dealt well with thy servant, O Lᴏʀᴅ, according unto thy word.

⁶⁶ Teach me good judgment and knowledge: for I have believed thy commandments.

⁶⁷ Before I was afflicted I went astray: but now have I kept thy word.

⁶⁸ Thou *art* good, and doest good: teach me thy statutes.

⁷⁶ Let, I pray thee, thy merciful kindness be for my comfort, according to thy word unto thy servant.

⁷⁷ Let thy tender mercies come unto me, that I may live: for thy law *is* my delight.

Psalm 119:64–68, 76–77

*I*t has been well said that "earthly cares are a heavenly discipline." But they are even something better than discipline,—they are God's chariots, sent to take the soul to its high places of triumph. . . .

Everything that comes to us becomes a chariot the moment we treat it as such; and on the other hand, even the smallest trials may be a Juggernaut car to crush us into misery or despair if we so consider them. It lies with each of us to choose which they shall be. . . .

Look upon your chastenings then, no matter how grievous they may be for the present, as God's chariots sent to carry your souls into the "high places" of spiritual achievement and uplifting, and you will find that they are, after all, "paved with love."

The Bible tells us that when God went forth for the salvation of His people, then He "did ride upon His horses and chariots of salvation." And it is the same now. Everything becomes a "chariot of salvation" when God rides upon it. He maketh even the "clouds his chariot," we are told, and "rideth on the wings of the wind." Therefore the clouds and storms that darken our skies and seem to shut out the shining of the sun of righteousness are really only God's chariots, into which we may mount with Him, and "ride prosperously" over all the darkness.

Hannah Whitall Smith

*H*ow well acquainted are you with the God Paul describes in 2 Corinthians 1:3? The next time you are ready to give up hope, why not trust the God of comfort to turn your troubles into triumphs of his making?

WEEKEND
The Healing Power of Forgiveness

2 Corinthians 1:18—3:3

*B*ut *as* God *is* true, our word toward you was not yea and nay.

¹⁹ For the Son of God, Jesus Christ, who was preached among you by us, *even* by me and Silvanus and Timothy, was not yea and nay, but in him was yea.

²⁰ For all the promises of God in him *are* yea, and in him Amen, unto the glory of God by us.

²¹ Now he which stablisheth us with you in Christ, and hath anointed us, *is* God;

²² who hath also sealed us, and given the earnest of the Spirit in our hearts.

²³ Moreover I call God for a record upon my soul, that to spare you I came not as yet unto Corinth.

²⁴ Not for that we have dominion over your faith, but are helpers of your joy: for by faith ye stand.

2 But I determined this with myself, that I would not come again to you in heaviness.

² For if I make you sorry, who is he then that maketh me glad, but the same which is made sorry by me?

³ And I wrote this same unto you, lest, when I came, I should have sorrow from them of whom I ought to rejoice; having confidence in you all, that my joy is *the joy* of you all.

⁴ For out of much affliction and anguish of heart I wrote unto you with many tears; not that ye should be grieved, but that ye might know the love which I have more abundantly unto you.

Forgive the Sinner

*B*ut if any have caused grief, he hath not grieved me, but in part: that I may not overcharge you all.

⁶ Sufficient to such a man *is* this punishment, which *was inflicted* of many.

⁷ So that contrariwise ye *ought* rather to forgive *him*, and comfort *him*, lest perhaps such a one should be swallowed up with overmuch sorrow.

⁸ Wherefore I beseech you that ye would confirm *your* love toward him.

⁹ For to this end also did I write, that I might know the proof of you, whether ye be obedient in all things.

¹⁰ To whom ye forgive any thing, I *forgive* also: for if I forgave any thing, to whom I forgave it, for your sakes *forgave I it* in the person of Christ;

¹¹ lest Satan should get an advantage of us: for we are not ignorant of his devices.

Paul's Concern in Troas

*F*urthermore, when I came to Troas to *preach* Christ's gospel, and a door was opened unto me of the Lord,

¹³ I had no rest in my spirit, because I found not Titus my brother; but taking my leave of them, I went from thence into Macedonia.

Victory Through Christ

*N*ow thanks *be* unto God, which always causeth us to triumph in Christ, and maketh manifest the savor of his knowledge by us in every place.

¹⁵ For we are unto God a sweet savor of Christ, in them that are saved, and in them that perish:

¹⁶ to the one *we are* the savor of death

unto death; and to the other the savor of life unto life. And who *is* sufficient for these things?

[17] For we are not as many, which corrupt the word of God: but as of sincerity, but as of God, in the sight of God speak we in Christ.

Servants of the New Covenant

3 Do we begin again to commend ourselves? or need we, as some *others,* epistles of commendation to you, or *letters* of commendation from you?

[2] Ye are our epistle written in our hearts, known and read of all men:

[3] *forasmuch as ye are* manifestly declared to be the epistle of Christ ministered by us, written not with ink, but with the Spirit of the living God; not in tables of stone, but in fleshy tables of the heart.

OLD TESTAMENT READING

*A*nd they sent a messenger unto Joseph, saying, Thy father did command before he died, saying,

[17] So shall ye say unto Joseph, Forgive, I pray thee now, the trespass of thy brethren, and their sin; for they did unto thee evil: and now, we pray thee, forgive the trespass of the servants of the God of thy father. And Joseph wept when they spake unto him.

[19] And Joseph said unto them, Fear not: for *am* I in the place of God?

[20] But as for you, ye thought evil against me; *but* God meant it unto good, to bring to pass, as *it is* this day, to save much people alive.

[21] Now therefore fear ye not: I will nourish you, and your little ones.

And he comforted them, and spake kindly unto them.

Genesis 50:16–17, 19–21

INSIGHTS

*F*orgiveness of sins is a great all-embracing gift of God. In His mercy, God sets the sinner free and receives him back into His love and favor. When we are forgiven, we have confidence toward God in prayer. We can be thankful every day of our lives because we are free and nothing stands between us and God. With the door open to communion with Him, God desires that we spend time with Him in His Word each day as people whose sins are forgiven. We need to live in the light of His countenance daily.

And God desires that this assurance affect our relationship with others. Those who are forgiven are free to forgive others. If it is difficult to forgive, we should consider how freely God has forgiven us of every offense toward Him. . . .

Remember these words daily: "As I need God's forgiveness each day, so let me be ready each day to forgive my brother." God grant you grace to do it!

Andrew Murray

APPLICATION

*W*hat healing has God's forgiveness accomplished in your life? What are the consequences when God's people don't forgive one another? Whom do you need to forgive? Pray that you will always follow God's merciful example in forgiving others.

MONDAY

*God's Spirit Brings
Glory and Understanding
to Those Who Believe*

2 Corinthians 3:4—4:15

*A*nd such trust have we through Christ to God-ward:

⁵ not that we are sufficient of ourselves to think any thing as of ourselves; but our sufficiency *is* of God;
⁶ who also hath made us able ministers of the new testament; not of the letter, but of the spirit: for the letter killeth, but the spirit giveth life.
⁷ But if the ministration of death, written *and* engraven in stones, was glorious, so that the children of Israel could not steadfastly behold the face of Moses for the glory of his countenance; which *glory* was to be done away;
⁸ how shall not the ministration of the spirit be rather glorious?
⁹ For if the ministration of condemnation *be* glory, much more doth the ministration of righteousness exceed in glory.
¹⁰ For even that which was made glorious had no glory in this respect, by reason of the glory that excelleth.
¹¹ For if that which is done away *was* glorious, much more that which remaineth *is* glorious.
¹² Seeing then that we have such hope, we use great plainness of speech:
¹³ and not as Moses, *which* put a vail over his face, that the children of Israel could not steadfastly look to the end of that which is abolished:
¹⁴ but their minds were blinded: for until this day remaineth the same vail untaken away in the reading of the old testament; which *vail* is done away in Christ.
¹⁵ But even unto this day, when Moses is read, the vail is upon their heart.
¹⁶ Nevertheless, when it shall turn to the Lord, the vail shall be taken away.
¹⁷ Now the Lord is that Spirit: and where the Spirit of the Lord *is*, there *is* liberty.
¹⁸ But we all, with open face beholding as in a glass the glory of the Lord, are changed into the same image from glory to glory, *even* as by the Spirit of the Lord.

Preaching the Gospel

4 Therefore, seeing we have this ministry, as we have received mercy, we faint not;
² but have renounced the hidden things of dishonesty, not walking in craftiness, nor handling the word of God deceitfully; but, by manifestation of the truth, commending ourselves to every man's conscience in the sight of God.
³ But if our gospel be hid, it is hid to them that are lost:
⁴ in whom the god of this world hath blinded the minds of them which believe not, lest the light of the glorious gospel of Christ, who is the image of God, should shine unto them.
⁵ For we preach not ourselves, but Christ Jesus the Lord; and ourselves your servants for Jesus' sake.
⁶ For God, who commanded the light to shine out of darkness, hath shined in our hearts, to *give* the light of the knowledge of the glory of God in the face of Jesus Christ.

Spiritual Treasure in Earthen Vessels

*B*ut we have this treasure in earthen vessels, that the excellency of the power may be of God, and not of us.

[8] *We are* troubled on every side, yet not distressed; we *are* perplexed, but not in despair;

[9] persecuted, but not forsaken; cast down, but not destroyed;

[10] always bearing about in the body the dying of the Lord Jesus, that the life also of Jesus might be made manifest in our body.

[11] For we which live are alway delivered unto death for Jesus' sake, that the life also of Jesus might be made manifest in our mortal flesh.

[12] So then death worketh in us, but life in you.

[13] We having the same spirit of faith, according as it is written, I believed, and therefore have I spoken; we also believe, and therefore speak;

[14] knowing that he which raised up the Lord Jesus shall raise up us also by Jesus, and shall present *us* with you.

[15] For all things *are* for your sakes, that the abundant grace might through the thanksgiving of many redound to the glory of God.

OLD TESTAMENT READING

*T*hey are of those that rebel against the light; they know not the ways thereof, nor abide in the paths thereof. [24] They are exalted for a little while, but are gone and brought low; they are taken out of the way as all *other*, and cut off as the tops of the ears of corn.

Job 24:13, 24

INSIGHTS

*G*lory, I've learned, is what God is all about. His essential being. Whenever you talk about His character or attributes—like holiness, love, compassion, justice, truth, or mercy—that's God's glory. . . .

So how is it that you and I can glorify God? It happens every time we reveal His attributes in the course of our daily lives. Every time you share the good news of Christ with another. Every time you reflect patience in the middle of an upsetting or perplexing problem. Every time you smile from the heart or offer an encouraging word. Whenever those around you see God's character displayed in your attitudes and responses, you are displaying His glory.

. . . God's glory isn't reserved for a temple of stone or some heavenly vista. It can shine out clearly while you're changing a flat on the freeway . . . or counseling an angry co-worker . . . or lying in a hospital bed . . . or balancing two crying babies in the church nursery.

Joni Eareckson Tada

APPLICATION

*H*ow is God's glory that is shown through believers different from that shown by Moses? How has God's Spirit opened up your mind? How is God's glory shining in your life?

TUESDAY

*The Righteous Will Receive
Eternal Glory*

2 Corinthians 4:16—6:2

Living by Faith

*F*or which cause we faint not; but though our outward man perish, yet the inward *man* is renewed day by day.

17 For our light affliction, which is but for a moment, worketh for us a far more exceeding *and* eternal weight of glory;

18 while we look not at the things which are seen, but at the things which are not seen: for the things which are seen *are* temporal; but the things which are not seen *are* eternal.

5 For we know that, if our earthly house of *this* tabernacle were dissolved, we have a building of God, a house not made with hands, eternal in the heavens.

2 For in this we groan, earnestly desiring to be clothed upon with our house which is from heaven:

3 if so be that being clothed we shall not be found naked.

4 For we that are in *this* tabernacle do groan, being burdened: not for that we would be unclothed, but clothed upon, that mortality might be swallowed up of life.

5 Now he that hath wrought us for the selfsame thing *is* God, who also hath given unto us the earnest of the Spirit.

6 Therefore *we are* always confident, knowing that, whilst we are at home in the body, we are absent from the Lord:

7 (for we walk by faith, not by sight:)

8 we are confident, *I say,* and willing rather to be absent from the body, and to be present with the Lord.

9 Wherefore we labor, that, whether present or absent, we may be accepted of him.

10 For we must all appear before the judgment seat of Christ; that every one may receive the things *done* in *his* body, according to that he hath done, whether it *be* good or bad.

Reconciled to God

*K*nowing therefore the terror of the Lord, we persuade men; but we are made manifest unto God; and I trust also are made manifest in your consciences.

12 For we commend not ourselves again unto you, but give you occasion to glory on our behalf, that ye may have somewhat to *answer* them which glory in appearance, and not in heart.

13 For whether we be beside ourselves, *it is* to God: or whether we be sober, *it is* for your cause.

14 For the love of Christ constraineth us; because we thus judge, that if one died for all, then were all dead:

15 and *that* he died for all, that they which live should not henceforth live unto themselves, but unto him which died for them, and rose again.

16 Wherefore henceforth know we no man after the flesh: yea, though we have known Christ after the flesh, yet now henceforth know we *him* no more.

17 Therefore if any man *be* in Christ, *he is* a new creature: old things are passed away; behold, all things are become new.

18 And all things *are* of God, who hath reconciled us to himself by Jesus

Christ, and hath given to us the ministry of reconciliation;

[19] to wit, that God was in Christ, reconciling the world unto himself, not imputing their trespasses unto them; and hath committed unto us the word of reconciliation.

[20] Now then we are ambassadors for Christ, as though God did beseech *you* by us: we pray *you* in Christ's stead, be ye reconciled to God.

[21] For he hath made him *to be* sin for us, who knew no sin; that we might be made the righteousness of God in him.

6 We then, as workers together *with him,* beseech *you* also that ye receive not the grace of God in vain.

[2] (For he saith, I have heard thee in a time accepted, and in the day of salvation have I succored thee: Behold, now *is* the accepted time; behold, now is the day of salvation.)

OLD TESTAMENT READING

*W*ho shall ascend into the hill of the Lord? or who shall stand in his holy place?

[4] He that hath clean hands, and a pure heart; who hath not lifted up his soul unto vanity, nor sworn deceitfully.

[5] He shall receive the blessing from the Lord, and righteousness from the God of his salvation.

[6] This *is* the generation of them that seek him, that seek thy face, O Jacob. Selah.

Psalm 24:3–6

INSIGHTS

*M*an's place in creation was very remarkable. The Psalmist says, "For thou hast made him a little lower than the angels, and hast crowned him with glory and honor. Thou madest him to have dominion over the works of thy hands; thou hast put all things under his feet: all sheep and oxen, yea, and the beasts of the field; the fowl of the air, and the fish of the sea, and whatsoever passeth through the paths of the seas." . . .

What a man will become we can scarcely tell when he is remade in the image of God, and made like unto our divine Lord who is "the firstborn among many brethren." Our bodies are to be developed into something infinitely brighter and better than the bodies of men here below: and as for the soul, we cannot guess to what an elevation it shall be raised in Christ Jesus. There is room for the largest expectation here, as we conjecture what will be the full accomplishment of the vast intent of eternal love, an intent which has involved the sacrifice of the only-begotten Son of God. That can be no mean design which has been carried on at the expense of the best that heaven itself possessed.

Charles Spurgeon

ACTION POINT

*S*top now and focus your eyes on what you cannot yet see. Imagine yourself standing in God's temple with clean hands and a pure heart. Imagine God as your glory and light forever. Praise him for his eternal glory that is to come!

WEDNESDAY

The Importance of Living a Pure Life

---

2 Corinthians 6:3—7:7

Giving no offense in any thing, that the ministry be not blamed:

4 but in all *things* approving ourselves as the ministers of God, in much patience, in afflictions, in necessities, in distresses,

5 in stripes, in imprisonments, in tumults, in labors, in watchings, in fastings;

6 by pureness, by knowledge, by long-suffering, by kindness, by the Holy Ghost, by love unfeigned,

7 by the word of truth, by the power of God, by the armor of righteousness on the right hand and on the left,

8 by honor and dishonor, by evil report and good report: as deceivers, and *yet* true;

9 as unknown, and *yet* well known; as dying, and, behold, we live; as chastened, and not killed;

10 as sorrowful, yet alway rejoicing; as poor, yet making many rich; as having nothing, and *yet* possessing all things.

11 O *ye* Corinthians, our mouth is open unto you, our heart is enlarged.

12 Ye are not straitened in us, but ye are straitened in your own bowels.

13 Now for a recompense in the same, (I speak as unto *my* children,) be ye also enlarged.

Warning About Unbelievers

Be ye not unequally yoked together with unbelievers: for what fellowship hath righteousness with unrighteousness? and what communion hath light with darkness?

15 And what concord hath Christ with Belial? or what part hath he that believeth with an infidel?

16 And what agreement hath the temple of God with idols? for ye are the temple of the living God; as God hath said, I will dwell in them, and walk in *them;* and I will be their God, and they shall be my people.

17 Wherefore come out from among them, and be ye separate, saith the Lord, and touch not the unclean *thing;* and I will receive you,

18 and will be a Father unto you, and ye shall be my sons and daughters, saith the Lord Almighty.

7 Having therefore these promises, dearly beloved, let us cleanse ourselves from all filthiness of the flesh and spirit, perfecting holiness in the fear of God.

Paul's Joy

Receive us; we have wronged no man, we have corrupted no man, we have defrauded no man.

3 I speak not *this* to condemn *you:* for I have said before, that ye are in our hearts to die and live with *you.*

4 Great *is* my boldness of speech toward you, great *is* my glorying of you: I am filled with comfort, I am exceeding joyful in all our tribulation.

5 For, when we were come into Macedonia, our flesh had no rest, but we were troubled on every side; without *were* fightings, within *were* fears.

6 Nevertheless God, that comforteth those that are cast down, comforted us by the coming of Titus;

7 and not by his coming only, but by the consolation wherewith he was comforted in you, when he told us your earnest desire, your mourning, your fervent mind toward me; so that I rejoiced the more.

OLD TESTAMENT READING

*E*nter not into the path of the wicked, and go not in the way of evil men.
15 Avoid it, pass not by it, turn from it, and pass away.

Proverbs 4:14–15

INSIGHTS

*S*omeone has said, "a belief is what you hold; a conviction is what holds you." A conviction is not truly a conviction unless it includes a commitment to live by what we claim to believe. A commitment is not a vow but a resolution—a determined purpose to live by God's word as he applies it to our lives. First, we need a commitment to holiness as a total way of life. We must decide that holiness is so important to God that it deserves priority attention in our lives. We must commit ourselves to obeying God in all of his commands. We cannot pick and choose according to our own values. A little bit of fudging on one's income tax return is sin just as much as outright theft; an unforgiving spirit toward someone else is sin just as much as murder. I am not suggesting that all sin is equally offensive to God; I am saying that all sin is offensive to God. The measure of sin is not just in its effect upon our neighbor, but in its affront to the majesty and holiness of a sovereign God.*

Sin is serious to God, and it becomes serious business to us when we reflect upon the fact that every sin, regardless of how seemingly insignificant it appears to us, is an expression of contempt toward the sovereign authority of God. . . .

The psalmist recognized the seriousness of any and all sin when he said, "You have laid down precepts that are to be fully obeyed" (Psalm 119:4). He recognized that partial obedience—for example, refraining from outright theft of our neighbor's property while allowing our heart to covet it—is actually disobedience. God's precepts are to be fully obeyed.

Jerry Bridges

APPLICATION

*L*ist the lifestyle traits that are to characterize those who serve God. Why is purity so important to God? Why must God's people seek purity? What is the way to live a pure life? Is your desire for purity a belief or a conviction?

THURSDAY

Godly Sorrow Leads Us to Repentance

2 Corinthians 7:8—8:15

*F*or though I made you sorry with a letter, I do not repent, though I did repent: for I perceive that the same epistle hath made you sorry, though *it were* but for a season.

⁹ Now I rejoice, not that ye were made sorry, but that ye sorrowed to repentance: for ye were made sorry after a godly manner, that ye might receive damage by us in nothing.

¹⁰ For godly sorrow worketh repentance to salvation not to be repented of: but the sorrow of the world worketh death.

¹¹ For behold this selfsame thing, that ye sorrowed after a godly sort, what carefulness it wrought in you, yea, *what* clearing of yourselves, yea, *what* indignation, yea, *what* fear, yea, *what* vehement desire, yea, *what* zeal, yea, *what* revenge! In all *things* ye have approved yourselves to be clear in this matter.

¹² Wherefore, though I wrote unto you, *I did it* not for his cause that had done the wrong, nor for his cause that suffered wrong, but that our care for you in the sight of God might appear unto you.

¹³ Therefore we were comforted in your comfort: yea, and exceedingly the more joyed we for the joy of Titus, because his spirit was refreshed by you all.

¹⁴ For if I have boasted any thing to him of you, I am not ashamed; but as we spake all things to you in truth,

even so our boasting, which *I made* before Titus, is found a truth.

¹⁵ And his inward affection is more abundant toward you, whilst he remembereth the obedience of you all, how with fear and trembling ye received him.

¹⁶ I rejoice therefore that I have confidence in you in all *things*.

Christian Giving

8 Moreover, brethren, we do you to wit of the grace of God bestowed on the churches of Macedonia;

² how that in a great trial of affliction, the abundance of their joy and their deep poverty abounded unto the riches of their liberality.

³ For to *their* power, I bear record, yea, and beyond *their* power *they were* willing of themselves;

⁴ praying us with much intreaty that we would receive the gift, and *take upon us* the fellowship of the ministering to the saints.

⁵ And *this they did*, not as we hoped, but first gave their own selves to the Lord, and unto us by the will of God.

⁶ Insomuch that we desired Titus, that as he had begun, so he would also finish in you the same grace also.

⁷ Therefore, as ye abound in every *thing, in* faith, and utterance, and knowledge, and *in* all diligence, and *in* your love to us, *see* that ye abound in this grace also.

⁸ I speak not by commandment, but by occasion of the forwardness of others, and to prove the sincerity of your love.

⁹ For ye know the grace of our Lord Jesus Christ, that, though he was rich, yet for your sakes he became poor, that ye through his poverty might be rich.

¹⁰And herein I give *my* advice: for this is expedient for you, who have begun before, not only to do, but also to be forward a year ago.

¹¹Now therefore perform the doing of it; that as *there was* a readiness to will, so *there may* be a performance also out of that which ye have.

¹²For if there be first a willing mind, *it is* accepted according to that a man hath, *and* not according to that he hath not.

¹³For *I mean* not that other men be eased, and ye burdened:

¹⁴but by an equality, *that* now at this time your abundance *may be a supply* for their want, that their abundance also may be *a supply* for your want; that there may be equality:

¹⁵as it is written, He that *had gathered* much had nothing over; and he that *had gathered* little had no lack.

OLD TESTAMENT READING

*N*ow when Ezra had prayed, and when he had confessed, weeping and casting himself down before the house of God, there assembled unto him out of Israel a very great congregation of men and women and children: for the people wept very sore.

²And Shechaniah the son of Jehiel, *one* of the sons of Elam, answered and said unto Ezra, We have trespassed against our God, and have taken strange wives of the people of the land: yet now there is hope in Israel concerning this thing.

³Now therefore let us make a covenant with our God to put away all the wives, and such as are born of them, according to the counsel of my lord, and of those that tremble at the commandment of our God.

Ezra 10:1–3a

INSIGHTS

*R*epentance is simply and precisely a change of mind. The original term denotes, a thinking again—a turning of the mind—as when one finds himself going wrong and turns about to pursue the opposite course. The term, when applied to evangelical repentance, means not merely a turning of the mind, but a change of the entire purposes of action, change in the entire attitude of the will. . . .

Conviction of sin as a wrong committed against God is implied in repentance. Without this there can be no rational repentance.

The sinner must become truly honest with God. He must honestly admit the truths affirmed by his reason and pressed on his soul by his conscience. Especially must he recognize God's rights: that he himself is God's property and belongs truly to God. . . .

Repentance implies a universal reformation of life, a reformation extending to all forms of sin. Penitent men turn from all sin as sin, because they regard it as sin, and therefore can have no sympathy with it. . . .

When I speak of abandoning sin, I do not imply that the penitent man never for even a moment relapses into it; but I imply that he sets himself against it in real honest earnestness.

Charles Finney

APPLICATION

*W*hat is the difference between godly sorrow and the world's sorrow? What feelings and actions does godly sorrow bring about?

FRIDAY

God Encourages Us to Share Liberally with Others

2 Corinthians 8:16—9:15

Titus and His Companions Help

*B*ut thanks *be* to God, which put the same earnest care into the heart of Titus for you.

¹⁷ For indeed he accepted the exhortation; but being more forward, of his own accord he went unto you.

¹⁸ And we have sent with him the brother, whose praise *is* in the gospel throughout all the churches;

¹⁹ and not *that* only, but who was also chosen of the churches to travel with us with this grace, which is administered by us to the glory of the same Lord, and *declaration* of your ready mind:

²⁰ avoiding this, that no man should blame us in this abundance which is administered by us:

²¹ providing for honest things, not only in the sight of the Lord, but also in the sight of men.

²² And we have sent with them our brother, whom we have oftentimes proved diligent in many things, but now much more diligent, upon the great confidence which *I have* in you.

²³ Whether *any do inquire* of Titus, *he is* my partner and fellowhelper concerning you: or our brethren *be inquired of, they are* the messengers of the churches, *and* the glory of Christ.

²⁴ Wherefore show ye to them, and before the churches, the proof of your love, and of our boasting on your behalf.

Help for Fellow Christians

9 For as touching the ministering to the saints, it is superfluous for me to write to you:

² for I know the forwardness of your mind, for which I boast of you to them of Macedonia, that Achaia was ready a year ago; and your zeal hath provoked very many.

³ Yet have I sent the brethren, lest our boasting of you should be in vain in this behalf; that, as I said, ye may be ready:

⁴ lest haply if they of Macedonia come with me, and find you unprepared, we (that we say not, ye) should be ashamed in this same confident boasting.

⁵ Therefore I thought it necessary to exhort the brethren, that they would go before unto you, and make up beforehand your bounty, whereof ye had notice before, that the same might be ready, as *a matter of* bounty, and not as *of* covetousness.

⁶ But this *I say,* He which soweth sparingly shall reap also sparingly; and he which soweth bountifully shall reap also bountifully.

⁷ Every man according as he purposeth in his heart, *so let him give;* not grudgingly, or of necessity: for God loveth a cheerful giver.

⁸ And God *is* able to make all grace abound toward you; that ye, always having all sufficiency in all *things,* may abound to every good work:

⁹ (as it is written, He hath dispersed abroad; he hath given to the poor: his righteousness remaineth for ever.

¹⁰ Now he that ministereth seed to the sower both minister bread for *your* food, and multiply your seed sown, and increase the fruits of your righteousness:)

[11] Being enriched in every thing to all bountifulness, which causeth through us thanksgiving to God.
[12] For the administration of this service not only supplieth the want of the saints, but is abundant also by many thanksgivings unto God;
[13] while by the experiment of this ministration they glorify God for your professed subjection unto the gospel of Christ, and for *your* liberal distribution unto them, and unto all *men;*
[14] and by their prayer for you, which long after you for the exceeding grace of God in you.
[15] Thanks *be* unto God for his unspeakable gift.

OLD TESTAMENT READING

*H*e that giveth unto the poor shall not lack: but he that hideth his eyes shall have many a curse.

Proverbs 28:27

*T*he desire of the slothful killeth him; for his hands refuse to labor.
[26] He coveteth greedily all the day long: but the righteous giveth and spareth not.

Proverbs 21:25–26

INSIGHTS

*W*e all know how subtle the materialistic temptations are and how convincing the rationalizations. Only by God's grace and with great effort can we escape the shower of luxuries which has almost suffocated our Christian compassion. All of us face this problem. Some years ago I spent about fifty dollars on an extra suit. That's not much of course. Besides, I persuaded myself, it was

a wise investment (thanks to the 75 percent discount). But that money would have fed a starving child in India for about a year. In all honesty we have to ask ourselves: Dare we care at all about current fashions if that means reducing our ability to help hungry neighbors? Dare we care more about obtaining a secure economic future for our family than for living an uncompromisingly Christian lifestyle? . . .

. . . We have been brainwashed to believe that bigger houses, more prosperous businesses, more luxurious gadgets, are worthy goals in life. As a result, we are caught in an absurd, materialistic spiral. The more we make, the more we think we need in order to live decently and respectably. Somehow we have to break this cycle because it makes us sin against our needy brothers and sisters and, therefore, against our Lord. And it also destroys us. Sharing with others is the way to real joy.

Ronald Sider

APPLICATION

*L*ist what God promises those who give generously. What do you think it means to be made "rich in every way so that you can always give freely"? Is your giving such that it brings praise to God from others?

WEEKEND

*Our Spiritual Weapons
Are Empowered by God*

2 Corinthians 10:1—11:4

Paul Defends His Ministry

10 Now I Paul myself beseech you by the meekness and gentleness of Christ, who in presence *am* base among you, but being absent am bold toward you:

2 but I beseech *you,* that I may not be bold when I am present with that confidence, wherewith I think to be bold against some, which think of us as if we walked according to the flesh.

3 For though we walk in the flesh, we do not war after the flesh:

4 (for the weapons of our warfare *are* not carnal, but mighty through God to the pulling down of strong holds;)

5 casting down imaginations, and every high thing that exalteth itself against the knowledge of God, and bringing into captivity every thought to the obedience of Christ;

6 and having in a readiness to revenge all disobedience, when your obedience is fulfilled.

7 Do ye look on things after the outward appearance? If any man trust to himself that he is Christ's, let him of himself think this again, that, as he *is* Christ's, even so *are* we Christ's.

8 For though I should boast somewhat more of our authority, which the Lord hath given us for edification, and not for your destruction, I should not be ashamed:

9 that I may not seem as if I would terrify you by letters.

10 For *his* letters, say they, *are* weighty and powerful; but *his* bodily presence *is* weak, and *his* speech contemptible.

11 Let such a one think this, that, such as we are in word by letters when we are absent, such *will we be* also in deed when we are present.

12 For we dare not make ourselves of the number, or compare ourselves with some that commend themselves: but they, measuring themselves by themselves, and comparing themselves among themselves, are not wise.

13 But we will not boast of things without *our* measure, but according to the measure of the rule which God hath distributed to us, a measure to reach even unto you.

14 For we stretch not ourselves beyond *our measure,* as though we reached not unto you: for we are come as far as to you also in *preaching* the gospel of Christ:

15 not boasting of things without *our* measure, *that is,* of other men's labors; but having hope, when your faith is increased, that we shall be enlarged by you according to our rule abundantly,

16 to preach the gospel in the *regions* beyond you, *and* not to boast in another man's line of things made ready to our hand.

17 But he that glorieth, let him glory in the Lord.

18 For not he that commendeth himself is approved, but whom the Lord commendeth.

Paul and the False Apostles

11 Would to God ye could bear with me a little in *my* folly: and indeed bear with me.

2 For I am jealous over you with godly jealousy: for I have espoused you to one husband, that I may present *you* as a chaste virgin to Christ.

3 But I fear, lest by any means, as the serpent beguiled Eve through his subtilty, so your minds should be corrupted from the simplicity that is in Christ.

4 For if he that cometh preacheth another Jesus, whom we have not preached, or *if* ye receive another spirit, which ye have not received, or another gospel, which ye have not accepted, ye might well bear with *him*.

OLD TESTAMENT READING

The Power of Faith

*A*nd they rose early in the morning, and went forth into the wilderness of Tekoa: and as they went forth, Jehoshaphat stood and said, Hear me, O Judah, and ye inhabitants of Jerusalem; Believe in the Lord your God, so shall ye be established; believe his prophets, so shall ye prosper.

21 And when he had consulted with the people, he appointed singers unto the Lord, and that should praise the beauty of holiness, as they went out before the army, and to say, Praise the Lord; for his mercy *endureth* for ever.

22 And when they began to sing and to praise, the Lord set ambushments against the children of Ammon, Moab, and mount Seir, which were come against Judah; and they were smitten.

2 Chronicles 20:20–22

INSIGHTS

*W*e have no enemies but the enemies of God. Our fights are not against men but against spiritual wickednesses. We war with the devil and the blasphemy and error and despair which he brings into the field of battle. We fight with all the armies of sin—impurity, drunkenness, oppression, infidelity, and ungodliness. With these we contend earnestly, but not with sword or spear; the weapons of our warfare are not carnal.

Jehovah, our God, abhors everything which is evil, and, therefore, He goeth with us to fight for us in this crusade. He will save us, and He will give us grace to war a good warfare and win the victory. We may depend upon it that if we are on God's side God is on our side. With such an august ally the conflict is never in the least degree doubtful. It is not that truth is mighty and must prevail but that might lies with the Father who is almighty, with Jesus who has all power in heaven and in earth, and with the Holy Spirit who worketh His will among men.

Soldiers of Christ, gird on your armor. Strike home in the name of the God of holiness, and by faith grasp His salvation. Let not this day pass without striking a blow for Jesus and holiness.

Charles Spurgeon

ACTION POINT

*A*gainst what enemy does the believer fight? What weapons are in your spiritual arsenal? Are your weapons ready for battle and armed with the power of God? Pray that you will faithfully obey God and diligently fight against the enemy.

MONDAY

*God Brings Good
out of Our Suffering*

---

2 Corinthians 11:5–33

For I suppose I was not a whit behind the very chiefest apostles.

⁶ But though *I be* rude in speech, yet not in knowledge; but we have been thoroughly made manifest among you in all things.

⁷ Have I committed an offense in abasing myself that ye might be exalted, because I have preached to you the gospel of God freely?

⁸ I robbed other churches, taking wages *of them,* to do you service.

⁹ And when I was present with you, and wanted, I was chargeable to no man: for that which was lacking to me the brethren which came from Macedonia supplied: and in all *things* I have kept myself from being burdensome unto you, and *so* will I keep *myself.*

¹⁰ As the truth of Christ is in me, no man shall stop me of this boasting in the regions of Achaia.

¹¹ Wherefore? because I love you not? God knoweth.

¹² But what I do, that I will do, that I may cut off occasion from them which desire occasion; that wherein they glory, they may be found even as we.

¹³ For such *are* false apostles, deceitful workers, transforming themselves into the apostles of Christ.

¹⁴ And no marvel; for Satan himself is transformed into an angel of light.

¹⁵ Therefore *it is* no great thing if his ministers also be transformed as the ministers of righteousness; whose end shall be according to their works.

Paul Tells About His Sufferings

I say again, Let no man think me a fool; if otherwise, yet as a fool receive me, that I may boast myself a little.

¹⁷ That which I speak, I speak *it* not after the Lord, but as it were foolishly, in this confidence of boasting.

¹⁸ Seeing that many glory after the flesh, I will glory also.

¹⁹ For ye suffer fools gladly, seeing ye *yourselves* are wise.

²⁰ For ye suffer, if a man bring you into bondage, if a man devour *you,* if a man take of *you,* if a man exalt himself, if a man smite you on the face.

²¹ I speak as concerning reproach, as though we had been weak. Howbeit, whereinsoever any is bold, (I speak foolishly,) I am bold also.

²² Are they Hebrews? so *am* I. Are they Israelites? so *am* I. Are they the seed of Abraham? so *am* I.

²³ Are they ministers of Christ? (I speak as a fool,) I *am* more; in labors more abundant, in stripes above measure, in prisons more frequent, in deaths oft.

²⁴ Of the Jews five times received I forty *stripes* save one.

²⁵ Thrice was I beaten with rods, once was I stoned, thrice I suffered shipwreck, a night and a day I have been in the deep;

²⁶ *in* journeyings often, *in* perils of waters, *in* perils of robbers, *in* perils by *mine own* countrymen, *in* perils by the heathen, *in* perils in the city, *in* perils in the wilderness, *in* perils in the sea, *in* perils among false brethren;

²⁷ in weariness and painfulness, in

watchings often, in hunger and thirst, in fastings often, in cold and nakedness.

28 Beside those things that are without, that which cometh upon me daily, the care of all the churches.

29 Who is weak, and I am not weak? who is offended, and I burn not?

30 If I must needs glory, I will glory of the things which concern mine infirmities.

31 The God and Father of our Lord Jesus Christ, which is blessed for evermore, knoweth that I lie not.

32 In Damascus the governor under Aretas the king kept the city of the Damascenes with a garrison, desirous to apprehend me:

33 and through a window in a basket was I let down by the wall, and escaped his hands.

OLD TESTAMENT READING

*A*nd Pharaoh charged all his people, saying, Every son that is born ye shall cast into the river, and every daughter ye shall save alive.

Exodus 1:22

*A*nd Pharaoh's daughter said unto her, Take this child away, and nurse it for me, and I will give *thee* thy wages. And the woman took the child, and nursed it.

10 And the child grew, and she brought him unto Pharaoh's daughter, and he became her son. And she called his name Moses: and she said, Because I drew him out of the water.

Exodus 2:9, 10

INSIGHTS

*W*e grow in our understanding through difficulties, as God opens to us that which we could not have understood with any other background or in any other set of circumstances. Our assurance as children of the Living God is that He is able to bring beauty from ashes and to give the "oil of joy" for the spirit of mourning (see Isaiah 61:3). And, in addition, He refines, purifies, proves, and causes to grow in us something very precious and lasting in our attitudes toward Him and in our actions to other human beings. As He removed the hedge protecting Job (or any one of us . . .) he is also able to give us the grace to come through the onslaught that follows. However, there is much more than just "coming through," still hanging on to our trust and love of God. There is a "coming through," with a shinier, more gleaming sheen on our surface. We have the possibility during the hard time to have skimmed off more of the specks and scum which are hindering the more beautiful reality of love, joy, peace, longsuffering, and meekness.

Edith Schaeffer

APPLICATION

*F*or Paul, preaching the Good News was "good" enough to willingly bear great suffering, wasn't it? Pray for total confidence that God is bringing about good through the suffering in your life, too.

TUESDAY

*God's Power Is Made
Perfect in Weakness*

---

2 Corinthians 12:1—13:4

A Special Blessing in Paul's Life

12 It is not expedient for me doubtless to glory. I will come to visions and revelations of the Lord.

[2] I knew a man in Christ above fourteen years ago, (whether in the body, I cannot tell; or whether out of the body, I cannot tell: God knoweth;) such a one caught up to the third heaven.

[3] And I knew such a man, (whether in the body, or out of the body, I cannot tell: God knoweth;)

[4] how that he was caught up into paradise, and heard unspeakable words, which it is not lawful for a man to utter.

[5] Of such an one will I glory: yet of myself I will not glory, but in mine infirmities.

[6] For though I would desire to glory, I shall not be a fool; for I will say the truth: but *now* I forbear, lest any man should think of me above that which he seeth me *to be,* or *that* he heareth of me.

[7] And lest I should be exalted above measure through the abundance of the revelations, there was given to me a thorn in the flesh, the messenger of Satan to buffet me, lest I should be exalted above measure.

[8] For this thing I besought the Lord thrice, that it might depart from me.

[9] And he said unto me, My grace is sufficient for thee: for my strength is made perfect in weakness. Most gladly therefore will I rather glory in my infirmities, that the power of Christ may rest upon me.

[10] Therefore I take pleasure in infirmities, in reproaches, in necessities, in persecutions, in distresses for Christ's sake: for when I am weak, then am I strong.

Paul's Love for the Christians

I am become a fool in glorying; ye have compelled me: for I ought to have been commended of you: for in nothing am I behind the very chiefest apostles, though I be nothing.

[12] Truly the signs of an apostle were wrought among you in all patience, in signs, and wonders, and mighty deeds.

[13] For what is it wherein ye were inferior to other churches, except *it be* that I myself was not burdensome to you? forgive me this wrong.

[14] Behold, the third time I am ready to come to you; and I will not be burdensome to you: for I seek not yours, but you: for the children ought not to lay up for the parents, but the parents for the children.

[15] And I will very gladly spend and be spent for you; though the more abundantly I love you, the less I be loved.

[16] But be it so, I did not burden you: nevertheless, being crafty, I caught you with guile.

[17] Did I make a gain of you by any of them whom I sent unto you?

[18] I desired Titus, and with *him* I sent a brother. Did Titus make a gain of you? walked we not in the same spirit? *walked we* not in the same steps?

[19] Again, think ye that we excuse ourselves unto you? we speak before God in Christ: but *we do* all things, dearly beloved, for your edifying.

[20] For I fear, lest, when I come, I shall not find you such as I would, and *that* I shall be found unto you such as ye would not: lest *there be* debates, envyings, wraths, strifes, backbitings, whisperings, swellings, tumults:

[21] *and* lest, when I come again, my God will humble me among you, and *that* I shall bewail many which have sinned already, and have not repented of the uncleanness and fornication and lasciviousness which they have committed.

Final Warnings and Greetings

13 This *is* the third *time* I am coming to you. In the mouth of two or three witnesses shall every word be established.

[2] I told you before, and foretell you, as if I were present, the second time; and being absent now I write to them which heretofore have sinned, and to all other, that, if I come again, I will not spare:

[3] since ye seek a proof of Christ speaking in me, which to you-ward is not weak, but is mighty in you.

[4] For though he was crucified through weakness, yet he liveth by the power of God. For we also are weak in him, but we shall live with him by the power of God toward you.

OLD TESTAMENT READING

*D*avid encouraged himself in the LORD his God.

[8] And David inquired at the LORD,

saying, Shall I pursue after this troop? shall I overtake them? And he answered him, Pursue: for thou shalt surely overtake *them*, and without fail recover *all*.

1 Samuel 30:6b, 8

INSIGHTS

*U*pon examining the life of the apostle Paul, one hardly gets the impression that he was a weak man. On the contrary, he debated against Christ's apostles over the question of gentile salvation, and he won! He spent his life preaching in the most hostile of circumstances. He planted churches throughout the major cities of Asia Minor and in the port cities along the Aegean Sea. Paul trained the first pastors and elders of these early congregations. And to top it all off, he wrote half of the New Testament! . . .

So how do we reconcile Paul's claim to weakness with his amazing accomplishments? Simple, the answer is in the phrase, "when I am weak, then I am strong." A paraphrase of his comment would go something like this: "When I, Paul, in and of my own strength, am weak, then I, Paul, relying of the power of Christ in me, become strong, capable of whatever the Lord requires of me, full of energy and zeal to accomplish His will."

Charles Stanley

APPLICATION

*W*hy does Paul say that God allowed him to become weak? How did Paul respond to his weakness? What does this example of faith teach you?

WEDNESDAY

God Has Plans for His Own

2 Corinthians 13:5—Galatians 1:20

*E*xamine yourselves, whether ye be in the faith; prove your own selves. Know ye not your own selves, how that Jesus Christ is in you, except ye be reprobates?

6 But I trust that ye shall know that we are not reprobates.

7 Now I pray to God that ye do no evil; not that we should appear approved, but that ye should do that which is honest, though we be as reprobates.

8 For we can do nothing against the truth, but for the truth.

9 For we are glad, when we are weak, and ye are strong: and this also we wish, *even* your perfection.

10 Therefore I write these things being absent, lest being present I should use sharpness, according to the power which the Lord hath given me to edification, and not to destruction.

11 Finally, brethren, farewell. Be perfect, be of good comfort, be of one mind, live in peace; and the God of love and peace shall be with you.

12 Greet one another with a holy kiss.

13 All the saints salute you.

14 The grace of the Lord Jesus Christ, and the love of God, and the communion of the Holy Ghost, *be* with you all. Amen.

Greetings from Paul

1 Paul, an apostle, (not of men, neither by man, but by Jesus Christ, and God the Father, who raised him from the dead;)

2 and all the brethren which are with me, unto the churches of Galatia:

3 Grace *be* to you and peace from God the Father, and *from* our Lord Jesus Christ,

4 who gave himself for our sins, that he might deliver us from this present evil world, according to the will of God and our Father:

5 to whom *be* glory for ever and ever. Amen.

The Only Gospel

I marvel that ye are so soon removed from him that called you into the grace of Christ unto another gospel:

7 which is not another; but there be some that trouble you, and would pervert the gospel of Christ.

8 But though we, or an angel from heaven, preach any other gospel unto you than that which we have preached unto you, let him be accursed.

9 As we said before, so say I now again, If any *man* preach any other gospel unto you than that ye have received, let him be accursed.

10 For do I now persuade men, or God? or do I seek to please men? for if I yet pleased men, I should not be the servant of Christ.

Paul's Authority Is from God

*B*ut I certify you, brethren, that the gospel which was preached of me is not after man.

12 For I neither received it of man, neither was I taught *it,* but by the revelation of Jesus Christ.

13 For ye have heard of my conversation in time past in the Jews' religion, how that beyond measure I

persecuted the church of God, and wasted it:

[14] and profited in the Jews' religion above many my equals in mine own nation, being more exceedingly zealous of the traditions of my fathers.

[15] But when it pleased God, who separated me from my mother's womb, and called *me* by his grace,

[16] to reveal his Son in me, that I might preach him among the heathen; immediately I conferred not with flesh and blood:

[17] neither went I up to Jerusalem to them which were apostles before me; but I went into Arabia, and returned again unto Damascus.

[18] Then after three years I went up to Jerusalem to see Peter, and abode with him fifteen days.

[19] But other of the apostles saw I none, save James the Lord's brother.

[20] Now the things which I write unto you, behold, before God, I lie not.

OLD TESTAMENT READING

*N*ow therefore thus shalt thou say unto my servant David, Thus saith the LORD of hosts, I took thee from the sheepcote, *even* from following the sheep, that thou shouldest be ruler over my people Israel:

[8] and I have been with thee whithersoever thou hast walked, and have cut off all thine enemies from before thee, and have made thee a name like the name of the great men that *are* in the earth.

[9] Also I will ordain a place for my people Israel, and will plant them, and they shall dwell in their place, and shall be moved no more: neither shall the children of wickedness waste them any more, as at the beginning,

[10] and since the time that I commanded judges *to be* over my people Israel.

1 Chronicles 17:7–10a

*A*nd when Samuel saw Saul, the LORD said unto him, Behold the man whom I spake to thee of ! this same shall reign over my people.

1 Samuel 9:17

INSIGHTS

*I*t is better we should not know our future. If we did, we should often spoil God's plan for our life. If we could see into tomorrow and know the troubles it will bring, we might be tempted to seek some way of avoiding them, while really they are God's way to new honor and blessing. God's thoughts for us are always thoughts of love, good, promotion; but sometimes the path to the hilltop lies through dark valleys or up rough paths. Yet to miss the hard bit of road is to fail of gaining the lofty height. It is better, therefore, to walk, not knowing, with God, than it would be to see the way and choose for ourselves. God's way for us is always better than our own.

J. R. Miller

ACTION POINT

*D*avid, Samuel, Saul, and Paul all knew that they were called by God to fulfill his plans. Is there any reason to believe that God has planned your life to a lesser degree? Are you willing to test yourself to see if you are following his plan for you? Pray that you will be faithful to his plan and calling for your life.

THURSDAY

"Remember the Poor"

Galatians 1:21—2:21

*A*fterwards I came into the regions of Syria and Cilicia.

²² And was unknown by face unto the churches of Judea which were in Christ:

²³ but they had heard only, That he which persecuted us in times past now preacheth the faith which once he destroyed.

²⁴ And they glorified God in me.

Other Apostles Accepted Paul

2 Then fourteen years after I went up again to Jerusalem with Barnabas, and took Titus with *me* also.

² and I went up by revelation, and communicated unto them that gospel which I preach among the Gentiles, but privately to them which were of reputation, lest by any means I should run, or had run, in vain.

³ But neither Titus, who was with me, being a Greek, was compelled to be circumcised:

⁴ and that because of false brethren unawares brought in, who came in privily to spy out our liberty which we have in Christ Jesus, that they might bring us into bondage:

⁵ to whom we gave place by subjection, no, not for an hour; that the truth of the gospel might continue with you.

⁶ But of these who seemed to be somewhat, (whatsoever they were, it maketh no matter to me: God accepteth no man's person:) for they who seemed *to be somewhat* in conference added nothing to me:

⁷ but contrariwise, when they saw that the gospel of the uncircumcision was committed unto me, as *the gospel* of the circumcision *was* unto Peter;

⁸ (for he that wrought effectually in Peter to the apostleship of the circumcision, the same was mighty in me toward the Gentiles:)

⁹ and when James, Cephas, and John, who seemed to be pillars, perceived the grace that was given unto me, they gave to me and Barnabas the right hands of fellowship; that we *should go* unto the heathen, and they unto the circumcision.

¹⁰ Only *they would* that we should remember the poor; the same which I also was forward to do.

Paul Confronts Peter

*B*ut when Peter was come to Antioch, I withstood him to the face, because he was to be blamed.

¹² For before that certain came from James, he did eat with the Gentiles: but when they were come, he withdrew and separated himself, fearing them which were of the circumcision.

¹³ And the other Jews dissembled likewise with him; insomuch that Barnabas also was carried away with their dissimulation.

¹⁴ But when I saw that they walked not uprightly according to the truth of the gospel, I said unto Peter before *them* all, If thou, being a Jew, livest after the manner of Gentiles, and not as do the Jews, why compellest thou the Gentiles to live as do the Jews?

¹⁵ We *who are* Jews by nature, and not sinners of the Gentiles,

¹⁶ knowing that a man is not justified by the works of the law, but by the

faith of Jesus Christ, even we have believed in Jesus Christ, that we might be justified by the faith of Christ, and not by the works of the law: for by the works of the law shall no flesh be justified.

17 But if, while we seek to be justified by Christ, we ourselves also are found sinners, *is* therefore Christ the minister of sin? God forbid.

18 For if I build again the things which I destroyed, I make myself a transgressor.

19 For I through the law am dead to the law, that I might live unto God.

20 I am crucified with Christ: nevertheless I live; yet not I, but Christ liveth in me: and the life which I now live in the flesh I live by the faith of the Son of God, who loved me, and gave himself for me.

21 I do not frustrate the grace of God: for if righteousness *come* by the law, then Christ is dead in vain.

OLD TESTAMENT READING

*W*hoso stoppeth his ears at the cry of the poor, he also shall cry himself, but shall not be heard.

Proverbs 21:13

*A*nd if thy brother be waxen poor, and fallen in decay with thee; then thou shalt relieve him: *yea, though he be* a stranger, or a sojourner; that he may live with thee.

36 Take thou no usury of him, or increase: but fear thy God; that thy brother may live with thee.

Leviticus 25:35–36

INSIGHTS

*T*he Bible specifically commands believers to imitate God's special concern for the poor and oppressed. In the Old Testament, Yahweh frequently reminded the Israelites of their former oppression in Egypt when he commanded them to care for the poor. . . .

When Paul took up the collection for the poor in Jerusalem, he pointedly reminded the Corinthians that the Lord Jesus became poor so that they might become rich (2 Cor. 8:9). When the author of 1 John called on Christians to share with the needy, he first mentioned the example of Christ: "By this we know love, that he laid down his life for us; and we ought to lay down our lives for the brethren" (1 John 3:16). Then, in the very next verse, he urged Christians to give generously to the needy. It is the amazing self-sacrifice of Christ which Christians are to imitate as they relate to the poor and oppressed.

. . . God's Word commands believers to care for the poor. In fact the Bible underlines the command by teaching that when God's people care for the poor, they imitate God himself. But that is not all. God's Word teaches that those who neglect the poor and oppressed are really not God's people at all—no matter how frequent their religious rituals or how orthodox their creeds and confessions.

Ronald Sider

ACTION POINT

*W*hat do these passages reveal to you about God's attitude toward the poor? Deep in your heart, do you really want to help the poor? What more can you do to show God's compassion for the poor? Will you do it?

FRIDAY

God Will Bless
Those Who Believe

Galatians 3:1–20

Blessing Comes Through Faith

3 O foolish Galatians, who hath bewitched you, that ye should not obey the truth, before whose eyes Jesus Christ hath been evidently set forth, crucified among you?

² This only would I learn of you, Received ye the Spirit by the works of the law, or by the hearing of faith?

³ Are ye so foolish? having begun in the Spirit, are ye now made perfect by the flesh?

⁴ Have ye suffered so many things in vain? if it *be* yet in vain.

⁵ He therefore that ministereth to you the Spirit, and worketh miracles among you, *doeth he it* by the works of the law, or by the hearing of faith?

⁶ Even as Abraham believed God, and it was accounted to him for righteousness.

⁷ Know ye therefore that they which are of faith, the same are the children of Abraham.

⁸ And the scripture, foreseeing that God would justify the heathen through faith, preached before the gospel unto Abraham, *saying*, In thee shall all nations be blessed.

⁹ So then they which be of faith are blessed with faithful Abraham.

¹⁰ For as many as are of the works of the law are under the curse: for it is written, Cursed *is* every one that continueth not in all things which are written in the book of the law to do them.

¹¹ But that no man is justified by the law in the sight of God, *it is* evident: for, The just shall live by faith.

¹² And the law is not of faith: but, The man that doeth them shall live in them.

¹³ Christ hath redeemed us from the curse of the law, being made a curse for us: for it *is* written, Cursed *is* every one that hangeth on a tree:

¹⁴ that the blessing of Abraham might come on the Gentiles through Jesus Christ; that we might receive the promise of the Spirit through faith.

The Law and the Promise

*B*rethren, I speak after the manner of men; Though *it be* but a man's covenant, yet *if it be* confirmed, no man disannulleth, or addeth thereto.

¹⁶ Now to Abraham and his seed were the promises made. He saith not, And to seeds, as of many; but as of one, And to thy seed, which is Christ.

¹⁷ And this I say, *that* the covenant, that was confirmed before of God in Christ, the law, which was four hundred and thirty years after, cannot disannul, that it should make the promise of none effect.

¹⁸ For if the inheritance *be* of the law, *it is* no more of promise: but God gave *it* to Abraham by promise.

¹⁹ Wherefore then *serveth* the law? It was added because of transgressions, till the seed should come to whom the promise was made; *and it was* ordained by angels in the hand of a mediator.

²⁰ Now a mediator is not a *mediator* of one, but God is one.

*A*nd the angel of the LORD called unto Abraham out of heaven the second time,

¹⁶ and said, By myself have I sworn, saith the LORD, for because thou hast done this thing, and hast not withheld thy son, thine only *son*,

¹⁷ that in blessing I will bless thee, and in multiplying I will multiply thy seed as the stars of the heaven, and as the sand which *is* upon the seashore.

Genesis 22:15–17a

---

*W*hen upon life's billows you are
   tempest tossed,
When you are discouraged,
   thinking all is lost,
Count your many blessings, name
   them one by one,
And it will surprise you what the
   Lord hath done.

Are you ever burdened with a load
   of care?
Does the cross seem heavy you are
   called to bear?
Count your many blessings, ev'ry
   doubt will fly,
And you will be singing as the
   days go by.

When you look at others with their
   lands and gold,
Think that Christ has promised
   you His wealth untold;
Count your many blessings, money
   cannot buy
Your reward in heaven, nor your
   home on high.

So, amid the conflict, whether
   great or small,
Do not be discouraged, God is over
   all;
Count your many blessings, angels
   will attend,
Help and comfort give you to your
   journey's end.

Count your blessings, name them
   one by one;
Count your blessings, see what
   God hath done;
Count your blessings, name them
   one by one;
Count your many blessings, see
   what God hath done.

Johnson Oatman, Jr.

---

*W*hat are the differences between obeying the law and believing the Good News? What was the purpose of the law? What is promised to all who believe? Name the blessings God has bestowed on you!

WEEKEND
We Are God's Children

Galatians 3:21—4:20

The Purpose of the Law of Moses

*I*s the law then against the promises of God? God forbid: for if there had been a law given which could have given life, verily righteousness should have been by the law.
²² But the scripture hath concluded all under sin, that the promise by faith of Jesus Christ might be given to them that believe.
²³ But before faith came, we were kept under the law, shut up unto the faith which should afterwards be revealed.
²⁴ Wherefore the law was our schoolmaster *to bring us* unto Christ, that we might be justified by faith.
²⁵ But after that faith is come, we are no longer under a schoolmaster.
²⁶ For ye are all the children of God by faith in Christ Jesus.
²⁷ For as many of you as have been baptized into Christ have put on Christ.
²⁸ There is neither Jew nor Greek, there is neither bond nor free, there is neither male nor female: for ye are all one in Christ Jesus.
²⁹ And if ye *be* Christ's, then are ye Abraham's seed, and heirs according to the promise.

4 Now I say, *That* the heir, as long as he is a child, differeth nothing from a servant, though he be lord of all;
² but is under tutors and governors until the time appointed of the father.
³ Even so we, when we were children, were in bondage under the elements of the world:
⁴ but when the fulness of the time was come, God sent forth his Son, made of a woman, made under the law,
⁵ to redeem them that were under the law, that we might receive the adoption of sons.
⁶ And because ye are sons, God hath sent forth the Spirit of his Son into your hearts, crying, Abba, Father.
⁷ Wherefore thou art no more a servant, but a son; and if a son, then an heir of God through Christ.

Paul's Love for the Christians

*H*owbeit then, when ye knew not God, ye did service unto them which by nature are no gods.
⁹ But now, after that ye have known God, or rather are known of God, how turn ye again to the weak and beggarly elements, whereunto ye desire again to be in bondage?
¹⁰ Ye observe days, and months, and times, and years.
¹¹ I am afraid of you, lest I have bestowed upon you labor in vain.
¹² Brethren, I beseech you, be as I *am;* for I *am* as ye *are:* ye have not injured me at all.
¹³ Ye know how through infirmity of the flesh I preached the gospel unto you at the first.
¹⁴ And my temptation which was in my flesh ye despised not, nor rejected; but received me as an angel of God, *even* as Christ Jesus.
¹⁵ Where is then the blessedness ye spake of? for I bear you record, that, if *it had been* possible, ye would have plucked out your own eyes, and have given them to me.
¹⁶ Am I therefore become your enemy, because I tell you the truth?

¹⁷They zealously affect you, *but* not well; yea, they would exclude you, that ye might affect them.

¹⁸But *it is* good to be zealously affected always in a good *thing,* and not only when I am present with you.

¹⁹My little children, of whom I travail in birth again until Christ be formed in you,

²⁰I desire to be present with you now, and to change my voice; for I stand in doubt of you.

OLD TESTAMENT READING

*B*ut now, O LORD, thou *art* our Father; we *are* the clay, and thou our potter; and we all *are* the work of thy hand.

⁹Be not wroth very sore, O LORD, neither remember iniquity for ever: behold, see, we beseech thee, we *are* all thy people.

Isaiah 64:8–9

*Y*et the number of the children of Israel shall be as the sand of the sea, which cannot be measured nor numbered; and it shall come to pass, *that* in the place where it was said unto them, Ye *are* not my people, *there* it shall be said unto them, *Ye are* the sons of the living God.

¹¹Then shall the children of Judah and the children of Israel be gathered together, and appoint themselves one head, and they shall come up out of the land: for great *shall be* the day of Jezreel.

Hosea 1:10–11

*F*or thou *art* a holy people unto the LORD thy God, and the LORD hath chosen thee to be a peculiar people unto himself, above all the nations that *are* upon the earth.

Deuteronomy 14:2

INSIGHTS

*A*doption, by its very nature, is an act of free kindness to the persons adopted. If you become a father by adopting a child, you do so because you choose to, not because you are bound to. Similarly, God adopts because he chooses to. He has no duty to do so. He need not have done anything about our sins save punish us as we deserved. But he loved us; he redeemed us, forgave us . . . gave himself to us as our Father.

Nor does his grace stop short with that initial act, any more than the love of human parents who adopt stops short with the completing of the legal process that makes the child theirs. The establishing of the child's status as a member of the family is only a beginning. The real task remains: to establish a filial relationship between your adopted child and yourself to win the child's love by loving it. You seek to excite affection by showing affection. And so it is with God. Throughout our life in this world, and to all eternity beyond, he will constantly be showing us in one way or another more and more of his love, and thereby increasing our love to him continually.

J. I. Packer

ACTION POINT

*T*hink carefully about the implications of being made a child of God. How does one live as a child of a living, holy God? Pray that you will live like a child of God, not like a child of the world.

MONDAY

Christ Gives Us Freedom

Galatians 4:21—5:15

The Example of Hagar and Sarah

*T*ell me, ye that desire to be under the law, do ye not hear the law?

²² For it is written, that Abraham had two sons, the one by a bondmaid, the other by a free woman.

²³ But he *who was* of the bondwoman was born after the flesh; but he of the free woman *was* by promise.

²⁴ Which things are an allegory: for these are the two covenants; the one from the mount Sinai, which gendereth to bondage, which is Hagar.

²⁵ For this Hagar is Mount Sinai in Arabia, and answereth to Jerusalem which now is, and is in bondage with her children.

²⁶ But Jerusalem which is above is free, which is the mother of us all.

²⁷ For it is written, Rejoice, thou barren that bearest not; break forth and cry, thou that travailest not: for the desolate hath many more children than she which hath a husband.

²⁸ Now we, brethren, as Isaac was, are the children of promise.

²⁹ But as then he that was born after the flesh persecuted him *that was born* after the Spirit, even so *it is* now.

³⁰ Nevertheless what saith the scripture? Cast out the bondwoman and her son: for the son of the bondwoman shall not be heir with the son of the free woman.

³¹ So then, brethren, we are not children of the bondwoman, but of the free.

Keep Your Freedom

5 Stand fast therefore in the liberty wherewith Christ hath made us free, and be not entangled again with the yoke of bondage.

² Behold, I Paul say unto you, that if ye be circumcised, Christ shall profit you nothing.

³ For I testify again to every man that is circumcised, that he is a debtor to do the whole law.

⁴ Christ is become of no effect unto you, whosoever of you are justified by the law; ye are fallen from grace.

⁵ For we through the Spirit wait for the hope of righteousness by faith.

⁶ For in Jesus Christ neither circumcision availeth any thing, nor uncircumcision; but faith which worketh by love.

⁷ Ye did run well; who did hinder you that ye should not obey the truth?

⁸ This persuasion *cometh* not of him that calleth you.

⁹ A little leaven leaveneth the whole lump.

¹⁰ I have confidence in you through the Lord, that ye will be none otherwise minded: but he that troubleth you shall bear his judgment, whosoever he be.

¹¹ And I, brethren, if I yet preach circumcision, why do I yet suffer persecution? then is the offense of the cross ceased.

¹² I would they were even cut off which trouble you.

¹³ For, brethren, ye have been called unto liberty; only *use* not liberty for an occasion to the flesh, but by love serve one another.

¹⁴ For all the law is fulfilled in one word, *even* in this; Thou shalt love thy neighbor as thyself.

¹⁵ But if ye bite and devour one an-

other, take heed that ye be not consumed one of another.

*A*nd the child grew, and was weaned: and Abraham made a great feast the *same* day that Isaac was weaned.

⁹ And Sarah saw the son of Hagar the Egyptian, which she had borne unto Abraham, mocking.

¹⁰ Wherefore she said unto Abraham, Cast out this bondwoman and her son: for the son of this bondwoman shall not be heir with my son, *even* with Isaac.

¹¹ And the thing was very grievous in Abraham's sight because of his son.

¹² And God said unto Abraham, Let it not be grievous in thy sight because of the lad, and because of thy bondwoman; in all that Sarah hath said unto thee, hearken unto her voice; for in Isaac shall thy seed be called.

Genesis 21:8–12

INSIGHTS

*F*reedom is the privilege of those who are willing to obey. It is a privilege which carries many responsibilities. It is not an automatic right. . . .

Jesus said, ". . . You shall know the truth, and the truth shall make you free" (John 8:32). Truth makes us free because it gives understanding. Understanding helps us accept the necessary conditions, restrictions, and discipline which must prevail if there is to be true freedom. To obey the truth of God's Word makes us free from the slavery of evil habits, desires which harm us, and behavior which dishonors the Lord. Liberty is not the result of human achievement. It is the result of obedience to God. Disobedience means loss of freedom.

If freedom is to be real and lasting, it must be controlled by love. Freedom to do as one pleases, without regard for others or for the circumstances, is destructive. Christian liberty is freedom to love and to serve. It is abused when it is made an excuse for loveless behavior or inconsiderate action.

Real freedom is found in serving God. With our minds centered on Christ and what He would have us do, the self-centered desires and degrading habits of life are crowded out. Life is complete and happy when we surrender ourselves to God, whose yoke is easy and burden is light (Matthew 11:30).

Lucille Sollenberger

PAUSE FOR REFLECTION

*W*hat are the differences between the children of the bondwoman and the free woman? Who gives true freedom? What privileges does freedom in Christ provide? Do you fully enjoy those privileges?

TUESDAY

We Harvest What We Plant

Galatians 5:16—6:18

The Spirit and the Flesh

*T*his I say then, Walk in the Spirit, and ye shall not fulfil the lust of the flesh.

¹⁷ For the flesh lusteth against the Spirit, and the Spirit against the flesh: and these are contrary the one to the other: so that ye cannot do the things that ye would.

¹⁸ But if ye be led of the Spirit, ye are not under the law.

¹⁹ Now the works of the flesh are manifest, which are *these*, adultery, fornication, uncleanness, lasciviousness,

²⁰ idolatry, witchcraft, hatred, variance, emulations, wrath, strife, seditions, heresies,

²¹ envyings, murders, drunkenness, revelings, and such like: of the which I tell you before, as I have also told *you* in time past, that they which do such things shall not inherit the kingdom of God.

²² But the fruit of the Spirit is love, joy, peace, long-suffering, gentleness, goodness, faith,

²³ meekness, temperance: against such there is no law.

²⁴ And they that are Christ's have crucified the flesh with the affections and lusts.

²⁵ If we live in the Spirit, let us also walk in the Spirit.

²⁶ Let us not be desirous of vainglory, provoking one another, envying one another.

Bear Each Other's Burdens

*6*Brethren, if a man be overtaken in a fault, ye which are spiritual, restore such a one in the spirit of meekness; considering thyself, lest thou also be tempted.

² Bear ye one another's burdens, and so fulfil the law of Christ.

³ For if a man think himself to be something, when he is nothing, he deceiveth himself.

⁴ But let every man prove his own work, and then shall he have rejoicing in himself alone, and not in another.

⁵ For every man shall bear his own burden.

⁶ Let him that is taught in the word communicate unto him that teacheth in all good things.

You Reap What You Sow

*B*e not deceived; God is not mocked: for whatsoever a man soweth, that shall he also reap.

⁸ For he that soweth to his flesh shall of the flesh reap corruption; but he that soweth to the Spirit shall of the Spirit reap life everlasting.

⁹ And let us not be weary in well doing: for in due season we shall reap, if we faint not.

¹⁰ As we have therefore opportunity, let us do good unto all *men*, especially unto them who are of the household of faith.

Paul Ends His Letter

*Y*e see how large a letter I have written unto you with mine own hand.

¹² As many as desire to make a fair show in the flesh, they constrain you

to be circumcised; only lest they should suffer persecution for the cross of Christ.

¹³ For neither they themselves who are circumcised keep the law; but desire to have you circumcised, that they may glory in your flesh.

¹⁴ But God forbid that I should glory, save in the cross of our Lord Jesus Christ, by whom the world is crucified unto me, and I unto the world.

¹⁵ For in Christ Jesus neither circumcision availeth any thing, nor uncircumcision, but a new creature.

¹⁶ And as many as walk according to this rule, peace *be* on them, and mercy, and upon the Israel of God.

¹⁷ From henceforth let no man trouble me: for I bear in my body the marks of the Lord Jesus.

¹⁸ Brethren, the grace of our Lord Jesus Christ *be* with your spirit. Amen.

OLD TESTAMENT READING

*F*or *God* giveth to a man that *is* good in his sight, wisdom, and knowledge, and joy: but to the sinner he giveth travail, to gather and to heap up, that he may give to *him that is* good before God. This also *is* vanity and vexation of spirit.

Ecclesiastes 2:26

INSIGHTS

*O*ur dividends in heaven are determined by what we invest in on earth. We can invest in eternal sureties, or we can invest in wind. . . .

. . . According to the law of the harvest you reap what you sow. If you sow wheat, you reap wheat; if you sow weeds, you reap weeds; if you sow wind, you reap wind. The law of the harvest operates in the spiritual and moral realms as well as the physical. "Do not be deceived, God is not mocked; for whatever a man sows, this he will also reap" (Galatians 6:7). . . . We should guard against sowing too much time, energy, and money on clothes and recreation and parties and other means of self-indulgence. We will reap nothing in terms of our eternal well-being from these seeds. No wonder growing Christians are exhorted to "guard yourselves from idols" (1 John 5:21). Idols are not just the wood and stone types that Israel turned to, but anything that steals our hearts and minds away from total commitment to the Lord. . . .

. . . If we invest our lives in the nothingness of what this world has to offer, we not only reap a harvest of nothing but we destroy our lives as well. Many Christians have lives that are disordered, chaotic, and shattered because of their investment in the wind of this world. . . .

. . . We must have a steady diet of the solid food of the Word of God now if we are going to avoid the stunted growth, starvation, and emptiness that are associated with feeding on wind.

David Reid

ACTION POINT

*E*xamine your life and list what you have sown. Does what you have sown please the Spirit (Gal. 5:16–25)? What do you need to sow on earth in order to receive the heavenly dividends you desire?

WEDNESDAY

*The Importance of Praying
for One Another*

Ephesians 1:1—2:3

1 Paul, an apostle of Jesus Christ by the will of God, to the saints which are at Ephesus, and to the faithful in Christ Jesus:
2 Grace *be* to you, and peace, from God our Father, and *from* the Lord Jesus Christ.

Spiritual Blessings in Christ

*B*lessed *be* the God and Father of our Lord Jesus Christ, who hath blessed us with all spiritual blessings in heavenly *places* in Christ:
4 according as he hath chosen us in him before the foundation of the world, that we should be holy and without blame before him in love:
5 having predestinated us unto the adoption of children by Jesus Christ to himself, according to the good pleasure of his will,
6 to the praise of the glory of his grace, wherein he hath made us accepted in the beloved:
7 in whom we have redemption through his blood, the forgiveness of sins, according to the riches of his grace;
8 wherein he hath abounded toward us in all wisdom and prudence;
9 having made known unto us the mystery of his will, according to his good pleasure which he hath purposed in himself:
10 that in the dispensation of the fulness of times he might gather together in one all things in Christ,

both which are in heaven, and which are on earth; *even* in him.
11 In whom also we have obtained an inheritance, being predestinated according to the purpose of him who worketh all things after the counsel of his own will:
12 that we should be to the praise of his glory, who first trusted in Christ.
13 In whom ye also *trusted,* after that ye heard the word of truth, the gospel of your salvation: in whom also, after that ye believed, ye were sealed with that Holy Spirit of promise,
14 which is the earnest of our inheritance until the redemption of the purchased possession, unto the praise of his glory.

Paul's Prayer

*W*herefore I also, after I heard of your faith in the Lord Jesus, and love unto all the saints,
16 cease not to give thanks for you, making mention of you in my prayers;
17 that the God of our Lord Jesus Christ, the Father of glory, may give unto you the spirit of wisdom and revelation in the knowledge of him:
18 the eyes of your understanding being enlightened; that ye may know what is the hope of his calling, and what the riches of the glory of his inheritance in the saints,
19 and what *is* the exceeding greatness of his power to us-ward who believe, according to the working of his mighty power,
20 which he wrought in Christ, when he raised him from the dead, and set *him* at his own right hand in the heavenly *places,*
21 far above all principality, and power, and might, and dominion, and every name that is named, not

only in this world, but also in that which is to come:

²² and hath put all *things* under his feet, and gave him *to be* the head over all *things* to the church,
²³ which is his body, the fulness of him that filleth all in all.

We Now Have Life

2 And you *hath he quickened,* who were dead in trespasses and sins;
² wherein in time past ye walked according to the course of this world, according to the prince of the power of the air, the spirit that now worketh in the children of disobedience:
³ among whom also we all had our conversation in times past in the lusts of our flesh, fulfilling the desires of the flesh and of the mind; and were by nature the children of wrath, even as others.

OLD TESTAMENT READING

*A*nd my servant Job shall pray for you: for him will I accept: lest I deal with you *after your* folly, in that ye have not spoken of me *the thing which is* right, like my servant Job.
⁹ So Eliphaz the Temanite and Bildad the Shuhite *and* Zophar the Naamathite went, and did according as the LORD commanded them: the LORD also accepted Job.

Job 42:8b–9

INSIGHTS

*C*ompassion lies at the heart of intercession. . . .

When we promise to pray for someone, how often do we truly enter into the reality of what that means? The story of the paralytic

borne by four friends to Jesus for healing is a powerful illustration of intercessory love. We 'carry' those for whom we pray (we even speak sometimes of having 'a burden' in prayer). Self is out of the picture, for we have become that other person experiencing his pain with him, suffering his fears for him, consumed with the same longings.

"Blessed are the merciful," said Jesus (Matt 5:7). Part of the meaning of being merciful is to get inside the skin of someone else, to feel as he feels, think as he thinks, see as he sees, to understand life the way he understands it. That, of course, is at the heart of the incarnation. It is precisely what Jesus did when he 'got inside the skin' of a human being and experienced life as we do.

This kind of intercession is contemplative rather than petitionary. It is gathered up in compassion and empathy more often than words— though words are sometimes helpful to us in focusing on a particular person or need. We can bear people to the Lord, as the friends of the paralytic did, and leave them with him. We do not need to inform him of all the facts or suggest how he should act. We are not able to pray, but the Holy Spirit can pray through and in us. We cannot heal, but God can heal through us.

Margaret Magdalen

PAUSE FOR REFLECTION

*D*o you feel the passion with which Paul prayed? Such prayers go far deeper than cursory "Lord bless" and "Lord forgive" prayers, don't they? Could your prayers perhaps flow from deeper in your heart?

THURSDAY

*God Gives Mercy and
Grace to His People*

Ephesians 2:4—3:6

*B*ut God, who is rich in mercy, for his great love wherewith he loved us, [5] even when we were dead in sins, hath quickened us together with Christ, (by grace ye are saved;) [6] and hath raised *us* up together, and made *us* sit together in heavenly *places* in Christ Jesus: [7] that in the ages to come he might show the exceeding riches of his grace in *his* kindness toward us, through Christ Jesus. [8] For by grace are ye saved through faith; and that not of yourselves: *it is* the gift of God: [9] not of works, lest any man should boast. [10] For we are his workmanship, created in Christ Jesus unto good works, which God hath before ordained that we should walk in them.

One in Christ

*W*herefore remember, that ye *being* in time past Gentiles in the flesh, who are called Uncircumcision by that which is called the Circumcision in the flesh made by hands; [12] that at that time ye were without Christ, being aliens from the commonwealth of Israel, and strangers from the covenants of promise, having no hope, and without God in the world: [13] but now in Christ Jesus ye who sometime were far off are made nigh by the blood of Christ.

[14] For he is our peace, who hath made both one, and hath broken down the middle wall of partition *between us;* [15] having abolished in his flesh the enmity, *even* the law of commandments *contained* in ordinances; for to make in himself of twain one new man, *so* making peace; [16] and that he might reconcile both unto God in one body by the cross, having slain the enmity thereby: [17] And came and preached peace to you which were afar off, and to them that were nigh. [18] For through him we both have access by one Spirit unto the Father. [19] Now therefore ye are no more strangers and foreigners, but fellow citizens with the saints, and of the household of God; [20] And are built upon the foundation of the apostles and prophets, Jesus Christ himself being the chief corner *stone;* [21] in whom all the building fitly framed together groweth unto a holy temple in the Lord: [22] in whom ye also are builded together for a habitation of God through the Spirit.

Paul's Work in Preaching the Gospel

3 For this cause I Paul, the prisoner of Jesus Christ for you Gentiles, [2] if ye have heard of the dispensation of the grace of God which is given me to you-ward: [3] how that by revelation he made known unto me the mystery; (as I wrote afore in few words, [4] whereby, when ye read, ye may understand my knowledge in the mystery of Christ,)

[5]which in other ages was not made known unto the sons of men, as it is now revealed unto his holy apostles and prophets by the Spirit;

[6]that the Gentiles should be fellow heirs, and of the same body, and partakers of his promise in Christ by the gospel.

OLD TESTAMENT READING

Who *is* a God like unto thee, that pardoneth iniquity, and passeth by the transgression of the remnant of his heritage? he retaineth not his anger for ever, because he delighteth *in* mercy.

[19]He will turn again, he will have compassion upon us.

Micah 7:18–19a

INSIGHTS

In my own life I am acutely aware that I am a roughhewn man. Because of my rather tough, rough upbringing in a frontier environment, I simply do not possess the polish of the "man about the town." There are characteristics in my makeup which may seem harsh and unyielding. But, despite this, my life has been deeply touched by the mercy of those who took the time to try and understand me—who cared enough to forgive so many faults and who in mercy made me their friend.

Often these were people to whom I had shown no special kindness. Their bestowal of mercy on me was something totally unexpected and undeserved. Because of this, it has been a double delight. More than that, it has been an enormous inspiration that lifted and challenged me to respond in a measure beyond my wildest dreams.

Mercy does just that to people. It excites and stimulates their hope. It reassures them that life can be beautiful. It convinces them that there is good reason to carry on and push for better things if others care that much.

This all implies that if someone has extended mercy to me, surely I, in turn, can and must extend mercy to others.

But, to really find the true source of inner inspiration for this sort of conduct, the Christian simply must look beyond his fellow man. He must look away to the mercy of God our Father. Nothing else in all the world will so humble us. Nothing else will so move our stony spirits to extend mercy. Nothing else will so powerfully induce us to do the proper thing in extending genuine mercy to our contemporaries.

W. Phillip Keller

PAUSE FOR REFLECTION

What has God's mercy, as described in Ephesians, accomplished for all people? How has God's mercy touched your life? What has been the result of his merciful touch? How will you thank him?

FRIDAY

Christ's Love Is Greater than Anyone Can Fathom

Ephesians 3:7—4:16

*W*hereof I was made a minister, according to the gift of the grace of God given unto me by the effectual working of his power.

⁸ Unto me, who am less than the least of all saints, is this grace given, that I should preach among the Gentiles the unsearchable riches of Christ;

⁹ and to make all *men* see what *is* the fellowship of the mystery, which from the beginning of the world hath been hid in God, who created all things by Jesus Christ:

¹⁰ To the intent that now unto the principalities and powers in heavenly *places* might be known by the church the manifold wisdom of God,

¹¹ according to the eternal purpose which he purposed in Christ Jesus our Lord:

¹² in whom we have boldness and access with confidence by the faith of him.

¹³ Wherefore I desire that ye faint not at my tribulations for you, which is your glory.

The Love of Christ

*F*or this cause I bow my knees unto the Father of our Lord Jesus Christ,

¹⁵ of whom the whole family in heaven and earth is named,

¹⁶ that he would grant you, according to the riches of his glory, to be strengthened with might by his Spirit in the inner man;

¹⁷ that Christ may dwell in your hearts by faith; that ye, being rooted and grounded in love,

¹⁸ may be able to comprehend with all saints what *is* the breadth, and length, and depth, and height;

¹⁹ and to know the love of Christ, which passeth knowledge, that ye might be filled with all the fulness of God.

²⁰ Now unto him that is able to do exceeding abundantly above all that we ask or think, according to the power that worketh in us,

²¹ unto him be glory in the church by Christ Jesus throughout all ages, world without end. Amen.

The Unity of the Body

4 I therefore, the prisoner of the Lord, beseech you that ye walk worthy of the vocation wherewith ye are called,

² with all lowliness and meekness, with long-suffering, forbearing one another in love;

³ endeavoring to keep the unity of the Spirit in the bond of peace.

⁴ *There is* one body, and one Spirit, even as ye are called in one hope of your calling;

⁵ one Lord, one faith, one baptism,

⁶ one God and Father of all, who *is* above all, and through all, and in you all.

⁷ But unto every one of us is given grace according to the measure of the gift of Christ.

⁸ Wherefore he saith, When he ascended up on high, he led captivity captive, and gave gifts unto men.

⁹ (Now that he ascended, what is it but that he also descended first into the lower parts of the earth?

¹⁰ He that descended is the same also that ascended up far above all heavens, that he might fill all things.)

¹¹ And he gave some, apostles; and some, prophets; and some, evangelists; and some, pastors and teachers;

¹² for the perfecting of the saints, for the work of the ministry, for the edifying of the body of Christ:

¹³ till we all come in the unity of the faith, and of the knowledge of the Son of God, unto a perfect man, unto the measure of the stature of the fulness of Christ:

¹⁴ That we *henceforth* be no more children, tossed to and fro, and carried about with every wind of doctrine, by the sleight of men, *and* cunning craftiness, whereby they lie in wait to deceive;

¹⁵ But speaking the truth in love, may grow up into him in all things, which is the head, *even* Christ:

¹⁶ from whom the whole body fitly joined together and compacted by that which every joint supplieth, according to the effectual working in the measure of every part, maketh increase of the body unto the edifying of itself in love.

OLD TESTAMENT READING

O give thanks unto the LORD; for *he is* good: for his mercy *endureth* for ever.

⁴ To him who alone doeth great wonders: for his mercy *endureth* for ever.

⁵ To him that by wisdom made the heavens: for his mercy *endureth* for ever.

²⁶ O give thanks unto the God of heaven: for his mercy *endureth* for ever.

Psalm 136:1, 4–5, 26

INSIGHTS

Before we can have any right idea of the love of Jesus, we must understand His previous glory in its height of majesty, and His incarnation upon the earth in all its depths of shame. But who can tell us the majesty of Christ? When He was enthroned in the highest heavens He was very God of very God; by Him were the heavens made, and all the hosts thereof. His own almighty arm upheld the spheres; the praises of cherubim and seraphim perpetually surrounded Him; the full chorus of the hallelujahs of the universe unceasingly flowed to the foot of his throne: He reigned supreme above all His creatures, God over all, blessed for ever. Who can tell His height of glory then? And who, on the other hand, can tell how low He descended? To be a man was something, to be a man of sorrows was far more; to bleed, and die, and suffer, these were much for Him who was the Son of God; but to suffer such unparalleled agony—to endure a death of shame and desertion by His Father, this is a depth of condescending love which the most inspired mind must utterly fail to fathom. Herein is love! and truly it is love that "passeth knowledge." O let this love fill our hearts with adoring gratitude, and lead us to practical manifestations of its power.

Charles Spurgeon

ACTION POINT

Describe, in your words, the extent of Christ's love. Pray that you will know the fullness of God's love in your life.

WEEKEND

Guard Against Greed

Ephesians 4:17—5:14

The Way You Should Live

*T*his I say therefore, and testify in the Lord, that ye henceforth walk not as other Gentiles walk, in the vanity of their mind,

[18] having the understanding darkened, being alienated from the life of God through the ignorance that is in them, because of the blindness of their heart:

[19] who being past feeling have given themselves over unto lasciviousness, to work all uncleanness with greediness.

[20] But ye have not so learned Christ;

[21] if so be that ye have heard him, and have been taught by him, as the truth is in Jesus:

[22] That ye put off concerning the former conversation the old man, which is corrupt according to the deceitful lusts;

[23] and be renewed in the spirit of your mind;

[24] and that ye put on the new man, which after God is created in righteousness and true holiness.

[25] Wherefore putting away lying, speak every man truth with his neighbor: for we are members one of another.

[26] Be ye angry, and sin not: let not the sun go down upon your wrath:

[27] Neither give place to the devil.

[28] Let him that stole steal no more: but rather let him labor, working with *his* hands the thing which is good, that he may have to give to him that needeth.

[29] Let no corrupt communication proceed out of your mouth, but that which is good to the use of edifying, that it may minister grace unto the hearers.

[30] And grieve not the Holy Spirit of God, whereby ye are sealed unto the day of redemption.

[31] Let all bitterness, and wrath, and anger, and clamor, and evil speaking, be put away from you, with all malice:

[32] And be ye kind one to another, tenderhearted, forgiving one another, even as God for Christ's sake hath forgiven you.

Living in the Light

5 Be ye therefore followers of God, as dear children;

[2] and walk in love, as Christ also hath loved us, and hath given himself for us an offering and a sacrifice to God for a sweetsmelling savor.

[3] But fornication, and all uncleanness, or covetousness, let it not be once named among you, as becometh saints;

[4] neither filthiness, nor foolish talking, nor jesting, which are not convenient: but rather giving of thanks.

[5] For this ye know, that no whoremonger, nor unclean person, nor covetous man, who is an idolater, hath any inheritance in the kingdom of Christ and of God.

[6] Let no man deceive you with vain words: for because of these things cometh the wrath of God upon the children of disobedience.

[7] Be not ye therefore partakers with them.

[8] For ye were sometime darkness, but now *are ye* light in the Lord: walk as children of light;

9 (for the fruit of the Spirit *is* in all goodness and righteousness and truth;)

10 proving what is acceptable unto the Lord.

11 And have no fellowship with the unfruitful works of darkness, but rather reprove *them*.

12 For it is a shame even to speak of those things which are done of them in secret.

13 But all things that are reproved are made manifest by the light: for whatsoever doth make manifest is light.

14 Wherefore he saith, Awake thou that sleepest, and arise from the dead, and Christ shall give thee light.

OLD TESTAMENT READING

*T*he horseleech hath two daughters, *crying*, Give, give. There are three *things that* are never satisfied, *yea*, four *things* say not, *It is* enough:
16 the grave; and the barren womb; the earth *that* is not filled with water; and the fire *that* saith not, *It is* enough.

Proverbs 30:15–16

INSIGHTS

*S*omeone has well said, "Our pocketbooks have more to do with heaven and hell than our hymnbooks." Jesus told the story of the rich man who had everything, and a beggar who had nothing. The rich man, blinded by his abundance, neither saw his need for righteousness nor prepared himself for eternity. Lazarus, who had received only bad things, "crumbs from the rich man's table," had prepared well for his future. And their roles in the future life were completely reversed! (Luke 16:19–31) . . .

Cyprian, the third-century bishop of Carthage, wrote an amazingly up-to-date description of the affluent:

Their property held them in chains . . . which shackled their courage and choked their faith and hampered their judgment and throttled their souls. . . . If they stored up their treasure in heaven, they would not now have an enemy and a thief within their household. . . . They think of themselves as owners, whereas it is they rather who are owned: enslaved as they are to their own property, they are not the masters of their money but its slaves.

How we need to hear the voice of the New Testament as it calls us to a life of responsible stewardship of our resources.

Art Beals

APPLICATION

*W*hy is greed such a hindrance to spiritual growth? What other lifestyle choices are wrong for God's holy people? Why? What does your handling of possessions reveal about your heart?

MONDAY

Mutual Love in Marriage

Ephesians 5:15—6:4

See then that ye walk circumspectly, not as fools, but as wise,

¹⁶ redeeming the time, because the days are evil.

¹⁷ Wherefore be ye not unwise, but understanding what the will of the Lord *is*.

¹⁸ And be not drunk with wine, wherein is excess; but be filled with the Spirit;

¹⁹ speaking to yourselves in psalms and hymns and spiritual songs, singing and making melody in your heart to the Lord;

²⁰ giving thanks always for all things unto God and the Father in the name of our Lord Jesus Christ;

Wives and Husbands

Submitting yourselves one to another in the fear of God.

²² Wives, submit yourselves unto your own husbands, as unto the Lord.

²³ For the husband is the head of the wife, even as Christ is the head of the church: and he is the saviour of the body.

²⁴ Therefore as the church is subject unto Christ, so *let* the wives *be* to their own husbands in every thing.

²⁵ Husbands, love your wives, even as Christ also loved the church, and gave himself for it;

²⁶ that he might sanctify and cleanse it with the washing of water by the word,

²⁷ that he might present it to himself a glorious church, not having spot, or wrinkle, or any such thing; but that it should be holy and without blemish.

²⁸ So ought men to love their wives as their own bodies. He that loveth his wife loveth himself.

²⁹ For no man ever yet hated his own flesh; but nourisheth and cherisheth it, even as the Lord the church:

³⁰ for we are members of his body, of his flesh, and of his bones.

³¹ For this cause shall a man leave his father and mother, and shall be joined unto his wife, and they two shall be one flesh.

³² This is a great mystery: but I speak concerning Christ and the church.

³³ Nevertheless let every one of you in particular so love his wife even as himself; and the wife *see* that she reverence *her* husband.

Children and Parents

6 Children, obey your parents in the Lord: for this is right.

² Honor thy father and mother; which is the first commandment with promise;

³ That it may be well with thee, and thou mayest live long on the earth.

⁴ And, ye fathers, provoke not your children to wrath: but bring them up in the nurture and admonition of the Lord.

OLD TESTAMENT READING

Let thy fountain be blessed: and rejoice with the wife of thy youth.

¹⁹ *Let her be as* the loving hind and the pleasant roe; let her breasts satisfy thee at all times; and be thou ravished always with her love.

Proverbs 5:18–19

*M*y beloved *is* mine, and I *am* his: he feedeth among the lilies.
¹⁷ Until the day break, and the shadows flee away, turn, my beloved, and be thou like a roe or a young hart upon the mountains of Bether.

Song of Solomon 2:16–17

*T*hen Laban and Bethuel answered and said, The thing proceedeth from the LORD: we cannot speak unto thee bad or good.
⁵¹ Behold, Rebekah *is* before thee; take *her*, and go, and let her be thy master's son's wife, as the LORD hath spoken.
⁶⁶ And the servant told Isaac all things that he had done.
⁶⁷ And Isaac brought her into his mother Sarah's tent, and took Rebekah, and she became his wife; and he loved her: and Isaac was comforted after his mother's *death.*

Genesis 24:50–51, 66–67

INSIGHTS

*I*f you could enter a time machine and emerge back in the first century when Paul's letters hit the culture of the day, you would be in for some real excitement. His instruction to husbands in Ephesians 5:25–27 must have caused a riot! They went contrary to the way men treated women at that time. Paul's writing called the husband to a ministry of loving servanthood to his wife in a culture which treated women as little better than household furnishings!

A husband is to love his wife with the same sacrificial self-abandonment that Christ adopted toward each of us. When a man considers hardship in marriage, he needs to look at the life of Jesus. Jesus said, "The Son of Man came not to be served, but to serve" (Matthew 20:28). Jesus is presented in Scripture as both Head and Servant. He is the "head over everything for the church" (Ephesians 1:22) who took "the very nature of a servant" (Philippians 2:7). And Jesus instructed us, "The greatest among you will be your servant" (Matthew 23:11).

As believers, we are all called to servanthood as an expression of our new life in Christ. However, when it comes to marriage, modeling this attribute of God's Son is a calling extended to husbands. A husband expresses love to his wife by regarding her as a completely equal partner in everything that concerns their life together. He asserts his headship to see that this equal partnership works. Loving headship affirms and defers; it encourages and stimulates. Loving headship delights to delegate without demanding.

H. Norman Wright

PAUSE FOR REFLECTION

*H*ow do Paul's instructions about marriage fit in with the broader scope of instructions on Christian living that he offers in this passage (Ephesians 5:15–21)? What do his instructions reveal about God's desired intent for marriage?

TUESDAY

We Are Involved in a Spiritual Battle!

Ephesians 6:5–24

Slaves and Masters

*S*ervants, be obedient to them that are *your* masters according to the flesh, with fear and trembling, in singleness of your heart, as unto Christ;

⁶ not with eyeservice, as men-pleasers; but as the servants of Christ, doing the will of God from the heart;

⁷ with good will doing service, as to the Lord, and not to men:

⁸ knowing that whatsoever good thing any man doeth, the same shall he receive of the Lord, whether *he be* bond or free.

⁹ And, ye masters, do the same things unto them, forbearing threatening: knowing that your Master also is in heaven; neither is there respect of persons with him.

Wear the Full Armor of God

*F*inally, my brethren, be strong in the Lord, and in the power of his might.

¹¹ Put on the whole armor of God, that ye may be able to stand against the wiles of the devil.

¹² For we wrestle not against flesh and blood, but against principalities, against powers, against the rulers of the darkness of this world, against spiritual wickedness in high *places*.

¹³ Wherefore take unto you the whole armor of God, that ye may be able to withstand in the evil day, and having done all, to stand.

¹⁴ Stand therefore, having your loins girt about with truth, and having on the breastplate of righteousness;

¹⁵ and your feet shod with the preparation of the gospel of peace;

¹⁶ above all, taking the shield of faith, wherewith ye shall be able to quench all the fiery darts of the wicked.

¹⁷ And take the helmet of salvation, and the sword of the Spirit, which is the word of God:

¹⁸ praying always with all prayer and supplication in the Spirit, and watching thereunto with all perseverance and supplication for all saints;

¹⁹ and for me, that utterance may be given unto me, that I may open my mouth boldly, to make known the mystery of the gospel,

²⁰ for which I am an ambassador in bonds; that therein I may speak boldly, as I ought to speak.

Final Greetings

*B*ut that ye also may know my affairs, *and* how I do, Tychicus, a beloved brother and faithful minister in the Lord, shall make known to you all things:

²² whom I have sent unto you for the same purpose, that ye might know our affairs, and *that* he might comfort your hearts.

²³ Peace *be* to the brethren, and love with faith, from God the Father and the Lord Jesus Christ.

²⁴ Grace *be* with all them that love our Lord Jesus Christ in sincerity. Amen.

OLD TESTAMENT READING

*N*ow there was a day when the sons of God came to present themselves before the LORD, and Satan came also among them.

⁷ And the LORD said unto Satan, Whence comest thou? Then Satan answered the LORD and said, From going to and fro in the earth, and from walking up and down in it.

⁸ And the LORD said unto Satan, Hast thou considered my servant Job, that *there is* none like him in the earth, a perfect and an upright man, one that feareth God, and escheweth evil?

⁹ Then Satan answered the LORD, and said, Doth Job fear God for nought?

¹⁰ Hast not thou made a hedge about him, and about his house, and about all that he hath on every side? thou hast blessed the work of his hands, and his substance is increased in the land.

Job 1:6–10

*A*nd thou shalt consume all the people which the LORD thy God shall deliver thee; thine eye shall have no pity upon them: neither shalt thou serve their gods; for that *will be* a snare unto thee.

Deuteronomy 7:16

INSIGHTS

*A*wareness that we are involved in a cosmic battle which is supernatural, personal, and futile if fought with natural weapons is the beginning of conquering wisdom. We must be convinced of these things if we are to succeed. We must go beyond evangelical lip service to a deep-souled conviction which bursts our simplistic religious shackles.

Paul is specific about the nature of our evil opponents: "our struggle is . . . against the rulers, against the authorities, against the powers of this dark world and against the spiritual forces of evil in the heavenly realms" (v. 12). . . .

The immediate implication is that Satan is terribly powerful. To be sure he does not possess anything near the power of God, but in God's inscrutable arrangement he temporarily dominates and drives the world, which on the whole is separated from God's grace. . . .

. . . If we are filled with the Spirit (5:18), Satan's forces cannot subdue us. But those of us who neglect our resources, and especially those who give the enemies room in our lives, place ourselves in harm's way. . . .

. . . We cannot fight Satan ourselves. All our own doing will be in vain. Nevertheless there is something we can do, and that is to avail ourselves of the Lord's strength. . . . We are to acknowledge our weakness and invite his power. We must imitate Gideon's going from 32,000 warriors to 10,000 to 300 armed only with trumpets and lanterns (Judges 7). This divestment of natural strength enabled the putting on of God's power—and a mighty victory!

R. Kent Hughes

APPLICATION

*W*hat does Scripture say you need in order to fight spiritual battles? Identify the spiritual battlefields in your life. List the battles you most frequently fail to recognize as spiritual. How can you better avail yourself of God's resources to fight those battles?

WEDNESDAY

Be Humble and
Give Honor to Others

Philippians 1:1—2:4

1 Paul and Timothy, the servants of Jesus Christ, to all the saints in Christ Jesus which are at Philippi, with the bishops and deacons:

2 Grace *be* unto you, and peace, from God our Father and from the Lord Jesus Christ.

Paul's Prayer

I thank my God upon every remembrance of you,

4 always in every prayer of mine for you all making request with joy,

5 for your fellowship in the gospel from the first day until now;

6 being confident of this very thing, that he which hath begun a good work in you will perform *it* until the day of Jesus Christ:

7 even as it is meet for me to think this of you all, because I have you in my heart; inasmuch as both in my bonds, and in the defense and confirmation of the gospel, ye all are partakers of my grace.

8 For God is my record, how greatly I long after you all in the bowels of Jesus Christ.

9 And this I pray, that your love may abound yet more and more in knowledge and *in* all judgment;

10 that ye may approve things that are excellent; that ye may be sincere and without offense till the day of Christ;

11 Being filled with the fruits of righteousness, which are by Jesus Christ, unto the glory and praise of God.

Paul's Troubles Help the Work

*B*ut I would ye should understand, brethren, that the things *which happened* unto me have fallen out rather unto the furtherance of the gospel;

13 So that my bonds in Christ are manifest in all the palace, and in all other *places*;

14 And many of the brethren in the Lord, waxing confident by my bonds, are much more bold to speak the word without fear.

15 Some indeed preach Christ even of envy and strife; and some also of good will:

16 the one preach Christ of contention, not sincerely, supposing to add affliction to my bonds:

17 but the other of love, knowing that I am set for the defense of the gospel.

18 What then? notwithstanding, every way, whether in pretense, or in truth, Christ is preached; and I therein do rejoice, yea, and will rejoice.

19 For I know that this shall turn to my salvation through your prayer, and the supply of the Spirit of Jesus Christ,

20 according to my earnest expectation and *my* hope, that in nothing I shall be ashamed, but *that* with all boldness, as always, so now also Christ shall be magnified in my body, whether *it be* by life, or by death.

21 For to me to live *is* Christ, and to die *is* gain.

22 But if I live in the flesh, this *is* the fruit of my labor: yet what I shall choose I wot not.

23 For I am in a strait betwixt two,

having a desire to depart, and to be with Christ; which is far better:

²⁴ nevertheless to abide in the flesh *is* more needful for you.

²⁵ And having this confidence, I know that I shall abide and continue with you all for your furtherance and joy of faith;

²⁶ that your rejoicing may be more abundant in Jesus Christ for me by my coming to you again.

²⁷ Only let your conversation be as it becometh the gospel of Christ: that whether I come and see you, or else be absent, I may hear of your affairs, that ye stand fast in one spirit, with one mind striving together for the faith of the gospel;

²⁸ and in nothing terrified by your adversaries: which is to them an evident token of perdition, but to you of salvation, and that of God.

²⁹ For unto you it is given in the behalf of Christ, not only to believe on him, but also to suffer for his sake;

³⁰ having the same conflict which ye saw in me, and now hear *to be* in me.

2 If *there be* therefore any consolation in Christ, if any comfort of love, if any fellowship of the Spirit, if any bowels and mercies,

² fulfil ye my joy, that ye be likeminded, having the same love, *being* of one accord, of one mind.

³ *Let* nothing *be done* through strife or vainglory; but in lowliness of mind let each esteem other better than themselves.

⁴ Look not every man on his own things, but every man also on the things of others.

OLD TESTAMENT READING

*H*e hath showed thee, O man, what *is* good; and what doth the LORD re-

quire of thee, but to do justly, and to love mercy, and to walk humbly with thy God?

Micah 6:8

INSIGHTS

*H*umility *inclines us to distrust ourselves and depend only upon God. The proud person has a high opinion of his own wisdom or strength or righteousness and is inordinately self-confident. The humble rely upon God and delight to cast themselves wholly on Him as their refuge, righteousness, and strength.*

The humble person will renounce all the glory of the good he has or does and give it all to God. If there is anything good in him or any good done by him, he is not disposed to glorify himself or boast about it before God. . . .

Humility tends to prevent an inordinate aspiring to wealth or position—in short, ambitious behavior among people. A humble person is content with such a situation among others as God is pleased to allot to him and is not greedy for honor. Nor does he try to appear uppermost and exalted above his neighbors.

Jonathan Edwards

PAUSE FOR REFLECTION

*W*hy *is God opposed to the proud? Why is humility necessary for Christian living? What does God promise to those who are humble? In what ways is humility part of obeying Christ's commandment to love one another?*

THURSDAY

Do Everything Without Complaining or Arguing

Philippians 2:5–30

Be Humble like Christ

*L*et this mind be in you, which was also in Christ Jesus:

⁶ who, being in the form of God, thought it not robbery to be equal with God:

⁷ but made himself of no reputation, and took upon him the form of a servant, and was made in the likeness of men:

⁸ and being found in fashion as a man, he humbled himself, and became obedient unto death, even the death of the cross.

⁹ Wherefore God also hath highly exalted him, and given him a name which is above every name:

¹⁰ that at the name of Jesus every knee should bow, of *things* in heaven, and *things* in earth, and *things* under the earth;

¹¹ and *that* every tongue should confess that Jesus Christ *is* Lord, to the glory of God the Father.

Be the People God Wants You to Be

*W*herefore, my beloved, as ye have always obeyed, not as in my presence only, but now much more in my absence, work out your own salvation with fear and trembling:

¹³ for it is God which worketh in you both to will and to do of *his* good pleasure.

¹⁴ Do all things without murmurings and disputings:

¹⁵ that ye may be blameless and harmless, the sons of God, without rebuke, in the midst of a crooked and perverse nation, among whom ye shine as lights in the world;

¹⁶ holding forth the word of life; that I may rejoice in the day of Christ, that I have not run in vain, neither labored in vain.

¹⁷ Yea, and if I be offered upon the sacrifice and service of your faith, I joy, and rejoice with you all.

¹⁸ For the same cause also do ye joy, and rejoice with me.

¹⁹ But I trust in the Lord Jesus to send Timothy shortly unto you, that I also may be of good comfort, when I know your state.

Timothy and Epaphroditus

*F*or I have no man likeminded, who will naturally care for your state.

²¹ For all seek their own, not the things which are Jesus Christ's.

²² But ye know the proof of him, that, as a son with the father, he hath served with me in the gospel.

²³ Him therefore I hope to send presently, so soon as I shall see how it will go with me.

²⁴ But I trust in the Lord that I also myself shall come shortly.

²⁵ Yet I supposed it necessary to send to you Epaphroditus, my brother, and companion in labor, and fellow-soldier, but your messenger, and he that ministered to my wants.

²⁶ For he longed after you all, and was full of heaviness, because that ye had heard that he had been sick.

²⁷ For indeed he was sick nigh unto death: but God had mercy on him; and not on him only, but on me also, lest I should have sorrow upon sorrow.

²⁸ I sent him therefore the more carefully, that, when ye see him again, ye may rejoice, and that I may be the less sorrowful.

²⁹ Receive him therefore in the Lord with all gladness; and hold such in reputation:

³⁰ because for the work of Christ he was nigh unto death, not regarding his life, to supply your lack of service toward me.

OLD TESTAMENT READING

*I*t is an honor for a man to cease from strife: but every fool will be meddling.

Proverbs 20:3

*P*leasant words *are as* a honeycomb, sweet to the soul, and health to the bones.

Proverbs 16:24

*H*e that is void of wisdom despiseth his neighbor: but a man of understanding holdeth his peace.

Proverbs 11:12

INSIGHTS

*W*hether we admit it or not, unbelief and disobedience are the underlying reasons for a complaining spirit.

God's Word is clear: "Do everything without complaining or arguing." This is a command, not an option. He doesn't qualify the statement and excuse us if things suddenly go wrong and it's not our fault. He says everything—and I take that to be all-inclusive. He is talking about every single circumstance whether desirable or not. When I complain, I am in essence saying, "I really don't believe God has arranged these circumstances or that He could change them if He desired." If I did believe it, I wouldn't need to complain. I'd know my only safety is in the center of His will no matter what happens.

The same God who told me not to complain also said, "In everything give thanks, for this is the will of God in Christ Jesus concerning you." How is it possible to give thanks and complain at the same time?

Is it hypocritical to say I'm thankful for my problems when I don't feel thankful? Not really, because God assures us that ". . . all things work together for good. . . ." Even when it looks disastrous, I can be certain that these self-same predicaments will be miraculously transformed under the skilled knife of the divine surgeon. He might do a little hurtful cutting on me through the process, but it will only be for my good.

Madalene Harris

PAUSE FOR REFLECTION

*D*id you realize that arguing and complaining are sins against God? Reread these Scripture passages and list the results of resisting the temptation to complain or argue—in your own life and in the lives of those around you.

FRIDAY

*Pursue God and
His Salvation*

Philippians 3:1–21

The Importance of Christ

3 Finally, my brethren, rejoice in the Lord. To write the same things to you, to me indeed *is* not grievous, but for you *it is* safe.

² Beware of dogs, beware of evil workers, beware of the concision.

³ For we are the circumcision, which worship God in the spirit, and rejoice in Christ Jesus, and have no confidence in the flesh.

⁴ Though I might also have confidence in the flesh. If any other man thinketh that he hath whereof he might trust in the flesh, I more:

⁵ circumcised the eighth day, of the stock of Israel, *of* the tribe of Benjamin, a Hebrew of the Hebrews; as touching the law, a Pharisee;

⁶ concerning zeal, persecuting the church; touching the righteousness which is in the law, blameless.

⁷ But what things were gain to me, those I counted loss for Christ.

⁸ Yea doubtless, and I count all things *but* loss for the excellency of the knowledge of Christ Jesus my Lord: for whom I have suffered the loss of all things, and do count them *but* dung, that I may win Christ,

⁹ and be found in him, not having mine own righteousness, which is of the law, but that which is through the faith of Christ, the righteousness which is of God by faith:

¹⁰ that I may know him, and the power of his resurrection, and the fellowship of his sufferings, being made conformable unto his death;

¹¹ if by any means I might attain unto the resurrection of the dead.

Continuing Toward Our Prize

Not as though I had already attained, either were already perfect: but I follow after, if that I may apprehend that for which also I am apprehended of Christ Jesus.

¹³ Brethren, I count not myself to have apprehended: but *this* one thing *I do*, forgetting those things which are behind, and reaching forth unto those things which are before,

¹⁴ I press toward the mark for the prize of the high calling of God in Christ Jesus.

¹⁵ Let us therefore, as many as be perfect, be thus minded: and if in any thing ye be otherwise minded, God shall reveal even this unto you.

¹⁶ Nevertheless, whereto we have already attained, let us walk by the same rule, let us mind the same thing.

¹⁷ Brethren, be followers together of me, and mark them which walk so as ye have us for an ensample.

¹⁸ (For many walk, of whom I have told you often, and now tell you even weeping, *that they are* the enemies of the cross of Christ:

¹⁹ whose end *is* destruction, whose God *is their* belly, and *whose* glory *is* in their shame, who mind earthly things.)

²⁰ For our conversation is in heaven; from whence also we look for the Saviour, the Lord Jesus Christ:

²¹ who shall change our vile body, that it may be fashioned like unto his glorious body, according to the

working whereby he is able even to subdue all things unto himself.

OLD TESTAMENT READING

*A*s the hart panteth after the water brooks, so panteth my soul after thee, O God.
[2] My soul thirsteth for God, for the living God: when shall I come and appear before God?

Psalm 42:1–2

O God, thou *art* my God; early will I seek thee: my soul thirsteth for thee, my flesh longeth for thee in a dry and thirsty land, where no water is;
[2] to see thy power and thy glory, so *as* I have seen thee in the sanctuary.
[3] Because thy loving-kindness *is* better than life, my lips shall praise thee.
[4] Thus will I bless thee while I live: I will lift up my hands in thy name.

Psalm 63:1–4

INSIGHTS

*R*ecently, I saw a young New Zealand cyclist win a grueling race in which he broke the national record. In a subsequent interview by the TV sports commentator, he was asked the question, "And what do you aim at for the future?" With not a moment's hesitation the reply came back: "I aim to be one of the best cyclists in the world."

In order to realize his ambition, he was prepared to pay any price in training—grueling discipline, forfeiture of social life, self-denial in many areas—and all for a piece of gold, or even bronze. Why is it that so few disciples have a similar, fixed ambition to excel for Christ? Are we "taking time and trouble to keep spiritually fit," or have we grown soft and flabby? . . .

. . . Winning a race makes great demands on the stamina and perseverance of the athlete.

Once the race has begun, the athlete cannot afford to look back. He must press on to the tape without distraction. His eyes must be fixed on the umpire's stand at the end of the track if he is to win the prize. . . .

So must the disciple run his race with eyes steadfastly fixed on his encouraging Lord, who is at once Judge, Umpire, and Awarder. He is not to look back either wistfully or hopelessly but to resolutely forget what is behind—failures and disappointments as well as successes and victories. He must strain forward to the tape with eyes fixed on his welcoming Lord. It was He who initiated our faith, and it is He who will strengthen us to complete the course.

J. Oswald Sanders

PAUSE FOR REFLECTION

*I*n what way does Paul say knowledge of Christ changes a person's thinking? How diligently are you pursuing God's calling? May the psalmist's words be your prayer and praise to the Lord!

WEEKEND

*Don't Worry About Anything;
Ask God for What You Need*

Philippians 4:1–23

What the Christians Are to Do

4 Therefore, my brethren dearly beloved and longed for, my joy and crown, so stand fast in the Lord, *my* dearly beloved.
2 I beseech Euodias, and beseech Syntyche, that they be of the same mind in the Lord.
3 And I entreat thee also, true yokefellow, help those women which labored with me in the gospel, with Clement also, and *with* other my fellow laborers, whose names *are* in the book of life.
4 Rejoice in the Lord always: *and* again I say, Rejoice.
5 Let your moderation be known unto all men. The Lord *is* at hand.
6 Be careful for nothing; but in every thing by prayer and supplication with thanksgiving let your requests be made known unto God.
7 And the peace of God, which passeth all understanding, shall keep your hearts and minds through Christ Jesus.
8 Finally, brethren, whatsoever things are true, whatsoever things *are* honest, whatsoever things *are* just, whatsoever things *are* pure, whatsoever things *are* lovely, whatsoever things *are* of good report; if *there be* any virtue, and if *there be* any praise, think on these things.
9 Those things, which ye have both learned, and received, and heard, and seen in me, do: and the God of peace shall be with you.

Paul Thanks the Christians

B ut I rejoiced in the Lord greatly, that now at the last your care of me hath flourished again; wherein ye were also careful, but ye lacked opportunity.
11 Not that I speak in respect of want: for I have learned, in whatsoever state I am, *therewith* to be content.
12 I know both how to be abased, and I know how to abound: every where and in all things I am instructed both to be full and to be hungry, both to abound and to suffer need.
13 I can do all things through Christ which strengtheneth me.
14 Notwithstanding ye have well done, that ye did communicate with my affliction.
15 Now ye Philippians know also, that in the beginning of the gospel, when I departed from Macedonia, no church communicated with me as concerning giving and receiving, but ye only.
16 For even in Thessalonica ye sent once and again unto my necessity.
17 Not because I desire a gift: but I desire fruit that may abound to your account.
18 But I have all, and abound: I am full, having received of Epaphroditus the things *which were sent* from you, an odor of a sweet smell, a sacrifice acceptable, well-pleasing to God.
19 But my God shall supply all your need according to his riches in glory by Christ Jesus.
20 Now unto God and our Father *be*

glory for ever and ever. Amen.
²¹ Salute every saint in Christ Jesus. The brethren which are with me greet you.
²² All the saints salute you, chiefly they that are of Caesar's household.
²³ The grace of our Lord Jesus Christ *be* with you all. Amen.

OLD TESTAMENT READING

*C*ast thy burden upon the LORD, and he shall sustain thee: he shall never suffer the righteous to be moved.

Psalm 55:22

*T*rust in the LORD, and do good; so shalt thou dwell in the land, and verily thou shalt be fed.
⁴ Delight thyself also in the LORD; and he shall give thee the desires of thine heart.
⁵ Commit thy way unto the LORD; trust also in him; and he shall bring *it* to pass.

Psalm 37:3–5

INSIGHTS

*D*uring the Great Depression the bank in which my father was an officer was forced to close. . . .

I was convinced my father would be out of work. I knew I had to get a job as a boy of twelve to help support the family. A nearby corner grocer hired me after school and Saturdays for a dollar a week to sweep the floors and deliver groceries.

When I told my father, he replied, "I appreciate your concern and desire to help, son, but I am trusting the Lord to meet our needs. We belong to Him and He will take care of His own."

God honored my father's faith. He never went a day without employment through the entire Depression.

With similar confidence Paul wrote to the Philippian Christians, "My God will meet all your needs" (4:19). This was the encouragement those believers needed because they were far from affluent (2 Cor. 8:1–5). Out of their meager resources they had sent an offering to Paul in Rome (Phil. 4:14–18). Paul assured them that God would reimburse them.

Two important details about this promise must be observed. First, God will meet "all your needs," not your desires. Jesus said, "Your Father knows what you need" (Matt. 6:8), and His understanding of our needs may be different from ours.

Second, God will meet our needs "according to His glorious riches in Christ Jesus." God's supply is not "out of" but "according to His glorious riches." God is "able to do immeasurably more than we ask or imagine" (Eph. 3:20). . . .

Whatever your needs are right now, trust God to meet them and look for His supply.

John Witmer

ACTION POINT

*W*hat does God's peace enable us to do? List the things on which God wants you to focus your thoughts. Will you ask God for what you need and trust him to care for you?

MONDAY

Christ's Preeminence in All of History

Colossians 1:1-23

1 Paul, an apostle of Jesus Christ by the will of God, and Timothy *our* brother,

2 To the saints and faithful brethren in Christ which are at Colossae: Grace *be* unto you, and peace, from God our Father and the Lord Jesus Christ.

3 We give thanks to God and the Father of our Lord Jesus Christ, praying always for you,

4 since we heard of your faith in Christ Jesus, and of the love *which ye have* to all the saints,

5 for the hope which is laid up for you in heaven, whereof ye heard before in the word of the truth of the gospel;

6 which is come unto you, as *it is* in all the world; and bringeth forth fruit, as *it doth* also in you, since the day ye heard *of it*, and knew the grace of God in truth:

7 as ye also learned of Epaphras our dear fellow servant, who is for you a faithful minister of Christ;

8 who also declared unto us your love in the Spirit.

9 For this cause we also, since the day we heard *it*, do not cease to pray for you, and to desire that ye might be filled with the knowledge of his will in all wisdom and spiritual understanding;

10 that ye might walk worthy of the Lord unto all pleasing, being fruitful in every good work, and increasing in the knowledge of God;

11 strengthened with all might, according to his glorious power, unto all patience and long-suffering with joyfulness;

12 giving thanks unto the Father, which hath made us meet to be partakers of the inheritance of the saints in light:

13 who hath delivered us from the power of darkness, and hath translated *us* into the kingdom of his dear Son.

14 In whom we have redemption through his blood, *even* the forgiveness of sins:

The Importance of Christ

Who is the image of the invisible God, the firstborn of every creature:

16 for by him were all things created, that are in heaven, and that are in earth, visible and invisible, whether *they be* thrones, or dominions, or principalities, or powers: all things were created by him, and for him:

17 and he is before all things, and by him all things consist.

18 and he is the head of the body, the church: who is the beginning, the firstborn from the dead; that in all things he might have the preeminence.

19 For it pleased *the Father* that in him should all fulness dwell;

20 and, having made peace through the blood of his cross, by him to reconcile all things unto himself; by him, *I say*, whether *they be* things in earth, or things in heaven.

21 And you, that were sometime alienated and enemies in *your* mind by wicked works, yet now hath he reconciled

22 in the body of his flesh through death, to present you holy and

unblamable and unreprovable in his sight:
23 if ye continue in the faith grounded and settled, and *be* not moved away from the hope of the gospel, which ye have heard, *and* which was preached to every creature which is under heaven; whereof I Paul am made a minister.

OLD TESTAMENT READING

*W*ho raised up the righteous *man* from the east, called him to his foot, gave the nations before him, and made *him* rule over kings?
4 Who hath wrought and done *it*, calling the generations from the beginning? I the LORD, the first, and with the last; I *am* he.

Isaiah 41:2a, 4

INSIGHTS

*R*ight through the Old Testament the conviction runs that God is managing all human history for the good of his people and that the climax will be the setting up of the kingdom of God under the Messiah, God's anointed King. In the New Testament, Jesus of Nazareth is shown to be that Messiah or Christ. But his role is not only a kingly one, but prophetic and priestly too. Jesus as prophet preached in God's name; as priest, he offered himself in sacrifice for the sins of the people; as king, having risen triumphantly from the dead, he now reigns at God's right hand. "All authority in heaven and on earth has been given to me," he told his disciples (Matt. 28:18). So the early Christians came to see Jesus of Nazareth as the Christ of God, their Teacher, Savior, and living Lord.

. . . As Christians we know that Christ is reigning until all things are put under his feet and that we are living in the last days—the period between his first coming, to bring salvation and set up his kingdom, and his second coming, to complete the work of his kingdom in royal triumph and final judgment.

There is increasing chaos and confusion as human history moves to its close, but as Christians we can find stability and hope in Jesus who is the sovereign Lord of history. The Father has promised the Son, "Thy throne, O God, is forever and ever" (Heb. 1:8), and the promise will never fail.

J. I. Packer

ACTION POINT

*H*ow does Christ's management of heaven and earth affect your view of history? Your hope for the future? Spend time in prayer, praising God for his incomparable greatness and his awesome love for you.

TUESDAY

*Be Strong in Your Faith
so No One Turns You
Away from God*

Colossians 1:24—2:15

Paul's Work for the Church

Who now rejoice in my sufferings for you, and fill up that which is behind of the afflictions of Christ in my flesh for his body's sake, which is the church:

25 whereof I am made a minister, according to the dispensation of God which is given to me for you, to fulfil the word of God;

26 *even* the mystery which hath been hid from ages and from generations, but now is made manifest to his saints:

27 to whom God would make known what is the riches of the glory of this mystery among the Gentiles; which is Christ in you, the hope of glory:

28 whom we preach, warning every man, and teaching every man in all wisdom; that we may present every man perfect in Christ Jesus:

29 whereunto I also labor, striving according to his working, which worketh in me mightily.

2 For I would that ye knew what great conflict I have for you, and *for* them at Laodicea, and *for* as many as have not seen my face in the flesh;

2 that their hearts might be comforted, being knit together in love, and unto all riches of the full assurance of understanding, to the acknowledgment of the mystery of God, and of the Father, and of Christ;

3 in whom are hid all the treasures of wisdom and knowledge.

4 And this I say, lest any man should beguile you with enticing words.

5 For though I be absent in the flesh, yet am I with you in the spirit, joying and beholding your order, and the steadfastness of your faith in Christ.

Continue to Live in Christ

As ye have therefore received Christ Jesus the Lord, *so* walk ye in him:

7 rooted and built up in him, and stablished in the faith, as ye have been taught, abounding therein with thanksgiving.

8 Beware lest any man spoil you through philosophy and vain deceit, after the tradition of men, after the rudiments of the world, and not after Christ.

9 For in him dwelleth all the fulness of the Godhead bodily.

10 And ye are complete in him, which is the head of all principality and power:

11 in whom also ye are circumcised with the circumcision made without hands, in putting off the body of the sins of the flesh by the circumcision of Christ:

12 buried with him in baptism, wherein also ye are risen with *him* through the faith of the operation of God, who hath raised him from the dead.

13 And you, being dead in your sins and the uncircumcision of your flesh, hath he quickened together with him, having forgiven you all trespasses;

14 blotting out the handwriting of ordinances that was against us, which was contrary to us, and took it out

of the way, nailing it to his cross; [15] *and* having spoiled principalities and powers, he made a show of them openly, triumphing over them in it.

I waited patiently for the LORD; and he inclined unto me, and heard my cry.
[2] He brought me up also out of a horrible pit, out of the miry clay, and set my feet upon a rock, *and* established my goings.
[3] And he hath put a new song in my mouth, *even* praise unto our God: many shall see *it*, and fear, and shall trust in the LORD.
[4] Blessed *is* that man that maketh the LORD his trust, and respecteth not the proud, nor such as turn aside to lies.

Psalm 40:1–4

*T*ake fast hold of instruction; let *her* not go: keep her; for she *is* thy life. [14] Enter not into the path of the wicked.

Proverbs 4:13–14a

It is a grand thing to have a faith which cannot be shaken. I saw one day a number of beech trees which had formed a wood: they had all fallen to the ground through a storm. The fact was they leaned upon one another to a great extent, and the thickness of the wood prevented each tree from getting a firm hold of the soil. They kept each other up and also constrained each other to grow up tall and thin, to the neglect of root growth. When the tempest forced down the first few trees the others readily followed one after the other. Close to that same spot I saw another tree in the open, bravely defying the blast, in solitary strength. The hurricane had beaten upon it but it had endured all its force unsheltered. That lone, brave tree seemed to be better rooted than before the storm.

I thought, "Is it not so with professors?" They often hold together, and help each other to grow up, but if they have not firm personal roothold, when a storm arises they fall in rows. A minister dies, or certain leaders are taken away, and over go the members by departure from the faith and from holiness. I would have you be self-contained, growing each man into Christ for himself, rooted and grounded in love and faith and every holy grace. Then when the worst storm that ever blew on mortal man shall come, it will be said of your faith, "It could not shake it."

Charles Spurgeon

*W*hy must believers know and understand God's truth? How deep and strong are your roots in the faith? Can you clearly separate the ideas of humans from the teachings of God? Are his teachings safe within your heart?

WEDNESDAY

*Put Away All Evil and Focus
on the Holy Things of God*

Colossians 2:16—3:17

Don't Let People Judge You

*L*et no man therefore judge you in meat, or in drink, or in respect of a holyday, or of the new moon, or of the sabbath *days*: ¹⁷ which are a shadow of things to come; but the body *is* of Christ.

¹⁸ Let no man beguile you of your reward in a voluntary humility and worshipping of angels, intruding into those things which he hath not seen, vainly puffed up by his fleshly mind, ¹⁹ and not holding the Head, from which all the body by joints and bands having nourishment ministered, and knit together, increaseth with the increase of God.

²⁰ Wherefore if ye be dead with Christ from the rudiments of the world, why, as though living in the world, are ye subject to ordinances, ²¹ (touch not; taste not; handle not; ²² which all are to perish with the using;) after the commandments and doctrines of men?

²³ which things have indeed a show of wisdom in will-worship, and humility, and neglecting of the body; not in any honor to the satisfying of the flesh.

Your New Life in Christ

3 If ye then be risen with Christ, seek those things which are above, where Christ sitteth on the right hand of God.

² Set your affection on things above, not on things on the earth.

³ For ye are dead, and your life is hid with Christ in God.

⁴ When Christ, *who is* our life, shall appear, then shall ye also appear with him in glory.

⁵ Mortify therefore your members which are upon the earth; fornication, uncleanness, inordinate affection, evil concupiscence, and covetousness, which is idolatry:

⁶ for which things' sake the wrath of God cometh on the children of disobedience:

⁷ in the which ye also walked some time, when ye lived in them.

⁸ But now ye also put off all these; anger, wrath, malice, blasphemy, filthy communication out of your mouth.

⁹ Lie not one to another, seeing that ye have put off the old man with his deeds;

¹⁰ and have put on the new *man*, which is renewed in knowledge after the image of him that created him:

¹¹ where there is neither Greek nor Jew, circumcision nor uncircumcision, Barbarian, Scythian, bond *nor* free: but Christ *is* all, and in all.

¹² Put on therefore, as the elect of God, holy and beloved, bowels of mercies, kindness, humbleness of mind, meekness, long-suffering;

¹³ forbearing one another, and forgiving one another, if any man have a quarrel against any: even as Christ forgave you, so also do ye.

¹⁴ And above all these things *put on* charity, which is the bond of perfectness.

¹⁵ And let the peace of God rule in your hearts, to the which also ye are

called in one body; and be ye thankful.

¹⁶ Let the word of Christ dwell in you richly in all wisdom; teaching and admonishing one another in psalms and hymns and spiritual songs, singing with grace in your hearts to the Lord.

¹⁷ And whatsoever ye do in word or deed, *do* all in the name of the Lord Jesus, giving thanks to God and the Father by him.

OLD TESTAMENT READING

Sanctify yourselves therefore, and be ye holy: for I *am* the LORD your God.

⁸ And ye shall keep my statutes, and do them: I *am* the LORD which sanctify you.

²⁶ And ye shall be holy unto me: for I the LORD *am* holy, and have severed you from *other* people, that ye should be mine.

Leviticus 20:7–8, 26

INSIGHTS

The New Testament leaves no doubt that holiness is our responsibility. If we are to pursue holiness, we must take some decisive action. . . .

The action we are to take is to put to death the misdeeds of the body (Romans 8:13). Paul uses the same expression in another book: "Put to death, therefore, whatever belongs to your earthly nature" (Colossians 3:5). . . . To put to death the misdeeds of the body, then, is to destroy the strength and vitality of sin as it tries to reign in our bodies.

It must be clear to us that mortification, though it is something we do, cannot be carried out in our own

strength. . . . *Mortification must be done by the strength and under the direction of the Holy Spirit. . . .*

. . . "How do we destroy the strength and vitality of sin?" If we are to work at this difficult task, we must first have conviction. We must be persuaded that a holy life of God's will for every Christian is important. . . .

Not only must we develop conviction for living a holy life in general, but we must also develop convictions in specific areas of obedience.

These convictions are developed through exposure to the Word of God. . . .

. . . Obedience is the pathway to holiness, but it is only as we have His commands that we can obey them. God's Word must be so strongly fixed in our minds that it becomes the dominant influence in our thoughts, our attitudes, and our actions.

Jerry Bridges

PAUSE FOR REFLECTION

What is the one and only reason that God's people are to be holy? What does a person need to know to be holy? What must a person do to be holy? How does a person have the strength to be holy? What do you need to focus on as you pursue holiness?

THURSDAY

Honor Your Parents

Colossians 3:18—4:18

Living with Other People

Wives, submit yourselves unto your own husbands, as it is fit in the Lord.

[19] Husbands, love *your* wives, and be not bitter against them.

[20] Children, obey *your* parents in all things: for this is well-pleasing unto the Lord.

[21] Fathers, provoke not your children *to anger*, lest they be discouraged.

[22] Servants, obey in all things *your* masters according to the flesh; not with eyeservice, as menpleasers; but in singleness of heart, fearing God:

[23] And whatsoever ye do, do *it* heartily, as to the Lord, and not unto men;

[24] knowing that of the Lord ye shall receive the reward of the inheritance: for ye serve the Lord Christ.

[25] But he that doeth wrong shall receive for the wrong which he hath done: and there is no respect of persons.

4 Masters, give unto *your* servants that which is just and equal; knowing that ye also have a Master in heaven.

What the Christians Are to Do

Continue in prayer, and watch in the same with thanksgiving;

[3] withal praying also for us, that God would open unto us a door of utterance, to speak the mystery of Christ, for which I am also in bonds:

[4] that I may make it manifest, as I ought to speak.

[5] Walk in wisdom toward them that are without, redeeming the time.

[6] Let your speech *be* always with grace, seasoned with salt, that ye may know how ye ought to answer every man.

The People with Paul

All my state shall Tychicus declare unto you, *who is* a beloved brother, and a faithful minister and fellow servant in the Lord:

[8] whom I have sent unto you for the same purpose, that he might know your estate, and comfort your hearts;

[9] with Onesimus, a faithful and beloved brother, who is *one* of you. They shall make known unto you all things which *are done* here.

[10] Aristarchus my fellow prisoner saluteth you, and Mark, sister's son to Barnabas, (touching whom ye received commandments: if he come unto you, receive him;)

[11] and Jesus, which is called Justus, who are of the circumcision. These only *are my* fellow workers unto the kingdom of God, which have been a comfort unto me.

[12] Epaphras, who is *one* of you, a servant of Christ, saluteth you, always laboring fervently for you in prayers, that ye may stand perfect and complete in all the will of God.

[13] For I bear him record, that he hath a great zeal for you, and them *that are* in Laodicea, and them in Hierapolis.

[14] Luke, the beloved physician, and Demas, greet you.

[15] Salute the brethren which are in Laodicea, and Nymphas, and the

church which is in his house.
¹⁶ And when this epistle is read among you, cause that it be read also in the church of the Laodiceans; and that ye likewise read the *epistle* from Laodicea.
¹⁷ And say to Archippus, Take heed to the ministry which thou hast received in the Lord, that thou fulfil it.
¹⁸ The salutation by the hand of me Paul. Remember my bonds. Grace *be* with you. Amen.

OLD TESTAMENT READING

*M*y son, keep thy father's commandment, and forsake not the law of thy mother:
²¹ bind them continually upon thine heart, *and* tie them about thy neck.
²² When thou goest, it shall lead thee; when thou sleepest, it shall keep thee; and *when* thou awakest, it shall talk with thee.

Proverbs 6:20–22

INSIGHTS

*M*uch is being said and written these days about the care of the elderly. But what is being done in practical ways to relieve them of their ongoing fears for their future? Such fears as:

- *financial problems in a day of rising costs and a fixed income*
- *fears of sickness with no one to take care of them, in a day when families can be so scattered as to be unavailable to one another . . .*

Each of us, whatever our age, needs to remind himself that we are of great worth in the sight of God, that He has plans for each one. Speaking of the righteous, the psalmist writes, "They shall still bring forth fruit in old age" (Psalm 92:14).

Ironically, some countries to which we send missionaries with the gospel message can teach us much about honoring our fathers and our mothers. For example, a woman whom I met on one of my teaching trips to Asian countries confided to me, "My sister, who is much wealthier than I, felt that she should have the pleasure of taking care of our aged mother. But, as the youngest daughter, it is my privilege.". . .

. . . God knows our heart and our intentions. Where we treat the elderly around us with love and care, it will be counted as our obeying the fifth commandment.

And obedience is its own reward.

The Lord Jesus Himself set the pattern. From the cross, in the midst of His own agony, He remembered His mother and committed her to the care of "the disciple . . . whom he loved" (John 19:26–27).

Jeanette Lockerbie

PAUSE FOR REFLECTION

*I*t is good to honor one's parents by caring for them, but Scripture reveals a broader perspective on what it means to honor one's parents. How does this reading expand your picture of honoring one's parents? How do you measure up?

FRIDAY

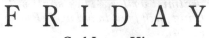

*God Loves His
Chosen People, Who May
Endure Suffering*

---

1 Thessalonians 1:1—2:16

1 Paul, and Silvanus, and Timothy, unto the church of the Thessalonians *which is* in God the Father and *in* the Lord Jesus Christ: Grace *be* unto you, and peace, from God our Father, and the Lord Jesus Christ.

The Faith of the Thessalonians

*W*e give thanks to God always for you all, making mention of you in our prayers;

[3] remembering without ceasing your work of faith, and labor of love, and patience of hope in our Lord Jesus Christ, in the sight of God and our Father;

[4] Knowing, brethren beloved, your election of God.

[5] For our gospel came not unto you in word only, but also in power, and in the Holy Ghost, and in much assurance; as ye know what manner of men we were among you for your sake.

[6] And ye became followers of us, and of the Lord, having received the word in much affliction, with joy of the Holy Ghost:

[7] so that ye were ensamples to all that believe in Macedonia and Achaia.

[8] For from you sounded out the word of the Lord not only in Macedonia and Achaia, but also in every place your faith to God-ward is spread abroad; so that we need not to speak any thing.

[9] For they themselves show of us what manner of entering in we had unto you, and how ye turned to God from idols to serve the living and true God;

[10] and to wait for his Son from heaven, whom he raised from the dead, *even* Jesus, which delivered us from the wrath to come.

Paul's Work in Thessalonica

2 For yourselves, brethren, know our entrance in unto you, that it was not in vain:

[2] but even after that we had suffered before, and were shamefully entreated, as ye know, at Philippi, we were bold in our God to speak unto you the gospel of God with much contention.

[3] For our exhortation *was* not of deceit, nor of uncleanness, nor in guile:

[4] but as we were allowed of God to be put in trust with the gospel, even so we speak; not as pleasing men, but God, which trieth our hearts.

[5] For neither at any time used we flattering words, as ye know, nor a cloak of covetousness; God *is* witness:

[6] nor of men sought we glory, neither of you, nor *yet* of others, when we might have been burdensome, as the apostles of Christ.

[7] But we were gentle among you, even as a nurse cherisheth her children:

[8] so being affectionately desirous of you, we were willing to have imparted unto you, not the gospel of God only, but also our own souls, because ye were dear unto us.

[9] For ye remember, brethren, our labor and travail: for laboring night and day, because we would not be chargeable unto any of you, we preached

unto you the gospel of God.

[10] Ye *are* witnesses, and God *also*, how holily and justly and unblamably we behaved ourselves among you that believe:

[11] as ye know how we exhorted and comforted and charged every one of you, as a father *doth* his children,

[12] that ye would walk worthy of God, who hath called you unto his kingdom and glory.

[13] For this cause also thank we God without ceasing, because, when ye received the word of God which ye heard of us, ye received *it* not *as* the word of men, but, as it is in truth, the word of God, which effectually worketh also in you that believe.

[14] For ye, brethren, became followers of the churches of God which in Judea are in Christ Jesus: for ye also have suffered like things of your own countrymen, even as they *have* of the Jews:

[15] who both killed the Lord Jesus, and their own prophets, and have persecuted us; and they please not God, and are contrary to all men:

[16] forbidding us to speak to the Gentiles that they might be saved, to fill up their sins always: for the wrath is come upon them to the uttermost.

OLD TESTAMENT READING

*T*he LORD did not set his love upon you, nor choose you, because ye were more in number than any people; for ye *were* the fewest of all people:

[8] but because the LORD loved you, and because he would keep the oath which he had sworn unto your fathers, hath the LORD brought you out with a mighty hand.

Deuteronomy 7:7–8a

INSIGHTS

If there be one place where our Lord Jesus most fully becomes the joy and comfort of His people, it is where He plunged deepest into the depths of woe. Come hither, gracious souls, and behold the Man in the garden of Gethsemane; behold His heart so brimming with love that He cannot hold it in—so full of sorrow that it must find a vent. Behold the Man as they drive the nails into His hands and feet. . . .

Most of us know what it is to be overwhelmed in heart. Disappointments and heartbreaks will do this when billow after billow rolls over us, and we are like a broken shell hurled to and fro by the surf. Blessed be God, at such seasons we are not without an all-sufficient solace; our Savior is the harbor of weatherbeaten sails, the hospice of forlorn pilgrims. Higher than we are is our God, His mercy higher than our sins, His love higher than our thoughts. A rock He is since He changes not, and a high rock, because the tempests which overwhelm us roll far beneath at His feet. O Lord, our God, by Your Holy Spirit, teach us your way of faith, lead us unto Your rest.

Charles Spurgeon

ACTION POINT

*H*ow do you think Paul's words encouraged the Thessalonians? When has someone encouraged you with the assurance of God's love? Who can you encourage today?

WEEKEND

God Requires Holy Living

1 Thessalonians 2:17—4:12

Paul Wants to Visit Them Again

*B*ut we, brethren, being taken from you for a short time in presence, not in heart, endeavored the more abundantly to see your face with great desire.

¹⁸ Wherefore we would have come unto you, even I Paul, once and again; but Satan hindered us.

¹⁹ For what *is* our hope, or joy, or crown of rejoicing? *Are* not even ye in the presence of our Lord Jesus Christ at his coming?

²⁰ For ye are our glory and joy.

3 Wherefore when we could no longer forbear, we thought it good to be left at Athens alone;

² and sent Timothy, our brother, and minister of God, and our fellow laborer in the gospel of Christ, to establish you, and to comfort you concerning your faith:

³ that no man should be moved by these afflictions: for yourselves know that we are appointed thereunto.

⁴ For verily, when we were with you, we told you before that we should suffer tribulation; even as it came to pass, and ye know.

⁵ For this cause, when I could no longer forbear, I sent to know your faith, lest by some means the tempter have tempted you, and our labor be in vain.

⁶ But now when Timothy came from you unto us, and brought us good tidings of your faith and charity, and

that ye have good remembrance of us always, desiring greatly to see us, as we also *to see* you:

⁷ therefore, brethren, we were comforted over you in all our affliction and distress by your faith:

⁸ for now we live, if ye stand fast in the Lord.

⁹ for what thanks can we render to God again for you, for all the joy wherewith we joy for your sakes before our God;

¹⁰ night and day praying exceedingly that we might see your face, and might perfect that which is lacking in your faith?

¹¹ Now God himself and our Father, and our Lord Jesus Christ, direct our way unto you.

¹² And the Lord make you to increase and abound in love one toward another, and toward all *men*, even as we *do* toward you:

¹³ to the end he may stablish your hearts unblamable in holiness before God, even our Father, at the coming of our Lord Jesus Christ with all his saints.

A Life that Pleases God

4 Furthermore then we beseech you, brethren, and exhort *you* by the Lord Jesus, that as ye have received of us how ye ought to walk and to please God, so ye would abound more and more.

² For ye know what commandments we gave you by the Lord Jesus.

³ For this is the will of God, *even* your sanctification, that ye should abstain from fornication:

⁴ that every one of you should know how to possess his vessel in sanctification and honor;

⁵ not in the lust of concupiscence,

even as the Gentiles which know not God:

[6] that no *man* go beyond and defraud his brother in *any* matter: because that the Lord *is* the avenger of all such, as we also have forewarned you and testified.

[7] For God hath not called us unto uncleanness, but unto holiness.

[8] He therefore that despiseth, despiseth not man, but God, who hath also given unto us his Holy Spirit.

[9] But as touching brotherly love ye need not that I write unto you: for ye yourselves are taught of God to love one another.

[10] And indeed ye do it toward all the brethren which are in all Macedonia: but we beseech you, brethren, that ye increase more and more;

[11] and that ye study to be quiet, and to do your own business, and to work with your own hands, as we commanded you;

[12] that ye may walk honestly toward them that are without, and *that* ye may have lack of nothing.

OLD TESTAMENT READING

*T*herefore shall ye keep my commandments, and do them: I *am* the LORD.

[32] Neither shall ye profane my holy name; but I will be hallowed among the children of Israel: I *am* the LORD which hallow you,

[33] that brought you out of the land of Egypt, to be your God: I *am* the LORD.

Leviticus 22:31–33

*F*or I *am* the LORD your God: ye shall therefore sanctify yourselves, and ye shall be holy; for I *am* holy.

[45] For I *am* the LORD that bringeth you up out of the land of Egypt, to be your God: ye shall therefore be holy, for I *am* holy.

Leviticus 11:44a–45

INSIGHTS

*O*ur daily expression of holiness is a reflection of our faith in Christ. If we have no desire to be holy, we should seriously question the genuineness of our faith in the Lord Jesus.

Christ not only died to save us from the punishment for our sins, but also from slavery to sin in this worldly culture. To continue to live in sin as a Christian is contradictory to the most basic meaning of Christianity. Christ died to save us from our sins, not to let us remain in our sins (Matthew 1:21; 1 John 1:6, 7). What kind of person would want to follow Christ and not desire to live a holy life? . . .

To trust Christ for salvation is to trust him for holiness. If there is no desire for holiness within, then it is doubtful that the Holy Spirit has come to dwell within. The Holy Spirit does not save us without giving us the desire to live a holy life.

Floyd McClung

APPLICATION

*W*hat instruction does Paul give to those who please God? How does Scripture define holy living? What is required of you to live a more holy life?

MONDAY

The Hope of Christ's Second Coming

1 Thessalonians 4:13—5:28

The Lord's Coming

*B*ut I would not have you to be ignorant, brethren, concerning them which are asleep, that ye sorrow not, even as others which have no hope. ¹⁴ For if we believe that Jesus died and rose again, even so them also which sleep in Jesus will God bring with him.
¹⁵ For this we say unto you by the word of the Lord, that we which are alive *and* remain unto the coming of the Lord shall not prevent them which are asleep.
¹⁶ For the Lord himself shall descend from heaven with a shout, with the voice of the archangel, and with the trump of God: and the dead in Christ shall rise first:
¹⁷ then we which are alive *and* remain shall be caught up together with them in the clouds, to meet the Lord in the air: and so shall we ever be with the Lord.
¹⁸ Wherefore comfort one another with these words.

Watch for the Lord's Coming

5 But of the times and the seasons, brethren, ye have no need that I write unto you.
² For yourselves know perfectly that the day of the Lord so cometh as a thief in the night.
³ For when they shall say, Peace and safety; then sudden destruction cometh upon them, as travail upon a woman with child; and they shall not escape.
⁴ But ye, brethren, are not in darkness, that that day should overtake you as a thief.
⁵ Ye are all the children of light, and the children of the day: we are not of the night, nor of darkness.
⁶ Therefore let us not sleep, as *do* others; but let us watch and be sober.
⁷ For they that sleep sleep in the night; and they that be drunken are drunken in the night.
⁸ But let us, who are of the day, be sober, putting on the breastplate of faith and love; and for a helmet, the hope of salvation.
⁹ For God hath not appointed us to wrath, but to obtain salvation by our Lord Jesus Christ,
¹⁰ who died for us, that, whether we wake or sleep, we should live together with him.
¹¹ Wherefore comfort yourselves together, and edify one another, even as also ye do.

Final Instructions and Greetings

*A*nd we beseech you, brethren, to know them which labor among you, and are over you in the Lord, and admonish you;
¹³ and to esteem them very highly in love for their work's sake. *And* be at peace among yourselves.
¹⁴ Now we exhort you, brethren, warn them that are unruly, comfort the feebleminded, support the weak, be patient toward all *men*.
¹⁵ See that none render evil for evil unto any *man*; but ever follow that which is good, both among yourselves, and to all *men*.
¹⁶ Rejoice evermore.

[17] Pray without ceasing.

[18] In every thing give thanks: for this is the will of God in Christ Jesus concerning you.

[19] Quench not the Spirit.

[20] Despise not prophesyings.

[21] Prove all things; hold fast that which is good.

[22] Abstain from all appearance of evil.

[23] And the very God of peace sanctify you wholly; and *I pray God* your whole spirit and soul and body be preserved blameless unto the coming of our Lord Jesus Christ.

[24] Faithful *is* he that calleth you, who also will do *it*.

[25] Brethren, pray for us.

[26] Greet all the brethren with a holy kiss.

[27] I charge you by the Lord, that this epistle be read unto all the holy brethren.

[28] The grace of our Lord Jesus Christ *be* with you. Amen.

OLD TESTAMENT READING

*F*or I know *that* my Redeemer liveth, and *that* he shall stand at the latter *day* upon the earth:

[26] and *though* after my skin *worms* destroy this *body*, yet in my flesh shall I see God:

[27] whom I shall see for myself, and mine eyes shall behold, and not another; *though* my reins be consumed within me.

Job 19:25–27

INSIGHTS

*W*hat would you say about a person who had made a hundred promises to you and kept ninety-nine of them? You probably would think that he was honest enough to fulfill the last promise as well, wouldn't you?

Jesus Christ has fulfilled every promise He ever made, except one. He has not yet returned. Will He?

In both the Old and New Testaments there are references to the return of the Lord. . . . Ezekiel tells of a Jerusalem which is to be restored, a temple which is to be rebuilt, and a land which is to be reclaimed and blessed with prosperity at the Lord's return. Zephaniah gives us the new song that He will teach to Israel and describes the overthrow of the false Christ.

In the New Testament, Matthew likens Christ to a bridegroom coming to receive His bride. Mark sees Him as a householder going on a long journey and entrusting certain tasks to his servants until his return. To Luke, Jesus is a nobleman going to a far country to transact business and leaving his possessions with his servants that they may trade with them until he comes.

John quotes Christ as saying, "I go to prepare a place for you. I will come again to receive you unto myself." The entire book of Revelation tells of the glorious return of Christ. And we can say with the apostle John, who wrote that book, "Amen, even so, come, Lord Jesus."

Billy Graham

PAUSE FOR REFLECTION

*W*hat about Christ's second coming gives you hope? What difference does Paul say the hope of Christ's second coming should make in the believer's life? What difference does that hope make in your life?

TUESDAY

*God's Righteous Judgment
Will Destroy Those Who
Refuse to Believe*

2 Thessalonians 1:1—2:12

1 Paul, and Silvanus, and Timothy, unto the church of the Thessalonians in God our Father and the Lord Jesus Christ:

² Grace unto you, and peace, from God our Father and the Lord Jesus Christ.

Paul Talks About God's Judgment

*W*e are bound to thank God always for you, brethren, as it is meet, because that your faith groweth exceedingly, and the charity of every one of you all toward each other aboundeth;

⁴ so that we ourselves glory in you in the churches of God for your patience and faith in all your persecutions and tribulations that ye endure:

⁵ *Which is* a manifest token of the righteous judgment of God, that ye may be counted worthy of the kingdom of God, for which ye also suffer:

⁶ Seeing *it is* a righteous thing with God to recompense tribulation to them that trouble you;

⁷ and to you who are troubled rest with us, when the Lord Jesus shall be revealed from heaven with his mighty angels,

⁸ in flaming fire taking vengeance on them that know not God, and that obey not the gospel of our Lord Jesus Christ:

⁹ who shall be punished with everlasting destruction from the presence of the Lord, and from the glory of his power;

¹⁰ when he shall come to be glorified in his saints, and to be admired in all them that believe (because our testimony among you was believed) in that day.

¹¹ Wherefore also we pray always for you, that our God would count you worthy of *this* calling, and fulfil all the good pleasure of *his* goodness, and the work of faith with power:

¹² that the name of our Lord Jesus Christ may be glorified in you, and ye in him, according to the grace of our God and the Lord Jesus Christ.

Evil Things Will Happen

2 Now we beseech you, brethren, by the coming of our Lord Jesus Christ, and *by* our gathering together unto him,

² that ye be not soon shaken in mind, or be troubled, neither by spirit, nor by word, nor by letter as from us, as that the day of Christ is at hand.

³ Let no man deceive you by any means: for *that day shall not come*, except there come a falling away first, and that man of sin be revealed, the son of perdition;

⁴ who opposeth and exalteth himself above all that is called God, or that is worshipped; so that he as God sitteth in the temple of God, showing himself that he is God.

⁵ Remember ye not, that, when I was yet with you, I told you these things?

⁶ And now ye know what withholdeth that he might be revealed in his time.

⁷ For the mystery of iniquity doth al-

ready work: only he who now letteth *will let*, until he be taken out of the way.

⁸ And then shall that Wicked be revealed, whom the Lord shall consume with the spirit of his mouth, and shall destroy with the brightness of his coming:

⁹ *even him*, whose coming is after the working of Satan with all power and signs and lying wonders,

¹⁰ and with all deceivableness of unrighteousness in them that perish; because they received not the love of the truth, that they might be saved.

¹¹ And for this cause God shall send them strong delusion, that they should believe a lie:

¹² that they all might be damned who believed not the truth, but had pleasure in unrighteousness.

OLD TESTAMENT READING

*Z*ion shall be redeemed with judgment, and her converts with righteousness.

²⁸ And the destruction of the transgressors and of the sinners *shall be* together, and they that forsake the LORD shall be consumed.

Isaiah 1:27–28

INSIGHTS

*D*eath is the "wages of sin." It is just what sin deserves. Labour earns wages, and creates a rightful claim to such remuneration. So men are conceived as earning wages when they sin. They become entitled to their pay. God deems Himself holden to give them their well-deserved wages. . . .

We are informed that in the final consummation of earthly scenes, "the judgment shall sit and the books shall be opened." We shall be there, and what is more, there to close up our account with our Lord and receive our allotment. Which will you have on that final settlement day? The wages of sin? . . .

. . . O, sinner, think of hell, and of yourself thrust into it. It pours forth its volumes of smoke and flame forever, never ceasing, never exhausted. Upon that spectacle the universe can look and read—"The wages of sin is death! O, sin not, since such is the doom of the unpardoned sinner!" Think what a demonstration this is in the government of God! What an exhibition of His holy justice, of His inflexible purpose to sustain the interests of holiness and happiness in all His vast dominions! . . .

Sinner, you may now escape this fearful doom. This is the reason why God has revealed hell in His faithful Word.

Charles Finney

PAUSE FOR REFLECTION

*W*hen will God punish those who don't know him? How can one escape God's punishment? How will God treat those who believe? What will happen before Jesus comes again? How are believers to live until he comes?

WEDNESDAY

Called to Work
for God's Service

2 Thessalonians 2:13—3:18

You Are Chosen for Salvation

*B*ut we are bound to give thanks always to God for you, brethren beloved of the Lord, because God hath from the beginning chosen you to salvation through sanctification of the Spirit and belief of the truth:

[14] Whereunto he called you by our gospel, to the obtaining of the glory of our Lord Jesus Christ.

[15] Therefore, brethren, stand fast, and hold the traditions which ye have been taught, whether by word, or our epistle.

[16] Now our Lord Jesus Christ himself, and God, even our Father, which hath loved us, and hath given *us* everlasting consolation and good hope through grace,

[17] comfort your hearts, and stablish you in every good word and work.

Pray for Us

3 Finally, brethren, pray for us, that the word of the Lord may have *free* course, and be glorified, even as *it is* with you:

[2] and that we may be delivered from unreasonable and wicked men: for all *men* have not faith.

[3] But the Lord is faithful, who shall stablish you, and keep *you* from evil.

[4] And we have confidence in the Lord touching you, that ye both do and will do the things which we command you.

[5] And the Lord direct your hearts into the love of God, and into the patient waiting for Christ.

The Duty to Work

*N*ow we command you, brethren, in the name of our Lord Jesus Christ, that ye withdraw yourselves from every brother that walketh disorderly, and not after the tradition which he received of us.

[7] For yourselves know how ye ought to follow us: for we behaved not ourselves disorderly among you;

[8] neither did we eat any man's bread for nought; but wrought with labor and travail night and day, that we might not be chargeable to any of you:

[9] not because we have not power, but to make ourselves an ensample unto you to follow us.

[10] For even when we were with you, this we commanded you, that if any would not work, neither should he eat.

[11] For we hear that there are some which walk among you disorderly, working not at all, but are busybodies.

[12] Now them that are such we command and exhort by our Lord Jesus Christ, that with quietness they work, and eat their own bread.

[13] But ye, brethren, be not weary in well doing.

[14] And if any man obey not our word by this epistle, note that man, and have no company with him, that he may be ashamed.

[15] Yet count *him* not as an enemy, but admonish *him* as a brother.

Final Words

*N*ow the Lord of peace himself give

you peace always by all means. The Lord *be* with you all.

¹⁷ The salutation of Paul with mine own hand, which is the token in every epistle: so I write.

¹⁸ The grace of our Lord Jesus Christ *be* with you all. Amen.

OLD TESTAMENT READING

*W*ho can find a virtuous woman? for her price *is* far above rubies.

¹¹ The heart of her husband doth safely trust in her, so that he shall have no need of spoil.

¹² She will do him good and not evil all the days of her life.

¹³ She seeketh wool, and flax, and worketh willingly with her hands.

¹⁴ She is like the merchants' ships; she bringeth her food from afar.

¹⁵ She riseth also while it is yet night, and giveth meat to her household, and a portion to her maidens.

¹⁶ She considereth a field, and buyeth it: with the fruit of her hands she planteth a vineyard.

Proverbs 31:10–16

INSIGHTS

*T*he common drudgery of daily life can be a Divine Calling. We often speak of a young man as "being called to the Ministry"; but it is as fitting to speak of a carpenter being called to the bench, the blacksmith to the forge, and the shoemaker to his last. "Brethren," said the Apostle, "let every man wherein he is called, therein abide with God."

Remember that your life has been appointed by God's wise providence. God as much sent Joseph to the drudgery and discipline of the prison as to the glory and responsibility of the palace. Nothing happens to us which is not included in His plan for us; and the incidents which seem most tiresome are often contrived to give us opportunities to become nobler, stronger characters.

We are called to be faithful in performing our assigned duties. Not brilliance, not success, not notoriety which attracts the world's notice, but the regular, quiet, and careful performance of trivial and common duties; faithfulness in that which is least is as great an attainment in God's sight as in the greatest. . . .

Take up your work, then, you who seem to be the nobodies, the drudges, the maid-of-all-work, the clerk, or shop assistant. Do it with a brave heart, looking up to Him who for many years toiled at the carpenter's bench. Amid the many scenes and actions of life, set the Lord always before your face. Do all as in His presence, and to win His smile; and be sure to cultivate a spirit of love to God and man. Look out for opportunities of cheering your fellow-workers. Do not murmur or grumble, but let your heart rise from your toil to God your Maker, Saviour, and Friend. So the lowliest service will glisten, as grass-blades do when sun and dewdrops garnish them.

F. B. Meyer

ACTION POINT

*S*tudy these readings and describe what it means to be a diligent and faithful worker for God's service today. How well do you measure up? What changes will you make to bring greater honor to God?

THURSDAY

*God Is Patient and
Merciful to Sinners*

1 Timothy 1:1–20

1 Paul, an apostle of Jesus Christ by the commandment of God our Saviour, and Lord Jesus Christ, *which is* our hope;
2 Unto Timothy, *my* own son in the faith: Grace, mercy, *and* peace, from God our Father and Jesus Christ our Lord.

Warning Against False Teaching

*A*s I besought thee to abide still at Ephesus, when I went into Macedonia, that thou mightest charge some that they teach no other doctrine,
4 neither give heed to fables and endless genealogies, which minister questions, rather than godly edifying which is in faith: *so do.*
5 Now the end of the commandment is charity out of a pure heart, and *of* a good conscience, and *of* faith unfeigned:
6 from which some having swerved have turned aside unto vain jangling;
7 desiring to be teachers of the law; understanding neither what they say, nor whereof they affirm.
8 But we know that the law *is* good, if a man use it lawfully;
9 knowing this, that the law is not made for a righteous man, but for the lawless and disobedient, for the ungodly and for sinners, for unholy and profane, for murderers of fathers and murderers of mothers, for manslayers,

10 for whoremongers, for them that defile themselves with mankind, for menstealers, for liars, for perjured persons, and if there be any other thing that is contrary to sound doctrine;
11 according to the glorious gospel of the blessed God, which was committed to my trust.

Thanks for God's Mercy

*A*nd I thank Christ Jesus our Lord, who hath enabled me, for that he counted me faithful, putting me into the ministry;
13 who was before a blasphemer, and a persecutor, and injurious: but I obtained mercy, because I did *it* ignorantly in unbelief.
14 And the grace of our Lord was exceeding abundant with faith and love which is in Christ Jesus.
15 This *is* a faithful saying, and worthy of all acceptation, that Christ Jesus came into the world to save sinners; of whom I am chief.
16 Howbeit for this cause I obtained mercy, that in me first Jesus Christ might show forth all long-suffering, for a pattern to them which should hereafter believe on him to life everlasting.
17 Now unto the King eternal, immortal, invisible, the only wise God, *be* honor and glory for ever and ever. Amen.
18 This charge I commit unto thee, son Timothy, according to the prophecies which went before on thee, that thou by them mightest war a good warfare;
19 holding faith, and a good conscience; which some having put away, concerning faith have made shipwreck:

20 of whom is Hymeneus and Alexander; whom I have delivered unto Satan, that they may learn not to blaspheme.

*L*et the wicked forsake his way, and the unrighteous man his thoughts: and let him return unto the LORD, and he will have mercy upon him; and to our God, for he will abundantly pardon.

Isaiah 55:7

*T*he LORD *is* merciful and gracious, slow to anger, and plenteous in mercy.
9 He will not always chide: neither will he keep *his anger* for ever.
10 He hath not dealt with us after our sins; nor rewarded us according to our iniquities.

Psalm 103:8–10

*I*n amateur baseball, there is a rule known as the "mercy rule." This rule terminates a game after a certain number of innings (usually seven) when one team is ahead by a certain number of runs (usually ten). The "mercy rule" has relieved the misery of many inferior teams or of a team that just had a bad day.

Mercy is an attribute of God for which we should be especially thankful. How wonderful that He has not given us what we really deserve! We all have our "bad days." So many times we've "blown it" with God. But He is merciful! His patience is astounding! It's hard to fathom God's mercy as He looks down upon this wicked world. How many chances He has given us! How many times we have failed to obey! . . .

. . . It is God's mercy that gives us hope for a continued relationship with Him.

Because of his mercy, we are still here! We should be so grateful that God is merciful toward His children. Our God promises to complete what He began in us (Philippians 1:6), and by His mercy He shows compassion toward us in our weaknesses. Psalms 103:14 says, "For He knows how we are formed, He remembers that we are dust." God sees us in our lowly estate and extends His mercy. Our hearts should praise the God of mercy. . . .

. . . It's only by His mercy that we are not destroyed totally and completely. Therefore, we . . . should be imitators of God and show mercy to those God brings our way.

Elliot Johnson
Al Schierbaum

*R*eview the evidence in these readings that God is not begrudgingly merciful, but abundantly merciful! The next time someone accuses God of being harsh or unforgiving, tell about the evidence you have found of God's awesome, unfailing mercy.

F R I D A Y

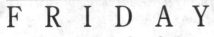

*There Is Only One God,
and He Alone Saves Us*

1 Timothy 2:1—3:13

Some Rules for Men and Women

2 I exhort therefore, that, first of all, supplications, prayers, intercessions, *and* giving of thanks, be made for all men;

[2] for kings, and *for* all that are in authority; that we may lead a quiet and peaceable life in all godliness and honesty.

[3] For this *is* good and acceptable in the sight of God our Saviour;

[4] who will have all men to be saved, and to come unto the knowledge of the truth.

[5] For *there is* one God, and one mediator between God and men, the man Christ Jesus;

[6] who gave himself a ransom for all, to be testified in due time.

[7] Whereunto I am ordained a preacher, and an apostle, (I speak the truth in Christ, *and* lie not,) a teacher of the Gentiles in faith and verity.

[8] I will therefore that men pray every where, lifting up holy hands, without wrath and doubting.

[9] In like manner also, that women adorn themselves in modest apparel, with shamefacedness and sobriety; not with braided hair, or gold, or pearls, or costly array;

[10] but (which becometh women professing godliness) with good works.

[11] Let the woman learn in silence with all subjection.

[12] But I suffer not a woman to teach, nor to usurp authority over the man, but to be in silence.

[13] For Adam was first formed, then Eve.

[14] And Adam was not deceived, but the woman being deceived was in the transgression.

[15] Notwithstanding she shall be saved in childbearing, if they continue in faith and charity and holiness with sobriety.

Elders in the Church

3 This *is* a true saying, If a man desire the office of a bishop, he desireth a good work.

[2] A bishop then must be blameless, the husband of one wife, vigilant, sober, of good behavior, given to hospitality, apt to teach;

[3] not given to wine, no striker, not greedy of filthy lucre; but patient, not a brawler, not covetous;

[4] one that ruleth well his own house, having his children in subjection with all gravity;

[5] (for if a man know not how to rule his own house, how shall he take care of the church of God?)

[6] not a novice, lest being lifted up with pride he fall into the condemnation of the devil.

[7] Moreover he must have a good report of them which are without; lest he fall into reproach and the snare of the devil.

Deacons in the Church

Likewise *must* the deacons *be* grave, not double-tongued, not given to much wine, not greedy of filthy lucre;

[9] holding the mystery of the faith in a pure conscience.

¹⁰ And let these also first be proved; then let them use the office of a deacon, being *found* blameless.

¹¹ Even so *must their* wives *be* grave, not slanderers, sober, faithful in all things.

¹² Let the deacons be the husbands of one wife, ruling their children and their own houses well.

¹³ For they that have used the office of a deacon well purchase to themselves a good degree, and great boldness in the faith which is in Christ Jesus.

OLD TESTAMENT READING

Or hath God assayed to go *and* take him a nation from the midst of *another* nation, by temptations, by signs, and by wonders, and by war, and by a mighty hand, and by a stretched out arm, and by great terrors, according to all that the LORD your God did for you in Egypt before your eyes?

³⁵ Unto thee it was showed, that thou mightest know that the LORD he is God; *there is* none else beside him.

³⁶ Out of heaven he made thee to hear his voice, that he might instruct thee: and upon earth he showed thee his great fire; and thou heardest his words out of the midst of the fire.

³⁷ And because he loved thy fathers, therefore he chose their seed after them, and brought thee out in his sight with his mighty power out of Egypt;

³⁸ to drive out nations from before thee greater and mightier than thou *art*, to bring thee in, to give thee their land *for* an inheritance, as *it is* this day.

Deuteronomy 4:34–38

INSIGHTS

*M*en have always stumbled over the simplicity of salvation. That is why there are so many cults. Each one has a unique slant on the doctrine of salvation, each corrupting the simplicity of the gospel revealed in God's Word (cf. 2 Corinthians 11:3) by espousing salvation by human works. . . .

From start to finish, God's Word disproves them all, and in a wonderfully consistent way. Its message, woven through sixty-six books, written over a span of fifteen hundred years by more than forty different authors, is marvelously unified and congruous. The message is simply that God graciously saves repentant sinners who come to Him in faith. There is no secret here, no mystery, no obscurity, no complexity. . . .

. . . Jesus is the only source of salvation. Those who do not believe in His name are condemned, excluded from eternal life. No matter how sincere, how religious, how immersed in good works, everyone must be born again. There is no promise of life—only a guarantee of condemnation—for those who will not . . . turn from sin in obedient faith to the One who was lifted up so that they would not have to perish.

John F. MacArthur, Jr.

APPLICATION

*W*hat truth does God want all people to know? What evidence does Scripture give that God is the only true God? What is the one way of salvation? Do you personally know that way?

WEEKEND

*Your Life Should Be
a Godly Example*

1 Timothy 3:14—4:16

The Mystery of God

*T*hese things write I unto thee, hoping to come unto thee shortly: ¹⁵ but if I tarry long, that thou mayest know how thou oughtest to behave thyself in the house of God, which is the church of the living God, the pillar and ground of the truth.

¹⁶ And without controversy great is the mystery of godliness: God was manifest in the flesh, justified in the Spirit, seen of angels, preached unto the Gentiles, believed on in the world, received up into glory.

A Warning About False Teachers

4 Now the Spirit speaketh expressly, that in the latter times some shall depart from the faith, giving heed to seducing spirits, and doctrines of devils;

² speaking lies in hypocrisy; having their conscience seared with a hot iron;

³ forbidding to marry, *and commanding* to abstain from meats, which God hath created to be received with thanksgiving of them which believe and know the truth.

⁴ For every creature of God *is* good, and nothing to be refused, if it be received with thanksgiving:

⁵ for it is sanctified by the word of God and prayer.

Be A Good Minister of Christ

*I*f thou put the brethren in remembrance of these things, thou shalt be a good minister of Jesus Christ, nourished up in the words of faith and of good doctrine, whereunto thou hast attained.

⁷ But refuse profane and old wives' fables, and exercise thyself *rather* unto godliness.

⁸ For bodily exercise profiteth little: but godliness is profitable unto all things, having promise of the life that now is, and of that which is to come.

⁹ This *is* a faithful saying, and worthy of all acceptation.

¹⁰ For therefore we both labor and suffer reproach, because we trust in the living God, who is the Saviour of all men, specially of those that believe.

¹¹ These things command and teach.

¹² Let no man despise thy youth; but be thou an example of the believers, in word, in conversation, in charity, in spirit, in faith, in purity.

¹³ Till I come, give attendance to reading, to exhortation, to doctrine.

¹⁴ Neglect not the gift that is in thee, which was given thee by prophecy, with the laying on of the hands of the presbytery.

¹⁵ Meditate upon these things; give thyself wholly to them; that thy profiting may appear to all.

¹⁶ Take heed unto thyself, and unto the doctrine; continue in them: for in doing this thou shalt both save thyself, and them that hear thee.

OLD TESTAMENT READING

*A*nd the king stood by a pillar, and made a covenant before the Lᴏʀᴅ, to

504

walk after the Lord, and to keep his commandments and his testimonies and his statutes with all *their* heart and all *their* soul, to perform the words of this covenant that were written in this book. And all the people stood to the covenant.

24 Moreover the *workers with* familiar spirits, and the wizards, and the images, and the idols, and all the abominations that were spied in the land of Judah and in Jerusalem, did Josiah put away, that he might perform the words of the law, which were written in the book that Hilkiah the priest found in the house of the Lord.

25 And like unto him was there no king before him, that turned to the Lord with all his heart, and with all his soul, and with all his might, according to all the law of Moses; neither after him arose there *any* like him.

2 Kings 23:3, 24–25

INSIGHTS

I frequently hear that the call to be holy and the call to demonstrate love to sinners are mutually exclusive. (As if love is the antithesis to holiness!) Jesus welcomed and loved sinners; he did not drive them away by too much affectation of righteousness. He showed genuine compassion for people, but he was also direct and uncompromising in denouncing sin. Jesus had compassion, but there was also toughness in this love. He won them without sacrificing the purity of his life.

The paradox of agape love is that we accept our neighbor unconditionally and with open arms and at the same time desire moral purity for their lives. If Jesus is our Lord, our compassion will be shaped by his moral absolutes. Christ both was merciful and made judgments. Some things, he said, were immoral and destructive, but he never ceased to love. Indeed, it was his love that prompted his judgment. The enemy of our age is our desire to be tolerant and open-minded. . . .

I know a Christian woman who has cared deeply for a non-Christian woman who has had every variety of sexual experience. One day the non-Christian woman said to the Christian, "It's funny, my non-Christian friends accept me. They say it doesn't matter what I do. I'm free. But it's only with you that I feel loved, that I know I could always come to you. But it's also only when I'm with you that I feel shame and remorse for what I'm doing."

That is holiness. It never abandons; it identifies deeply with individual people. But it also brings the reality of God's presence, the purity of his holiness.

Rebecca Pippert

PAUSE FOR REFLECTION

*L*ist the areas of life in which the believer ought to be an example. What happens when people have a godly example before them? To whom are you an example of godly living? Do you know what impact your example is having?

MONDAY

The Importance of Account-
ability Among God's People

1 Timothy 5:1–25

Rules for Living with Others

5 Rebuke not an elder, but entreat *him* as a father; *and* the younger men as brethren;

² the elder women as mothers; the younger as sisters, with all purity.

³ Honor widows that are widows indeed.

⁴ But if any widow have children or nephews, let them learn first to show piety at home, and to requite their parents: for that is good and acceptable before God.

⁵ Now she that is a widow indeed, and desolate, trusteth in God, and continueth in supplications and prayers night and day.

⁶ But she that liveth in pleasure is dead while she liveth.

⁷ And these things give in charge, that they may be blameless.

⁸ But if any provide not for his own, and specially for those of his own house, he hath denied the faith, and is worse than an infidel.

⁹ Let not a widow be taken into the number under threescore years old, having been the wife of one man,

¹⁰ well reported of for good works; if she have brought up children, if she have lodged strangers, if she have washed the saints' feet, if she have relieved the afflicted, if she have diligently followed every good work.

¹¹ But the younger widows refuse: for when they have begun to wax wanton against Christ, they will marry;

¹² having damnation, because they have cast off their first faith.

¹³ And withal they learn *to be* idle, wandering about from house to house; and not only idle, but tattlers also and busybodies, speaking things which they ought not.

¹⁴ I will therefore that the younger women marry, bear children, guide the house, give none occasion to the adversary to speak reproachfully.

¹⁵ For some are already turned aside after Satan.

¹⁶ If any man or woman that believeth have widows, let them relieve them, and let not the church be charged; that it may relieve them that are widows indeed.

¹⁷ Let the elders that rule well be counted worthy of double honor, especially they who labor in the word and doctrine.

¹⁸ For the Scripture saith, Thou shalt not muzzle the ox that treadeth out the corn. And, The laborer *is* worthy of his reward.

¹⁹ Against an elder receive not an accusation, but before two or three witnesses.

²⁰ Them that sin rebuke before all, that others also may fear.

²¹ I charge *thee* before God, and the Lord Jesus Christ, and the elect angels, that thou observe these things without preferring one before another, doing nothing by partiality.

²² Lay hands suddenly on no man, neither be partaker of other men's sins: keep thyself pure.

²³ Drink no longer water, but use a little wine for thy stomach's sake and thine often infirmities.

²⁴ Some men's sins are open beforehand, going before to judgment; and some *men* they follow after.

²⁵ Likewise also the good works *of*

some are manifest beforehand; and they that are otherwise cannot be hid.

*A*nd Nathan said to David, Thou *art* the man. Thus saith the LORD God of Israel, I anointed thee king over Israel, and I delivered thee out of the hand of Saul;

⁸ and I gave thee thy master's house, and thy master's wives into thy bosom, and gave thee the house of Israel and of Judah; and if *that had been* too little, I would moreover have given unto thee such and such things.

⁹ Wherefore hast thou despised the commandment of the LORD, to do evil in his sight? thou hast killed Uriah the Hittite with the sword, and hast taken his wife *to be* thy wife, and hast slain him with the sword of the children of Ammon.

¹³ And David said unto Nathan, I have sinned against the LORD. And Nathan said unto David, The LORD also hath put away thy sin; thou shalt not die.

¹⁴ Howbeit, because by this deed thou hast given great occasion to the enemies of the LORD to blaspheme, the child also *that is* born unto thee shall surely die.

2 Samuel 12:7–9, 13–14

*T*oo often I have seen marriages go down the drain, relationships deteriorate to the point of destruction, people with glaring personal limitations go unchecked—all because Christians who know precisely what is wrong will not love sufficiently to tackle the problem.

"I was afraid I would hurt their future," is one lame excuse. But that is exactly what happens.

My mind recalls the words of our Lord to Peter when he veered off course; it seems a harsh slash to the disciple who had a short time before confessed him as Lord. "Out of my sight, Satan! You are a stumbling block to me; you do not have in mind the things of God, but the things of men." (Matthew 16:23) These words came from the lips of the One who loves with everlasting love.

A former pastor told me about his experience of sinking into an illicit sexual relationship. He said he felt like an exhausted swimmer battling alone in the pounding surf, unable to escape the strong undertow, about to go down for the last time. On shore he could see all the people of his church. Some were shaking their heads in weeping and despair; others were shouting and shaking their fists in anger and frustration. There were words of encouragement and gestures of good will. There they were, all lined up, watching and waiting for something to happen. Only one man stepped forward and risked everything to plunge into the water and help the victim to safety.

Howard and Jeanne Hendricks

*I*n what ways does Paul urge Christians to hold one another accountable? What are the results of a proper response to correction? Who holds you accountable to live in obedience to God?

TUESDAY

A Godly Attitude Toward Riches

1 Timothy 6:1–21

6 Let as many servants as are under the yoke count their own masters worthy of all honor, that the name of God and *his* doctrine be not blasphemed.

[2] And they that have believing masters, let them not despise *them*, because they are brethren; but rather do *them* service, because they are faithful and beloved, partakers of the benefit. These things teach and exhort.

False Teaching and True Riches

*I*f any man teach otherwise, and consent not to wholesome words, *even* the words of our Lord Jesus Christ, and to the doctrine which is according to godliness;

[4] he is proud, knowing nothing, but doting about questions and strifes of words, whereof cometh envy, strife, railings, evil surmisings,

[5] perverse disputings of men of corrupt minds, and destitute of the truth, supposing that gain is godliness: from such withdraw thyself.

[6] But godliness with contentment is great gain.

[7] For we brought nothing into *this* world, *and it is* certain we can carry nothing out.

[8] And having food and raiment, let us be therewith content.

[9] But they that will be rich fall into temptation and a snare, and *into* many foolish and hurtful lusts, which drown men in destruction and perdition.

[10] For the love of money is the root of all evil: which while some coveted after, they have erred from the faith, and pierced themselves through with many sorrows.

Some Things to Remember

*B*ut thou, O man of God, flee these things; and follow after righteousness, godliness, faith, love, patience, meekness.

[12] Fight the good fight of faith, lay hold on eternal life, whereunto thou art also called, and hast professed a good profession before many witnesses.

[13] I give thee charge in the sight of God, who quickeneth all things, and *before* Christ Jesus, who before Pontius Pilate witnessed a good confession;

[14] That thou keep *this* commandment without spot, unrebukable, until the appearing of our Lord Jesus Christ:

[15] which in his times he shall show, *who is* the blessed and only Potentate, the King of kings, and Lord of lords;

[16] who only hath immortality, dwelling in the light which no man can approach unto; whom no man hath seen, nor can see: to whom *be* honor and power everlasting. Amen.

[17] Charge them that are rich in this world, that they be not high-minded, nor trust in uncertain riches, but in the living God, who giveth us richly all things to enjoy;

[18] that they do good, that they be rich in good works, ready to distribute, willing to communicate;

[19] laying up in store for themselves a good foundation against the time to come, that they may lay hold on eternal life.

[20] O Timothy, keep that which is committed to thy trust, avoiding profane

and vain babblings, and oppositions of science falsely so called: [21] which some professing have erred concerning the faith. Grace *be* with thee. Amen.

OLD TESTAMENT READING

*B*eware that thou forget not the LORD thy God, in not keeping his commandments, and his judgments, and his statutes, which I command thee this day: [12] lest *when* thou hast eaten and art full, and hast built goodly houses, and dwelt *therein;* [13] and *when* thy herds and thy flocks multiply, and thy silver and thy gold is multiplied, and all that thou hast is multiplied, [14] then thine heart be lifted up, and thou forget the LORD thy God, which brought thee forth out of the land of Egypt, from the house of bondage. [17] And thou say in thine heart, My power and the might of *mine* hand hath gotten me this wealth. [18] But thou shalt remember the LORD thy God: for *it is* he that giveth thee power to get wealth, that he may establish his covenant which he sware unto thy fathers, as *it is* this day.

Deuteronomy 8:11–14, 17–18

*E*very man also to whom God hath given riches and wealth, and hath given him power to eat thereof, and to take his portion, and to rejoice in his labor; this *is* the gift of God. [20] For he shall not much remember the days of his life; because God answereth *him* in the joy of his heart.

Ecclesiastes 5:19–20

INSIGHTS

*T*here will be this difference between the rich that loves his riches and the poor that hates his poverty. When they die, the heart of the one will still be crowded with things and their pleasures, while the heart of the other will be relieved of their lack. The one has had his good things; the other, his sorrowful things.

But the rich man, on the other hand, who held his things lightly and who did not let them nestle in his heart, who was a channel and not a cistern, who was ever and always forsaking his money—this rich man starts in the new world side by side with the man who accepted, not hated, his poverty. Each will say, "I am free."

George MacDonald

*G*od often allows people to accumulate property so they may have an opportunity to extend the cause of truth and righteousness in the earth. . . . Professing Christians acknowledge themselves to be but stewards for God, that everything they possess is His; consequently, their possessions are at His disposal. Now, is it a fact that these people act in harmony with what they profess? Well, God often tries them to see if they are hypocrites or not.

Charles Finney

PAUSE FOR REFLECTION

*W*hat traps await those who accumulate riches? Who is the source of wealth? Write down what it means for you to have a godly attitude toward riches. In what ways do riches tempt you? How well are you handling what God has given to you?

WEDNESDAY

*Disciple One Another
in the Teachings of God*

2 Timothy 1:1—2:13

1 Paul, an apostle of Jesus Christ by the will of God, according to the promise of life which is in Christ Jesus,

2 To Timothy, *my* dearly beloved son: Grace, mercy, *and* peace, from God the Father and Christ Jesus our Lord.

Encouragement for Timothy

I thank God, whom I serve from *my* forefathers with pure conscience, that without ceasing I have remembrance of thee in my prayers night and day;

4 greatly desiring to see thee, being mindful of thy tears, that I may be filled with joy;

5 when I call to remembrance the unfeigned faith that is in thee, which dwelt first in thy grandmother Lois, and thy mother Eunice; and I am persuaded that in thee also.

6 Wherefore I put thee in remembrance, that thou stir up the gift of God, which is in thee by the putting on of my hands.

7 For God hath not given us the spirit of fear; but of power, and of love, and of a sound mind.

8 Be not thou therefore ashamed of the testimony of our Lord, nor of me his prisoner: but be thou partaker of the afflictions of the gospel according to the power of God;

9 who hath saved us, and called *us* with a holy calling, not according to our works, but according to his own purpose and grace, which was given us in Christ Jesus before the world began;

10 but is now made manifest by the appearing of our Saviour Jesus Christ, who hath abolished death, and hath brought life and immortality to light through the gospel:

11 whereunto I am appointed a preacher, and an apostle, and a teacher of the Gentiles.

12 For the which cause I also suffer these things: nevertheless I am not ashamed; for I know whom I have believed, and am persuaded that he is able to keep that which I have committed unto him against that day.

13 Hold fast the form of sound words, which thou hast heard of me, in faith and love which is in Christ Jesus.

14 That good thing which was committed unto thee keep by the Holy Ghost which dwelleth in us.

15 This thou knowest, that all they which are in Asia be turned away from me; of whom are Phygellus and Hermogenes.

16 The Lord give mercy unto the house of Onesiphorus; for he oft refreshed me, and was not ashamed of my chain:

17 but, when he was in Rome, he sought me out very diligently, and found *me*.

18 The Lord grant unto him that he may find mercy of the Lord in that day: and in how many things he ministered unto me at Ephesus, thou knowest very well.

A Loyal Soldier of Christ Jesus

2 Thou therefore, my son, be strong in the grace that is in Christ Jesus.

2 And the things that thou hast heard of me among many witnesses, the same commit thou to faithful men, who shall be able to teach others also.

3 Thou therefore endure hardness, as a good soldier of Jesus Christ.

4 No man that warreth entangleth himself with the affairs of *this* life; that he may please him who hath chosen him to be a soldier.

5 And if a man also strive for masteries, *yet* is he not crowned, except he strive lawfully.

6 The husbandman that laboreth must be first partaker of the fruits.

7 Consider what I say; and the Lord give thee understanding in all things.

8 Remember that Jesus Christ of the seed of David was raised from the dead, according to my gospel:

9 wherein I suffer trouble, as an evildoer, *even* unto bonds; but the word of God is not bound.

10 Therefore I endure all things for the elect's sake, that they may also obtain the salvation which is in Christ Jesus with eternal glory.

11 *It is* a faithful saying: For if we be dead with *him*, we shall also live with *him*:

12 if we suffer, we shall also reign with *him*: if we deny *him*, he also will deny us:

13 if we believe not, *yet* he abideth faithful: he cannot deny himself.

OLD TESTAMENT READING

*O*nly take heed to thyself, and keep thy soul diligently, lest thou forget the things which thine eyes have seen, and lest they depart from thy heart all the days of thy life: but teach them thy sons, and thy sons' sons;

10 *specially* the day that thou stoodest before the LORD thy God in Horeb, when the LORD said unto me, Gather me the people together, and I will make them hear my words, that they may learn to fear me all the days that they shall live upon the earth, and *that* they may teach their children.

Deuteronomy 4:9–10

INSIGHTS

*T*he discipling ministry lacks the glamour and excitement of the platform or large meeting type of ministry. But we can hardly overemphasize the importance of investing the right kind of person, one of vision and discipline, totally committed to Jesus Christ, willing to pay any price to have the will of God fulfilled in his life. . . .

. . . The Great Commission . . . says, "Go therefore, and teach [make disciples of] all nations." It takes a disciple-maker to make disciples. Historically, the Church has believed that the Great Commission was . . . to all believers. If this is true, then all believers can be disciple-makers. . . .

. . . If you are not a disciple-maker, then I would suggest that you . . . make yourself available to a disciple-maker. . . . Latch on to them. Learn from them the "how to" involved . . . to spiritually reproduce yourself in the lives of others.

Walter Henrichsen

PAUSE FOR REFLECTION

*W*hat principles of discipleship did Moses outline for the Israelites? In what ways do those principles apply today?

THURSDAY

Those Who Follow God Must Flee Evil

2 Timothy 2:14—3:11

A Worker Pleasing to God

*O*f these things put *them* in remembrance, charging *them* before the Lord that they strive not about words to no profit, *but* to the subverting of the hearers.

[15] Study to show thyself approved unto God, a workman that needeth not to be ashamed, rightly dividing the word of truth.

[16] But shun profane *and* vain babblings: for they will increase unto more ungodliness.

[17] And their word will eat as doth a canker: of whom is Hymeneus and Philetus;

[18] who concerning the truth have erred, saying that the resurrection is past already; and overthrow the faith of some.

[19] Nevertheless the foundation of God standeth sure, having this seal, The Lord knoweth them that are his. And, Let every one that nameth the name of Christ depart from iniquity.

[20] But in a great house there are not only vessels of gold and of silver, but also of wood and of earth; and some to honor, and some to dishonor.

[21] If a man therefore purge himself from these, he shall be a vessel unto honor, sanctified, and meet for the master's use, *and* prepared unto every good work.

[22] Flee also youthful lusts: but follow righteousness, faith, charity, peace, with them that call on the Lord out of a pure heart.

[23] But foolish and unlearned questions avoid, knowing that they do gender strifes.

[24] And the servant of the Lord must not strive; but be gentle unto all *men*, apt to teach, patient;

[25] in meekness instructing those that oppose themselves; if God peradventure will give them repentance to the acknowledging of the truth;

[26] And *that* they may recover themselves out of the snare of the devil, who are taken captive by him at his will.

The Last Days

3 This know also, that in the last days perilous times shall come.

[2] For men shall be lovers of their own selves, covetous, boasters, proud, blasphemers, disobedient to parents, unthankful, unholy,

[3] without natural affection, trucebreakers, false accusers, incontinent, fierce, despisers of those that are good,

[4] traitors, heady, high-minded, lovers of pleasures more than lovers of God;

[5] having a form of godliness, but denying the power thereof: from such turn away.

[6] For of this sort are they which creep into houses, and lead captive silly women laden with sins, led away with divers lusts,

[7] ever learning, and never able to come to the knowledge of the truth.

[8] Now as Jannes and Jambres withstood Moses, so do these also resist the truth: men of corrupt minds, reprobate concerning the faith.

⁹ But they shall proceed no further: for their folly shall be manifest unto all *men*, as theirs also was.

Obey the Teachings

*B*ut thou hast fully known my doctrine, manner of life, purpose, faith, long-suffering, charity, patience, ¹¹ persecutions, afflictions, which came unto me at Antioch, at Iconium, at Lystra; what persecutions I endured: but out of *them* all the Lord delivered me.

OLD TESTAMENT READING

I will sing of mercy and judgment: unto thee, O LORD, will I sing.
² I will behave myself wisely in a perfect way. O when wilt thou come unto me? I will walk within my house with a perfect heart.
³ I will set no wicked thing before mine eyes: I hate the work of them that turn aside; *it* shall not cleave to me.
⁴ A froward heart shall depart from me: I will not know a wicked *person*.
⁵ Whoso privily slandereth his neighbor, him will I cut off: him that hath a high look and a proud heart will not I suffer.

Psalm 101:1–5

INSIGHTS

*T*he practice of godliness involves the pursuit of holiness because God has said, "Be holy, because I am holy" (1 Peter 1:16). Paul tells us that we have been called to a holy life; we have been redeemed for that purpose. Any Christian who is not earnestly pursuing holiness in every aspect of his life is flying in the face of God's purpose in saving him.

What is holiness? The best practical definition that I have heard is simply "without sin." . . .

John said he wrote his first letter so that his readers would not sin (1 John 2:1). Most Christians seem content not to sin very much, but John's goal was that we not sin at all. Every sin, no matter how small it may seem to us, is an affront to God's authority, a disregard for his law, a spurning of his love. Because of this, sin cannot be tolerated in any form, to any degree. . . .

. . . When Paul was instructing the Ephesian Christians about the importance of holiness he said, "So I tell you this, and insist on it in the Lord, that you must no longer live as the Gentiles do" (4:17). He insisted on holiness, and he did so with the Lord's authority. Holiness is not an option but a must for every Christian. . . .

. . . If we want to train ourselves to be godly, it must be holiness in every area of our lives.

Jerry Bridges

PAUSE FOR REFLECTION

*W*hat must everyone who believes in God stop doing—and start doing? How important is this teaching for Christians today? In what ways do you share the psalmist's delight in innocence and pure living expressed in Psalm 101?

F R I D A Y

*God Gave Us Scripture
to Teach Us How to Live*

2 Timothy 3:12—4:22

Yea, and all that will live godly in Christ Jesus shall suffer persecution. [13] But evil men and seducers shall wax worse and worse, deceiving, and being deceived.

[14] But continue thou in the things which thou hast learned and hast been assured of, knowing of whom thou hast learned *them*;

[15] and that from a child thou hast known the holy Scriptures, which are able to make thee wise unto salvation through faith which is in Christ Jesus.

[16] All Scripture *is* given by inspiration of God, and *is* profitable for doctrine, for reproof, for correction, for instruction in righteousness:

[17] that the man of God may be perfect, thoroughly furnished unto all good works.

4 I charge *thee* therefore before God, and the Lord Jesus Christ, who shall judge the quick and the dead at his appearing and his kingdom;

[2] preach the word; be instant in season, out of season; reprove, rebuke, exhort with all long-suffering and doctrine.

[3] For the time will come when they will not endure sound doctrine; but after their own lusts shall they heap to themselves teachers, having itching ears;

[4] and they shall turn away *their* ears from the truth, and shall be turned unto fables.

[5] But watch thou in all things, endure afflictions, do the work of an evangelist, make full proof of thy ministry.

[6] For I am now ready to be offered, and the time of my departure is at hand.

[7] I have fought a good fight, I have finished *my* course, I have kept the faith:

[8] henceforth there is laid up for me a crown of righteousness, which the Lord, the righteous judge, shall give me at that day: and not to me only, but unto all them also that love his appearing.

Personal Words

Do thy diligence to come shortly unto me:

[10] for Demas hath forsaken me, having loved this present world, and is departed unto Thessalonica; Crescens to Galatia, Titus unto Dalmatia.

[11] Only Luke is with me. Take Mark, and bring him with thee: for he is profitable to me for the ministry.

[12] And Tychicus have I sent to Ephesus.

[13] The cloak that I left at Troas with Carpus, when thou comest, bring *with thee*, and the books, *but* especially the parchments.

[14] Alexander the coppersmith did me much evil: the Lord reward him according to his works:

[15] of whom be thou ware also; for he hath greatly withstood our words.

[16] At my first answer no man stood with me, but all *men* forsook me: *I pray God* that it may not be laid to their charge.

[17] Notwithstanding the Lord stood with me, and strengthened me; that by me the preaching might be fully

known, and *that* all the Gentiles might hear: and I was delivered out of the mouth of the lion.

[18] And the Lord shall deliver me from every evil work, and will preserve *me* unto his heavenly kingdom: to whom *be* glory for ever and ever. Amen.

Final Greetings

Salute Prisca and Aquila, and the household of Onesiphorus.

[20] Erastus abode at Corinth: but Trophimus have I left at Miletus sick.

[21] Do thy diligence to come before winter. Eubulus greeteth thee, and Pudens, and Linus, and Claudia, and all the brethren.

[22] The Lord Jesus Christ *be* with thy spirit. Grace *be* with you. Amen.

OLD TESTAMENT READING

So they read in the book in the law of God distinctly, and gave the sense, and caused *them* to understand the reading.

[14] And they found written in the law which the LORD had commanded by Moses, that the children of Israel should dwell in booths in the feast of the seventh month:

[15] and that they should publish and proclaim in all their cities, and in Jerusalem, saying, Go forth unto the mount, and fetch olive branches, and pine branches, and myrtle branches, and palm branches, and branches of thick trees, to make booths, as *it is* written.

Nehemiah 8:8, 14–15

INSIGHTS

There are few joys like the joy of sudden discovery. Instantly, there is

forgotten the pain and expense of the search, the inconveniences, the hours, the sacrifices. Bathed in the ecstasy of discovery, time stands still. . . .

Solomon talks about the greatest discovery of all. . . .

"My son, if you will receive my sayings,
And treasure my commandments within you,
Make your ear attentive to wisdom,
Incline your heart to understanding;
For if you cry for discernment,
Lift your voice for understanding;
If you seek her as silver,
And search for her as for hidden treasures;
Then you will discern the fear of the LORD,
And discover the knowledge of God."

(Proverbs 2:1–5)

Talk about a discovery! Hidden in the Scriptures are priceless verbal vaults. Silent. Hard to find. Easy to miss if you're in a hurry. But they are there, awaiting discovery. God's Word, like a deep, deep mine, stands ready to yield its treasures.

Charles Swindoll

PAUSE FOR REFLECTION

What are the results of learning and obeying God's Word? What are the results of rejecting it? Have you discovered the rich treasures of God's Word for yourself?

WEEKEND

*God's Teachers Must Be
Blameless and Trustworthy*

Titus 1:1—2:8

1 Paul, a servant of God, and an apostle of Jesus Christ, according to the faith of God's elect, and the acknowledging of the truth which is after godliness;

2 in hope of eternal life, which God, that cannot lie, promised before the world began;

3 but hath in due times manifested his word through preaching, which is committed unto me according to the commandment of God our Saviour;

4 To Titus, *mine* own son after the common faith: Grace, mercy, *and* peace, from God the Father and the Lord Jesus Christ our Saviour.

Titus' Work in Crete

*F*or this cause left I thee in Crete, that thou shouldest set in order the things that are wanting, and ordain elders in every city, as I had appointed thee:

6 if any be blameless, the husband of one wife, having faithful children not accused of riot or unruly.

7 For a bishop must be blameless, as the steward of God; not self-willed, not soon angry, not given to wine, no striker, not given to filthy lucre;

8 but a lover of hospitality, a lover of good men, sober, just, holy, temperate;

9 holding fast the faithful word as he hath been taught, that he may be able by sound doctrine both to ex-

hort and to convince the gainsayers.

10 For there are many unruly and vain talkers and deceivers, specially they of the circumcision:

11 whose mouths must be stopped, who subvert whole houses, teaching things which they ought not, for filthy lucre's sake.

12 One of themselves, *even* a prophet of their own, said, The Cretians *are* always liars, evil beasts, slow bellies.

13 This witness is true. Wherefore rebuke them sharply, that they may be sound in the faith;

14 not giving heed to Jewish fables, and commandments of men, that turn from the truth.

15 Unto the pure all things *are* pure: but unto them that are defiled and unbelieving *is* nothing pure; but even their mind and conscience is defiled.

16 They profess that they know God; but in works they deny *him*, being abominable, and disobedient, and unto every good work reprobate.

Following Sound Doctrine

2 But speak thou the things which become sound doctrine:

2 that the aged men be sober, grave, temperate, sound in faith, in charity, in patience.

3 The aged women likewise, that *they be* in behavior as becometh holiness, not false accusers, not given to much wine, teachers of good things;

4 that they may teach the young women to be sober, to love their husbands, to love their children,

5 *to be* discreet, chaste, keepers at home, good, obedient to their own husbands, that the word of God be not blasphemed.

⁶Young men likewise exhort to be soberminded.

⁷In all things showing thyself a pattern of good works: in doctrine *showing* uncorruptness, gravity, sincerity,

⁸sound speech, that cannot be condemned; that he that is of the contrary part may be ashamed, having no evil thing to say of you.

OLD TESTAMENT READING

*T*hey shall therefore keep mine ordinance, lest they bear sin for it, and die therefore, if they profane it: I the LORD do sanctify them.

Leviticus 22:9

*F*or the priest's lips should keep knowledge, and they should seek the law at his mouth: for he *is* the messenger of the LORD of hosts.

⁸But ye are departed out of the way; ye have caused many to stumble at the law; ye have corrupted the covenant of Levi, saith the LORD of hosts.

⁹Therefore have I also made you contemptible and base before all the people according as ye have not kept my ways, but have been partial in the law.

Malachi 2:7–9

INSIGHTS

*L*uke recorded that believers from Lystra and Iconium "spoke well of him" (Acts 16:2). In other words Timothy had a good reputation as a Christian. He was "blameless" in the eyes of those in the Christian community. There were no specific flaws in his life that would bring reproach to the cause of Christ. So Paul invited Timothy to be his missionary companion, and this resulted in a deep, lasting relationship and ministry together.

Titus was also this kind of man. Mature in many ways, he maintained pure motives, evidencing compassion and concern for people (2 Cor. 8:16) and demonstrating a positive attitude toward the ministry (v. 17). There is no better way in which to develop a good reputation among Christians and non-Christians alike.

Be blameless. This quality and the other qualifications for elders are standards all of us should strive for, whether we are in positions of church leadership or not.

Gene Getz

ACTION POINT

*W*hy is it essential that those who teach others in the ways of God be blameless? How much do you want to be the kind of Christian Paul describes as an 'elder'? What changes must you make to be blameless and trustworthy? Are you willing?

MONDAY

Our Lives Are
a Testimony to God

Titus 2:9—3:15

*E*xhort servants to be obedient unto their own masters, *and* to please *them* well in all things; not answering again;

¹⁰ not purloining, but showing all good fidelity; that they may adorn the doctrine of God our Saviour in all things.

¹¹ For the grace of God that bringeth salvation hath appeared to all men,

¹² teaching us that, denying ungodliness and worldly lusts, we should live soberly, righteously, and godly, in this present world;

¹³ looking for that blessed hope, and the glorious appearing of the great God and our Saviour Jesus Christ;

¹⁴ who gave himself for us, that he might redeem us from all iniquity, and purify unto himself a peculiar people, zealous of good works.

¹⁵ These things speak, and exhort, and rebuke with all authority. Let no man despise thee.

The Right Way to Live

3 Put them in mind to be subject to principalities and powers, to obey magistrates, to be ready to every good work,

² to speak evil of no man, to be no brawlers, *but* gentle, showing all meekness unto all men.

³ For we ourselves also were sometimes foolish, disobedient, deceived, serving divers lusts and pleasures, living in malice and envy, hateful, *and* hating one another.

⁴ But after that the kindness and love of God our Saviour toward man appeared,

⁵ not by works of righteousness which we have done, but according to his mercy he saved us, by the washing of regeneration, and renewing of the Holy Ghost;

⁶ which he shed on us abundantly through Jesus Christ our Saviour;

⁷ that being justified by his grace, we should be made heirs according to the hope of eternal life.

⁸ *This is* a faithful saying, and these things I will that thou affirm constantly, that they which have believed in God might be careful to maintain good works. These things are good and profitable unto men.

⁹ But avoid foolish questions, and genealogies, and contentions, and strivings about the law; for they are unprofitable and vain.

¹⁰ A man that is a heretic, after the first and second admonition, reject;

¹¹ knowing that he that is such is subverted, and sinneth, being condemned of himself.

Some Things to Remember

*W*hen I shall send Artemas unto thee, or Tychicus, be diligent to come unto me to Nicopolis: for I have determined there to winter.

¹³ Bring Zenas the lawyer and Apollos on their journey diligently, that nothing be wanting unto them.

¹⁴ And let ours also learn to maintain good works for necessary uses, that they be not unfruitful.

¹⁵ All that are with me salute thee. Greet them that love us in the faith. Grace *be* with you all. Amen.

*T*hen said Daniel unto the king, O king, live for ever.

22 My God hath sent his angel, and hath shut the lions' mouths, that they have not hurt me: forasmuch as before him innocency was found in me; and also before thee, O king, have I done no hurt.

25 Then king Darius wrote unto all people, nations, and languages, that dwell in all the earth; Peace be multiplied unto you.

26 I make a decree, That in every dominion of my kingdom men tremble and fear before the God of Daniel: for he *is* the living God, and steadfast for ever, and his kingdom *that* which shall not be destroyed, and his dominion *shall be even* unto the end.

27 He delivereth and rescueth, and he worketh signs and wonders in heaven and in earth, who hath delivered Daniel from the power of the lions.

Daniel 6:21–22, 25–27

INSIGHTS

*I*f you are a publisher or a pastor, a ditch-digger or a pilot, a fisherman or a fruit grower, a garage mechanic or a furniture maker, a writer or a homemaker, an office worker or a congressman . . . there are unique things involved in your moment-by-moment work since you are a child of the Creator of the universe. . . .

You are to do well, whatever you are doing, to the glory of God (see 1 Peter 4:11). Just as flowers that grow on the Alpine peaks, beauty in the cracks of rocks with perhaps no one ever passing that way, are not growing in vain because God sees

them, so it is true of the human being. A person may live alone, walk alone, and feel that no one is recognizing that he or she is being patient in the tribulation of loneliness . . . but God does know, and is aware of the whisper, "I love you, God. Please accept my praise as I walk alone today." This is true of people in prisons, in concentration camps, in hospital beds, or in wheelchairs. . . . "Work" to the glory of God can be done in every part of life . . . which is what makes it all so fair. No one gets a bigger opportunity than another. And no one is "out of work"!

Edith Schaeffer

PAUSE FOR REFLECTION

*W*hat kind of people are we without Jesus? What kind of people does his death make us? How are believers supposed to use their lives? Who do you know who truly lives like a servant of the living God?

TUESDAY

All People Are Valuable in God's Eyes

Philemon 1–25

A Slave Becomes a Christian

1 Paul, a prisoner of Jesus Christ, and Timothy *our* brother, unto Philemon our dearly beloved, and fellow laborer,

2 and to *our* beloved Apphia, and Archippus our fellow soldier, and to the church in thy house:

3 Grace to you, and peace, from God our Father and the Lord Jesus Christ.

Philemon's Love and Faith

I thank my God, making mention of thee always in my prayers,

5 hearing of thy love and faith, which thou hast toward the Lord Jesus, and toward all saints;

6 that the communication of thy faith may become effectual by the acknowledging of every good thing which is in you in Christ Jesus.

7 For we have great joy and consolation in thy love, because the bowels of the saints are refreshed by thee, brother.

Accept Onesimus as a Brother

*W*herefore, though I might be much bold in Christ to enjoin thee that which is convenient,

9 yet for love's sake I rather beseech *thee*, being such a one as Paul the aged, and now also a prisoner of Jesus Christ.

10 I beseech thee for my son Ones-imus, whom I have begotten in my bonds:

11 which in time past was to thee unprofitable, but now profitable to thee and to me:

12 whom I have sent again: thou therefore receive him, that is, mine own bowels:

13 whom I would have retained with me, that in thy stead he might have ministered unto me in the bonds of the gospel:

14 but without thy mind would I do nothing; that thy benefit should not be as it were of necessity, but willingly.

15 For perhaps he therefore departed for a season, that thou shouldest receive him for ever;

16 not now as a servant, but above a servant, a brother beloved, specially to me, but how much more unto thee, both in the flesh, and in the Lord?

17 If thou count me therefore a partner, receive him as myself.

18 If he hath wronged thee, or oweth *thee* ought, put that on mine account;

19 I Paul have written *it* with mine own hand, I will repay *it*: albeit I do not say to thee how thou owest unto me even thine own self besides.

20 Yea, brother, let me have joy of thee in the Lord: refresh my bowels in the Lord.

21 Having confidence in thy obedience I wrote unto thee, knowing that thou wilt also do more than I say.

22 But withal prepare me also a lodging: for I trust that through your prayers I shall be given unto you.

Final Greetings

*T*here salute thee Epaphras, my fellow prisoner in Christ Jesus;

24 Mark, Aristarchus, Demas, Luke, my fellow laborers.

²⁵ The grace of our Lord Jesus Christ *be* with your spirit. Amen.

*A*nd Pharaoh said unto Joseph, Forasmuch as God hath showed thee all this, *there is* none so discreet and wise as thou *art*:
⁴⁰ thou shalt be over my house, and according unto thy word shall all my people be ruled: only in the throne will I be greater than thou.
⁴² And Pharaoh took off his ring from his hand, and put it upon Joseph's hand, and arrayed him in vestures of fine linen, and put a gold chain about his neck;
⁴³ and he made him to ride in the second chariot which he had; and they cried before him, Bow the knee: and he made him *ruler* over all the land of Egypt.

Genesis 41:39–40, 42–43

*A*nd Joseph said unto his brethren, Come near to me, I pray you. And they came near. And he said, I *am* Joseph your brother, whom ye sold into Egypt.
⁵ Now therefore be not grieved, nor angry with yourselves, that ye sold me hither: for God did send me before you to preserve life.
⁹ Haste ye, and go up to my father, and say unto him, Thus saith thy son Joseph, God hath made me lord of all Egypt: come down unto me, tarry not:
¹⁰ and thou shalt dwell in the land of Goshen, and thou shalt be near unto me, thou, and thy children, and thy children's children, and thy flocks, and thy herds, and all that thou hast:
¹¹ and there will I nourish thee; for yet *there are* five years of famine; lest

thou, and thy household, and all that thou hast, come to poverty.
¹⁵ Moreover he kissed all his brethren, and wept upon them: and after that his brethren talked with him.

Genesis 45:4–5, 9–11, 15

INSIGHTS

*A*re you still running around trying to milk acceptance and self-esteem out of the world like lost people when you've already got both? Are you still employing the same old methods, such as trying to perform up to your flesh's standards to generate and maintain self-esteem moment by moment? You are of infinite worth. You are accepted. Not by people, perhaps, but of God! If you're rejected by certain people, welcome to the club. So was Jesus. But He didn't go around with His head down. Why? Because He knew it's not a feeling that matters; it's what you know. He knew He was accepted.

Do you know that? . . . You are not to strive to get love; we don't live that way. We live from a posture of knowing that we are loved.

. . . You can accept yourself now as the new person you truly are in Him, just as the Father accepts you—perfectly.

Bill Gillham

PAUSE FOR REFLECTION

*I*n biblical times, who had less value than a slave? In what ways did God affirm the value of Joseph and Onesimus? How was each one received? Who do you need to accept as a beloved brother or sister before God?

WEDNESDAY

God Has Given Us a Great Salvation

Hebrews 1:1—2:4

God Spoke Through His Son

1 God, who at sundry times and in divers manners spake in time past unto the fathers by the prophets,

2 hath in these last days spoken unto us by *his* Son, whom he hath appointed heir of all things, by whom also he made the worlds;

3 who being the brightness of *his* glory, and the express image of his person, and upholding all things by the word of his power, when he had by himself purged our sins, sat down on the right hand of the Majesty on high;

4 being made so much better than the angels, as he hath by inheritance obtained a more excellent name than they.

5 For unto which of the angels said he at any time, Thou art my Son, this day have I begotten thee? And again, I will be to him a Father, and he shall be to me a Son?

6 And again, when he bringeth in the first-begotten into the world, he saith, And let all the angels of God worship him.

7 And of the angels he saith, Who maketh his angels spirits, and his ministers a flame of fire.

8 But unto the Son *he saith*, Thy throne, O God, *is* for ever and ever: a sceptre of righteousness *is* the sceptre of thy kingdom.

9 Thou hast loved righteousness, and hated iniquity; therefore God, *even*

thy God, hath anointed thee with the oil of gladness above thy fellows.

10 And, Thou, Lord, in the beginning hast laid the foundation of the earth; and the heavens are the works of thine hands.

11 They shall perish, but thou remainest: and they all shall wax old as doth a garment;

12 and as a vesture shalt thou fold them up, and they shall be changed: but thou art the same, and thy years shall not fail.

13 But to which of the angels said he at any time, Sit on my right hand, until I make thine enemies thy footstool?

14 Are they not all ministering spirits, sent forth to minister for them who shall be heirs of salvation?

Our Salvation Is Great

2 Therefore we ought to give the more earnest heed to the things which we have heard, lest at any time we should let *them* slip.

2 For if the word spoken by angels was steadfast, and every transgression and disobedience received a just recompense of reward;

3 how shall we escape, if we neglect so great salvation; which at the first began to be spoken by the Lord, and was confirmed unto us by them that heard *him*;

4 God also bearing *them* witness, both with signs and wonders, and with divers miracles, and gifts of the Holy Ghost, according to his own will?

OLD TESTAMENT READING

I will sing unto the LORD, for he hath triumphed gloriously: the horse and

his rider hath he thrown into the sea.
[2] The LORD *is* my strength and song, and he is become my salvation: he *is* my God, and I will prepare him a habitation; my father's God, and I will exalt him.

Exodus 15:1b–2

*T*each me thy way, O LORD; I will walk in thy truth: unite my heart to fear thy name.
[12] I will praise thee, O Lord my God, with all my heart: and I will glorify thy name for evermore.
[13] For great *is* thy mercy toward me: and thou hast delivered my soul from the lowest hell.

Psalm 86:11–13

INSIGHTS

*O*ur salvation is good reason to rejoice. Hannah rejoiced because of salvation in a song that Mary echoed when Jesus was born and salvation had come. The magi rejoiced when they saw the star that led them to the infant Jesus and salvation (Matthew 2:10). The Ethiopian eunuch rejoiced in the discovery of salvation through Philip's ministry of the Word (Acts 8:39). Christians rejoice in hope and even in suffering since they have peace with God (Romans 5:2–3).

Rejoicing and salvation belong together. The coming of Jesus into this world can never be a matter of academic aloofness or objective study. Because it is real and because it means so much it goes right to the heart to make it leap with joy. It is the emotion felt when a woman finds a lost coin or a shepherd finds a lost sheep or a waiting Father sees his lost son on the horizon (read

Luke 15). It is not like a student poring over a book in the library. It is more like a student with a thousand others, rejoicing over a touchdown on the field. It is like oil drillers watching their first wild fountain of black gold after days of hard and fruitless labor. It is a soldier seeing a light in the window or a returning prisoner finding yellow ribbons tied all over the tree. In prayer let us remember all the joy we have drawn from the wells of salvation. It should make quite a list.*

William Stoddard

ACTION POINT

*I*f you risk living as if salvation were unimportant, take notice! What makes salvation great? Who revealed it? Who has proven it? Throughout the ages, God's people have rejoiced and celebrated his salvation. Go ahead, be amazed, and join them in praising God for his salvation!*

THURSDAY

*Jesus, Our Savior,
Makes His People Holy*

Hebrews 2:5—3:6

Christ Became like Humans

*F*or unto the angels hath he not put in subjection the world to come, whereof we speak.

[6] But one in a certain place testified, saying, What is man, that thou art mindful of him? or the son of man, that thou visitest him?

[7] Thou madest him a little lower than the angels; thou crownedst him with glory and honor, and didst set him over the works of thy hands:

[8] thou hast put all things in subjection under his feet. For in that he put all in subjection under him, he left nothing *that is* not put under him. But now we see not yet all things put under him.

[9] But we see Jesus, who was made a little lower than the angels for the suffering of death, crowned with glory and honor; that he by the grace of God should taste death for every man.

[10] For it became him, for whom *are* all things, and by whom *are* all things, in bringing many sons unto glory, to make the captain of their salvation perfect through sufferings.

[11] For both he that sanctifieth and they who are sanctified *are* all of one: for which cause he is not ashamed to call them brethren,

[12] saying, I will declare thy name unto my brethren, in the midst of the church will I sing praise unto thee.

[13] And again, I will put my trust in him. And again, Behold I and the children which God hath given me.

[14] Forasmuch then as the children are partakers of flesh and blood, he also himself likewise took part of the same; that through death he might destroy him that had the power of death, that is, the devil;

[15] and deliver them who through fear of death were all their lifetime subject to bondage.

[16] For verily he took not on *him the nature of* angels; but he took on *him* the seed of Abraham.

[17] Wherefore in all things it behooved him to be made like unto *his* brethren, that he might be a merciful and faithful high priest in things *pertaining* to God, to make reconciliation for the sins of the people.

[18] For in that he himself hath suffered being tempted, he is able to succor them that are tempted.

Jesus Is Greater than Moses

3 Wherefore, holy brethren, partakers of the heavenly calling, consider the Apostle and High Priest of our profession, Christ Jesus;

[2] who was faithful to him that appointed him, as also Moses *was faithful* in all his house.

[3] For this *man* was counted worthy of more glory than Moses, inasmuch as he who hath builded the house hath more honor than the house.

[4] For every house is builded by some *man*; but he that built all things *is* God.

[5] And Moses verily *was* faithful in all his house as a servant, for a testimony of those things which were to be spoken after;

[6] but Christ as a son over his own house; whose house are we, if we hold fast the confidence and the rejoicing of the hope firm unto the end.

*A*nd I will make them one nation in the land upon the mountains of Israel; and one king shall be king to them all: and they shall be no more two nations, neither shall they be divided into two kingdoms any more at all:

23b but I will save them out of all their dwelling places, wherein they have sinned, and will cleanse them: so shall they be my people, and I will be their God.

24 And David my servant *shall be* king over them; and they all shall have one shepherd: they shall also walk in my judgments, and observe my statutes, and do them.

25 And they shall dwell in the land that I have given unto Jacob my servant, wherein your fathers have dwelt; and they shall dwell therein, *even* they, and their children, and their children's children for ever: and my servant David *shall be* their prince for ever.

26 Moreover I will make a covenant of peace with them; it shall be an everlasting covenant with them: and I will place them, and multiply them, and will set my sanctuary in the midst of them for evermore.

27 My tabernacle also shall be with them: yea, I will be their God, and they shall be my people.

28 And the heathen shall know that I the LORD do sanctify Israel, when my sanctuary shall be in the midst of them for evermore.

Ezekiel 37:22, 23b–28

INSIGHTS

*C*hrist in us can manifest His holiness if we will yield our flesh to Him. This is not a human operation; it is a spiritual one. Jesus installs His holiness in us by grace. Not a once-for-all-time transaction, this is a daily, moment-by-moment striving to live more by the Spirit and less by the flesh.

Though becoming more holy is God's work in us, it is not a passive enterprise. Our part is active, to strive and strain toward the high calling we have received. God's part is to forgive our failings based on the merit of Christ's atoning death.

His will is that we become holy. . . . This kind of holiness is not the result of our own best effort. . . .

The forgiveness of Christ makes us holy; He washed away our sin. In reality, God in us—the Holy Spirit—makes us holy. There is no possibility of holiness apart from His grace. He calls us, He justifies us, He sanctifies us (makes us holy), and He will glorify us—all by His grace.

Our part is to surrender in faith; God's part is to implant the sanctifying Holy Spirit in us. "So I say, live by the Spirit, and you will not gratify the desires of the sinful nature" (Galatians 5:16). Because of His everlasting love, we know Him, and He is faithful to mold us into the character of His Son Jesus Christ—to make us holy.

Patrick Morley

ACTION POINT

*M*editate on what Jesus did to make his people holy. How significant is it that Jesus considers his holy people to be his family—his brothers? How do these truths inspire you to yield to his holiness?

FRIDAY

*God Demands Obedience
and Punishes Unbelief*

Hebrews 3:7—4:13

We Must Continue to Follow God

Wherefore as the Holy Ghost saith, Today if ye will hear his voice, [8] harden not your hearts, as in the provocation, in the day of temptation in the wilderness:

[9] when your fathers tempted me, proved me, and saw my works forty years.

[10] Wherefore I was grieved with that generation, and said, They do always err in *their* heart; and they have not known my ways.

[11] So I sware in my wrath, They shall not enter into my rest.

[12] Take heed, brethren, lest there be in any of you an evil heart of unbelief, in departing from the living God.

[13] But exhort one another daily, while it is called Today; lest any of you be hardened through the deceitfulness of sin.

[14] For we are made partakers of Christ, if we hold the beginning of our confidence steadfast unto the end;

[15] while it is said, Today if ye will hear his voice, harden not your hearts, as in the provocation.

[16] For some, when they had heard, did provoke: howbeit not all that came out of Egypt by Moses.

[17] But with whom was he grieved forty years? *was it* not with them that had sinned, whose carcasses fell in the wilderness?

[18] And to whom sware he that they should not enter into his rest, but to them that believed not?

[19] So we see that they could not enter in because of unbelief.

4 Let us therefore fear, lest, a promise being left *us* of entering into his rest, any of you should seem to come short of it.

[2] For unto us was the gospel preached, as well as unto them: but the word preached did not profit them, not being mixed with faith in them that heard *it*.

[3] For we which have believed do enter into rest, as he said, As I have sworn in my wrath, if they shall enter into my rest: although the works were finished from the foundation of the world.

[4] For he spake in a certain place of the seventh *day* on this wise, And God did rest the seventh day from all his works.

[5] And in this *place* again, If they shall enter into my rest.

[6] Seeing therefore it remaineth that some must enter therein, and they to whom it was first preached entered not in because of unbelief:

[7] again, he limiteth a certain day, saying in David, Today, after so long a time; as it is said, Today if ye will hear his voice, harden not your hearts.

[8] For if Jesus had given them rest, then would he not afterward have spoken of another day.

[9] There remaineth therefore a rest to the people of God.

[10] For he that is entered into his rest, he also hath ceased from his own works, as *God* did from his.

[11] Let us labor therefore to enter into that rest, lest any man fall after the same example of unbelief.

[12] For the word of God *is* quick, and

powerful, and sharper than any two-edged sword, piercing even to the dividing asunder of soul and spirit, and of the joints and marrow, and *is* a discerner of the thoughts and intents of the heart.

[13] Neither is there any creature that is not manifest in his sight: but all things *are* naked and opened unto the eyes of him with whom we have to do.

OLD TESTAMENT READING

*I*f the LORD delight in us, then he will bring us into this land, and give it us; a land which floweth with milk and honey.

[9] Only rebel not ye against the LORD, neither fear ye the people of the land; for they *are* bread for us: their defense is departed from them, and the LORD *is* with us: fear them not.

[20] And the LORD said, I have pardoned according to thy word:

[21] but *as* truly *as* I live, all the earth shall be filled with the glory of the LORD.

[22] Because all those men which have seen my glory, and my miracles, which I did in Egypt and in the wilderness, and have tempted me now these ten times, and have not hearkened to my voice;

[23] surely they shall not see the land which I sware unto their fathers, neither shall any of them that provoked me see it.

Numbers 14:8–9, 20–23

INSIGHTS

*H*ow do we find God and grow in him? Jesus was adamant at this point. He said we must do what he says. We must put into practical obe-dience the knowledge that we have. He continually asked people to drop their nets, to sell all they had and to follow him.

We might say that Jesus had a theology of obedience. And the object of this obedience was a living person, not a historical norm, not a code of laws, but himself. He called people to be accountable to God whether they were believers or skeptics who were searching. For example, he told his disciples, "What is the point of calling me, 'Lord, Lord,' without doing what I tell you to do?" (Lk. 6:46 Phillips). . . .

Jesus knew that obedience to his and his Father's words yielded faith. . . . If I had to sum up one's response to the gospel message, I would say as William Pannell has said, "It's paint—or get off the ladder." Jesus approached people exactly like that. He told them to pick up their brush and paint something.

Do you want to discover who Jesus is and deal honestly with your doubts? Jesus' style is not to suggest that you go and ponder the virgin birth for three months but to begin doing what he says.

Rebecca Pippert

APPLICATION

*W*hat does an unbelieving heart lead us to do? What is the relationship between obedience and belief? When our life is over, what will God ask us to explain? Are you ready to answer him?

WEEKEND

Jesus Is Our High Priest

Hebrews 4:14—6:8

Seeing then that we have a great high priest, that is passed into the heavens, Jesus the Son of God, let us hold fast *our* profession.

15 For we have not a high priest which cannot be touched with the feeling of our infirmities; but was in all points tempted like as *we are, yet* without sin.

16 Let us therefore come boldly unto the throne of grace, that we may obtain mercy, and find grace to help in time of need.

5 For every high priest taken from among men is ordained for men in things *pertaining* to God, that he may offer both gifts and sacrifices for sins:

2 who can have compassion on the ignorant, and on them that are out of the way; for that he himself also is compassed with infirmity.

3 And by reason hereof he ought, as for the people, so also for himself, to offer for sins.

4 And no man taketh this honor unto himself, but he that is called of God, as *was* Aaron.

5 So also Christ glorified not himself to be made a high priest; but he that said unto him, Thou art my Son, today have I begotten thee.

6 As he saith also in another *place*, Thou *art* a priest for ever after the order of Melchizedek.

7 Who in the days of his flesh, when he had offered up prayers and supplications with strong crying and tears unto him that was able to save him from death, and was heard in that he feared;

8 though he were a Son, yet learned he obedience by the things which he suffered;

9 and being made perfect, he became the author of eternal salvation unto all them that obey him;

10 called of God an high priest after the order of Melchizedek.

Warning Against Falling Away

Of whom we have many things to say, and hard to be uttered, seeing ye are dull of hearing.

12 For when for the time ye ought to be teachers, ye have need that one teach you again which *be* the first principles of the oracles of God; and are become such as have need of milk, and not of strong meat.

13 For every one that useth milk *is* unskilful in the word of righteousness: for he is a babe.

14 But strong meat belongeth to them that are of full age, *even* those who by reason of use have their senses exercised to discern both good and evil.

6 Therefore leaving the principles of the doctrine of Christ, let us go on unto perfection; not laying again the foundation of repentance from dead works, and of faith toward God,

2 of the doctrine of baptisms, and of laying on of hands, and of resurrection of the dead, and of eternal judgment.

3 And this will we do, if God permit.

4 For *it is* impossible for those who were once enlightened, and have tasted of the heavenly gift, and were made partakers of the Holy Ghost,

5 and have tasted the good word of

God, and the powers of the world to come,

⁶ if they shall fall away, to renew them again unto repentance; seeing they crucify to themselves the Son of God afresh, and put *him* to an open shame.

⁷ For the earth which drinketh in the rain that cometh oft upon it, and bringeth forth herbs meet for them by whom it is dressed, receiveth blessing from God:

⁸ but that which beareth thorns and briers *is* rejected, and *is* nigh unto cursing; whose end *is* to be burned.

OLD TESTAMENT READING

God Chooses Priests for His Holy Work

*A*nd take thou unto thee Aaron thy brother, and his sons with him, from among the children of Israel, that he may minister unto me in the priest's office, *even* Aaron, Nadab and Abihu, Eleazar and Ithamar, Aaron's sons.

² And thou shalt make holy garments for Aaron thy brother, for glory and for beauty.

³ And thou shalt speak unto all *that are* wise-hearted, whom I have filled with the spirit of wisdom, that they may make Aaron's garments to consecrate him, that he may minister unto me in the priest's office.

Exodus 28:1–3

INSIGHTS

*A*t one time in history a "NO ACCESS" sign was posted at the gates of Paradise. Even in the Old Testament temple there was no access to the throne of God by the ordinary person. Even for the High Priest his access was "limited" to once a year under very guarded circumstances. A thick veil separated the Holy of Holies from the rest of the temple. It was off-limits. Restricted. No admission was permitted to the rank-and-file believer.

The moment Jesus was slain, the instant the Just One died for the unjust, the veil in the temple was torn. The presence of God became accessible to us. For the Christian the "NO ACCESS" sign was removed from the gates of Paradise. We may now trespass freely on holy ground. We have access to His grace, but even more, we have access to Him. Justified men need no longer say to the Holy, "Depart from me, for I am a sinful man." Now we can be comfortable in the presence of a holy God. We can take our questions to Him. He is not too remote to hear our cries. We come as those covered by the righteousness of Christ. I repeat: We can be comfortable in the presence of God. To be sure we still come in awe, in a spirit of reverence and adoration, but the tremendous news is that we can . . . approach the throne of grace with confidence.

R. C. Sproul

PAUSE FOR REFLECTION

*F*rom the Old Testament reading, do you begin to sense the vital role of God's priests? In what ways does your understanding of Christ's role as high priest (explained in Hebrews) help you realize how much he has done to save us?

529

MONDAY

God's Word Is True:
He Keeps His Promises

Hebrews 6:9—7:10

*B*ut, beloved, we are persuaded better things of you, and things that accompany salvation, though we thus speak.

[10] For God *is* not unrighteous to forget your work and labour of love, which ye have showed toward his name, in that ye have ministered to the saints, and do minister.

[11] And we desire that every one of you do show the same diligence to the full assurance of hope unto the end:

[12] that ye be not slothful, but followers of them who through faith and patience inherit the promises.

[13] For when God made promise to Abraham, because he could swear by no greater, he sware by himself,

[14] saying, Surely blessing I will bless thee, and multiplying I will multiply thee.

[15] And so, after he had patiently endured, he obtained the promise.

[16] For men verily swear by the greater: and an oath for confirmation *is* to them an end of all strife.

[17] Wherein God, willing more abundantly to show unto the heirs of promise the immutability of his counsel, confirmed *it* by an oath:

[18] that by two immutable things, in which *it was* impossible for God to lie, we might have a strong consolation, who have fled for refuge to lay hold upon the hope set before us:

[19] which *hope* we have as an anchor of the soul, both sure and steadfast, and which entereth into that within the veil;

[20] whither the forerunner is for us entered, *even* Jesus, made an high priest for ever after the order of Melchizedek.

The Priest Melchizedek

7 For this Melchizedek, king of Salem, priest of the most high God, who met Abraham returning from the slaughter of the kings, and blessed him;

[2] to whom also Abraham gave a tenth part of all; first being by interpretation King of righteousness, and after that also King of Salem, which is, King of peace;

[3] without father, without mother, without descent, having neither beginning of days, nor end of life; but made like unto the Son of God; abideth a priest continually.

[4] Now consider how great this man *was*, unto whom even the patriarch Abraham gave the tenth of the spoils.

[5] And verily they that are of the sons of Levi, who receive the office of the priesthood, have a commandment to take tithes of the people according to the law, that is, of their brethren, though they come out of the loins of Abraham:

[6] but he whose descent is not counted from them received tithes of Abraham, and blessed him that had the promises.

[7] And without all contradiction the less is blessed of the better.

[8] And here men that die receive tithes; but there he *receiveth them*, of whom it is witnessed that he liveth.

[9] And as I may so say, Levi also, who receiveth tithes, paid tithes in Abraham.

¹⁰ For he was yet in the loins of his father, when Melchizedek met him.

OLD TESTAMENT READING

*A*nd the LORD your God, he shall expel them from before you, and drive them from out of your sight; and ye shall possess their land, as the LORD your God hath promised unto you.

⁶ Be ye therefore very courageous to keep and to do all that is written in the book of the law of Moses, that ye turn not aside therefrom *to* the right hand or *to* the left.

¹⁴ And, behold, this day I *am* going the way of all the earth: and ye know in all your hearts and in all your souls, that not one thing hath failed of all the good things which the LORD your God spake concerning you; all are come to pass unto you, *and* not one thing hath failed thereof.

¹⁵ Therefore it shall come to pass, *that* as all good things are come upon you, which the LORD your God promised you; so shall the LORD bring upon you all evil things, until he have destroyed you from off this good land which the LORD your God hath given you.

¹⁶ When ye have transgressed the covenant of the LORD your God, which he commanded you, and have gone and served other gods, and bowed yourselves to them; then shall the anger of the LORD be kindled against you, and ye shall perish quickly from off the good land which he hath given unto you.

Joshua 23:5–6, 14–16

INSIGHTS

*T*he Bible is filled with the promises of God. We need to claim each one by faith and activate its truth in our lives. Some folks like to say, "If God said it, I believe it, and that settles it!" The fact of the matter is, if God said it, that settles it, whether we believe it or not.

Someone will question, "How can I be sure God really said this?" or, "How can I be sure this is what it means?" I realize we must interpret each promise in its proper context. But I also believe that we need to take those promises which apply to us and activate them by faith.

In Hebrews 4:3, we read an amazing truth. It says there that God's works were "finished from the foundation of the world." In other words, God had already provided the answer to your every need before the world was ever formed. With His divine foreknowledge He looked down the corridor of time to come, saw your coming problem and provided just exactly what you would need. . . .

. . . Think on the majesty and magnitude of God. Focus on the promises He has given you in His Word. Turn your attention to fulfilling His purpose for your life. Live in the confidence that He is in control. Now you can relax, for there is nothing to worry about. God cares and He keeps His promises to help.

Richard Lee

APPLICATION

*W*hat about God's character encourages us to trust in his promises? Of what did Joshua remind the Israelites before he died? Why is it important to remember that God keeps his promises? Will you remember to live by his promises?

TUESDAY

Jesus Is the High Priest of God's New Covenant

Hebrews 7:11—8:6

*I*f therefore perfection were by the Levitical priesthood, (for under it the people received the law,) what further need *was there* that another priest should rise after the order of Melchizedek, and not be called after the order of Aaron?
¹² For the priesthood being changed, there is made of necessity a change also of the law.
¹³ For he of whom these things are spoken pertaineth to another tribe, of which no man gave attendance at the altar.
¹⁴ For *it is* evident that our Lord sprang out of Judah; of which tribe Moses spake nothing concerning priesthood.

Jesus Is like Melchizedek

*A*nd it is yet far more evident: for that after the similitude of Melchizedek there ariseth another priest,
¹⁶ who is made, not after the law of a carnal commandment, but after the power of an endless life.
¹⁷ For he testifieth, Thou *art* a priest for ever after the order of Melchizedek.
¹⁸ For there is verily a disannulling of the commandment going before for the weakness and unprofitableness thereof.
¹⁹ For the law made nothing perfect, but the bringing in of a bet-

ter hope *did*; by the which we draw nigh unto God.
²⁰ And inasmuch as not without an oath *he was made priest*:
²¹ (for those priests were made without an oath; but this with an oath by him that said unto him, The Lord sware and will not repent, Thou *art* a priest for ever after the order of Melchizedek:)
²² by so much was Jesus made a surety of a better testament.
²³ And they truly were many priests, because they were not suffered to continue by reason of death:
²⁴ but this *man*, because he continueth ever, hath an unchangeable priesthood.
²⁵ Wherefore he is able also to save them to the uttermost that come unto God by him, seeing he ever liveth to make intercession for them.
²⁶ For such a high priest became us, *who is* holy, harmless, undefiled, separate from sinners, and made higher than the heavens;
²⁷ who needeth not daily, as those high priests, to offer up sacrifice, first for his own sins, and then for the people's: for this he did once, when he offered up himself.
²⁸ For the law maketh men high priests which have infirmity; but the word of the oath, which was since the law, *maketh* the Son, who is consecrated for evermore.

Jesus Is Our High Priest

8 Now of the things which we have spoken *this is* the sum: We have such a high priest, who is set on the right hand of the throne of the Majesty in the heavens;

[2] a minister of the sanctuary, and of the true tabernacle, which the Lord pitched, and not man.

[3] For every high priest is ordained to offer gifts and sacrifices: wherefore *it is* of necessity that this man have somewhat also to offer.

[4] For if he were on earth, he should not be a priest, seeing that there are priests that offer gifts according to the law:

[5] who serve unto the example and shadow of heavenly things, as Moses was admonished of God when he was about to make the tabernacle: for, See, saith he, *that* thou make all things according to the pattern showed to thee in the mount.

[6] But now hath he obtained a more excellent ministry, by how much also he is the mediator of a better covenant, which was established upon better promises.

OLD TESTAMENT READING

*T*he LORD said unto my Lord, Sit thou at my right hand, until I make thine enemies thy footstool.

[2] The LORD shall send the rod of thy strength out of Zion: rule thou in the midst of thine enemies.

[3] Thy people *shall be* willing in the day of thy power, in the beauties of holiness from the womb of the morning: thou hast the dew of thy youth.

[4] The LORD hath sworn, and will not repent, Thou *art* a priest for ever after the order of Melchizedek.

Psalm 110:1–4

*B*ut this *shall be* the covenant that I will make with the house of Israel; After those days, saith the LORD, I will put my law in their inward parts, and write it in their hearts; and will be their God, and they shall be my people.

Jeremiah 31:33

INSIGHTS

*W*e need a priest such as Jesus is, to represent us in heaven. Although we are so completely absolved from guilt, and so fully "accepted in the beloved", yet in ourselves, while down here, we are still erring, sinning, feeble, needy creatures, exposed to trials and temptations, liable to stumble, and encompassed by infirmities. How we need the high priestly mediation of our dear heavenly Advocate, whose presence yonder keeps us in all the benefits of the New Covenant, maintains our standing in grace, and releases to us the paraclete ministries of the Holy Spirit. It has been well said, "We could not stand for a moment down here, if He were not living for us up there."

Thank God, "we have such an high priest"!

J. Sydlow Baxter

ACTION POINT

*I*dentify the unique aspects of Christ's priesthood and describe why his unique role as high priest is significant. Pray now and thank God that he has sent a high priest— like no other— to offer the only perfect sacrifice for your sins.

WEDNESDAY
Jesus Takes Away Our Sins Forever

Hebrews 8:7—9:12

*F*or if that first *covenant* had been faultless, then should no place have been sought for the second.

⁸ For finding fault with them, he saith, Behold, the days come, saith the Lord, when I will make a new covenant with the house of Israel and with the house of Judah:

⁹ not according to the covenant that I made with their fathers, in the day when I took them by the hand to lead them out of the land of Egypt; because they continued not in my covenant, and I regarded them not, saith the Lord.

¹⁰ For this *is* the covenant that I will make with the house of Israel after those days, saith the Lord; I will put my laws into their mind, and write them in their hearts: and I will be to them a God, and they shall be to me a people:

¹¹ and they shall not teach every man his neighbor, and every man his brother, saying, Know the Lord: for all shall know me, from the least to the greatest.

¹² For I will be merciful to their unrighteousness, and their sins and their iniquities will I remember no more.

¹³ In that he saith, A new *covenant*, he hath made the first old. Now that which decayeth and waxeth old *is* ready to vanish away.

The Old Covenant

9 Then verily the first *covenant* had also ordinances of divine service, and a worldly sanctuary.

² For there was a tabernacle made; the first, wherein *was* the candlestick, and the table, and the showbread; which is called the sanctuary.

³ And after the second veil, the tabernacle which is called the holiest of all;

⁴ which had the golden censer, and the ark of the covenant overlaid round about with gold, wherein *was* the golden pot that had manna, and Aaron's rod that budded, and the tables of the covenant;

⁵ and over it the cherubims of glory shadowing the mercy seat; of which we cannot now speak particularly.

⁶ Now when these things were thus ordained, the priests went always into the first tabernacle, accomplishing the service *of God*.

⁷ But into the second *went* the high priest alone once every year, not without blood, which he offered for himself, and *for* the errors of the people:

⁸ the Holy Ghost this signifying, that the way into the holiest of all was not yet made manifest, while as the first tabernacle was yet standing:

⁹ which *was* a figure for the time then present, in which were offered both gifts and sacrifices, that could not make him that did the service perfect, as pertaining to the conscience;

¹⁰ which stood only in meats and drinks, and divers washings, and carnal ordinances, imposed *on them* until the time of reformation.

The New Covenant

*B*ut Christ being come a high priest of good things to come, by a greater and more perfect tabernacle, not made with hands, that is to say, not of this building; ¹²neither by the blood of goats and calves, but by his own blood he entered in once into the holy place, having obtained eternal redemption *for us.*

*Y*et it pleased the LORD to bruise him; he hath put *him* to grief: when thou shalt make his soul an offering for sin, he shall see *his* seed, he shall prolong *his* days, and the pleasure of the LORD shall prosper in his hand. ¹¹He shall see of the travail of his soul, *and* shall be satisfied: by his knowledge shall my righteous servant justify many; for he shall bear their iniquities.

Isaiah 53:10–11

*I*f we confess our sins, he is faithful and just and will forgive us our sins and purify us from all unrighteousness" (1 John 1:9). This verse tells us what to do when we've sinned—we must confess that we have sinned and need forgiveness.

Then if we confess, God promises to forgive. He takes care of that sin once and for all. He restores our relationship with him. . . .

. . . At the center of forgiveness is always the cross of Christ. Without his body on the cross, forgiveness would not even be available. Forgiveness is costly, and we need to see it from that perspective. There is no forgiveness without tears, without a price to be paid, without the sacrifice of Christ.

Because of Christ's sacrifice, sin need not defeat us. . . .

Though we cannot eliminate the temptation to sin, we are not left without redemptive resources. God is on our side, Jesus is advocating for us, and the Holy Spirit is making us aware of our weaknesses as our Teacher and Guide.

David McKenna

*D*escribe the many differences between the old and new covenants. What difference does it make that Jesus is now our high priest? Pray and thank God that the blood of Jesus takes away our sins forever.

THURSDAY

Christ's Blood:
The Perfect Sacrifice

Hebrews 9:13—10:10

*F*or if the blood of bulls and of goats, and the ashes of a heifer sprinkling the unclean, sanctifieth to the purifying of the flesh:

¹⁴ how much more shall the blood of Christ, who through the eternal Spirit offered himself without spot to God, purge your conscience from dead works to serve the living God? ¹⁵ And for this cause he is the mediator of the new testament, that by means of death, for the redemption of the transgressions *that were* under the first testament, they which are called might receive the promise of eternal inheritance.

¹⁶ For where a testament *is*, there must also of necessity be the death of the testator.

¹⁷ For a testament *is* of force after men are dead: otherwise it is of no strength at all while the testator liveth.

¹⁸ Whereupon neither the first *testament* was dedicated without blood.

¹⁹ For when Moses had spoken every precept to all the people according to the law, he took the blood of calves and of goats, with water, and scarlet wool, and hyssop, and sprinkled both the book and all the people,

²⁰ saying, This *is* the blood of the testament which God hath enjoined unto you.

²¹ Moreover he sprinkled with blood both the tabernacle, and all the vessels of the ministry.

²² And almost all things are by the law purged with blood; and without shedding of blood is no remission.

Christ's Death Takes Away Sins

*I*t *was* therefore necessary that the patterns of things in the heavens should be purified with these; but the heavenly things themselves with better sacrifices than these.

²⁴ For Christ is not entered into the holy places made with hands, *which are* the figures of the true; but into heaven itself, now to appear in the presence of God for us:

²⁵ nor yet that he should offer himself often, as the high priest entereth into the holy place every year with blood of others;

²⁶ for then must he often have suffered since the foundation of the world: but now once in the end of the world hath he appeared to put away sin by the sacrifice of himself.

²⁷ And as it is appointed unto men once to die, but after this the judgment:

²⁸ so Christ was once offered to bear the sins of many; and unto them that look for him shall he appear the second time without sin unto salvation.

10 For the law having a shadow of good things to come, *and* not the very image of the things, can never with those sacrifices which they offered year by year continually make the comers thereunto perfect.

² For then would they not have ceased to be offered? because that the worshippers once purged should have had no more conscience of sins.

³ But in those *sacrifices there is* a remembrance again *made* of sins every year.

4 For *it is* not possible that the blood of bulls and of goats should take away sins.

5 Wherefore, when he cometh into the world, he saith, Sacrifice and offering thou wouldest not, but a body hast thou prepared me:

6 in burnt offerings and *sacrifices* for sin thou hast had no pleasure.

7 Then said I, Lo, I come (in the volume of the book it is written of me) to do thy will, O God.

8 Above when he said, Sacrifice and offering and burnt offerings and *offering* for sin thou wouldest not, neither hadst pleasure *therein*; which are offered by the law;

9 then said he, Lo, I come to do thy will, O God. He taketh away the first, that he may establish the second.

10 By the which will we are sanctified through the offering of the body of Jesus Christ once *for all.*

OLD TESTAMENT READING

*T*hen shall he kill the goat of the sin offering, that *is* for the people, and bring his blood within the veil, and do with that blood as he did with the blood of the bullock, and sprinkle it upon the mercy seat, and before the mercy seat.

17 And there shall be no man in the tabernacle of the congregation when he goeth in to make an atonement in the holy *place*, until he come out, and have made an atonement for himself, and for his household, and for all the congregation of Israel.

34 And this shall be an everlasting statute unto you, to make an atonement for the children of Israel for all their sins once a year. And he did as the LORD commanded Moses.

Leviticus 16:15, 17, 34

INSIGHTS

*W*hen we sin, our only option is repentance. Without repentance there is no forgiveness. We must come before God in contrition. David put it this way:

"For thou has no delight in sacrifice. . . . The sacrifice acceptable to God is a broken spirit; a broken and contrite heart, O God, thou wilt not despise" [Psalm 51:16, 17].

Here David's profound thoughts reveal his understanding of what many Old Testament persons failed to grasp—that the offering of sacrifices in the temple did not gain merit for the sinner. Sacrifices pointed beyond themselves to the perfect Sacrifice. The perfect atonement was offered by the perfect Lamb without blemish. The blood of bulls and goats does not take away sin. The blood of Jesus does. To avail ourselves of the atonement of Christ, to gain that covering, requires that we come before God in brokenness and contrition. The true sacrifices of God are a broken spirit and a contrite heart.

R. C. Sproul

APPLICATION

*W*hat does the sacrifice of Christ's blood accomplish that no other sacrifice can do? What kind of sacrifice does God want from his people? What has Christ's sacrifice done for you personally?

FRIDAY

The Lord Will
Judge His People

Hebrews 10:11–39

*A*nd every priest standeth daily ministering and offering oftentimes the same sacrifices, which can never take away sins:

[12] but this man, after he had offered one sacrifice for sins for ever, sat down on the right hand of God;

[13] from henceforth expecting till his enemies be made his footstool.

[14] For by one offering he hath perfected for ever them that are sanctified.

[15] *Whereof* the Holy Ghost also is a witness to us: for after that he had said before,

[16] This *is* the covenant that I will make with them after those days, saith the Lord; I will put my laws into their hearts, and in their minds will I write them;

[17] and their sins and iniquities will I remember no more.

[18] Now where remission of these *is*, *there is* no more offering for sin.

Keep the Faith

*H*aving therefore, brethren, boldness to enter into the holiest by the blood of Jesus,

[20] by a new and living way, which he hath consecrated for us, through the veil, that is to say, his flesh;

[21] and *having* a high priest over the house of God;

[22] Let us draw near with a true heart in full assurance of faith, having our hearts sprinkled from an evil con-science, and our bodies washed with pure water.

[23] Let us hold fast the profession of *our* faith without wavering; for he *is* faithful that promised;

[24] and let us consider one another to provoke unto love and to good works:

[25] not forsaking the assembling of ourselves together, as the manner of some *is*; but exhorting *one another*: and so much the more, as ye see the day approaching.

[26] For if we sin wilfully after that we have received the knowledge of the truth, there remaineth no more sacrifice for sins,

[27] but a certain fearful looking for of judgment and fiery indignation, which shall devour the adversaries.

[28] He that despised Moses' law died without mercy under two or three witnesses:

[29] of how much sorer punishment, suppose ye, shall he be thought worthy, who hath trodden under foot the Son of God, and hath counted the blood of the covenant, wherewith he was sanctified, an unholy thing, and hath done despite unto the Spirit of grace?

[30] For we know him that hath said, Vengeance *belongeth* unto me, I will recompense, saith the Lord. And again, The Lord shall judge his people.

[31] *It is* a fearful thing to fall into the hands of the living God.

[32] But call to remembrance the former days, in which, after ye were illuminated, ye endured a great fight of afflictions;

[33] partly, whilst ye were made a gazingstock both by reproaches and afflictions; and partly, whilst ye became companions of them that were so used.

³⁴ For ye had compassion of me in my bonds, and took joyfully the spoiling of your goods, knowing in yourselves that ye have in heaven a better and an enduring substance.
³⁵ Cast not away therefore your confidence, which hath great recompense of reward.
³⁶ For ye have need of patience, that, after ye have done the will of God, ye might receive the promise.
³⁷ For yet a little while, and he that shall come will come, and will not tarry.
³⁸ Now the just shall live by faith: but if *any man* draw back, my soul shall have no pleasure in him.
³⁹ But we are not of them who draw back unto perdition; but of them that believe to the saving of the soul.

OLD TESTAMENT READING

*F*or by fire and by his sword will the LORD plead with all flesh: and the slain of the LORD shall be many.

Isaiah 66:16

*S*eek good, and not evil, that ye may live: and so the LORD, the God of hosts, shall be with you, as ye have spoken.

Amos 5:14

INSIGHTS

*W*ithout a physical order in the universe, there could be no science.

Much of the genius of our space program involves achieving the most precise knowledge and conformity to this order. Failure means disaster.

*Tens of thousands of man-hours, the most sophisticated technology, and the latest advances in space sci-*ence are involved. . . . But all of it is helpless without an orderly universe to count on, and conform to.

God, who ordained physical order, also ordained moral and spiritual order.

Conformity guarantees fulfillment. Disobedience spells destruction. . . .

One can reject God's moral absolutes. But that does not get rid of them. The law of sin and death is just as inviolable as the law of gravity. Morality isn't arbitrary. It's part of the natural law of the universe. God's law stands whether we like it or not.

We ignore this fact to our doom. Violating God's physical law is destructive, but violating His moral law is infinitely more serious—for it has eternal consequences.

Every malfunction of the social order in America derives from our transgression of God's moral law. If we refuse to turn to God for mercy and grace, we condemn ourselves to His inexorable justice and judgment.

Richard Halverson

APPLICATION

*W*hat will happen to everyone who lives against God? What is promised to those who continue living by faith? Pray for the courage to live as God wants his people to live.

WEEKEND

Faith Pleases God

Hebrews 11:1–22

What Is Faith?

11 Now faith is the substance of things hoped for, the evidence of things not seen.

2 For by it the elders obtained a good report.

3 Through faith we understand that the worlds were framed by the word of God, so that things which are seen were not made of things which do appear.

4 By faith Abel offered unto God a more excellent sacrifice than Cain, by which he obtained witness that he was righteous, God testifying of his gifts: and by it he being dead yet speaketh.

5 By faith Enoch was translated that he should not see death; and was not found, because God had translated him: for before his translation he had this testimony, that he pleased God.

6 But without faith *it is* impossible to please *him*: for he that cometh to God must believe that he is, and *that* he is a rewarder of them that diligently seek him.

7 By faith Noah, being warned of God of things not seen as yet, moved with fear, prepared an ark to the saving of his house; by the which he condemned the world, and became heir of the righteousness which is by faith.

8 By faith Abraham, when he was called to go out into a place which he should after receive for an inheritance, obeyed; and he went out, not knowing whither he went.

9 By faith he sojourned in the land of promise, as *in* a strange country, dwelling in tabernacles with Isaac and Jacob, the heirs with him of the same promise:

10 for he looked for a city which hath foundations, whose builder and maker *is* God.

11 Through faith also Sarah herself received strength to conceive seed, and was delivered of a child when she was past age, because she judged him faithful who had promised.

12 Therefore sprang there even of one, and him as good as dead, *so many* as the stars of the sky in multitude, and as the sand which is by the sea shore innumerable.

13 These all died in faith, not having received the promises, but having seen them afar off, and were persuaded of *them*, and embraced *them*, and confessed that they were strangers and pilgrims on the earth.

14 For they that say such things declare plainly that they seek a country.

15 And truly, if they had been mindful of that *country* from whence they came out, they might have had opportunity to have returned.

16 But now they desire a better *country*, that is, a heavenly: wherefore God is not ashamed to be called their God: for he hath prepared for them a city.

17 By faith Abraham, when he was tried, offered up Isaac: and he that had received the promises offered up his only begotten *son*,

18 of whom it was said, That in Isaac shall thy seed be called:

19 accounting that God *was* able to raise *him* up, even from the dead;

from whence also he received him in a figure.

²⁰ By faith Isaac blessed Jacob and Esau concerning things to come.

²¹ By faith Jacob, when he was a dying, blessed both the sons of Joseph; and worshipped, *leaning* upon the top of his staff.

²² By faith Joseph, when he died, made mention of the departing of the children of Israel; and gave commandment concerning his bones.

OLD TESTAMENT READING

*A*nd he brought him forth abroad, and said, Look now toward heaven, and tell the stars, if thou be able to number them: and he said unto him, So shall thy seed be.

⁶ And he believed in the LORD; and he counted it to him for righteousness.

Genesis 15:5–6

INSIGHTS

*F*aith is my deliberate and positive response to the good in another to the extent that I will act on his behalf in a personal, powerful way. . . .

. . . It means that I am willing to share my life along with all its capacities (time, strength, attention, talents, means, energy, affection, acceptance) with another. It means that I actively, energetically give of my best to another outside of and apart from myself.

To speak of faith in any other way than this is to indulge in mere "believism." It is to play around with pious platitudes that pack no punch at all. This sort of superficial spirituality is actually the great bane of Christianity. Literally hundreds of thousands of people claim they trust in God; they claim to have faith in Christ; they claim to be believers, yet their lives and personal conduct are a denial and travesty of true faith. . . .

. . . When our Lord lived amongst us He was continually looking for this dynamic trust and response to Himself. Whenever He found even the tiniest fragment of faith being exercised in Him He was delighted.

W. Phillip Keller

ACTION POINT

*I*s faith for things in the past, present, or future? In what ways is faith a catalyst in your life? Pray that your faith will be a delight to God.

MONDAY

God Corrects Those He Loves

Hebrews 11:23—12:6

*B*y faith Moses, when he was born, was hid three months of his parents, because they saw *he was* a proper child; and they were not afraid of the king's commandment.

24 By faith Moses, when he was come to years, refused to be called the son of Pharaoh's daughter;

25 choosing rather to suffer affliction with the people of God, than to enjoy the pleasures of sin for a season;

26 esteeming the reproach of Christ greater riches than the treasures in Egypt: for he had respect unto the recompense of the reward.

27 By faith he forsook Egypt, not fearing the wrath of the king: for he endured, as seeing him who is invisible.

28 Through faith he kept the passover, and the sprinkling of blood, lest he that destroyed the firstborn should touch them.

29 By faith they passed through the Red sea as by dry *land*: which the Egyptians assaying to do were drowned.

30 By faith the walls of Jericho fell down, after they were compassed about seven days.

31 By faith the harlot Rahab perished not with them that believed not, when she had received the spies with peace.

32 And what shall I more say? for the time would fail me to tell of Gideon, and *of* Barak, and *of* Samson, and *of* Jephthah; *of* David also, and Samuel, and *of* the prophets:

33 who through faith subdued kingdoms, wrought righteousness, obtained promises, stopped the mouths of lions,

34 quenched the violence of fire, escaped the edge of the sword, out of weakness were made strong, waxed valiant in fight, turned to flight the armies of the aliens.

35 Women received their dead raised to life again: and others were tortured, not accepting deliverance; that they might obtain a better resurrection:

36 and others had trial of *cruel* mockings and scourgings, yea, moreover of bonds and imprisonment:

37 they were stoned, they were sawn asunder, were tempted, were slain with the sword: they wandered about in sheepskins and goatskins; being destitute, afflicted, tormented;

38 of whom the world was not worthy: they wandered in deserts, and *in* mountains, and *in* dens and caves of the earth.

39 And these all, having obtained a good report through faith, received not the promise:

40 God having provided some better thing for us, that they without us should not be made perfect.

Follow Jesus' Example

12 Wherefore, seeing we also are compassed about with so great a cloud of witnesses, let us lay aside every weight, and the sin which doth so easily beset *us*, and let us run with patience the race that is set before us,

2 looking unto Jesus the author and finisher of *our* faith; who for the joy that was set before him endured the cross, despising the shame, and is

set down at the right hand of the throne of God.

³ For consider him that endured such contradiction of sinners against himself, lest ye be wearied and faint in your minds.

God Is like a Father

Ye have not yet resisted unto blood, striving against sin.

⁵ And ye have forgotten the exhortation which speaketh unto you as unto children, My son, despise not thou the chastening of the Lord, nor faint when thou art rebuked of him: ⁶ for whom the Lord loveth he chasteneth, and scourgeth every son whom he receiveth.

OLD TESTAMENT READING

My son, despise not the chastening of the LORD; neither be weary of his correction:

¹² for whom the LORD loveth he correcteth; even as a father the son *in whom* he delighteth.

Proverbs 3:11–12

INSIGHTS

Most of us don't want to be broken in the storms of life. We much prefer to protect our personalities from the stresses and strains of our days. We would rather, much rather, be tough and rugged and self-assured than contrite before Christ, repentant in soul before His Spirit. . . .

Many of us would like to avoid the mills of God. We are tempted to ask Him to deliver us from the upsetting, tumbling tides of time that knock off our rough corners and shape us to His design. We plead for release from the discipline of difficulties, the rub of routine responsibilities, the polish that comes from long perseverance.

We are a restless generation. We of the West want and insist on instant results. We demand a quick fix. We look for shortcuts and immediate results. We are quite sure we can be a rough slab of stone today and a polished gemstone tomorrow.

But God's ways and our ways are not the same. His patience is persistent. His work is meticulous. His years know no end. His perception of time is that one day is as a thousand years and a thousand years as but a single day.

The shattering of rock, the smoothing of stone, the polishing of a jewel in the sea requires eons of time. Can I then expect the breaking of my hard heart, the smoothing of my spirit, the shaping of my character as it is conformed to His own to be any less time-consuming?

W. Phillip Keller

APPLICATION

What is the relationship between having faith and receiving God's correction? In what way does correction help us remove sin from our lives? Pray that you will feel God's great love as he corrects you!

TUESDAY

*Accept God's Correction
so You Will Learn
the Right Way to Live*

Hebrews 12:7–29

*I*f ye endure chastening, God dealeth with you as with sons; for what son is he whom the father chasteneth not?

⁸ But if ye be without chastisement, whereof all are partakers, then are ye bastards, and not sons.

⁹ Furthermore we have had fathers of our flesh which corrected *us*, and we gave *them* reverence: shall we not much rather be in subjection unto the Father of spirits, and live?

¹⁰ For they verily for a few days chastened *us* after their own pleasure; but he for *our* profit, that *we* might be partakers of his holiness.

¹¹ Now no chastening for the present seemeth to be joyous, but grievous: nevertheless, afterward it yieldeth the peaceable fruit of righteousness unto them which are exercised thereby.

Be Careful How You Live

*W*herefore lift up the hands which hang down, and the feeble knees;

¹³ and make straight paths for your feet, lest that which is lame be turned out of the way; but let it rather be healed.

¹⁴ Follow peace with all *men*, and holiness, without which no man shall see the Lord:

¹⁵ looking diligently lest any man fail of the grace of God; lest any root of bitterness springing up trouble *you*, and thereby many be defiled;

¹⁶ Lest there be any fornicator, or profane person, as Esau, who for one morsel of meat sold his birthright.

¹⁷ For ye know how that afterward, when he would have inherited the blessing, he was rejected: for he found no place of repentance, though he sought it carefully with tears.

¹⁸ For ye are not come unto the mount that might be touched, and that burned with fire, nor unto blackness, and darkness, and tempest,

¹⁹ and the sound of a trumpet, and the voice of words; which *voice* they that heard entreated that the word should not be spoken to them any more:

²⁰ (for they could not endure that which was commanded, And if so much as a beast touch the mountain, it shall be stoned, or thrust through with a dart:

²¹ and so terrible was the sight, *that* Moses said, I exceedingly fear and quake:)

²² but ye are come unto mount Zion, and unto the city of the living God, the heavenly Jerusalem, and to an innumerable company of angels,

²³ to the general assembly and church of the firstborn, which are written in heaven, and to God the Judge of all, and to the spirits of just men made perfect,

²⁴ and to Jesus the mediator of the new covenant, and to the blood of sprinkling, that speaketh better things than *that of* Abel.

²⁵ See that ye refuse not him that speaketh: For if they escaped not who refused him that spake on earth, much more *shall not* we *escape*, if we turn away from him that *speaketh* from heaven:

²⁶ whose voice then shook the earth: but now he hath promised, saying,

Yet once more I shake not the earth only, but also heaven.
²⁷ And this *word*, Yet once more, signifieth the removing of those things that are shaken, as of things that are made, that those things which cannot be shaken may remain.
²⁸ Wherefore we receiving a kingdom which cannot be moved, let us have grace, whereby we may serve God acceptably with reverence and godly fear:
²⁹ for our God *is* a consuming fire.

OLD TESTAMENT READING

*A*nd David's heart smote him after that he had numbered the people. And David said unto the Lord, I have sinned greatly in that I have done: and now, I beseech thee, O Lord, take away the iniquity of thy servant; for I have done very foolishly.
¹⁵ᵃ So the Lord sent a pestilence upon Israel from the morning even to the time appointed.
¹⁷ And David spake unto the Lord when he saw the angel that smote the people, and said, Lo, I have sinned, and I have done wickedly: but these sheep, what have they done? let thine hand, I pray thee, be against me, and against my father's house.
¹⁸ And Gad came that day to David, and said unto him, Go up, rear an altar unto the Lord in the threshingfloor of Araunah the Jebusite.
¹⁹ And David, according to the saying of Gad, went up as the Lord commanded.
²⁵ᵇ So the Lord was entreated for the land, and the plague was stayed from Israel.

2 Samuel 24:10, 15a, 17–19, 25b

INSIGHTS

*J*ust as a caring parent will lovingly discipline and train his child, so God lovingly disciplines us. We live in a world of mystery and unexplained enigmas, so it is not surprising that the element of mystery should invade this realm too. Indeed, our Lord indicated that it would be so. "What I do you do not realize now; but you shall understand hereafter" (John 13:7). If we are to experience serenity in this turbulent world, we will need to take firmer grasp of God's sovereignty and trust His love even when we cannot discern His purpose. We must remember that the hand molding the clay is nail-pierced, and that our God's sovereignty will never clash with His paternity. "But now, O Lord, Thou art our Father, we are the clay, and Thou our potter" (Isa. 64:8). If we are to enjoy a deepening intimacy with God, we must react to His providential dealings in a spiritual way, even though they may be inscrutable. These dealings may take various forms, but all are planned in love, and with a view to cultivating a deeper intimacy with God.

J. Oswald Sanders

PAUSE FOR REFLECTION

*W*hy does God punish his people? What did God's punishment accomplish in David's life (2 Samuel 24)? Do you think David realized how seriously he had sinned before God punished him? What causes you to recognize the seriousness of your sin?

WEDNESDAY

Live in a Way
that Pleases God

Hebrews 13:1–25

13 Let brotherly love continue.
² Be not forgetful to entertain strangers: for thereby some have entertained angels unawares.

³ Remember them that are in bonds, as bound with them; *and* them which suffer adversity, as being yourselves also in the body.

⁴ Marriage *is* honorable in all, and the bed undefiled: but whoremongers and adulterers God will judge.

⁵ *Let your* conversation *be* without covetousness; *and be* content with such things as ye have: for he hath said, I will never leave thee, nor forsake thee.

⁶ So that we may boldly say, The Lord *is* my helper, and I will not fear what man shall do unto me.

⁷ Remember them which have the rule over you, who have spoken unto you the word of God: whose faith follow, considering the end of *their* conversation.

⁸ Jesus Christ the same yesterday, and today, and for ever.

⁹ Be not carried about with divers and strange doctrines: for *it is* a good thing that the heart be established with grace; not with meats, which have not profited them that have been occupied therein.

¹⁰ We have an altar, whereof they have no right to eat which serve the tabernacle.

¹¹ For the bodies of those beasts, whose blood is brought into the sanctuary by the high priest for sin, are burned without the camp.

¹² Wherefore Jesus also, that he might sanctify the people with his own blood, suffered without the gate.

¹³ Let us go forth therefore unto him without the camp, bearing his reproach.

¹⁴ For here have we no continuing city, but we seek one to come.

¹⁵ By him therefore let us offer the sacrifice of praise to God continually, that is, the fruit of *our* lips, giving thanks to his name.

¹⁶ But to do good and to communicate forget not: for with such sacrifices God is well pleased.

¹⁷ Obey them that have the rule over you, and submit yourselves: for they watch for your souls, as they that must give account, that they may do it with joy, and not with grief: for that *is* unprofitable for you.

¹⁸ Pray for us: for we trust we have a good conscience, in all things willing to live honestly.

¹⁹ But I beseech *you* the rather to do this, that I may be restored to you the sooner.

²⁰ Now the God of peace, that brought again from the dead our Lord Jesus, that great shepherd of the sheep, through the blood of the everlasting covenant,

²¹ make you perfect in every good work to do his will, working in you that which is well-pleasing in his sight, through Jesus Christ; to whom *be* glory for ever and ever. Amen.

²² And I beseech you, brethren, suffer the word of exhortation: for I have written a letter unto you in few words.

²³ Know ye that *our* brother Timothy is set at liberty; with whom, if he come shortly, I will see you.

24 Salute all them that have the rule over you, and all the saints. They of Italy salute you.

25 Grace *be* with you all. Amen.

---

*A*nd now, Israel, what doth the LORD thy God require of thee, but to fear the LORD thy God, to walk in all his ways, and to love him, and to serve the LORD thy God with all thy heart and with all thy soul,

13 to keep the commandments of the LORD, and his statutes, which I command thee this day for thy good?

16 Circumcise therefore the foreskin of your heart, and be no more stiffnecked.

18 He doth execute the judgment of the fatherless and widow, and loveth the stranger, in giving him food and raiment.

19 Love ye therefore the stranger: for ye were strangers in the land of Egypt.

20 Thou shalt fear the LORD thy God; him shalt thou serve, and to him shalt thou cleave, and swear by his name.

21 He *is* thy praise, and he *is* thy God, that hath done for thee these great and terrible things, which thine eyes have seen.

Deuteronomy 10:12–13, 16, 18–21

---

*I*n recent decades the phrase "easy believism" has surfaced. Unfortunately, it describes a large number of contemporary Christians who have received Christ as Savior but do not, in practice, regard Him as Lord. They seem to have received Him in order to reach heaven some-

day or to get help for their problems, but they have never fully committed to trust, obey, honor and serve Him as a way of life.

Our Lord never intended that we be His casual acquaintances. He wants us to be His disciples, fully dedicated to following Him and lifting up His holy name to the world. . . . Our Lord is repulsed by mediocre commitment. . . .

. . . When we acknowledge Christ as our Lord, we affirm that He is our Master for life and that we are dedicated to serving and glorifying Him. In all things, large and small, our deepest desire is to do what our Lord would want us to do. We ask for His guidance—not for our gain, but for His glory. We discipline ourselves in studying and obeying His written Word. We proclaim His love to the world around us. We try to think, speak and act in a way that will attract others to Him.

The misguided person who thinks all this is too difficult or irrelevant misses the point. The Christian life is far more than a fire escape from hell; it is the life of submission and obedience which result in joy and victory.

Bill Bright

---

*D*escribe the kind of life God has called his people to live (in both Old and New Testaments). Pray that living such a life will be of utmost importance to you. Make that commitment today!

THURSDAY

God Gives Wisdom
to Those Who Ask for It

James 1:1–27

1 James, a servant of God and of the Lord Jesus Christ, to the twelve tribes which are scattered abroad, greeting.

Faith and Wisdom

My brethren, count it all joy when ye fall into divers temptations;
3 knowing *this*, that the trying of your faith worketh patience.
4 But let patience have *her* perfect work, that ye may be perfect and entire, wanting nothing.
5 If any of you lack wisdom, let him ask of God, that giveth to all *men* liberally, and upbraideth not; and it shall be given him.
6 But let him ask in faith, nothing wavering: for he that wavereth is like a wave of the sea driven with the wind and tossed.
7 For let not that man think that he shall receive any thing of the Lord.
8 A double-minded man *is* unstable in all his ways.

True Riches

Let the brother of low degree rejoice in that he is exalted:
10 but the rich, in that he is made low: because as the flower of the grass he shall pass away.
11 For the sun is no sooner risen with a burning heat, but it withereth the grass, and the flower thereof falleth, and the grace of the fashion of it perisheth: so also shall the rich man fade away in his ways.

Temptation Is Not from God

Blessed *is* the man that endureth temptation: for when he is tried, he shall receive the crown of life, which the Lord hath promised to them that love him.
13 Let no man say when he is tempted, I am tempted of God: for God cannot be tempted with evil, neither tempteth he any man:
14 but every man is tempted, when he is drawn away of his own lust, and enticed.
15 Then when lust hath conceived, it bringeth forth sin; and sin, when it is finished, bringeth forth death.
16 Do not err, my beloved brethren.
17 Every good gift and every perfect gift is from above, and cometh down from the Father of lights, with whom is no variableness, neither shadow of turning.
18 Of his own will begat he us with the word of truth, that we should be a kind of firstfruits of his creatures.

Listening and Obeying

Wherefore, my beloved brethren, let every man be swift to hear, slow to speak, slow to wrath:
20 for the wrath of man worketh not the righteousness of God.
21 Wherefore lay apart all filthiness and superfluity of naughtiness, and receive with meekness the engrafted word, which is able to save your souls.
22 But be ye doers of the word, and not hearers only, deceiving your own selves.
23 For if any be a hearer of the word,

and not a doer, he is like unto a man beholding his natural face in a glass: ²⁴ for he beholdeth himself, and goeth his way, and straightway forgetteth what manner of man he was. ²⁵ But whoso looketh into the perfect law of liberty, and continueth *therein*, he being not a forgetful hearer, but a doer of the work, this man shall be blessed in his deed.

Pure Religion

*I*f any man among you seem to be religious, and bridleth not his tongue, but deceiveth his own heart, this man's religion *is* vain. ²⁷ Pure religion and undefiled before God and the Father is this, To visit the fatherless and widows in their affliction, *and* to keep himself unspotted from the world.

OLD TESTAMENT READING

*A*nd the speech pleased the LORD, that Solomon had asked this thing. ¹¹ And God said unto him, Because thou hast asked this thing, and hast not asked for thyself long life; neither hast asked riches for thyself, nor hast asked the life of thine enemies; but hast asked for thyself understanding to discern judgment; ¹² behold, I have done according to thy word: lo, I have given thee a wise and an understanding heart; so that there was none like thee before thee, neither after thee shall any arise like unto thee. ¹³ And I have also given thee that which thou hast not asked, both riches, and honor: so that there shall not be any among the kings like unto thee all thy days.

1 Kings 3:10–13

INSIGHTS

It has been said that the wisest man in the world is the man who knows he doesn't know.

In the midst of trials how often we say, "If only I knew what to do"; or we may say, "I don't know which way to turn or what to do."

God has promised to give us His wisdom. "If any of you is deficient in wisdom, let him ask of the giving God [Who gives] to every one liberally and ungrudgingly, without reproaching or faultfinding, and it will be given him" (Amplified). . . .

Not only are we to ask God for wisdom but we are to ask in faith. Someone has said, "Doubt is a nonconductor of grace."

We are not to be double-minded, wanting partly our way and partly God's way.

As we ask of God and ask in faith, God has promised to give liberally. We are to ask for wisdom to face serenely the trials of today, unwaveringly trusting in Him. We are to ask for wisdom to meet each trial of life and to face it triumphantly.

Millie Stamm

PAUSE FOR REFLECTION

*F*or what reasons did Solomon ask for God's wisdom? Did God's answer meet or exceed his expectations? For what in your life do you need God's wisdom? Have you asked him for it?

FRIDAY

*Love Your Neighbor
as Yourself*

James 2:1–26

Love All People

2 My brethren, have not the faith of our Lord Jesus Christ, *the Lord* of glory, with respect of persons.

² For if there come unto your assembly a man with a gold ring, in goodly apparel, and there come in also a poor man in vile raiment;

³ and ye have respect to him that weareth the gay clothing, and say unto him, Sit thou here in a good place; and say to the poor, Stand thou there, or sit here under my footstool:

⁴ are ye not then partial in yourselves, and are become judges of evil thoughts?

⁵ Hearken, my beloved brethren, Hath not God chosen the poor of this world rich in faith, and heirs of the kingdom which he hath promised to them that love him?

⁶ But ye have despised the poor. Do not rich men oppress you, and draw you before the judgment seats?

⁷ Do not they blaspheme that worthy name by the which ye are called?

⁸ If ye fulfil the royal law according to the Scripture, Thou shalt love thy neighbor as thyself, ye do well:

⁹ but if ye have respect to persons, ye commit sin, and are convinced of the law as transgressors.

¹⁰ For whosoever shall keep the whole law, and yet offend in one *point*, he is guilty of all.

¹¹ For he that said, Do not commit adultery, said also, Do not kill. Now if thou commit no adultery, yet if thou kill, thou art become a transgressor of the law.

¹² So speak ye, and so do, as they that shall be judged by the law of liberty.

¹³ For he shall have judgment without mercy, that hath showed no mercy; and mercy rejoiceth against judgment.

Faith and Good Works

What *doth it* profit, my brethren, though a man say he hath faith, and have not works? can faith save him?

¹⁵ If a brother or sister be naked, and destitute of daily food,

¹⁶ and one of you say unto them, Depart in peace, be *ye* warmed and filled; notwithstanding ye give them not those things which are needful to the body; what *doth it* profit?

¹⁷ Even so faith, if it hath not works, is dead, being alone.

¹⁸ Yea, a man may say, Thou hast faith, and I have works: show me thy faith without thy works, and I will show thee my faith by my works.

¹⁹ Thou believest that there is one God; thou doest well: the devils also believe, and tremble.

²⁰ But wilt thou know, O vain man, that faith without works is dead?

²¹ Was not Abraham our father justified by works, when he had offered Isaac his son upon the altar?

²² Seest thou how faith wrought with his works, and by works was faith made perfect?

²³ And the Scripture was fulfilled which saith, Abraham believed God, and it was imputed unto him for righteousness: and he was called the Friend of God.

²⁴ Ye see then how that by works a man is justified, and not by faith only.

25 Likewise also was not Rahab the harlot justified by works, when she had received the messengers, and had sent *them* out another way? 26 For as the body without the spirit is dead, so faith without works is dead also.

OLD TESTAMENT READING

*T*hou shouldest not have entered into the gate of my people in the day of their calamity; yea, thou shouldest not have looked on their affliction in the day of their calamity, nor have laid *hands* on their substance in the day of their calamity; 14 neither shouldest thou have stood in the crossway, to cut off those of his that did escape; neither shouldest thou have delivered up those of his that did remain in the day of distress.

Obadiah 13–14

INSIGHTS

*M*y life has been deeply touched by the mercy of those who took the time to try and understand me—who cared enough to forgive so many of my faults and who in mercy made me their friend.

Often these were people to whom I had shown no special kindness. Their bestowal of mercy on me was something totally unexpected and undeserved. Because of this, it has been a double delight. More than that, it has been an enormous inspiration that lifted and challenged me to respond in a measure beyond my wildest dreams. . . .

. . . To really find the true source of inner inspiration for this sort of conduct, the Christian simply must look beyond his fellow man. He must look away to the mercy of God our Father. Nothing else in all the world will so humble us. Nothing else will so move our stony spirits to extend mercy. Nothing else will so powerfully induce us to do the proper thing in extending genuine mercy to our contemporaries. . . .

Christ calls us to be merciful. He calls us to be forgiving and compassionate. This does not mean we wink at wrong and sweep sin under the carpet. Rather it demands that we care enough to bring others to the God of all mercy. And it is He who will cleanse, re-create, and renew them in His loving-kindness and tender mercy. Bless His dear name!

W. Phillip Keller

ACTION POINT

*I*n what situations does James plead for believers to show mercy? What lack of mercy does God condemn in Obadiah 13–14? In what ways does your normal human behavior lack God's mercy? How will you seek to demonstrate his mercy?

WEEKEND

*Train Your Tongue
for God's Service*

James 3:1—4:10

Taming the Tongue

3 My brethren, be not many masters, knowing that we shall receive the greater condemnation.
² For in many things we offend all. If any man offend not in word, the same *is* a perfect man, *and* able also to bridle the whole body.
³ Behold, we put bits in the horses' mouths, that they may obey us; and we turn about their whole body.
⁴ Behold also the ships, which though *they be* so great, and *are* driven of fierce winds, yet are they turned about with a very small helm, whithersoever the governor listeth.
⁵ Even so the tongue is a little member, and boasteth great things. Behold, how great a matter a little fire kindleth!
⁶ And the tongue *is* a fire, a world of iniquity: so is the tongue among our members, that it defileth the whole body, and setteth on fire the course of nature; and it is set on fire of hell.
⁷ For every kind of beasts, and of birds, and of serpents, and of things in the sea, is tamed, and hath been tamed of mankind:
⁸ but the tongue can no man tame; *it is* an unruly evil, full of deadly poison.
⁹ Therewith bless we God, even the Father; and therewith curse we men, which are made after the similitude of God.
¹⁰ Out of the same mouth proceedeth blessing and cursing. My brethren, these things ought not so to be.
¹¹ Doth a fountain send forth at the same place sweet *water* and bitter?
¹² Can the fig tree, my brethren, bear olive berries? either a vine, figs? so *can* no fountain both yield salt water and fresh.

True Wisdom

Who *is* a wise man and endued with knowledge among you? let him show out of a good conversation his works with meekness of wisdom.
¹⁴ But if ye have bitter envying and strife in your hearts, glory not, and lie not against the truth.
¹⁵ This wisdom descendeth not from above, but *is* earthly, sensual, devilish.
¹⁶ For where envying and strife *is*, there *is* confusion and every evil work.
¹⁷ But the wisdom that is from above is first pure, then peaceable, gentle, *and* easy to be entreated, full of mercy and good fruits, without partiality, and without hypocrisy.
¹⁸ And the fruit of righteousness is sown in peace of them that make peace.

Be Humble

4 From whence *come* wars and fightings among you? *come they* not hence, *even* of your lusts that war in your members?
² Ye lust, and have not: ye kill, and desire to have, and cannot obtain: ye fight and war, yet ye have not, because ye ask not.
³ Ye ask, and receive not, because ye ask amiss, that ye may consume *it* upon your lusts.

⁴ Ye adulterers and adulteresses, know ye not that the friendship of the world is enmity with God? whosoever therefore will be a friend of the world is the enemy of God.

⁵ Do ye think that the Scripture saith in vain, The spirit that dwelleth in us lusteth to envy?

⁶ But he giveth more grace. Wherefore he saith, God resisteth the proud, but giveth grace unto the humble.

⁷ Submit yourselves therefore to God. Resist the devil, and he will flee from you.

⁸ Draw nigh to God, and he will draw nigh to you. Cleanse *your* hands, *ye* sinners; and purify *your* hearts, *ye* double-minded.

⁹ Be afflicted, and mourn, and weep: let your laughter be turned to mourning, and *your* joy to heaviness.

¹⁰ Humble yourselves in the sight of the Lord, and he shall lift you up.

OLD TESTAMENT READING

A man's belly shall be satisfied with the fruit of his mouth; *and* with the increase of his lips shall he be filled. ²¹ Death and life *are* in the power of the tongue: and they that love it shall eat the fruit thereof.

Proverbs 18:20–21

INSIGHTS

No man can tame the tongue, but the Word of God encourages us to recognize that the Holy Spirit can transform and tie the tongue. . . .

. . . The tongue is the temperature gauge on the heart's engine. If the engine overheats, then the temperature gauge warns us of engine trouble. If the tongue gets out of con-

trol, it is a sure sign that we need to check our heart. . . . We need to constantly fill the heart with good things from God's Word in order to tie our tongues.

One must also concede to the Spirit's control to tie the tongue successfully. It always interested me that when James describes the tongue as a horse's bit that controls the horse or a ship's rudder that directs the ship, he, perhaps purposefully, fails to mention that a horse's bit must, in reality, be controlled by the rider and the ship's rudder must be controlled by the helmsman. I daily remind myself that the Lord, through the Holy Spirit, must be the rider or the helmsman controlling my tongue. Who is your helmsman?

If you have difficulty yielding control to the Lord, ask Him for the desire to give Him control. . . . When you have the willingness to concede control of your tongue, you'll soon discover you also have the strength to do it as well.

Vicki Lake

PAUSE FOR REFLECTION

What does your tongue reveal about your heart? Think about your experiences with the good and evil things people have said, and write your own proverb about the tongue.

MONDAY

God Answers the Prayers of His People

James 4:11—5:20

You Are Not the Judge

*S*peak not evil one of another, brethren. He that speaketh evil of *his* brother, and judgeth *his* brother, speaketh evil of the law, and judgeth the law: but if thou judge the law, thou art not a doer of the law, but a judge. ¹²There is one lawgiver, who is able to save and to destroy: who art thou that judgest another?

Let God Plan Your Life

*G*o to now, ye that say, Today or tomorrow we will go into such a city, and continue there a year, and buy and sell, and get gain: ¹⁴whereas ye know not what *shall* be on the morrow. For what *is* your life? It is even a vapor, that appeareth for a little time, and then vanisheth away. ¹⁵For that ye *ought* to say, If the Lord will, we shall live, and do this, or that. ¹⁶But now ye rejoice in your boastings: all such rejoicing is evil. ¹⁷Therefore to him that knoweth to do good, and doeth *it* not, to him it is sin.

A Warning to the Rich

5 Go to now, *ye* rich men, weep and howl for your miseries that shall come upon *you*. ²Your riches are corrupted, and your garments are moth-eaten. ³Your gold and silver is cankered; and the rust of them shall be a witness against you, and shall eat your flesh as it were fire. Ye have heaped treasure together for the last days. ⁴Behold, the hire of the laborers who have reaped down your fields, which is of you kept back by fraud, crieth: and the cries of them which have reaped are entered into the ears of the Lord of sabaoth. ⁵Ye have lived in pleasure on the earth, and been wanton; ye have nourished your hearts, as in a day of slaughter. ⁶Ye have condemned *and* killed the just; *and* he doth not resist you.

Be Patient

*B*e patient therefore, brethren, unto the coming of the Lord. Behold, the husbandman waiteth for the precious fruit of the earth, and hath long patience for it, until he receive the early and latter rain. ⁸Be ye also patient; stablish your hearts: for the coming of the Lord draweth nigh. ⁹Grudge not one against another, brethren, lest ye be condemned: behold, the judge standeth before the door. ¹⁰Take, my brethren, the prophets, who have spoken in the name of the Lord, for an example of suffering affliction, and of patience. ¹¹Behold, we count them happy which endure. Ye have heard of the patience of Job, and have seen the end of the Lord; that the Lord is very pitiful, and of tender mercy.

Be Careful What You Say

*B*ut above all things, my brethren, swear not, neither by heaven, neither by the earth, neither by any other oath: but let your yea be yea; and *your* nay, nay; lest ye fall into condemnation.

The Power of Prayer

*I*s any among you afflicted? let him pray. Is any merry? let him sing psalms.
[14] Is any sick among you? let him call for the elders of the church; and let them pray over him, anointing him with oil in the name of the Lord:
[15] and the prayer of faith shall save the sick, and the Lord shall raise him up; and if he have committed sins, they shall be forgiven him.
[16] Confess *your* faults one to another, and pray one for another, that ye may be healed. The effectual fervent prayer of a righteous man availeth much.
[17] Elijah was a man subject to like passions as we are, and he prayed earnestly that it might not rain: and it rained not on the earth by the space of three years and six months.
[18] And he prayed again, and the heaven gave rain, and the earth brought forth her fruit.

Saving a Soul

*B*rethren, if any of you do err from the truth, and one convert him;
[20] let him know, that he which converteth the sinner from the error of his way shall save a soul from death, and shall hide a multitude of sins.

OLD TESTAMENT READING

*T*hen Esther bade *them* return Mordecai *this answer,*
[16] Go, gather together all the Jews

that are present in Shushan, and fast ye for me, and neither eat nor drink three days, night or day: I also and my maidens will fast likewise; and so will I go in unto the king, which *is* not according to the law: and if I perish, I perish.

Esther 4:15–16

INSIGHTS

*G*od honors prayer. . . . *He longs to demonstrate His power in the tremendous trials that jar us like thunder, and in the pinprick troubles that annoy us. Giant needs are never too great for His power; dwarf-sized ones are never too small for His love. . . .*

God can answer prayer because He is the supreme ruler of all. . . . He governs both world events and our individual lives, ready at our request to act, to intervene, to overrule for our good, His glory, and the progress of the gospel. He has decreed that prayer is the way to secure His aid and move His mighty hand. Therefore even in sickness, failure, rejection, or financial distress, we can pray and experience His peace which transcends human understanding. Through prayer we can open a window to let God's love shine into our lives; we can open our hands to receive His riches.

Warren Myers

PAUSE FOR REFLECTION

*W*hat great powers does James attribute to prayer? Do you believe God answers prayer—enough to risk your life on the power of prayer as Esther did?

TUESDAY

God Will Purify Our Faith

1 Peter 1:1–21

1 Peter, an apostle of Jesus Christ, to the strangers scattered throughout Pontus, Galatia, Cappadocia, Asia, and Bithynia,

2 elect according to the foreknowledge of God the Father, through sanctification of the Spirit, unto obedience and sprinkling of the blood of Jesus Christ: Grace unto you, and peace, be multiplied.

We Have a Living Hope

*B*lessed *be* the God and Father of our Lord Jesus Christ, which according to his abundant mercy hath begotten us again unto a lively hope by the resurrection of Jesus Christ from the dead,

4 to an inheritance incorruptible, and undefiled, and that fadeth not away, reserved in heaven for you,

5 who are kept by the power of God through faith unto salvation ready to be revealed in the last time.

6 Wherein ye greatly rejoice, though now for a season, if need be, ye are in heaviness through manifold temptations:

7 that the trial of your faith, being much more precious than of gold that perisheth, though it be tried with fire, might be found unto praise and honor and glory at the appearing of Jesus Christ:

8 whom having not seen, ye love; in whom, though now ye see *him* not, yet believing, ye rejoice with joy unspeakable and full of glory:

9 receiving the end of your faith, *even* the salvation of *your* souls.

10 Of which salvation the prophets have inquired and searched diligently, who prophesied of the grace *that should come* unto you:

11 searching what, or what manner of time the Spirit of Christ which was in them did signify, when it testified beforehand the sufferings of Christ, and the glory that should follow.

12 Unto whom it was revealed, that not unto themselves, but unto us they did minister the things, which are now reported unto you by them that have preached the gospel unto you with the Holy Ghost sent down from heaven; which things the angels desire to look into.

A Call to Holy Living

*W*herefore gird up the loins of your mind, be sober, and hope to the end for the grace that is to be brought unto you at the revelation of Jesus Christ;

14 as obedient children, not fashioning yourselves according to the former lusts in your ignorance:

15 but as he which hath called you is holy, so be ye holy in all manner of conversation;

16 because it is written, Be ye holy; for I am holy.

17 And if ye call on the Father, who without respect of persons judgeth according to every man's work, pass the time of your sojourning *here* in fear:

18 forasmuch as ye know that ye were not redeemed with corruptible things, *as* silver and gold, from your vain conversation *received* by tradition from your fathers;

19 but with the precious blood of

Christ, as of a lamb without blemish and without spot:

20 who verily was foreordained before the foundation of the world, but was manifest in these last times for you,

21 who by him do believe in God, that raised him up from the dead, and gave him glory; that your faith and hope might be in God.

OLD TESTAMENT READING

*A*nd I will bring the third part through the fire, and will refine them as silver is refined, and will try them as gold is tried: they shall call on my name, and I will hear them: I will say, It *is* my people: and they shall say, The LORD *is* my God.

Zechariah 13:9

INSIGHTS

*W*hat is trouble but that very influence that brings you nearer to the heart of God than prayers or hymns? I think sorrows usually bring us closer to God than joys do. But sorrows, to be of use, must be borne, as Christ's were, victoriously, carrying with them intimations and sacred prophecies to the heart of hope. This is not only so we will not be overcome by them, but also so we will be strengthened and ennobled and enlarged by them. . . .

. . . By fire, by anvil-strokes, by the hammer that breaks the flinty rock, you are made what you are. You were gold in the rock, and God played miner, and blasted you out of the rock. Then He played stamper, and crushed you. Then He played smelter, and melted you.

Now you are gold, free from the rock by the grace of God's severity to you. As you look back upon those experiences of 5, 10, or 20 years ago and see what they have done for you, and what you are now, you say, "I would not exchange what I learned from these things for all the world.". . .

When God comes to you wrapped and wreathed in clouds, and in storms, why should we not recognize Him, and say, "I know you, God; and I will not flee you; though you slay me, I will trust thee"? If a man could see God in his troubles and take sorrow to be the . . . sweet discipline of a bitter medicine that brings health, though the taste is not agreeable—if one could so look upon his God, how sorrows would make him strong!

Henry Beecher

APPLICATION

*W*hat is the value of a pure faith? What are its rewards? How does our faith become pure? How is God purifying your faith today? Welcome his testing!

WEDNESDAY

*The Lives of God's People
Bring Glory to Him*

1 Peter 1:22—2:17

Seeing ye have purified your souls in obeying the truth through the Spirit unto unfeigned love of the brethren, *see that ye* love one another with a pure heart fervently:

23 being born again, not of corruptible seed, but of incorruptible, by the word of God, which liveth and abideth for ever.

24 For all flesh *is* as grass, and all the glory of man as the flower of grass. The grass withereth, and the flower thereof falleth away:

25 but the word of the Lord endureth for ever. And this is the word which by the gospel is preached unto you.

Jesus Is the Living Stone

2 Wherefore laying aside all malice, and all guile, and hypocrisies, and envies, and all evil speakings,

2 as newborn babes, desire the sincere milk of the word, that ye may grow thereby:

3 if so be ye have tasted that the Lord *is* gracious.

4 To whom coming, *as unto* a living stone, disallowed indeed of men, but chosen of God, *and* precious,

5 ye also, as lively stones, are built up a spiritual house, a holy priesthood, to offer up spiritual sacrifices, acceptable to God by Jesus Christ.

6 Wherefore also it is contained in the Scripture, Behold, I lay in Zion a chief corner stone, elect, precious:

and he that believeth on him shall not be confounded.

7 Unto you therefore which believe *he is* precious: but unto them which be disobedient, the stone which the builders disallowed, the same is made the head of the corner,

8 and a stone of stumbling, and a rock of offence, *even to them* which stumble at the word, being disobedient: whereunto also they were appointed.

9 But ye *are* a chosen generation, a royal priesthood, a holy nation, a peculiar people; that ye should show forth the praises of him who hath called you out of darkness into his marvelous light:

10 which in time past *were* not a people, but *are* now the people of God: which had not obtained mercy, but now have obtained mercy.

Live for God

Dearly beloved, I beseech *you* as strangers and pilgrims, abstain from fleshly lusts, which war against the soul;

12 having your conversation honest among the Gentiles: that, whereas they speak against you as evildoers, they may by *your* good works, which they shall behold, glorify God in the day of visitation.

Yield to Every Human Authority

Submit yourselves to every ordinance of man for the Lord's sake: whether it be to the king, as supreme;

14 or unto governors, as unto them that are sent by him for the punishment of evildoers, and for the praise of them that do well.

¹⁵ For so is the will of God, that with well doing ye may put to silence the ignorance of foolish men:

¹⁶ as free, and not using *your* liberty for a cloak of maliciousness, but as the servants of God.

¹⁷ Honor all *men*. Love the brotherhood. Fear God. Honor the king.

OLD TESTAMENT READING

*T*hen Nebuchadnezzar spake, and said, Blessed *be* the God of Shadrach, Meshach, and Abednego, who hath sent his angel, and delivered his servants that trusted in him, and have changed the king's word, and yielded their bodies, that they might not serve nor worship any god, except their own God.

²⁹ Therefore I make a decree, That every people, nation, and language, which speak any thing amiss against the God of Shadrach, Meshach, and Abednego, shall be cut in pieces, and their houses shall be made a dunghill; because there is no other God that can deliver after this sort.

Daniel 3:28–29

INSIGHTS

*G*od considers himself honored by the high attainments of His children and dishonored by their low attainments. He is honored in the fact that their graces so shine forth that it shall be seen by all around that they have partaken largely of His Spirit.

Exalted piety is honorable to God. Manifestations of great grace and spirituality of mind honor God. He is greatly honored by the fruits of righteousness His people bring forth. Christ himself says, "Herein is my Father glorified that ye bring

forth much fruit." Ministers should be greatly fruitful. They should bring forth the fruits of the Spirit in their tempers, in their lives, in the strength of their faith and labors of love. Can you doubt that God has great interest in these things? Indeed His great desire, that you should bring forth fruit to His glory, is shown in the fact that He says, "open thy mouth wide, and I will fill it."

Charles Finney

PAUSE FOR REFLECTION

*W*hat do you think it means to "have purified your souls in obeying the truth"? What purpose is served when believers live good lives? What have you learned from the lives of those who honor God in such a way? Are you willing to get rid of everything in your life that doesn't bring honor to the King?

THURSDAY

Live in Peace!

1 Peter 2:18—3:12

Follow Christ's Example

Servants, *be* subject to *your* masters with all fear; not only to the good and gentle, but also to the froward.

¹⁹ For this *is* thankworthy, if a man for conscience toward God endure grief, suffering wrongfully.

²⁰ For what glory *is it*, if, when ye be buffeted for your faults, ye shall take it patiently? but if, when ye do well, and suffer *for it*, ye take it patiently, this *is* acceptable with God.

²¹ For even hereunto were ye called: because Christ also suffered for us, leaving us an example, that ye should follow his steps:

²² who did no sin, neither was guile found in his mouth:

²³ who, when he was reviled, reviled not again; when he suffered, he threatened not; but committed *himself* to him that judgeth righteously:

²⁴ who his own self bare our sins in his own body on the tree, that we, being dead to sins, should live unto righteousness: by whose stripes ye were healed.

²⁵ For ye were as sheep going astray; but are now returned unto the Shepherd and Bishop of your souls.

Wives and Husbands

3 Likewise, ye wives, *be* in subjection to your own husbands; that, if any obey not the word, they also may without the word be won by the conversation of the wives;

² while they behold your chaste conversation *coupled* with fear.

³ Whose adorning, let it not be that outward *adorning* of plaiting the hair, and of wearing of gold, or of putting on of apparel;

⁴ but *let it be* the hidden man of the heart, in that which is not corruptible, *even the ornament* of a meek and quiet spirit, which is in the sight of God of great price.

⁵ For after this manner in the old time the holy women also, who trusted in God, adorned themselves, being in subjection unto their own husbands:

⁶ even as Sarah obeyed Abraham, calling him lord: whose daughters ye are, as long as ye do well, and are not afraid with any amazement.

⁷ Likewise, ye husbands, dwell with *them* according to knowledge, giving honor unto the wife, as unto the weaker vessel, and as being heirs together of the grace of life; that your prayers be not hindered.

Suffering for Doing Right

Finally, *be ye* all of one mind, having compassion one of another, love as brethren, *be* pitiful, *be* courteous:

⁹ not rendering evil for evil, or railing for railing: but contrariwise blessing; knowing that ye are thereunto called, that ye should inherit a blessing.

¹⁰ For he that will love life, and see good days, let him refrain his tongue from evil, and his lips that they speak no guile:

¹¹ let him eschew evil, and do good; let him seek peace, and ensue it.

¹² For the eyes of the Lord *are* over

the righteous, and his ears *are open* unto their prayers: but the face of the Lord *is* against them that do evil.

OLD TESTAMENT READING

*T*hen Abimelech went to him from Gerar, and Ahuzzath one of his friends, and Phichol the chief captain of his army.
²⁷ And Isaac said unto them, Wherefore come ye to me, seeing ye hate me, and have sent me away from you?
²⁸ And they said, We saw certainly that the LORD was with thee: and we said, Let there be now an oath betwixt us, *even* betwixt us and thee, and let us make a covenant with thee;
²⁹ that thou wilt do us no hurt, as we have not touched thee, and as we have done unto thee nothing but good, and have sent thee away in peace: thou *art* now the blessed of the LORD.
³⁰ And he made them a feast, and they did eat and drink.
³¹ And they rose up betimes in the morning, and sware one to another: and Isaac sent them away, and they departed from him in peace.

Genesis 26:26–31

INSIGHTS

*I*f the life is opened to receive the divine presence of the risen Christ, He comes in, speaking peace—just as He came again and again to His distraught disciples after His resurrection, saying, "Peace be unto you!"

He comes into our lives there to shed abroad a new love, His own life, that expresses itself in peace.

When He enters my experience; when He penetrates my personality; when He becomes Sovereign in my spirit, I in turn become a person of peace. It is then that I begin to know what it means to be at peace with God, at peace with others, at peace with myself.

Increasingly as He is given control of my life the entire complexion of my character, conduct, and conversation alters. I discover that He can change me dramatically. Peace, good will, good cheer, and serenity replace animosity, bitterness, hostility, belligerence, jealousy, bad temper, quarreling, and rivalry. . . .

. . . The peace of God, which is self-sacrificing and self-foregoing, produces healing. It comes to bind up the wounds; to pour in the oil of consolation; to bring repose and quietness; to still the troubled soul; to speak peace to stormy spirits. This peace comes only from Christ. It is one of the genuine, indisputable marks of God's presence in a person's life.

W. Phillip Keller

ACTION POINT

*W*ho set the standard for living in peace? What does living in peace look like? How full of Christ's peace is your life? Pray that God will give you a fuller love and more intimate understanding of his peace and that it will touch every area of your life.

FRIDAY

*Always Be Ready to Explain the
Hope of Your Salvation*

---

1 Peter 3:13—4:11

*A*nd who *is* he that will harm you, if ye be followers of that which is good?

¹⁴ But and if ye suffer for righteousness' sake, happy *are ye*: and be not afraid of their terror, neither be troubled;

¹⁵ but sanctify the Lord God in your hearts: and *be* ready always to *give* an answer to every man that asketh you a reason of the hope that is in you, with meekness and fear:

¹⁶ having a good conscience; that, whereas they speak evil of you, as of evildoers, they may be ashamed that falsely accuse your good conversation in Christ.

¹⁷ For *it is* better, if the will of God be so, that ye suffer for well doing, than for evil doing.

¹⁸ For Christ also hath once suffered for sins, the just for the unjust, that he might bring us to God, being put to death in the flesh, but quickened by the Spirit:

¹⁹ by which also he went and preached unto the spirits in prison;

²⁰ which sometime were disobedient, when once the longsuffering of God waited in the days of Noah, while the ark was a preparing, wherein few, that is, eight souls were saved by water.

²¹ The like figure whereunto *even* baptism doth also now save us, (not the putting away of the filth of the flesh, but the answer of a good conscience toward God,) by the resurrection of Jesus Christ:

²² who is gone into heaven, and is on the right hand of God; angels and authorities and powers being made subject unto him.

Change Your Lives

4 Forasmuch then as Christ hath suffered for us in the flesh, arm yourselves likewise with the same mind: for he that hath suffered in the flesh hath ceased from sin;

² that he no longer should live the rest of *his* time in the flesh to the lusts of men, but to the will of God.

³ For the time past of *our* life may suffice us to have wrought the will of the Gentiles, when we walked in lasciviousness, lusts, excess of wine, revelings, banquetings, and abominable idolatries:

⁴ wherein they think it strange that ye run not with *them* to the same excess of riot, speaking evil of *you*:

⁵ who shall give account to him that is ready to judge the quick and the dead.

⁶ For, for this cause was the gospel preached also to them that are dead, that they might be judged according to men in the flesh, but live according to God in the spirit.

Use God's Gifts Wisely

*B*ut the end of all things is at hand: be ye therefore sober, and watch unto prayer.

⁸ And above all things have fervent charity among yourselves: for charity shall cover the multitude of sins.

⁹ Use hospitality one to another without grudging.

¹⁰ As every man hath received the

gift, *even so* minister the same one to another, as good stewards of the manifold grace of God.

¹¹ If any man speak, *let him speak* as the oracles of God; if any man minister, *let him do it* as of the ability which God giveth; that God in all things may be glorified through Jesus Christ: to whom be praise and dominion for ever and ever. Amen.

OLD TESTAMENT READING

O God, be not far from me: O my God, make haste for my help.

¹³ Let them be confounded *and* consumed that are adversaries to my soul; let them be covered *with* reproach and dishonor that seek my hurt.

¹⁴ But I will hope continually, and will yet praise thee more and more.

¹⁵ My mouth shall show forth thy righteousness *and* thy salvation all the day; for I know not the numbers *thereof.*

¹⁶ I will go in the strength of the Lord GOD: I will make mention of thy righteousness, *even* of thine only.

Psalm 71:12–16

INSIGHTS

*C*hristians have a corner on hope. Why? Because the basis of all hope is knowing who God is. There is no hope without a God who controls the universe and promises to bring us to heaven.

Hope designates a future—that is what we hope in. Time, our period on this earth, can be seen in various ways, but only one way offers hope. Some see time as cyclical: history repeats itself and will continue to repeat itself only to get worse (and fi-nally burn itself up). Others see time in the modern secular view that immortality exists as each generation gives birth to the next, which then gives birth to the next. But Christians see time in a straight line— God began time, has a specific purpose for each person within his divine plan, and he will bring it to an end when he returns as he promised.

Hope is not in most of the things our fellow humans hope in. It cannot be found in possessions, in our own strength or supposed "immortality," in people's love, in the past. Neither can it be found in human achievement, in who we are or what we have done, or in this life itself.

So where is hope? Our hope lies in our Christian growth here on earth—that we are doing what God wants for us in our particular place in time. We hope in the new heaven and new earth God has promised for us (Hebrews 13:14). We hope in Christ's second coming, in eternal life, and in resurrection (1 John 3:2, 3). We hope in the fact that this world is not all there is (Revelation 21:2, 3). And the great thing about our hope is that it is based on fact. It will happen because our hope is based on God, not on us.

YFC Editors

ACTION POINT

*D*escribe the hope of your salvation. Be specific. How might your hope affect the heart of an unbeliever? What should be your purpose in everything you do? Ask God to fulfill his purpose through you.

WEEKEND

*Give All Your Worries to God;
He Cares for You*

1 Peter 4:12—5:14

Suffering as a Christian

*B*eloved, think it not strange concerning the fiery trial which is to try you, as though some strange thing happened unto you:

¹³ but rejoice, inasmuch as ye are partakers of Christ's sufferings; that, when his glory shall be revealed, ye may be glad also with exceeding joy.

¹⁴ If ye be reproached for the name of Christ, happy are *ye*; for the spirit of glory and of God resteth upon you: on their part he is evil spoken of, but on your part he is glorified.

¹⁵ But let none of you suffer as a murderer, or *as* a thief, or *as* an evildoer, or *as* a busybody in other men's matters.

¹⁶ Yet if *any man suffer* as a Christian, let him not be ashamed; but let him glorify God on this behalf.

¹⁷ For the time *is come* that judgment must begin at the house of God: and if *it* first *begin* at us, what shall the end *be* of them that obey not the gospel of God?

¹⁸ And if the righteous scarcely be saved, where shall the ungodly and the sinner appear?

¹⁹ Wherefore, let them that suffer according to the will of God commit the keeping of their souls *to him* in well doing, as unto a faithful Creator.

The Flock of God

5 The elders which are among you I exhort, who am also an elder, and a witness of the sufferings of Christ, and also a partaker of the glory that shall be revealed:

² Feed the flock of God which is among you, taking the oversight *thereof*, not by constraint, but willingly; not for filthy lucre, but of a ready mind;

³ neither as being lords over *God's* heritage, but being ensamples to the flock.

⁴ And when the chief Shepherd shall appear, ye shall receive a crown of glory that fadeth not away.

⁵ Likewise, ye younger, submit yourselves unto the elder. Yea, all *of you* be subject one to another, and be clothed with humility: for God resisteth the proud, and giveth grace to the humble.

⁶ Humble yourselves therefore under the mighty hand of God, that he may exalt you in due time:

⁷ casting all your care upon him; for he careth for you.

⁸ Be sober, be vigilant; because your adversary the devil, as a roaring lion, walketh about, seeking whom he may devour:

⁹ whom resist steadfast in the faith, knowing that the same afflictions are accomplished in your brethren that are in the world.

¹⁰ But the God of all grace, who hath called us unto his eternal glory by Christ Jesus, after that ye have suffered a while, make you perfect, stablish, strengthen, settle *you*.

¹¹ To him *be* glory and dominion for ever and ever. Amen.

Final Greetings

*B*y Silvanus, a faithful brother unto you, as I suppose, I have written briefly, exhorting, and testifying that this is the true grace of God wherein ye stand.

¹³ The *church that is* at Babylon, elected together with *you*, saluteth you; and *so doth* Mark my son.

¹⁴ Greet ye one another with a kiss of charity. Peace *be* with you all that are in Christ Jesus. Amen.

OLD TESTAMENT READING

*A*nd the word of the Lord came unto him, saying,

³ Get thee hence, and turn thee eastward, and hide thyself by the brook Cherith, that *is* before Jordan.

⁴ And it shall be, *that* thou shalt drink of the brook; and I have commanded the ravens to feed thee there.

⁶ And the ravens brought him bread and flesh in the morning, and bread and flesh in the evening; and he drank of the brook.

⁷ And it came to pass after a while, that the brook dried up, because there had been no rain in the land.

⁸ And the word of the Lord came unto him, saying,

⁹ Arise, get thee to Zarephath, which *belongeth* to Zidon, and dwell there: behold, I have commanded a widow woman there to sustain thee.

1 Kings 17:2-4, 6-9

INSIGHTS

*O*ne winter I worked as secretary and receptionist at a mortuary. . . .

My husband had just been affected by a large company layoff, so I had needed to work. One particularly dark and dreary day I sat all by myself in the large office of the mortuary. While I typed a letter, my thoughts drifted to the house payment and utility bills. I soon felt overwhelmed. Tears came as I thought about the fact that we also needed groceries. Furthermore, Christmas was coming.

Suddenly, my thoughts were interrupted by a noise at the window. I walked over to see what it was. Through my tears, I saw that a sparrow had flown into the window and, stunned by the blow, had fallen to the ground.

This little incident reminded me of what God has to say in His Word about the birds of the air. He's aware of and provides for all of their needs. How much more is He aware of His children in need.

I felt so encouraged as I recalled sermons on this topic. I could almost hear the gospel singer: "His Eye Is On the Sparrow." I hummed the song the rest of the day. My faith increased, as I learned to trust God for my every need.

Then one morning a friend stood at the front door. "The Lord laid it on my heart to give you this money," he said. He didn't know it, but it was our house payment. Later, several checks came in the mail from a loving friend, signed, "Love, Jesus." One week we were invited out to dinner every night. And the children ended up having a delightful Christmas.

Barbara Hyatt

APPLICATION

*W*hat worry did Peter's readers face? For what reasons does he tell them not to worry? What reassurance of God's loving care does the Old Testament reading provide? Will you trust in his care?

MONDAY

Add Knowledge to Your Faith

2 Peter 1:1–21

1 Simon Peter, a servant and an apostle of Jesus Christ, to them that have obtained like precious faith with us through the righteousness of God and our Saviour Jesus Christ: ² Grace and peace be multiplied unto you through the knowledge of God, and of Jesus our Lord.

God Has Given Us Blessings

*A*ccording as his divine power hath given unto us all things that *pertain* unto life and godliness, through the knowledge of him that hath called us to glory and virtue: ⁴ whereby are given unto us exceeding great and precious promises; that by these ye might be partakers of the divine nature, having escaped the corruption that is in the world through lust. ⁵ And besides this, giving all diligence, add to your faith virtue; and to virtue, knowledge; ⁶ and to knowledge, temperance; and to temperance, patience; and to patience, godliness; ⁷ And to godliness, brotherly kindness; and to brotherly kindness, charity. ⁸ For if these things be in you, and abound, they make *you that ye shall* neither *be* barren nor unfruitful in the knowledge of our Lord Jesus Christ. ⁹ But he that lacketh these things is blind, and cannot see afar off, and hath forgotten that he was purged from his old sins. ¹⁰ Wherefore the rather, brethren, give diligence to make your calling and election sure: for if ye do these things, ye shall never fall: ¹¹ for so an entrance shall be ministered unto you abundantly into the everlasting kingdom of our Lord and Saviour Jesus Christ. ¹² Wherefore I will not be negligent to put you always in remembrance of these things, though ye know *them*, and be established in the present truth. ¹³ Yea, I think it meet, as long as I am in this tabernacle, to stir you up by putting *you* in remembrance; ¹⁴ knowing that shortly I must put off *this* my tabernacle, even as our Lord Jesus Christ hath showed me. ¹⁵ Moreover I will endeavor that ye may be able after my decease to have these things always in remembrance.

We Saw Christ's Majesty

*F*or we have not followed cunningly devised fables, when we made known unto you the power and coming of our Lord Jesus Christ, but were eyewitnesses of his majesty. ¹⁷ For he received from God the Father honor and glory, when there came such a voice to him from the excellent glory, This is my beloved Son, in whom I am well pleased. ¹⁸ And this voice which came from heaven we heard, when we were with him in the holy mount. ¹⁹ We have also a more sure word of prophecy; whereunto ye do well that ye take heed, as unto a light that shineth in a dark place, until the day dawn, and the day-star arise in your hearts:

20 knowing this first, that no prophecy of the Scripture is of any private interpretation.

21 For the prophecy came not in old time by the will of man: but holy men of God spake *as they were* moved by the Holy Ghost.

OLD TESTAMENT READING

*F*or the LORD giveth wisdom: out of his mouth *cometh* knowledge and understanding.

Proverbs 2:6

*T*he proverbs of Solomon the son of David, king of Israel.

3 To receive the instruction of wisdom, justice, and judgment, and equity.

7 The fear of the LORD *is* the beginning of knowledge: *but* fools despise wisdom and instruction.

Proverbs 1:1, 3, 7

INSIGHTS

*W*e are to make every effort to increase our faith, knowledge, self-control, steadfastness and brotherly affection. Each of us is expected to be spiritually self-sustaining. We cannot rely on pastors or Christian leaders to keep our faith propped up.

Some Christians live from Sunday to Sunday. They start their week ready for action, but by Saturday are drained of their enthusiasm and can barely drag themselves to church the next day for another boost. Paul talks of digesting the milk of the Word (1 Cor 3:2). Babies need someone to feed them milk, and in the same way, new Christians need someone to help them understand biblical truth. Yet, we have all seen retarded adults who are incapable of feeding themselves. Behavior that is natural and cute in an infant is saddening to watch in these adults. Sadly, there are Christians who have not made "every effort to supplement their faith," and they too are retarded in their spiritual development.

Prayer and Bible study are important in supplementing our faith. God reveals himself to us in the Bible, and through prayer we have direct access to him with our problems and questions. . . .

. . . Once Bible study is a regular part of our lives, we will begin to reap the rewards of a more stable and mature relationship with the Lord. We will also have the personal confidence to go to the Bible and find our own answers to life's questions.

God does not want us to be spiritually retarded and unable to sustain the new life he has given us. He wants us to reach a place of maturity where we can spiritually feed ourselves and be able to stand firm in the face of any adversity.

Floyd McClung

PAUSE FOR REFLECTION

*W*hat things does Peter say to add to your faith? What is the purpose and the result of doing these things? Consider your own life, and write down what you think will be accomplished if you add each of these things to your faith. Be specific.

TUESDAY

*God Condemns False Teachers
Who Lead People into Evil*

2 Peter 2:1–22

False Teachers

2 But there were false prophets also among the people, even as there shall be false teachers among you, who privily shall bring in damnable heresies, even denying the Lord that bought them, and bring upon themselves swift destruction. ² And many shall follow their pernicious ways; by reason of whom the way of truth shall be evil spoken of. ³ And through covetousness shall they with feigned words make merchandise of you: whose judgment now of a long time lingereth not, and their damnation slumbereth not. ⁴ For if God spared not the angels that sinned, but cast *them* down to hell, and delivered *them* into chains of darkness, to be reserved unto judgment; ⁵ And spared not the old world, but saved Noah the eighth *person*, a preacher of righteousness, bringing in the flood upon the world of the ungodly; ⁶ and turning the cities of Sodom and Gomorrah into ashes condemned *them* with an overthrow, making *them* an ensample unto those that after should live ungodly; ⁷ and delivered just Lot, vexed with the filthy conversation of the wicked: ⁸ (for that righteous man dwelling among them, in seeing and hearing, vexed *his* righteous soul from day to day with *their* unlawful deeds;)

⁹ the Lord knoweth how to deliver the godly out of temptation, and to reserve the unjust unto the day of judgment to be punished: ¹⁰ but chiefly them that walk after the flesh in the lust of uncleanness, and despise government. Presumptuous *are they*, selfwilled, they are not afraid to speak evil of dignities. ¹¹ Whereas angels, which are greater in power and might, bring not railing accusation against them before the Lord. ¹² But these, as natural brute beasts made to be taken and destroyed, speak evil of the things that they understand not; and shall utterly perish in their own corruption; ¹³ and shall receive the reward of unrighteousness, *as* they that count it pleasure to riot in the daytime. Spots *they are* and blemishes, sporting themselves with their own deceivings while they feast with you; ¹⁴ having eyes full of adultery, and that cannot cease from sin; beguiling unstable souls: a heart they have exercised with covetous practices; cursed children: ¹⁵ which have forsaken the right way, and are gone astray, following the way of Balaam *the son* of Beor, who loved the wages of unrighteousness; ¹⁶ but was rebuked for his iniquity: the dumb ass speaking with man's voice forbade the madness of the prophet. ¹⁷ These are wells without water, clouds that are carried with a tempest; to whom the mist of darkness is reserved for ever. ¹⁸ For when they speak great swelling words of vanity, they allure through the lusts of the flesh, *through much* wantonness, those

that were clean escaped from them who live in error.

¹⁹ While they promise them liberty, they themselves are the servants of corruption: for of whom a man is overcome, of the same is he brought in bondage.

²⁰ For if after they have escaped the pollutions of the world through the knowledge of the Lord and Saviour Jesus Christ, they are again entangled therein, and overcome, the latter end is worse with them than the beginning.

²¹ For it had been better for them not to have known the way of righteousness, than, after they have known *it*, to turn from the holy commandment delivered unto them.

²² But it is happened unto them according to the true proverb, The dog *is* turned to his own vomit again; and the sow that was washed to her wallowing in the mire.

OLD TESTAMENT READING

*Y*ea, *they are* greedy dogs *which* can never have enough, and they *are* shepherds *that* cannot understand: they all look to their own way, every one for his gain, from his quarter.

Isaiah 56:11

INSIGHTS

*D*eception is on the rise within the Christian church and we ignore it to our peril.

Sometimes it is difficult—even for a Christian—to recognize the deceivers. Jesus spoke of false prophets who "perform great signs and miracles to deceive even the elect." . . .

Satan does not want to build a church and call it "The First Church of Satan." He is far too clever for that. He invades the Sunday school, the youth department, the Christian education program, the pulpit and the seminary classroom.

The apostle Paul warned that many will follow false teachers, not knowing that in feeding upon what these people say they are taking the devil's poison into their own lives. Thousands of uninstructed Christians are being deceived today. False teachers use high-sounding words that seem like the height of logic, scholarship and culture. They are intellectually clever and crafty in their sophistry. They are adept at beguiling thoughtless, untaught men and women. . . .

The best advice against deception that I can give is to urge you to spend your time looking at the real Christ. Then, when a counterfeit appears, you'll have less trouble spotting him.

Billy Graham

ACTION POINT

*L*ist the lifestyle patterns that serve as clues that a false teacher is at work. How can a person guard against the practiced deception of false teachers? How do you plan to learn God's truth?

WEDNESDAY

*You May Be Mocked, but
Be Strong in Your Faith*

2 Peter 3:1–18

Jesus Will Come Again

3 This second epistle, beloved, I now write unto you; in *both* which I stir up your pure minds by way of remembrance:

2 that ye may be mindful of the words which were spoken before by the holy prophets, and of the commandment of us the apostles of the Lord and Saviour:

3 knowing this first, that there shall come in the last days scoffers, walking after their own lusts,

4 and saying, Where is the promise of his coming? for since the fathers fell asleep, all things continue as *they were* from the beginning of the creation.

5 For this they willingly are ignorant of, that by the word of God the heavens were of old, and the earth standing out of the water and in the water:

6 whereby the world that then was, being overflowed with water, perished:

7 but the heavens and the earth, which are now, by the same word are kept in store, reserved unto fire against the day of judgment and perdition of ungodly men.

8 But, beloved, be not ignorant of this one thing, that one day *is* with the Lord as a thousand years, and a thousand years as one day.

9 The Lord is not slack concerning his promise, as some men count slackness; but is longsuffering to usward, not willing that any should perish, but that all should come to repentance.

10 But the day of the Lord will come as a thief in the night; in the which the heavens shall pass away with a great noise, and the elements shall melt with fervent heat, the earth also and the works that are therein shall be burned up.

11 *Seeing* then *that* all these things shall be dissolved, what manner *of persons* ought ye to be in *all* holy conversation and godliness,

12 looking for and hasting unto the coming of the day of God, wherein the heavens being on fire shall be dissolved, and the elements shall melt with fervent heat?

13 Nevertheless we, according to his promise, look for new heavens and a new earth, wherein dwelleth righteousness.

14 Wherefore, beloved, seeing that ye look for such things, be diligent that ye may be found of him in peace, without spot, and blameless.

15 And account *that* the long-suffering of our Lord *is* salvation; even as our beloved brother Paul also according to the wisdom given unto him hath written unto you;

16 as also in all *his* epistles, speaking in them of these things; in which are some things hard to be understood, which they that are unlearned and unstable wrest, as *they do* also the other Scriptures, unto their own destruction.

17 Ye therefore, beloved, seeing ye know *these things* before, beware lest ye also, being led away with the error of the wicked, fall from your own steadfastness.

18 But grow in grace, and *in* the

knowledge of our Lord and Saviour Jesus Christ. To him *be* glory both now and for ever. Amen.

*B*ut thou *art* holy, *O thou* that inhabitest the praise of Israel.

⁴ Our fathers trusted in thee: they trusted, and thou didst deliver them.

⁵ They cried unto thee, and were delivered: they trusted in thee, and were not confounded.

⁶ But I *am* a worm, and no man; a reproach of men, and despised of the people.

⁷ All they that see me laugh me to scorn: they shoot out the lip, they shake the head *saying,*

⁸ He trusted on the LORD *that* he would deliver him: let him deliver him, seeing he delighted in him.

Psalm 22:3–8

*T*hey laughed at me and made fun of me because I wouldn't participate in what they were doing."

"I lost the promotion at work because I refused to take my clients to that sleazy nightclub."

"I lost several 'friends' because I didn't go along with their gossiping when we got together."

Modern day persecution because of our faith? Perhaps. It hurts to be misunderstood and not accepted. Believers in China and other parts of the world still face intense persecution. They lose their homes, some end up in prison, and many are killed because of their faith.

Most of us have never really felt the piercing sting of persecution. It could happen to us as it does in other countries like China. It could happen in ways hard to imagine if our democratic society were overturned. You never know. But whatever type of persecution you experience, do you know how Jesus wants you to respond? It's quite simple. Rejoice and be glad. That's all. Be glad. Don't retaliate. Don't sulk. Don't complain. Don't just grin and bear it. Rejoice and actually "leap for joy" (Luke 6:23).

. . . Expect opposition to your Christian stance. That's normal. If you are persecuted because of your stance for Jesus Christ, it means you are really committed to Him and your commitment is evident to others. You are having an impact in the world around you. Isn't it strange that living for Him brings discomfort? But why not? Living for Christ means confronting a world that is living contrary to the way God intended. Your Christian life bothers them. It's convicting. So they will react to you. But I guess Jesus understands that pretty well, doesn't He? Look at what it cost Him.

H. Norman Wright

*W*hat perspective does Peter offer to help his readers bear persecution? Will God hurry to fulfill his plan for anyone? In what ways does focusing on God—his eternal timelessness and omnipotent power—help you face the challenges of unbelievers?

THURSDAY

Live in the Light!

1 John 1:1—2:14

1 That which was from the beginning, which we have heard, which we have seen with our eyes, which we have looked upon, and our hands have handled, of the Word of life;

2 (for the life was manifested, and we have seen *it*, and bear witness, and show unto you that eternal life, which was with the Father, and was manifested unto us;)

3 that which we have seen and heard declare we unto you, that ye also may have fellowship with us: and truly our fellowship *is* with the Father, and with his Son Jesus Christ.

4 And these things write we unto you, that your joy may be full.

God Forgives Our Sins

*T*his then is the message which we have heard of him, and declare unto you, that God is light, and in him is no darkness at all.

6 If we say that we have fellowship with him, and walk in darkness, we lie, and do not the truth:

7 but if we walk in the light, as he is in the light, we have fellowship one with another, and the blood of Jesus Christ his Son cleanseth us from all sin.

8 If we say that we have no sin, we deceive ourselves, and the truth is not in us.

9 If we confess our sins, he is faithful and just to forgive us *our* sins, and to cleanse us from all unrighteousness.

10 If we say that we have not sinned, we make him a liar, and his word is not in us.

Jesus Is Our Advocate

2 My little children, these things write I unto you, that ye sin not. And if any man sin, we have an advocate with the Father, Jesus Christ the righteous:

2 and he is the propitiation for our sins: and not for ours only, but also for *the sins of* the whole world.

3 And hereby we do know that we know him, if we keep his commandments.

4 He that saith, I know him, and keepeth not his commandments, is a liar, and the truth is not in him.

5 But whoso keepeth his word, in him verily is the love of God perfected: hereby know we that we are in him.

6 He that saith he abideth in him ought himself also so to walk, even as he walked.

The Command to Love Others

*B*rethren, I write no new commandment unto you, but an old commandment which ye had from the beginning. The old commandment is the word which ye have heard from the beginning.

8 Again, a new commandment I write unto you, which thing is true in him and in you: because the darkness is past, and the true light now shineth.

9 He that saith he is in the light, and hateth his brother, is in darkness even until now.

10 He that loveth his brother abideth in the light, and there is none occasion of stumbling in him.

¹¹ But he that hateth his brother is in darkness, and walketh in darkness, and knoweth not whither he goeth, because that darkness hath blinded his eyes.

¹² I write unto you, little children, because your sins are forgiven you for his name's sake.

¹³ I write unto you, fathers, because ye have known him *that is* from the beginning. I write unto you, young men, because ye have overcome the wicked one. I write unto you, little children, because ye have known the Father.

¹⁴ I have written unto you, fathers, because ye have known him *that is* from the beginning. I have written unto you, young men, because ye are strong, and the word of God abideth in you, and ye have overcome the wicked one.

OLD TESTAMENT READING

O send out thy light and thy truth: let them lead me; let them bring me unto thy holy hill, and to thy tabernacles.

⁴ Then will I go unto the altar of God, unto God my exceeding joy: yea, upon the harp will I praise thee, O God my God.

Psalm 43:3–4

---

*A*nd from the wicked their light is withholden.

Job 38:15a

INSIGHTS

*S*ervants of Christ shine with His light in a society that is hopelessly lost. . . .

We pose a weird phenomenon to those in darkness. They cannot figure us out! And that is exactly as Jesus planned it. Think of some distinctive characteristics of light:

• *Light is silent.* No noise, no big splash, no banners—light simply shines. It's like a single lighthouse along a rugged shoreline. All it does is shine as it turns.

• *Light gives direction.* No words, no sermon. Jesus says that others "see" our actions—but nothing is said of their hearing.

• *Light attracts attention.* You don't have to ask people to look at you when you turn a light on in a dark room. It happens automatically. . . . If you are a Christian family in a non-Christian neighborhood, you are the light in that darkness. The same is true if you are the only Christian nurse on your floor, or student in your school, or professional in your firm or group, or salesman in your district. You are a light in darkness—a servant of God who is being watched, who gives off a very distinct message . . . often with hardly a word being said. . . . Let it shine! Don't attempt to show off how bright and sparkling you are, just shine!

Charles Swindoll

APPLICATION

*W*hat feelings does the God of light bring into your life? Describe what it means for you to "live in the light." What corners of darkness in your life do you need to open up to God's cleansing light?

FRIDAY

*You Have Been Forgiven,
so Don't Love the World's
Fleeting Pleasures*

1 John 2:15—3:10

*L*ove not the world, neither the things *that are* in the world. If any man love the world, the love of the Father is not in him. [16] For all that *is* in the world, the lust of the flesh, and the lust of the eyes, and the pride of life, is not of the Father, but is of the world. [17] And the world passeth away, and the lust thereof: but he that doeth the will of God abideth for ever.

Reject the Enemies of Christ

*L*ittle children, it is the last time: and as ye have heard that antichrist shall come, even now are there many antichrists; whereby we know that it is the last time. [19] They went out from us, but they were not of us; for if they had been of us, they would *no doubt* have continued with us: but *they went out*, that they might be made manifest that they were not all of us. [20] But ye have an unction from the Holy One, and ye know all things. [21] I have not written unto you because ye know not the truth, but because ye know it, and that no lie is of the truth. [22] Who is a liar but he that denieth that Jesus is the Christ? He is antichrist, that denieth the Father and the Son. [23] Whosoever denieth the Son, the same hath not the Father: [*but*] *he*

that acknowledgeth the Son hath the Father also. [24] Let that therefore abide in you, which ye have heard from the beginning. If that which ye have heard from the beginning shall remain in you, ye also shall continue in the Son, and in the Father. [25] And this is the promise that he hath promised us, *even* eternal life. [26] These things have I written unto you concerning them that seduce you. [27] But the anointing which ye have received of him abideth in you, and ye need not that any man teach you: but as the same anointing teacheth you of all things, and is truth, and is no lie, and even as it hath taught you, ye shall abide in him. [28] And now, little children, abide in him; that, when he shall appear, we may have confidence, and not be ashamed before him at his coming. [29] If ye know that he is righteous, ye know that every one that doeth righteousness is born of him.

We Are God's Children

3 Behold, what manner of love the Father hath bestowed upon us, that we should be called the sons of God: therefore the world knoweth us not, because it knew him not. [2] Beloved, now are we the sons of God, and it doth not yet appear what we shall be: but we know that, when he shall appear, we shall be like him; for we shall see him as he is. [3] And every man that hath this hope in him purifieth himself, even as he is pure. [4] Whosoever committeth sin transgresseth also the law: for sin is the transgression of the law.

⁵ And ye know that he was manifested to take away our sins; and in him is no sin.

⁶ Whosoever abideth in him sinneth not: whosoever sinneth hath not seen him, neither known him.

⁷ Little children, let no man deceive you: he that doeth righteousness is righteous, even as he is righteous.

⁸ He that committeth sin is of the devil; for the devil sinneth from the beginning. For this purpose the Son of God was manifested, that he might destroy the works of the devil.

⁹ Whosoever is born of God doth not commit sin; for his seed remaineth in him: and he cannot sin, because he is born of God.

¹⁰ In this the children of God are manifest, and the children of the devil: whosoever doeth not righteousness is not of God, neither he that loveth not his brother.

OLD TESTAMENT READING

I said in mine heart, Go to now, I will prove thee with mirth; therefore enjoy pleasure: and, behold, this also *is* vanity.

¹⁰ And whatsoever mine eyes desired I kept not from them, I withheld not my heart from any joy; for my heart rejoiced in all my labor: and this was my portion of all my labor.

¹¹ Then I looked on all the works that my hands had wrought, and on the labor that I had labored to do: and, behold, all *was* vanity and vexation of spirit, and *there was* no profit under the sun.

Ecclesiastes 2:1, 10–11

INSIGHTS

When I look back on my life nowa-

days, which I sometimes do, what strikes me forcibly about it is that what seemed at the time most significant and seductive, seems now most futile and absurd. For instance, success in all of its various guises; being known and being praised; ostensible pleasures, like acquiring money or seducing women, or travelling, going to and fro in the world and up and down in it like Satan, exploring and experiencing whatever Vanity Fair has to offer.

In retrospect all these exercises in self-gratification seem pure fantasy, what Pascal called "licking the earth." They are diversions designed to distract our attention from the true purpose of our existence in this world, which is, quite simply, to look for God, and, in looking, to find Him, and having found Him, to love Him, thereby establishing a harmonious relationship with His purposes for His creation.

Malcolm Muggeridge

ACTION POINT

Write down what you believe to be your true purpose in life. What things are important according to that purpose? Pray that God will help you focus on the important things and put aside everything else—no matter how tempting it may appear!

WEEKEND

*God's People Must Show Their
Love for One Another*

1 John 3:11—4:12

We Should Love One Another

*F*or this is the message that ye heard from the beginning, that we should love one another.

¹² Not as Cain, *who* was of that wicked one, and slew his brother. And wherefore slew he him? Because his own works were evil, and his brother's righteous.

¹³ Marvel not, my brethren, if the world hate you.

¹⁴ We know that we have passed from death unto life, because we love the brethren. He that loveth not *his* brother abideth in death.

¹⁵ Whosoever hateth his brother is a murderer: and ye know that no murderer hath eternal life abiding in him.

¹⁶ Hereby perceive we the love *of God*, because he laid down his life for us: and we ought to lay down *our* lives for the brethren.

¹⁷ But whoso hath this world's good, and seeth his brother have need, and shutteth up his bowels *of compassion* from him, how dwelleth the love of God in him?

¹⁸ My little children, let us not love in word, neither in tongue; but in deed and in truth.

¹⁹ And hereby we know that we are of the truth, and shall assure our hearts before him.

²⁰ For if our heart condemn us, God is greater than our heart, and knoweth all things.

²¹ Beloved, if our heart condemn us not, *then* have we confidence toward God.

²² And whatsoever we ask, we receive of him, because we keep his commandments, and do those things that are pleasing in his sight.

²³ And this is his commandment, That we should believe on the name of his Son Jesus Christ, and love one another, as he gave us commandment.

²⁴ And he that keepeth his commandments dwelleth in him, and he in him. And hereby we know that he abideth in us, by the Spirit which he hath given us.

Warning Against False Teachers

4 Beloved, believe not every spirit, but try the spirits whether they are of God: because many false prophets are gone out into the world.

² Hereby know ye the Spirit of God: Every spirit that confesseth that Jesus Christ is come in the flesh is of God:

³ and every spirit that confesseth not that Jesus Christ is come in the flesh is not of God: and this is that *spirit* of antichrist, whereof ye have heard that it should come; and even now already is it in the world.

⁴ Ye are of God, little children, and have overcome them: because greater is he that is in you, than he that is in the world.

⁵ They are of the world: therefore speak they of the world, and the world heareth them.

⁶ We are of God: he that knoweth God heareth us; he that is not of God heareth not us. Hereby know we the spirit of truth, and the spirit of error.

Love Comes from God

*B*eloved, let us love one another: for love is of God; and every one that loveth is born of God, and knoweth God.

⁸ He that loveth not, knoweth not God; for God is love.

⁹ In this was manifested the love of God toward us, because that God sent his only begotten Son into the world, that we might live through him.

¹⁰ Herein is love, not that we loved God, but that he loved us, and sent his Son *to be* the propitiation for our sins.

¹¹ Beloved, if God so loved us, we ought also to love one another.

¹² No man hath seen God at any time. If we love one another, God dwelleth in us, and his love is perfected in us.

OLD TESTAMENT READING

*A*nd the king said, *Is* there not yet any of the house of Saul, that I may show the kindness of God unto him? And Ziba said unto the king, Jonathan hath yet a son, *which is* lame on *his* feet.

⁵ Then king David sent, and fetched him out of the house of Machir, the son of Ammiel, from Lo-debar.

⁶ Now when Mephibosheth, the son of Jonathan, the son of Saul, was come unto David, he fell on his face, and did reverence. And David said, Mephibosheth. And he answered, Behold thy servant!

⁷ And David said unto him, Fear not: for I will surely show thee kindness for Jonathan thy father's sake, and will restore thee all the land of Saul thy father; and thou shalt eat bread at my table continually.

2 Samuel 9:3, 5–7

INSIGHTS

*T*here is more to becoming a Christian than accepting a set of doctrines and striving to live out a particular lifestyle. Being a Christian involves allowing God to become a living presence in your life. . . . A Christian is a person who is possessed by Christ in such a way that feelings, thoughts, and attitudes are all changed. For the Christian person, loving becomes a spiritual exercise because God is love, and the Christian knows that "every one that loveth is born of God." God wants to indwell you and affect your consciousness for many reasons, but above them all is His desire to be able to reach other people with His love through you. . . . If you will pray and ask Him to be an indwelling reality and if you are willing to yield to His will in all things, He will enter into your consciousness and begin to effect a transformation in your life. Most important, you will, little by little, begin to relate to other people as He would relate to them. You will recognize that being a Christian involves a commitment to treat others as He would treat them. . . .

If you want to do something that will cause you to become a more loving person, surrender yourself to Jesus. He has a way of making lovers out of people.

Tony Campolo

APPLICATION

*W*hy is love characteristic of God's children? What does a lack of love reveal about a person's heart?

MONDAY

*God Listens to the
Prayers of His People*

1 John 4:13—5:21

*H*ereby know we that we dwell in him, and he in us, because he hath given us of his Spirit.

¹⁴ And we have seen and do testify that the Father sent the Son *to be* the Saviour of the world.

¹⁵ Whosoever shall confess that Jesus is the Son of God, God dwelleth in him, and he in God.

¹⁶ And we have known and believed the love that God hath to us. God is love; and he that dwelleth in love dwelleth in God, and God in him.

¹⁷ Herein is our love made perfect, that we may have boldness in the day of judgment: because as he is, so are we in this world.

¹⁸ There is no fear in love; but perfect love casteth out fear: because fear hath torment. He that feareth is not made perfect in love.

¹⁹ We love him, because he first loved us.

²⁰ If a man say, I love God, and hateth his brother, he is a liar: for he that loveth not his brother whom he hath seen, how can he love God whom he hath not seen?

²¹ And this commandment have we from him, That he who loveth God love his brother also.

Faith in the Son of God

5 Whosoever believeth that Jesus is the Christ is born of God: and every one that loveth him that begat loveth him also that is begotten of him.

² By this we know that we love the children of God, when we love God, and keep his commandments.

³ For this is the love of God, that we keep his commandments: and his commandments are not grievous.

⁴ For whatsoever is born of God overcometh the world: and this is the victory that overcometh the world, *even* our faith.

⁵ Who is he that overcometh the world, but he that believeth that Jesus is the Son of God?

⁶ This is he that came by water and blood, *even* Jesus Christ; not by water only, but by water and blood. And it is the Spirit that beareth witness, because the Spirit is truth.

⁷ For there are three that bear record in heaven, the Father, the Word, and the Holy Ghost: and these three are one.

⁸ And there are three that bear witness in earth, the spirit, and the water, and the blood: and these three agree in one.

⁹ If we receive the witness of men, the witness of God is greater: for this is the witness of God which he hath testified of his Son.

¹⁰ He that believeth on the Son of God hath the witness in himself: he that believeth not God hath made him a liar; because he believeth not the record that God gave of his Son.

¹¹ And this is the record, that God hath given to us eternal life, and this life is in his Son.

¹² He that hath the Son hath life; *and* he that hath not the Son of God hath not life.

We Have Eternal Life Now

*T*hese things have I written unto you that believe on the name of the

Son of God; that ye may know that ye have eternal life, and that ye may believe on the name of the Son of God.

14 And this is the confidence that we have in him, that, if we ask any thing according to his will, he heareth us: 15 and if we know that he hear us, whatsoever we ask, we know that we have the petitions that we desired of him.

16 If any man see his brother sin a sin *which is* not unto death, he shall ask, and he shall give him life for them that sin not unto death. There is a sin unto death: I do not say that he shall pray for it. 17 All unrighteousness is sin: and there is a sin not unto death.

18 We know that whosoever is born of God sinneth not; but he that is begotten of God keepeth himself, and that wicked one toucheth him not.

19 *And* we know that we are of God, and the whole world lieth in wickedness.

20 And we know that the Son of God is come, and hath given us an understanding, that we may know him that is true, and we are in him that is true, *even* in his Son Jesus Christ. This is the true God, and eternal life.

21 Little children, keep yourselves from idols. Amen.

OLD TESTAMENT READING

But verily God hath heard *me*; he hath attended to the voice of my prayer. 20 Blessed *be* God, which hath not turned away my prayer, nor his mercy from me.

Psalm 66:19–20

INSIGHTS

PLEASE INTERRUPT

Sometimes I feel like an interruption, and then I want to shrink back into my shell and never come out again. I want to walk away and say, "I'm sorry I took your time."

Being an interruption hurts. It tells me something is more important than I am. It tells me to hurry up and move along. It tells me you are looking but don't see me. It tells me you are listening but don't hear me. And so I move along.

But, God says, "Don't hurry away. Stick around. Tell me how it is with you. Tell me what you're feeling right this minute. Tell me why you feel that way. I want to know you. You count with me. I care about you. Tell me what I can do for you."

And I go away feeling He was glad I called.

Ruth Senter

PAUSE FOR REFLECTION

Who listens to you every time you speak? How do you know that God hears your prayers? What would you tell others that he has done for you?

TUESDAY

*Encourage and Support
One Another in the Faith*

2 John 1—3 John 14

1 The elder unto the elect lady and her children, whom I love in the truth; and not I only, but also all they that have known the truth;

2 for the truth's sake, which dwelleth in us, and shall be with us for ever.

3 Grace be with you, mercy, *and* peace, from God the Father, and from the Lord Jesus Christ, the Son of the Father, in truth and love.

4 I rejoiced greatly that I found of thy children walking in truth, as we have received a commandment from the Father.

5 And now I beseech thee, lady, not as though I wrote a new commandment unto thee, but that which we had from the beginning, that we love one another.

6 And this is love, that we walk after his commandments. This is the commandment, That, as ye have heard from the beginning, ye should walk in it.

7 For many deceivers are entered into the world, who confess not that Jesus Christ is come in the flesh. This is a deceiver and an antichrist.

8 Look to yourselves, that we lose not those things which we have wrought, but that we receive a full reward.

9 Whosoever transgresseth, and abideth not in the doctrine of Christ, hath not God. He that abideth in the doctrine of Christ, he hath both the Father and the Son.

10 If there come any unto you, and bring not this doctrine, receive him not into *your* house, neither bid him God-speed:

11 for he that biddeth him God-speed is partaker of his evil deeds.

12 Having many things to write unto you, I would not *write* with paper and ink: but I trust to come unto you, and speak face to face, that our joy may be full.

13 The children of thy elect sister greet thee. Amen.

Help Christians Who Teach Truth

1 The elder unto the well-beloved Gaius, whom I love in the truth.

2 Beloved, I wish above all things that thou mayest prosper and be in health, even as thy soul prospereth.

3 For I rejoiced greatly, when the brethren came and testified of the truth that is in thee, even as thou walkest in the truth.

4 I have no greater joy than to hear that my children walk in truth.

5 Beloved, thou doest faithfully whatsoever thou doest to the brethren, and to strangers;

6 which have borne witness of thy charity before the church: whom if thou bring forward on their journey after a godly sort, thou shalt do well:

7 Because that for his name's sake they went forth, taking nothing of the Gentiles.

8 We therefore ought to receive such, that we might be fellow helpers to the truth.

9 I wrote unto the church: but Diotrephes, who loveth to have the preeminence among them, receiveth us not.

10 Wherefore, if I come, I will remember his deeds which he doeth, prating against us with malicious words: and not content therewith, neither

doth he himself receive the brethren, and forbiddeth them that would, and casteth *them* out of the church.
[11] Beloved, follow not that which is evil, but that which is good. He that doeth good is of God: but he that doeth evil hath not seen God.
[12] Demetrius hath good report of all *men*, and of the truth itself: yea, and we *also* bear record; and ye know that our record is true.
[13] I had many things to write, but I will not with ink and pen write unto thee:
[14] but I trust I shall shortly see thee, and we shall speak face to face. Peace *be* to thee. *Our* friends salute thee. Greet the friends by name.

OLD TESTAMENT READING

*A*nd Moses called unto Joshua, and said unto him in the sight of all Israel, Be strong and of a good courage: for thou must go with this people unto the land which the LORD hath sworn unto their fathers to give them; and thou shalt cause them to inherit it.
[8] And the LORD, he *it is* that doth go before thee; he will be with thee, he will not fail thee, neither forsake thee: fear not, neither be dismayed.

Deuteronomy 31:7–8

INSIGHTS

I decided to take a break and hit the slopes (emphasis on hit, since it was my first time in all my life to attempt to ski). . . .

It was unbelievable! You have heard of the elephant man? On skis, I'm the rhinoceros man. It is doubtful that anyone else on planet earth has ever come down any ski slope more ways than I did. Or landed in more positions. . . .

Working with me that humiliating day was the world's most encouraging ski instructor (yes, I had an instructor!) who set the new record in patience. . . .

Never once did she lose her cool.
Never once did she laugh at me.
Never once did she yell, scream, threaten, or swear.
Never once did she call me "dummy.". . .

. . . That day God gave me a living, never-to-be-forgotten illustration of the value of encouragement. . . .

What is true for a novice on the snow once a year is all the more true for the people we meet every day. Harassed by demands and deadlines; bruised by worry, adversity, and failure; broken by disillusionment; and defeated by sin, they live somewhere between dull discouragement and sheer panic. Even Christians are not immune! We may give off this "I've got it all together" air of confidence, much like I did when I first snapped on the skis. But realistically, we also struggle, lose our balance, slip and slide, tumble, and fall flat on our faces.

All of us need encouragement—somebody to believe in us. To reassure and reinforce us. To help us pick up the pieces and go on.

Charles Swindoll

APPLICATION

*D*escribe the kinds of encouragement in faith revealed through these Scripture readings.

WEDNESDAY

God Will Punish Everyone Who Is Against Him

Jude 1–13

1 Jude, the servant of Jesus Christ, and brother of James, to them that are sanctified by God the Father, and preserved in Jesus Christ, *and* called:

2 Mercy unto you, and peace, and love, be multiplied.

God Will Punish Sinners

*B*eloved, when I gave all diligence to write unto you of the common salvation, it was needful for me to write unto you, and exhort *you* that ye should earnestly contend for the faith which was once delivered unto the saints.

4 For there are certain men crept in unawares, who were before of old ordained to this condemnation, ungodly men, turning the grace of our God into lasciviousness, and denying the only Lord God, and our Lord Jesus Christ.

5 I will therefore put you in remembrance, though ye once knew this, how that the Lord, having saved the people out of the land of Egypt, afterward destroyed them that believed not.

6 And the angels which kept not their first estate, but left their own habitation, he hath reserved in everlasting chains under darkness unto the judgment of the great day.

7 Even as Sodom and Gomorrah, and the cities about them in like manner, giving themselves over to fornication, and going after strange flesh, are set forth for an example, suffering the vengeance of eternal fire.

8 Likewise also these *filthy* dreamers defile the flesh, despise dominion, and speak evil of dignities.

9 Yet Michael the archangel, when contending with the devil he disputed about the body of Moses, durst not bring against him a railing accusation, but said, The Lord rebuke thee.

10 But these speak evil of those things which they know not: but what they know naturally, as brute beasts, in those things they corrupt themselves.

11 Woe unto them! for they have gone in the way of Cain, and ran greedily after the error of Balaam for reward, and perished in the gainsaying of Korah.

12 These are spots in your feasts of charity, when they feast with you, feeding themselves without fear: clouds *they are* without water, carried about of winds; trees whose fruit withereth, without fruit, twice dead, plucked up by the roots;

13 raging waves of the sea, foaming out their own shame; wandering stars, to whom is reserved the blackness of darkness for ever.

OLD TESTAMENT READING

*H*owl ye; for the day of the LORD *is* at hand; it shall come as a destruction from the Almighty.

7 Therefore shall all hands be faint, and every man's heart shall melt:

8 and they shall be afraid: pangs and sorrows shall take hold of them; they shall be in pain as a woman that travaileth: they shall be amazed one at another; their faces *shall be as* flames.

⁹Behold, the day of the LORD cometh, cruel both with wrath and fierce anger, to lay the land desolate: and he shall destroy the sinners thereof out of it.

¹⁰For the stars of heaven and the constellations thereof shall not give their light: the sun shall be darkened in his going forth, and the moon shall not cause her light to shine.

¹¹And I will punish the world for *their* evil, and the wicked for their iniquity; and I will cause the arrogancy of the proud to cease, and will lay low the haughtiness of the terrible.

Isaiah 13:6–11

INSIGHTS

You have a "lake of fire and brimstone," and you see lost sinners thrown into its waves of rolling fire; and they lash its burning shore, and gnaw their tongues for pain. There the worm dieth not, and their fire is not quenched, and "not one drop of water" can reach them to "cool their tongues"—"tormented in that flame."

What think you? Has God said these things to frighten our poor souls? Did He mean to play on our fears for His own amusement? Can you think so? Nay, does it not rather grieve His heart that He must build such a hell, and must plunge therein the sinners who will not honour His law—will not embrace salvation from sinning through His grace? Ah, the waves of death roll darkly under the eye of the Holy and compassionate One! He has no pleasure in the death of the sinner! But He must sustain His throne, and save His loyal subjects if He can. . . .

God would have us understand what an awful thing sin is, and what fearful punishment it deserves. He would fain show us by such figures how terrible must be the doom of the determined sinner.

Charles Finney

PAUSE FOR REFLECTION

Why must God punish those who are against him? List the sins of those who are against God. How can God's people stand strong against them? How are God's people to treat those who have doubts?

THURSDAY

God Is a
Merciful Judge

Jude 14–25

*A*nd Enoch also, the seventh from Adam, prophesied of these, saying, Behold, the Lord cometh with ten thousands of his saints,

[15] to execute judgment upon all, and to convince all that are ungodly among them of all their ungodly deeds which they have ungodly committed, and of all their hard *speeches* which ungodly sinners have spoken against him.

[16] These are murmurers, complainers, walking after their own lusts; and their mouth speaketh great swelling *words*, having men's persons in admiration because of advantage.

A Warning and Things to Do

*B*ut, beloved, remember ye the words which were spoken before of the apostles of our Lord Jesus Christ;

[18] how that they told you there should be mockers in the last time, who should walk after their own ungodly lusts.

[19] These be they who separate themselves, sensual, having not the Spirit.

[20] But ye, beloved, building up yourselves on your most holy faith, praying in the Holy Ghost,

[21] keep yourselves in the love of God, looking for the mercy of our Lord Jesus Christ unto eternal life.

[22] And of some have compassion, making a difference:

[23] and others save with fear, pulling *them* out of the fire; hating even the garment spotted by the flesh.

Praise God

*N*ow unto him that is able to keep you from falling, and to present *you* faultless before the presence of his glory with exceeding joy,

[25] to the only wise God our Saviour, *be* glory and majesty, dominion and power, both now and ever. Amen.

The Truth About Bragging

*T*hus saith the LORD, Let not the wise *man* glory in his wisdom, neither let the mighty *man* glory in his might, let not the rich *man* glory in his riches:

[24] but let him that glorieth glory in this, that he understandeth and knoweth me, that I *am* the LORD which exercise loving-kindness, judgment, and righteousness, in the earth: for in these *things* I delight, saith the LORD.

Jeremiah 9:23–24

Those Who Have Faith in God
Will Receive His Mercy

*R*ejoice the soul of thy servant: for unto thee, O Lord, do I lift up my soul.

[5] For thou, Lord, *art* good, and ready to forgive; and plenteous in mercy unto all them that call upon thee.

[11] Teach me thy way, O LORD; I will walk in thy truth: unite my heart to fear thy name.

[12] I will praise thee, O Lord my God, with all my heart: and I will glorify thy name for evermore.

¹³ For great *is* thy mercy toward me: and thou hast delivered my soul from the lowest hell.

¹⁴ O God, the proud are risen against me, and the assemblies of violent *men* have sought after my soul; and have not set thee before them.

¹⁶ O turn unto me, and have mercy upon me.

Psalm 86:4–5, 11–14, 16a

INSIGHTS

*G*od is a just God, One who shows no partiality. Outside of grace, God's penalty falls on all. "The wages of sin is death" (Romans 6:23). Sin is sin. The consequences have been posted; He gives fair warning. No excuses accepted. No variations on the rules. Man is accountable. Rebellion, be it active or passive, calls for justice.

I understand God's justice because I remember rebellion—ten-year-old rebellion. My father was the dispenser of justice. "No swimming in the creek today," he said. I had plenty of excuses: "Jimmy went in." "I was so hot." "It isn't fair when everybody else's dad lets them go."

Excuses didn't matter because the standard had been violated. The penalty was swift and sure. Justice was done. But then the father who had just administered justice reached for his big white handkerchief and wiped the tears from his eyes. That day, justice and love were forever linked in my mind.

My father's actions pointed me toward a heavenly Father who sits in the hall of justice, calls His creation to accountability, but weeps over waywardness even as He pronounces sentence. "Oh, Jerusalem,

Jerusalem . . . how often I have longed to gather your children together, as a hen gathers her chicks under her wings, but you were not willing!" (Luke 13:34, NIV). Justice and love exist in the same person.

. . . I can be at peace about God's system of justice, for I have confidence in the Judge. There will be no payoffs. He judges clean.

As a sinner who knew where to find grace, I know God today not as my judge but as a loving Father who continually calls me to accountability. One day He was my judge. But I can almost see a white handkerchief dabbing tears as He wept over my rebellion, issued the sentence, and then took my penalty upon Himself. I am acquitted. Justice has been done. My debt has been paid. I can rest my case. . . .

"God is fair," I said to myself, "whether or not I understand His ways. For He is a God of justice."

Ruth Senter

APPLICATION

*H*ow does God want his people to treat those who have doubts? Do you have complete trust in God, who is both Judge and Savior? Are you at rest in his love?

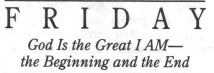

FRIDAY

*God Is the Great I AM—
the Beginning and the End*

Revelation 1:1–20

John Tells About This Book

1 The Revelation of Jesus Christ, which God gave unto him, to show unto his servants things which must shortly come to pass; and he sent and signified it by his angel unto his servant John:

2 who bare record of the word of God, and of the testimony of Jesus Christ, and of all things that he saw.

3 Blessed *is* he that readeth, and they that hear the words of this prophecy, and keep those things which are written therein: for the time *is* at hand.

Jesus' Message to the Churches

*J*ohn to the seven churches which are in Asia: Grace *be* unto you, and peace, from him which is, and which was, and which is to come; and from the seven Spirits which are before his throne;

5 and from Jesus Christ, *who is* the faithful witness, *and* the first-begotten of the dead, and the prince of the kings of the earth. Unto him that loved us, and washed us from our sins in his own blood,

6 and hath made us kings and priests unto God and his Father; to him *be* glory and dominion for ever and ever. Amen.

7 Behold, he cometh with clouds; and every eye shall see him, and they *also* which pierced him: and all kindreds of the earth shall wail because of him. Even so, Amen.

8 I am Alpha and Omega, the beginning and the ending, saith the Lord, which is, and which was, and which is to come, the Almighty.

9 I John, who also am your brother, and companion in tribulation, and in the kingdom and patience of Jesus Christ, was in the isle that is called Patmos, for the word of God, and for the testimony of Jesus Christ.

10 I was in the Spirit on the Lord's day, and heard behind me a great voice, as of a trumpet,

11 saying, I am Alpha and Omega, the first and the last: and, What thou seest, write in a book, and send *it* unto the seven churches which are in Asia; unto Ephesus, and unto Smyrna, and unto Pergamos, and unto Thyatira, and unto Sardis, and unto Philadelphia, and unto Laodicea.

12 And I turned to see the voice that spake with me. And being turned, I saw seven golden candlesticks;

13 and in the midst of the seven candlesticks *one* like unto the Son of man, clothed with a garment down to the foot, and girt about the paps with a golden girdle.

14 His head and *his* hairs *were* white like wool, as white as snow; and his eyes *were* as a flame of fire;

15 and his feet like unto fine brass, as if they burned in a furnace; and his voice as the sound of many waters.

16 And he had in his right hand seven stars: and out of his mouth went a sharp two-edged sword: and his countenance was as the sun shineth in his strength.

17 And when I saw him, I fell at his feet as dead. And he laid his right

hand upon me, saying unto me, Fear not; I am the first and the last:
[18] *I am* he that liveth, and was dead; and, behold, I am alive for evermore, Amen; and have the keys of hell and of death.
[19] Write the things which thou hast seen, and the things which are, and the things which shall be hereafter; [20] the mystery of the seven stars which thou sawest in my right hand, and the seven golden candlesticks. The seven stars are the angels of the seven churches: and the seven candlesticks which thou sawest are the seven churches.

OLD TESTAMENT READING

*H*earken unto me, O Jacob and Israel, my called; I *am* he; I *am* the first, I also *am* the last.
[13] Mine hand also hath laid the foundation of the earth, and my right hand hath spanned the heavens: *when* I call unto them they stand up together.

Isaiah 48:12–13

INSIGHTS

I am the beginning;
I am the end.
You are very concerned with beginnings.
You hesitate to reach
the end.
The Alpha / beginning,
the Omega / end,
means that I am your all-in-all.
Do you want to stay
an Alpha person—
always at the starting line of
faith?
That is a safe place—
where you say you believe Me,

where you champion truth,
but you don't move.

Move, I say!
Feel the wind of trials and
victories in Me.
I am the Finisher, the Omega.
Lift your eyes from the starting
line
and focus on all that lies before
you—
on the intelligent golden faith
awaiting you at the finish.

Learn of me; digest My Word,
always in communion with Me.
I am your health, your energy:
I bring you to a "finish"
that is not the end of all things;
not a place where you collapse,
emptied out, done.
It is the place where you
allow Me freely
to live through you.

My finish means new development,
new discoveries,
new victories,
new holy charges.
My dearest and most effective servants
are those who move
in "finished" faith.

Marie Chapian

APPLICATION

*A*s you read about the awesome power and greatness of God, the I AM, fear seems to be an appropriate response. Yet when John fell down in fear before God, God gently reached out and told him what to do (Rev. 1:17–20). What is the great I AM moving you to do?

WEEKEND

*Repent and Regain
Your Love for Christ*

Revelation 2:1–17

To the Church in Ephesus

2 Unto the angel of the church of Ephesus write; These things saith he that holdeth the seven stars in his right hand, who walketh in the midst of the seven golden candlesticks.

2 I know thy works, and thy labor, and thy patience, and how thou canst not bear them which are evil: and thou hast tried them which say they are apostles, and are not, and hast found them liars:

3 and hast borne, and hast patience, and for my name's sake hast labored, and hast not fainted.

4 Nevertheless I have *somewhat* against thee, because thou hast left thy first love.

5 Remember therefore from whence thou art fallen, and repent, and do the first works; or else I will come unto thee quickly, and will remove thy candlestick out of his place, except thou repent.

6 But this thou hast, that thou hatest the deeds of the Nicolaitans, which I also hate.

7 He that hath an ear, let him hear what the Spirit saith unto the churches; To him that overcometh will I give to eat of the tree of life, which is in the midst of the paradise of God.

To the Church in Smyrna

And unto the angel of the church

in Smyrna write; These things saith the first and the last, which was dead, and is alive.

9 I know thy works, and tribulation, and poverty, (but thou art rich) and *I know* the blasphemy of them which say they are Jews, and are not, but *are* the synagogue of Satan.

10 Fear none of those things which thou shalt suffer: behold, the devil shall cast *some* of you into prison, that ye may be tried; and ye shall have tribulation ten days: be thou faithful unto death, and I will give thee a crown of life.

11 He that hath an ear, let him hear what the Spirit saith unto the churches; He that overcometh shall not be hurt of the second death.

To the Church in Pergamos

And to the angel of the church in Pergamos write; These things saith he which hath the sharp sword with two edges.

13 I know thy works, and where thou dwellest, *even* where Satan's seat *is*: and thou holdest fast my name, and hast not denied my faith, even in those days wherein Antipas *was* my faithful martyr, who was slain among you, where Satan dwelleth.

14 But I have a few things against thee, because thou hast there them that hold the doctrine of Balaam, who taught Balak to cast a stumblingblock before the children of Israel, to eat things sacrificed unto idols, and to commit fornication.

15 So hast thou also them that hold the doctrine of the Nicolaitans, which thing I hate.

16 Repent; or else I will come unto thee quickly, and will fight against them with the sword of my mouth.

¹⁷ He that hath an ear, let him hear what the Spirit saith unto the churches; To him that overcometh will I give to eat of the hidden manna, and will give him a white stone, and in the stone a new name written, which no man knoweth saving he that receiveth *it*.

OLD TESTAMENT READING

Jeremiah Delivers a Message of Repentance

*G*o and proclaim these words toward the north, and say, Return, thou backsliding Israel, saith the LORD; *and* I will not cause mine anger to fall upon you: for I *am* merciful, saith the LORD, *and* I will not keep *anger* for ever.

Jeremiah 3:12

INSIGHTS

A few years ago, in a commencement address at Harvard University, Alexander Solzhenitsyn tried to summarize the root problem facing capitalism and Marxism. He said that the trouble with both systems is that men have forgotten God. One system does it by its materialist philosophy; the other system by its materialist economy.

But "the sin of forgetting God" is not just the sin of economics and governments. It can be the sin of religion as well. Religious people forget God by setting up a religious system in His place.

Stephen was up against such a system in Acts 7. Stephen charged that the religion of Jerusalem had turned bad. The supreme court of that city did not take Stephen's

words lightly. They were furious. They tried to silence him by running him out of town, and finally they killed him by stoning. Stephen's hot piety was a threat to the council's cold religion.

A fire dies unless it is fed. The most natural thing in this world is for a person to lose his zeal, fervor, and drive. . . .

Each of us forgets too soon. We all have the inherent tendency to drift from God.

The constant call of the Bible is to be on guard—to remember! Continually we are told to turn around, to repent, to draw near to God and submit to Him. . . .

The first lesson we must learn is the one Stephen tried to teach the Sanhedrin: "The Most High does not dwell in houses [or structures, or systems] made by human hands" (v. 48). He is God, Maker of heaven and earth, Alpha and Omega. He is the One to whom every man shall one day give account.

The second lesson that Stephen preached, by his words and life, is that God wants a personal relationship with His people. He does not want a system or a dead religion. He wants you. He wants to be your God and your friend. He wants a partnership with His creatures. He wants them to love Him and enjoy Him forever.

George Sweeting
Donald Sweeting

ACTION POINT

*H*ow much does God treasure the faithful love of his followers? What does he promise to those who love him faithfully?

MONDAY
God Calls Us to Get Rid of Sin and Walk with Him

Revelation 2:18—3:6

To the Church in Thyatira

*A*nd unto the angel of the church in Thyatira write; These things saith the Son of God, who hath his eyes like unto a flame of fire, and his feet *are* like fine brass.

19 I know thy works, and charity, and service, and faith, and thy patience, and thy works; and the last *to be* more than the first.

20 Notwithstanding I have a few things against thee, because thou sufferest that woman Jezebel, which calleth herself a prophetess, to teach and to seduce my servants to commit fornication, and to eat things sacrificed unto idols.

21 And I gave her space to repent of her fornication; and she repented not.

22 Behold, I will cast her into a bed, and them that commit adultery with her into great tribulation, except they repent of their deeds.

23 And I will kill her children with death; and all the churches shall know that I am he which searcheth the reins and hearts: and I will give unto every one of you according to your works.

24 But unto you I say, and unto the rest in Thyatira, as many as have not this doctrine, and which have not known the depths of Satan, as they speak; I will put upon you none other burden.

25 But that which ye have *already,* hold fast till I come.

26 And he that overcometh, and keepeth my works unto the end, to him will I give power over the nations:

27 and he shall rule them with a rod of iron; as the vessels of a potter shall they be broken to shivers: even as I received of my Father.

28 And I will give him the morning star.

29 He that hath an ear, let him hear what the Spirit saith unto the churches.

To the Church in Sardis

3 And unto the angel of the church in Sardis write; These things saith he that hath the seven Spirits of God, and the seven stars; I know thy works, that thou hast a name that thou livest, and art dead.

2 Be watchful, and strengthen the things which remain, that are ready to die: for I have not found thy works perfect before God.

3 Remember therefore how thou hast received and heard, and hold fast, and repent. If therefore thou shalt not watch, I will come on thee as a thief, and thou shalt not know what hour I will come upon thee.

4 Thou hast a few names even in Sardis which have not defiled their garments; and they shall walk with me in white: for they are worthy.

5 He that overcometh, the same shall be clothed in white raiment; and I will not blot out his name out of the book of life, but I will confess his name before my Father, and before his angels.

6 He that hath an ear, let him hear what the Spirit saith unto the churches.

*A*nd now, Israel, what doth the LORD thy God require of thee, but to fear the LORD thy God, to walk in all his ways, and to love him, and to serve the LORD thy God with all thy heart and with all thy soul.

Deuteronomy 10:12

*T*hou hast avouched the LORD this day to be thy God, and to walk in his ways, and to keep his statutes, and his commandments, and his judgements, and to hearken unto his voice:
[18] and the LORD hath avouched thee this day to be his peculiar people, as he hath promised thee, and that *thou* shouldest keep all his commandments.

Deuteronomy 26:17–18

*I*f there arise among you a prophet, or a dreamer of dreams, and giveth thee a sign or a wonder,
[2] and the sign or the wonder come to pass, whereof he spake unto thee, saying, Let us go after other gods, which thou hast not known, and let us serve them.
[5] And that prophet, or that dreamer of dreams, shall be put to death; because he hath spoken to turn *you* away from the LORD your God, which brought you out of the land of Egypt, and redeemed you out of the house of bondage, to thrust thee out of the way which the LORD thy God commanded thee to walk in. So shalt thou put the evil away from the midst of thee.

Deuteronomy 13:1–2, 5

INSIGHTS

*T*he older I get and the better acquainted I am with Christ, the more I'm aware of His insistence on holiness. This seems to be a matter about which He's not open to negotiation even in the slightest.

I guess somebody could consider bringing up this subject for discussion, "Ah, Jesus, I feel You're a bit too stubborn on this righteousness issue. I mean, I figure I've made some pretty big concessions Your way. On the matter of this one pet sin, couldn't You compromise a little? Accommodate me? Maybe 3 or 4 percent darkness allowable, and all the rest light?"

I warn you, the Lord won't budge even one millimeter. . . .

The absolute truth is: Anyone who wants to be close friends with Christ needs to achieve this victory-over-sin mindset, needs to learn to keep short accounts with God, needs to refuse to allow sins of long standing to go unconfessed day after day, week after week, even year after year. . . .

The hour must come when the church as a body and the individuals who compose the corporate entity reach for holiness. We must ask God for determination to overcome sin; we must pray for conviction for our unrighteousness. We must understand that we will never experience that overwhelming sense of the presence of Christ if we are not intent on striving to be 100 percent light-walkers.

David Mains

APPLICATION

*W*hat attitude do these readings say God's people must have toward sin? What action does he require? What does God promise to those who win the victory?

TUESDAY

*God Saves and Honors Those
Who Follow Him Faithfully*

Revelation 3:7—4:5

To the Church in Philadelphia

*A*nd to the angel of the church in Philadelphia write; These things saith he that is holy, he that is true, he that hath the key of David, he that openeth, and no man shutteth; and shutteth, and no man openeth.

⁸ I know thy works: behold, I have set before thee an open door, and no man can shut it: for thou hast a little strength, and hast kept my word, and hast not denied my name.

⁹ Behold, I will make them of the synagogue of Satan, which say they are Jews, and are not, but do lie; behold, I will make them to come and worship before thy feet, and to know that I have loved thee.

¹⁰ Because thou hast kept the word of my patience, I also will keep thee from the hour of temptation, which shall come upon all the world, to try them that dwell upon the earth.

¹¹ Behold, I come quickly: hold that fast which thou hast, that no man take thy crown.

¹² Him that overcometh will I make a pillar in the temple of my God, and he shall go no more out: and I will write upon him the name of my God, and the name of the city of my God, *which is* new Jerusalem, which cometh down out of heaven from my God: and *I will write upon him* my new name.

¹³ He that hath an ear, let him hear what the Spirit saith unto the churches.

To the Church in Laodicea

*A*nd unto the angel of the church of the Laodiceans write; These things saith the Amen, the faithful and true witness, the beginning of the creation of God.

¹⁵ I know thy works, that thou art neither cold nor hot: I would thou wert cold or hot.

¹⁶ So then because thou art lukewarm, and neither cold nor hot, I will spew thee out of my mouth.

¹⁷ Because thou sayest, I am rich, and increased with goods, and have need of nothing; and knowest not that thou art wretched, and miserable, and poor, and blind, and naked:

¹⁸ I counsel thee to buy of me gold tried in the fire, that thou mayest be rich; and white raiment, that thou mayest be clothed, and *that* the shame of thy nakedness do not appear; and anoint thine eyes with eyesalve, that thou mayest see.

¹⁹ As many as I love, I rebuke and chasten: be zealous therefore, and repent.

²⁰ Behold, I stand at the door, and knock: if any man hear my voice, and open the door, I will come in to him, and will sup with him, and he with me.

²¹ To him that overcometh will I grant to sit with me in my throne, even as I also overcame, and am set down with my Father in his throne.

²² He that hath an ear, let him hear what the Spirit saith unto the churches.

John Sees Heaven

4 After this I looked, and, behold, a door *was* opened in heaven: and the first voice which I heard *was* as it

were of a trumpet talking with me; which said, Come up hither, and I will show thee things which must be hereafter.

2 And immediately I was in the Spirit: and, behold, a throne was set in heaven, and *one* sat on the throne.

3 And he that sat was to look upon like a jasper and a sardine stone: and *there was* a rainbow round about the throne, in sight like unto an emerald.

4 And round about the throne *were* four and twenty seats: and upon the seats I saw four and twenty elders sitting, clothed in white raiment; and they had on their heads crowns of gold.

5 And out of the throne proceeded lightnings and thunderings and voices: and *there were* seven lamps of fire burning before the throne, which are the seven Spirits of God.

OLD TESTAMENT READING

God Will Save and Honor His People

*A*nd at that time shall Michael stand up, the great prince which standeth for the children of thy people: and there shall be a time of trouble, such as never was since there was a nation *even* to that same time: and at that time thy people shall be delivered, every one that shall be found written in the book.

2 And many of them that sleep in the dust of the earth shall awake, some to everlasting life, and some to shame *and* everlasting contempt.

3 And they that be wise shall shine as the brightness of the firmament; and they that turn many to righteousness, as the stars for ever and ever.

Daniel 12:1–3

INSIGHTS

*R*ay Stedman tells the story of an old missionary couple who had been working in Africa for many years and were returning to New York City to retire. With no pension and broken in health, they were discouraged, fearful of the future.

They happened to be booked on the same ship as Teddy Roosevelt, who was returning from a big-game hunting expedition. . . .

At the dock in New York a band was waiting to greet the President. . . . But the missionary couple slipped off the ship unnoticed.

That night, in a cheap flat they found on the East Side, the man's spirit broke. He said to his wife, "I can't take this; God is not treating us fairly." His wife suggested he go in the bedroom and tell the Lord.

A short time later he came out of the bedroom with a face completely changed. His wife asked, "Dear, what happened?"

"The Lord settled it with me," he said. "I told him how bitter I was that the President should receive this tremendous homecoming, when no one met us as we returned home. And when I finished, it seemed as though the Lord put his hand on my shoulder and simply said, 'But you're not home yet!' "

Donald McCullough

APPLICATION

*T*o whom does Jesus promise salvation? What kind of a 'homecoming' does he promise to those who belong to him? Ask God to help you, like the old missionary, keep perspective on what is to come!

WEDNESDAY

*A Glimpse of
Heaven's Holiness*

Revelation 4:6—6:2

*A*nd before the throne *there was* a sea of glass like unto crystal: and in the midst of the throne, and round about the throne, *were* four beasts full of eyes before and behind.

⁷ And the first beast *was* like a lion, and the second beast like a calf, and the third beast had a face as a man, and the fourth beast *was* like a flying eagle.

⁸ And the four beasts had each of them six wings about *him*; and *they were* full of eyes within: and they rest not day and night, saying, Holy, holy, holy, Lord God Almighty, which was, and is, and is to come.

⁹ And when those beasts give glory and honor and thanks to him that sat on the throne, who liveth for ever and ever,

¹⁰ the four and twenty elders fall down before him that sat on the throne, and worship him that liveth for ever and ever, and cast their crowns before the throne, saying,

¹¹ Thou art worthy, O Lord, to receive glory and honor and power: for thou hast created all things, and for thy pleasure they are and were created.

5 And I saw in the right hand of him that sat on the throne a book written within and on the backside, sealed with seven seals.

² And I saw a strong angel proclaiming with a loud voice, Who is worthy to open the book, and to loose the seals thereof?

³ And no man in heaven, nor in earth, neither under the earth, was able to open the book, neither to look thereon.

⁴ And I wept much, because no man was found worthy to open and to read the book, neither to look thereon.

⁵ And one of the elders saith unto me, Weep not: behold, the Lion of the tribe of Judah, the Root of David, hath prevailed to open the book, and to loose the seven seals thereof.

⁶ And I beheld, and, lo, in the midst of the throne and of the four beasts, and in the midst of the elders, stood a Lamb as it had been slain, having seven horns and seven eyes, which are the seven Spirits of God sent forth into all the earth.

⁷ And he came and took the book out of the right hand of him that sat upon the throne.

⁸ And when he had taken the book, the four beasts and four *and* twenty elders fell down before the Lamb, having every one of them harps, and golden vials full of odors, which are the prayers of saints.

⁹ And they sung a new song, saying, Thou art worthy to take the book, and to open the seals thereof: for thou wast slain, and hast redeemed us to God by thy blood out of every kindred, and tongue, and people, and nation;

¹⁰ and hast made us unto our God kings and priests: and we shall reign on the earth.

¹¹ And I beheld, and I heard the voice of many angels round about the throne, and the beasts, and the elders: and the number of them was ten thousand times ten thousand, and thousands of thousands;

¹² saying with a loud voice, Worthy

is the Lamb that was slain to receive power, and riches, and wisdom, and strength, and honor, and glory, and blessing.

¹³ And every creature which is in heaven, and on the earth, and under the earth, and such as are in the sea, and all that are in them, heard I saying, Blessing, and honor, and glory, and power, *be* unto him that sitteth upon the throne, and unto the Lamb for ever and ever.

¹⁴ And the four beasts said, Amen. And the four *and* twenty elders fell down and worshipped him that liveth for ever and ever.

And I saw when the Lamb opened one of the seals, and I heard, as it were the noise of thunder, one of the four beasts saying, Come and see.

² And I saw, and behold a white horse: and he that sat on him had a bow; and a crown was given unto him: and he went forth conquering, and to conquer.

OLD TESTAMENT READING

*I*n the year that king Uzziah died I saw also the Lord sitting upon a throne, high and lifted up, and his train filled the temple.

² Above it stood the seraphim: each one had six wings; with twain he covered his face, and with twain he covered his feet, and with twain he did fly.

³ And one cried unto another, and said, Holy, holy, holy, *is* the LORD of hosts: the whole earth *is* full of his glory.

⁴ And the posts of the door moved at the voice of him that cried, and the house was filled with smoke.

⁵ Then said I, Woe *is* me! for I am undone; because I *am* a man of unclean lips, and I dwell in the midst of a people of unclean lips: for mine eyes have seen the King, the LORD of hosts.

Isaiah 6:1–5

INSIGHTS

*F*or this one moment in time, the old apostle was ushered into the presence of the Mystery behind the universe. There is no way to describe God. John could only describe the response to God. . . . Even as he stood before Him, God remained a mystery to John and to us—the Mystery who was and is and will always be, the Mystery behind our creation and our preservation, the Mystery worthy of our glory and honor and power.

The risen Christ had called John into the presence of God so that the old man could know, and through him we could know, this fact: Behind the universe there is a Power worthy of our praise and of our trust. In spite of rumors to the contrary, we are not creatures abandoned on a planet spinning madly through the universe. . . . We are the children of a great and wonderful God who even now sits in power accomplishing His purposes in His creation.

Billy Graham

APPLICATION

*R*eread each detail John uses to describe heaven's holiness. Imagine the sights, the sounds, and magnitude of God's powerful holiness! Praise God for his holiness. Seek to live in his holiness.

THURSDAY

*Who Can Stand Against
the Lord's Anger?*

Revelation 6:3—7:8

*A*nd when he had opened the second seal, I heard the second beast say, Come and see.

4 And there went out another horse *that was* red: and *power* was given to him that sat thereon to take peace from the earth, and that they should kill one another: and there was given unto him a great sword.

5 And when he had opened the third seal, I heard the third beast say, Come and see. And I beheld, and lo a black horse; and he that sat on him had a pair of balances in his hand.

6 And I heard a voice in the midst of the four beasts say, A measure of wheat for a penny, and three measures of barley for a penny; and *see* thou hurt not the oil and the wine.

7 And when he had opened the fourth seal, I heard the voice of the fourth beast say, Come and see.

8 And I looked, and behold a pale horse: and his name that sat on him was Death, and Hell followed with him. And power was given unto them over the fourth part of the earth, to kill with sword, and with hunger, and with death, and with the beasts of the earth.

9 And when he had opened the fifth seal, I saw under the altar the souls of them that were slain for the word of God, and for the testimony which they held:

10 and they cried with a loud voice, saying, How long, O Lord, holy and true, dost thou not judge and avenge our blood on them that dwell on the earth?

11 And white robes were given unto every one of them; and it was said unto them, that they should rest yet for a little season, until their fellow servants also and their brethren, that should be killed as they *were*, should be fulfilled.

12 And I beheld when he had opened the sixth seal, and, lo, there was a great earthquake; and the sun became black as sackcloth of hair, and the moon became as blood;

13 and the stars of heaven fell unto the earth, even as a fig tree casteth her untimely figs, when she is shaken of a mighty wind.

14 And the heaven departed as a scroll when it is rolled together; and every mountain and island were moved out of their places.

15 And the kings of the earth, and the great men, and the rich men, and the chief captains, and the mighty men, and every bondman, and every free man, hid themselves in the dens and in the rocks of the mountains;

16 and said to the mountains and rocks, Fall on us, and hide us from the face of him that sitteth on the throne, and from the wrath of the Lamb:

17 for the great day of his wrath is come; and who shall be able to stand?

The 144,000 People of Israel

7 And after these things I saw four angels standing on the four corners of the earth, holding the four winds of the earth, that the wind should not blow on the earth, nor on the sea, nor on any tree.

2 And I saw another angel ascend-

ing from the east, having the seal of the living God: and he cried with a loud voice to the four angels, to whom it was given to hurt the earth and the sea,

³ saying, Hurt not the earth, neither the sea, nor the trees, till we have sealed the servants of our God in their foreheads.

⁴ And I heard the number of them which were sealed: *and there were* sealed a hundred *and* forty *and* four thousand of all the tribes of the children of Israel.

⁵ Of the tribe of Judah *were* sealed twelve thousand. Of the tribe of Reuben *were* sealed twelve thousand. Of the tribe of Gad *were* sealed twelve thousand.

⁶ Of the tribe of Asher *were* sealed twelve thousand. Of the tribe of Naphtali *were* sealed twelve thousand. Of the tribe of Manasseh *were* sealed twelve thousand.

⁷ Of the tribe of Simeon *were* sealed twelve thousand. Of the tribe of Levi *were* sealed twelve thousand. Of the tribe of Issachar *were* sealed twelve thousand.

⁸ Of the tribe of Zebulun *were* sealed twelve thousand. Of the tribe of Joseph *were* sealed twelve thousand. Of the tribe of Benjamin *were* sealed twelve thousand.

⁶ Who can stand before his indignation? and who can abide in the fierceness of his anger? his fury is poured out like fire, and the rocks are thrown down by him.

Nahum 1:2a, 5–6

INSIGHTS

The Sixth Seal Judgment (Rev. 6:12–17) . . . unleashes universal havoc on the earth. . . .

These judgments will produce terror in the hearts of all living men. Their hearts will be filled with fear—not primarily because of the physical disturbances or the awful wars and pestilences, but because they will see God on His throne. Men will plead to be hidden "from the face of Him that sitteth on the throne, and from the wrath of the Lamb." They will go to any length to avoid facing their Creator and Judge, even to seeking death under the rocks and mountains in which they will try to hide. All classes of people (v. 15) will be affected. As has been true throughout history, there will be no general or mass turning to God in repentance, but only a turning from God's face.

Charles Ryrie

OLD TESTAMENT READING

God Declares His Anger Against Nineveh

God *is* jealous, and the LORD revengeth.

⁵ The mountains quake at him, and the hills melt, and the earth is burned at his presence, yea, the world, and all that dwell therein.

ACTION POINT

What does God promise to those who are guilty of sin? When their time of punishment comes, how can they escape and who can save them? Pray that you will be faithful so you will not hide from God's presence.

FRIDAY

The Glorious Reward of Those Washed Clean by the Blood of the Lamb

Revelation 7:9—8:13

The Multitude Worships God

*A*fter this I beheld, and, lo, a great multitude, which no man could number, of all nations, and kindreds, and people, and tongues, stood before the throne, and before the Lamb, clothed with white robes, and palms in their hands;

10 and cried with a loud voice, saying, Salvation to our God which sitteth upon the throne, and unto the Lamb.

11 And all the angels stood round about the throne, and *about* the elders and the four beasts, and fell before the throne on their faces, and worshipped God,

12 saying, Amen: Blessing, and glory, and wisdom, and thanksgiving, and honor, and power, and might, *be* unto our God for ever and ever. Amen.

13 And one of the elders answered, saying unto me, What are these which are arrayed in white robes? and whence came they?

14 And I said unto him, Sir, thou knowest. And he said to me, These are they which came out of great tribulation, and have washed their robes, and made them white in the blood of the Lamb.

15 Therefore are they before the throne of God, and serve him day and night in his temple: and he that sitteth on the throne shall dwell among them.

16 They shall hunger no more, neither thirst any more; neither shall the sun light on them, nor any heat.

17 For the Lamb which is in the midst of the throne shall feed them, and shall lead them unto living fountains of waters: and God shall wipe away all tears from their eyes.

The Seventh Seal

8 And when he had opened the seventh seal, there was silence in heaven about the space of half an hour.

2 And I saw the seven angels which stood before God; and to them were given seven trumpets.

3 And another angel came and stood at the altar, having a golden censer; and there was given unto him much incense, that he should offer *it* with the prayers of all saints upon the golden altar which was before the throne.

4 And the smoke of the incense, *which came* with the prayers of the saints, ascended up before God out of the angel's hand.

5 And the angel took the censer, and filled it with fire of the altar, and cast *it* into the earth: and there were voices, and thunderings, and lightnings, and an earthquake.

The Seven Angels and Trumpets

*A*nd the seven angels which had the seven trumpets prepared themselves to sound.

7 The first angel sounded, and there followed hail and fire mingled with blood, and they were cast upon the earth: and the third part of trees was burnt up, and all green grass was burnt up.

⁸ And the second angel sounded, and as it were a great mountain burning with fire was cast into the sea: and the third part of the sea became blood;

⁹ and the third part of the creatures which were in the sea, and had life, died; and the third part of the ships were destroyed.

¹⁰ And the third angel sounded, and there fell a great star from heaven, burning as it were a lamp, and it fell upon the third part of the rivers, and upon the fountains of waters;

¹¹ and the name of the star is called Wormwood: and the third part of the waters became wormwood; and many men died of the waters, because they were made bitter.

¹² And the fourth angel sounded, and the third part of the sun was smitten, and the third part of the moon, and the third part of the stars; so as the third part of them was darkened, and the day shone not for a third part of it, and the night likewise.

¹³ And I beheld, and heard an angel flying through the midst of heaven, saying with a loud voice, Woe, woe, woe, to the inhabiters of the earth by reason of the other voices of the trumpet of the three angels, which are yet to sound!

OLD TESTAMENT READING

I will greatly rejoice in the LORD, my soul shall be joyful in my God; for he hath clothed me with the garments of salvation, he hath covered me with the robe of righteousness, as a bridegroom decketh *himself* with ornaments, and as a bride adorneth *herself* with her jewels.

Isaiah 61:10

INSIGHTS

How many achievements and how many blessings for men the Scripture ascribes to the power of the Blood of the Lord Jesus! By the power of His Blood peace is made between man and God. By its power there is forgiveness of sins and eternal life for all who put their faith in the Lord Jesus. By the power of His Blood Satan is overcome. By its power there is continual cleansing from all sin for us. By the power of His Blood we may be set free from the tyranny of an evil conscience to serve the living God. By its infinite power with God the most unworthy have liberty to enter the Holy of Holies of God's presence and live there all the day. . . .

. . . That which gives the precious Blood its power with God for men is the lamb-like disposition of the One who shed it. . . . The title "the Lamb" so frequently given to the Lord Jesus in Scripture is first of all descriptive of His work—that of being a sacrifice for our sin. . . . But the title "the Lamb" has a deeper meaning. It describes His character. He is the Lamb in that He is meek and lowly in heart, gentle and unresisting, and all the time surrendering His own will to the Father's for the blessing and saving of men.

Roy and Revel Hession

ACTION POINT

Who is the Lamb of God? What does the blood of the Lamb do? List the ways God will bless those who are washed clean by the blood of the Lamb.

WEEKEND

God Sends Punishment in Order to Turn People from Sin

Revelation 9:1—10:4

9 And the fifth angel sounded, and I saw a star fall from heaven unto the earth: and to him was given the key of the bottomless pit.

2 And he opened the bottomless pit; and there arose a smoke out of the pit, as the smoke of a great furnace; and the sun and the air were darkened by reason of the smoke of the pit.

3 And there came out of the smoke locusts upon the earth: and unto them was given power, as the scorpions of the earth have power.

4 And it was commanded them that they should not hurt the grass of the earth, neither any green thing, neither any tree; but only those men which have not the seal of God in their foreheads.

5 And to them it was given that they should not kill them, but that they should be tormented five months: and their torment *was* as the torment of a scorpion, when he striketh a man.

6 And in those days shall men seek death, and shall not find it; and shall desire to die, and death shall flee from them.

7 And the shapes of the locusts *were* like unto horses prepared unto battle; and on their heads *were* as it were crowns like gold, and their faces *were* as the faces of men.

8 And they had hair as the hair of women, and their teeth were as *the teeth* of lions.

9 And they had breastplates, as it were breastplates of iron; and the sound of their wings *was* as the sound of chariots of many horses running to battle.

10 And they had tails like unto scorpions, and there were stings in their tails: and their power *was* to hurt men five months.

11 And they had a king over them, *which is* the angel of the bottomless pit, whose name in the Hebrew tongue *is* Abaddon, but in the Greek tongue hath *his* name Apollyon.

12 One woe is past; *and*, behold, there come two woes more hereafter.

13 And the sixth angel sounded, and I heard a voice from the four horns of the golden altar which is before God,

14 saying to the sixth angel which had the trumpet, Loose the four angels which are bound in the great river Euphrates.

15 And the four angels were loosed, which were prepared for an hour, and a day, and a month, and a year, for to slay the third part of men.

16 And the number of the army of the horsemen *were* two hundred thousand thousand: and I heard the number of them.

17 And thus I saw the horses in the vision, and them that sat on them, having breastplates of fire, and of jacinth, and brimstone: and the heads of the horses *were* as the heads of lions; and out of their mouths issued fire and smoke and brimstone.

18 By these three was the third part of men killed, by the fire, and by the smoke, and by the brimstone, which issued out of their mouths.

19 For their power is in their mouth, and in their tails: for their tails *were* like unto serpents, and had heads,

and with them they do hurt.
[20] And the rest of the men which were not killed by these plagues yet repented not of the works of their hands, that they should not worship devils, and idols of gold, and silver, and brass, and stone, and of wood: which neither can see, nor hear, nor walk:
[21] neither repented they of their murders, nor of their sorceries, nor of their fornication, nor of their thefts.

The Angel and the Little Book

10 And I saw another mighty angel come down from heaven, clothed with a cloud: and a rainbow *was* upon his head, and his face *was* as it were the sun, and his feet as pillars of fire:
[2] and he had in his hand a little book open: and he set his right foot upon the sea, and *his* left *foot* on the earth,
[3] and cried with a loud voice, as *when* a lion roareth: and when he had cried, seven thunders uttered their voices.
[4] And when the seven thunders had uttered their voices, I was about to write: and I heard a voice from heaven saying unto me, Seal up those things which the seven thunders uttered, and write them not.

OLD TESTAMENT READING

*L*et all the inhabitants of the land tremble: for the day of the LORD cometh, for *it is* nigh at hand.
[10] The earth shall quake before them; the heavens shall tremble: the sun and the moon shall be dark, and the stars shall withdraw their shining:
[11] and the LORD shall utter his voice before his army: for his camp *is* very great: for *he is* strong that executeth his word: for the day of the LORD *is* great and very terrible; and who can abide it?
[12] Therefore also now, saith the LORD, turn ye *even* to me with all your heart, and with fasting, and with weeping, and with mourning.

Joel 2:1b, 10–12

INSIGHTS

*H*ow terrible it is to witness the approach of a tempest: to note the forewarnings of the storm; to mark the birds of heaven as they droop their wings; to see the cattle as they lay their heads low in terror . . . and the heavens which are angry and frowning! . . . And yet, sinner, this is your present position. No hot drops have as yet fallen, but a shower of fire is coming. No terrible winds howl around you, but God's tempest is gathering its dread artillery. As yet the water-floods are dammed up by mercy, but the flood-gates shall soon be opened: the thunderbolts of God are yet in His storehouse, but lo! the tempest hastens, and how awful shall that moment be when God, robed in vengeance, shall march forth in fury! Where, where, where, O sinner, wilt thou hide thy head, or whither wilt thou flee? O that the hand of mercy may now lead you to Christ!

Charles Spurgeon

PAUSE FOR REFLECTION

*W*hat is the sole reason for the horrible punishment that is promised on God's day of judgment?

MONDAY

God's Prophets Are Empowered to Deliver His Message

Revelation 10:5—11:14

*A*nd the angel which I saw stand upon the sea and upon the earth lifted up his hand to heaven,

[6] and sware by him that liveth for ever and ever, who created heaven, and the things that therein are, and the earth, and the things that therein are, and the sea, and the things which are therein, that there should be time no longer:

[7] but in the days of the voice of the seventh angel, when he shall begin to sound, the mystery of God should be finished, as he hath declared to his servants the prophets.

[8] And the voice which I heard from heaven spake unto me again, and said, Go *and* take the little book which is open in the hand of the angel which standeth upon the sea and upon the earth.

[9] And I went unto the angel, and said unto him, Give me the little book. And he said unto me, Take *it*, and eat it up; and it shall make thy belly bitter, but it shall be in thy mouth sweet as honey.

[10] And I took the little book out of the angel's hand, and ate it up; and it was in my mouth sweet as honey: and as soon as I had eaten it, my belly was bitter.

[11] And he said unto me, Thou must prophesy again before many peoples, and nations, and tongues, and kings.

The Two Witnesses

11 And there was given me a reed like unto a rod: and the angel stood, saying, Rise, and measure the temple of God, and the altar, and them that worship therein.

[2] But the court which is without the temple leave out, and measure it not; for it is given unto the Gentiles: and the holy city shall they tread under foot forty *and* two months.

[3] And I will give *power* unto my two witnesses, and they shall prophesy a thousand two hundred *and* threescore days, clothed in sackcloth.

[4] These are the two olive trees, and the two candlesticks standing before the God of the earth.

[5] And if any man will hurt them, fire proceedeth out of their mouth, and devoureth their enemies: and if any man will hurt them, he must in this manner be killed.

[6] These have power to shut heaven, that it rain not in the days of their prophecy: and have power over waters to turn them to blood, and to smite the earth with all plagues, as often as they will.

[7] And when they shall have finished their testimony, the beast that ascendeth out of the bottomless pit shall make war against them, and shall overcome them, and kill them.

[8] And their dead bodies *shall lie* in the street of the great city, which spiritually is called Sodom and Egypt, where also our Lord was crucified.

[9] And they of the people and kindreds and tongues and nations shall see their dead bodies three days and a half, and shall not suf-

fer their dead bodies to be put in graves.

[10] And they that dwell upon the earth shall rejoice over them, and make merry, and shall send gifts one to another; because these two prophets tormented them that dwelt on the earth.

[11] And after three days and a half the Spirit of life from God entered into them, and they stood upon their feet; and great fear fell upon them which saw them.

[12] And they heard a great voice from heaven saying unto them, Come up hither. And they ascended up to heaven in a cloud; and their enemies beheld them.

[13] And the same hour was there a great earthquake, and the tenth part of the city fell, and in the earthquake were slain of men seven thousand: and the remnant were affrighted, and gave glory to the God of heaven.

[14] The second woe is past; *and*, behold, the third woe cometh quickly.

OLD TESTAMENT READING

*A*nd Elijah the Tishbite, *who was* of the inhabitants of Gilead, said unto Ahab, *As* the LORD God of Israel liveth, before whom I stand, there shall not be dew nor rain these years, but according to my word.

[1] And it came to pass *after* many days, that the word of the LORD came to Elijah in the third year, saying, Go, show thyself unto Ahab; and I will send rain upon the earth.

[2] And Elijah went to show himself unto Ahab. And *there was* a sore famine in Samaria.

1 Kings 17:1; 18:1–2

INSIGHTS

*D*uring the darkest ages, men have been raised up to testify against the prevailing corruption of their time, and especially the corruption of the apostate church. Their opponents have endeavored to silence their voice and blacken their character, but God has ever vindicated them and given life out of death. Always when the enemies of the truth have deemed themselves triumphant, there has been a rekindling of gospel testimony. A few years before Luther appeared, a medal was struck to commemorate the extinction of so-called heresy. Such witness-bearing as is suggested by the comparison with Zechariah's vision is fed from the heart of Christ. He is the root of the martyr line; his Spirit is the life-breath of his witnesses. All through the centuries, commonly called Christian though generally very un-Christian, there has been an unbroken succession of pure and noble souls who have stood for Jesus Christ even unto death. Let us dare to stand with them and our Lord, that he may not be ashamed of us at his coming.

F. B. Meyer

ACTION POINT

*A*t what times does God call special prophets? What powers does he give them? Who controls their fate? What has God called you to do? Pray that you will trust him to care for you and enable you to accomplish his work.

TUESDAY

Satan Is Defeated by Christ's Coming

Revelation 11:15—12:12

The Seventh Trumpet

*A*nd the seventh angel sounded; and there were great voices in heaven, saying, The kingdoms of this world are become *the kingdoms* of our Lord, and of his Christ; and he shall reign for ever and ever.

16 And the four and twenty elders, which sat before God on their seats, fell upon their faces, and worshipped God,

17 saying, We give thee thanks, O Lord God Almighty, which art, and wast, and art to come; because thou hast taken to thee thy great power, and hast reigned.

18 And the nations were angry, and thy wrath is come, and the time of the dead, that they should be judged, and that thou shouldest give reward unto thy servants the prophets, and to the saints, and them that fear thy name, small and great; and shouldest destroy them which destroy the earth.

19 And the temple of God was opened in heaven, and there was seen in his temple the ark of his testament: and there were lightnings, and voices, and thunderings, and an earthquake, and great hail.

The Woman and the Dragon

12 And there appeared a great wonder in heaven; a woman clothed with the sun, and the moon under her feet, and upon her head a crown of twelve stars:

2 and she being with child cried, travailing in birth, and pained to be delivered.

3 And there appeared another wonder in heaven; and behold a great red dragon, having seven heads and ten horns, and seven crowns upon his heads.

4 And his tail drew the third part of the stars of heaven, and did cast them to the earth: and the dragon stood before the woman which was ready to be delivered, for to devour her child as soon as it was born.

5 And she brought forth a man child, who was to rule all nations with a rod of iron: and her child was caught up unto God, and *to* his throne.

6 And the woman fled into the wilderness, where she hath a place prepared of God, that they should feed her there a thousand two hundred *and* threescore days.

7 And there was war in heaven: Michael and his angels fought against the dragon; and the dragon fought and his angels,

8 and prevailed not; neither was their place found any more in heaven.

9 And the great dragon was cast out, that old serpent, called the Devil, and Satan, which deceiveth the whole world: he was cast out into the earth, and his angels were cast out with him.

10 And I heard a loud voice saying in heaven, Now is come salvation, and strength, and the kingdom of our God, and the power of his Christ: for the accuser of our brethren is cast down, which accused them before our God day and night.

11 And they overcame him by the

blood of the Lamb, and by the word of their testimony; and they loved not their lives unto the death. [12] Therefore rejoice, *ye* heavens, and ye that dwell in them. Woe to the inhabiters of the earth and of the sea! for the devil is come down unto you, having great wrath, because he knoweth that he hath but a short time.

OLD TESTAMENT READING

I beheld, and the same horn made war with the saints, and prevailed against them; [22] until the Ancient of days came, and judgment was given to the saints of the Most High; and the time came that the saints possessed the kingdom.

Daniel 7:21–22

INSIGHTS

What is this celestial conflict all about? The fact that Michael led God's angels to victory is significant, because Michael is identified with the nation Israel. . . . Apparently, the devil's hatred of Israel will spur him to make one final assault against the throne of God, but he will be defeated by Michael and a heavenly host. . . .

How does this future war apply to the church today? The same serpent who accuses the saints in heaven also deceives . . . the nations into thinking that the people of God are dangerous, deluded, even destructive. . . . God's people in every age must expect the world's opposition, but the church can always defeat the enemy by being faithful to Jesus Christ. . . .

. . . Satan is not equal to God; he is not omnipotent, omnipresent, or omniscient. His power is limited and his tactics must fail when God's people trust the power of the blood and of the Word. . . .

Believers in any age or situation can rejoice in this victory, no matter how difficult their experiences may be. Our warfare is not against flesh and blood, but against the spiritual forces of the wicked one; and these have been defeated by our Saviour (Eph. 6:10ff; note also 1:15–23).

Warren Wiersbe

ACTION POINT

What persepective do you gain on your struggles today from this account of ultimate struggle in heaven? Thank God he has already won the battle! Pray that you will remain faithful to him as you fight the battles in your life.

WEDNESDAY

*God's People Must Fight Satan
with Patience and Faith*

Revelation 12:13—13:18

*A*nd when the dragon saw that he was cast unto the earth, he persecuted the woman which brought forth the man *child*.

14 And to the woman were given two wings of a great eagle, that she might fly into the wilderness, into her place, where she is nourished for a time, and times, and half a time, from the face of the serpent.

15 And the serpent cast out of his mouth water as a flood after the woman, that he might cause her to be carried away of the flood.

16 And the earth helped the woman; and the earth opened her mouth, and swallowed up the flood which the dragon cast out of his mouth.

17 And the dragon was wroth with the woman, and went to make war with the remnant of her seed, which keep the commandments of God, and have the testimony of Jesus Christ.

The Two Beasts

13 And I stood upon the sand of the sea, and saw a beast rise up out of the sea, having seven heads and ten horns, and upon his horns ten crowns, and upon his heads the name of blasphemy.

2 And the beast which I saw was like unto a leopard, and his feet were as *the feet* of a bear, and his mouth as the mouth of a lion: and the dragon gave him his power, and his seat, and great authority.

3 And I saw one of his heads as it were wounded to death; and his deadly wound was healed: and all the world wondered after the beast.

4 And they worshipped the dragon which gave power unto the beast: and they worshipped the beast, saying, Who *is* like unto the beast? who is able to make war with him?

5 And there was given unto him a mouth speaking great things and blasphemies; and power was given unto him to continue forty *and* two months.

6 And he opened his mouth in blasphemy against God, to blaspheme his name, and his tabernacle, and them that dwell in heaven.

7 And it was given unto him to make war with the saints, and to overcome them: and power was given him over all kindreds, and tongues, and nations.

8 And all that dwell upon the earth shall worship him, whose names are not written in the book of life of the Lamb slain from the foundation of the world.

9 If any man have an ear, let him hear.

10 He that leadeth into captivity shall go into captivity: he that killeth with the sword must be killed with the sword. Here is the patience and the faith of the saints.

11 And I beheld another beast coming up out of the earth; and he had two horns like a lamb, and he spake as a dragon.

12 And he exerciseth all the power of the first beast before him, and causeth the earth and them which dwell therein to worship the first beast, whose deadly wound was healed.

13 And he doeth great wonders, so that he maketh fire come down from

heaven on the earth in the sight of men,

[14] and deceiveth them that dwell on the earth by *the means of* those miracles which he had power to do in the sight of the beast; saying to them that dwell on the earth, that they should make an image to the beast, which had the wound by a sword, and did live.

[15] And he had power to give life unto the image of the beast, that the image of the beast should both speak, and cause that as many as would not worship the image of the beast should be killed.

[16] And he causeth all, both small and great, rich and poor, free and bond, to receive a mark in their right hand, or in their foreheads:

[17] and that no man might buy or sell, save he that had the mark, or the name of the beast, or the number of his name.

[18] Here is wisdom. Let him that hath understanding count the number of the beast: for it is the number of a man; and his number *is* Six hundred threescore *and* six.

OLD TESTAMENT READING

*I*f *it had* not *been* the LORD who was on our side, when men rose up against us:

[3] then they had swallowed us up quick, when their wrath was kindled against us:

[4] then the waters had overwhelmed us, the stream had gone over our soul:

[5] then the proud waters had gone over our soul.

[6] Blessed *be* the LORD, who hath not given us *as* a prey to their teeth.

[7] Our soul is escaped as a bird out of the snare of the fowlers: the snare is broken, and we are escaped.

[8] Our help *is* in the name of the LORD, who made heaven and earth.

Psalms 124:2–8

INSIGHTS

*W*e must be entrenched in the strength of the Lord. We must be enclosed "in the power of his might," or, as one has paraphrased it, "in the energy of him, the strong." It is in vain we engage in the conflict if that preliminary condition has not been fulfilled. In earthly warfare the soldier does not provide his own means of defense or weapons of assault. So in Christian conflict our whole equipment is divinely provided for us. He gives us a position that is impregnable—strength in the Lord; an armor that is impenetrable; and a weapon that is infallible—"the sword of the Spirit." We have by faith to take that position and continually to abide in it. We have by faith to put on that armor and wear it constantly.

Evan Hopkins

ACTION POINT

*W*hat difficulties will God's people face in the end times? How must they respond to Satan? What are their weapons, and what must they be prepared to give up? What will be accomplished by those who remain strong? Pray that your faith will be purified through the battles you face!

THURSDAY

God Will Pour Out His Holy Anger Against the Wicked

Revelation 14:1–20

The Song of the Saved

14 And I looked, and, lo, a Lamb stood on the mount Zion, and with him a hundred forty *and* four thousand, having his Father's name written in their foreheads.

² And I heard a voice from heaven, as the voice of many waters, and as the voice of a great thunder: and I heard the voice of harpers harping with their harps:

³ and they sung as it were a new song before the throne, and before the four beasts, and the elders: and no man could learn that song but the hundred *and* forty *and* four thousand, which were redeemed from the earth.

⁴ These are they which were not defiled with women; for they are virgins. These are they which follow the Lamb whithersoever he goeth. These were redeemed from among men, *being* the firstfruits unto God and to the Lamb.

⁵ And in their mouth was found no guile: for they are without fault before the throne of God.

The Three Angels

*A*nd I saw another angel fly in the midst of heaven, having the everlasting gospel to preach unto them that dwell on the earth, and to every nation, and kindred, and tongue, and people,

⁷ saying with a loud voice, Fear God, and give glory to him; for the hour of his judgment is come: and worship him that made heaven, and earth, and the sea, and the fountains of waters.

⁸ And there followed another angel, saying, Babylon is fallen, is fallen, that great city, because she made all nations drink of the wine of the wrath of her fornication.

⁹ And the third angel followed them, saying with a loud voice, If any man worship the beast and his image, and receive *his* mark in his forehead, or in his hand,

¹⁰ the same shall drink of the wine of the wrath of God, which is poured out without mixture into the cup of his indignation; and he shall be tormented with fire and brimstone in the presence of the holy angels, and in the presence of the Lamb:

¹¹ and the smoke of their torment ascendeth up for ever and ever: and they have no rest day nor night, who worship the beast and his image, and whosoever receiveth the mark of his name.

¹² Here is the patience of the saints: here *are* they that keep the commandments of God, and the faith of Jesus.

¹³ And I heard a voice from heaven saying unto me, Write, Blessed *are* the dead which die in the Lord from henceforth: Yea, saith the Spirit, that they may rest from their labors; and their works do follow them.

The Earth Is Harvested

*A*nd I looked, and behold a white cloud, and upon the cloud *one* sat like unto the Son of man, having on his head a golden crown, and in his hand a sharp sickle.

15 And another angel came out of the temple, crying with a loud voice to him that sat on the cloud, Thrust in thy sickle, and reap: for the time is come for thee to reap; for the harvest of the earth is ripe.

16 And he that sat on the cloud thrust in his sickle on the earth; and the earth was reaped.

17 And another angel came out of the temple which is in heaven, he also having a sharp sickle.

18 And another angel came out from the altar, which had power over fire; and cried with a loud cry to him that had the sharp sickle, saying, Thrust in thy sharp sickle, and gather the clusters of the vine of the earth; for her grapes are fully ripe.

19 And the angel thrust in his sickle into the earth, and gathered the vine of the earth, and cast it into the great winepress of the wrath of God.

20 And the winepress was trodden without the city, and blood came out of the winepress, even unto the horse bridles, by the space of a thousand and six hundred furlongs.

26b And all the kingdoms of the world, which are upon the face of the earth: and the king of Sheshach shall drink after them.

Jeremiah 25:15–17, 26b

INSIGHTS

The sinner's peace is that terribly prophetic calm that the traveler occasionally experiences on the higher Alps. Everything is still. The birds suspend their notes, fly low, and cower down with fear. The hum of bees among the flowers is hushed. A horrible stillness rules the hour, as if death had silenced all things by stretching his awful scepter over them. But the tempest is preparing—the lightning will soon cast abroad its flames of fire. Earth will rock with thunder-blasts; granite peaks will be dissolved. All nature will tremble beneath the fury of the storm. That calm is what the sinner is experiencing. He should not rejoice in it, because the hurricane of wrath is coming, the whirlwind and the tribulation that can sweep him away and utterly destroy him.

Charles Spurgeon

OLD TESTAMENT READING

*F*or thus saith the LORD God of Israel unto me; Take the winecup of this fury at my hand, and cause all the nations, to whom I send thee, to drink it.

16 And they shall drink, and be moved, and be mad, because of the sword that I will send among them.

17 Then took I the cup at the LORD's hand, and made all the nations to drink, unto whom the LORD had sent me.

PAUSE FOR REFLECTION

*I*n light of these Scripture readings, the "sinner's peace" that Spurgeon refers to certainly is ominous, isn't it? What does God's merciful forgiveness that he repeatedly offers to all people, contrasted with his guarantee of final, unchangeable punishment, teach you about the divine nature?

FRIDAY

God's People Praise Their Righteous and Faithful God

Revelation 15:1—16:11

The Last Plagues

15And I saw another sign in heaven, great and marvelous, seven angels having the seven last plagues; for in them is filled up the wrath of God.

² And I saw as it were a sea of glass mingled with fire: and them that had gotten the victory over the beast, and over his image, and over his mark, *and* over the number of his name, stand on the sea of glass, having the harps of God.

³ And they sing the song of Moses the servant of God, and the song of the Lamb, saying, Great and marvellous *are* thy works, Lord God Almighty; just and true *are* thy ways, thou King of saints.

⁴ Who shall not fear thee, O Lord, and glorify thy name? for *thou* only *art* holy: for all nations shall come and worship before thee; for thy judgments are made manifest.

⁵ And after that I looked, and, behold, the temple of the tabernacle of the testimony in heaven was opened:

⁶ and the seven angels came out of the temple, having the seven plagues, clothed in pure and white linen, and having their breasts girded with golden girdles.

⁷ And one of the four beasts gave unto the seven angels seven golden vials full of the wrath of God, who liveth for ever and ever.

⁸ And the temple was filled with smoke from the glory of God, and from his power; and no man was able to enter into the temple, till the seven plagues of the seven angels were fulfilled.

The Bowls of God's Wrath

16And I heard a great voice out of the temple saying to the seven angels, Go your ways, and pour out the vials of the wrath of God upon the earth.

² And the first went, and poured out his vial upon the earth; and there fell a noisome and grievous sore upon the men which had the mark of the beast, and *upon* them which worshipped his image.

³ And the second angel poured out his vial upon the sea; and it became as the blood of a dead *man*: and every living soul died in the sea.

⁴ And the third angel poured out his vial upon the rivers and fountains of waters; and they became blood.

⁵ And I heard the angel of the waters say, Thou art righteous, O Lord, which art, and wast, and shalt be, because thou hast judged thus.

⁶ For they have shed the blood of saints and prophets, and thou hast given them blood to drink; for they are worthy.

⁷ And I heard another out of the altar say, Even so, Lord God Almighty, true and righteous *are* thy judgments.

⁸ And the fourth angel poured out his vial upon the sun; and power was given unto him to scorch men with fire.

⁹ And men were scorched with great heat, and blasphemed the name of God, which hath power over these

plagues: and they repented not to give him glory.

¹⁰ And the fifth angel poured out his vial upon the seat of the beast; and his kingdom was full of darkness; and they gnawed their tongues for pain,

¹¹ and blasphemed the God of heaven because of their pains and their sores, and repented not of their deeds.

OLD TESTAMENT READING

*A*nd when the LORD saw *it*, he abhorred *them*, because of the provoking of his sons, and of his daughters. ²⁰ And he said, I will hide my face from them, I will see what their end *shall be*: for they *are* a very froward generation, children in whom *is* no faith.

²³ I will heap mischiefs upon them; I will spend mine arrows upon them. ²⁴ *They shall be* burnt with hunger, and devoured with burning heat, and with bitter destruction: I will also send the teeth of beasts upon them, with the poison of serpents of the dust.

Deuteronomy 32:19–20, 23–24

INSIGHTS

*H*ow glorious must He [Christ] have been in the eyes of seraphs, when a cloud received Him out of mortal sight, and He ascended up to heaven! Now He wears the glory which He had with God or ever the earth was, and yet another glory above all—that which He has well earned in the fight against sin, death, and hell. As victor He wears the illustrious crown. . . . He wears the glory of an Intercessor

who can never fail, of a Prince who can never be defeated, of a Conqueror who has vanquished every foe, of a Lord who has the heart's allegiance of every subject. Jesus wears all the glory which the pomp of heaven can bestow upon Him, which ten thousand times ten thousand angels can minister to Him. You cannot with your utmost stretch of imagination conceive His exceeding greatness; yet there will be a further revelation of it when He shall descend from heaven in great power, with all the holy angels—"Then shall He sit upon the throne of His glory." Oh, the splendour of that glory! It will ravish His people's hearts. Nor is this the close, for eternity shall sound His praise, "Thy throne, O God, is for ever and ever!" Reader, if you would joy in Christ's glory hereafter, He must be glorious in your sight now. Is He so?

Charles Spurgeon

APPLICATION

*S*tudy the contrasts between the praises of God's people and the evil of those who reject God and his salvation. On which side of the battle will you stand firm? Do you delight to sing God's praises?

WEEKEND

*God Reveals His Holiness
Through His Anger
Against Evil*

Revelation 16:12—17:8

*A*nd the sixth angel poured out his vial upon the great river Euphrates; and the water thereof was dried up, that the way of the kings of the east might be prepared.

[13] And I saw three unclean spirits like frogs *come* out of the mouth of the dragon, and out of the mouth of the beast, and out of the mouth of the false prophet.

[14] For they are the spirits of devils, working miracles, *which* go forth unto the kings of the earth and of the whole world, to gather them to the battle of that great day of God Almighty.

[15] Behold, I come as a thief. Blessed *is* he that watcheth, and keepeth his garments, lest he walk naked, and they see his shame.

[16] And he gathered them together into a place called in the Hebrew tongue Armageddon.

[17] And the seventh angel poured out his vial into the air; and there came a great voice out of the temple of heaven, from the throne, saying, It is done.

[18] And there were voices, and thunders, and lightnings; and there was a great earthquake, such as was not since men were upon the earth, so mighty an earthquake, *and* so great.

[19] And the great city was divided into three parts, and the cities of the nations fell: and great Babylon came in remembrance before God, to give unto her the cup of the wine of the fierceness of his wrath.

[20] And every island fled away, and the mountains were not found.

[21] And there fell upon men a great hail out of heaven, *every stone* about the weight of a talent: and men blasphemed God because of the plague of the hail; for the plague thereof was exceeding great.

The Woman on the Beast

[17] And there came one of the seven angels which had the seven vials, and talked with me, saying unto me, Come hither; I will show unto thee the judgment of the great whore that sitteth upon many waters:

[2] with whom the kings of the earth have committed fornication, and the inhabitants of the earth have been made drunk with the wine of her fornication.

[3] So he carried me away in the spirit into the wilderness: and I saw a woman sit upon a scarlet-colored beast, full of names of blasphemy, having seven heads and ten horns.

[4] And the woman was arrayed in purple and scarlet color, and decked with gold and precious stones and pearls, having a golden cup in her hand full of abominations and filthiness of her fornication:

[5] and upon her forehead *was* a name written, MYSTERY, BABYLON THE GREAT, THE MOTHER OF HARLOTS AND ABOMINATIONS OF THE EARTH.

[6] And I saw the woman drunken with the blood of the saints, and with the blood of the martyrs of Jesus: and when I saw her, I wondered with great admiration.

[7] And the angel said unto me, Where-

fore didst thou marvel? I will tell thee the mystery of the woman, and of the beast that carrieth her, which hath the seven heads and ten horns. [8] The beast that thou sawest was, and is not; and shall ascend out of the bottomless pit, and go into perdition: and they that dwell on the earth shall wonder, whose names were not written in the book of life from the foundation of the world, when they behold the beast that was, and is not, and yet is.

OLD TESTAMENT READING

*A*nd it shall come to pass at the same time when Gog shall come against the land of Israel, saith the Lord GOD, *that* my fury shall come up in my face.

[19] For in my jealousy *and* in the fire of my wrath have I spoken, Surely in that day there shall be a great shaking in the land of Israel;

[20] so that the fishes of the sea, and the fowls of the heaven, and the beasts of the field, and all creeping things that creep upon the earth, and all the men that *are* upon the face of the earth, shall shake at my presence, and the mountains shall be thrown down, and the steep places shall fall, and every wall shall fall to the ground.

[21] And I will call for a sword against him throughout all my mountains, saith the Lord GOD: every man's sword shall be against his brother.

[22] And I will plead against him with pestilence and with blood; and I will rain upon him, and upon his bands, and upon the many people that *are* with him, an overflowing rain, and great hailstones, fire, and brimstone.

[23] Thus will I magnify myself, and sanctify myself; and I will be known in the eyes of many nations, and they shall know that I *am* LORD.

Ezekiel 38:18–23

INSIGHTS

*I*f men and women will not yield to the love of God, and be changed by the grace of God, then there is no way for them to escape the wrath of God.

Rank and wealth will not deliver anyone in that terrible day. John's list included kings, captains, and slaves, the rich and the poor. "Who shall be able to stand?"

. . . We are so accustomed to emphasizing the meekness and gentleness of Christ (Matt. 11:28–30) that we forget His holiness and justice. The same Christ who welcomed the children in the temple also drove merchants from that same temple. God's wrath is not like a child's temper tantrum or punishment meted out by an impatient parent. God's wrath is the evidence of His holy love for all that is right and His holy hatred for all that is evil. Only a soft and sentimental person would want to worship a God who did not deal justly with evil in the world.

Warren Wiersbe

PAUSE FOR REFLECTION

*W*hat are God's purposes in punishing the evil nations? How will the people on earth respond when the last of God's angels pours out his anger? Pray that God will give you greater insight into his perfect holiness as you study these passages.

MONDAY

God Calls His People to Run Away from Evil

Revelation 17:9—18:10

And here *is* the mind which hath wisdom. The seven heads are seven mountains, on which the woman sitteth.

10 And there are seven kings: five are fallen, and one is, *and* the other is not yet come; and when he cometh, he must continue a short space.

11 And the beast that was, and is not, even he is the eighth, and is of the seven, and goeth into perdition.

12 And the ten horns which thou sawest are ten kings, which have received no kingdom as yet; but receive power as kings one hour with the beast.

13 These have one mind, and shall give their power and strength unto the beast.

14 These shall make war with the Lamb, and the Lamb shall overcome them: for he is Lord of lords, and King of kings: and they that are with him *are* called, and chosen, and faithful.

15 And he saith unto me, The waters which thou sawest, where the whore sitteth, are peoples, and multitudes, and nations, and tongues.

16 And the ten horns which thou sawest upon the beast, these shall hate the whore, and shall make her desolate and naked, and shall eat her flesh, and burn her with fire.

17 For God hath put in their hearts to fulfil his will, and to agree, and give their kingdom unto the beast, until the words of God shall be fulfilled.

18 And the woman which thou sawest is that great city, which reigneth over the kings of the earth.

Babylon Is Destroyed

18 And after these things I saw another angel come down from heaven, having great power; and the earth was lightened with his glory.

2 And he cried mightily with a strong voice, saying, Babylon the great is fallen, is fallen, and is become the habitation of devils, and the hold of every foul spirit, and a cage of every unclean and hateful bird.

3 For all nations have drunk of the wine of the wrath of her fornication, and the kings of the earth have committed fornication with her, and the merchants of the earth are waxed rich through the abundance of her delicacies.

4 And I heard another voice from heaven, saying, Come out of her, my people, that ye be not partakers of her sins, and that ye receive not of her plagues.

5 For her sins have reached unto heaven, and God hath remembered her iniquities.

6 Reward her even as she rewarded you, and double unto her double according to her works: in the cup which she hath filled, fill to her double.

7 How much she hath glorified herself, and lived deliciously, so much torment and sorrow give her: for she saith in her heart, I sit a queen, and am no widow, and shall see no sorrow.

8 Therefore shall her plagues come

in one day, death, and mourning, and famine; and she shall be utterly burned with fire: for strong *is* the Lord God who judgeth her.

⁹ And the kings of the earth, who have committed fornication and lived deliciously with her, shall bewail her, and lament for her, when they shall see the smoke of her burning,

¹⁰ standing afar off for the fear of her torment, saying, Alas, alas, that great city Babylon, that mighty city! for in one hour is thy judgment come.

OLD TESTAMENT READING

*A*nd when the morning arose, then the angels hastened Lot, saying, Arise, take thy wife, and thy two daughters, which are here; lest thou be consumed in the iniquity of the city.

Genesis 19:15

INSIGHTS

*T*hrough our union with Christ in His death we are delivered from the dominion of sin. But we still find sin struggling to gain mastery over us. . . . We may not like the fact that we have this lifelong struggle with sin, but the more we realize and accept it, the better equipped we will be to deal with it. . . .

The Bible tells us that the heart is deceitful and unsearchable to any but God alone (Jeremiah 17:9–10). Even as believers we do not know our own hearts (1 Corinthians 4:3–5). . . .

Knowing that indwelling sin occupies a heart that is deceitful and unsearchable should make us extremely wary. . . .

. . . Though sin no longer has

dominion over us, it wages its guerrilla warfare against us. If left unchecked, it will defeat us. Our recourse against this warfare is to deal swiftly and firmly with the first motions of indwelling sin. . . .

. . . We must never consider that our fight against sin is at an end. The heart is unsearchable, our evil desires are insatiable, and our reason is constantly in danger of being deceived. Well did Jesus say, "Watch and pray so that you will not fall into temptation" (Matthew 26:41).

Jerry Bridges

APPLICATION

*W*hy is it important for God's people to do everything they can to separate themselves from sin? What punishment will come to those who linger when God tells them to run? Are you listening for his warning?

TUESDAY

God Will Punish Babylon

Revelation 18:11–24

Judgment on the Great City of Babylon

*A*nd the merchants of the earth shall weep and mourn over her; for no man buyeth their merchandise any more:

¹²the merchandise of gold, and silver, and precious stones, and of pearls, and fine linen, and purple, and silk, and scarlet, and all thyine wood, and all manner vessels of ivory, and all manner vessels of most precious wood, and of brass, and iron, and marble,

¹³and cinnamon, and odors, and ointments, and frankincense, and wine, and oil, and fine flour, and wheat, and beasts, and sheep, and horses, and chariots, and slaves, and souls of men.

¹⁴And the fruits that thy soul lusted after are departed from thee, and all things which were dainty and goodly are departed from thee, and thou shalt find them no more at all.

¹⁵The merchants of these things, which were made rich by her, shall stand afar off for the fear of her torment, weeping and wailing,

¹⁶and saying, Alas, alas, that great city, that was clothed in fine linen, and purple, and scarlet, and decked with gold, and precious stones, and pearls!

¹⁷For in one hour so great riches is come to nought. And every shipmaster, and all the company in ships, and sailors, and as many as trade by sea, stood afar off,

¹⁸and cried when they saw the smoke of her burning, saying, What *city* is like unto this great city!

¹⁹And they cast dust on their heads, and cried, weeping and wailing, saying, Alas, alas, that great city, wherein were made rich all that had ships in the sea by reason of her costliness! for in one hour is she made desolate.

²⁰Rejoice over her, *thou* heaven, and *ye* holy apostles and prophets; for God hath avenged you on her.

²¹And a mighty angel took up a stone like a great millstone, and cast *it* into the sea, saying, Thus with violence shall that great city Babylon be thrown down, and shall be found no more at all.

²²And the voice of harpers, and musicians, and of pipers, and trumpeters, shall be heard no more at all in thee; and no craftsman, of whatsoever craft *he be*, shall be found any more in thee; and the sound of a millstone shall be heard no more at all in thee;

²³and the light of a candle shall shine no more at all in thee; and the voice of the bridegroom and of the bride shall be heard no more at all in thee: for thy merchants were the great men of the earth; for by thy sorceries were all nations deceived.

²⁴And in her was found the blood of prophets, and of saints, and of all that were slain upon the earth.

OLD TESTAMENT READING

*B*ehold, I *am* against thee, O destroying mountain, saith the Lᴏʀᴅ, which destroyest all the earth: and I will stretch out mine hand upon thee, and roll thee down from the rocks, and will make thee a burnt mountain.

²⁶ And they shall not take of thee a stone for a corner, nor a stone for foundations; but thou shalt be desolate for ever, saith the LORD.

³⁶ Therefore thus saith the LORD; Behold, I will plead thy cause, and take vengeance for thee.

Jeremiah 51:25–26, 36a

INSIGHTS

In spite of what people often think, no one is getting away with anything. Payday someday! God's vengeance will be revealed, even against false religion in whose name and under whose influence millions have suffered and died. God's judgment will fall and vindicate His people. . . .

The extent of Babylon's payment: The law of retribution is applied; what we sow, we shall reap. It is doubled to emphasize the enormity of the woman's sins and the justice behind her judgment and fall. The "cup which she has mixed," containing the wine of her wrath against the people of God, is now mixed for her with a double portion of God's wrath (14:10).

The experience of Babylon's sorrow: Like so many unbelievers today, this woman believes she will never experience sorrow or torment for her lifestyle and luxurious living. She boasts "I sit as queen, and am no widow." After all, she reasons, the kings of the earth are her lovers. But she is a widow in that God has forsaken her. . . .

Two things characterize the harlot's lifestyle: self-glorification and sensuous living. For this, she *will receive torment and sorrow. So will all who choose to follow her path. . . .*

The hunger for achievement and accumulation of wealth remains as the dominant factor of people's lifestyles and desires. The "fools" of this world are found daily in every marketplace and place of business. . . . But judgment day is coming! The merchants of the world, along with the kings of the earth, will mourn the sudden destruction of the woman who helped them become prosperous.

David Hocking

PAUSE FOR REFLECTION

Why is God against Babylon? Why will the people of earth mourn the destruction of Babylon? What does her defeat symbolize? Where is your heart's loyalty? Will you shed even one tear over Babylon's loss?

WEDNESDAY

All the People of Heaven Worship God!

Revelation 19:1–16

People in Heaven Praise God

19 And after these things I heard a great voice of much people in heaven, saying, Alleluia; Salvation, and glory, and honor, and power, unto the Lord our God:

2 for true and righteous *are* his judgments: for he hath judged the great whore, which did corrupt the earth with her fornication, and hath avenged the blood of his servants at her hand.

3 And again they said, Alleluia. And her smoke rose up for ever and ever.

4 And the four and twenty elders and the four beasts fell down and worshipped God that sat on the throne, saying, Amen; Alleluia.

5 And a voice came out of the throne, saying, Praise our God, all ye his servants, and ye that fear him, both small and great.

6 And I heard as it were the voice of a great multitude, and as the voice of many waters, and as the voice of mighty thunderings, saying, Alleluia: for the Lord God omnipotent reigneth.

7 Let us be glad and rejoice, and give honor to him: for the marriage of the Lamb is come, and his wife hath made herself ready.

8 And to her was granted that she should be arrayed in fine linen, clean and white: for the fine linen is the righteousness of saints.

9 And he saith unto me, Write, Blessed *are* they which are called unto the marriage supper of the Lamb. And he saith unto me, These are the true sayings of God.

10 And I fell at his feet to worship him. And he said unto me, See *thou do it* not: I am thy fellow servant, and of thy brethren that have the testimony of Jesus: worship God: for the testimony of Jesus is the spirit of prophecy.

The Rider on the White Horse

*A*nd I saw heaven opened, and behold a white horse; and he that sat upon him *was* called Faithful and True, and in righteousness he doth judge and make war.

12 His eyes *were* as a flame of fire, and on his head *were* many crowns; and he had a name written, that no man knew, but he himself.

13 And he *was* clothed with a vesture dipped in blood: and his name is called The Word of God.

14 And the armies *which were* in heaven followed him upon white horses, clothed in fine linen, white and clean.

15 And out of his mouth goeth a sharp sword, that with it he should smite the nations: and he shall rule them with a rod of iron: and he treadeth the winepress of the fierceness and wrath of Almighty God.

16 And he hath on *his* vesture and on his thigh a name written, KING OF KINGS, AND LORD OF LORDS..

OLD TESTAMENT READING

*W*ho *is* like unto thee, O LORD, among the gods? Who *is* like thee, glorious in holiness, fearful *in* praises, doing wonders?

¹²Thou stretchedst out thy right hand, the earth swallowed them.

¹³Thou in thy mercy hast led forth the people *which* thou hast redeemed: thou hast guided *them* in thy strength unto thy holy habitation.

¹⁷Thou shalt bring them in, and plant them in the mountain of thine inheritance, *in* the place, O LORD, *which* thou hast made for thee to dwell in; *in* the sanctuary, O LORD, *which* thy hands have established.

¹⁸The LORD shall reign for ever and ever.

Exodus 15:11–13, 17–18

INSIGHTS

There is a party in heaven because the party that meant destruction for so many has been ended. A new celebration sponsored by God has gotten under way. According to this scripture, those allied with the Lamb of God cannot help but shout, "Hallelujah!" at this incredible turn of events. . . .

. . . Many of the most credible biblical scholars have agreed that Babylon in the Book of Revelation always refers to the dominant society in which Christians have to live. . . .

. . . When our Babylon falls (and it, like all Babylons, will one day fall), how will you react? Will you react like the merchants described in Revelation 18:3 who "grew rich from her excessive luxuries" and those political potentates who conspired with her to exploit the weak and the poor? Or will you be able to join the angels on that day and sing praises to God?

. . . Have you given your time and energy to get those things that go with living in Babylon so that, when it falls, all that you have ever worked for will fall with it? Or have you so invested your life in the Kingdom of God that, even if heaven and earth shall pass away, what is important to you will endure? In the end, will you be able to shout and sing in that eternal party that will be shared by those who have laid up their treasures in heaven (Matt. 6:19–21)?

Tony Campolo

PAUSE FOR REFLECTION

Reread the praises to God in these passages—several times, if you'd like. Can you imagine anything more wonderful than praising God in heaven? Have you accepted your invitation to join his everlasting party?

THURSDAY

*God's Triumph over Satan and
Sin Is Complete*

Revelation 19:17—20:15

*A*nd I saw an angel standing in the sun; and he cried with a loud voice, saying to all the fowls that fly in the midst of heaven, Come and gather yourselves together unto the supper of the great God;

18 that ye may eat the flesh of kings, and the flesh of captains, and the flesh of mighty men, and the flesh of horses, and of them that sit on them, and the flesh of all *men, both* free and bond, both small and great.

19 And I saw the beast, and the kings of the earth, and their armies, gathered together to make war against him that sat on the horse, and against his army.

20 And the beast was taken, and with him the false prophet that wrought miracles before him, with which he deceived them that had received the mark of the beast, and them that worshipped his image. These both were cast alive into a lake of fire burning with brimstone.

21 And the remnant were slain with the sword of him that sat upon the horse, which *sword* proceeded out of his mouth: and all the fowls were filled with their flesh.

The Thousand Years

20 And I saw an angel come down from heaven, having the key of the bottomless pit and a great chain in his hand.

2 And he laid hold on the dragon, that old serpent, which is the Devil, and Satan, and bound him a thousand years,

3 and cast him into the bottomless pit, and shut him up, and set a seal upon him, that he should deceive the nations no more, till the thousand years should be fulfilled: and after that he must be loosed a little season.

4 And I saw thrones, and they sat upon them, and judgment was given unto them: and *I saw* the souls of them that were beheaded for the witness of Jesus, and for the word of God, and which had not worshipped the beast, neither his image, neither had received *his* mark upon their foreheads, or in their hands; and they lived and reigned with Christ a thousand years.

5 But the rest of the dead lived not again until the thousand years were finished. This *is* the first resurrection.

6 Blessed and holy *is* he that hath part in the first resurrection: on such the second death hath no power, but they shall be priests of God and of Christ, and shall reign with him a thousand years.

7 And when the thousand years are expired, Satan shall be loosed out of his prison,

8 and shall go out to deceive the nations which are in the four quarters of the earth, Gog and Magog, to gather them together to battle: the number of whom *is* as the sand of the sea.

9 And they went up on the breadth of the earth, and compassed the camp of the saints about, and the beloved city: and fire came down from God out of heaven, and devoured them.

10 And the devil that deceived them was cast into the lake of fire and brimstone, where the beast and the false prophet *are*, and shall be tormented day and night for ever and ever.

People of the World Are Judged

*A*nd I saw a great white throne, and him that sat on it, from whose face the earth and the heaven fled away; and there was found no place for them.

¹² And I saw the dead, small and great, stand before God; and the books were opened: and another book was opened, which is *the book* of life: and the dead were judged out of those things which were written in the books, according to their works.

¹³ And the sea gave up the dead which were in it; and death and hell delivered up the dead which were in them: and they were judged every man according to their works.

¹⁴ And death and hell were cast into the lake of fire. This is the second death.

¹⁵ And whosoever was not found written in the book of life was cast into the lake of fire.

OLD TESTAMENT READING

*T*herefore, thou son of man, prophesy against Gog, and say, Thus saith the Lord GOD; Behold, I *am* against thee, O Gog, the chief prince of Meshech and Tubal.

⁴ Thou shalt fall upon the mountains of Israel, thou, and all thy bands, and the people that *is* with thee: I will give thee unto the ravenous birds of every sort, and *to* the beasts of the field, to be devoured.

⁵ Thou shalt fall upon the open field: for I have spoken *it*, saith the Lord GOD.

⁶ And I will send a fire on Magog, and among them that dwell carelessly in the isles: and they shall know that I *am* the LORD.

⁷ So will I make my holy name known in the midst of my people Israel; and I will not *let them* pollute my holy name any more: and the heathen shall know that I *am* the LORD, the Holy One in Israel.

⁸ Behold, it is come, and it is done, saith the Lord GOD; this *is* the day whereof I have spoken.

Ezekiel 39:1, 4–8

INSIGHTS

*F*or thousands of years, Satan has seduced nations and people into thinking that they can build a world of peace and love without Christ. Sometimes he has deceived people into thinking that education or money would solve personal problems. But his dirty work is over, for a time. At the end of the thousand years "he must be set free for a short time" (Revelation 20:3). . . .

When Satan is released for a time, he will gather some of his old cohorts, Gog and Magog, the nations that hated Israel, and march on Jerusalem once more. This battle will not last long, for fire will come down from heaven and zap them. Then Satan will have his final place of unrest; he will be thrown "into the lake of burning sulfur, where the beast and the false prophet had been thrown. They will be tormented day and night for ever and ever" (Revelation 20:10).

David Jeremiah

APPLICATION

*W*hat amazing events are promised for future times in this portion of Scripture? What is the penalty for those who are not faithful to God?

FRIDAY

*God Makes All Things New
and Comes to Live
with His People*

Revelation 21:1–27

The New Jerusalem

21 And I saw a new heaven and a new earth: for the first heaven and the first earth were passed away; and there was no more sea.

2 And I John saw the holy city, new Jerusalem, coming down from God out of heaven, prepared as a bride adorned for her husband.

3 And I heard a great voice out of heaven saying, Behold, the tabernacle of God *is* with men, and he will dwell with them, and they shall be his people, and God himself shall be with them, *and be* their God.

4 And God shall wipe away all tears from their eyes; and there shall be no more death, neither sorrow, nor crying, neither shall there be any more pain: for the former things are passed away.

5 And he that sat upon the throne said, Behold, I make all things new. And he said unto me, Write: for these words are true and faithful.

6 And he said unto me, It is done. I am Alpha and Omega, the beginning and the end. I will give unto him that is athirst of the fountain of the water of life freely.

7 He that overcometh shall inherit all things; and I will be his God, and he shall be my son.

8 But the fearful, and unbelieving, and the abominable, and murderers, and whoremongers, and sorcerers, and idolaters, and all liars, shall have their part in the lake which burneth with fire and brimstone: which is the second death.

9 And there came unto me one of the seven angels which had the seven vials full of the seven last plagues, and talked with me, saying, Come hither, I will show thee the bride, the Lamb's wife.

10 And he carried me away in the spirit to a great and high mountain, and showed me that great city, the holy Jerusalem, descending out of heaven from God,

11 having the glory of God: and her light was like unto a stone most precious, even like a jasper stone, clear as crystal;

12 and had a wall great and high, *and* had twelve gates, and at the gates twelve angels, and names written thereon, which are *the names* of the twelve tribes of the children of Israel:

13 on the east three gates; on the north three gates; on the south three gates; and on the west three gates.

14 And the wall of the city had twelve foundations, and in them the names of the twelve apostles of the Lamb.

15 And he that talked with me had a golden reed to measure the city, and the gates thereof, and the wall thereof.

16 And the city lieth foursquare, and the length is as large as the breadth: and he measured the city with the reed, twelve thousand furlongs. The length and the breadth and the height of it are equal.

17 And he measured the wall thereof, a hundred *and* forty *and* four cubits, *according to* the measure of a man, that is, *of* the angel.

18 And the building of the wall of it

was *of* jasper: and the city *was* pure gold, like unto clear glass.

¹⁹ And the foundations of the wall of the city *were* garnished with all manner of precious stones. The first foundation *was* jasper; the second, sapphire; the third, a chalcedony; the fourth, an emerald;

²⁰ the fifth, sardonyx; the sixth, sardius; the seventh, chrysolite; the eighth, beryl; the ninth, a topaz; the tenth, a chrysoprasus; the eleventh, a jacinth; the twelfth, an amethyst.

²¹ And the twelve gates *were* twelve pearls; every several gate was of one pearl: and the street of the city *was* pure gold, as it were transparent glass.

²² And I saw no temple therein: for the Lord God Almighty and the Lamb are the temple of it.

²³ And the city had no need of the sun, neither of the moon, to shine in it: for the glory of God did lighten it, and the Lamb *is* the light thereof.

²⁴ And the nations of them which are saved shall walk in the light of it: and the kings of the earth do bring their glory and honor into it.

²⁵ And the gates of it shall not be shut at all by day: for there shall be no night there.

²⁶ And they shall bring the glory and honor of the nations into it.

²⁷ And there shall in no wise enter into it any thing that defileth, neither *whatsoever* worketh abomination, or *maketh* a lie: but they which are written in the Lamb's book of life.

OLD TESTAMENT READING

Sing and rejoice, O daughter of Zion: for, lo, I come, and I will dwell in the midst of thee, saith the Lord.

¹¹ And many nations shall be joined to the Lord in that day, and shall be my people: and I will dwell in the midst of thee, and thou shalt know that the Lord of hosts hath sent me unto thee.

¹² And the Lord shall inherit Judah his portion in the holy land, and shall choose Jerusalem again.

¹³ Be silent, O all flesh, before the Lord: for he is raised up out of his holy habitation.

Zechariah 2:10–13

INSIGHTS

The longing for a future glorious city of God can be traced back as far as the Old Testament patriarchs. Abraham ". . . was looking forward to the city with foundations, whose architect and builder is God" (Hebrews 11:10).

Paul mentioned this city in his letter to the Galatians. He called it "the Jerusalem which is above" (Galatians 4:26).

The "New Jerusalem" (Revelation 21:2; 3:12) is just one of the several names given to this future city of God. It is also called The Holy City, the Heavenly Jerusalem, and Mount Zion. Whatever it is named, it will be a holy and beautiful place, more perfect than the Garden of Eden. . . .

David Jeremiah

ACTION POINT

Study what God promises to his children in the New Jerusalem. Do you have any doubts that God deeply loves you and fully knows your every pain and sorrow?

WEEKEND

*Come to the Water of Life,
for Jesus Is Coming Soon*

Revelation 22:1–21

22 And he showed me a pure river of water of life, clear as crystal, proceeding out of the throne of God and of the Lamb.

² In the midst of the street of it, and on either side of the river, *was there* the tree of life, which bare twelve *manner of* fruits, *and* yielded her fruit every month: and the leaves of the tree *were* for the healing of the nations.

³ And there shall be no more curse: but the throne of God and of the Lamb shall be in it; and his servants shall serve him:

⁴ and they shall see his face; and his name *shall be* in their foreheads.

⁵ And there shall be no night there; and they need no candle, neither light of the sun; for the Lord God giveth them light: and they shall reign for ever and ever.

⁶ And he said unto me, These sayings *are* faithful and true: and the Lord God of the holy prophets sent his angel to show unto his servants the things which must shortly be done.

⁷ Behold, I come quickly: blessed *is* he that keepeth the sayings of the prophecy of this book.

⁸ And I John saw these things, and heard *them*. And when I had heard and seen, I fell down to worship before the feet of the angel which showed me these things.

⁹ Then saith he unto me, See *thou do it* not: for I am thy fellow servant, and of thy brethren the prophets, and of them which keep the sayings of this book: worship God.

¹⁰ And he saith unto me, Seal not the sayings of the prophecy of this book: for the time is at hand.

¹¹ He that is unjust, let him be unjust still: and he which is filthy, let him be filthy still: and he that is righteous, let him be righteous still: and he that is holy, let him be holy still.

¹² And, behold, I come quickly; and my reward *is* with me, to give every man according as his work shall be.

¹³ I am Alpha and Omega, the beginning and the end, the first and the last.

¹⁴ Blessed *are* they that do his commandments, that they may have right to the tree of life, and may enter in through the gates into the city.

¹⁵ For without *are* dogs, and sorcerers, and whoremongers, and murderers, and idolaters, and whosoever loveth and maketh a lie.

¹⁶ I Jesus have sent mine angel to testify unto you these things in the churches. I am the root and the offspring of David, *and* the bright and morning star.

¹⁷ And the Spirit and the bride say, Come. And let him that heareth say, Come. And let him that is athirst come. And whosoever will, let him take the water of life freely.

¹⁸ For I testify unto every man that heareth the words of the prophecy of this book, If any man shall add unto these things, God shall add unto him the plagues that are written in this book:

¹⁹ and if any man shall take away from the words of the book of this prophecy, God shall take away his part out of the book of life, and out of the holy city, and *from* the things which are written in this book.

[20] He which testifieth these things saith, Surely I come quickly. Amen. Even so, come, Lord Jesus.

[21] The grace of our Lord Jesus Christ *be* with you all. Amen.

OLD TESTAMENT READING

*H*o, every one that thirsteth, come ye to the waters, and he that hath no money; come ye, buy, and eat; yea, come, buy, wine and milk without money and without price.

[3] Incline your ear, and come unto me: hear, and your soul shall live.

Isaiah 55:1, 3a

*T*here *is* a river, the streams whereof shall make glad the city of God, the holy *place* of the tabernacles of the Most High.

[5] God *is* in the midst of her; she shall not be moved.

Psalm 46:4–5a

INSIGHTS

*C*ome celebrate the living water that flows for you from an eternal spring. You need not fear stagnation. You need only draw nearer—put your roots down deep, settle in, and be at home in My love. Then every day will be a new day. Every day you will wonder at the richness of life that has come to you by My grace. Every day you will watch eagerly for My sunrise, search eagerly for My presence in the mundane activities of your world. Every day you will know Me better, and every day you will want to know Me more.

And every day you will live in joyful anticipation of My presence. You will think of My love for you as it is now, and as it will be on that day when I carry you across the threshold into the New Jerusalem—the home I am preparing for you.

Every day you will count the days until the wedding, when you and I will sit down together at the marriage supper of the Lamb. . . .

On that day, child, I will call you by a new name. You will be a crown of splendor in My hand, a royal diadem in the hand of your God. I will delight in you, I will rejoice over you as a bridegroom rejoices over his bride.

Come to the spring and drink deeply of My love. Let it flow over you, bringing a foretaste of that day when the river of life will flow for you through the New Jerusalem and love will be forever fresh.

Until then, turn from your fears and relax in My love. Here at the source you will find your renewal.

Ruth Senter

PAUSE FOR REFLECTION

*W*hat to you is the most meaningful aspect of God's salvation, of his endless river of life? Meditate on this glorious gift. Thank him for what he has done for you and for anyone who will forsake sin and come to him.

INDEX

God's Spirit Brings Glory and Under-
standing to Those Who Believe, 434
God Demands Obedience and Punishes
Unbelief, 526

Warfare, Spiritual (See Spiritual Warfare)

Will, God's
Jesus Sought the Will of the Fa-
ther, 212
God's Will Can't Be Thwarted, 296
God Has Plans for His Own, 450

Wisdom
There Is Wisdom and Goodness in
Walking in God's Ways, 16
Not Everyone Who Hears Under-
stands, 32
Jesus Understands the Hearts of
Spiritually Closed People, 164
God Gives His Wisdom and Power to
His Servants, 174
God's Wisdom Defies Human Wis-
dom, 398

God Is the Source of Wisdom, 400
God Gives Wisdom to Those Who Ask
for It, 548
Add Knowledge to Your Faith, 566

Word of God
Hide God's Teachings in Your
Heart, 34
Jesus Offers Real Food, 42
God Wants to Teach Us His Ways, 110
God's Word Brings Joy to Those Who
Understand It, 306
It's Important to Know God's Powerful
Word, 330
God Gave Us Scripture to Teach Us
How to Live, 514
God's Word Is True: He Keeps His
Promises, 530

Worship
God Seeks Sincere Worship, 56
All the People of Heaven Worship
God! 618

ACKNOWLEDGMENTS

Alcorn, Randy C., taken from *Sexual Temptation*. © 1989 by Randy Alcorn. Used by permission of InterVarsity Press, P.O. Box 1400, Downers Grove, IL 60515.

Anderson, Lynn, *Finding the Heart to Go On,* Here's Life Publishers, San Bernadino, CA, © 1991.

Arnold, Duane W. H., taken from the book *Prayers of the Martyrs*. Copyright © 1991 by Duane W. H. Arnold. Used by permission of Zondervan Publishing House.

Augsburger, David W., taken from *Freedom of Forgiveness*. Copyright ©1970, 1988. Moody Bible Institute of Chicago. Moody Press. Used by permission.

Avila, St. Theresa of, from the book *A Life of Prayer,* copyright 1983 by Multnomah Press. Published by Multnomah Press, Portland, Oregon, 97206. Used by permission.

Babcock, Maltbie, *This Is My Father's World* in *The Hymnal for Worship and Celebration,* copyright © 1986, Word Music, Waco, Texas.

Barna, George, *The Frog in the Kettle,* copyright © 1990 by Regal Books, a division of Gospel Light Publications. Used by permission.

Baxter, J. Sidlow, taken from the book *Awake My Heart*. Copyright © 1959 by J. Sidlow Baxter. Used by permission of the Zondervan Publishing House.

Beals, Art, *Beyond Hunger,* copyright © 1985, Multnomah Press, Portland, Oregon 97266.

Beckwith, Mary, *Still Moments,* copyright © 1989 by Regal Books, a division of Gospel Light Publications. Used by permission.

Blue, Ron, *Master Your Money,* copyright © 1986, Thomas Nelson Publishers, Nashville, TN.

Boice, James Montgomery, taken from *The Parables of Jesus*. Copyright © 1983. Moody Bible Institute of Chicago. Moody Press. Used by permission.

Bridges, Jerry, *The Practice of Godliness,* copyright © 1983 by Jerry Bridges, NavPress, Colorado Springs, Colorado.

Bridges, Jerry, *The Pursuit of Holiness,* copyright © 1978 by the Navigators, NavPress, Colorado Springs, Colorado.

Bright, Bill, *Promises — A Daily Guide to Supernatural Living,* Here's Life Publishers, San Bernadino, CA, © 1983.

Bright, Bill, *The Secret: How to Live with Purpose and Power,* Here's Life Publishers, San Bernadino, CA, © 1989.

Briscoe, Jill, *Running on Empty,* copyright © 1988, Word, Inc., Dallas, Texas.

Bruce, F. F., taken from *The Hard Sayings of Jesus*. © 1983 by F. F. Bruce. Used by permission of InterVarsity Press, P.O. Box 1400, Downers Grove, IL 60515. Worldwide permission granted by Hodder & Stoughton Limited, England.

Bryant, Al, (Compiler) *Day By Day With C. H. Spurgeon,* copyright © 1980, Word, Inc., Dallas, Texas.

Bryant, Al, *Keep in Touch,* copyright © 1981, Word, Inc., Dallas, Texas.

Bryant, Al, *Strength for the Day: Daily Meditations with F. B. Meyer,* copyright © 1979, Word, Inc., Dallas, Texas.

Buechner, Frederick, excerpt from *Wishful Thinking*. Copyright © 1973 by Frederick Buechner. Reprinted by permission of HarperCollins Publishers.

Calkins, Ruth Harms, from *Tell Me Again Lord, I Forget,* © 1974. Used by permission of Tyndale House Publishers, Inc. All rights reserved.

Campolo, Anthony, *The Kingdom of God is a Party,* copyright © 1990, Word, Inc., Dallas, Texas.

Campolo, Anthony, *Who Switched the Price Tags?,* copyright © 1986, Word, Inc., Dallas, Texas.

Chapian, Marie, *Discovering Joy,* Bethany House Publishers, © 1990.

Chisholm, Thomas O. (Words) and Runyan, William M. (Music), *Great Is Thy Faithfulness* in *The Hymnal for Worship and Celebration,* copyright © 1923. Renewal 1951 by Hope Publishing Co., Carol Stream, IL 60188. All rights reserved. Used by permission.

Crabb, Rachael, *The Personal Touch,* copyright © 1990 by Rachael Crabb and Raeann Hart, NavPress, Colorado Springs, Colorado.

Evans, Anthony T., taken from *America's Only Hope.* Copyright © 1990. Moody Bible Institute of Chicago. Moody Press. Used by permission.

Fickett, Harold L., *Walking What You're Talking (Principles of James),* copyright © 1988 by Regal Books, a division of Gospel Light Publications. Used by permission.

Finney, Charles G., *God's Love for a Sinning World.* © 1966 by Kregel Publications: Grand Rapids, Michigan. Used by permission.

Finney, Charles G., *Principles of Consecration,* Bethany House Publishers, © 1990.

Finney, Charles Grandison, *Principles of Devotion,* Bethany House Publishers, © 1987.

Finney, Charles G., *Victory Over the World.* © 1966 by Kregel Publications: Grand Rapids, Michigan. Used by permission.

Fletcher, William M., *The Second Greatest Commandment.* Copyright © 1983. NavPress, Colorado Springs, Colorado. (Dr. William M. Fletcher is Minister-at-Large, Rocky Mountain Conservative Baptist Association.)

Foster, Richard J., excerpts from *Celebration of Discipline.* Copyright © 1978 by Richard J. Foster. Reprinted by permission of HarperCollins Publishers.

Foster, Richard J., excerpts from *Money, Sex and Power.* Copyright © 1985 by Richard J. Foster. Reprinted by permission of HarperCollins Publishers.

Fullham, Terry L., *Thirsting,* copyright © 1989, Thomas Nelson Publishers, Nashville, TN.

Gaither, Gloria, *We Have This Moment,* copyright © 1988, Word, Inc., Dallas, Texas.

Geisler, Norman L., (Editor), *What Augustine Says,* Baker Book House, © 1982.

Gillham, Bill, *Lifetime Guarantee,* Wolgemuth & Hyatt, Publishers, Inc. Used by permission.

Graham, Billy, *Answers to Life's Problems,* copyright © 1960, 1988, Word, Inc., Dallas, Texas.

Graham, Billy, *Approaching Hoofbeats,* copyright © 1983, Word, Inc., Dallas, Texas.

Graham, Billy, *The Holy Spirit,* copyright © 1978, 1988, Word, Inc., Dallas, Texas.

Graham, Billy, *Unto the Hills: A Devotional Treasury from Billy Graham,* copyright © 1986, Word, Inc., Dallas, Texas.

Gregory, Joel C., *Growing Pains of the Soul,* copyright © 1987, Word, Inc., Dallas, Texas.

Guiness, Os, taken from *The Devil's Gauntlet.* © 1989 by Os Guiness. Used by permission of InterVarsity Press, P.O. Box 1400, Downers Grove, IL 60515.

Halverson, Richard C., *No Greater Power,* copyright © 1986, Multnomah Press, Portland, Oregon 97266.

Harris, Madalene, *Climbing Higher,* Here's Life Publishers, San Bernadino, CA, © 1989.

Hayford, Jack, from *Daybreak,* © 1984. Used by permission of Tyndale House Publishers, Inc. All rights reserved.

Hendrichson, Walter A., Reprinted by permission from *Disciples are Made — Not Born.* Published by Victor Books and © 1974 by SP Publications, Inc., Wheaton, IL.

Hendricks, Howard G. and Jeanne W., from the book *Footprints,* copyright © 1981, Multnomah Press, Portland, Oregon, 97266. (Howard Hendricks is a distinguished professor at Dallas Theological Seminary; Jeanne Hendricks is an author, mother of four, and grandmother of six.)

Hession, Roy, from *The Calvary Road,* copyright 1952 Christian Literature Crusade, London (Ft. Washington, PA and Alresford, Hants: Christian Literature Crusade). Used by permission.

Hocking, David L., from the book *The Coming World Leader,* copyright 1988 by Calvary Communications, Inc. Published by Multnomah Press, Portland, Oregon 97266. Used by permission.

Hughes, R. Kent, taken from *Ephesians,* copyright 1990. Used with permission by Good News Publishers/Crossway Books, Wheaton, IL.

Hybels, Bill, *Seven Wonders of the Spiritual World,* copyright © 1988, Word, Inc., Dallas, Texas.

Hybels, Bill, taken from *Too Busy Not to Pray.* © 1988 by Bill Hybels. Used by permission of InterVarsity Press, P.O. Box 1400, Downers Grove, IL 60515.

Jeremiah, David and Carlson, Carole C., *Escape the Coming Night,* copyright © 1990, Word, Inc., Dallas, Texas.

Johnson, Elliott and Schierbaum, Al, *Our Great and Awesome God: Meditations for Athletes.* Wolgemuth & Hyatt, Publishers, Inc. Used by permission.

Keller, W. Phillip, *A Gardener Looks at the Fruits of the Spirit,* copyright © 1986, Word, Inc., Dallas, Texas.

Keller, W. Phillip, *Salt for Society,* copyright © 1981, Word, Inc., Dallas, Texas.

Keller, W. Phillip, *Songs of My Soul,* copyright © 1989, Word, Inc., Dallas, Texas.

Keller, W. Phillip, *Taming Tension,* Baker Book House, © 1979.

Kempis, Thomas à, taken from *The Imitation of Christ.* Copyright © 1984. Moody Bible Institute of Chicago. Moody Press. Used by permission.

Kroll, Woodrow Michael, *Early in the Morning, Book Two.* Used by permission of Loizeaux Brothers, Inc., Neptune, New Jersey.

Lake, Vicki, reprinted by permission from *Firming Up Your Flabby Faith.* Published by Victor Books and © 1990 by SP Publications, Inc., Wheaton, IL.

Larson, Bruce, reprinted from *A Call to Holy Living,* copyright © 1988 Augsburg Publishing House. Used by permission of Augsburg Fortress.

Lee, Richard, *The Unfailing Promise,* copyright © 1988, Word, Inc., Dallas, Texas.

Lockerbie, Jeanette, taken from *Springtime of Faith.* Copyright © 1990. Moody Bible Institute of Chicago. Moody Press. Used by permission.

Lockyer, Herbert, *Satan: His Person and Power,* copyright © 1980, Word, Inc., Dallas, Texas.

Lucado, Max, *The Applause of Heaven,* copyright © 1990, Word, Inc., Dallas, Texas.

Lucado, Max, from the book *God Came Near,* copyright 1987 by Max Lucado. Published by Multnomah Press, Portland, Oregon 97266. Used by permission.

Lucado, Max, from *On the Anvil,* © 1985. Used by permission of Tyndale House Publishers, Inc. All rights reserved.

Luther, Martin, *A Mighty Fortress Is Our God* in *The Hymnal for Worship and Celebration,* copyright © 1986, Word Music, Waco, Texas.

MacArthur, John Jr., taken from the book *The Gospel According to Jesus.* Copyright © 1988 by John F. MacArthur, Jr. Used by permission of Zondervan Publishing House.

MacDonald, George, *Knowing the Heart of God,* Bethany House Publishers, © 1990.

MacDonald, Gordon, *Ordering Your Private World,* copyright © 1984, 1985, Thomas Nelson Publishers, Nashville, TN.

MacDonald, Gordon, *Rebuilding Your Broken World,* copyright © 1988, 1990, Thomas Nelson Publishers, Nashville, TN.

McClung, Floyd, *Holiness and the Spirit of the Age.* Copyright © 1990 by Harvest House Publishers, Eugene, OR 97402.

McClung, Floyd, taken from *Wholehearted.* © 1988, 1990 by Floyd McClung. Used by permission of InterVarsity Press, P.O. Box 1400, Downers Grove, IL 60515. Worldwide permission granted by HarperCollins Publishers, London, England.

McCullough, Donald W., taken from *Finding Happiness in the Most Unlikely Places.* © 1990 by Donald W. McCullough. Used by permission of InterVarsity Press, P.O. Box 1400, Downers Grove, IL 60515.

McKenna, David, from *Practical Christianity*; LaVonne Neff, Ron Beers, Bruce Barton, Linda Taylor, Dave Veerman, and Jim Galvin (Compilers and Editors), © 1987 by Youth for Christ/USA. Used by permission of Tyndale House Publishers. All rights reserved.

Magdalen, Margaret, taken from *Jesus, Man of Prayer.* © 1987 by Sister Margaret Magdalen. Used by permission of InterVarsity Press, P.O. Box 1400, Downers Grove, IL 60515. Worldwide permission granted by Hodder & Stoughton Limited, England.

Mains, David R., *The Sense of His Presence,* copyright © 1988, Word, Inc., Dallas, Texas.

Mains, Karen Burton, taken from the book *You Are What You Say.* Copyright © 1988 by Karen Burton Mains. Used by permission of the Zondervan Publishing House.

Merritt, James Gregory, reprinted by permission from *God's Prescription for a Healthy*

Christian. Published by Victor Books and © 1990 by SP Publications, Inc., Wheaton, IL.

Meyer, F. B., from *Devotional Commentary by F. B. Meyer* (1989) Tyndale House Publishers, Inc. Used by permission. All rights reserved.

Meyer, F. B., taken from *Our Daily Walk.* Copyright © 1951, 1972 by the Zondervan Publishing House. Used by permission.

Miley, Jeanie, *Creative Silence: Keys to the Deeper Life,* copyright © 1989, Word, Inc., Dallas, Texas.

Mitchell, John G., from the book *An Everlasting Love,* copyright 1982 by Multnomah Press. Published by Multnomah Press, Portland, Oregon 97206. Used by permission.

Moody, D. L., taken from *The Way to God and How to Find It.* Copyright © 1983. Moody Bible Institute of Chicago. Moody Press. Used by permission.

Morley, Patrick, *I Surrender.* Wolgemuth & Hyatt, Publishers, Inc. Used by permission.

Mote, Edward, *The Solid Rock* in *The Hymnal for Worship and Celebration,* copyright © 1986, Word Music, Waco, Texas.

Muggeridge, Malcolm, from *The End of Christendom,* copyright 1980 by William B. Eerdmans Publishing Co., pp. 51-54. Used by permission.

Muggeridge, Malcolm, *A Twentieth Century Testimony,* copyright © 1978, Thomas Nelson Publishers, Nashville, TN.

Murray, Andrew, from *Abide in Christ* (Ft. Washington, PA: Christian Literature Crusade).

Murray, Andrew, *The Believer's Secret of Living Like Christ,* Bethany House Publishers, © 1985.

Murray, Andrew, *The Believer's Secret of Waiting on God,* Bethany House Publishers, © 1986.

Murray, Andrew, taken from *The True Vine.* Copyright © 1983. Moody Bible Institute of Chicago. Moody Press. Used by permission.

Murray, Andrew, and Edwards, Jonathan; Parkhurst, Louis Gifford (Compiler and Editor), *The Believer's Secret of Christian Love,* Bethany House Publishers, © 1990.

Murray, Andrew, and Finney, Charles G.; Parkhurst, L. G. (Compiler and Editor), *The Believer's Secret of Spiritual Power,* Bethany House Publishers, © 1987.

Myers, Warren and Ruth, *Pray: How to Be Effective in Prayer,* copyright © 1983, Navpress, Colorado Springs, Colorado.

Oatman, Johnson Jr., *Count Your Blessings* in *The Hymnal for Worship and Celebration,* copyright © 1986, Word Music, Waco, Texas.

Ogilvie, Lloyd, *Enjoying God,* copyright © 1989, Word, Inc., Dallas, Texas.

Ogilvie, Lloyd John, taken from *Silent Strength for My Life.* Copyright © 1990 by Harvest House Publishers, Eugene, OR 97402. Used by permission.

Ortlund, Anne, *Disciplines of the Home,* copyright © 1990, Word, Inc., Dallas, Texas.

Packer, J. I., taken from *Knowing God.* © 1973 by J. I. Packer. Used by permission of InterVarsity Press, P.O. Box 1400, Downers Grove, IL 60515. Worldwide permission granted by Hodder & Stoughton Limited, England.

Packer, James and Watson, Jean, reprinted from *Your Father Loves You,* © 1986 by James Packer and Jean Watson. Used by permission of Harold Shaw Publishers, Wheaton, IL. Worldwide permission granted by Hodder & Stoughton Limited, England.

Palau, Luis, reprinted by permission from *Time to Stop Pretending.* Published by Victor Books and © 1985 by SP Publications, Inc., Wheaton, IL.

Pinnock, Clark H., from *Practical Christianity*; LaVonne Neff, Ron Beers, Bruce Barton, Linda Taylor, Dave Veerman, and Jim Galvin (Compilers and Editors), © 1987 by Youth for Christ/USA. Used by permission of Tyndale House Publishers. All rights reserved.

Pippert, Rebecca Manley, taken from *Out of the Saltshaker and Into the World.* © 1979 by Inter-Varsity Christian Fellowship of the USA. Used by permission of InterVarsity Press, P.O. Box 1400, Downers Grove, IL 60515.

Reid, David, *Devotions for Growing Christians.* Used by permission of Loizeaux Brothers, Inc., Neptune, New Jersey.

Ryrie, Charles C., reprinted by permission from *The Final Countdown.* Published by Victor Books and © 1982 by SP Publications, Inc., Wheaton, IL.

Sanders, J. Oswald, taken from *Enjoying Intimacy With God.* Copyright © 1980. Moody Bible Institute of Chicago. Moody Press. Used by permission.

Sanders, J. Oswald, taken from *Just Like Us.* Copyright © 1978. Moody Bible Institute of Chicago. Moody Press. Used by permission.

Sanders, J. Oswald, taken from *Shoe Leather Commitment.* Copyright © 1990. Moody Bible Institute of Chicago. Moody Press. Used by permission.

Schaeffer, Edith, from the book *Affliction,* copyright © 1978 by Edith Schaeffer. Used by permission of Fleming H. Revell Company.

Schaeffer, Edith, *Common Sense Christian Living,* copyright © 1983, Thomas Nelson Publishers, Nashville, TN.

Schmidt, Thomas E., taken from the book *Trying to Be Good.* Copyright © 1990 by Thomas E. Schmidt. Used by permission of the Zondervan Publishing House.

Senter, Ruth, taken from *The Attributes of God.* Copyright © 1987. Moody Bible Institute of Chicago. Moody Press. Used by permission.

Senter, Ruth, *Longing for Love,* copyright © 1991 by Ruth Senter, NavPress, Colorado Springs, Colorado.

Senter, Ruth, taken from the book *Startled by Silence.* Copyright © 1986 by Ruth Senter. Used by permission of the Zondervan Publishing House.

Shaw, Luci, reprinted from *Postcard from the Shore,* © 1985 by Luci Shaw. Used by permission of Harold Shaw Publishers, Wheaton, IL.

Sherman, Doug and Hendricks, William, *How to Succeed Where It Really Counts,* copyright © 1989 by Doug Sherman and William Hendricks, NavPress, Colorado Springs, Colorado.

Sider, Ronald J., *Rich Christians in an Age of Hunger,* copyright © 1990, Word, Inc., Dallas, Texas.

Simpson, A. B., taken from the book *Days of Heaven on Earth.* Copyright © 1984 by Christian Publications. Used by permission of the Zondervan Publishing House.

Smith, F. LaGard, *The Daily Gospels* (formerly *The Intimate Jesus*). Copyright © 1988 by Harvest House Publishers, Eugene, OR 97402.

Smith, Hannah Whitall, from the book *The Christian's Secret of a Happy Life.* Copyright © 1952 by Fleming H. Revell Company. Used by permission of Fleming H. Revell Company.

Sollenberger, Lucille Fern, *My Daily Appointment with God,* copyright © 1988, Word, Inc., Dallas, Texas.

Sproul, R. C., from *Effective Prayer,* © 1984. Used by permission of Tyndale House Publishers, Inc. All rights reserved.

Sproul, R. C., from *The Holiness of God,* © 1985. Used by permission of Tyndale House Publishers, Inc. All rights reserved.

Sproul, R. C., *One Holy Passion,* copyright © 1987, Thomas Nelson Publishers, Nashville, TN.

Spurgeon, C. H., taken from *All of Grace.* Copyright © 1984. Moody Bible Institute of Chicago. Moody Press. Used by permission.

Spurgeon, Charles H., taken from *Faith's Checkbook.* Copyright © 1987. Moody Bible Institute of Chicago. Moody Press. Used by permission.

Spurgeon, Charles H., *Morning and Evening,* copyright © 1991, Hendrickson Publishers, Inc. Peabody, MA.

Spurgeon, C. H., reprinted from *The Quotable Spurgeon,* © 1990 by Harold Shaw Publishers, Wheaton, IL. Used by permission.

Stamm, Mildred, taken from the book *Meditation Moments for Women.* Copyright © 1967 by the Zondervan Publishing House. Used by permission.

Stamm, Millie, taken from the book *Beside Still Waters.* Copyright © 1984 by Christian Women's Club. Used by permission of the Zondervan Publishing House.

Stamm, Millie, taken from the book *Be Still and Know.* Copyright © 1978 by Millie Stamm. Used by permission of the Zondervan Publishing House.

Stanley, Charles, *How to Handle Adversity,* copyright © 1989, Thomas Nelson Publishers, Nashville, TN.

Steer, Roger, reprinted from *Spiritual Secrets of George Müller,* © 1985 by Roger Steer. U.S.A. rights granted by permission of Harold Shaw Publishers, Wheaton, IL. Worldwide permission granted by Hodder & Stoughton Limited, England.

Steinberger, G., *In the Footprints of the Lamb,* Bethany House Publishers, © 1936.

Stoddard, William S., from the book *First Light,* copyright 1990 by Multnomah Press. Published by Multnomah Press, Portland, Oregon 97266. Used by permission.

Stott, John, from *Basic Christianity.* Copyright 1958, 1971. Inter-Varsity Press, London. Published in the U.S.A. by William B. Eerdmans Publishing Co. and in the U.K. by InterVarsity Press. Used by permission. Worldwide permission granted by InterVarsity Press, London, England. Second edition.

Sweeting, George, taken from *The Acts of God.* Copyright © 1986. Moody Bible Institute of Chicago. Moody Press. Used by permission.

Swindoll, Charles R., *The Grace Awakening,* copyright © 1990, Word, Inc., Dallas, Texas.

Swindoll, Charles R., *Improving Your Serve: The Art of Unselfish Living,* copyright © 1981, Word, Inc., Dallas, Texas.

Swindoll, Charles R., *Living Above the Level of Mediocrity: A Commitment to Excellence.* Copyright © 1987, Word, Inc., Dallas, Texas.

Swindoll, Charles R., from the book *Make Up Your Mind,* copyright 1981. Published by Multnomah Press, Portland, Oregon 97266. Used by permission.

Swindoll, Charles R., *Strengthening Your Grip: Essentials in an Aimless World,* copyright © 1982, Word, Inc., Dallas, Texas.

Tada, Joni Eareckson, from the book *Secret Strength,* copyright 1988 by Joni, Inc. Published by Multnomah Press, Portland, Oregon 97266. Used by permission.

Tamasy, Robert J., (General Editor), *The Complete Christian Businessman,* Wolgemuth & Hyatt, Publishers, Inc. Used by permission.

Tucker, Ruth A., taken from the book *Stories of Faith.* Copyright © 1989 by Ruth A. Tucker. Used by permission of Zondervan Publishing House.

Webber, Robert, *Worship is a Verb,* copyright © 1985, Word, Inc., Dallas, Texas. (Second edition by Abbott Martyn Press, Nashville, TN).

Wenham, David, taken from *The Parables of Jesus.* © 1989 by David Wenham. Used by permission of InterVarsity Press, P.O. Box 1400, Downers Grove, IL 60515. Worldwide permission granted by Hodder & Stoughton Limited, England.

White, John, taken from *The Fight.* © 1976 by Inter-Varsity Christian Fellowship of the U.S.A. Used by permission of InterVarsity Press, P.O. Box 1400, Downers Grove, IL 60515.

Wiersbe, Warren W., Reprinted by permission from *Be Alert.* Published by Victor Books and © 1984 by SP Publications, Inc., Wheaton, IL.

Wiersbe, Warren W., Reprinted by permission from *Be Victorious.* Published by Victor Books and © by 1985 SP Publications, Inc., Wheaton, IL.

Wiersbe, Warren W. (Compiler), *Classic Sermons on the Attributes of God.* © 1989 by Kregel Publications: Grand Rapids, Michigan. Used by permission.

Wiersbe, Warren W., taken from *Thoughts for Men on the Move.* Copyright © 1970, 1988. Moody Bible Institute of Chicago. Moody Press. Used by permission.

Wiersbe, Warren W., Reprinted by permission from *Windows on the Parables.* Published by Victor Books and © 1979 by SP Publications, Inc., Wheaton, IL.

Wirt, Sherwood E., *Your Mighty Fortress: Cultivating Your Inner Life With God,* Here's Life Publishers, San Bernadino, CA, © 1989.

Wright, H. Norman, *Quiet Times for Couples.* Copyright © 1990 by Harvest House Publishers, Eugene, OR 97402.

YFC Editors, from *Practical Christianity*; LaVonne Neff, Ron Beers, Bruce Barton, Linda Taylor, Dave Veerman, and Jim Galvin (Compilers and Editors), © 1987 by Youth for Christ/USA. Used by permission of Tyndale House Publishers. All rights reserved.

Yancey, Philip, taken from the book *Where Is God When It Hurts?* Copyright © 1990, 1977 by Philip Yancey. Used by permission of the Zondervan Publishing House.

Yohn, Rick, *Finding Time,* copyright © 1984, Word, Inc., Dallas, Texas.

Zuck, Roy B. (Editor), reprinted by permission from *Devotions for Kindred Spirits.* Published by Victor Books and © 1990 by SP Publications, Inc., Wheaton, IL.